Opportunities for Media and Information Literacy in the Middle East and North Africa

Editors:
Magda Abu-Fadil, Jordi Torrent & Alton Grizzle

The International Clearinghouse on
CHILDREN, YOUTH & MEDIA
at NORDICOM, University of Gothenburg

Yearbook 2016

Opportunities for Media and Information Literacy in the Middle East and North Africa

Editors: Magda Abu-Fadil, Jordi Torrent & Alton Grizzle

A collaboration between the United Nations Alliance of Civilization (UNAOC), UNESCO and the International Clearinghouse on Children, Youth and Media at Nordicom, University of Gothenburg

ISBN 978-91-87957-33-8

Published by:
The International Clearinghouse on Children, Youth and Media
Series editor: Ingela Wadbring

Nordicom
University of Gothenburg
Box 713
SE 405 30 Göteborg
Sweden

Cover by: Karin Persson

Printed by: Billes Tryckeri AB, Mölndal, Sweden 2016

3014 0129

Contents

Preface

It is with great pleasure that this volume *Opportunities for Media and Information Literacy in the Middle East and North Africa* is presented as Yearbook 2016 from the International Clearinghouse on Children, Youth and Media, at Nordicom. The Yearbook is published in cooperation with UNESCO and UNAOC.

The aim of the International Clearinghouse on Children, Youth and Media is to increase awareness and knowledge about children, youth and media. Providing information and knowledge about new research findings and positive examples will hopefully offer a solid basis for relevant policy-making, contributions to a constructive public debate, and an enhancement of children's and young people's media literacy and media competence.

The rapid advances in information and communication technology, the opportunities that, for example, social media provide for citizens to engage, have transformed how and at what pace information is spread and circulated. In a time when almost everyone can be a publisher, the abundance of media content gives us increased opportunities to find information, but also disinformation. Hence, this development has also brought forward new challenges. The need for information and education about media and information literacy (MIL) has become more and more urgent. With MIL competencies, citizens may be empowered and able to fully exercise fundamental human rights such as freedom of information and freedom of expression, and be able to scrutinize media content with a critical eye.

Opportunities for Media and Information Literacy in the Middle East and North Africa is the seventeenth Yearbook published by the Clearinghouse and fills a gap in the existing body of literature about the progress of media and information literacy work in different parts of the world. We believe it is of particular interest to shed light on a region, the MENA region, where young citizens' engagement with media has been in focus in news reporting all over the world in recent years and awareness of MIL competencies is gaining ground.

All books published by the Clearinghouse aim to stimulate further research on children, youth and media. Various groups of users are targeted, such as researchers, policy-makers, media professionals, voluntary organizations, teachers, students and interested individuals. It is our hope that this Yearbook will provide new insights to these targeted groups all over the globe.

Ingela Wadbring

Director at Nordicom, University of Gothenburg
and The International Clearinghouse on Children, Youth and Media

Foreword

This publication is one of the outcomes of a series of media and information literacy teacher training workshops that the UNAOC co-organized in 2013 and 2014 in Fez (Morocco) and in Cairo (Egypt).[1]

From early on, the UNAOC recognized the paramount importance that MIL has in building peaceful societies, where individuals from different cultural and religious backgrounds live side by side in harmony. As the UNAOC High Level-Group Report acknowledged:

> The constant exposure of populations to media presents an educational challenge, which has increased in the electronic and digital age. Evaluating information sources requires skills and critical thinking and is an educational responsibility the importance of which is often underestimated. Separating fact from opinion, evaluating text and image for bias, as well as constructing and deconstructing a text based on principles of logic are teachable skills. Media literacy instruction is not widely recognized for its importance as an aspect of civic and peace education and therefore few instructional programs have been developed as part of basic modern education.

The Report recommends that

> Media literacy programs should be implemented in schools, particularly at the secondary level, to help develop a discerning and critical approach to news coverage by media consumers and to promote media awareness and development of Internet literacy to combat misperceptions, prejudices and hate speech.[2]

Today, the need to implement media and information literacy in schools has only increased in extraordinary proportions, the pervasive power of social media has caught the attention not only of the publicists of consumer goods, but – tragically so – of the digital propaganda engines of groups spreading hate, polarization and extreme violence across the world. Media and information literacy should be understood as a fundamental piece in the efforts towards building resilience to the narratives of violent extremists. Media and information literacy, not as censorship, but as a platform for the development of critical thinking skills, creating counter narratives to the speech that glorifies death and violence.

We hope this book will inspire and become a resource for educators in the Middle East and North Africa region looking for opportunities to bring to their classrooms elements of MIL education, with the hope that it will facilitate the development of better understanding among individuals from different religious and cultural backgrounds.

We would like to thank the government of Spain for providing the funding for the above-mentioned workshops and facilitating this publication. We would also like to thank all the contributors of this book, particularly Magda Abu-Fadil for her double task by being the main editor in English and Arabic. Our gratitude as well goes to Alton Grizzle and UNESCO for joining forces with the UNAOC and making this book possible. A very special thank you to The International Clearinghouse on Children, Youth and Media at NORDICOM for their support in publishing this book and ensuring its global distribution.

Jordi Torrent

Project Manager
Media and Information Literacy Initiatives
United Nations Alliance of Civilizations

Notes
1. These workshops tested and discussed with secondary level educators the opportunities and challenges for the implementation of UNESCO's "MIL Curriculum for Teachers." Please see http://unesco.mil-for-teachers.unaoc.org
2. Please see http://www.unaoc.org/who-we-are/high-level-group

I.
General Perspectives on
Media and Information Literacy in the MENA Region

1. Introduction

Magda Abu-Fadil

There has never been a more propitious time than the present to promote, teach, and engage with media and information literacy (MIL) in all its permutations across the Middle East/North Africa region, notably the Arab states that are undergoing tectonic changes. The very notion of MIL is nascent in most of the countries surveyed herein and the application of programs falling under the MIL umbrella varies from almost non-existent to relatively dynamic, albeit on a limited scale. That is due, in great measure, to the variety of educational systems across the Arab world, although there is also common ground in that the top-down imparting of information (not always knowledge) has been the rule rather than the exception and can still be seen in schools and universities. Critical thinking has yet to take root across the board. There are examples of educational institutions where it has been encouraged but various factors come into play in its application.

Religious and social traditions in the region have dictated norms where certain figures such as parents and teachers are treated with respect and high regard and whose views and knowledge should not be questioned. Religious figures sometimes also double as educators and are supposed to be held in high esteem, so their approach to media and information literacy is likely colored by their moralistic and more conservative slant on the topic.

Then there is the matter of the different educational systems that exist in the region. There are public, private, and religious schools (that could be either publicly funded or privately subsidized) and learning is acquired mostly in Arabic (the common language in the Arab countries), French (where the French colonized), and English (where the British Empire spread its influence). This has also been complemented by the influence of the American entry into the educational and religious panorama through missionaries establishing their foothold in several countries, as well as teaching in local and/or ethnic languages like Amazigh in North African states, Kurdish in some parts of the Middle

East, and Armenian in Lebanon and Syria where an Armenian minority has lived for over a century. All of these elements have become part of the intertwined, integrated and multimedia content, interaction, and audiences/producers in the region.

Since media and information literacy as a field of study is relatively new, it continues to be explored and built upon worldwide, and is still taking baby steps in the Middle East and North Africa region. Quite often media literacy and information literacy are used interchangeably. For those with more academic backgrounds, information literacy takes precedence, with media literacy acting as an appendage. Those more in tune with the media landscape tend to focus on that aspect of the literacy spectrum. Ideally, those who have worked in media and have been involved in academia and are familiar with the latter's structures, tend to better straddle those two cultures through their comprehension of what exists and what needs to be done, provided, they, too, keep up with the fast changing technologies and priorities.

The book's authors shed light on this promising landscape with the hope that their enterprising work will provide the building blocks on which to erect a solid, yet flexible, structure. The following lineup sheds light on different national, local and individual efforts to create more awareness, show the existing shortcomings, and expand the circle of stakeholders involved in MIL.

In his *Preliminary Comparative Analysis of Media and Information Literacy in the MENA Region*, UNESCO's Alton Grizzle explored what is transpiring in the Middle East and North Africa. Grizzle provided a roadmap to the region, with an overview of its demographics and information and media environments in light of the large number of young citizens in the Arab countries. He also stressed that the conceptualization of media and information literacy had direct bearing on how MIL programs were designed, implemented, and monitored and their impact on the lives of youth, and citizens in general. The author's underlying rationale is that MIL in the Arab states is treated as a means to achieve a broad spectrum of social, political, and economic development goals. "On the other hand, it is also an end in itself, insofar as MIL enables people to acquire personal competencies, self-awareness, creativity and self-actualization" he said.

Meanwhile in Lebanon, Jad Melki, an associate professor of media studies at the American University of Beirut, and Lubna Maaliki, the director of the Media and Digital Literacy Academy of Beirut (MDLAB), shed light on the academy, its activities, and its evolution. MDLAB was launched in 2013 by a group of Arab and international academics "with the explicit aim of advancing digital and media literacy education in the region through training Arab media educators and developing digital and media literacy curricula, not only in Arabic, but also grounded in Arabic cultures and concerns." The academy has since been convened in summers to host academics, graduate students and media practitioners from different Arab countries wishing to hone their digital skills and gain better understanding of how those skills tie in with an understanding of media and information literacy. According to Melki: "Media and digital literacy is media education for the masses. It is the silent revolution that can counter the ideologies of greed, hate and death and fight for generalizing and globalizing social justice and egalitarian systems". The authors conclude their chapter by stressing that digital and media literacy cannot be only available for the shrinking pool of students who can afford a university education: "We need to create more accessible online and offline courses and workshops in Arabic to reach a broader audience. What's more, media and digital literacy needs to move into schools, all the way down to elementary teaching and beyond. We need to develop a critical mass of well-networked teachers, academics and researchers capable of taking digital and media literacy teaching and research to the next level."

Jordi Torrent, Project Manager of Media and Information Literacy at the United Nations Alliance of Civilizations (UNAOC), turned his attention to youth and digital media, with particular focus on workshops involving middle and high school educators in Egypt and Morocco. "The workshops were an opportunity for most of the educators to discuss for the first time the main concepts and building blocks of MIL pedagogy, understanding that traditional concepts of literacy (writing and reading print texts) are no longer enough skills for individuals to properly function as active participant citizens in contemporary societies," he said. While digital technology skills are an important prerequisite to succeed in today's world, Torrent stressed that media and information literacy was more 'humanities' than 'technology.' The educators in Cairo and Fez conducted a simple survey to gauge their students' media habits and discovered that television was the young respondents' favorite medium. Torrent wrote: "I put watching TV in quotes because youth today do not only watch TV (this is no longer the captive audience of the pre-Internet era), they consume other forms of media while watching TV." That includes uploading photos and videos to social media, sending text messages, and using multi platforms for multi purposes.

A very difficult scenario is the one presented by Lucy Nuseibeh and Mohammed Abu Arqoub on the concept of MIL in the occupied Palestinian territories of the West Bank, East Jerusalem and the Gaza Strip, why it is composite, and why it has to be on empowerment. The authors said the concept of 'information literacy' was more prevalent than 'media literacy.' What is particularly striking is that Palestinians have had to live in those territories under the control of Jordan and Egypt at one point, then under Israeli military occupation, and under their own form of government that has been divided between pro-Palestine Liberation Organization's (PLO, or Fateh in Arabic) supporters mostly on the West Bank of the Jordan River and annexed East Jerusalem, and the pro-Hamas advocates mostly in the Gaza Strip. The divisions have created their own set of challenges, not least of which are restrictions on Palestinians' movements, individual and collective punishment of those opposing the occupation, shortages of basic needs such as water, a chaotic media scene where conflicting jurisdictions of ministries play out in the control, licensing, airwaves rentals and fees of the media, and, a diet of crackdowns on the media. Against this backdrop, Nuseibeh and Abu Arqoub explained that MIL is still a relatively new concept in Palestine, both in the education system and in civil society. "There is also growing realization of the need to raise the general level of awareness on how to interact and deal with the media," they said. "These activities are being organized across all sectors of society: civil society, academia, government and the private sector." "But," they added, "more than developments in technology, is the prolonged Arab-Israeli conflict that has had, and continues to have, the most impact on everything to do with media, including media literacy, for Palestinians."

In tackling prospects, Dr. Abdul Ameer Al-Faisal noted that one might not be able to frame the information scene in Iraq, as it is evolving in a country that is swiftly turning to expanded use of information at all levels via unrestrained Internet access. "Iraq has kept pace with the current boom in terms of the evolution and proliferation of information into which individuals and organizations tap, to promote advanced technological developments to monitor, collect, process, store, retrieve, transfer and use information via computers, microfilm techniques, and telecommunications, to name a few, and their coupling and association to form what we call 'information technology,'" he said. There is more focus on Information and Communication Technologies (ICTs) than on an actual MIL mechanism, despite the emergence of a national information policy in Iraq. Dr. Al-Faisal concentrated on the role of libraries in Iraq as they have evolved over the years and technology is the predominant interest in this particular MIL equation. "In a nutshell, Iraq's information technology footprint began in 2003, and has witnessed quantum leaps," he wrote. "It has managed to make clear changes in the IT's general performance."

On the other side of the Arab world, Dr. Redouane Boujemaa, a research professor at the University of Algiers, addressed the issue of media literacy in Algeria and its correlation with various historical developments the educational system has been undergoing since the country's independence. Boujemaa acknowledged that Algeria had suffered from high illiteracy rates due to colonialism and its negative consequences and that at independence in 1962 the rate stood at 86 per cent. Since then and the country had not yet achieved the goal of integrating media and communication into the education system by using ICTs. Algeria has also gone through a transition of self-definition, where the educated few had functioned in French, the language of the former colonists, and where the need to recognize Arab and African roots required a re-examination of the educational system, and, by extension, the media landscape. In this chapter, the author zeroed in on the introduction and promotion of ICTs, as opposed to MIL since the concept has yet to take hold in Algeria and where teachers and students require extensive training and immersion into its multiple strata. "However, the introduction of technologies alone will not have a significant impact unless it is associated with new educational practices along with other educational activities and a new dynamic; a dynamic which will pave the way for a collective knowledge-building process," he concluded.

Abdelhamid Nfissi, from Sidi Mohamed Ben Abdellah University in Fez, Morocco and Drissia Chouit from Moulay Ismail University in Meknes, Morocco, examine the state of the art of media and information literacy in their country. They study how MIL was introduced in Morocco, the actions undertaken to promote it to better prepare citizens for the information age, and the main action plans and initiatives which will be undertaken in the future. According to Nfissi and Chouit, "media and information literacy is still in its infancy in Morocco. It is not included in the educational system.

It is not on the agenda of activists, policy makers and educators. People are not even informed about it to consider it. For many Moroccans, 'literacy' means the ability to read, write, and interpret printed messages." Media literacy was incorporated into Moroccan media studies courses, they wrote, but information literacy per se had not been integrated into university curricula. So there was a missing component. "After teaching ML and IL separately in semester 2, the course on Studies in Media and Cyber Culture taught in semester 4 involved the combination of ML and IL since it included both 'studies in media' and 'cyber-culture,'" they said. Since MIL was not on anyone's radar screen in Morocco, and believing strongly that it is important for youth, parents and every citizen, they decided to organize an international conference on the topic to make it known to Moroccan academics and to raise individuals' awareness of its importance in their lives. They have since engaged in other activities, detailed in their chapter, and are well on their way to developing a more rooted understanding and implementation of MIL.

Egypt, at the heart of the Arab countries, also boasts the largest population in the region, with 95 percent of some 85 million Egyptians occupying a mere three percent of the landmass. Urban congestion in most cities alongside an overloaded free public school system with woefully underpaid teachers, an over-priced private school network beyond the reach of average Egyptians, and a mix of private and state-controlled print, broadcast and online media marching to different drummers need qualified media interpreters to ensure citizens comprehend what they're consuming. Samy Tayie, a department head at Cairo University's Faculty of Mass Communication, admits his country is a bit of a latecomer to the world of media and information literacy despite the proliferation of news and entertainment outlets following transformative years after recent revolutions triggered by the 'Arab Spring' in 2010 and several changes of governments in Egypt. Tayie said his faculty had introduced a course on media and information literacy for undergraduate students in 2005 and that other public and private universities had followed suit. Moreover, his efforts included workshops, conferences and the creation of a kit aimed at making available resources for university professors to use in their teaching of MIL courses at different public and private institutions. But stumbling blocks abounded, as he explained: "The main challenge to media and information literacy in Egypt lies with policy makers. There is no policy on the matter. Some scholars and experts tried to include representatives from the Ministry of Education and Ministry of Higher Education in most of these activities but the problems and obstacles usually came from policy makers and those working at the Ministry of Education."

Yasar Durra of the Jordan Media Institute (JMI) admitted he first learned of MIL at a UNESCO conference in 2012 and that prior to that it was a series of fragmented values and goals taught within different media training curricula that did not include young school children. "In the past three years, however, the term has become part of the jargon used by staff and students at JMI and has assumed ever-greater momentum as students are regularly invited to take part in MIL workshops," he said. Durra said "that the most extensive and long-term MIL-focused training in Jordan took place in

2006 as part of the Newspapers in Education NIE Development Project, an initiative by the World Association of Newspapers and News Publishers (WAN-IFRA)." While schools in urban areas were more fortunate to receive the attention of, and funds from, policymakers, those in remote regions of Jordan, where they have had to host a steady flow of Syrian refugees escaping that war-torn country, lack the resources needed to help make the country more media and information literate. "In the present unsettled climate in the region where blame is laid on the failure of education systems to address the issues of pluralism, freedom of expression, and the right to information, it is imperative for the Ministry of Education to integrate MIL in the national curriculum as a matter of priority," said Durra who recommended an action plan to put Jordan on the international MIL map.

In the Sultanate of Oman, Dr. Naifa Eid Saleem, an assistant professor in the Department of Information Studies, found that the development of ICTs and the huge flow of information has made it easier for civil society actors to share information with each other, which the country's leader, Sultan Qaboos, had addressed in November 2008. Referring to the role of the Omani Ministry of Information and the Ministry of Heritage and Culture, in addition to an IT body whose aim is to turn the Sultanate into a sustainable knowledge society through ICTs, Saleem said these entities' goals were to provide citizens and residents with accurate information in addition to helping people process information and develop critical and analytical thinking. She also called for the introduction of a curriculum on media and information literacy in schools, urging the Ministry of Education to implement it, given the ministry's experience with learning resource centers that are the equivalent of school libraries. "If the content of the proposed 'media and information literacy' course does not correspond with the Ministry of Education's specific guidelines and benchmarks, the Learning Resources Center is expected to provide the course as it is directly linked to the media and information programs following approval by the Ministry," she wrote. Saleem further offered alternatives to those centers, saying that if they did not provide the MIL course, private and public universities should incorporate it within their education plans and make it a requirement for all students.

Magda Abu-Fadil, a veteran international journalist, academic and blogger, was an early adopter and proponent of the concepts of media literacy. In 1999, as the coordinator of a journalism program at a university in Lebanon, she participated with her students in a virtual media exchange project with a professor and students from the University of Missouri's School of Journalism. Through it, they were all part of an experiment in cross-cultural communication, values, newsworthiness, the use of nascent technology (notably the Internet in Lebanon), and finding out what really mattered in a media environment to people on two different continents. As a multilingual foreign correspondent who covered news from different capitals around the world, Abu-Fadil was also too well aware of the impact media had on audiences and was particularly sensitized to their often harmful effects on children and young people. With the proliferation of online, digital and social media across various platforms, Abu-Fadil became a strong advocate of media ethics and the need to create awareness about deconstructing messages, processes, outcomes and repercussions of all the interactivity, integration, convergence, and the overwhelming flow of communications that keeps morphing into new shapes at incredible speeds. "Subliminal messages tucked into programs may influence purchasing patterns. Conflict-filled episodes or video games could incite violence and lead to aggressive behavior. Even innocuous-seeming serials could traumatize young people into confusing fantasy with reality. All with the end result that an unsophisticated approach to the consumption of news, entertainment, and even the more popular 'edutainment' may contribute to dysfunctional societies and individuals, or, at the very least, confusion about how to react to the cacophony of messages overloading our sensory circuits," she wrote. Abu-Fadil has since been writing extensively on the subject, speaking at conferences on the need to adopt national MIL programs and training educators, students and media practitioners on the pros and cons of the media.

Carmilla Floyd and Gabriella Thinz present a refreshing hands-on approach in their chapter on empowering children and youth in Tunisia by fusing media and education. They took on the task of training students and teachers on how media and information literacy can help them find meaning in their lives, particularly in post-revolution Tunisia, following the self-immolation of street vendor Mohamed Bouazizi in December 2010 that marked what the media termed the 'Arab Spring.' Floyd and Thinz wrote:

> Picture this: A regime that unscrupulously controlled the media was forced to give up power. Before the revolution, censorship was commonplace. Journalists were often subjected to harassment. [1] For the first time, during the revolution Tunisian journalists went out on the streets and reported live – letting the public voice their opinion without any censorship.
>
> With the fall of the regime, the Ministry of Information, a once-feared instrument of media control, was abolished. Suddenly there was free speech. An explosion of new radio stations, TV channels and online news sites followed, while state broadcasters re-organized, and an endless stream of information and news was shared through online news services and social networks.

Enter the authors, who between them have extensive experience working with young people in Sweden and elsewhere, to provide capacity building through a series of workshops for youngsters, educators and media producers in different parts of the country aimed at helping children and young people become active and have a voice in matters of human rights and a democratic Tunisia. "To achieve this, we believe that adults also need to become media and information literate – teachers, youth leaders and parents. In addition we were determined to reach out to those who produce the media: journalists, editors, newsroom managers, TV producers and bloggers," they wrote.

Some Arab countries are making fast inroads and aiming to ascend to the next levels. These countries have the economic resources and/or a certain modicum of freedom, where creativity and vision are encouraged. In the United Arab Emirates, the Dubai

Foundation for Women and Children has been active in calling for the inclusion of media literacy in school curricula in a bid to mitigate the negative impact of television and online content on young people and lessen the effects of violence that various media can promote. The Mohammad Bin Rashid Program for Smart Learning – named after the UAE's vice president and ruler of Dubai – launched in 2012 has also been pro-active in promoting the latest high tech tools and equipping classrooms with digital tablets to replace traditional textbooks, cut down on paper use, and foster awareness on the need to protect the environment. A young Emirati illustrator has created an iPad book app for children. The Smart Learning Program has helped school students enjoy, and become more involved in, the learning process; better interact with their teachers and classmates in class and wherever they are thanks to high speed mobile connectivity; and, develop their curiosity to search for information via the Internet and other online channels. It is part of the Emirates' *Vision 2021* initiative. The program was awarded a prize for capacity building projects at the World Summit on the Information Society (WSIS) in Geneva, Switzerland in 2014. The *twofour54* media and entertainment hub in Abu Dhabi, a tax-free media zone that provides television and film services, is also home to a creative lab and training center available to students and professionals. In 2014 it began collaborating with major Arab media and entertainment organizations to support young media producers, gaming developers and platforms that conform to the country's norms and traditions.

In Saudi Arabia, progress on media and information literacy has been slower. Despite tremendous wealth, the country's education system has been more traditional and its teachers less attuned to the digital knowledge society. Smart learning has taken a back seat to the more classical methodologies but the desert kingdom is pressing ahead trying to catch up with other countries in the region. Distance learning is catching on and teachers are encouraged to adopt it as one of several teaching/learning methods. While command of foreign languages has proven a key to better understanding and interaction with media and information, the Saudi public educational system has failed to produce up-to-date English language curricula as well as qualified instructors who use creative teaching methods, as opposed to subjecting their charges to learning by rote. But all is not lost. There have been efforts underway to turn the tide, if only incrementally, in accordance with religious and cultural traditions. Ultimately, there's much ground to cover and MIL in the MENA region remains a work in progress.

2. Preliminary Comparative Analysis of Media and Information Literacy in the MENA Region

Alton Grizzle

Media and information literacy (MIL) is coming of age. It should no longer be overlooked by governments and policy makers of the world given the emerging huge body of academic literature supporting the relevance of MIL. MIL is a necessary subject of learning, a way of learning and self-awareness, self-guided socialization or self-regulation. It is a tool that can be applied to all forms of development issues and contexts. Finally, MIL is a set of 21st Century competencies that can ultimately lead to citizens' empowerment, self-expression and intercultural and interreligious dialogue.

In marked similarity, the UNESCO *Education for All Global Monitoring Report 2006*, drawing on years of work of many academic scholars, proposes four ways to understand literacy and has evolved based on disciplinary traditions. First, literacy is considered a separate set of tangible skills such as reading, writing and numeracy, that is independent of context and that extends to skills to access information and knowledge. Second, literacy is viewed as reliant on context, going beyond acquisition of skills to bringing to the fore the use and application of these skills to real-life situations. Third, literacy is seen as a learning process. As persons learn, they gradually and actively become literate. In this sense literacy is both a means and an end. Finally, literacy is considered as 'text' or 'subject matter' – located in communication, politics and power that can take on multiple forms. Written language is one form of text through which learning is communicated. But there are other texts, such as oral communication, media (radio, television, and newspaper), technological, art and artifacts. Media and technology are associated with all four traditions of literacy. In the 21st Century, more than in any other period of history, learning, socialization, cultural exchange, political, and social activism are being mediated by media, technology, the Internet and the flood of information they bring. Media and information literacy can empower all citizens to understand what new dimensions media and technology bring to their experiences. In the 21st Century more than ever before, citizens are learning more about themselves and the world around them outside the classroom (Watt, 2012; See also Macedo, 2007[1]). Media and information literacy is that bridge between learning in the classroom and learning that takes place outside of the classroom enabling both to enrich each other. This calls for new pedagogy of learning and a greater focus on non-traditional literacy competencies. MIL is as relevant to the Middle East and North Africa as it is to every other region of the world.

Abu-Fadil (2007) wrote, "Media literacy and awareness have long been neglected in the Arab world... Media literacy as a subject is rarely taught in schools in any organized way and is often couched in vague terminologies within university courses that fail to address the raison d'etre of mass communication tools..." (p.1). Six years later, etching Lebanon and Qatar as case studies, she acknowledged that there is slow progress with respect to the existence and development of media literacy programs in the Middle East and North Africa and that "critical thinking is not embedded in the education systems of many of the countries [though many experts would agree that this phenomenon is common in all regions of the world]..." but many inventive educators and other actors are implementing projects that enable students to think critically and to explore multi-modal learning through multiple media platforms (Abu-Fadil, 2013). Watt (2012) cited Mihailidis (2009, p. 65) as arguing, "it is not enough to focus on media content alone, but also on citizens as the nexus of the information world."

The articulation of MIL as an area that deserves the attention of the development community and national governments, the depth of awareness and implementation of MIL initiatives vary from region to region. The depth and breadth of what has changed in media and information literacy awareness and implementation in the Middle East/ North Africa since the first international meeting on media literacy in the region – the Riyadh International Conference on Media Education in March 2007 – is the subject of this chapter, and indeed this entire book. I first give a sketch of the media and information environment in the region. I then navigate a basic framework for a preliminary critical comparative analysis of MIL in the region using four questions:

- How do experts in the MENA region conceptualize MIL?

- What is the underlying rationale for MIL in the Arab States?

- Are these countries harmonizing the field?

- Do they have national policies and strategies on MIL?

Overview – demographics, information and media environments

The Middle East and North Africa (MENA), often erroneously used interchangeably with the Arab States, covers the region that includes countries from northern and north-eastern Africa and southwest Asia[2]. The Middle East includes Iran and Turkey, two non-Arab countries. The 22 countries in the MENA, according to the League of Arab States, in alphabetical order are Algeria, Bahrain, the Comoros, Djibouti, Egypt,

Table 1. Media Characteristics in the MENA Countries

| Country | Population[8] | Proportion of population on the Internet (%)[9] | Number of Libraries[9] | Radio stations, television stations[10] and newspapers | | | | |
				Radio stations	Proportion of households with radios (%)[11]	Television stations	Proportion of households with television sets (%)	Number of Newspaper-titles[12]
Algeria	39 667 000	17	760	34	60 (2009)	46	...	17
Bahrain	1 377 000	97	209	5	32 (2013)	4	99 (2013)	6
Comoros	788 000	7	3	6	...	...	...	1
Djibouti	888 000	9	4	3	50 (2004)	1	...	...
Egypt	91 508 000	48	11 048	65	20 (2013)	64	97 (2013)	...
Iraq	36 423 000	8	11 395	55	...	28	...	...
Jordan	7 595 000	45	5 687	29	...	4	...	4
Kuwait	3 892 000	87	132	18	...	13	...	8
Lebanon	5 851 000	67	642	54	...	12	...	15
Libya	6 278 000	22	41	22	...	12	...	4
Mauritania	4 068 000	11	38	16	...	1	...	3
Morocco	34 378 000	60	735	15	67 (2009)	8	100 (2011)	24
Oman	4 491 000	66	1 121	14	36 (2010)	13	94 (2011)	6
Qatar	2 235 000	97	208	12	25 (2013)	1	95 (2013)	5
Saudi Arabia	31 540 000	59	5 317	76	...	117	...	12
Somalia	10 787 000	2	4	12	...	4	...	...
State of Palestine	4 668 000	1		...	3	...	...	3
Sudan	40 235 000	24	4 851	14	...	4	...	22
Syria	18 502 000	27	1 760	55	...	44	...	...
Tunisia	11 254 000	45	947	47	67 (2012)	26	98 (2012)	10
United Arab Emirates	9 157 000	93	1 364	23	53 (2012)	15	95 (2012)	55
Yemen	26 832 000	19	12	9	...	3	...	6

Note: Readers should use this table carefully when making comparison given the unavailability of complete data from a single source and in some cases data are not available for the same set of dates.

Iraq, Jordan, Kuwait, Lebanon, Libya, Mauritania, Morocco, Oman, Qatar, Saudi Arabia, Somalia, the State of Palestine, Sudan, Syria, Tunisia, the United Arab Emirates, and Yemen. This configuration varies from source to source. For instance, the World Bank references a configuration that consists of 14 countries including Israel[3]. The United Nations Human Rights/Office of the High Commissioner for Human Rights lists 19 countries as part of the MENA region[4]. This configuration also includes Israel but excludes the Comoros, Somalia and Sudan and Djibouti.

The region has an estimated population of 416,000,000[5]. Approximately 20 per cent of the population of the MENA region, one in five people, are youth between the ages of 15 and 24 (Assaad and Roudi-Fahimi, 2007). The number of youth in the region stood at 95 million in 2005 (ibid). The youth population is almost evenly distributed across Arab countries ranging from 15 per cent to 23 per cent with only four countries having less than 18 per cent of youth as a percentage of their population. "The extent to which this large group of young people will become healthy and productive members of their societies depends on how well governments and civil societies invest in social, economic, and political institutions that meet the current needs of young people." (ibid)

Thirty-seven percent of the MENA population have access to the Internet[6]. At the time of this writing, the author could not find sources providing the number of archives in the region as a whole or by country. Public, academic and special libraries stood at over 47,364. Radio stations, television stations and newspapers stood at 584, 420 and 201, respectively in MENA (See details and sources in Table 1).

Conceptualization of MIL by experts in the MENA region

Those who follow my writings on information literacy, media literacy, digital literacy or media and information literacy would know that I go through pains to stress the necessity of a coherent approach, focusing on key commonalities and interrelated competencies, rather than a disjointed definitional approach. This is not to belabor a point but, the conceptualization of media and information literacy has direct bearing on how MIL programs are designed, implemented, monitored and ultimately their impact on the lives of youth, and citizens in general. In a September 2015 meeting with Dr. Fahad Sultan Alsultan, Deputy Secretary-General, King Abdul Aziz Centre for National Dialogue, he reminded me of the transformative potential of creating knowledge in a local language (in this case – Arabic) as opposed to simply translating knowledge or concepts from one language to another. Dr Alsultan is a senior representative from Saudi Arabia, which is one of the lead partners and supporters of UNESCO's media and information literacy thrust in MENA. He was right. He also acknowledged that when translation of knowledge from one language to another takes place adaptation should be in the mix. By saying this he recognized that to create new knowledge, it is often necessary to borrow and adapt from other sources and languages. As Jenkins (Jenkins et al., 2009: 32) posits, "most of the classics we teach in the schools are themselves the product of appropriation and transformation, or what we would call sampling and remixing." As

Professor Redouane Boudjema said in his chapter when reporting on ICTs and media literacy in Algeria, "Traditionally, knowledge and culture were at the core of several philosophical debates as well as various social, political and ideological conflicts. The current education systems and institutions were no exception. Since the second decade of the last century, mass communication has played at least a pivotal role in either overestimating or underestimating the importance of education." All the authors of this book employed that approach here or in other articles written by them; they directly or indirectly sampled and remixed concepts of information literacy, media literacy, digital literacy or media and information literacy in their discourses.

Jad Melki and Lubna Maaliki, Lebanon: Here and in and other academic writings a strong leaning to critical digital competencies, 'digital media literacy.' (See Melki, 2013)

Jordi Torrent, Morocco and Egypt: Presents MIL as a composite concept based on the UNESCO model.

Lucy Nusseibeh and Mohammed Abu Arqoub, Palestine: In this chapter, the authors focus primarily on media literacy. They propose that media literacy is teaching about how media work as well as how citizens can effectively engage with media. It is both protective and proactive. Protective in connection with enabling people to "analyze media content and read between the lines, understand the messages behind the images, and therefore become less vulnerable" and proactive to the extent that people are empowered to "to work creatively – not as technicians, but again in regard to content, so they can produce their own media messages." In their conceptualization, Internet literacy, citizen journalism as well as Master of Arts and Bachelor of Arts degrees in media are connected to media literacy.

Abdul Ameer Al-Faisal, Iraq: Abdul Ameer Al-Faisal in his chapter focused on information and an understanding of how information is created and disseminated as being central to development in Iraq. The author used the word information 41 times and information technology 9 times. He mentioned computer literacy only once in referring to the objectives of the National Information Technology Strategy in Iraq. While he highlighted the revolutionary impact that new technologies have had on media and freedom of expression in Iraq and the centrality of libraries and documentation centres – media literacy, information or MIL as concepts was not mentioned though evidently implicit in his arguments.

Redouane Boudjemaa, Algeria: The very title of this chapter suggests a particular focus. The author juxtaposes ICTs in education, media literacy and education and communication. He defines media literacy as "the process of optimally using means of communication in order to meet the goals stated in the state's education and communication policy. Another definition is that the process consists of teaching and training students as well as teachers on how to deal with media content selectively and consciously in order to avoid their negative impact, leading to an awareness in dealing with media messages and images."

Abdelhamid Nfissi and Drissia Chouit, Morocco: These authors note, "the potentials of media and information cannot be realized if people lack the ability to access, analyze, evaluate and create media content." They also posit that media and information literacy is "providing individuals with the skills and tools to critically evaluate, process and interpret the content of messages, sounds and powerful images of our multimedia culture." As they see it, information literacy and media literacy are natural transitions from basic literacy given the proliferation of media and technology. In their analysis, information literacy is being able to assess authority, credibility, and reliability of information, identify information needs in cyberspace, how to visit the relevant websites and to use ICTs effectively. Based on their experiences in teaching media studies and cyber culture in the Department of English, they see the necessity for the combination of information literacy and media literacy as media and information literacy (see also Nfissi, 2014 and Nfissi, 2013).

Samy Tayie, Egypt: While no particular reference is made to conceptualization of MIL in this chapter, in describing MIL activities in Egypt, the author alludes to the need for young people to understand media and to effectively use social media.

Yasar Durra, Jordan: The author made no reference to what MIL entails. Having first encountered the concept through the UNESCO MIL Curriculum, the concept quickly became central to the work of the Jordan Media Institute. He thus aptly used this umbrella concept to describe a series of activities related to youth engagement in political accountability, storytelling, simulation exercises for youth as a platform for opinion and expression, news in education, and, "mentoring and training journalists, journalism students and representatives of civil society organizations on the power of data to help make this dialogue more effective and informed."

Naifa Eid Saleem, Oman: Dr. Saleem, based on her background in information sciences, places emphasis on the data and information aspect of MIL. She writes that there is a need to "provide citizens with the right skills and information or the so-called 'Media and Information Culture' covering knowledge as well as attitudes. Access to knowledge is about the data needed, their timing, how and where to get them, how to analyze them, criticize them, arrange them, and most importantly, how to use them ethically." She outlines MIL as described by UNESCO and embraces MIL as a composite concept.

Magda Abu-Fadil, Lebanon: Magda Abu-Fadil used the term MIL throughout her discourse though she has used the terms media literacy and media education in other articles (Abu-Fadil, 2013). She ties MIL closely to journalism education and media ethics. She underlines the mixed media environment that exists in Lebanon, games, applications, animated cartoons, comic books, posters and street signs, newspaper, television, digital and mobile media, radio, and multimedia online and offline. Magda Abu-Fadil writes, "In Lebanon, MIL is tied to education, pedagogy, religion, and media in the general sense. Information is often brought in as an adjunct, with technology playing a supportive role."

Carmilla Floyd and Gabriella Thinz, Tunisia: These authors, while using the term media and information literacy, did not offer a specific or explicit definition. However they pointed to MIL as a tool for youth empowerment and civic engagement. They noted that MIL initiatives in Tunisia received inspiration from similar projects in Palestine, Belarus and Sweden where MIL is used to combat gender stereotypes, promote respect for human rights and "sustainable development that improves conditions for peace, stability…."

Other experts from the region have also presented important perspectives on MIL. Only two are noted here for the sake of brevity. Saleh (2011: 35) argues that media education (media literacy or MIL) should necessarily begin in primary school when fundamental knowledge skills and habits are formed. "Children must learn how to question the reliability and validity of decisions and to offer criticism and alternatives, as well as to understand that there exist other viewpoints, solutions or perspectives in addition to their own." For Gomaa (2014: 33), media literacy or MIL includes being able to think critically, be creative, as well as "exercising one's duties and rights as an active citizen rather than be [a subject] subjects of the state." Moghtar, Majiid et al. (2008: 196) purports, "…Teaching information literacy does not merely involve library and bibliographic instructions or the ability to use different information sources effectively. It also includes teaching critical and analytical thinking skills regarding information, as well as the ability to generate new ideas from current information and prior knowledge. Most importantly, it includes what students will be able to know, think or do as a result…".

What is clear from the above analysis is that there are a variety of viewpoints about how MIL should be conceptualized in the MENA region. However one cannot help but notice the convergence and complementarity of perspectives offered. MENA is no different from the rest of the world in grappling with ensuring clarity to delineating the field and process of media and information literacy.

Underlying rationale for MIL in the Arab States

The purpose or rationale for media and information literacy is to some extent implicit in, or at the very least, grows out of the myriad of conceptualizations of the field. Based on the contribution of authors in this book, other sources, preliminary analysis of the findings of research that I am undertaking, MIL is treated as a means to achieve a broad spectrum of social, political, and economic development goals. On the other hand, it is also an end in itself, insofar as MIL enables people to acquire personal competencies, self-awareness, creativity and self-actualization (Grizzle, 2013)[13]. Some experts question the overemphasis of the 'instrumentalization' of MIL over citizens' acquisition of these competencies for personal use, enjoyment and creativity (see Madrenas, 2014). Frau-Meigs (2011: 334) posits, "For now, media education [MIL] is seen as a kind of panacea by all partners (private, public and civic) but in many ways it is being instrumentalized as the sweet wrapper around the bitter pill of neo-liberal polices…".

These rationales include:

- Combatting stereotypes and promoting intercultural understanding (Saudi Arabia, Qatar, many Arab States) (See Abu-Fadil, 2007).

- Promoting press freedom and understanding of the news.

- Increasing access to information and easing the free flow of ideas (Qatar, Lebanon) (ibid).

- Combatting the influence of media in the lives of youth (Egypt) (See Tayie, 2011[14], 2013 and 2014; See also Saleh, 2009)

- Journalists needing digital skills to compete with the influx of news from outside and within the country (Lebanon)

- Enabling young people to use social networks for productive and development purposes other than entertainment (Lebanon, Egypt).

- Advocating for media ethics (Lebanon).

- For young people, challenging world views in media and being critical of the tendency towards monolithic secular and religious media in the Middle East (Lebanon, Egypt, Morocco, Palestine).

- Protecting and preserving local cultures and intercultural dialogue (Morocco, Saudi Arabia, and Egypt) (Nfissi, 2013 and 2014).

- Establishing a basis for citizen journalism (Tunisia, Egypt Jordan, Lebanon, and Qatar).

- Enhancing quality education (Algiers, Oman).

- Improving quality research and decision-making (Morcco, Algieria, Oman).

- Promoting peace and non-violence (Palestine, Egypt, and Tunisia).

Trends towards national policies on MIL in the MENA region

There is no country in the Arab States Region with a national policy on MIL. Countries like Morocco and Qatar are perhaps heading in that direction, given related decisions taken by these governments and national initiatives supported by them. However, most Arab States have related policies and laws based on constitutions and information and broadcast regulations. These include ICT policies and strategies, access to information laws, education policies, cultural policies (all countries in MENA), and media and communication policies and national youth policies. See Table 2 below.

Table 2. Strategies on Information-, ICT-, and media policies/media laws in the MENA Region

Country	National Information Policies/Strategy	National ICT Policies/Strategy	National Communication/ Media Policies/Laws
Algeria	Yes	Yes	Yes
Bahrain	Yes	Yes[15]	Yes[16]
The Comoros	N/A	N/A	N/A
Djibouti	N/A	Yes[17] (Evidence of this online but not full version)	N/A
Egypt	Yes	Yes[18]	Yes
Iraq	N/A	In Draft or being prepared	Yes
Jordan	Yes[19]	Yes	Yes
Kuwait	Yes	Yes	Yes
Lebanon	N/A	Yes[20]	Yes
Libya	N/A	N/A	N/A
Mauritania	N/A	Yes[21]	N/A
Morocco	Yes	Yes[22]	Yes
Oman	Yes	Yes[23]	N/A
Qatar	Yes	Yes[24]	Yes
Saudi Arabia	Yes[25]	Yes[26]	N/A
Somalia	N/A	No[27]	N/A
State of Palestine	N/A	Yes	N/A
Sudan	N/A	Yes[28]	N/A
Syria	In Draft	Yes	N/A
Tunisia	Yes	Yes[29]	N/A
United Arab Emirates	No	Yes	N/A
Yemen	Yes	Yes	N/A

Source (if not indicated): National Profiles of the Information Society http://www.escwa.un.org/wsis/profiles.html

A summary and analysis of as well as recommendations concerning media related laws in Bahrain, Kuwait Saudi Arabia, United Arab Emerate, Qatar, and Oman was carried out by the Doha Centre for Media Freedom and written by Dr. Matt J. Duffy[30]. A broad analysis of these existing policies, strategies or laws is needed to ascertain the extent to which they cover elements to ensure media and information literacy for all. For instance, are there provisions in these policies that promote, direct and guide the design and implementation of programs to enable citizens' acquisition of critical thinking competencies about information, media and ICTs? This is the subject of another paper and comprehensive research. However, contemplating these policies has implications for the future articulation of national MIL policies in the MENA region and elsewhere. One implication is whether these policies, strategies or laws are geared towards citizens' empowerment in contrast to a focus on institutions, business or government processes, opens the possibility for the articulation of media and information literacy policies. Menou (2002), for example gives an insightful analysis of how information literacy (IL) could be integrated in national ICTs policies referring to cases from Latin America.

While it is clear that citizens can be, and are often, reached through institutions, policies that serve institutions may not necessarily serve citizens. Media and information literacy policies should not be developed in isolation. Rather, they should be placed in the broader ecology and seen as an enabler to the efficacy of other related policies that may include youth, cultural and educational policies (Grizzle, Moore et al., 2013).

Figure 1 below shows the interrelationship of various national policies. Purposeful collaboration across government ministries or entities is necessary to lead to multilateral policy development, a sort of crossing of policies that embeds MIL in relevant aspects of public policies (cf. idem). It is crucial to note here that national MIL policies and strategies are not only the remit of national governments. All information providers such as libraries, archives, media organizations, telecommunication organizations, publishers, Internet service providers, museums, etc., should engage in internal MIL policy formulation and outreach strategies to benefit their audiences and users.

Figure 1. UNESCO Media and Information Literacy Policy and Strategy Guidelines

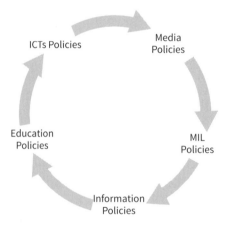

Source: Grizzle, Moore et al., 2013.

The articulation and application of national/regional MIL policies and strategies should consider five interwoven approaches:

1) Convergence – a joined-up approach as described in Figure 1 above;

2) Rights-based approach – recognizing that MIL is a direct offshoot of the right to quality education, the right to access to information, the right to freedom of expression, and the right to peace and security;

3) A shift from a focus only on protecting citizens from potentially negative aspects of information, media and technology to empowering them to self-regulate as well as appropriate the benefits of the information, technology and media-driven age (Mihailidis, 2008);

4) Building an inclusive knowledge society/communication and information for development, including a culture and linguistic diversity approach.

5) A gender-based approach – underscoring equal access, participation and leadership of women and men in the information life cycle, media and technology development, and providing men and women equal access to MIL education (see detail analysis in ibid).

National strategies on MIL and their implementation

There are no systemized national MIL strategies. In the main, there are many important, but often fragmented, workshops and conferences. Pockets of success, mostly led by universities and in some cases libraries and NGOs, are highlighted here:

- MENTOR Project, Cairo University, Egypt – MENTOR International Media Education Association.

- Alexandria Library, High-level colloquium on information literacy and lifelong learning, Alexandria, Egypt.

- American University in Cairo, information literacy instruction labs[31].

- Sidi Mohamed Ben Abdellah Univeristy, Morocco – International Institute on MIL.

- Birzeit University´s Media Development Center, Palestine – Media Education (MIL) Program – Cooperation with Ministry of Education and development of materials for teachers and students[32].

- Doha Centre for Media Freedom – MIL Program involving 10 per cent of public and private elementary schools in Qatar, with projections to implement it in all 150 elementary schools.

- Qatar University Library, Information literacy program and the Qatar chapter of the Information Literacy Network of the Gulf[33].

- MENTOR/Cairo University taking steps to set-up a Master of Arts in MIL.

- MIL Toolkit for the Arab States supported by UNESCO.

- Ministry of Education in Morocco leading the national integration of MIL in teacher education supported by UNESCO.

- Magda Abu-Fadil conducted workshops at the Two Sacred Hearts School and International College for high school seniors (Lebanon), as well as for teachers and coordinators at International College (Lebanon), for teachers and coordinators of dozens of schools in Qatar, for journalists in Morocco, Tunisia and Mauritania, and in a remote media literacy (ML) program with the University of Missouri School of Journalism, to name a few.

- Information Literacy Program in a Private School in Lebanon[34].

- The Interactive Cultures research group is working in partnership with the US-based technology company Meedan on *Developing Citizen Journalists in the Arab region*, (Tunisia, Egypt Jordan, Lebanon).

- Maghreb network of media and information literacy (IL) experts launched by UNESCO[35].

Where governments are involved, there is evidence of possibly more sustained or long and broad-based MIL programs. This is evident in Qatar, through the government's MIL program at the Doha Centre for Media Freedom.[36]

Are MIL Programs in These Countries Harmonizing the Field?

- Activities are generally either ML- or IL-related.

- In some cases, ML or IL includes digital/ICT skills.

- In a few cases, MIL is being considered (the use of the UNESCO MIL Curriculum for Teachers) in countries recently taking systematic actions to promote media and information literacy. These countries include Morocco, Egypt, Qatar, Lebanon, Tunisia, and Jordan.

Do many MIL experts/practitioners live and work in the region?

At the time of this writing, I was in the middle of initial analysis of research, one component of which was to ascertain the existence and levels of media and information literacy experts globally. The research explores criteria such a level and area of qualification, level and period of involvement in MIL, academic writings in MIL, etc. In the MENA region, over 150 experts from various disciplines such information, media, communication, education and other practitioners, were invited to complete the questionnaire. Preliminary analysis indicated that library and information specialists, media and communication specialists, and journalists were the main drivers of media and information literacy education. With respect to experts who spend more than half their professional time on MIL-related activities, Table 3 depicts how the MENA region compares to the rest of the world.

Table 3.   Arab States Compared to Other Regions on MIL Experts

MENA	Other Regions of the World
Less than or equal to	Sub-Sahara Africa
Less than	Latin America
Less than	Asia Pacific
Less than	Caribbean
Less than	Europe
Less than	North America

Using the UNESCO Media and Information Literacy Policy and Strategy Guidelines and the Media and Information Literacy Assessment Framework as a basis, literature review of MIL in the MENA region, including chapters in this book, as well as preliminary analysis of the primary research that I am undertaking, Table 4 offers an initial classification of the take-up of MIL in MENA countries across four possible scenarios.

Table 4.   Initial Classification of the Take-Up of MIL in MENA Countries

Scenario	Countries
MIL is largely unknown and undeveloped	Bahrain, Libya, Iraq, Kuwait, Somalia, Sudan, Syria, the Comoros, Yemen, Mauritania, Palestine, and Oman.
MIL is nascent and quite novel as a concept	Djibouti, Algeria and the United Arab Emirates.
MIL is somewhat established within specialist programs and institutions and some citizens benefit from access to these initiatives	Qatar, Jordan, Lebanon, Morocco, Saudi Arabia, Tunisia and Egypt.
MIL is widely understood and MIL programs are available to most citizens	

Systemizing MIL in the MENA region and standing together through regional and international alliances

The future for MIL in the MENA region is dependent on all stakeholders, individuals, private and public organizations or institutions, international development organizations, and civil society in general. This preliminary analysis attempted to illuminate some first steps that should be considered such as a harmonized approach in conceptualizing and articulating MIL competencies, recognizing that there already exist related public policies in the MENA region on which MIL policies can be built, and the need to create consensus around MIL diffusion. There is undoubtedly meaningful experience in the region on which to build. A main challenge for the region – lack of policy – has been noted by Samy Tayie, a leading expert, in various regional and international conferences. A key starting point then is to raise the awareness about MIL among policy makers and educators and to strengthen concrete partnerships among actors in the region to accelerate MIL for all. This was the subject of the *Regional Forum on Media and Information Literacy (MIL) in the Arab States* in Cairo, Egypt, held April 22-23, 2015 and organized by UNESCO in collaboration with the League of Arab States, the Swedish International Development Corporation Agency (SIDA), Al Ahram Canadian University, and the Egyptian National Commission for UNESCO.

It grouped some 140 participants from Algeria, Bahrain, Egypt, Jordan, Kuwait, Lebanon, Libya, Morocco, Oman, Palestine, Sudan, Tunisia, Yemen, and the UAE. Participants included policy makers, curriculum experts, educators, and media and information experts. Ms. Zainab Al-Wakeel, Assistant Secretary-General of the Egyptian

National Commission for UNESCO, representing Prof. El Sayed Abdel-Khalek, Minister of Higher Education of Egypt, Dr. Haifa Abu Ghazaleh, the Assistant Secretary-General, League of Arab States, Dr. Farouk Ismail, President of Ahram Canadian University, underlined the importance of media and information literacy in the Arab states in the present social and political context. They also stressed the need to introduce literacies at an early stage of the students', and citizens in general, lives in schools and clubs, work, on the Internet or social media, and other places (cf.[37]).

In connection with enhancing partnerships among MIL actors in the region, in 2013 UNESCO launched the Global Alliance for Partnerships on MIL (GAPMIL) with three objectives: 1) articulating concrete partnerships to drive media and information literacy (MIL) development and impact; 2) enabling the MIL community to speak as one voice on certain critical matters, particularly as it relates to policies; and 3) further deepening the strategy for MIL by providing a common platform for MIL-related networks and associations. A formal call for membership in the alliance was carried through an on-going survey in English, French and Spanish. While this is anecdotal, since then only 13 organizations from the MENA region have joined the alliance which now has over 600 members (See Table 5).

Table 5.   GAPMIL Members from the MENA region

Name of Organization	City	Country
Doha Centre for Media Freedom	Doha	Qatar
Delta University for Science and Technology	Mansoura	Egypt
Search For Common Ground Morocco	Rabat	Morocco
Zayed University	Abu Dhabi	United Arab Emirates
Supreme Council for Information and Communication Technology (ict QATAR)	DOHA	Qatar
Editore libri e comunicazione (Book Publisher)	Cairo	Egypt
International Centre of Film for Children and Youth (CIFEJ) Headquarters	Tehran	Iran
Petra University	Amman	Jordan
Al-Hussein Bin Talal University	Ma'an	Jordan
Hashemite University	Zarqa	Jordan
Regional Centre for Media and Information Literacy and Intercultural Dialogue	Fez	Morocco
Jordan Media Institute	Amman	Jordan

The Arab States' Chapter of the Global Alliance on Partnerships on Media and Information Literacy was launched at the Forum. A detailed action plan for the Arab States GAPMIL Chapter was finalized along with committee members from 14 countries.

UNESCO has developed four vital international resources that, through adaptation, can help to systemize national MIL policies and programs in the MENA region. In the area of *curriculum*, there is the Media and Information Literacy Curriculum for Teachers. This is adaptable to all levels of society and is available in Arabic.[38] In the area of *policy and strategy*, countries can access the model Media and Information Literacy Policy and Strategy resource[39] which will be available in Arabic by the first quarter of 2016 through the UNESCO and Saudi Arabia Culture of Peace Project. In the area of *monitoring and assessment*, UNESCO has produced the Global Media and Information Literacy Assessment Framework: Country Readiness and Competencies.[40] In the area of *teaching resources*, to make these more accessible to teachers and trainers, UNESCO has partnered with the United Nations Alliance of Civilizations (UNAOC), also in connection with the UNESCO and Saudi Arabia Culture of Peace Project, to set up an international online multimedia, intercultural MIL teaching resources tool. This online platform, while available to the public, is still under development with components in Arabic, French, and other languages.

Finally, systemizing national MIL policies and strategies requires capitalizing on new forms and modes of educating citizens. To increase access to media and information literacy among youth in the Arab States, UNESCO has partnered with the American University of Beirut and is preparing the first Massive Open Online Course (MOOC) in media and information literacy in Arabic. It is an adaptation of an international MIL and intercultural MOOC developed by UNESCO. The Arabic version will include cooperation among many other universities in the MENA region. The reader of this article should recognize that the traditional information literacy part is not as rich as the traditional media literacy characteristic. This is due to a general absence of relevant literature. Attempts will be made to address this in a future article. This article and indeed the entire book, attempts to put stakeholders in the know about MIL in the MENA region. When one does not know and thus does nothing, a certain course of action is required. When one knows and still does nothing, other questions are raised. In June 2015, I was browsing through the latest book published by the renowned expert Paul Zurkowski, who coined the concept 'Information Literacy.' The book is titled, *Action Literacy – Empowering "We the People" in the information age.* During my reading of this book I learned of a new form of literacy called 'Action Literacy.' According to Zurkowski, Action Literacy means "the ability to transform good information into ethical action. Being action literate means that one's ethical actions are firmly rooted in good information." He goes on to say "the actions are helpful. The actions are good. Right actions are carried out even when difficult." There are many inferences we could draw from this definition of action literacy.

Here, UNESCO and I propose two points for reflection:

One, Action Literacy is part of media and information literacy (MIL). When we are fully media and information literate we should take positive and purposeful actions concerning how we use, engage with, act upon the positive and negative impact of information, media and technology in our personal, economic and social life.

Two, armed with information about MIL in the MENA region, UNESCO encourages all stakeholders to consider the challenges facing the region. We first need the commitment of all players. We can do this together but we must first commit and take action.

Like the 13-year-old girl, who was determined to tackle cyberbullying by creating the innovation software, ReThink,[41] we must rethink the relevance of media and information literacy in the MENA region and globally. We must take rapid and innovative actions to fuel change.

Notes

1. Editors note: Not in list of references.
2. An independent view of the Arab World website, http://www.arableagueonline.org. Accessed on September 7, 2015. (NB: This is not the official website of the League of Arab States. See http://www.arableagueonline.org/remark. The official website is http://www.lasportal.org/ar/Pages/default.aspx and there is no English equivalent).
3. http://www.worldbank.org/en/region/mena. Accessed on 26 October 2015.
4. http://www.ohchr.org/EN/Countries/MenaRegion/Pages/MenaRegionIndex.aspx. Accessed on 26 October 2015.
5. This is based on the configuration of MENA by the League of Arab States.
6. ITU ICT Facts And Figures – The World In 2015. Geneva: International Telecommunication Union, 2015. http://www.itu.int/en/ITU-D/Statistics/Pages/facts/default.aspx Accessed on September 16, 2015.
7. United Nations, Department of Economic and Social Affairs, Population Division (2015). World Population Prospects: The 2015 Revision. http://esa.un.org/unpd/wpp/ or directly at, http://esa.un.org/unpd/wpp/publications/files/key_findings_wpp_2015.pdf. Accessed on September 16, 2015.
8. Internetlivestats.com, "Internet Users By Country (2014) – Internet Live Stats." http://www.internetlivestats.com/. Accessed on September 16, 2015.
9. Oclc.org, "Global Library Statistics." www.oclc.org/content/dam/oclc/globallibrarystats/globalstats_countrydataset_oclcweb.xlsx Accessed on September 16, 2015.
10. Cia.gov, *The World Factbook*. https://www.cia.gov/library/publications/the-world-factbook/. Accessed on September 16, 2015.
11. https://www.quandl.com/collections/society/households-with-a-radio-by-country. Accessed on November 7, 2015.
12. Data.uis.unesco.org, 'Communication and Information: Newspapers'. http://data.uis.unesco.org/. Accessed on September 16, 2015.
13. Editors note: Reference not found.
14. Editors note: Reference not found.
15. Bahrain eGovernment Programme 'Looking Beyond the Obvious', 2009, http://www.ega.gov.bh/ Accessed on November 7, 2015.
16. The five-year strategic plan (2013- 2018) seeks to support professionalism in media practice and production and to contribute to the spreading of awareness and knowledge throughout the community. National Profiles of the Information Society in Bahrain (2013), p. 31.
17. Djibouti National ICT Strategy and accompanying Action Plan (has disappeared from site. It is mentioned on the following link which may not be reputable given the disclaimer, http://www.hartford-hwp.com/archives/33/index-bc.html).
18. National ICTs Strategy: 2005-Present, a very elaborate plan focused on infrastructure and governance of ICT networks. http://www.mcit.gov.eg/ict_sector.

Acknowledgement

This article is connected to research on analyses of MIL globally and citizens' responses to media and information literacy competencies in relation to personal, social, economic, political, cultural, and religious challenges and opportunities on and offline after having acquired MIL-related competencies through different kinds of on-line courses. The research is being carried out at the Autonomous University of Barcelona under the supervision of Professor Jose Manuel Pérez Tornero.

19. Freedom of Access to Information Law No. 47/2007.

20. The National eStrategy for Lebanon, Document 4: The ICT Policies and the Seven Initiatives (2003), http://siteresources.worldbank.org/EDUCATION/Resources/WorldBankMasterICT-EdPolicyDocumentList-Draft_June2011_for-external-site.pdf Access on November 7, 2015.

21. Plan de Développement de l'Infrastructure Nationale d'Information et de Communication 1999-2002 (Available in French language, 2000). http://www.uneca.org/AISI/NICI/Documents/Mauritanie_NICI_PLan.html

22. Généralisation des Technologies de l'Information et de la Communication (TIC) dans l'enseignement (GENIE, French/Arabic); National Strategy for Information Society and Digital Economy «Digital Morocco 2013.» http://www.men.gov.ma/sites/fr/SiteCollectionDocuments/G%C3%A9n%C3%A9ralisation_TICEnseignement_Vf2.pdf Accessed on November 7, 2015.

23. National IT Strategy titled "Digital Oman" Strategy 2002 http://www.ita.gov.om (Available in Arabic here)

24. The Supreme Council of Information and Communication Technology (ictQATAR) developed a comprehensive strategic ICT Plan in 2010, http://www.ictqatar.qa/en/news-events/news/ictqatar-releases-2010-annual-report. Accessed on November 8, 2015.

25. The Universal Access and Universal Service Policy, siteresources.worldbank.org/.../2012-02-29-AndrewDymond.pptx . Accessed on November 8, 2015.

26. The National Information and Communications Technology Plan (NICTP), www.kacst.edu.sa/en/research/Documents/InformationTechnology.pdf and www.mcit.gov.sa. Accessed on November 8, 2015.

27. Survey of ICT and Education in Africa: Somalia Country Report https://www.infodev.org/infodev-files/resource/InfodevDocuments_428.pdf.

28. Survey of ICT and Education in Africa: Sudan Country Report https://openknowledge.worldbank.org/handle/10986/10660.

29. Tunisia – Information and Communications Technology (ICT) contribution to growth and employment generation (Vol. 2) : Technical report, http://documents.banquemondiale.org/ Accessed on November 8, 2015.

30. Media laws and regulations of the GCC countries: Summary, analysis and recommendations By Dr. Matt J. Duffy, http://www.dc4mf.org/sites/default/files/gcc_media_law_en_0.pdf. Accessed on November 7, 2015.

31. http://library.aucegypt.edu/dept/infoliteracy/index.htm. Access on November 7, 2015.

32. http://mdc.birzeit.edu/en/, Accessed on October 4, 2015.

33. International Federation of Library Associations, http://blogs.ifla.org/literacy-reading/2014/03/16/qatar-information-literacy-network-meeting/ and University of Qatar, http://library.qu.edu.qa/index.php/services/faculty/information-literacy-program. Access on November 7, 2015.

34. See excerpt of academic article Description and Evaluation of the Information Literacy Program in a Private School in Lebanon: A Case Study, https://www.questia.com/library/journal/1P3-1741798951/description-and-evaluation-of-the-information-literacy. Access on November 7, 2015.

35. UNESO website, http://www.unesco.org/new/en/media-services/single-view/news/unesco_launches_maghreb_network_of_media_and_information_literacy/#.Vj-UXfxdHIU. Accessed on November 7, 2015

36. http://www.dc4mf.org/en/content/media-literacy-another-vision-teaching, Accessed on October 4, 2015.

37. See news article published on the UNESCO website and written by Hara Padhy, Advisor for Communication and Information, UNESCO Cairo Office, and Alton Grizzle, UNESCO, Paris, http://www.unesco.org/new/en/communication-and-information/resources/news-and-in-focus-articles/all-news/news/unesco_gave_boost_to_media_and_information_literacy_for_arab_states/#.VhCtj_yhfIU Accessed on October 4, 2015. The title of some of these officials might have changed by the time this book is published.

38. Wilson et al., 2011.

39. Grizzle et al., 2013.

40. UNESCO, 2013.

41. http://rethinkwords.com/, Accessed on October 4, 2015.

References

Abu-Fadil, M. (2013). Qatar educators learn to integrate media literacy into curricula, pp. 381-386, in *Media and Information Literacy and Intercultural Dialogue*. U. Carlsson & S.H. Culver (Eds.). MILID Yearbook 2013, Nordicom, University of Gothenburg, Sweden. Available online at www.nordicom.gu.se/clearinghouse

Abu-Fadil, M. (2007). Media Literacy – a tool to combat stereotypes and promote intercultural dialogue. Research paper prepared for the UNESCO regional conference in support of global literacy. Doha, 12-14 March 2007.

Abu-Fadil, M. (2006). Lebanese youth and the Media – social and political influences, pp. 183-195, in *In the Service of Young People? Studies and Reflections on Media in the Digital Age*. U. Carlsson & C. von Feilitzen (Eds.). Yearbook 2005/2006, The International Clearinghouse on Children, Youth and Media, Nordicom, University of Gothenburg, Sweden.

Assaad, R., & Roudi-Fahimi, F. (2007). Youth in the Middle East and North Africa: Demographic opportunity or challenge? http://www.prb.org/pdf07/youthinmena.pdf Accessed on September 7, 2015.

Degani, A. & Degani R. (2015). Survey of young adults' perceptions and attitudes regarding media coverage in Israel. Research commissioned by UNESCO to Geocartography Group.

Fahmy, E.I., & Rifaat, N.M. (2010). Middle East information literacy awareness and indigenous Arabic content challenges, pp. 111-123. *The International Information and Library Review* Vol. 42(2).

Frau-Meigs, D. (2011). *Media Matters in the Cultural Contradictions of the 'Information Society' –Towards a human rights-based governance*, pp. 334. Council of Europe, Strasbourg, France.

Gomaa, E.H. (2014). Video production as a tool to reinforce media literacy and citizenship in Egypt, pp. 33-43, in *Global Citizenship in a Digital World*. S.H. Culver & P. Kerr (Eds.). MILID Yearbook, Nordicom, University of Gothenburg, Sweden. Available online at www.nordicom.gu.se/clearinghouse

Grizzle, A. (2015). Measuring media and information literacy: Implications for the sustainable development goals, pp.107-129, in *Media and Information Literacy for the Sustainable Development Goals*. J. Singh, A. Grizzle, S. J. Yee and S. H. Culver (Eds.). MILID Yearbook 2015, Nordicom, University of Gothenburg, Sweden. Available online at www.nordicom.gu.se/clearinghouse

Grizzle, A. (2009). Media Literacy-global perspective. Keynote presentation given at the Euromeduc seminar on Media literacy and appropriation of Internet by young people. Faro, Portugal.

Grizzle, A., Moore, P., Dezuanni, M., Asthana, S., Wilson, C., Banda, F., & Onumah, C. (2013). *Media and information literacy policy and strategy guidelines*. UNESCO, Paris, France. Available online at www.unesco.org

Horton, F.W. (2013). Overview of Information Literacy resources worldwide. UNESCO, Paris, France.

Ito, M. (2013). Integration of media and information literacy into the national teacher-training curriculum in Morocco, pp. 275-276, in *Media and Information Literacy and Intercultural Dialogue*. U. Carlsson & S. H. Culver (Eds.). MILID Yearbook 2013, Nordicom, University of Gothenburg, Sweden. Available online at www.nordicom.gu.se/clearinghouse

Jenkins, H., Clinton, K., Purushotma, R., Robison, A.J. & Weigel, M. (2009). *Confronting the challenges of participatory culture: Media education for the 21st century*. MIT Press, London, England.

Kamerer, D. (2013). Media Literacy. *Communication Research Trends* – Centre for the study of Communication and Culture Vol. 32(1).

Kellner, D., & Share, J. (2007). Critical media literacy, democracy, and the reconstruction of education, pp. 3-23 in *Media literacy: A reader*. D. Macedo & S. R. Steinberg (Eds.). Peter Lang Publishing, New York, USA.

Madrenas, C. R., "Media Literacy and the English as a Second Language Curriculum: A Curricular Critique and Dreams for the Future" (2014). Electronic Thesis and Dissertation Repository. Paper 2529.

Masmoudi, M. (2006). The Arab child and the information society, pp. 77-100, in *In the Service of Young People? Studies and Reflections on Media in the Digital Age*. U. Carlsson & C. von Feilitzen (Eds.). Nordicom, University of Gothenburg, Sweden.

Melki, J. P. (2013). Sowing the Seeds of Digital and Media Literacy in Lebanon and the Arab World, pp. 77-86, in *Media Literacy Education in Action: Theoretical and pedagogical perspectives*. B. S. De Abreu and P. Mihailidis (Eds.). Routledge, New York, USA.

Menou, J. M. (2002). Information literacy in national information and communications technology (ICT) policies: The missed dimension, information culture. White Paper prepared for UNESCO, the U.S. National Commission on Libraries and Information Science, and the National Forum on Information

Literacy, for use at the Information Literacy Meeting of Experts, Prague, the Czech Republic. Available at: http://www.nclis.gov/libinter/infolitconf&meet/papers/menou-fullpaper.pdf.

Mihailidis, P. (2008). Beyond cynicism: How media literacy can make students more engaged citizens. Dissertation submitted to the Faculty of the Graduate School of the University of Maryland, USA.

Moghtar, I. A., Majiid, S., and Foo, S. (2008). Information literacy education: Applications of mediated learning and multiple intelligences. *Library and Information Science Research*. Vol. 30 pp. 195 -206.

Mohamed, M. & El Moniem, N.A. (2013). Evaluating the effect of outdoor ads on urban coordination in Egypt's historical spots, pp. 115-123, in *Media and Information Literacy and Intercultural Dialogue*. U. Carlsson & S. H. Culver (Eds.). MILID Yearbook 2013, Nordicom, University of Gothenburg, Sweden. Available online at www.nordicom.gu.se/clearinghouse

Nfissi, A. (2014). Information literacy in the digital age: Morocco as a case study, pp. 389-399, in *Global Citizenship in a Digital World*. S. H. Culver and P. Kerr (Eds.). MILID Yearbook 2014, Nordicom, University of Gothenburg, Sweden. Available online at www.nordicom.gu.se/clearinghouse

Nfissi, A. (2013). The state of the art of media and information literacy in Morocco, pp. 87-96, in *Media and Information Literacy and Intercultural Dialogue*. U. Carlsson & S. H. Culver (Eds.). MILID Yearbook 2013, Nordicom, University of Gothenburg, Sweden. Available online at www.nordicom.gu.se/clearinghouse

Orhon, E.N. (2009). Media education in Turkey: toward a multi-stakeholder framework, pp. 211-224, in *Mapping Media Education Policies in the World – Visions, Programmes and Challenges*. D. Frau-Meigs and J. Torrent (Eds.). UN-Alliance of Civilizations, USA.

Sakr, R., Nabhani, M. & Osta, I. (2009). Description and evaluation of the information literacy program in a private school in Lebanon: A case study, pp. 28-44. *School Libraries Worldwide* Vol. 15(1).

Saleh, I. (2015). From living rooms to classrooms: "Turn on the lights" of mobile learning in MENA, pp. 83-89, in *Media and Information Literacy for the Sustainable Development Goals*. J. Singh, A. G., S. J. Yee & S. H. Culver (Eds.). MILID Yearbook 2015, Nordicom, University of Gothenburg, Sweden. Available online at www.nordicom.gu.se/clearinghouse

Saleh, I. (2013). Convergence culture and youth activism in Egypt – new social movements on the block, pp. 201-214, in *Media and Information Literacy and Intercultural Dialogue*. U. Carlsson & S. H. Culver (Eds.). MILID Yearbook 2013, Nordicom, University of Gothenburg, Sweden. Available online at www. nordicom.gu.se/clearinghouse

Saleh, I. (2011). What underlies children, media and democracy in the Middle East and North Africa (MENA)?, pp. 29-37, in *New Questions, New Insights, New Approaches*. C. von Feilitzen, U. Carlsson & C. Bucht (Eds.). Yearbook 2011, The International Clearinghouse on Children, Youth and Media, Nordicom, University of Gothenburg, Sweden.

Saleh, I. (2009). Media literacy in the MENA: moving beyond the vicious cycle of oxymora, pp. 155-174, in *Mapping Media Education Policies in the World – Visions, Programmes and Challenges*. D. Frau-Meigs and J. Torrent (Eds.). UN-Alliance of Civilizations, USA.

Tayie, S. (2014). Towards an increased awareness about media and information literacy in Egypt, pp. 347-354, in *Global Citizenship in a Digital World* ,S. H. Culver & P. Kerr (Eds.). MILID Yearbook 2014, Nordicom, University of Gothenburg, Sweden. Available online at www.nordicom.gu.se/clearinghouse

Tayie, S. S. (2015). Impact of social media on political participation of Egyptian youth, pp.169-178, in *Media and Information Literacy for the Sustainable Development Goals*. J. Singh, A. Grizzle, S. J. Yee and S. H. Culver (Eds.). MILID Yearbook 2015, Nordicom, University of Gothenburg, Sweden. Available online at www.nordicom.gu.se/clearinghouse

UNESCO (2013). *Global Media and Information Literacy Assessment Framework: Country Readiness and Competencies*. UNESCO, Paris, France. Available online at www.unesco.org

UNESCO (1998). Statistics on children in the world, pp. 289-299, in *Children and Media Violence*. U. Carlsson and C. von Feilitzen (Eds.). Yearbook 1998, The International Clearinghouse on Children, Youth and Media, Nordicom, University of Gothenburg, Sweden.

UNESCO (1998). Statistics on media in the world, pp. 261-285, in *Children and Media Violence*. U. Carlsson and C. von Feilitzen (Eds.). Yearbook 1998, The International Clearinghouse on Children, Youth and Media, Nordicom, University of Gothenburg, Sweden.

UNESCO (2006). *Literacy for Life. Education for All Global Monitoring Report*. UNESCO, Paris, France.

Watt, D. (2012). The urgency of visual media literacy in our post-9/11 world: reading images of Muslim women in the print news media. *Journal of Media Literacy Education*. Vol. 4(1) pp. 32-43.

Wilson, C., Grizzle, A., Tuazon, R., Akyempong, K. & Cheung, C. (2011). *Media and Information Literacy Curriculum for Teachers*. UNESCO, Paris, France. Available online at www.unesco.org

Yildiz, M.N. (2014). Different cultures, similar challenges – integrating multilingual, multicultural, multimedia in media literacy education, pp. 259-270, in *Global Citizenship in a Digital World*. S. H. Culver and P. Kerr (Eds.). MILID Yearbook 2014, Nordicom, University of Gothenburg, Sweden. Available online at www.nordicom.gu.se/clearinghouse

Zurkowski, P. (2014). *Action Literacy – Empowering "We the People" in the Information Age*. All Good Literacies Press, Laurel, MD, USA.

3. Helping Arab Digital and Media Literacy Blossom

Three Years of the Media and Digital Literacy Academy of Beirut (MDLAB)

Jad Melki & Lubna Maaliki

Realizing the importance of educating youth about ubiquitous media systems and messages that surround every aspect of their lives, many countries across the globe have embraced media and information literacies as core components of university curricula, and in some cases middle- and high-school programs. Unfortunately, the Arab region has been a latecomer to this realization (Melki, 2009, 2011).

Even as social media fuel Arab uprisings, most Arab higher education systems remain oblivious to the merits of incorporating digital and media literacies within their core teaching requirements, and in most cases critical media literacy competencies remain absent even from journalism and communication programs. In fact, up until recently, most digital and media literacy initiatives in the Arab region have been individually driven or promoted transiently by a few civil society groups through training workshops and awareness campaigns (Melki, 2013b, 2015b). But even the individual academic initiatives – mostly at private elite Arab universities – have faced opposition and discouragement from entrenched interests of traditional Arab media academics who have resisted innovations that threaten their turfs and have clung to outdated media theories that view the digital media revolution as an insignificant matter. In addition, many Arab academics who would otherwise have championed digital and media literacy at their universities faced a dearth in Arabic curricular material and an absence of the necessary facilities and equipment. Many of them were also uncertain about their own skills and knowledge to develop and teach digital and media literacy. In the past few years, multiple efforts to advance digital and media literacy in the Arab world have been launched by academic coalitions and international institutions, such as the UNESCO-initiated International Network on Media and Information Literacy and Intercultural Dialogue (MILID), the Doha Center for Media Freedom (DCMF), and the Association of Kuwaiti Teachers and the Kuwait Centre for Media Literacy (KCML). These admirable efforts have had mixed outcomes so far. Both DCMF and KCML seem to be mainly nationally focused and have yet to produce significant, tangible and long-lasting outcomes (DCMF has had an outreach program involving workshops in Jordan, Morocco and other countries). MILID remains the most promising international initiative that will hopefully bear fruit soon for the Arab region.

Launch of the Media and Digital Literacy Academy of Beirut

Another institutional initiative that has tried to address this situation and fill the gap is the Media and Digital Literacy Academy of Beirut (MDLAB). Sponsored by the Open Society Foundations (OSF), al-Monitor news, and the Arab-European Association for Media and Communication Researchers (AREACORE) through the German Academic Exchange Service, MDLAB launched in 2013 by a group of Arab and international academics with the explicit aim of advancing digital and media literacy education in the region through training Arab media educators and developing digital and media literacy curricula, not only in Arabic, but also grounded in Arabic cultures and concerns.

Building on the model of the Salzburg Academy on Media and Global Change – an international partnership of over a dozen universities from around the world – MDLAB runs an annual summer academy that brings together 50 Arab media faculty and graduate students, in addition to Arab and international media literacy trainers and experts, particularly from the Salzburg Academy network. The academy also works year-round to develop curricula, support media literacy initiatives in the region, and acts as a hub for a network of Arab media literacy educators. MDLAB's missions encompass five objectives:

(1) To diffuse the knowledge and teaching of digital and media literacy education and promote its importance among Arab universities.

(2) To train each year young Arab university instructors and graduate students on digital and media literacy concepts and competencies.

(3) To develop annually university-level curricula that include lesson plans, curricular modules, training manuals, case studies, and multimedia content.

(4) To establish a hub for a network of regional universities and media educators centering on the development and promotion of digital and media literacy education.

(5) To create and maintain an open online space for the dissemination of curricular material and the connection of the academy's alumni and potential contributors and collaborators.

The Academy

The idea of MDLAB first emerged as a recommendation of the 2011 conference of the Arab-US Association of Communication Educators (AUSACE) themed "Digital and Media Literacy: New Directions" and the OSF-sponsored global study on Mapping Digital Media (Melki et al., 2012). Both projects recommended the expansion and generalization of digital and media literacy education in the Arab region. By providing the needed training, curricular material and resources, and motivating faculty to transfer what they learned to their institutions, the academy aims to spread such knowledge throughout Arab universities, creating a multiplier effect. MDLAB focuses mainly on junior educators and graduate students who have the highest potential and flexibility to learn advanced digital skills and accept innovative ideas, in addition to being closely in touch with the largest Arab demographic that today is leading change in the region. Three years after the launch of MDLAB, some two-dozen Arab universities teach digital and media literacy in a variety of formats based on curricula developed at the academy. Some have introduced full courses. Others have used the modules to infuse their traditional media courses with digital and media literacy concepts and competencies, while they continue to battle with tedious government and institutional bureaucracies and obstacles that have delayed the approval of standalone digital and media literacy courses. Nevertheless, today nine Arab universities have been able to offer full digital and media literacy courses: Damascus University, American University in Sharjah, American University of Beirut, Ahram Canadian University, Lebanese American University, Rafik Hariri University, Notre Dame University, Birzeit University, and Azm University. The number is expected to double next year, especially after the Iraqi Ministry of Education approves a proposed national curriculum that includes a required digital and media literacy course.

Although the first two years of the academy focused on Eastern Arab countries – namely Lebanon, Syria, Palestine, Jordan and Iraq, the 2015 MDLAB academy had participants from Egypt, Oman, Yemen, Qatar, Sudan, the UAE, and Iran. The same year, MDLAB included three schoolteachers from the International College (IC) in Lebanon, the first Arab school to officially name media literacy as a strategic priority. Future plans include expanding to the rest of the Arab region, adding more schoolteachers, and other international participants. MDLAB's resolution is to get each Arab country by the end of this decade to have at least one school and one university offer digital and media literacy as a core curriculum.

Curriculum and methods used

When it comes to curriculum, teaching and learning methods, MDLAB has striven to go beyond the classic definition of media literacy, "the ability to access, analyze, evaluate and create media in a variety of forms" (Center for Media Literacy, 1992). Digital and media literacy, in this conception, transcends the mission of training students to become critical media consumers. In an era of infinite digital media potential and globalized communication, digital and media literacy becomes most essential for survival in the information age and more critical for our globalized cultures and economic systems. Hence, digital and media literacy not only offers competencies to critically read, listen and watch diverse media content and decipher its underlying ideologies, assess its embedded commercialism, propagandistic intentions, and harmful hidden consequences. Digital and media literacy also empowers individuals and communities. It helps people intelligently manage their media uses, effectively utilize digital and social media tools for personal and communal advancement, and proactively engage in collaborative global discussions and civic action. Digital and media literacy offers the requisite knowledge and competencies for marginalized individuals and disenfranchised communities to gain back the initiative and balance the powers of big business, concentrated wealth, and unbridled authoritarian systems. "Media and digital literacy is media education for the masses. It is the silent revolution that can counter the ideologies of greed, hate and death and fight for generalizing and globalizing social justice and egalitarian systems" (Melki, 2015b). MDLAB's curriculum covers diverse social, political and economic topics, integrated with essential digital competencies and research skills, all of which are guided by studies that inquire into the media uses and digital activism of Arab youth and prevalent media-related disorders and trends in the region (Hitti et al., 2014; Melki, 2013a, 2015a; Melki and Mallat, 2014a, 2014b; Melki et al., 2014). Core conceptual modules include the influences of corporate ownership and business practices on media production, the politics of news construction and control, the persuasive power of images, advertising and its devastating effects on body image and self-worth, media representation of gender, race, and sexuality, and, deconstructing propaganda messages and institutions.

The curriculum strives to integrate critical media analysis with digital production competencies and scientific research skills in a seamless and coherent fashion (Melki, 2013a). Weaved into the conceptual lectures are a set of research methods and digital composition workshops that both concretize the media literacy theories and offer students an array of exciting technologies to learn and use creatively. Core digital and research competencies cover blogging, photo manipulation, audio and video editing, digital curation, comparative media analysis, social network analysis, and the effective use of digital research tools. The curriculum tries hard to tie each of these digital and research competencies to corresponding theoretical and critical media literacy concepts. For example, teaching photo manipulation using free applications such as *Pixlr* are closely tied to lectures about the power of images in news and the representation of the body in advertising, while learning digital curation and comparative news analysis with applications such as *Storify* and *Meograph* are linked to lessons about news construction and the role of media in war. While the teaching of theoretical and critical media literacy concepts is delivered through a series of lectures and discussions moderated by renowned digital and media literacy academics, a team of digital media production experts dubbed the 'digital squad' runs the digital media workshops. The digital workshops follow a carefully designed learning approach based on four guidelines: Visual demonstrations, one-on-one guidance, non-linear exercises, and scaffolding (Melki, 2013a). The non-linear approach allows participants with a higher level of technical skills to skip to a different task while they await the teacher's help, which saves time and lowers frustration levels. In addition, these advanced participants can offer great help during the workshop. Whenever a participant finishes the exercise quickly, we recruit him/her to help other participants during the lab exercise, which also offers the participant a chance to test his/her teaching skills. A digital workshop session usually starts with a 15-minute lecture about, for instance, digital audio formats and the concept of push technology used by podcasting applications. Then, the digital squad delivers a short demo on how to use a digital audio recording application, such as *Audacity*, to record, edit, and export an audio file. Immediately after that, participants follow a written exercise that guides them step-by-step through a specific task, such as creating a 60-second audio interview with one sound bite. The detailed written instructions are posted online along with all curricula, lectures and exercises created at the academy for participants to use in the future when they plan to teach digital and media literacy at their universities. Such integrative teaching and learning approaches were developed and tested over several years in collaboration with international academics within the Salzburg Academy circle (Mihailidis, 2011, 2014; Shumow, 2014). The methods have consistently shown great promise:

> Effectively integrating digital and research skills into media and news literacy teaching builds on the critical reading skills traditional media literacy classes produce, and helps students transition from media consumer to adept and critical producers of information and knowledge and empowered global citizens engaged in important discussions and able to organize in networks better positioned to shape societies and regions and enhance the statuses of marginalized individuals and disenfranchised groups. (Melki, 2013a)

Building on experiences

The hard work of MDLAB participants has helped us refocus the academy's curriculum and better deal with the priorities of Arab societies. Thanks to extensive feedback from participants through discussion sessions and focus groups, the core curriculum now includes such topics as media and terrorism, sectarianism, extremism and war and emphasizes human rights, tolerance, civic activism and global citizenship. Other recommendations include strengthening the training components on social network analysis, digital media research, and data literacy competencies, as well as more networking opportunities and ongoing activities throughout the year, such as conferences and shorter workshops conducted on the campuses of each participating university. Moreover, the academy offers intentional social integration activities, as well as cultural excursions and networking events to help participants from various countries and cultures better assimilate and build long-lasting relationships. Such activities were enhanced after the inaugural academy when we observed participants clustering in national and even sectarian groups with little interaction between groups.

During that first year, in at least one recorded case, some participants felt being derided by individuals from another national group. The matter was effectively addressed in the following academy by ensuring that each working group and team – as well as hotel roommates – included participants from various countries and by incorporating several 'speed meets' where participants spend time meeting with other individuals and ask about their lives and professional backgrounds. In addition, the screening of applicants became more rigorous in the second and third years, including phone interviews that asked questions about openness to other cultures and tolerance of difference. What also helped tremendously in raising the quality of participants was the increase in the pool of applications from fewer than 70 in the first year (70 per cent acceptance rate) to over 200 in the third year (25 per cent acceptance rate).

We anticipate even further improvement in this area and expect the number of applicants to exceed 250 in the fourth year, as the academy continues to build a strong reputation regionally and internationally and as digital and media literacy courses become more common on Arab campuses. But MDLAB's long-term goals for the region are far from being reached. Promoting the teaching of digital and media literacy courses on Arab campuses is a positive step in the right direction but not enough. Arab media and communication curricula – regardless of specialty – should become grounded in the theories, concepts and skills of digital and media literacy.

Whether it is journalism, advertising, public relations, political communication, health communication or any subspecialty within this field, all its courses and curricula should incorporate critical media literacy concepts and applied digital literacy competencies. For example, teaching advertising should never be devoid of critical teaching about the negative effects of advertising and consumerism on society. Journalism training must incorporate the formidable competencies of citizen journalism, data journalism, and digital activism, as well as the latest knowledge on propaganda strategies and tactics, especially those used in war and conflict by extremists and terrorists. Questions examining gender, sexuality, race and religion should become embedded within any communication training and research, while civic engagement, global citizenship, social justice and tolerance should guide their purpose. In addition, digital and media literacy cannot be only available for the shrinking pool of students who can afford a university education. We need to create more accessible online and offline courses and workshops in Arabic to reach a broader audience. What's more, media and digital literacy needs to move into schools, all the way down to elementary teaching and beyond. We need to develop a critical mass of well-networked teachers, academics and researchers capable of taking digital and media literacy teaching and research to the next level.

References

Center for Media Literacy. (1992). Aspen Media Literacy Conference Report. Available at: http://www.medialit. org/reading-room/what-media-literacy-definitionand-more

Hitti, E., Melki, J., and Mufarrij, A. (2014). The Prevalence and Determinants of Anabolic Steroids Use among Fitness Center Attendees in Lebanon. *International SportMed Journal, 15*(4), 391-401.

Hobbs, R. (1998). The seven great debates in the media literacy movement. *Journal of Communication, 48*(1), 16-32.

Jones-Kavalier, B. R., and Falannigan, S. L. (2006). Connecting the Digital Dots: Literacy of the 21st Century. *Educause Quarterly, 2*.

Livingstone, S. (2004). Media Literacy and the Challenge of New Information and Communication Technologies. *The Communication Review*, 7, 3-14.

Melki, Jad. (2009). Journalism and Media Studies in Lebanon. *Journalism Studies, 10*(5), 672-690.

Melki, J. (2011). The Plight of Media Education and Research in Arab Higher Education. In Chi-Kim Cheung (Ed.), *Research in Media Education* (pp. 83-108). New York: Nova Science.

Melki, J. (2013a). Incorporating In-Depth Research Methodologies and Digital Competencies with Media Literacy Pedagogies. In P. Mihailidis (Ed.), *News Literacy: Global Perspectives for the Newsroom and the Classroom* (pp. 139-160). Mass Communication and Journalism series, New York: Peter Lang Publishing.

Melki, J. (2013b). Sowing The Seeds Of Digital And Media Literacy In Lebanon And The Arab World: The importance of a locally grown and sustainable curriculum. In B. De Abreu and P. Mihailidis (Eds.), *Media Literacy Education in Action: Theoretical and Pedagogical Perspectives*. Routledge.

Melki, J. (2015a). Guiding digital and media literacy development in Arab curricula through understanding media uses of Arab youth. *Journal of Media Literacy Education, 6*(3), 14-28.

Melki, J. (2015b). Media Literacy Offers the Arab World a Way Forward. *Al-Fanar*. http://www.al-fanarmedia. org/2015/07/media-literacy-offers-the-arab-world-a-way-forward/

Melki, J., Dabbous, Y., Nasser, K., and Mallat, S.. (2012). Mapping Digital Media: Lebanon. In *Mapping Digital Media, a multiple country study, a report by the Open Society Foundations Media Program*. Available at www.opensocietyfoundations.org

Melki, J., Hitti, E., Oghia, M., and Mufarrij, A. (2014). Media Exposure, Mediated Social Comparison to Idealized Images of Muscularity, and Anabolic Steroid Use. *Health Communication 30*(5), 473-84.

Melki, J., and Mallat, S. (2014a). Block her entry, keep her down, and push her out: gender discrimination, sexual harassment, and the disenabling legal and social environments that face women journalists in the Arab world. *Journalism Studies 17*(1).

Melki, J., and Mallat, S. (2014b). Digital Activism: Efficacies and burdens of digital and social media for civic activism. *Arab Media and Society* (Special Edition), 19 (Fall).

Mihailidis, P. (2009). Beyond Cynicism: Media education and civic learning outcomes in the university. *International Journal of Media and Learning, 1*(3).

Mihailidis, P. (2011). *News Literacy: Global Perspectives for the Newsroom and the Classroom*. New York: Peter Lang Publishing.

Mihailidis, P. (2014). *Media Literacy and the Emerging Citizen: Youth Engagement and Participation in Digital Culture*. New York: Peter Lang Publishing.

Shumow, M. (2014). *Mediated Communities: Civic Voices, Empowerment and Media Literacy in the Digital Era*. New York: Peter Lang Publishing.

4. Youth and Digital Media

Drafting a Landscape from Fez and Cairo

Jordi Torrent

In November 2013 and February 2014, the United Nations Alliance of Civilizations (UNAOC) organized two workshops on Media and Information Literacy (MIL) for educators in Cairo, Egypt, and Fez, Morocco. In Egypt, the local organizer was Cairo University[1], and in Morocco it was the Sidi Mohamed Ben Abdellah University[2]. Both universities are partners of the UNESCO-UNITWIN UNAOC Global University Network on Media and Information Literacy and Intercultural Dialogue.[3] Both universities were able to gain the support and engage with their respective country's Ministry of Education, facilitating in this way the participation of middle and high school educators in the MIL training during these workshops (presented as an opportunity for professional development). Other partners of these workshops included UNESCO, the Doha Center for Media Freedom, and, for the ones organized in Fez, Search for Common Ground.[4] A total of 36 educators in Cairo and 27 in Fez participated; the workshops were conducted in Arabic.

The main purpose of the workshops was to introduce MIL concepts and a framework to the educators, mostly using UNESCO's Arabic version of the *Media and Information Literacy Curriculum for Teachers*[5] as well as the Doha Center for Media Freedom's teacher resources on MIL.[6] The workshops were an opportunity for most of the educators to discuss for the first time the main concepts and building blocks of MIL pedagogy, understanding that traditional concepts of literacy (writing and reading print texts) are no longer enough skills for individuals to properly function as active participant citizens in contemporary societies. During the workshops it was also stressed that teaching merely 'digital technology skills' (how to use a computer, build a blog, basic coding, etc.) is not MIL education per se. Developing critical thinking skills applied to media messages, introducing the analysis of media representations of historical events in social studies, encouraging students to produce relevant and ethical media messages, etc., is part of MIL education.

Making it clear that MIL is in many ways more 'humanities' than 'technology', that MIL education is a good platform to re-introduce humanistic themes in an educational framework that currently – across the world – tends to prioritize science and technology over philosophy, history and social studies. Questions of state power, media control, freedom of speech, citizens' ethical responsibilities as media producers, censorship, hate speech in social media platforms, etc., were also discussed during the workshops. Given the challenging political and social movements that certain countries from the MENA region are experiencing, some of the educators expressed concerns that teaching MIL in their schools could be interpreted as a form of social activism with political implications that could jeopardize the safety and future of their students. Others responded that while it is true MIL education has aspects of social criticism, it is also true that learning to read and write is already a political act. In that sense, MIL education is no more a 'political activist' pedagogy than teaching to read and write – it is only a better, more relevant, way to teach 'literacy' in the mediatized world that we inhabit.

Survey of media use

At the end of the workshops, the educators were asked to distribute in their classrooms a questionnaire aimed at assessing the media habits of their students.[7]

Looking at the results of the research we acknowledge that television continues to be the favorite medium for these young people, over 60 per cent of youth (in Cairo and in Fez) spend between 1 and 3 hours a day watching TV. Some 18 per cent in Cairo spend 4-6 hours a day in front of the TV screen. Not dissimilar to youth of the same age from other countries. A 2015 Nielsen study reported that North-American youth of the same age watch television an average of 2.8 hours a day.[8] This being an average calculation, we can infer that at least 18 per cent, if not more, of American teenagers are also spending 4-6 hours a day "watching TV." I put watching TV in quotes because youth today do not only watch TV (this is no longer the captive audience of the pre-Internet era), they consume other forms of media while watching TV. We found that 16 per cent of the young people from Fez and Cairo who participated in the questionnaire spend 4 to 6 hours a day surfing the Net. Youth watch TV while surfing the Internet as well as sending SMS with their phones to their friends, and some listening to music as well. This being the so-called multi-tasking phenomenon: multi-media (multi platforms, multi screens) simultaneously used. This occurrence is also global; other countries experience similar youth interactions with media.[9] The study also showed that youth from Fez and Cairo upload photos and/or videos to their Internet social media of choice at least once a week, in Cairo 31 per cent of them do this daily. In Fez, 30 per cent send more than 10 SMS to their friends each day. In contrast 16 per cent have conversations with their family only once a week. In both cities 40 per cent spend 30 minutes or less a day doing school homework. And only a quarter read from a book each day. It is clear then that media have a great stake in their socialization development as well as in their identity-

Table 1. Media Use Among Youth in Egypt and Morocco (per cent)

Youth 10 to 20 years of age	Cairo, Egypt	Fez, Morocco
Television watching 1-3 hours a day	67	62
Television watching 4-6 hours a day	18	11
Internet surfing from school	13	4
Internet surfing from home	65	32
Internet surfing using a cellphone	39	16
Internet surfing 1-3 hours a day	45	38
Internet surfing 4-6 hours a day	16	15
Internet use for social media & fun	90	36
Internet use for news	15	5
Uploading photos & videos on social media	78	49
Uploading photos & videos on social media, each day	31	7
Uploading photos & videos on social media, once a week	42	40
Have a cellphone	92	70
Using a cellphone for photos	80	90
Using a cellphone for videos	39	80
Using a cellphone for SMS, more than 10 messages a day	13	30
Reading books, each day	21	25
Reading books, once a month	10	34
School homework, less than 15 minutes a day	16	9
School homework, about 30 minutes a day	25	34
Meeting with friends after school, each day	57	30
Meeting with friends after school, once a week	8	44
Having conversations with family, once a week	22	16
Having conversations with family, once in a while	20	12

Note: The number of respondents in Morocco was 201 students and 233 students from Egypt. The gender balance was about 50/50. The respondents were between 10 to 20 years old.

personality formation. That it is through media consumption and production that their social persona is created, that the understanding of themselves, their community, the world at large, and 'the other' is shaped and constructed.

It is precisely because of this that MIL education needs to be included in the mandatory curriculum of middle and high school education. We were pleased that the representatives of the Ministries of Education of Morocco and Egypt present during the workshops understood the scope and importance of MIL education. We trust they conveyed to their supervisors information and knowledge that will soon be developed into new educational policies where MIL education is not only acknowledged but, more importantly, included in the school curricula of their countries. Recognizing that many educators need to be trained on MIL concepts, we also hope that these workshops were but a pilot for a much larger MIL teacher-training program in the region. We welcome the efforts of many organizations that are actively involved in promoting MIL education in the MENA region, many mentioned in the introduction and chapters of this publication.

The UNAOC understands that a media literate individual is less prone to be violently polarized when finding on his/her media options messages that might be insulting to his or her creed. A media literate citizen develops opportunities to engage in conversation, not in violent confrontation. It is for these reasons that from its origins the UNAOC identified media literacy as one educational initiative to be supported, encouraged and developed – as it is clearly stated in the initial UNAOC's High Level Group Report.[10]

Notes

1. Special thanks to Professor Dr. Samy Tayie from Cairo University
2. Special thanks to Professor Dr. Abdelhamid Nfissi, from Sidi Mohamed Ben Abdellah University
3. Please see http://milunesco.unaoc.org/unitwin
4. Other instructors included Ayman Bardawil, Youssef Omar, Foad Helmy, Adly Reda, Hassan Emad, Amal El Shafie, Drissia Chouit, Khalid Aoutail, Rawia Alhumaidan, Ahmad Al Mohanadi, Mohamed Fawbar, Soufiana El Hamdi, Mohamed Azami, and Youssef Benabderazzak.
5. Please see http://www.unesco.org/new/en/communication-and-information/resources/publications-and-communication-materials/publications/full-list/media-and-information-literacy-curriculum-for-teachers
6. Please see http://www.dc4mf.org/en/content/media-literacy-another-vision-teaching
7. Special thanks to Mohamed Samy Abdel Raouf and Nora S. Abdel Raouf Mohamed (Cairo) and Mohamed Faoubar (Fez) for their support on this research
8. Please see http://www.adweek.com/news/television/infographic-look-kids-media-consumption-163087.
9. Please see "2015 Ofcom Report on Media use and Attitudes" http://stakeholders.ofcom.org.uk/binaries/research/media-literacy/media-lit-10years/2015_Adults_media_use_and_attitudes_report.pdf
10. Please see http://www.unaoc.org/repository/report.htm

II.
Media and Information Literacy in the MENA Region
From State Policies to Action Research

5. An Overview from the Occupied Palestinian Territories

Lucy Nuseibeh & Mohammed Abu Arqoub

This article gives a brief overview of the state of Media and Information Literacy (MIL) in the Occupied Palestinian Territories (oPt), starting with a brief look at the concept, including why it is has to be composite, and why the focus has to be on empowerment. It focuses on MIL among the Palestinian population in the West Bank and Gaza Strip (the Occupied Palestinian Territory), including East Jerusalem, among schoolchildren, university students, and among the general public. It also examines briefly the overall media context and situation, various MIL activities, and the most urgent needs of the Palestinian population with regard to MIL.

MIL as concept

MIL is a two-way concept. It includes both educating about how media work, how emotions and images can be manipulated, and how to work actively with media including new media and technology. MIL is a subject that is still settling, with the definition and scope still the subject of hot debates, but as a composite concept, comprising the technological (information literacy) along with the analytical skills (media literacy), it combines and underpins what is needed for full participation in today's world. In the words of the United Nations Educational, Scientific and Cultural Organization (UNESCO) Media and Information Literacy Policy and Strategy Guidelines[1], "Media and Information Literacy (MIL) is a basis for enhancing access to information and knowledge, freedom of expression, and quality education. It describes skills and attitudes that are needed to value the functions of media and other information providers, including those on the Internet, in societies, and to find, evaluate and produce information and media content; in other words, it covers the competencies that are vital for people to be effectively engaged in all aspects of development." As different forms of media have proliferated during the past 20 years, so have the different names and different forms of literacy, such as digital literacy, Internet literacy, even social networking literacy, with new terms accompanying the new developments in technology. These can be taken as included in the overall umbrella of MIL.[2] While media literacy is sometimes opposed to information or digital literacy, which are more concerned with skills and with Internet navigation, it is the combination of the two that has the most force. The UNESCO MIL policy and strategy paper gives clear details of how the two separate concepts combine: "Information Literacy focuses on the purposes of engaging with information and the process of becoming informed."[3] "While the concept of information literacy focuses on the information user as an autonomous decision-maker, citizen and learner, media literacy examines the ways in which the media environment facilitates, shapes, enables and, in some cases, constrains engagement with information and the communication process, be it for intentional or indirect learning, social participation or simply for entertainment."[4]

In the context of the occupied Palestinian territories, "information literacy" is more present and more known than "media literacy" or the composite, MIL. In the case of libraries, training is taking place on information literacy: "Changes in technology are having a considerable impact on libraries and their instruction programmes. These changes require information literacy programmes for users to become more effective, efficient and independent in their information searching."[5] There is general appreciation of the importance of information literacy: all the 13 Palestinian universities offer ICT courses, as do many smaller community colleges, and in the revised Palestinian school curriculum, grades 5 to 10 are supposed to include technology education as part of the science and maths overall "STEM" (Science, Technology, Engineering and Mathematics) approach. However, it is the composite concept, MIL, with emphasis on media literacy as well as the information component, that is most relevant for the oPt, a nation that, regardless of the frustrating situation of prolonged occupation (in fact also because of this), that needs to move towards becoming a learning society, with a knowledge base, to build a viable democracy. "When addressed jointly, media and information literacy do not only interact, but add value in promoting participation in future knowledge societies."[6]

In addition to the debate about the actual term, (which kind of literacy?) there has also been considerable debate as to whether MIL is protective or empowering (proactive). It can be seen as protective in so far as people are taught to analyze media content and read between the lines, understand the messages behind the images, and therefore become less vulnerable, less easy prey. This is especially in relation to children and media, where research has tended to focus on the possible negative impacts, even dangers from unfiltered media. But it is the proactive empowering element of MIL that really makes it essential for all sectors of society. Renee Hobbs, for instance, describes how: "we look to digital and media literacy to help us more deeply engage with ideas and information to make decisions and participate in cultural life"[7] MIL is proactive and empowering in so far as people are taught to read, listen, watch, perhaps interact, with an active critical approach, not simply a passive receptivity. It is also proactive in so far as people are taught to work creatively – not as technicians, but again in regard to content, so they can choose, develop and produce their own media messages.

UNESCO again, sums this up well:

> The 'everywhereness' of information, media, Internet and other information providers requires a greater emphasis on citizens' empowerment by ensuring that they have the skills, attitudes and knowledge that will enable them to critically and effectively interact with content in all forms of media and with all information providers. The digital age thus calls for a shift from a "protectionism only" approach to a focus on citizen empowerment. This does not necessarily imply that protection, for instance Internet safety, should be abandoned, but the emphasis should be on empowerment. Emphasis on only protectionism may lead to excessive restrictions being placed on media and other information providers. Further, children who do not acquire the competencies to be critical of media and information will be more susceptible to the potential negative influence of information and media content and less equipped to capitalize on opportunities when they become adults.[8]

By encouraging greater awareness of the various forces in society, such as media owners, business, special interests, MIL programs encourage civic engagement. "MIL has the citizen as its starting point. In addressing the status of the citizen, MIL is underpinned by human rights…." However, people are not regarded as inactive from an MIL perspective. Rather, they are actively involved in constructing their own realities. "Thus, the purpose of MIL becomes one of empowering people to actively take part in determining the conditions under which they live."[9] What is more, MIL becomes its own engine of empowerment: "…There is strong evidence to support the hypothesis that if young people gain greater media literacy and access to the internet, they will use it to obtain information about and express their views on political and other public debates."[10]

The examples of media literacy projects in the oPt, such as those teaching children to become "Media Smart" or enhancing the rule of law, or participatory video, are all in fact examples of MIL as empowerment. MIL as protection can contribute to awareness around the manipulation of words, images and general propaganda, thereby giving some protection against manipulation, scaremongering and divisiveness, although even this is in a way also a form of empowerment. Too much of a protective approach would risk being yet another restriction on already restricted lives, where human rights are lacking. Both the protection and the empowerment elements are relevant in the context of conflict. MIL "enables diversity, dialogue and tolerance."[11] What is more, MIL can also be considered an important component of peace building as it shapes self-awareness, awareness of others and awareness of bias and stereotyping, thereby building resistance to them, and generally to propaganda.[12]

Brief background on the political situation and media landscape

The oPt (East Jerusalem, the West Bank and the Gaza Strip) are roughly 6,220 square kilometres (2,402 square miles), with a population of just over 4.5 million in 2014 (2,790,000 in the West Bank, including East Jerusalem, and 1,760,000 in the Gaza Strip) of whom nearly 70 per cent are under 30 years old.[13] Since June 1967, for nearly 50 years, Palestinians in the West Bank and Gaza Strip have been living under Israeli military occupation, and in East Jerusalem, which was annexed by Israel, where the Palestinians are also directly subject to Israeli laws. Israel retains control over every aspect of Palestinian lives.

The current state of affairs for Palestinians in the oPt is summed up by the United Nations Office for the Coordination of Humanitarian Affairs (OCHA):[14]

> Palestinian civilians living in the occupied Palestinian territory (oPt) continue to bear the brunt of ongoing conflict and Israeli occupation. A lack of respect for international humanitarian and human rights law has resulted in a protection crisis with serious and negative humanitarian consequences. In the Gaza Strip, Israel continues to impose a land, sea and air blockade that has significantly undermined livelihoods, seriously diminished the quality of, and access to, basic services, and which amounts to collective punishment of the population of the Gaza Strip. In the West Bank, East Jerusalem is isolated from the rest of the West Bank. Communities in Area C face a range of pressures, including demolitions, settler violence, and movement and access restrictions, that make meeting basic needs increasingly difficult and threaten Palestinian presence in the area. Bedouin and herder communities are particularly vulnerable. Unlawful Israeli settlement activity lies at the heart of many of the humanitarian difficulties facing Palestinians in the West Bank. Overall, the lack of accountability for violations of human rights and humanitarian law, along with a failure to effectively enforce the rule of law when it comes to attacks on Palestinians and their property by Israeli military forces or Israeli settlers, has created a climate of impunity that contributes to further violence.

History

The first Palestinian newspaper was published on September 18, 1908,[15] with a license from the Ottoman rulers, rapidly followed by licences for 15 more newspapers and magazines. Apart from a brief hiatus during World War I, the media continued to develop and thrive first under the Ottomans and then under the British Mandate (1922-48). The first radio station, Honaalquds ("This is Jerusalem Calling") was launched in March 1936. From 1948 to 1967, the Gaza Strip was under the control of Egypt, and the West Bank of the River Jordan was under the control of Jordan, with the media continuing under their respective auspices, while the rest of British Mandate Palestine became the Israeli state. In June 1967, the "Six-Day War" left Israel in control of the West Bank and the Gaza Strip, as well as Egypt's Sinai Peninsula and Syria's Golan Heights. Israel imposed a military occupation on the West Bank and the Gaza Strip and annexed East Jerusalem, and, immediately clamped down on Palestinian media. In 1968, some newspapers, such as Al-Quds, As-Shaab, An-Nahar and Al-Fajr, representing different Palestinian factions, and all printed in Jerusalem, were allowed, but only with heavy censorship, and often with large glaring blanks on the pages.[16] No Palestinian television or radio stations were allowed. Therefore, in those days before widespread satellite access, Palestinians under occupation would mostly watch either Jordanian or Israeli television. They did however have access to a broad range of international radio stations, and several monthly magazines, including those published within Israel.[17]

Less traditional media were prominent, too. In the "Intifada," the Palestinian uprising against the Israeli occupation in 1987, the main form of media that gave the instructions for the forms of nonviolent resistance (such as what days to strike, what hours shops should be closed) and therewith drove the uprising, was leaflets, distributed in the name of the Unified Leadership of the Intifada. Graffiti were also used a lot at that stage and are still very much part of the Palestinian media landscape, generally expressing political affiliation. It was only after the Oslo Peace accords of 1993 and 1995 that Palestinian radio and TV stations were allowed to operate. This time, apart from the original newspapers, they were allowed only in the West Bank and Gaza and not in Jerusalem, as the Palestinian Authority was not allowed to operate in Jerusalem. Despite rapid proliferation of media outlets, the situation remains complex in relation to freedom of expression, frequencies, and other core matters, and is still essentially under Israeli control.

The media landscape

The media environment in the West Bank and Gaza is, at best, a confusing one. Three ministries control licensing, airwave rentals, and fees, and they were in conflict until late 2005. The media law is at odds with the basic law. The press and publications law is currently being reworked. Many say there are too many media outlets.[18]

The main media outlet is the Palestine Broadcasting Corporation (PBC) set up in 1995 with "Palestine TV" as the national satellite (and originally also terrestrial) television, the "Voice of Palestine," the national radio station, and the national news and information agency "WAFA" (in Arabic, English, French and Hebrew). Originally broadcasting from Gaza, the PBC moved to Ramallah in 2007, when there was a split between the two main Palestinian factions, Fatah and Hamas, leading to separate governments in the West Bank and the Gaza Strip. In a survey published by Internews in 2014,[19] "in the West Bank alone, there are 17 terrestrial TV stations and 72 radio stations…the majority of stations are in [the main cities] Hebron Nablus, Ramallah." According to the UNESCO Assessment of Media Development in Palestine, published in 2014, there are: "85 radio stations – 70 in the West Bank and 15 in the Gaza Strip – and 17 local TV stations, which broadcast from the West Bank. There are also four satellite channels: Maan and Falastiniat in the West Bank and Al-Aqsa and Al-Kittab from Gaza."[20]

In addition to the local media, Palestinians watch Aljazeera (established in 1996) and Al Arabiya (established in 2003) and any of the wide variety of available satellite channels.[21]

There are three main newspapers in the West Bank, Al Quds (published in Jerusalem), Al Ayyam (published in Ramallah) and Al Hayat Al Jadida (also published in Ramallah). There is one newspaper published in Gaza called Al Resala. "There are approximately 18 local news agencies with locations in Gaza and the West Bank."[22] The newspapers also have online versions. According to the Palestine Central Bureau of Statistics, about one-fifth of Palestinian households take a daily newspaper and more than half prefer to listen to the news: "The percentage of households in Palestine who obtain a daily newspaper was 20 per cent distributed as 24 per cent in the West Bank and 14 per cent in the Gaza Strip compared with 32 per cent in 2009. Also, 23 per cent of persons aged 10 years and above in Palestinian society read newspapers: 27 per cent of males and 18 per cent of females." The percentage of households who listen to radio stations was 61 per cent, including 57 per cent in the West Bank and 68 per cent in the Gaza strip. With regard to the households' first choice of programs, news ranked the highest followed by religious programs and music and songs.[23]

New media are developing fast. In the decade preceding 2014, the number of young people with access to mobile phones has doubled – 75 per cent of young people own a mobile phone (79 per cent in the West Bank against 69 per cent in the Gaza Strip) compared to 35 per cent in 2004. For 28 per cent of youth ages 18-35, the Internet is now their primary source of information while 25 per cent of people use the Internet daily. Some 50 per cent of youth aged 15-29 in the Palestinian Territory do not read newspapers or magazines at all – 40 per cent in the West Bank and 65 per cent in the Gaza Strip (Palestinian Central Bureau of Statistics, 2013). In 2013, 68 per cent of young people in the age group 15-29 used a computer (70 per cent in the West Bank and 63 per cent in the Gaza Strip) and 43 per cent used e-mail (PCBS, 2013). The landscape is changing and moving to younger users as shown by figures from the Palestinian Central Bureau of Statistics (PCBS) indicating that in 2014, 60 per cent of the population aged 10 or over used a computer and 54 per cent used the Internet. (PCBS 2014).[24] This should facilitate MIL programs with schools. Even in 2012, UNESCO reported that the percentage of Internet users in the oPt, 58 per cent, was almost 20 per cent higher than the average (40 per cent) for the MENA region.

UNESCO draws attention to the development of community media, noting that "despite having limited access to the Internet, community media use the available ICTs to convey their message to the community and encourage public interaction through the existing means of communication, such as mobile phones and land lines."[25] Two radio stations (Ajyal and Raya) have developed apps to broadcast their programs to smart phones in areas out of range of frequencies. UNESCO also mentions another example of community media, Honaalquds, a community radio and news agency in the Old City of Jerusalem that targets the Jerusalemite community and broadcasts via the Internet.[26] However, social media are the most popular method of communication among

Palestinians, and Facebook is far and away the most prevalent form (used primarily for chatting and by nearly half the entire population,[27] according to Socialbakers (a social media analysis and publicity company for Facebook.)[28] "The number of Facebook users is the third highest in the region with over 1,987,000 making it #81 in the ranking of all Facebook statistics by country in an area with a population of approximately 4 million." Again, according to Socialbakers, "Although Twitter has been slow to catch among Palestinians, the interest and usage has increased in the three years since the Arab uprising. In 2013, the total number of active Twitter users reached 36,800."

Use of broadcast media

UNESCO sums it up: "The conditions of Palestine's use of broadcasting frequencies were decided by the Oslo Accords of 1993 and 1995. Frequencies have been granted to Palestinian governmental radio and TV media outlets only and not formally to the private or community broadcast media. The PA has not, to date, devised a plan for spectrum allocation and management. The PA is now looking to develop a plan for digital transition to be implemented mid-2015 as per the road map set out by the International Telecommunication Union (ITU). The lack of a proper legal basis renders the Palestinian spectrum management unclear and unstable."[29] "Unclear and unstable" means that Israel can close down Palestinian stations whenever it wants, on the pretext that they are interfering with its communications. This will soon change however, as in relation to traditional media, especially radio and television, the media landscape is set to change between 2015 and 2020, as throughout the Arab world TV and radio frequencies are moving from analogue to digital.[30] Mamoun Mattar, a Palestinian expert who has been working on this, states that: "One of the biggest advantages of going digital will be that the current spectrum will be freed of frequencies that can have other usages. It will allow for the use of 4G technologies for local cell phone companies and therefore allow us to skip the problems over 3G, which Israel is refusing to give to the Palestinian cell phone companies, using the excuse that the frequency spectrum for 3G is already full."[31] This fogginess over frequencies is part of the Palestinian media landscape, which includes attacks both on the infrastructure and on journalists themselves.[32]

Lack of safety for Palestinian journalists, and problems over freedom of expression

While problems of safety and freedom of expression for journalists are not directly connected to MIL, they still have an impact on the overall media scene in Palestine. The Israeli occupation permeates the media landscape as it does the political scene, and "Where there is an environment of fear the media cannot effectively carry out their role of disseminating information to the public and fostering democracy. Safety standards for journalists in Palestine are poor. Numerous assaults have been recorded by international and local institutions that monitor violations against Palestinian journalists."[33] Journalists are often affected by Israeli restrictions on movement (including the denial of access to Jerusalem) just as much as the rest of the population. The Israeli army also sometimes deliberately targets journalists, so they are generally discouraged from moving around. The violations against Palestinian journalists by the Israelis are escalating according to a 2014 report by the Palestinian Center for Development and Media Freedoms (MADA):[34]

> The violations monitored by MADA escalated in the West Bank including East Jerusalem, and the Gaza Strip in 2014, compared to the violations against journalists and media freedoms in Palestine monitored during the previous years. The total number of crimes and violations in the West Bank, the Gaza Strip and Jerusalem reached 465 in 2014. The IOF [*Israel Occupying Forces*] committed the most serious and dangerous violations: 351 cases, i.e. 75 per cent of the total of violations. The Palestinian side committed 114 violations, i.e. 25 per cent of the total. The number of the Israeli violations was double of the violations committed in 2013, with the Israeli violations rising from 151 violations in 2013 to 351 assaults in 2014, which means an escalation of 132 per cent.

MADA also pointed out that half the Israeli attacks directly threatened the lives of journalists. Moreover, 17 Palestinian journalists and media workers were killed in the summer of 2014 alone in the Israeli operation "Protective Edge."[35]

The impact of the conflict on media for Palestinians is, therefore, like other aspects of the occupation, oppressive and restrictive. The impact on MIL is to hold it back along with all other developments that could take place in a more enabling environment. In an atmosphere of fear and insecurity, it is even more essential than in an atmosphere of peace and safety, to be able both to distinguish truth from falsehood and the real from the unreal, and to be able to engage in action, including media actions, that could perhaps improve the situation. It is not only the Israeli occupation that has a negative impact on the Palestinian media landscape. Specifically, the rift between the two main factions Fatah and Hamas that began in May 2007, has severely negatively affected the Palestinian media scene.

Although since 2014 there is an official reconciliation and "unity government" made up of members from Fatah and Hamas, it is not clear how long this will last and the situation remains tense. As the extreme factionalism and aggressive divisions encourage media being both used and perceived as propaganda and attack tools rather than reliable sources of information, the Palestinian media environment, by extension, tends to have a negative impact on media and media literacy. Rather than encourage pluralism and respect for human rights, the media climate encourages divisions, bias and even violence, and pushes people away from mutual understanding. As for MIL, Palestinians primarily watch Palestine TV (Fatah) or Al-Aqsa TV (Hamas) with varying levels of credulity. There is little criticism or analysis, with little tolerance for contrarian views. The preceding overview of the media landscape in Palestine is of specific relevance to local media literacy in so far as the bias in the coverage of news has become more and more extreme. "No doubt that the internal Palestinian division negatively impacted Palestinian media," says Adel Zanoun, a reporter with Agence France-Presse in Gaza. "The most important impact was the gradual retreat among journalists from ethical, professional and objective values and standards to political agendas, and the consequent exploitation of the news outlets in the respective areas. As such, many of the news outlets contributed, by agreeing to be a tool of the division, in strengthening the division itself."[36] The increase in partisan attitudes as expressed in the Palestinian media were not limited to them, but were also manifested in attacks on the press, and on journalists and bloggers. The figures from MADA's report (above) give evidence of this.[37] The problem of the Fatah-Hamas rift and the decline in media ethics is also linked to freedom of expression and the question of pluralism and diversity in the media[38] – the rift affects the laws as there cannot be elections and, therefore, the entire system is paralyzed.

Freedom of expression is part of the Palestinian constitution (article 19): "Freedom of opinion may not be prejudiced. Every person shall have the right to express his opinion and to circulate it orally, in writing or in any form of expression or art, with due consideration to the provisions of the law."[39] But it is not so simple. There are in fact many contradictory laws. There are various press laws that guarantee freedom of opinion and expression for each Palestinian and freedom of the press, such as Article 4 of the Palestinian Press and Publications Law, while Article 7 stipulates that it is "illegal to publish anything that goes against the general system," without defining what this means. Indeed, the law institutes a number of sweeping restrictions on the content of what may be published, many of which are unacceptably broad or vague."[40] In fact the legal situation is extremely unclear, with laws still in force from Ottoman times, from the British Mandate and from Jordan.[41] For instance, Jordanian Criminal Law No 16 of 1960 applied in the West Bank defines slander as: "The attribution of a specific statement about someone – even as a suspicion or a question – that may damage his honour or dignity or expose him to derision, whether the crime requires punishment or not."[42] This allows any number of restrictions and arrests on the grounds of slander or libel, and as criminal offenses they are punishable by imprisonment. UNESCO states that "Both the Palestinian Authority (PA) and the de facto authorities in Gaza exercise tight control over the information disseminated by the media. There have been cases of media content being censored and journalists being detained and persecuted for voicing political opinions and for reporting on human rights violations."[43] It goes on to say that, "Official bodies prosecute most often in response to published material that allegedly defames political figures, damages national security, incites hatred or includes inaccurate information."[44] In addition to the external constraints on freedom of expression, there is also a serious problem with self-censorship.

In a study released in December 2014, showing that 80 per cent of interviewed journalists practice self-censorship, MADA's General Director Musa Rimawi pointed out that the spread of self-censorship seriously impacts the quality of Palestinian journalism, in addition to hampering freedom of expression and citizens' right to information. He explained that self-censorship obstructs the role that journalism must play in a democratic society.[45] The question of pluralism and diversity in the media is clear from the problems with the Fatah-Hamas rift and the extreme bias in some of the media outlets. But, as the sheer number of outlets shows, there is open access to these opposing views.

In general the media reflect the tradition of openness and tolerance prevalent in Palestinian society towards different groups. The problem is more with the perception of bias in media outlets, not in their being dominated by any one group. UNESCO states that "there does not necessarily appear to be much trust in media outlets overall,"[46] and that "a number of Palestinian media outlets tend to be biased towards one political orientation and are reported to design their programmes on the basis of their political leaning rather than the needs of their audiences."[47]

Background for Media and Information Literacy

MIL, as such, is still a relatively new concept in Palestine, both in the education system and in civil society. The writers of this chapter were introduced to media literacy outside the context of Palestine – via work with nonviolence and gender, the United Nations Alliance of Civilizations (UNAOC), and media activities in Jordan. Since 2009, there has been growing appreciation of MIL's importance. There has also been an increasing number of activities related to information and media literacy, as there have been a number of projects, i.e. developing skills, and how to navigate today's digital world.

There is also growing realization of the need to raise the general level of awareness on how to interact and deal with the media. These activities are being organized across all sectors of society: civil society, academia, government and the private sector. For instance, "In relation to schools, and information literacy, the Ministry of Education has had several initiatives regarding e-learning since 1995, and several projects were conducted such as 'Intel teach' that was related to training teachers on the use of ICT in education and training them on basic computer skills, involving more than 10,000 teachers. Other major projects related to the use of ICT in education were 'world links' funded by the European Union (EU), 'SEED' funded by the Japanese International Cooperation Fund (JICA), as well as smaller projects."[48] More than developments in technology, however, it is the prolonged conflict that has had, and continues to have, the most impact on everything to do with media, including media literacy, for Palestinians. One aspect of the occupation, for instance, is the severe restriction on movement imposed on the Palestinian population. Media is one of the ways that can help to overcome these. From teaching children through televised classes (in Hebron), to Facebook, to meetings via digital videoconference between the West Bank and the Gaza Strip, although they are often not possible due to the lack of sufficient electricity.[49]

The current situation is one of frustration and fragmentation among the Palestinian population, as the Israeli occupation continues, and becomes increasingly entrenched, and as the level of human security decreases and hopes for a just solution fade. The occupation remains the dominating feature of all Palestinians' lives. It also keeps the bulk of the population constantly focused on media to keep up with what is happening around them. MIL is especially important for Palestinians. With more media awareness, their sources and messages, along with an ability to anaylze them, Palestinians could perhaps take more control of their lives and the process of conflict, "actively determining the conditions under which they live,"[50] and start to improve their human security. Given the intensity of the international focus on the Israeli-Palestinian conflict, Palestinians are used to seeing themselves represented in the media. Foreign journalists covering the conflict regularly number in the hundreds. But this representation of Palestinians all too often is negative, whether as victims or as violent actors and terrorists, thus feeding into existing stereotypes. What is more, these negative images affect self-image and lead to disempowerment and demoralization among Palestinians. MIL could help Palestinians escape from some of these chains as they communicate more and better with the outside world; as they build up internal freedom and democracy within Palestinian society, and become sure of their own battered and bruised identity.

Media literacy and universities

It is via universities that various projects on media literacy, as opposed to just information literacy, have begun to be implemented and to have an impact. Some 300 students graduate every year from the 10 Palestinian universities in the West Bank, East Jerusalem and Gaza that currently offer BAs in various forms of media studies, though only Birzeit and Al-Quds Universities do additional work on media literacy. The Islamic University in Gaza is so far the only Palestinian institution to offer an MA in Journalism and Media.

Media literacy is not a separate major or emphasis area under the umbrella of media studies, although it is included in a general way in courses across the board from the theoretical "Introduction to Media" and "International Media," to a variety of practical courses on different media techniques. Al Quds Open University (a completely different entity from Al-Quds University in Jerusalem, owned and funded by the Palestinian Authority and with a very large virtual student body, in the tens of thousands, as it has offices in all major population centers), through collaboration with the Palestinian Ministry of Information, has provided training and education in the media as a general course for its students. This has included field visits to Palestinian and other media institutions to draw students' attention to the media as a means of influencing and bringing about change in the community. It provides an introduction to MIL as a means of empowerment.

Finally, and only tangentially connected with media literacy, starting in 2013, Al-Quds University developed a series of training manuals on investigative journalism, for professional journalists, for civil society (including training 30 NGO representatives), and undergraduates. Since February 2014, the course was approved and has been included as a requirement for all undergraduates. This is part of a project funded by the United Nations Democracy Education Fund (UNDEF), which has included the production of 36 investigative reports, partly with the aim of raising the standard of expectations on the part of the public regarding Palestinian media. While this is not specifically media and information literacy, by raising expectations regarding reporting, it indirectly encourages media literacy, as audiences will start to look for more depth and accuracy and in general view news reports with a more critical eye.

Media literacy projects

Both Al-Quds University and Bir Zeit University have worked specifically on MIL projects. Birzeit, in conjuction with FOJO of Sweden, spearheaded a project on media literacy education in secondary schools. Al-Quds has introduced MIL via community and school projects, such as training the "popular resistance" nonviolent activists, (groups of Palestinians who since 2005 have been organising weekly nonviolent demonstrations in their villages, to try to change the route of the Israeli separation wall) both in how to use and how to analyse the media. The Media Development Center of Birzeit University implemented the first specific MIL project, "Helping Palestinian Children Become Media Smart," in 2007. Its goal was to deepen the understanding of children and adolescents, to inform them and to provide them with tools for analysis and critique of the various types of media messages, as well as encourage them to undertake their own media productions.[51] "It included a new media literacy toolkit for Palestinian schools to help children become "media smart." The toolkit was the result of a joint project between the Birzeit University Media Development Center (MDC), in Ramallah, and Sweden's FOJO, the Institute for Further Education of Journalists. Some of the activities were tested in a pilot workshop for Palestinian schoolchildren in the Ramallah area – 21 children aged 9-14 and three teachers spent a day at the BZU Media Center, discussing what makes media tick and how they influence our lives. The children analyzed all kinds of media, from newspapers to the Internet to graffiti. After a lively discussion, the workshop ended with the children producing their own "fanzine."Participating children's comments were enthusiastic:

> I learned in the workshop how to differentiate between important news and unimportant news that does not touch our lives or our concerns, but unfortunately it fills the newspapers. I dream of an integrated Palestinian newspaper or magazine that meets the tastes and needs of children and adolescents and the family in general. (Aya Jayousi – sixth grade, 12 years old)

The first stage of this project, in 2008/2009, involved producing a toolkit: a manual for seventh grade school children along with a manual for their teachers. The preparation of these manuals was based on a large number of interviews, meetings and workshops that included specialized institutions working with children, as well as media, teachers, writers and intellectuals, in addition to children themselves and their parents. Altogether, 2,000 hard copies were published. They are not available online. In 2009 the manuals were tested in eight schools; a combination of government, private, and the United Nations Refugee and Works Agency (UNWRA)[52] schools. An evaluation of this stage, and further consultations resulted in the inclusion of an additional chapter on the art of journalistic writing, and the inclusion of practical exercises in media work. The manuals were based on nationwide input and expertise, and more importantly, on local Palestinian input and models. There were additional worksheets produced for training in media literacy, based on a comprehensive range of interviews and thorough testing and preparation. The project continued for two years with the development and distribution of manuals, and 17 schools involved. The project was very participatory in nature, working continuously with the manuals as drafts, and regularly soliciting and incorporating feedback. Despite plans to continue with the project, the most recent meeting was in February 2011. The significance of this project notwithstanding at the formal education level in schools, there are always constraints due to constant pressure to focus on the official curriculum for each year, and to complete it during the allotted time. In the Occupied Palestinian territory, this can be quite challenging as there are often disruptions to the school year, due to "normal" interference by the Israeli occupation, such as road closures, incursions, and exacerbation of the overall conflict. There is officially one class per week allocated for "activities" such as MIL, citizen education, or drama, but to work effectively with the formal education system, it would be essential to integrate media literacy into the formal curriculum via the Ministry of Education, and especially to include it as a subject in the final school exams. This means much of the current work with schoolchildren on MIL has to be done via non-formal education, through projects with media institutions or NGOs.

In fact, it is through civil society that the bulk of MIL takes place. There are tens of projects (there are more than 2,400 NGOs in the oPt, according to an estimate from 2010[53]) that include some element of media training and empowerment, such as a radio discussion or a film, as well as blogs or elements of social media. Fewer, however, include a specific element of media literacy such as media awareness, though these also exist. Youth organizations often implement projects, funded primarily by the United States Agency for International Development (USAID) and the European Union (EU), that include media training and production. As an example of a youth empowerment project, Al-Quds University in 2013-14 implemented a project funded via the United States Middle East Partnership Initiative (MEPI)) that consisted of training 30 marginalized youth from East Jerusalem, many of whom had not completed their schooling, to become "citizen journalists." This resulted in a group of confident and empowered young people, several of whom were able to find work, and all of whom are now able to express themselves on camera and via all forms of modern media. Their training focused on media literacy as well as on specific skills and competencies.

An example of a current very wide-reaching youth-centred project,[54] also funded via USAID, is one that began in 2009 with the training of three groups of youth in media skills and the establishment of youth media centers in three key city centers. Again, this is more closely related to media skills and information literacy than specifically to media literacy. However, the project was restarted in 2015 by the International Research and Exchanges Board (IREX) as the "Partnership with Youth." As part of the project, youth in the West Bank were to develop pre-employment and marketable employability skills through engagement in media activities, information communications technology (ICT) programs, and other areas such as the English language, sports, drama, and the environment. This involves extensive practical training in new media techniques and the project has included the production of a media training manual for the youth, with some media literacy components. One of the more interesting projects on MIL that actually focused as much on literacy as on skills, combined learning about the law with learning about media. In January 2012 Al-Quds University's Institute of Modern Media engaged in MIL education via a series of projects to promote justice and the rule of law through the use of media. The projects were funded by USAID's Palestinian Justice Enhancement program (PEJP) with the aim of raising the levels of knowledge and awareness among school children and teachers in the Palestinian governorates on the principles of the rule of law, and as a way to combat internal community violence (20 schoolchildren and 10 teachers).[55] The children and teachers attended workshops on how to create media messages and analyze them. They were also trained in the use and questioning of media with regard to many issues of concern to both the community and individuals in Palestinian society. They produced three documentaries, four talk shows, five radio reports, and 20 written reports. The training included many different pedagogical methods to ensure the children's attention and interaction with the trainer and the taught material. The trainer's feedback on the teachers training was very positive; he mentioned that the teachers' session included a very interesting and lively discussion on the current lack of law enforcement, its obstacles and possibilities to overcome them.

Jana Hamarsheh, a 15-year-old student from Jenin was one of the workshop participants. In her interview she said she was very happy during her participation in the training, as it was a very special experience for her and enhanced her understanding of the law, the justice sector and the role of media as an informant of society, which can be used to strengthen the rule of law. Jana stated that she personally enjoyed the part in which participants were trained on how to produce TV and radio reports. She added that the trainers asked the school children to give examples from their daily lives, such as the issue of school dropouts or the right to vote, and used this example to explain how the rule of law can help solve this problem as well as how media can be used to spread information and awareness on the subject. Jana said she plans to share her experiences with classmates. As an example of empowerment through MIL, another project implemented by Al-Quds University in 2008, "All Children Together" (ACT), funded by the Canadian International Development Agency (CIDA), taught children with special needs how to use media to create and report via programs catering to their needs. It empowered them to speak up on their need for inclusion in the general education system from which they are frequently excluded.

Media literacy and civil society

At the level of civil society, as opposed to universities, The Foundation for the Future has focused on training Palestinians to promote community accountability through the use of media. The foundation organized a program in partnership with the Maan News Network in Bethlehem, which started in 2011, during which participants were trained on how to use media to monitor the performance of various institutions operating in the community, and to hold accountable those responsible for mistakes and corruption. The project was named "Empowering Citizens, Civil Society and Media to Demand Accountability and Good Governance in the Occupied Palestinian Territories" (OPt). Its main focus was on training 10 Palestinian journalists and civil society actors on how to act as strong and independent interlocutors between the Palestinian population and those in positions of power in the Palestinian National Authority. Specifically, training was designed to focus on utilizing innovative media activities and strengthening awareness of best practices.

Another civil society approach is that of "participatory video," a form of empowerment through the teaching of video/film techniques to small groups of ordinary people – often marginalized groups, such as women and youth – whereby they learn both to film and be filmed and to become aware of their own image. This method has been used particularly by Middle East Nonviolence and Democracy (MEND) in projects supported by the United Nations Development Programme (UNDP), the United Nations Development Fund for Women (UNIFEM), and more recently with the Institute of Development Studies at Sussex University.[56] The MEND project with Sussex University was undertaken in the context of research on change, and the importance of participation as an element in creating change, with the aim of proving how a participatory approach is crucial to formulating the next set of sustainable development goals. The films were shown at the United Nations Children's Fund (UNICEF) in September 2013, as part of a campaign to influence policy makers towards a more participatory approach regarding sustainable development goals. The short films were designed and produced by two groups of rural women from villages on the outskirts of Jerusalem that have been totally cut off from the city by the Israeli separation wall. With no media background, after 52 hours of training[57] the women were directly responsible for every stage of each film; they chose their own subjects, wrote their own storyboards, did their own filming. Everything short of editing. But they also worked with the editor for the day given to each film.

The above examples come from the West Bank and East Jerusalem, where despite the many problems and restrictions on human rights due to the occupation, there is still some level of media freedom. However, efforts towards education on MIL in the Gaza Strip have been considerably fewer, due to appalling security conditions and the Israeli-imposed siege since 2007. Nevertheless, there have been some attempts at MIL in a few schools. These were carried out by the Ministry of Youth and Sports in the Gaza Strip in 2010, as part of a project on media education for children. The project was implemented at the ministry's headquarters, with the participation of 20 children, some of them very young, one even described as a "baby." The ministry organized an additional workshop with experts to discuss a vision for the activation of school sports and how to work with it via media. This workshop involved 12 hours of training, included a simplified definition of the concepts of the press and news reports and interviews, as well as how to develop websites, how to analyze, how to implement and how to develop good interactions with the media. Sadly, with the deterioration of conditions in Gaza, especially since the war in the summer of 2014, the focus switched to urgent basic needs.[58]

Media literacy in the context of peace building

Living under occupation is often humiliating, whether directly or indirectly. This damage to dignity and self-respect is also harmful to the sense of self. MIL, through its empowerment, can help rebuild self-respect and a strong sense of identity. These are also an essential base for being able to engage in cross-cultural dialogue and peace building. This process of self-identity formation is critical to intercultural dialogue, enabling people to understand their own cultural points of departure, and thus engage in dialogue on the basis of an "authentic communication" in which they "have an awareness of the ways in which they might be manipulated or coerced and an awareness of the ways in which differential power is operative in the society."[59] What is more, MIL can also be considered an important component of peace building as it shapes self-awareness, awareness of others and awareness of bias and stereotyping, thereby building resistance to them, and generally to propaganda.[60]

Projects using MIL as a peace building tool could have a lot of potential, and could be a way to shift some of the negative stereotyping that contributes (directly or indirectly) to the perpetuation of the occupation, and to work towards overcoming some of the psychological obstacles to peace. There has been one attempt at working with media literacy as an approach to peace-making, funded by the European Union and implemented on the Palestinian side by the Israel–Palestine Journal, which has a joint Israeli-Palestinian editorial board and staff. As a joint project, with an emphasis on reaching the Israeli side, it is on the very edge of the scope of this chapter, but it did work with some young Palestinians and did focus specifically on media "to encourage students to apply critical thinking to the functioning of older and newer media, and to offer alternative approaches to, and messages about conflict coverage. "The project, funded by the EU as part of their 'Peace Education Through Media,'" featured three expert roundtable discussions (15-20 participants) in Jerusalem in 2010 and 2011, and included a detailed policy paper on "Media Guidelines for Covering the Middle East Conflict"[61] modelled on the theoretical bases of critical media literacy for the purpose of developing students' critical analysis and evaluation of media frames of the Israeli-Palestinian conflict. It is based on the experimental resources of three academic colleges in Israel (two of them teacher training institutions), which encourage students to apply critical thinking to the functioning of older and newer media, and to offer alternative approaches to and messages about conflict coverage. In this way it offers students the experience, both as consumers and producers, of being critical citizens of current digital new media."[62]

The other joint project: Middle East Entrepreneurs of Tomorrow (MEET) focuses on information literacy. Established in 2005 under the auspices of the Massachusetts Institute of Technology, MEET works with Palestinian and Israeli secondary school children in a three-year program that "enables its participants to acquire advanced technological and leadership tools while empowering them to create positive social change within their own communities."[63] The teaching takes place at the Hebrew University, and, as it is in East Jerusalem, due to the Israeli restrictions on Palestinian access, is only open to Palestinian children from Jerusalem.

Educational needs

Education is one of the areas frequently suffering from the negative effects of the Israeli occupation, due to closures of schools, of roads, or to settler violence, as well as from flare-ups of the conflict.[64] The only locally produced publication specifically on media literacy is via the FOJO/Birzeit project. The IREX project includes a training manual in Arabic, but more focused on practical media skills than on the analytical approach of media and information literacy. While there is an excellent training manual for teachers in Arabic produced by UNESCO,[65] unfortunately this is not widely known, compared with the many resources on the topic in English. This reflects a real problem in that many of the educational institutions would like to provide media literacy, but have difficulty in finding educational and training materials for the reliable implementation of their programs. The authors of this chapter, for instance, were both introduced via materials in translation and via other projects.

In general, the Palestinian educational environment discourages media literacy by discouraging all forms of critical thinking and enquiry. The final high school exam, the Tawjihi, is based on rote learning in all subjects.[66] Even in science it is possible to achieve a grade of 99 per cent without ever having performed a scientific experiment.[67] Media literacy, by contrast, as a skill that develops a curious, critical and analytical approach, could and should ideally be taught even in primary schools.[68] It includes familiarity and "literacy" with the Internet. But while Internet literacy might seem to provide a possible entry point, unfortunately the vast majority of government and UNRWA, despite the introduction of technology as a compulsory subject from grades 5 to 10, many public schools do not have enough computers or Internet bandwidth. Many will only have one computer at most for the school principal, and none for the children. Schools often cannot afford to maintain an Internet connection (a cost of some $40 per month). Despite major progress in the provision of materials, equipment and ICT, the challenge is to get evidence on their actual levels of use in schools and classrooms.[69] This means exploring to what extent they are really used, how intensively and in which subjects, what the level of curriculum integration is, and, most importantly, the impact on student performance and learning outcomes. All are key elements for the future agenda of improving quality and relevance of education in the West Bank and Gaza.

The issue of MIL in the Palestinian curriculum is essentially non-existent. There have not been any discussions or debates of MIL at the national level. Nor has there been any decision to incorporate the subject in the curriculum in spite of the huge and rapid developments in the media, and the growing presence of social media and their increasing impact on students and schools. There is an urgent need to identify and develop sound approaches and teaching tools to deal with these new developments and to teach young people to analyze the mass of information in all the various media. While media literacy is much needed and is highly relevant in today's world for Palestinians as for all in the MENA region, it will take time and dedicated work with the Ministry of Education to convince policy makers of its importance as a separate subject of focus in the school curriculum before it can be mainstreamed.

Recommendations

MIL in its sense of understanding the media and being able to analyze and criticize, and in its sense of knowing how to use media and participate, especially via the use of digital tools, is crucial for the development and empowerment of individuals and societies.[70] The authors believe it essential to be included in the formal education system in the oPt, from primary schools through universities. The process of mainstreaming MIL can perhaps be done most effectively by a combination of a bottom-up and top-down approach. Bottom-up to make sure the needs of the general public, and especially women and youth and marginalized groups, are heard and addressed in any program. Top-down, to make sure that the process can be implemented throughout the education systems – primary, secondary and tertiary, and both formal and non-formal.

We therefore make the following specific recommendations:

1. A high-level multi-stakeholder consultation

One of the best ways to initiate and give immediate momentum to MIL would be to organize a high-level consultation with representatives from the UNAoC, UNESCO, and other development agencies with expertise in MIL and could thereby engage high-level officials from the Palestinian Authority and educational community in the appreciation of the importance of MIL and the formulation of a national strategy.

It would be important to incorporate monitoring and evaluation from the outset to make sure the project takes place as planned and that schools and teachers don't just put it to one side. It would be better to start small and prove the effectiveness of MIL.

2. Regarding primary and secondary education

MIL should be introduced to the main (compulsory) curriculum for primary and secondary schools, starting from first grade. It should be treated as an essential form of literacy in this day and age. The focus should be on practical exercises, not on theories, and on encouraging children to ask questions, not just learn by heart.

It is not enough to have it as an option. It needs to be included from primary school through to the final "Tawjihi" (terminal high school) exam.

The first step could be a workshop/consultation under the auspices of the UN, and especially in conjunction with the Global Alliance for Partnerships on Media and

Information Literacy (GAPMIL)[71] to raise awareness of the success in other contexts, and to share the tools such as the MIL curriculum for teachers, and the system for evaluation. In particular, it would be relevant for Palestinians to hear about the example of Argentina and work with young children in that country. Such a workshop would need to include all the local stakeholders, especially the UNRWA, that is responsible for roughly half the Palestinian schools. Since UNRWA has an extensive psycho-social program, it could contribute to how the MIL may help address these needs both in the oPt, and for other countries in the MENA region.

Teachers and officials would need to be trained, or at least given a thorough introduction to MIL. Monitoring and evaluation would be essential throughout the process.

3. Regarding universities/higher education

MIL should be a requirement for ALL university students (along with basic courses such as Islamic culture, etc.), and the emphasis should be on the practical not the theoretical.

A first step for higher education could be, in addition to the high-level consultation, a major conference under UN auspices, bringing international speakers and securing media coverage to get the subject into the discourse. There could be two days of conference and one day of very practical discussion on course building to help each participating university devise its own course for its specific student body.

Again, monitoring and evaluation should be built into the courses and participating universities and other higher education institutions would meet every few years for a follow-up conference to analyze the impact and results.

4. Regarding civil society

A manual should be produced – a Practical Guide for Civil Society – on how to deal with local and international media. This could also come out of the UN conference, and should include questions that arise during the conference. Ideally there would be a questionnaire and base-line study first. This would help with raising awareness about the subject and would help with both the conference and the production of relevant teaching and training materials. The survey would also provide a baseline for measurements and evaluation of various proposed programs.

Specific media literacy training programs for civil society should be developed and implemented by, and for, NGOs, based on the survey's responses.

The donor community should support such developments and training and other related projects, to raise awareness and establish at least a basic level of consciousness regarding the media. It would be important to include them in the conference and in the training to make it a really multi-stakeholder effort.

5. Regarding media outlets

There also needs to be training for media outlets to learn how to deal with feedback, to share in producing media, and to encourage people with media awareness to work with them towards more openness, encourage media accountability and media ethics.[72] One of the conference panels should deal with problems facing media outlets in the oPt, and media outlets should be included at all stages in both the consultation and the conference.

In addition, media outlets could participate in a national (even MENA-wide) campaign to promote MIL, via a series of radio/TV spots, apps, games, etc. This could be discussed initially at the consultation and the conference and would use the findings of the questionnaires. Perhaps one of the media outlets could develop cartoon characters, one male, one female, who learn, make mistakes, and are easily identifiable, to bring out the importance and relevance of MIL.

6. Regarding Palestinian society as a whole

Start establishing a more critical approach among civil society, media, and the general public, and promote the concept of media accountability. The conference could help by raising awareness and should produce an interactive page for the general public, perhaps linked with the GAPMIL initiative, to keep up an ongoing discussion.

For youth, MIL summer camps could be an attractive option, especially if they are international. Youth who have been trained in MIL could then become mentors and perhaps help with the development and rapid expansion of the program in primary and secondary schools.

Notes and References

1. UNESCO (2013): *Media and Information Literacy Policy and Strategy Guidelines,* A. Grizzle and M. C. Torras Calvo (Eds). http://unesdoc.unesco.org/images/0022/002256/225606e.pdf p. 8
2. UNESCO (2013), p. 53, 54
3. UNESCO (2013), p. 47
4. UNESCO (2013), p. 48
5. Dr. Rashid Jayoousi, E-learning consultant Palestinian Ministry of Education
6. UNESCO (2013), p. 54
7. R. Hobbs (2010): *Digital and Media Literacy: A Plan of Action,* The Aspen Institute: http://www.knightcomm.org/wp-content/uploads/2010/12/Digital_and_Media_Literacy_A_Plan_of_Action.pdf
8. UNESCO (2013), p. 22
9. UNESCO (2013), p. 151
10. Mercy Corps (2012): *Civic Engagement of Youth in the Middle East and North Africa: An Analysis of Key Drivers and Outcomes,* p. 16 http://www.mercycorps.org/sites/default/files/mena_youth_civic_engagement_study_-_final.pdf
11. UNESCO (2013), p. 18
12. UNESCO (2013), ibid
13. Palestinian Central Bureau of Statistics (2014) http://www.pcbs.gov.ps/site/881/default.aspx. .
14. https://www.ochaopt.org/documents/ochaopt_atlas_opt_general_december2011.pdf. OCHA give excellent weekly updates on the situation as well as producing detailed reports and fact sheets, for instance on the problems of "Area C" (60per cent of the West Bank) https://www.ochaopt.org/documents/ocha_opt_area_c_factsheet_august_2014_english.pdf
15. M. Hanania (2007): Jurji Habib Hanania, History of the Earliest Press in Palestine, 1908-1914, *Journal of Palestine Studies,* Issue 32, p. 51, http://www.palestine-studies.org/jq/fulltext/77872

16. R. I. Friedman (1983): , Israeli Censorship of the Palestinian Press, *Journal of Palestine Studies*, Vol. 13, no 1: http://www.jstor.org/stable/2536927?seq=1#page_scan_tab_contents

17. P. Mattar (Ed.) (2000): *Encyclopedia of the Palestinians*, p. 321, Routledge.

18. Internews: *Palestinians and the Media: usage, trust and effectiveness*: http://www.internews.org/sites/default/files/resources/Palestinians%26Media070314.pdf

19. For more details see: http://www.internews.org/research-publications/media-landscape-west-bank-gaza#sthash.Vug7Iu3c.dpuf, also UNESCO (2014), listed below.

20. UNESCO (2014): *Assessment of media development in Palestine*, Available at http://www.unesco.org/new/en/communication-and-information/resources/publications-and-communication-materials/publications/full-list/assessment-of-media-development-in-palestine/ ,p. 31

21. "About the satellite TV channel, 48per cent watch Al Jazeera channel, 15per cent watch Al Arabiya and Palestine TV, 7per cent said that they watch other Arab channels, and 4per cent watch Al Mannar, 2per cent watch Al Aqsa and BBC, while 7per cent watch other channels." (Near East Consulting, report April May 2010); http://www.neareastconsulting.com/press/

22. Internews, ibid.

23. http://www.pcbs.gov.ps/site/512/default.aspx?tabID=512&lang=en&ItemID=1342&mid=3171&wversion=Staging

24. http://www.pcbs.gov.ps/site/881/default.aspx#InformationSociety

25. UNESCO, IPDC, ibid, p. 103 (Editors note: insufficient reference)

26. Ibid (Editors note: insufficient reference)

27. *Arab Social Media Report 2015*, p. 24 www.wpp.com/govtpractice/~/.../arabsocialmediareport-2015.pdf

28. Internews,as above and www.socialbakers.com

29. See UNESCO (2014) above, p. 12

30. Switch to digital television faces bumpy road in Palestine, Daoud Kuttab, May 4, 2015: http://www.al-monitor.com/pulse/originals/2015/05/palestinian-television-digital-media-independent.html#ixzz3er6gyFzQ "For most Palestinians, July 17, 2015, means very little. But for those who have long been working toward the migration of all Palestinian TV frequencies from analogue to digital, the date has been etched in stone. Mandated by the International Telecommunications Union and approved by the Arab League, all Arab states agreed in 2006 to turn off the analogue TV signals by this date."

31. Al-Monitor, ibid.

32. The unclarity of frequencies also impacts the ability to broadcast as in February 2011, the AQTV and Watan TV had their transmitters seized by the Israelis on the grounds they were interfering with air traffic.

33. UNESCO (2014), p. 76

34. Mada, The Palestinian Center for Development and Media Freedoms: *Media Freedoms Violations in Palestine, Annual Report for 2014*, pp. 5 and 6: http://www.madacenter.org/images/text_editor/annualrepE14.pdf

35. Mada, ibid.

36. Interview with for the Survey of Palestinian Media, Near East Consulting (2010) – for further details on this in Arabic: http://www.madacenter.org/images/text_editor/Study%20pdf.pdf

37. http://www.madacenter.org/images/text_editor/Study%20pdf.pdf and the annual reports.

38. http://mdc.birzeit.edu/files/English_Report_for_wessed.pdf p. 85

39. Palestine Basic Law, Article 19.

40. http://www.med-media.eu/wp-content/uploads/2014/07/palestine-media-framework.pdf

41. As decreed by Yasser Arafat in 1994 with the establishment of the Palestinian Authority: "Laws, regulations, and orders that were in force prior to 5/6/67 in the West Bank and Gaza Strip remain in effect." *Palestinian Gazette*: No.1 20/11/1994

42. Jordanian Criminal Law No. 16 of 1960, Article 188 (1) – this law was established when the West Bank was ruled by Jordan and seems more relevant to monarchy than a modern state.

43. UNESCO – IPDC, ibid, p. 11 (Editors note: insufficient reference)

44. UNESCO (2014), p. 38.

45. http://www.madacenter.org/news.php?lang=1&id=161

46. UNESCO (2014), p. 75.

47. UNESCO (2014), p. 31.
48. Rashid Jayousi, e-mail communication.
49. For details, especially regarding Gaza, see the OCHA reports referred to above.
50. UNESCO – MIL – p. 151 second – p. 107 (Editors note: insufficient reference)
51. http://milunesco.unaoc.org/helping-palestinian-children-become-media-smart/
52. UNRWA is the UN body responsible for the basic needs, notably the health and education of the Palestinian refugee population. This means it is responsible for roughly half the schools in the occupied territories.
53. http://www.palestine.rosalux.org/fileadmin/ab_palestine/pdf/RLF_newsletters_EN/RLF_PAL_Gerster_PNGOs.pdf
54. https://www.irex.org/projects/partnerships-with-youth
55. Project report – Annex 6b Milestone report No 1.
56. Sussex University published a book on this which includes a chapter on participatory video and another on the power of digital story telling: *'Knowledge from the Margins: An anthology from a global network on participatory practice and policy influence'*. The publication is available here: http://opendocs.ids.ac.uk/opendocs/handle/123456789/4199#.U8aGllGfj2s
57. The links for the films:
    https://www.youtube.com/watch?v=nHs3otiFHfA (Unhappy Birthday)
    https://www.youtube.com/watch?v=HZiFSBZfezw (The Swing)
    https://www.youtube.com/watch?v=81pcETn6sxI (I Need Work)
    https://www.youtube.com/watch?v=EWTFunqqicE (Blue I.D. Green I.D.)
    http://www.youtube.com/watch?v=48W2j1sN8Ag&feature=youtu.be (A Day in Nebi Samuel)
58. The OCHA reports give details on these – how even before the Israeli "Protective Edge" operation, there was a shortage of 200 schools in Gaza. https://www.ochaopt.org/documents/gaza_mira_report_9september.pdf
59. UNESCO (2013), p.18.
60. UNESCO (2013) ibid.
61. http://www.pij.org/policypapers/PETMed_PolicyPaper.pdf
62. A second phase of this project, also funded by the EU, worked only with Israelis, included the development of a teacher training manual.
63. http://meet.mit.edu/
64. Outside the scope of this article, reports by NGOs such as the Sharek Youth Forum provide additional information: www.youthpolicy.org/national/Palestine_2009_Youth_Study.pdf
65. http://unesdoc.unesdoc.org/images/0019/001929/192971a.pdf
66. See note 65, Sharek Youth Forum, p.23
67. Many schools do not have labs. "Despite the undeniable overall success of the process of design and development of the new Palestinian curriculum, evidence from the first few years of implementation reveals a serious problem of overload. Principals and teachers, parents and students, supervisors and teacher trainers concur that the new curriculum is "too long" and "too demanding." Opportunity to learn is undermined when there is too little time devoted to many of the key subjects; the fact that teachers and students voluntarily extend their classroom time in some schools to be able to cover the curriculum. A traditional approach emphasizing facts, descriptive knowledge and abstract theory does not leave curriculum space – or classroom time – to develop cognitive and citizenship skills required from graduates in the 21st century.
    For more information, including details on the numbers of science or ICT labs, see http://unispal.un.org/pdfs/ESASept06.pdf The World Bank Group; Education Sector Analysis 2006 pp. 28 and 29
68. Personal communication from Dr. Rawan Assali, educational consultant, Faisal Husseini Foundation (an NGO that specializes in work with Palestinian schools).
69. An attempt to work with "Twig," a British-based innovative educational institution producing three-minute educational films to clarify and supplement high school curricula and enhance the classroom environment fell through. Twig had hoped to work with their films in Palestinian schools, but could not even get started as tests, showed the schools lacked the Internet capacity to show the films in the classrooms.
70. UNESCO (2013) as earlier.

71. http://www.unesco.org/new/en/communication-and-information/media-development/media-literacy/global-alliance-for-partnerships-on-media-and-information-literacy/ and for plans: http://www.unesco.org/new/fileadmin/MULTIMEDIA/HQ/CI/CI/pdf/Events/gapmil_framework_and_plan_of_action.pdf

72. As an important step in building a code of conduct in May and June 2015, in Gaza and the West Bank. http://www.unesco.org/new/en/member-states/single-view/news/introducing_best_practices_for_code_of_conduct_and_ethics_among_journalists/#.VZrKR6bvs7A

6. An Iraqi Perspective

Abdul Ameer Al-Faisal

Knowledge and cognition are key pillars to any country's growth and development, since information is considered a primary aspect of knowledge building and cognitive skills enrichment. Information is also a key tool of performance that contributes to the decision-making process. Hence, the failure and success of any administrative organization in achieving its goals hinges on the validity, credibility and accuracy of information used for drafting and decision-making by higher administrations. This, in turn, was the main impetus for many countries in the world to give increased attention to information and allocate funds to guarantee access to it. Iraq was not isolated from the rest of the world as is still witnessing a radical shift at all levels and in all fields. At the forefront of these changes comes the scientific and technological progress occurring in Iraq. All the more so with libraries, research centers and public opinion polls becoming the vital inexhaustible wellspring feeding progress to the scientific and technological movement. One might not be able to frame the information scene in Iraq, as it is evolving in a country that is swiftly turning to expanded use of information at all levels via unrestrained Internet access. The more developed societies become, the more complicated lifestyles get, the more information is accumulated and used, the more our need for additional data to help us make sound decisions.

The field of 'information' has been subjected to vital and fast-paced developments, dictated by cultural needs, coupled with a technological revolution that put forward the role of information as a cornerstone to various aspects of human activity, and as an effective primary resource which constitutes an integral part of social and economic development plans and programs. Hence, the current era is known as *The Age of Information*, given its prominence. To many observers today, we live in an information society as an alternative to the 'industrial society' which we experienced for most of the 20th century, with proof that working in the field of information has increased from 10 per cent to about 30 per cent of the workforce. In parallel, the size of the labor force in agricultural professions has dropped to less than 4 per cent. Iraq has kept pace with the current boom in terms of the evolution and proliferation of information into which individuals and organizations tap, to promote advanced technological developments to monitor, collect, process, store, retrieve, transfer and use information via computers, microfilm techniques, and telecommunications, to name a few, and their coupling and association to form what we call 'information technology'.

The Internet and the media

Like previous new discoveries in Information and Communication Technologies (ICTs), Internet technology has had an impact on media, with every medium preserving its character, strength and popularity. In the media industry, the Internet has caused a massive revolution in the Iraqi press, where the majority of newspapers booked sites on the Net, to present their outlets to readers online. This called for creativity and innovation as well as avoiding what was familiar and traditional. In short, the network imposed a new rationale that profoundly changed the news industry, with 134 (Iraqi) newspaper sites 47 magazines and thousands of electronic websites across Iraq. The Iraqi press has become increasingly interested in serious analyses, studies and comments. The Internet is considered a pivotal source and tool at the service of these journalistic genres that as it contains hundreds of newspapers, magazines, radio and TV stations, and news agencies, all of which are important sources of information sought by newspapers to present to the public.

The media at the service of the Iraqi national plan

Major changes in Iraq at all political, economic, social and security levels following April 2003 (U.S. invasion) required the emergence of an energetic national media movement able to accommodate those variables and based on high professional standards and mechanisms. That period saw an unusual proliferation of media and mass communication means, marked by the emergence of hundreds of newspapers and publications, satellite TV channels and online radio stations. This was made possible through the appropriation of a billion dollars by the U.S. government in 2004 to support the Iraqi media sector.

Successive Iraqi governments have focused on building a media framework aimed at ensuring news coverage in broadcast and print media, to highlight the country's social, economic and political issues and promote purposeful media. Iraq has undergone an unprecedented media experience as a result of the change that affected the philosophy of the new political system based on freedom of expression and democratic practices. These were approved by the Constitution in Article (2) of the fundamental principles – Section I, paragraph (b) stating that no law may be enacted contradicting the principles of democracy, provided such a law does not violate public order and morality, as per Article (36):

First: Freedom of expression by all means.

Second: Freedom of the press, publishing, advertising and media.

Third: Freedom of assembly and peaceful protest organized by law.

The National Information Technology Strategy in Iraq

The National Public Information Technology Strategy in Iraq includes a set of goals that can be summarized as follows:

1. To keep on developing the legal and regulatory environment to control, regulate and protect working and dealing in this field in line with developments related to information technology applications and systems.

2. To rehabilitate human resources and to allow them to plan, manage, operate and make optimal use of ICT applications.

3. To mainstream an IT culture and enhance the ability to own and use modern technologies among all segments of society, and to achieve computer literacy.

4. To enhance and encourage academic research capabilities and support innovation.

5. To disseminate and promote the culture of the use and development of open source software (Open Sources), mainly those that can be used in the development of new software packages.

6. To facilitate access to information and the use of the Internet by all segments of society.

7. To adopt the concept of true partnership between the public and private sectors in the development and implementation of plans for the transfer and localization of information technology applications and knowledge sources.

8. To protect individual data and institutional databases.

9. To protect the intellectual property rights of digital categories of works.

Information and national development strategy in Iraq

Information is at the core of all work, so success or failure in reaching key goals depend on understating it, organizing it and the ability to use it. Additionally, information is a source of economic wealth as the strategic plan to the planning operation depends mostly on correct information that leads to taking right decisions that achieve accurate results. Information has economic, social, cultural and political dimensions disseminated via libraries, information centers and systems. They serve as channels to market data and develop sources of information and their delivery to benefit researchers, workers and scholars in the field of development and the use of available technologies. A joint study was undertaken by the World Bank and United Nations to assess Iraq's needs and presented at the Madrid Conference in line with Iraq's national strategy that incorporates a comprehensive economic and social development program. The estimated cost of investments for the reconstruction of Iraq was set at about 136 billion dollars, but components of the national strategy did not address the design of a strategy for information policies or ICT infrastructure in the country, as it falls under the jurisdiction of the Iraqi Ministry of Science and Technology that is leading the transformation to information technology applications.

National information policy components

The components of the National Information Policy confirm the value of information and the legal and regulatory framework set for its promotion and management, including the government's role in this area. These elements include the policy on ICT infrastructure in order to develop it. Cultural aspects and the human factor are important elements of the national information policies, as is regional and international cooperation in this vital domain. They also represent the general framework of the national policy for information in Iraq, which supports all activities aimed at:

1. Identifying, using and promoting common standards in IT developments.
2. Pooling information sources to utilize them in the process of comprehensive decision-making.
3. Overcoming barriers that prevent information sharing, in conformity with the responsibilities of individuals and institutions, and that emphasize the privacy and unity of information.
4. Encouraging participatory approach within a favorable coordination mechanism that deals with social, sectoral and regulatory issues.
5. Encouraging efforts to create an information and communication infrastructure considered urgent to link and exchange data.
6. Promoting efforts aimed at making Iraq a regional information center.

The stunning progress in all scientific and technological fields coupled with modern developments have resulted in an enormous increase in published information. This has had a direct impact on the economic and social development in each country, which has led to the establishment of institutions specializing in the collection, sorting, storage and retrieval of information before delivering it to researchers, scholars, decision-makers, scientists and others in a timely fashion.

Information technology infrastructure and communications in Iraq

At the beginning of the 19th and the 20th centuries, there were many libraries in mosques, as well as private libraries in the homes of dignitaries. Shortly thereafter, libraries spread in large cities, districts, and counties. The first such public structure in Baghdad, the *Peace Library*, was established in 1920. Other libraries followed suit in Mosul, Basra and other Iraqi cities, with publications donated by people. A cultural and scientific embargo was imposed on Iraq as a result of various wars. But the resolve of those working in the field of information never faltered as conferences, seminars, workshops and meetings have been held on several occasions since 1995. A conference was held at the University of Mosul that included the role of information among other topics. The university's Department of Information and Libraries at the Faculty of Arts approved theses related to that topic. On the Arab and international fronts, the efforts materialized in the preparation for the World Summit on Information Society, initiated in stages in Geneva in December 2003. Similarly, ESCWA (United Nations Economic and Social Commission for Western Asia) held an experts meeting on the Promotion of the Digital Arabic Content, in June 2005 at the United Nations House in Beirut, aimed at empowering Arab states in general and Asian countries in particular to raise Arab online standards and specify the most efficient strategies and mechanisms in this field.

Information institutions in Iraq

Public libraries proliferated in Iraq in the mid-1950s, following the enactment of legislation on local provincial administrations in 1945 in a bid to support libraries and provide them with books and magazines, and in recruiting professionals to manage, organize and support them with the necessary funding. However, due to the uncertain jurisdiction of, and affiliation with, the Ministry of Local Government and the Ministry of Interior, the libraries became ineffective and did not provide proper services. The exceptions were the National Library and the National Archives and Books that provide services to researchers such as professors, students and others. Public libraries numbered 54 in the province of Baghdad and 176 in other provinces of the country.

Having a *school library* in every school should be the goal of the Ministry of Education, especially at the secondary level, since a library is an integral part of the objectives of educational curricula to which the state aspires. Curricula cannot be enhanced without cooperation between the librarian, who is a member of the teaching body and of the school's administration. Cooperation with the Directorate of School Libraries is also a must to select the resources, according to school directives and curricula, and in line with students' aspirations, to allow them to compare, have extensive access to information, and the opportunity to connect academic subjects and prepare them for life, good citizenship, and aware of all aspects of their economic, social and political lives. School library activities provide students with the means to understand the situation of their countries, its history and its realities through information sources and modern technology. The table below lists the number and types of school libraries:

Table 1. Number of libraries in schools in Iraq per year (1971, 1988, 2005 and 2013)

Year	Number of primary school libraries	Number of secondary school libraries	Number of vocational school libraries
1971	358	648	305
1988	5 692	1 524	-
2005	1 783	217	-
2013	2 371	7 543	2 156

Table 1 shows that the number of school libraries does not meet the aspirations of the teaching body's aspirations, as indicated in Table 2.

Table 2. Number of schools, students and number of teachers members for all academic levels in Iraq

Levels	Number of schools	Number of students	Number of the personnel of the teaching body
Primary education	9 115	3 507 975	165 738
Secondary education (Middle and lower secondary education)	3 138	1 132 106	65 681
Vocational education	234	65 377	6 636
Teacher training institutes	151	42 669	1 620
Open colleges	18	6 000	369

As for the availability of audio-visual materials and modern technologies like computers and CD-ROMs and telecommunications, i.e. the Internet and online access to information, it is a different matter, since their use spread widely especially among the youth and students. But since Iraq has over 12,600 elementary, vocational and secondary schools, about 4.75 million students, and nearly a quarter of a million teaching staff members, 13 million of them need access to information and education to provide their services to Iraq.

The number of *academic libraries*, colleges and research centers affiliated with the Ministry of Higher Education and Scientific Research, according to statistics shown in table 3. Table 4 shows Iraqi universities in the province of Kurdistan. According to tables 3 and 4, there are 59 research centers, 240 colleges and 1,342 departments affiliated with the Ministry of Higher Education and Scientific Research. In the Province of Kurdistan, there are 71 colleges and 234 departments. This means 1,946 libraries in Iraqi public universities, in addition to more recently established community college libraries that need to be supplied with modern facilities such as the Internet, necessary hardware and the training of specialized and qualified personnel to operate all the resources.

It is known that *specialized libraries* are interested in specialized intellectual products in particular subjects, based on the goals and functions of the parent institution. Some libraries serve industrial or commercial companies, others serve ministries, hospitals, mosques, museums, and prisons as well as specialized professional associations.

Specialized libraries are as follows:

Table 3.   Iraqi universities

No.	Universities	Centers	Colleges	Depts	Number of teachers	Number of students in primary education	Ratio of teachers to students	Number of students in higher education	Year founded
1	Baghdad	11	24	100	4 391	63 289	15:1	1 556	1956
2	Basra	8	17	61	1 728	32 877	13:1	55	1963
3	Mosul	5	21	71	2 548	26 802	11:1	418	1964
4	Mustansiriya	6	11	48	1 788	39 137	22:1	225	1965
5	Technology	7	13	As faculties	832	13 660	17:1	264	1975
6	Kufa	2	10	29	549	10 399	19:1	152	1987
7	Tikrit	1	11	41	674	7 728	12:1	248	1987
8	El-Qadisiya	1	12	31	492	11 947	24:1	52	1987
9	Al-Anbar	1	12	47	596	9 343	16:1	89	1987
10	Mesopotamia	3	6	13	324	1 676	5:1	454	1988
11	Al-Iraqia	0	4	10	74	2 315	31:1	83	1989
12	Babylon	4	13	39	648	13 625	21:1	198	1991
13	Diyala	2	9	33	374	12 608	34:1	77	1999
14	Karbala	2	6	13	223	4 564	21:1	4	2001
15	Kar	1	6	14	245	4 858	20:1	10	2001
16	Kirkuk	1	7	18	154	4 502	29:1	11	2002
17	Waset	0	4	14	130	4 901	38:1	18	2002
18	Central Technical Education Authority	4	36	280	2 300	13 000	6:1	129	1969
19	Iraqi Council for Medical Specializations	-	-	-	16	-	-	438	-
20	Iraqi Computers and IT Authority	-	-	-	47	-	-	12	-
21	Community Colleges	-	18	89	671	24 719	-	1 988	-
	Total	59	240	1 342	18 804	291 950	-	4 493	-

Table 4.   Iraqi universities in the Province of Kurdistan

No.	Universities	Centers	Colleges	Depts	Teachers	Number of students (in thousands) Morning	Night	Higher education	Year founded
1	Salahuddin	-	19	49	1 023	12 741	-	-	1968
2	Sulaymaniyah	-	16	41	486	8 197	1 795	-	1992
3	Dohuk	-	11	34	377	4 041	408	-	1992
4	Koya	-	10	23	122	1 522	426	-	2005
5	Technical Education Authority, Erbil	-	8	45	-	-	-	-	-
6	Technical Education Authority, Sulaymaniyah	-	7	42	12	410	-	-	-
	Total		71	234	2 020	26 911	2 629		

- At research institutions such as the Center for Arab World Studies at Al-Mustan-siriya University.

- Industrial and commercial enterprises such as the Library of the Baghdad Chamber of Commerce.

- Ministries and their government departments.

- Professional and grassroots organizations such as the Iraqi Women's Association or the Iraqi Engineers Association (Ministry of State).

- Museums and historical archives.

- Disabled people and people with special needs

The Iraqi Academy of Sciences library is one of the best in social sciences and humanities in the country, notably on the Arabic, Kurdish, and Syriac languages and literature, history, geography, expeditions, Arab and Islamic heritage, providing academics and researchers with information. The library is divided into five sections, the largest being the Arabic section, which includes (160,000) books and volumes. Collections of books are obtained by purchase or dedication, and more than 30 magazines arrive monthly at the library.

Private libraries, such as the libraries of mosques, hussaynias (Shiite Muslim gathering halls), churches, monasteries, and parishes, have been the main source of knowledge for scholars and researchers for the preservation of Arab, Islamic and other religious heritage, since ancient times. The state was in charge of their construction and maintenance. These libraries were fed with rare books and manuscripts. Most of the collections relate to religions, languages, literature, philosophy, and history. Some of them were previously affiliated with the Ministry of Religious Endowments, others to dignitaries as part of private libraries, but mostly rare resources from donations, dedications, endowments and purchases.

The National Manuscript Center is considered one of the libraries that specializes in manuscripts on various topics and languages. It includes the rarest and most expensive manuscripts, totaling 42,146, and dating back to the history of Iraq and the Islamic nation. The manuscripts were either purchased or received as gifts from institutions, noted figures, or seizure and confiscation of libraries, mosques and religious schools.

Conclusion

In a nutshell, Iraq's information technology footprint began in 2003, and has witnessed quantum leaps. It has managed to make clear changes in the IT's general performance.

Note
No references available in this article.

7. An Algerian Perspective

Redouane Boujemaa

Traditionally, knowledge and culture were at the core of several philosophical debates as well as various social, political and ideological conflicts. The current education systems and institutions were no exception. Since the second decade of the last century mass communication has played at least a pivotal role in either overestimating or underestimating the importance of education. The same applies more or less to Algerian society, which has greatly suffered from high rates of illiteracy due to colonialism and its negative consequences. However, since its independence, Algeria has sought to build an education system, with the aim of expanding and spreading education, a goal, which has been relatively achieved, according to available quantitative data and statistics; however, the quality challenge has not yet been met, especially in terms of integrating media and communication into the education system by using ICTs. Since 2001, the education system has failed to address one of its main concerns, namely digitizing schools. Before sharing some figures and statistics on training and equipment which are part of a strategy on integrating ICTs in the education system – training teachers and students on various types of ICTs – it is essential, from a methodological perspective, to refer to some theories on media literacy as well as the relationship between education and media in general.

Media literacy:
evolution of a concept and the explosion of new technologies

The concept of education through means of communication deserves a separate study as a result of a wide and rich academic debate on education and on media and communication. However, in order not to lose sight of this dilemma, only the main concepts of this subject are to be discussed in the present article. The term 'media literacy' may be defined as the process of optimally using means of communication in order to meet the goals stated in the state's education and communication policy. Another definition is that the process consists of teaching and training students as well as teachers on how to deal with media content selectively and consciously in order to avoid their negative impact, leading to an awareness in dealing with media messages and images. The concept of media literacy has received special attention from various international organizations and institutions, which produced dozens of reports in this field. The Thomas report (1990), for example, has defined media literacy as "the ability to read and process information in order to be fully involved in one's community." The *ED-MEDIA 1999 World Conference on Educational Multimedia, Hypermedia & Telecommunications* defined it as "education specialized in dealing with all media and communication means including printed words and illustrations, audio, silent and motion pictures presented through any genre of technologies." This definition encompasses evolutions in modern ICTs especially that such evolutions have brought structural changes into both the communication and education systems. These changes increased the existing competition between ICTs and education, a competition that will escalate the theoretical and conceptual debate on education and communication and on media literacy where education goes beyond time and space especially with its evolution through the Web.

Education and communication in Algeria: the triangle of competition, contradiction and homogeneity

The majority of societies have recognized the increased competition and even contradiction in some cases between education and communication systems where competition has led to various contradictions in individuals' perceptions and ways of thinking. While the education system is based on competition in terms of attainment and achievement and on teaching critical individual thinking, the information system is based on mass communication where disseminating what is new is valued, without stopping to contemplate its content, while presenting, while presenting enjoyable entertainment programs that are easy to understand, regardless of their weakness in style and linguistic structure, all of which indicates clearly the contradiction between education and communication.

This contradiction has produced a confrontational relationship between educational institutions and the media where a clear discrepancy emerged between the academic knowledge-based schooling culture and media-based information culture, which revolves around promotion, entertainment, pleasure and publicity, which in turn reflect the existing relationship between media organizations and commercial, political and security bodies. Despite their contradictions, education and media share a kind of homogeneity and similarity that cannot be overlooked. Both institutions take part in the communication process and contribute to social development of individuals who spend much time exposed to media or as learners in classrooms, although many indicators confirmed since the end of the last century that a child in France, for example, spends an average of 1,200 hours a year watching TV against an average of 900 hours in the classroom. Studies in sociology of communication as well as cultural studies have concluded that the effects of mass media on the new generations' behavior, values, habits and trends, have greatly increased especially with uninterrupted satellite broadcasts. This has led the media and educators to end their estrangement by seeking to cooperate and put media at the service of education and vice versa. Thanks to modern technology and since the end of the 1990s, education and communication have become more homogeneous with media and ICTs becoming an integral part of the education process. Teachers began resorting to multimedia and the Internet in preparation of learning materials. Distance education, e-learning, the virtual university, and education websites have become important areas for educational institutions in technologically advanced and a real challenge in developing countries like Algeria.

Post-Independence illiteracy in Algeria exceeds 86 per cent

We cannot understand media literacy in Algeria without examining the reality of education and the history of the country, which was under colonial rule that imposed a racist educational system. In 1962 – the year of liberation from French colonialism – illiteracy exceeded 86 percent. This figure is essential if we are to understand the lack of media literacy and the qualitative deficiencies in the inclusion of new communication technologies in education. In 1962, education covered only 20 percent of children who reached school age. Algeria also inherited only a few educational institutions where the French language dominated. Education was limited to specific groups and categories. Since then, Algeria has been trying to address this intolerable situation by seeking alternatives and different reform measures. Reform measures and policies can be summarized in three major phases: The first phase from 1962 to 1976, a transition phase with several shortcomings where progressive adjustments were made as a prelude to the establishment of an educational system commensurate with development requirements. The priority was to systemize education by establishing facilities to be extended to remote areas while gradually introducing the Arabic language. These measures increased the enrollment percentage of school age children from 20 per cent in 1962 to 70 per cent by the end of 1976.

The second phase from 1976 to 1999 witnessed the execution of Decree 76-35 of April 16, 1976, which organized education and training in Algeria. The decree introduced educational reforms to keep pace with economic and social transformations, which manifested themselves in the consecration of compulsory free education. The decree was implemented in the academic year 1980-1981, and was called the 'basic school system' with a scientific and technological scope.

The third phase has been ongoing since 2000. It is the period of major reforms, which matters most for us since it coincides with the use of modern communication technologies and the school digitization projects, at the recommendations of experts overseeing reforms workshops calling for the use of modern teaching tools in education.

Quantitative developments and the challenge of quality

It is only natural that the demographic growth rate, which is relatively high in Algeria, associated with the principle of democratizing education, has contributed to increasing the school enrollment rate by more than ten times; the number of enrolled children during the academic year 2014-2015 exceeded 8,600,000. The number of successful candidates in the baccalaureate degree increased from 42 per cent in 1962 to 23 per cent in 1976, 23 per cent in 1979, 25 per cent in 1999, and to nearly 59 per cent in 2012. To counter the rise in the number of pupils, it was natural that the employment rate of teachers increase significantly – a rise of 16 times from 1962 to the present, reaching 326,000 in 2000, with 170,000 at the elementary level, 101,000 in basic education and 55,000 in secondary education.

The supervision percentage at the national level (number of pupils per teacher) was estimated at 54 per cent in primary schools, 97 per cent in intermediate schools, and 10 per cent at the secondary level. It is worth noting, from a sociological point of view, the progressive rise in the feminization of the teaching profession, with 130 women versus 100 men in 2010-2011, throughout the various grades, against 89 females in 2000-2001, with 121, 149 and 117 women in primary, intermediate and secondary education consecutively against 100 men, while it was completely non-existent in the wake of independence.

As far as education facilities are concerned, since 1962, Algeria has managed to build more than 24,932 institutions (elementary schools, intermediate and secondary schools) against an estimated number of 21,000 institutions in the year 2000 i.e. 355 primary, 79 complementary (intermediate) and 32 secondary schools every year.

Table 1.   Number of educational institutions in Algeria 1964 and 2000

Type of institution	1964	2000
Primary schools	3 050	19 040
Secondary schools	49	1 218
Total	3 099	20 258

But these figures, which were often a source of pride for Algerian officials, hide another reality manifested in a crisis of quality. Experts talk about a sick and stricken school from the perspective of quality. This diagnosis opened the door to a reform process in 2000, which aimed at mainstreaming modern communication technologies in the various stages of education.

ICTs at all levels of education and training in Algeria

Algeria embarked on comprehensive and in-depth reforms of the educational system in 2000 following work undertaken by the National Commission for the Reform of the Educational System, established May 13, 2000. The Commission conducted a number of workshops, namely the *training of trainers, radical pedagogical renewal, strengthening and supporting the Arabic language, upgrading the Amazigh language (Berber language) and openness to foreign languages, civic, moral and religious education to make citizens feel proud of their values and their country while being open to the world,* in addition to the inclusion of new ICTs at all levels of education and training. The commission also came up with a number of proposals, namely: Improving the level of teacher training, review of curricula and teaching materials, specifying a new policy for school textbooks, establishing an evaluation system, modernization of education's management system, and introducing modern ICTs in schools.

In order to improve the level of teachers, a new policy for the training of trainers was conceived as a means to teach academic knowledge in parallel with professional skills. The content of curricula was also reviewed, as were teaching methods, to keep pace with the evolution of technological or pedagogical scientific knowledge to ensure schools' openness to the outside world. The aim is to respond to the needs of the new Algerian society generated by profound political, economic and social transformations in Algeria. The commission concluded that it is a priority to use ICTS if the educational system is to be reformed.

School digitization

Therefore, bearing in mind the need to optimize the use of ICTs, the Ministry of Education introduced IT in the education process as part of comprehensive reforms. The official discourse, as well as resolutions related to education, confirms that IT literacy is indeed a strategic goal and that the targeted groups differ from one grade to another. In primary education, for example, students should learn how to use the basic functions of a computer and how to produce an electronic document. In intermediate school, students should be able to process and exploit data. Such capacities are to be developed for students to be ready for university and scientific research. The introduction of IT in education and the development of modern ICTs is an integral part of 'the school digitization' strategy that is divided into three levels: e-Education, equipment for school facilities and the digitization of the pedagogical and administrative content. In order to achieve the objectives of this strategy, a plan was developed as follows below.

Continuous training: recycling over 200,000 teachers

A training program was developed for teachers in primary, intermediate and secondary schools and has been applied since 2001. It targeted 50,000 teachers from secondary schools between 2001 and 2003, and over 18,000 teachers in the primary and intermediate school between 2003 and 2004. The sector succeeded in the period from 2006 to 2008 in training and recycling more than 102,000 teachers in primary education, 63,000 in intermediate schools, and 36,000 at the secondary level. The training sessions addressed four educational topics: introduction to the use of new technologies, inclusion of new IT rules while incorporating them in distance learning. These figures are expected to multiply significantly by 2020, as it is likely that the training will become more specialized, notably since the Ministry of Education plans to use smart boards and make ICTs accessible in all levels of education.

Equipping school facilities: one computer for every 15 students

The Ministry of Education earmarked a portfolio of 800 million dinars to equip educational institutions to connect to 'intranet' and 'Internet' networks. It is a project of major importance for public authorities that are seeking to achieve a so-called 'modernized education system,' notably in administrative and pedagogical management. This project consists of three phases: 1) Connecting the Ministry of Education with all its relevant institutions; 2) connecting 2,000 secondary and 5,000 intermediate schools; and, 3) introducing the 'intranet' and 'Internet' into all 15, 000 primary schools. Education officials in Algeria have ascertained that the aim of the project is to introduce the "video conferencing" system to allow schools in the south of the country to benefit from the lessons provided by schools in the north. It will also store data, post, digitize and record all lessons and lectures on the Web to make them accessible to students and teachers.

It is worth noting that 68 educational institutions have so far been connected to the official website of the ministry, with 84 per cent Internet connectivity in secondary schools, 77 per cent in intermediate schools and 23 per cent in primary schools. Significant amounts of money have been allocated to equip secondary and intermediate schools with computer labs. Figures indicate there is one computer for every 44 students in secondary schools as opposed to one computer for every 120 students in intermediate schools. However the short-term goal is to have one computer for every 15 secondary students and one for every 30 intermediate students, as well as connecting all educational institutions to the Internet in the short term.

Digitization of pedagogical and administrative content

The training of human resources was not limited to teachers since it also covered inspectors, directors and administrators of educational institutions. The plan aims at developing a network, which would connect central bodies to the various directorates of education, a process that has made significant progress so far. The plan also seeks to link the administration as a whole to training institutes, the aim being to digitize the pedagogical content, particularly the curricula. This is a huge process given that the education sector in Algeria employs about 650,000 people, 400,000 of whom are teachers who cover 25,000 educational institutions.

Digitization will create a kind of flexibility in the education system, which can, in turn, contribute to improving the level of students and compensate for deficiencies in training. Digitization should help students in the training process and will enable them to take advantage of the digital bag, so they won't have to carry and bear the burden of traditional books and copybooks, which exceed 15 kg.

Conclusion

One can conclude that media and information literacy in Algeria never received much attention until the end of the 1990s, due to historical and structural circumstances in Algerian society. Illiteracy in 1962, the year of liberation from French colonialism, exceeded 86 percent, which explains the failure of introducing communication means in the educational system and how attention to it has helped introduce ICTs into the learning process.

However, the challenges are many, mainly the quality of education, as experts acknowledge the existence of a deep crisis in a 'sick and stricken' school.

The education sector in Algeria currently employs about 650,000 people, among them 400,000 teachers in 25,000 institutions. Therefore, the introduction of modern ICTs will create a kind of flexibility in the system, which can, in turn, contribute to improving the level of students and compensate for deficiencies in training. Digitization should help students in the training process and will enable them to take advantage of the digital bag, so that they won't have to carry traditional books and pamphlets whose weight exceeds 15 kg.

However, the introduction of technologies alone will not have a significant impact unless it is associated with new educational practices along with other educational activities and a new dynamic; a dynamic which will pave the way for a collective knowledge-building process. Such a process is a good summary of the challenges facing the education system in Algeria through communication means and modern ICTs. Quality challenges as opposed to quantity.

References

Adel, F. (2005). L'élaboration des nouveaux programmes scolaires in *La refonte de la pédagogie en Algérie*, Bureau International de l'éducation. UNESCO. Ministère de l'éducation nationale. Algérie; 2005, pp. 45-56.

Chinapah, V. (1997). *Handbook on Monitoring Learning Achievement – Towards capacity building*. UNESCO – UNICEF

De Ketele, J.-M. & Hanssens, C. (1999). *L'évolution du statut de la connaissance. Des idées et des hommes : Pour construire l'avenir de la Wallonie et de Bruxelles*. Louvain-la-Neuve : Académia – Bruylants.

De Ketele, J.-M. (1996). L'évaluation des acquis scolaires: quoi? pourquoi? pour quoi?, *Revue Tunisienne des Sciences de l'Éducation*, 23, p. 17-36.

Gerard, F.-M. & Roegiers, X. (1993 ; 2003). Des manuels scolaires pour apprendre. Bruxelles: De Boeck Université.

Le Boterf, G. (1994). De la compétence: essai sur un attracteur étrange. Paris: Éditions d'Organisation.

Perrenoud, P. (1997). Construire des compétences dès l'école. Paris: ESF.

Rey, B. (1996). Les compétences transversales en question. Paris: ESF.

Roegiers, X. (2000). Une pédagogie de l'intégration. Bruxelles: De Boeck Université.

Roegiers, X. (2003). Des situations pour intégrer les acquis scolaires. Bruxelles: De Boeck.

Roegiers, X. (2004). L'école et l'évaluation. Bruxelles: De Boeck.

Tawil, S. (2005). Introduction aux enjeux et aux défis de la refonte pédagogique en Algérie in *La refonte de la pédagogie en Algérie*, Bureau International de l'éducation. UNESCO. Ministère de l'Education nationale. Algérie; 2005, pp. 33-44.

Toualbi-Thaalibi, N. (2005). Changement social, représentation identitaire et refonte de l'éducation en Algérie in *La refonte de la pédagogie en Algérie*, Bureau International de l'éducation. UNESCO. Ministère de l'Education Nationale. Algérie; 2005, pp. 19-32.

Fahed Ben Abdul Rahman Al Chmeimery: Information and Communication in Education: How to Deal With the Media – Riyadh 2010.

8. A Moroccan Perspective

Abdelhamid Nfissi & Drissia Chouit

Images in the media shape understanding, interpretation, and interaction amongst and between people, nations and groups in an increasingly globalized world. Media messages may be harmful, conflicting, confusing and confounding and may not often be uniformly understood or acted upon by their heterogeneous audiences. In this context, media and information literacy (MIL) becomes imperative to empower audiences to be more critical and discriminating in their reception, evaluation and use of information and media. Media ethics are often violated by journalists and media organizations, which may have a big impact on people if they are not media and information literate consumers. This is why it is of prime importance to develop high critical and analytical skills to be active and responsible media consumers and to understand how to demystify media and information as they depict social realities. MIL enjoys a very important status and is integrated in curricula in some developed countries. However, it is unknown or poorly developed in developing countries. This chapter examines the state of the art of MIL in Morocco, highlighting the actions undertaken by Sidi Mohamed Ben Abdellah University in this field.

Media and new information and communication technologies are a means for social and economic development. However, the potentials of media and information cannot be realized if people lack the ability to access, analyze, evaluate and create media content. Increasingly, media literacy and information literacy are viewed as operators for the acquisition of such skills and knowledge, and compulsory elements for all levels of education and every member of society. Yet, media literacy and information literacy (henceforth MIL) is still in its infancy in many developing countries and faces many challenges. The aim of this article is to examine the state of the art of media and information literacy in Morocco. It addresses the following issues: (1) it shows how media and information literacy is introduced in Morocco; (2) it highlights the actions undertaken by Morocco to promote MIL to better prepare citizens for the information age, and (3) it intends to inform the national and international reader of the main action plans and initiatives which will be undertaken in the future.

Media and information literacy in Morocco

Media and information literacy is still in its infancy in Morocco. It is not included in the educational system. It is not on the agenda of activists, policy makers and educators. People are not even informed about it to consider it. For many Moroccans, 'literacy' means the ability to read, write, and interpret printed messages. Yet, in today's multimedia world, it is not sufficient to teach this form of literacy only. We know that the information about what happens in the world comes to us not only through print but also through sounds and powerful images. So, providing individuals with the skills and tools to critically evaluate, process and interpret the content of messages, sounds and powerful images of our multimedia culture becomes a must. In fact, new information communication technologies and media culture have been shaping people's lives and reframing the way they reconstruct societies at the national and international levels. That's why we have to equip ourselves with the necessary skills to know how to use media and information contents in our lives.

Integrating media studies in the Moroccan educational system

Aware of the importance of the Internet in our daily lives, and aware of the challenges posed by the information age, the Moroccan Emergency Plan for Higher Education introduced in 2009 Media Studies and Cyber Culture in the curriculum of all departments of English at the faculties of Arts and Humanities in Morocco to help students understand the functions of media and their impact on society.

The course is taught in semesters 2 and 4, introducing students to the world of new and old media and cyber culture. The objective of this course is to help students learn how media work. This provides for us a good opportunity to include media and information literacy in the curriculum to enable students to critically interpret the media messages, information and the images we are bombarded with in our daily lives.

Teaching MIL at the Faculty of Arts Sais-Fez (Faculté des Lettres et des Sciences Humaines Sais-Fes): Personal experience

When I started teaching the course of introduction to media studies in semester 2 and media studies and cyber culture in semester 4, four years ago, my students expressed their dissatisfaction with Moroccan media programs, which, according to them, constitute a threat to their identity and culture. The first thing I did was to integrate MIL in the curriculum. MIL added value to media studies by equipping students with analytical skills to become responsible viewers, readers and users of different media and information content.

Media literacy

My students were introduced to media literacy (ML) by understanding the following key concepts:

1. Media messages are constructed to gain profit and power.

2. Critical thinking is vital to identify erroneous beliefs fostered by media content.

3. The media have an impact on individuals by shaping their values and points of view.

4. It is important to ask questions about the contents of media messages such as:
   Who is the target audience?
   What techniques are used to convey specific information?
   What values and lifestyles are promoted in this message?
   What is the credibility of information conveyed in a specific message?

5. It is important not to be addicted to one source of information since the media use different ways to present information about a topic.

6. It is important to go beyond the surface and be able to detect prejudice, stereotype, defamation, manipulation, misinformation, disinformation and distortion of information for specific purposes.

7. How can we invest in media for sustainable development and for world of peace?

These issues have helped my students know for the first time that there are skills to take into consideration when reading print, watching media formats and surfing the Net. They recognized that these skills provided them with reflective learning on the dynamics of mass media: the nature of the media landscape, its processes and functions, which raised their awareness on how the media shape the frames of reference of individuals, their value systems, attitudes and behaviors. It also provided them with the capacity to access, decipher, evaluate, interpret and make informed and responsible use of media forms and hence become active and responsible consumers of media content.

Information literacy

Information literacy (IL) has not yet been fully integrated into the Moroccan university curriculum. Information literacy includes library skills, computer literacy, thinking skills, visual literacy and culture literacy, in addition to research skills and evaluation of print and online sources. The exposure to a rich variety of information resources requires the acquisition of novel skills and competencies to evaluate information and media content to become competent readers and researchers able to make informed decisions. These skills provided the framework for students to learn how to find, critically evaluate, seek, check and use information in a variety of forms and in different contexts. Through IL, students were taught to:

1. Evaluate the authority, credibility and the accuracy of the materials required while carrying out academic research;

2. Question the reliability of online sources because they are much less controlled than the resources available in a library;

3. Identify their needs for information in cyberspace;

4. Check the accuracy of a piece of information retrieved from the Internet;

5. Know how to visit the right and useful website;

6. Know how to use information and communication technologies effectively. One obstacle to the efficient use of these technologies in developing countries is the lack of information literacy.

My students discovered that information literacy empowered them (1) to be competent and responsible researchers in their academic studies; (2) to be active consumers and creators of information; (3) to ethically use information to participate in building a culture of peace in their society and in the world community; and (4) to use ICTs effectively and efficiently.

MIL combined

After teaching ML and IL separately in semester 2, the course on Studies in Media and Cyber Culture taught in semester 4 involved the combination of ML and IL since it included both *studies in media* and *cyber-culture*. We seized the opportunity to highlight that the United Nations Educational, Scientific and Cultural Organization (UNESCO) took the lead in combining media and information literacy and encouraging its integration in educational systems as a set of competencies, aiming to equip individuals of all ages and genders with the skills and competencies to be more critical in their reception, evaluation, and use of media and information. The UNESCO Media and Information Literacy Curriculum for Teachers, launched at the First International Forum on Media and Information Literacy on June 15, 2011, puts teachers at the center of this process, towards achieving the goals of the Grünwald Declaration (1982), the Alexandria Declaration (2005) and the UNESCO Paris Agenda (2007).

We can conclude that MIL is taught in the departments of English at the faculties of Arts only. It is imperative to extend its teaching to all faculties and institutions. In this case, MIL will be most effective to teachers, parents, youth, decision-makers, etc. What is important to know is that the main working languages in Morocco are Arabic and French. The first step is to translate the main documents on MIL into Arabic to make everyone take advantage from these literacies. Since MIL is not known in Morocco, and believing strongly that it is important for youth, parents and for every citizen, we decided to organize an international conference on the topic to make it known to Moroccan academics and to raise individuals' awareness of its importance in their lives.

Conclusion

In recent years the Internet and other network technologies have emerged as a major issue for development worldwide. They have shown their potential to increase productivity and competitiveness in the economy, to create new ways to deliver education and health services, and to be driving forces for the modernization of public services. They also facilitate easy access to information.

Due to the explosion of information, media and information literacy becomes a must to help citizens handle and tailor this information to their personal, academic and social benefits. This article focused on the importance of media and information literacy in the digital age and highlighted the plans and actions taken by Sidi Mohamed Ben Abdellah University to promote MIL in Morocco.

We are at the stage of setting a network of Moroccan and Arab universities interested to work with us as associate members to promote MIL in Morocco, the Maghreb and Arab region. But, there are major challenges facing us, notably:

1. We need to adapt MIL actions and research to the Moroccan and Arab contexts and to serve in the best way the needs of Moroccan youth and people of the region;

2. The illiteracy rate in Morocco is high, which prevents people from taking advantage of MIL.

3. Poor mastery of foreign languages and lack of references on MIL in Arabic constitute a real handicap.

4. Libraries in Morocco still operate in traditional ways.

5. Users of the Internet cannot fully profit from this medium because they are neither media literate nor information literate.

Activities undertaken by Sidi Mohamed Ben Abdellah University in media and information literacy

First International Forum on Media and Information Literacy

Under the Auspices of King Mohammed VI, the First International Forum on Media and Information Literacy was organized by the Research Group on Mass Communication, Culture and Society; the Laboratory of Discourse, Creativity and Society: Perception and Implications; the Faculty of Arts and Humanities, Sais-Fes; and Sidi Mohamed Ben Abdellah University, Fez, Morocco, June 15-17, 2011 at the Faculty of Medicine and Pharmacy in Fez, with the collaboration of UNESCO as lead partner, the Islamic Educational, Scientific and Cultural Organization (ISESCO), the Arab Bureau of Education for the Gulf States (ABEGS), and the United Nations Alliance of Civilizations (UNAoC).

Project leaders

The project was conceptualized by Dr. Abdelhamid Nfissi, Chair, International Forum on Media and Information Literacy, Faculty of Arts and Humanities, Sidi Mohamed Ben Abdellah University, Fez, Morocco; and Dr. Drissia Chouit, Vice Chair, International Forum on Media and Information Literacy, Faculty of Arts and Humanities, Moulay Ismail University, Meknes, Morocco.

Rationale of the Forum: Grounds for combining media and information literacy

The Forum examined both media and information literacy because in the digital age and convergence of communications, these literacies should go hand in hand to achieve full human development, to build civic societies, and to lay the foundations for world peace and constructive intercultural dialogue. The Forum was the first of this magnitude since UNESCO initiated the blending of the two concepts to empower audiences to be aware of the functions of media and other information providers, and to be more critical and discriminating in their reception, evaluation and use of information and media.

Objectives

The Forum aimed: (1) to raise awareness and understanding about the importance of MIL in the information and communication age as a prerequisite to human and economic development; (2) to draw up plans to integrate MIL in the national educational programs to encourage the development of media and information literate users/audiences/producers, thereby maximizing the potentials of the media and information at the service of democracy, justice, sustainable economic models, and development at all levels of society; (3) to sensitize participants to legal, political, economic and ethical issues in information and media literacy, and to discuss scientific approaches for media and information sourcing, sharing, evaluation and utilization; (4) to examine conceptual issues regarding verbal, visual and digital literacy; (5) to focus discussion on media and information literacy from cross-cultural perspectives, giving voice to the concerns, preoccupations and aspirations of countries of the South and stressing the importance not only of North/South cooperation but also South/South to promote MIL, and (6) to come up with the Fez Declaration on MIL and Plan of Action to this effect.

Outcomes of the forum: Fez Declaration on media and information literacy
The First International Forum on Media and Information Literacy came up with the Fez Declaration on MIL. Participants urged UNESCO, UNAoC, ISESCO, ABEGS, and other stakeholders worldwide to:

1. Reaffirm their commitment to initiatives relating to Media and Information Literacy for all and consider this International Forum on MIL an international platform for MIL;

2. Dedicate a week as World Media and Information Literacy Week to highlight to all stakeholders the value of promoting and pursuing Media and Information Literacy throughout the world. It was proposed that this should be celebrated on 15-21 June every year;

3. Integrate media and information literacy in educational curricula both in the formal and non-formal systems, to (i) ensure the right of each and every citizen to this new civic education, (ii) capitalize on the multiplier effect of educators to train learners for critical thinking and analysis, (iii) endow both teachers and learners with MIL competencies to build up media and information literate societies, setting the stage for knowledge societies;

4. Include the production and distribution of user-generated content (UGC), particularly youth-produced media, as part of the overall framework of MIL;

5. Conduct research on the state of media and information literacy in different countries so that MIL experts and practitioners would be able to design more effective initiatives;

6. Pursue appropriate follow-up to the regional consultations for the adaptation of the MIL Curriculum for Teachers and the promotion of MIL and Intercultural Dialogue;

7. Expand the UNESCO-UNITWIN-UNAoC Media and Information Literacy and Intercultural Dialogue (UNESCO-UNITWIN-UNAoC-MILID) Network to include other universities representing all regions of the world; and encourage the setting up of national, regional and international institutes or centers or clearing

houses on media and information literacy in all regions to support media and information literacy initiatives worldwide; making this network a driving force for fostering MIL throughout societies at large, thus contributing to building sustainable peace around the world;

8. Foster media and information literacy for development of local cultures and as a platform for intercultural dialogue, mutual knowledge and understanding;

9. Ensure that media and information ethics are embedded in all curricula, and advocate for ethical values on the part of communication, information, and media providers;

10. Endorse the setting up of a regional MIL Institute or Center that will operate under the umbrella of Sidi Mohamed Ben Abdellah University, Fez, Morocco, and cooperate with this Institute/Center to enhance its international relevance within the framework of the UNESCO-UNITWIN-UNAOC-MILID Network;

11. Convene biennial meetings of the International Forum on Media and Information Literacy to provide a venue for continuing interactions on MIL across borders, cultures, fields of study and professional practice. The Second Edition of the International Forum on Media and Information Literacy is proposed to take place in 2013. The exact dates will be specified in consultation with all partners.

International seminar on media and information literacy at the university level

In celebration of the first anniversary of the Fez Declaration on Media and Information Literacy, the Research Group on "Mass Communication, Culture and Society;" the Laboratory of Discourse, Creativity and Society: Perception and Implications; the Faculty of Arts and Humanities Sais Fes; and Sidi Mohamed Ben Abdellah University organized an International Seminar on "Media and Information Literacy at the University Level" June 19-20, 2012 at the Faculty of Arts and Humanities Sais Fes, Morocco.

Objectives of the seminar

The seminar grouped teachers, activists, media specialists, journalists, librarians, and archivists to raise students' awareness of the vital importance of Media and Information Literacy in their academic and professional lives. It also emphasized the idea that in an increasingly digitalized world, and in view of the explosion of information, information literacy and media literacy form the basis for lifelong learning.

Regional Center for Media and Information Literacy and Intercultural Dialogue

The regional Center for MIL and Intercultural Dialogue endorsed in the Fez Declaration operates under the umbrella of Sidi Mohamed Ben Abdellah University, Fez, Morocco, and cooperates with the UNESCO-UNITWIN-UNAOC-MILID Network. The objective of the center is to:

1. Promote MIL in Morocco and the Arab World;

2. Highlight the critical role media and information literacy can play in building a culture of peace towards intercultural dialogue, mutual knowledge and understanding among civilizations;

3. Emphasize the importance of media and information literacy for social, economic and cultural development;

4. Promote the principal that media and information literacy is a fundamental human right, particularly in the digital age of explosion of information and convergence of communication technologies;

5. Highlight the importance of MIL in developing countries and its effects in the age of knowledge societies;

6. Reinforce the role of universities both as centers of knowledge and vectors of sustainable development.

Workshops on media and information literacy for future educators

The research group on "Mass Communication, Culture and Society" affiliated with the Laboratory of "Discourse, Creativity and Society: Perception and Implications" organized two workshops for future and current educators February 18-19, 2013 and March 26-27, 2014 at the Faculty of Letters and Human Sciences, Fez, Morocco with the collaboration of the United Nations Alliance of Civilizations (UNAOC), Moulay Ismail University, Morocco, and the Doha Centre for Media Freedom.

First workshop on media and information literacy for future and current educators
It is evident that today students live and learn in a world that is constantly changing. This workshop provided support for teachers to help students think critically about using and evaluating the vast amounts of information available to them for solving real-life problems, abilities and knowledge that will be vital for living productively in the 21st century.

The objective was to train teachers to be able to teach media and information literacy to primary and secondary schools students. This workshop aimed to:

1. Show current and future educators the importance of media and information literacy in the media-saturated world of the 21st Century;

2. Explain to them the basic media processes,

3. Introduce them to media and information providers and the world of information communication technologies for a better understanding of how traditional and new media work, what impact they have on individuals and society, and how they shape attitudes and behaviors.

4. Focus on analysis and critical thinking to make current teachers informed citizens, active users of mass media, able to read between the lines and decipher tendencies to manipulation and distortion of information.

5. Make them aware that media and information literacy is important given the amount of information available in contemporary society. Being exposed to a great deal of information will not make people informed citizens; they need to learn how to use it effectively.

6. A society that is capable to access, evaluate, use and communicate information in an effective and efficient manner is called a media and information literate society. When we educate our children with the necessary information literacy skills, society becomes information literate.

The papers presented at the event were diverse in subject matter, theoretical orientation, and methodological approach. A number of key common themes and issues were raised and discussed by different speakers and members of the audience.

Second workshop on media and information literacy

The rapid growth of media and information and communication technologies and the explosion of information make it imperative that MIL be taught at schools as young people are easily influenced by media and information content.

Enhancing MIL among students requires that teachers become media and information literate. In this context, the second workshop was devoted to exploring the main modules of the *Media and Information Literacy Curriculum for Teachers* published by UNESCO in 2011. This publication is designed to equip teachers with the skills and methodology to teach MIL in class.

Study day on information literacy in the information age

The research group on "Mass communication, Culture and Society" affiliated with the Laboratory of "Discourse, Creativity and Society: Perception and Implications" organized a Study Day on *Information literacy in the Digital Age* February 20, 2014 at the Faculty of Letters and Human Sciences Fez, Morocco.

The study day grouped teachers, researchers, activist, information specialists and librarians to raise people's awareness to the importance of information literacy in the digital age.

The Internet and other communication technologies are the greatest media of information for all people in the world. The information we are exposed to on the Internet determines and shapes our attitudes, our understanding, our interpretation, our beliefs, and our views about the world. Although the Internet and ICTs are a means for social and economic development, there are equally unprecedented numbers of mistakes, prejudice, stereotypes, propaganda, defamation, manipulation, misinformation, and many types of distortion of information.

In this context, information literacy becomes imperative to empower audiences to be more critical and discriminating in their reception, evaluation and use of information and to develop highly critical and analytical skills to be active and responsible information consumers. The study day tackled important issues such as key aspects of information literacy, integrating information literacy in the classroom, citizens' role in the digital age, cultural literacy, computer literacy, cinema literacy and news literacy.

Study day on cultural literacy

The growing use of information technology is increasing the demand for programs that address information and culture literacy. Such programs in the West are developed, as the rate of literacy in these countries is high. Besides, these countries enjoy economic and political stability, which provides a healthy platform for MIL.

However, the use of ICTs in the developing countries is very complex and suffers from many drawbacks. Today, in the Arab world, lack of literacy, lack of political security, and lack of economic stability are a handicap for the Arabs to be media and information literate as the programs of MIL cannot be easily implemented.

The objective is this study on culture literacy is two-fold:

1. To examine how to effectively and efficiently use ICTs in the Arab states.
2. To raise awareness on the right to access to information, the value of information and the right of freedom of speech.
3. To foster media and information literacy for development of local cultures and as a platform for intercultural dialogue, mutual knowledge and understanding.

References

Agger-Gupta, N. and Agger-Gupta, E. D. (2003). "Knowledge Economy." In A. Distefano, K. E. Rudestam & R. J. Silverman (Eds) *Encyclopedia of Distributed Learning. London:* SAGE Publications.

Alloway, N. and Gilbert, P. (1998). "Video game culture: playing with masculinity, violence and pleasure," in S. Howard (Ed.). *Wired-Up: Young People and Electronic Media.* London: UCL Press, p. 95-114.

Barry, D. S. (1999). "Growing Up Violent" in R. E. Hiebert: *The Impact of Mass Media: Current Issues.*Longman.

Bentivegna, S. (2002). "Politics and New Media." In L. A. Lievrouw & S. Livingstone: *The Handbook of New Media. London: SAGE Publications.*p. 50-61.

Berger, A. A. (2003). *Media and Society: A Critical Perspective.* New York: Rowman & Littlefield Publishers.

Buckingham, D. (2002). "The Electronic Generation? Children and New Media". In L. A. Lievrouw & S. Livingstone: *The Handbook of New Media. London: SAGE Publications.* p. 77-89.

Degler, D. and Battle, L. (2000). *"Knowledge Management in Pursuit of Performance: The Challenge of Context". Performance Improvement* (EPSS Special Edition). ISPI, 39(6), July 2000. Online: www.ipgems. com/writing/kmcontext.htm.

Gauntlett, D. (2002) *Media, Gender, and Identity. An Introduction.* London: Routledge.

Gorman, L. and McLean, D. (2003). *Media and Society in the Twentieth Century*: A Historical Introduction. UK: Blackwell.

Herman, E. S. and McChesney, R. W. (1997). *The Global Media: The New Missionaries of Corporate Capitalism.* London: Cassel.

Kellner, D. (2002). "New Media and New Literacies." In L. A. Lievrouw & S. Livingstone: *The Handbook of New Media. London: SAGE Publications.*p. 90-104.

Lamberton, D. (2002). "Economics of Information and Industrial Change." In L. A. Lievrouw & S. Livingstone: *The Handbook of New Media. London: SAGE Publications.*p. 334-349.

Morreale, S., Spitzberg, B. H. and Barge, J.K. (2007). *Human Communication: Motivation, Knowledge and Skills.* Canada: Thomson Learning.

9. An Egyptian Perspective

Samy Tayie

Egypt lies in North East Africa with part of the country, the Sinai Desert, jutting into Asia. It has long borders on both the Red Sea in the east, and the Mediterranean in the north. Egypt has the largest population in the Arab World, exceeding 85 million (Statistics published by the National Population Centre, 2014), living mainly along the banks of the Nile River, which crosses vertically the heart of the country. It is estimated that 95 per cent of the population live on only 3 per cent of the land. The capital Cairo is home to about 18 million. Young people under the age of 25 represent two-thirds of the population, with some 17 million being students at schools and universities.

Education in Egypt is compulsory for all children who attend government or private schools until the age of 12. Public schools provide almost free education. Children have to pay only a small amount of money for fees (sometimes about 10 dollars for the whole school year). If they cannot afford these fees, they may be waved. Textbooks are also provided for free. Children are admitted to public schools at the age of six. They represent nearly 1.5 million students (National Population Centre, 2014). Some private schools' fees are quite elevated. They can go up to 20,000 US Dollars a year, as is the case with most American and British schools in Egypt. Such institutions provide quality education. Most public schools lack quality education because classes are overcrowded and teachers are not highly qualified. Private and international schools follow the American, French, British or German systems. Egyptian students usually spend up to 12 academic years in school.

Media in Egypt

Egypt has a wide range of public and private media. The Egyptian Radio and Television Union (ERTU), which is a part of the Ministry of Information, oversees and 'controls' radio and television. There are three national TV channels and six local stations. National channels broadcast to the whole country whereas local outlets broadcast to only specific areas such as certain governorates. Channel Two, a national station, broadcasts mainly in English and French. It is meant to serve expatriates living in Egypt. There are more than 20 private TV channels that sometimes compete with the official (state-run) stations and have a higher viewership than the national channels. Viewers in the Arab World are exposed to hundreds of satellite channels. In addition to the TV stations, there are as many as 696 satellite outlets: governments own 97 while 599 are private (Arab League, Statistics, 2014)[1]. They broadcast through 17 satellites orbiting the Arab World. Among the state-run channels, 49 offer the usual mix of news and entertainment fare and 48 broadcast specialized programs like education or entertainment. Egyptians are also exposed to European, North American, Turkish and other channels. Egypt has seven radio networks drawing listeners from across the country. One network, Overseas Radio, broadcasts in more than 40 languages. There are local radio stations in all parts of the country as well as private FM radio stations that broadcast mainly light fare and music programs. They are the most listened to by young people.

On the print media front, there are three important state-run publishing houses that produce dozens of newspapers and magazines in Arabic, English, French and German. Private entities and political parties also publish newspapers such as Al Wafd and Al Ahaly. It is estimated there are over 600 newspapers and magazines in Egypt, according to Higher Press Council figures for 2011. Issuance of private and political party newspapers is subject to the approval of the Higher Press Council, which is the regulatory organization for print media. Egypt's film industry and its reach in the Arab World is similar to that of Hollywood in the West. Egyptian films and TV programs are very popular. Most Arab TV channels rely on these programs. In other media, subscriptions to mobile phone services total 125 per cent of the total population of Egypt, as subscribers often have more than one line, and the number of Internet users exceeds 40 million (Ministry of Telecommunications, 2013).

Young people in Egypt are in tune with new technology. They have been keen to use the Internet since 2002 when the Ministry of Communications launched an initiative to provide free service for all Egyptians. According to an agreement between the Ministry of Communications and Internet Service Providers (ISPs), Internet service was made available for all with the cost of normal telephone calls – (30 per cent of a call's cost went to the Egyptian Company for Communications and 70 per cent to the ISPs (Morad, 2012, p. 76). In 2004, the government launched high-speed Internet service (ADSL), placing Egypt first among Middle Eastern and North African (MENA) countries in terms of Internet users. Social media soon became the most important communication vehicle among young people (Tayie, 2014).

Since 2004, the number of young online political activists and human rights advocates has increased rapidly and the role of social media has changed. They became important tools to mobilize young people against the misconduct and corruption of the ousted government of then president Hosni Mubarak. Social media have become important and effective tools because of their speed and efficiency in enabling mobilization, instant feedback, and rapid actions by large numbers of people in response to socio-political issues. Media outlets' convergence and the ubiquity of multimedia have also contributed to the changing scenario and landscape. For young Egyptian activists inside and outside Egypt, social media provided an opportunity to express their views, join groups, and engage in discussions on current events and political issues. Such discussions paved the way for the January 25, 2011 events that took the form of uprisings to protest against unemployment, rising prices and corruption.

Social media:

- Made it easy to reach a large number of people and keep them engaged in discussions about political issues.

- Made it possible to participate in groups and discussions without the need to reveal one's identity. This was a crucial issue at a time when Egyptian authorities were paying close attention to political activities and when marshal law was enforced for 30 years (Chebib & Sohail, 2011, p. 140).

- Enabled Egyptian youths' political participation, which was prominently highlighted in April 2008. Egyptian activists created a page on Facebook to plan and organize a general strike of workers in textile factories at Al Mahalla Al Kobra (a governorate north of Cairo) to protest against their low wages and deteriorating working conditions. Thanks to the use of social media, more than 70,000 protesters participated in the action that was terminated decisively by security forces who used tear gas to quell the demonstration. It is worth noting that the number of Internet users jumped from 1.5 million in 2004 to 13.6 million in 2008.

In 2009 a young Egyptian university student and activist called Mahmoud Al Heeta created a group on Facebook called *Al Baradei for President in Egypt*. Tens of thousands of young Egyptians joined the group that was transformed into a popular movement to support Mohamed Al Baradei to be Egypt's new leader. Al Baradei was a famous political activist who was admired by many young people. He was the head of International Atomic Energy Agency (IAEA) for more than eight years and when he retired he came back to Egypt and form an opposition movement against the Mubarak regime. He succeeded in recruiting supporters among young people who were fed up with corruption and deteriorating economic conditions.

In 2010, Wael Ghoneim, another young Egyptian activist, who worked for Google, created a new pro-Al Baradei website. The number of young followers exceeded 100,000. When Al Baradei created an account on Twitter, he attracted more than 10,000 followers in a short period of time (ibid). In June 2010, Ghoneim created another Facebook page entitled *We Are All Khalid Saeed* in the wake of Egyptian police's torturing to death of a young man from the port city of Alexandria, and aimed at persuading people to rebel against police brutality and corruption. Ghoneim then expanded the page's activities and discussions to protest against violations of human rights in Egypt and police misconduct. Followers of the page exceeded a quarter of a million in September 2010. The followers reported news, exchanged information, and shared photos and video clips in support of an uprising. This page had more of an impact than any other medium or source of information in Egypt. Young followers relied on this website to organize gatherings and street demonstrations. When the number of followers reached 365,000, they called for street protests to rebel against injustice and police brutality (Masin, 2011, p. 19). Young people responded with fervor.

During the events the Egyptian government shut down the Internet and mobile phone connections from January 28 to February 1, 2011, a clear admission of the strength of social media and the Internet in mobilizing young people. Despite these measures, the number of followers of the webpage *We Are All Khalid Saeed* jumped from 365 000 to 640 000. After January 25, 2011, the number of Internet users in Egypt increased by 1.9 million in 2011 (Tayie, 2014), reaching 23.1 million, and the number of Facebook users also rose by a million, reaching 5.2 million for that period. Meanwhile, the number of Twitter users in Egypt jumped from 26 800 to 44 200 in 2011. More than 8.7 million webpages on YouTube were viewed during the last week of January 2011 (Lou, 2011, p. 2).

Media and information literacy in Egypt: late initiatives

Media and information literacy in the Arab world lags behind many other countries. By the turn of 21st Century, university students began knowing about this concept. More than 1,200 international participants, including representatives of the United Nations Educational, Scientific and Cultural Organization (UNESCO) and the European Commission attended a conference organized by the Mentor International Association for Media Education and sponsored and launched by the late Saudi King Abdullah Bin Abdel Aziz. Participants, mostly from the fields of academia and the media, took part in the event that introduced the "new" concept of *media literacy* in the Arab world.

The more inclusive *media and information literacy* (MIL) concept is still not very well known. It is more common to use 'media literacy' than 'media and information literacy'. Following this key regional event, a few initiatives emerged in the Arab world, promoted by the Arab Bureau of Education for the Gulf States, the Doha Centre for Media Freedom, and, universities and schools of journalism in the MENA region.

In the last few years, from the turn of the 21st century, a few initiatives related to media and information literacy took place in Egypt. Five important initiatives from the event worth are mentioning:

1. The introduction of MIL as a curriculum in university education

In 2005, the Faculty of Mass Communication at Cairo University introduced a course on Media and Information Literacy for undergraduate students. Other public and private universities followed suit. From the year 2000, I believe MIL has been taught at all 18 public and 29 private universities in Egypt. Additionally, a few M.A. and Ph.D. theses were conducted in the field of MIL.

2. The introduction of MIL to young journalists, information specialists, and researchers

In line with UNESCO's policy to promote media and information literacy globally, Cairo University organized a workshop for young journalists, information specialists and researchers in collaboration with the Autonomous University of Barcelona and with support from UNESCO. The three-day workshop (February 14-17, 2013) was initially planned for 25 participants, but because of high demand from the target groups, it was expanded to accommodate 65 persons from different Arab countries. Two trainees from Afghanistan and Ghana were also among the participants. An important outcome was extensive media coverage of the event and media and information literacy in print, radio and television outlets.

3. The production of a MIL teaching kit

Cairo University, in collaboration with the Autonomous University of Barcelona and support of the UNESCO Office in Cairo, produced a kit aimed at making available resources for university professors to use in their teaching of MIL courses at different public and private institutions.

The kit includes materials on the following:

Intercultural Dialogue and MIL (cultural diversity and MIL, stereotyping, reconstructing stereotypes, media cooperation);

New Media and Young People (the use of media, social media, risk and advantages);

Global Experiences in MIL;

Media and Information Literacy: Curriculum for Teachers (the UNESCO Curriculum, Media and Information Curriculum around the world: case studies);

An Introduction to Media and Information Literacy (definition, historical perspective, global framework, media and information literacy in formal learning);

Media Values and MIL (analyzing the news, entertainment, advertising, political persuasion);

How to implement Media and Information Literacy Curriculum (Methodology and Resources);

Freedom of expression and MIL;

MIL in the school (New languages and codes, new learning spaces, new learning approach, MIL competencies);

 Impact of status of Freedom of Expression and Press freedom on MIL in MENA countries;

Eleven teaching videos;

List of available resources.

4. MIL for secondary school teachers

The Faculty of Mass communication at Cairo University, in cooperation with the United Nations Alliance of Civilizations (UNAOC), organized a two-day workshop (November

19-20, 2103) for secondary school teachers in Egypt that was attended by 34 participants from different parts of the country. Representatives from the Ministry of Education also attended the workshop that dealt with different areas of Media and Information Literacy (MIL). The first day included three sessions on the concept of MIL, and planning for media and information literacy in schools' curricula (the strategies and the challenges).

The second day included four sessions. The first was about the media and information literacy and representing media from different cultures. The second session was about applying the media literacy program in schools. The third session was on who is to produce media material for children. The fourth session dealt with training and basic media production. The closing session was open for discussion and questions from participants as well as suggestions on how to improve the education process in Egypt using the media literacy program.

5. MIL for senior students at Cairo University's Faculty of Mass Communication

In collaboration with Filmpedagogerna of Sweden (an associate member of UNITWIN), a network of universities was created in Fez (Morocco) in 2009. The network's main goal is to encourage collaboration among member universities. Cairo University organized a two-day workshop for senior students. They were trained on MIL and the production of media materials, some of which were presented on Media Education Day in Sweden on January 29, 2014. The materials were well received by the Swedish audience.

Challenges to, recommendations for, the future of MIL in Egypt

The main challenge to media and information literacy in Egypt lies with policy makers. There is no policy on the matter. Some scholars and experts tried to include representatives from the Ministry of Education and Ministry of Higher Education in most of these activities but the problems and obstacles usually came from policy makers and those working at the Ministry of Education. Another challenge is related to the lack of awareness about media and information literacy. So there is a need to work closely with media people, to encourage them to publish and broadcast more information about the matter and to engage with them. It is hoped international organizations such as UNESCO and UNAOC will try to influence the Egyptian government to adopt policies on MIL.

Note
1.   Editors note: reference not found.

References
Chebib, N.K. & Sohail, R. M. (2011). "The Reasons Social Media Contributed to the 2011 Egyptian Revolution," *International Journal of Business Research and Management* (IJBRM), 2.3.
Higher Press Council (2011). Statistics Issued on the Media Situation in Egypt.

Lou, L. L. (2011). "Loneliness, Friendship and Self-Esteem: First Year College Students Experience of Using Facebook," Unpublished Ph.D. thesis: State University of New York.

Masin, R. (2011). "The Effects of Facebook Use on College Students' Interpersonal Development." Unpublished M.A. thesis: Oklahoma State University.

Ministry of Telecommunications (2013). Statistics on Mobile Use in Egypt.

Morad, M. (2012). "Use of Information Online Through Social Media and Its Effects on Young Egyptians' Political Awareness." *Egyptian Journal of Communication. 42* : 73-146.

National Population Centre. (2014). Statistics on Population, (Cairo).

Tayie, S. (2008). "Children and Media Use in The Arab World: A Second Level Analysis" in Carlsson, U. et al., (Eds.), *Empowerment Through Media Education: An Intercultural Dialogue*, Nordicom: University of Gothenburg.

Tayie, Sally. (2014). "Impact of Social Media on Political Participation of Egyptian Youth." Unpublished M.A. Thesis, (Cairo, American University in Cairo).

10. A Jordanian Perspective

Yasar Durra

My first encounter with the term MIL (Media and Information Literacy) was during discussions with UNESCO in 2012, while working on developing ideas for a series of European Union-funded training workshops to enhance professional and accurate media reporting on the electoral process in Jordan[1]. Prior to that, MIL for me was a series of fragmented values and goals taught within different media training curricula that did not include young school children. The term has now become part of the jargon used by staff and students at the Jordan Media Institute (JMI) and has assumed ever-greater momentum as students are regularly invited to take part in MIL Workshops. JMI's training programs were aimed at mid-career journalists and young users of social media. Such training comprised most of the values, if not all, presently grouped under MIL.

In 2013, the term assumed even greater weight and importance for me. I was invited by UNESCO to participate in the Abuja, Nigeria, 2013 launch of the Media and Information Literacy Global Network (GFPML), a/k/a the Global Forum for Partnership on Media and Information Literacy)[2]. The Forum's theme was "Promoting Media and Information Literacy as a Means to Cultural Diversity." The presentations and discussions at the conference sessions and outside were an eye opener and revealed the extent of work needed in the part of the world I represented. Unfortunately, other more immediate training priorities due to the technological upheaval the media were undergoing, and the absence of a MIL platform in Jordan, reduced the topic to a serious aspiration. The extent of my involvement in MIL training programs at that stage was confined to promoting the concept and asserting the great urgency with which it needed to be embraced by educators and parents. I made it a point to underscore the importance of the issue in every interview, meeting or talk I gave to students and visitors to the Jordan Media Institute. Since I started searching for evidence of MIL in Jordan, I came across United Nations Alliance of Civilizations (UNAOC) training manuals in the Arabic language. They were well written in user friendly Arabic and did not vary much from the manuals we use to train young journalists except in being more comprehensive and extensive.

Furthermore, following interviews I conducted with Ghada Kakish who is currently involved in MIL educational programs, her response can only be described as passionate engagement in the subject. She finds the manuals to be most adequate. She described the fulfillment and great satisfaction of the teachers, students and parents involved in the MIL programs she supervises.[3] Although there is no national database or reference to seek information on MIL programs implemented in Jordan, UNESCO-Amman and active NGOs led to a trail of limited activities and programs carried out in the country.

The Ministry of Education does not implement a MIL curriculum. However, a positive indicator was the comments by ministry officials that appeared in the press in 2007 supportive of MIL programs and values.[4] Inquiries made by phone to the ministry were met with encouraging replies of positive intentions to integrate MIL in the curriculum but without a definite date.[5]

Integrating MIL in the curriculum

During the last few years, successful MIL training initiatives took place. In May 2013, The National Commission for UNESCO and the Arab Women Media Center collaborated to incorporate media and information literacy into the Jordanian school curriculum by providing high school teachers and students the training to gather, analyze and utilize information.[6] The project targeted 40 male and female students aged 16 and 17 from four UNESCO Associated Schools representing the northern, central and southern regions of Jordan. Officially titled "Integrating Media and Information Literacy into Jordanian Schools," the project consisted of two phases. The first was training teachers who would be involved in the project, followed by a second phase during which specialists and teachers provided hands-on training to the students on journalistic writing skills, debating techniques, web search, website development, and, management and dissemination of information through modern media tools.

The aim of the project was to demonstrate a MIL activity and raise the profile of the topic to support a curriculum planner in its adoption in the Jordanian curriculum so that it can be taught on a sustainable and impactful basis. The project was funded by the Swedish International Development Cooperation Agency (SIDA) in its goal to promote an enabling environment for freedom of expression, with a special focus on the Arab region. The highlight was a public event marking the end of the program in which two teams competed in an open debate that was attended by high-ranking officials from the Ministry of Education, observers, representatives of NGOs, and members of the public. As a witness to the event, the enthusiasm displayed by teachers, trainers, students and the audience underscored the importance of MIL to the ministry officials attending the event and the public at large. The success achieved demonstrated the positive impact it had on the students who took part in the exercise and who displayed remarkable open mindedness and tolerance in their debating skill.

MIL training and workshops

UNESCO's efforts extended to encompass training of journalists and young social media activists in partnership with the Jordan Media Institute in a project to enhance the quality of media reporting for the 2013 parliamentary elections. The workshops, which were EU funded, concentrated on training journalists on independent media coverage of elections. They covered key topics such as understanding Jordan's elections laws, as well as a review of elections and democracy practices in Egypt and Lebanon. The training also focused on comparison of Jordan's election laws with international standards, elections from a gender sensitive perspective, and guidelines to independent and professional election coverage.

For the young activists in the governorates, the workshops focused on basic news writing and other journalistic skills in covering elections, interviewing techniques, and examination of candidates' election manifestos' credibility, requiring basic research skills to help pose informed authoritative questions. The training involved brainstorming with the participants and helped them focus on urgent priorities in their respective local communities. Other partners were involved in different components of the project such as Arab Reporters for Investigative Journalism (ARIJ) and Community Media Network (CMN), a not-for profit organization aimed at raising the level of cooperation within the same society and stimulating the development of communications between citizens within it. The combined effort gave impetus to enhanced independent coverage of the elections in a more professional manner than in previous elections.[8]

UNAOC also contributed to the training activities in Jordan with a two-day workshop in April of 2013. The theme was *Digital Tools for Newsgathering and Reporting Across Cultures* and was held at JMI, for a group of editors, journalists and bloggers from the Middle East North Africa (MENA) region. UNAOC and Google, in partnership with the World Bank Institute, created an environment during the workshop, for the participants to interact and acquire new skills and tools that strengthened their ability to communicate across different cultures. They learned many supplementary skills and approaches to online journalism using Google tools, Google maps, infographics and advanced browsing and search skills.[7] It was a good learning experience in view of the number of expert speakers and trainers who over the course of the two days introduced new skills and tools that participants could make use of and impart to their colleagues and trainees.[8]

The most extensive and long-term MIL-focused training in Jordan, however, took place in 2006 as part of the Newspapers in Education NIE Development Project. It was supported by Norske Skog, the Norway-based newsprint producer and was implemented by the World Association of Newspapers and News Publishers (WAN-IFRA). The Center for Defending Freedom of Journalists in Jordan (CDFJ), also in partnership with the Jordanian Ministry of Education and three leading daily newspapers, Ad Dustour, Al-Rai, Al Ghad, and the mobile telephone service provider Zain also cooperated for the most serious MIL program yet. Twenty teachers were selected from 25 participating schools at the initial phase of the project (five schools eventually opted out leaving 20 active members). Teachers were trained for a period of three days on the use of tools prepared by WAN-IFRA. A weekly period was dedicated to NIE in each of the 20 schools participating in the program. The newspapers supplied the schools with daily editions for the use of students participating in the NIE classes. A "Press Club" was established in each of the schools, and a wall newspaper and school morning broadcast became a part of the club's responsibility.

In one of the participating girls' schools in Amman, the students purchased a video camera and production of videos started almost immediately. Topics ranged from female harassment to other gender-related issues. Another school composed a special *Press Anthem*. Enthusiasm was huge and the learning curve of participating students improved greatly according to parents interviewed after the program ended. WAN-IFRA also organized a Training of Trainers (T.O.T.) program for teachers. The new trainers held eight workshops, attended by teachers from different parts of Jordan. The topics designed for training were drawn from local issues. Three teachers collaborated in writing a guidebook for NIE, which was distributed to teachers. The reaction of some students who participated in the program, as recorded in the video report they produced, indicated a heightened sense of curiosity and a growing-up experience as a result of sharing a product thought to be the domain of adults. Parents of participating students reported that their children had matured and the project's coordinator, Ghaith Shoqairi, said they had improved their reading skills. Aralynn MacMane, WAN-IFRA's project coordinator said: "What began with 25 government schools in and around Amman has now expanded to 170 governmental and private schools all over Jordan. By 2010, more than 6,000 classrooms were doing NIE." The project also created a national team of teachers who could train their colleagues in NIE. Two of those teachers, Raja'a Al Khatieb and Ghada Kakish, became WAN-IFRA Teacher Ambassadors and explained NIE to media executives attending WAN-IFRA's Arab Free Press Forum. "Media are no longer only used by politicians and politics, all people use media as a source of know-ledge and to engage in the political scene," said Nidal Mansour, executive president of the CDFJ, who led the project. "Media are now present everywhere – in homes, cafés, at work – and they should also be present in schools and in classrooms."[9]

Private schools were the principal long-term beneficiary of the program. Almost all major private schools have introduced MIL classes and show great commitment to its sustainability and values. The Jubilee School is one of the success models for MIL implementation in Jordan. The staff has embraced the ideals and the idea as they noted marked improvement in students' reading skills, general knowledge and critical thinking, according to MIL teacher Ghada Kakish. To this end, the school uses a variety of tools to reinforce MIL values. It also supports and promotes musical activities and school plays that enable students to gain profound understanding of various forms of expression. During student council elections in September 2014, students simulated campaign activities of a real election. Candidates published their manifestos and engaged in serious mature debates to explain or defend what they had declared to be their action plan if elected. Advertisements and posters carrying slogans were posted around the school.

Parents were invited as observers to ensure the fairness of the process.[10] Other private schools have also conducted similar exercises successfully. However, the vast majority of schools and particularly those in remote parts of the country can barely offer the most basic services to students due to limited resources and rapidly expanding student numbers given the unprecedented population growth and an influx of refugees from Syria.

Democratic Empowerment Program

By virtue of its precarious geo-strategic position and location, Jordan is extremely sensitive to developments in neighboring countries, which can best be characterized at this juncture of history as unstable and dangerously volatile. The steady flow of refugees, whose numbers vary from one day to the next and depending on how the calculations are made, are in excess of 615,000 for those registered, according to the United Nations High Commission for Refugees (UNHCR). Substantial unregistered numbers have settled outside refugee camps in towns and villages. Schools in northern Jordan, in the vicinity of the Syrian frontier, have suffered the most as their infrastructure and resources were never designed to withstand such a population explosion.[11] The already limited resources have been stretched to the limit, altering priorities and shifting attention to daily survival issues.

However, a major initiative by the King Abdallah II Fund for Economic Development has launched programs whose goals converge with those of MIL. The Fund's activities include debating clubs in schools, democratic empowerment programs, responsible citizenship through active participation, and embracing open minded approaches to culture, the arts and philosophy, which were considered necessary educational luxuries in recent years. According to Yousour Hassan, the Democratic Empowerment Program manager, 1,800 students in the 14-17 years age group participated in the debating clubs. The pilot program, which comprised 92 schools, was based on guidelines drawn after 23 brainstorming sessions with teachers. The Ministry of Education supported the pilot project by dedicating two class periods weekly, for a whole semester. They revolved around values of tolerance, enlightened intellectual discussion, and meaningful debate where emphasis on disagreement and constructive opposition were based on positions grounded in fact, not impressions, hearsay, or populism. The program also targeted 6,500 students with poor reading skills during the same period and yielded satisfactory results.

During the summer of 2014, 44 Ministry of Education summer camps provided a healthy environment for youth to discuss wide-ranging issues. They touched on matters that covered local pressing issues in the framework of nurturing democratic practices to broad cultural topics such as poetry, music and the arts. One thousand three hundred and twenty students participated in the discussions over the summer period. The experience provided program officers a valuable opportunity to appreciate the issues that mattered most to students and served as an indicator for planning similar future events to meet the program's objectives. Students had someone listening attentively to what they were saying for a change, instead of being at the receiving end of lectures from grownups. Many felt a certain degree of fulfillment and some felt empowered, having learned about their rights. Others felt the experience had turned them into responsible grownups able to participate in making decisions that affect their lives when electing competent candidates to represent them in local councils and municipalities. Under the same program, other initiatives were launched such as *Khan Al Funoun*, a festival activity designed to stimulate appreciation of the arts. Artists, poets, musicians from different parts of the country and the region were invited to perform. Young people who live in remote parts of the country and who were unable to participate were bused from their towns and villages for the day to attend the events and interact with young people from different parts of the country.

Another novel activity was the *Hakawaty Festival*, an enabling environment for people with special narrative skills to entertain the public with stories from their heritage or improvise and develop stories based on heritage themes. The events were well attended and held in busy and much frequented parts of the capital that attract a young age group. The events and activities created a positive atmosphere where people communicated through a medium that was the domain of the television screen. In another bold experiment, a *Speakers Corner* was established at Al Hashimiyah University in Zarka. A blog with guidelines was set up by the students. The topics were announced in the blog and once a week, students gathered and spoke freely to a crowd of curious *Speakers Corner* listeners. The event picked up momentum and became a regular feature of student life at the university. It enforced the principle of free expression, encouraged enlightened debate and fostered an ambience of friendly cordial challenges instead of violence and confrontation, a feature that had plagued some universities in recent years and resulted in the occasional loss of life.[12]

NGO's Building MIL skills

On the NGO front, activities take place on a regular basis. Unfortunately there are no surveys or data available on the number of activities, their precise nature, or numbers of participants. The NGOs selected are the most visible at the national level. However, It is hoped that the work which the Information Research Center (IRC), the King Hussein Fund on a National Youth Survey of Jordan, with funding from the United Nations Children's Fund (UNICEF), will be nearing completion after over a year of focus groups and the careful creation of survey tools to ensure quality assurance of the research conducted. The survey tools will be available for the collection by Jordan's Department of Statistics: this important contribution will provide credible and representative information on the diverse issues that Jordanian youth face today. The tools were redeveloped in the context of the post-Arab Spring world, so the survey will provide insight on youth civic engagement, political awareness, job readiness after education, and other elements related to their aspirations, perceptions, and opportunities in today's world.[13]

One of the innovative and active NGOs is MO7AKA, meaning *Leaders of Tomorrow* – a youth-led independent non-profit organization, active since 2007 in Jordan and regionally. In the absence of a national MIL policy or program, it works energetically on different initiatives that deliver a number of MIL objectives. The most relevant MIL initiatives are *Fadfed*,[14] meaning "Let it Out," and MO7AKA. Fadfed is a youth initiative that provides an open, low-key and free platform to encourage citizens to creatively express their opinions on sensitive issues on white papers in public places. By live-tweeting these opinions to decision makers, experts and officials, the citizens bridge the gap between the offline and online communities, hold decision makers accountable and keep experts in touch with the grassroots. Citizens also document public opinion, analyze it and write qualitative scientific research and reports. MO7AKA is a creative initiative that gets youth in an intense, mind-changing experience and builds their critical thinking and problem-solving capacity through a simulation and role-playing environment that provides eye-opening experience on human rights issues and contentious social and political subjects in an unconventional public space.[15]

In October 2014, Jordan Media Institute (JMI) trained 30 young students in a program funded by the Jordan River Foundation on basic social media and journalism skills. It incorporated components consistent with MIL culture. The participants who came from remote communities, received intensive training in critical thinking, evaluation of media and information sources, narrative skills that enabled them to produce basic reports using their mobile phones, in addition to simple slide shows and blogging on community issues. The program also focused on elections culture and democracy and how to evaluate and report on local municipal affairs. In the course of their stay, they visited a newspaper, a television station and a high-tech computer and IT facility where video games are designed. It is hoped that such a program will empower the participants and raise their awareness of local issues in their communities and empower them to blog and produce reports for social media outlets. JMI, in collaboration with Journalists for Human Rights (JHR), launched the Amman-based project *Expanding Public Dialogue on Human Rights Issues*. The project, which is supported by the U.S. Middle East Partnership Initiative (MEPI), includes mentoring and training journalists, journalism students and representatives of civil society organizations on the power of data to help "make this dialogue more effective and informed." Designed and managed by JHR, Canada's leading media development organization, and implemented by the JMI, the project was meant to engage two more local partners: Community Media Network (CMN), a media and community radio organization, and the Centre for Defending the Freedom of Journalists (CDFJ), a regional press freedom organization based in Amman.

At the core of the project is the use of data journalism tools to run major investigations on human rights issues. The initiative is supported by the use of "a citizen reporting crowd-sourcing tool developed by CMN – the first in the Arab world – which aims to help a more informed and participatory public dialogue on these issues." CDFJ will be facilitating the communications training and public engagement elements of the project. This project will support journalists through training and tools, including closely tracking a breaking story, reaching out to the public via snap polls, gauging civil society's mood about key issues. On the research and training side, the project will develop curricula to increase data-driven reporting on human rights, and monitoring media coverage of human rights issues.[16] JMI's involvement in the implementation of this program will give momentum to its leadership of MIL campaigns along with its active partners The launch of its fact-check website *Akeed* with the support of the King Abdallah II Fund for Economic Development, will equip more students and journalists with tools and skills to consolidate future MIL programs. The website has already contributed to creating a culture of awareness of the need for accountability, the right of access to information, and the application of professional criteria in content analysis, thus contributing to raising media standards and underscoring the importance of good journalistic practices.[17]

Recommendations

In the present unsettled climate in the region where blame is laid on the failure of education systems to address the issues of pluralism, freedom of expression, and the right to information, it is imperative for the Ministry of Education to integrate MIL in the national curriculum as a matter of priority. Such a move, accompanied by a visibility campaign in the national media expounding MIL's attributes and impact on youth in the promotion of harmony and tension reduction will go a long way towards preparing young people to play their part in the democratization of society. A vigorous campaign to mobilize parents and civil society organizations to take interest in supporting MIL programs would accelerate its implementation and encourage its adoption by teachers and schools. The impact will manifest itself in improved reading skills, expanded horizons, critical thinking and the development of an inquisitive mind. It will enhance acceptance of differences of opinion, and encourage free uninhibited self-expression and respect of human rights. The Jordan Media Institute, the Press Syndicate, media departments at universities, private schools that already implement MIL programs as well as NGOs and UNESCO, would be natural partners in such an endeavor. Their united drive would support the Ministry of Education in its efforts to introduce MIL and in securing additional financial appropriations needed to this end. The national media: principal newspapers, news websites, social media, radio and television stations, should all be lobbied to provide sustained exposure and support to the project.

UNAOC curricula and modules provide a rich and ready-to-use resource of material for schools and teachers. In areas where there is limited connectivity, NGOs and civil society volunteers can be invited to help. Poor Internet coverage in some areas should not be a pretext for delaying decisions to accelerate the introduction and institutionalization of MIL in schools. The current crisis in the Middle East gives impetus and urgency to decision makers and major donors interested in peace and stability in the region to support the scheme.

T.O.T. and training programs for teachers and administrators will need to be addressed. There is no shortage of innovative means to achieve tangible outputs. Criteria for the assessment of outputs and the program's impact should be developed simultaneously.

Schools with established experience in MIL should be invited to share their experience and contribute their know-how in the development and implementation of the project. Their achievements should be lauded and given a high profile and acknowledged by the local media and civil society. The public should be made aware of the value of their pioneering efforts to give them further encouragement and incentive to consolidate and expand their existing programs.

The setting up of an MIL digital teaching platform by the Ministry of Education would be a cost effective means to launch the program. It would provide resources needed for its efficient implementation by making needed educational material readily available to schools throughout the country. It would also help the program's administrators measure and evaluate its impact and provide a feedback channel for comments and constructive suggestions from students and teachers. The student discussion topics would be carefully selected and designed to nurture the generation and formulation of questions that enrich and enlighten. The skill of formulating questions would create awareness of the drawbacks of intransigence, hate and bigotry.

The daily school broadcast, part of Jordanian students' diet, is an opportunity that should not be missed by the ministry to promote MIL education. It is an opportunity to weave MIL values into the content of the schools' broadcast with content designed to inform, stimulate and inspire with narratives that fire the imagination. Resources can be dedicated so that schools can access new ideas and fresh material for the daily broadcasts with a leitmotif of human rights, freedom of expression, the bounty of pluralism, and responsible citizenship.

A new dynamic format for these broadcasts incorporating content streaming from different parts of the country, with MIL in the foreground, would turn these broadcasts into an agent for change that would, hopefully, chart the way for young generations to live in peace and harmony with themselves, "the other," and the rest of the world.

A report on the state of education in Jordan released to the national daily Al Rai on October 4, 2014[18] presents a huge challenge to the people, the government and international community to allocate resources to save the present generation.

Notes and references

1. http://www.unesco.org/new/en/media-services/single-view/news/unesco_and_partners_launched_global_alliance_for_partnerships_on_media_and_information_literacy/back/18256/#.VC2LBL6OlBs
2. http://www.unesco.org/new/en/communication-and-information/media-development/media-literacy/mil-events/global-forum-for-partnership-on-mil-gfpmil
3. Interview with Ghada Kakish.
4. http://classic.aawsat.com/details.asp?section= Asharq Al-Awsat issue number 9159 dated 26 December 2003
6. http://www.unesco.org/new/en/amman/about-this-office/single-view/news/integrating_media_and_information_literacy_into_jordanian_schools/#.VC8MNr6OlBs
7. http://www.unesco.org/new/en/amman/about-this-office/single-view/news/unesco_and_jmi_hold_training_workshop_for_journalists_on_independent_media_coverage_of_elections/#.VBSL9Uvx9Bs
8. http://www.unaoc.org/2013/04/google-the-united-nations-alliance-of-civilizations-and-the-world-bank-institute-jointly-organized-a-unique-digital-journalism-training-for-arab-media-professionals

9. http://www.wan-ifra.org/articles/2011/01/09/jordan-marks-fifth-year-of-using-newspapers-in-class
10. http://www.jubilee.edu.jo
11. http://www.fletcherforum.org/2014/04/07/siam
12. http://www.kafd.jo/node/77
13. http://www.kinghusseinfoundation.org/index.php?pager=end&task=view&type=news&pageid=200
14. www.fadfed.org
15. http://www.youtube.com/watch?v=ZuwWobdx_4g
16. http://www.jmi.edu.jo/en/details/3069/The-Announcement-of--Launching-Expanding-Public-Dialogue-on-Human-Rights-Issues-Project
17. http://www.akeed.jo
18. http://www.alrai.com/article/673265.html

11. An Omani Perspective

Naifa Eid Saleem

At a time when the importance of the media's role is being increasingly felt in modern times by society and peoples it is important to develop Omani media to undertake their mission of developing citizens' capabilities and enlightening them about their key role in building their nation.

In some instances, information may be undeclared, costly to assimilate, or difficult to interpret (Shinnick & Ryan, 2008).

Today information plays a key role in strengthening and reinforcing rulings by decision-makers. Without the appropriate information for the right person at the right time, decision making can be off track as the process of taking decisions is no longer dependent on experience or hunches alone but on the availability of reliable data from diverse sources. In today's ubiquitous information environment, no institution can afford to do without modern sources of data. Rather, most institutions compete to establish in-situ libraries and centers to provide and deliver accurate and appropriate sources of information for decision-makers and other beneficiaries.

According to the International Federation of Library Associations and Institutions (IFLA), access to information is possible through three steps: 1) observation and experimentation; 2) conversation, dialogue and communication with other people; and, 3) consultation of data storage and memory vehicles, namely data centers and institutions as well as libraries (IFLA, 2014). Not long ago accurate and important data were kept secret from citizens, notably concerning health, consumption and salaries. Failing to inform citizens led them to lose confidence in higher authorities. Citizens were denied the right to express themselves freely. The development of ICTs and the huge flow of information has made it easier for civil society actors to share information with each other, which Sultan Qaboos addressed at the Council of Oman in November 2008 when he said: "Information and communication technology have now become the key engine propelling development in the third millennium, which is why we have focused our attention on finding a national strategy to develop the skills and abilities of citizens in this domain with the aim of furthering eGovernment services."[1]

In the wake of the Arab Spring in 2010, with citizens in most Arab countries implementing what they considered their fundamental right to freedom of expression and to livelihood, some of them did not express their legitimate rights in a proper and systematic way, and instead became unruly, as noted by Calkins (2013). He believes the Arab Spring provided the Arabs with the first opportunity in decades to have their voices heard, but that the establishment of new governments and constitutions is ongoing and several countries are facing a backlash regarding freedom of speech. The correct and effective way to provide citizens benefiting from government services with appropriate skills and information is through Media and Information Literacy" (MIL). MIL includes knowledge and behaviors as well as the skills to:

1) Access needed data;

2) knowing when to obtain them;

3) how and where to get them;

4) how to analyze them, criticize them, and arrange them;

5) and, most importantly, how to use them ethically.

The MIL concept goes beyond information and communication technology to include learning, critical thinking, analysis and interpretation skills inside and outside the scope of learning and teaching. As for sources of information, the concept includes oral, printed and digital data from various sources (IFLA, 2014; Van de Vord, 2010). To help Arab and other countries learn and properly implement Media and Information Literacy by empowering citizens, the United Nations Educational, Scientific and Cultural Organization (UNESCO) produced the *Media and Information Literacy Curriculum for Teachers*[2] that covers the following:

Key elements of information literacy:

1) Define and articulate information needs
2) Locate and access information
3) Assess information
4) Organize information
5) Make ethical use of information
6) Communicate information
7) Use ICT skills for information processing

Key elements of media literacy:

1) Understand the role and functions of media in democratic societies
2) Understand the conditions under which media can fulfill their functions

3) Critically evaluate media content in the light of media functions

4) Engage with media for self-expression and democratic participation

5) Review skills (including ICTs) needed to produce user-generated content

The objective of this article is to shed light on the following points:

1) Media and information in the Sultanate of Oman and their links to the *Media and Information Literacy* curriculum.

2) The Ministry of Education and its role in promoting media and information literacy initiatives.

3) The Ministry of Higher Education's institutions and the culture of media and information literacy.

4) Introduction to the *Media and Information Literacy* curriculum.

5) Arab intellectual output and the culture of media and information literacy.

6) Convergence of the *Media and Information Literacy* curriculum and the Sultan Qaboos University curriculum.

Media and information in the Sultanate of Oman and its link to the *Media and Information Literacy* curriculum

Most Arab countries have a Ministry of Information, which is separated from the Ministry of Culture. In Saudi Arabia it is called the Ministry of Culture and Information, in the United Arab Emirates it is the Ministry of Information and Culture, in Qatar the appellation is Ministry of Culture, Arts and Heritage, in the Kingdom of Bahrain it is called the Ministry of Culture. In Oman, there is a Ministry of Information and another entity called the Ministry of Heritage and Culture, in addition to an IT body whose aim is to "transform the Sultanate into a sustainable Knowledge Society by leveraging Information and Communication Technologies to enhance government services, enrich businesses, and empower individuals."[3]

Regardless of their names, the ultimate goal of Oman's ministries and public agencies is to provide citizens and residents with accurate information in addition to helping people process information and develop critical and analytical thinking. On closer inspection of proposals and initiatives launched by the above-mentioned ministries and agencies, it seems none ever suggested adoption of a systematic curriculum on media and information literacy. Arming citizens with media and information literacy is a fundamental human right and one of the civil rights that have emerged in recent times supported by digital technology. The importance of this curriculum is its call for social integration and the bridging of the information gap between rich and poor (IFLA, 2014).

The Ministry of Education and its role in media and information literacy initiatives

In addition to the Ministry of Information, the Ministry of Heritage and Culture and the IT body, the role and mission of educational institutions should not be overlooked. The latter provide information and communication literacy skills, namely where to find and how to select information. If a media and information literacy curriculum is absent from the early stages of education, it should be incorporated into undergraduate, not graduate, studies. It is recommended that the curriculum accompany the student from the first educational stages without delay. What matters is to introduce it sooner or later. Despite the absence of a curriculum on media and information literacy, probably because its content does not match any existing program, the institutions and the schools of the Ministry of Education are equipped with so-called learning resource centers that are an equivalent of school libraries.

Since he came to power, Oman's Sultan Qaboos has paid special attention to the development and modernization of education, notably the establishment of school libraries. From nine school libraries in 1977, the number increased to 134 in 1990 spread across the country's provinces and regions (Ministry of Education, 1990). In the academic year 1998-1999, the Ministry of Education implemented the primary education system in 17 schools aimed at providing a quantum leap in education, to ensure quality outcomes and keep up with the explosion of knowledge and technological developments (Al Hanai 2007[4]). The new education system consisted of allocating resources to establish a learning center in each school to replace the traditional library and provide a technological environment and a variety of information sources. If the content of the proposed 'Media and Information Literacy' course does not correspond with the Ministry of Education's specific guidelines and benchmarks, the Learning Resources Center is expected to provide the course as it is directly linked to the media and information programs following approval by the Ministry. It appears from the above-mentioned key elements of media and information literacy that they help individuals effectively process information and have a clear picture about media, as the curriculum focuses on providing technological skills as well as the capacity to ethically evaluate, organize and use information. A survey of undergraduates by the author on the ethical use of the Internet revealed that students had no reservations about exchanging passwords to access online content despite their awareness of their unethical behavior (Saleem 2013).

The Ministry of Higher Education's institutions and media and information literacy

If learning resource centers affiliated with the Ministry of Education do not offer this curriculum, Sultan Qaboos University – the only public university – or private institutions such as Sohar University, Nizwa University, Dhofar University, the German

University of Technology or other institutions of higher education, should incorporate the curriculum within their education plans and make it a requirement for all students. The study plans of those universities were reviewed.

Both departments offer requirements related to media and society, and media and technology. At Sultan Qaboos University, the Media Department offers the following required courses:

Table 1. Required courses related to media and information at the Sultan Qaboos University Media Department

Required Course	Course Name	Semester	Credit Hours
1	News in the Media	2	3
2	Radio & TV Technology	4	3
3	Media Law & Ethics	7	3

Table 2. Required courses related to media and information at the Sohar University Journalism and Media Department

Required Course	Course Name	Semester	Credit Hours
1	Media & Society	2	3
2	Institutions & the Role of Media in Society	2	3
3	Communications & New Media & Society	2	3

The Department of Information Studies at Sultan Qaboos University offers a course called *Information Awareness*. Sadly, despite its importance in introducing students to accessing, organizing, evaluating, and using information through different sources, it is an elective, not a required, course. No private universities mentioned above include a Department of Information Studies, hence the need for such an entity to play a role in providing society with the requisite information awareness skills.

Mohamed (2008) undertook a study on universities that offer information awareness courses namely, Maricopa Community Colleges in the U.S. State of Arizona, Dakota State University, and Oregon State University in the United States of America. These institutions demonstrate their commitment to the inclusion of information awareness skills within the academic plan where instructors are required to teach the course in an effective way in collaboration with information experts.

There is no real course on media and information literacy at Sultan Qaboos University or private institutions. Required courses in the Media or Information Studies Departments at that university focus on each major's specialty separately. There is no single course that combines contents and components from both.

Introduction to the UNESCO Media and Information Literacy Curriculum

This researcher was introduced to the *Media and Information Literacy* curriculum in June 2011 while attending the first International Forum on Media and Information Literacy, organized by UNESCO in cooperation with the Educational, Scientific, Islamic Organization and Cultural Organization (ISESCO), and the Arab Bureau of Education for the Gulf States in Fez, Morocco.

During the forum, the curriculum was distributed to the teachers. The curriculum focuses on information and media from the perspective of understanding the role and functions of the media in democratic societies, critically evaluating media content in light of their functions as well as engaging with media for self-expression and democratic participation. Additionally, it is good to have a well thought out curriculum that addresses the use of information and communication technology skills in information processing. We need for our teachers and students to be aware of how to communicate information, to know its sources, to assess it, to define it, and most importantly, to make ethical use of it. Unfortunately, I could not, in my capacity as a researcher interested in the elements and basics of media and information, undertake research related to the curriculum. But in one instance I addressed ethics in dealing with the Internet, and in another examined the various behaviors of undergraduate students in dealing with information in a changing technological era.

Arab Iintellectual output and media and information literacy

There is a shortage of intellectual content in the Arab world addressing this curriculum, its basics and its components. The author could only find a conference held in Qatar in June 2013 that recommended the teaching of sound media literacy in a comprehensive way to help young generations avoid the negative consequences of the media[5].

Convergence between the curriculum on *Media and Information Literacy* and the requirements at Sultan Qaboos University

Sultan Qaboos University is the only public institution in the Sultanate of Oman, and the only university that hosts a department of Information Studies offering a course called *Information Awareness*.

Media and Information Literacy is a comprehensive course offering components of two majors, media and information, so it is fitting to adopt it after 'Omanizing' it, i.e. adapting it to fit the reality and nature of Omani society in a bid to turn out students aware of information and media and their issues.

Recommendations

The author, therefore, recommends the following:

1. Implementation of a *Media and Information Literacy* curriculum.

2. Incorporation of a *Media and Information Literacy* curriculum in the plans and curricula of the Ministry of Education at the early levels of education and later during university studies.

3. Addition of the curriculum to the educational plans of Sultan Qaboos University by setting it as requirement for all university students, the aim being to ensure the transfer of knowledge and skills to everyone.

Notes

1. http://www.itu.int/wsis/review/inc/docs/rcreports/WSIS10_Country_Reporting-OMA.pdf
2. http://unesdoc.unesco.org/images/0019/001929/192971e.pdf
3. http://www.ita.gov.om/ITAPortal/ITA/ITA_Vision_Mission.aspx?NID=3
4. Editors note: reference not found.
5. http://www.aljazeera.net/news/cultureandart/2013/6/13/

Arabic References

Aljazeera.net (2014). Recommendations at an experts meeting in Doha, Qatar to include media and information literacy in educational curricula. www.aljazeera.net

Saleem, Naifa Eid, Ethics of Undergraduate Students in Positive Utilization of the Internet at Sultan Qaboos University in Oman. 2013-14. Study available through the King Fahd National Library in Saudi Arabia. www.kfnl.org.sa/

Digital Oman. (2014). Vision and Mission of the ITA. Available at Mission.aspx?NID=3.

Oman. Ministry of Education. (1990). School libraries in the Sultanate of Oman.

Mohammed, Maha. (2008). Dimensions of information awareness among graduate students majoring in Library and Information Studies at Saudi universities: A study of realities and future trends. Mohammed bin Saud University, Saudi Arabia.

UNESCO. (2011). *Media and Information Literacy: Curriculum for Teachers.* Wilson, C. et al. (Eds) Available at: http://unesdoc.unesco.org/images/0019/001929/192971a.pdf

English References

Al-Saleem, N. (2014). Understanding Students Information Behavior in the Changing Technologies Era: An Investigation of Sultan Qaboos University, Oman. In M. Al-Suqri; L. L. Lillard & N. E. Al- Saleem (Eds.), Information Access and Library User Needs in Developing Countries. Hershey, PA: IGI Globa. pp. 211-226.

Calkins, A. (2013). A Rude Awakening: Free Speech and the Arab Spring. The Vanderbilt Political Review. Available at http://www.vanderbiltpoliticalreview.com/a-rude-awakening-free-speech-and-the-arab-spring-2/#

College of Arts and Social Science. (2015). Mass Communication. http://wwwdev.squ.edu.om/cass/Departments/MassCommunication.aspx

Dhofar University. (2015). Academic programme. Available at http://www.du.edu.om/index.php?lang=en&name=College%20of%20Arts%20and%20Applied%20Sciences%20%28CAAS%29&itemid=28

IFLA. (2014). IFLA Media and Information Literacy Recommendations. Available at http://www.ifla.org/publications/ifla-media-and-information-literacy-recommendations.

Information Technology Authority: Sultanate of Oman. (2013). Sultanate of Oman progress report on the information society 2003-2013. Available at http://www.itu.int/wsis/review/inc/docs/rcreports/WSIS10_Country_Reporting-OMA.pdf

Information Technology Authority: Sultanate of Oman: eOman. (2015). Vision and Mission. Available at http://www.ita.gov.om/ITAPortal/ITA/ITA_Vision_Mission.aspx?NID=3

German University of Technology in Oman: GUtech. (2015). Available at http://www.gutech.edu.om/Default.aspx#

Shinnick, E. & Ryan, G. (2008). The Role of Information in Decision Making. In F. Adam & P. Humphreys (Eds): *Encyclopedia of Decision Making and Decision Support Technologies*. Hershey & New York: Information Science Reference.

Sohar University. (2013). Faculty of English & English Language Studies. Available at http://www.soharuni.edu.om/fels/index.php/en/component/content/article?layout=edit&id=56-

Sultanate of Oman: Ministry of Information. (2015). Available at http://www.omaninfo.om/english/

Van de Vord, R. (2010). Distance students and online research: Promoting information literacy through media literacy. *The Internet and Higher Education,* 13(3), 170-175. Available at http://ac.els-cdn.com/S1096751610000266/1-s2.0-S1096751610000266-main.pdf?_tid=f1c99c30-5b4a-11e4-855e00000aab0f02&acdnat=1414133997_faa53a6d20095afe5261dbf9c8ef116c.

University of Nizwa: College of Arts and Sciences. (2015). Departments. Available at http://www.unizwa.edu.om/index.php?contentid=283&lang=en

12. A Lebanese Perspective

Magda Abu-Fadil

Do Middle East/North Africa (MENA) consumers and producers of media in all their permutations and across countless platforms fully comprehend what they are doing and how they fit in the larger scheme of things?

Do various groups and individuals take the time to deconstruct messages, processes, outcomes and repercussions of all the interactivity, integration, convergence and overwhelming flow of communications that keeps morphing into new shapes at speeds we can hardly keep up with?

It's as dizzying as Mork from the planet Ork, American comedian Robin Williams' famous TV character, credited in part with paving the way to our truncated media consumption habits from back in the 1970s. "Robin Williams Was An Unwitting Prophet of the Internet Era," headlined *Business Insider* to a story about Williams' frenetic and breathtaking influence on us.[1] According to writer Aaron Gell, Williams channeled culture; his cut-and-paste style echoed what rappers were doing with samples, and like them, he occasionally got into trouble for borrowing material. "It's only now, in retrospect – in the era of broadband and 'an app for that,' Twitter and subreddits, and binge-watching and channel-surfing and emojis and Google Now and instant everything everywhere at all times – that we can really see where he was coming from, acknowledge the debt we owe him and spot the warning flares he was sending up," Gell said. When news went viral of Williams' suicide in August 2014, media and citizen journalists worldwide were all over the map reporting it – many in very poor taste.[2] A day later Lebanon's *Future TV*'s website upped the ante by showing a photo[3] purportedly of Williams' corpse with the mark of the belt he used to hang himself around his neck, which several websites later said was a fake.[4] Such sights and other earlier violations got this writer interested in the 1990s in media ethics (or the lack thereof), explaining the media's role and power, demonstrating how to use media to create better engaged and more tolerant citizens, as well as developing awareness about the need for media and information literacy on all fronts.

A Lebanese MIL chronology

While serving as coordinator of the journalism program, director of university publications and eventually director of the Institute for Professional Journalists (wearing three hats) at the Lebanese American University, I participated in a virtual cross-cultural academic and journalistic experiment with a professor and students from the University of Missouri's School of Journalism. It was entitled *Internationalizing a Journalism Curriculum Using Distance Education Technology: A Pilot Project Between Lebanese American University and the University of Missouri – Columbia (Missouri School of Journalism)*. A paper about it is available online.[5] It was a rich exercise in cross-cultural communication, values, newsworthiness, the use of nascent technology (notably the Internet in Lebanon) and finding out what really mattered in a media environment to people on two different continents.

Fast forward to 2002 when I examined how Lebanese and Middle East media covered the September 11, 2001 attacks on the U.S. in an article for the (defunct) *Lebanon Journalism Review's* Spring 2002 issue entitled *Keep Kids in Mind When Writing that Story: Are Detailed Graphics Really Worth It?*:[6]

> Children were glued to TV sets, along with adults, when passenger jets slammed into the World Trade Center Towers in New York, the Pentagon in Washington and into a field outside Pittsburgh, Pennsylvania, on September 11, 2001.

> Reactions were varied, but often based on their own experiences with violent TV shows, epic Hollywood movies, or, science-fiction video or computer games. But when the reality began to sink in, thanks to the endless replay of the horrific footage, fear and incredulity also took hold.[7]

In May 2004, this author presented a paper entitled *Media Literacy: Awareness vs. Ignorance* at the seminar *Young People & the Media* organized by the Swedish Institute in Alexandria, Egypt.[8] In it, I asked if children knew what they received as information, if they evaluated content, if their parents and teachers were helpful in selecting programming, or if they let young people judge for themselves what was suitable for reading, listening, watching or browsing:

> Subliminal messages tucked into programs may influence purchasing patterns. Conflict-filled episodes or video games could incite violence and lead to aggressive behavior. Even innocuous-seeming serials could traumatize young people into confusing fantasy with reality. All with the end result that an unsophisticated approach to the consumption of news, entertainment, and even the more popular "edutainment" may contribute to dysfunctional societies and individuals, or, at the very least, confusion about how to react to the cacophony of messages overloading our sensory circuits.

It may then be worthwhile exploring the realm of media literacy to help young people – and their parents, teachers, counselors – understand the impact of the media and how their values and views are shaped by them.[9]

In November 2004, I delivered a lecture entitled *Lebanese Youth & the Media: Social & Political Influences* at the *German-Arab Media Dialogue* a conference organized by the German Foreign Ministry and Institute for Foreign and Cultural Affairs in Berlin.

In any country, when the state is a key partner in the media, or somehow linked to them, there's no hope for liberal media to operate," wrote Lebanese media professor and analyst Jean Karam.

He added that regardless of the state's liberalism, openness and democratic stance, there was no hope it would give up its hegemonic attitude, notably when it senses its political or economic plans or diplomacy are threatened by every journalist's legitimate free expression. (Media Pot Boiling, Jean Karam, Ink and Moons, An-Nahar, 29-10-2004).

Nordicom's Clearinghouse in Sweden published it as a chapter in the book *In The Service of Young People? Studies and Reflections on Media in the Digital Age* in September 2005[10]. This writer hammered on the theme again in a lecture entitled *Obstacles & Prospects for Women & Youth in the MENA Media Landscape* delivered at the seminar/workshop *Media, Women & Youth in the Middle East & North Africa* organized by the Olof Palme International Center at the Swedish Institute in Alexandria, Egypt in February 2005.

In March 2007, I presented a research paper for the UNESCO Regional Conference in Support of Global Literacy in Doha, Qatar entitled *Media Literacy: A Tool to Combat Stereotypes and Promote Intercultural Understanding:*[11]

Media literacy and awareness have long been neglected in the Arab world, often leading to unfavorable consequences and exacerbating a volatile situation spawned by political, economic and social unrest, not to mention lack of leadership. Media literacy as a subject is rarely taught in schools in any organized way and is often couched in vague terminology within university courses that fail to address the raison d'être of mass communication tools, their financial support systems and the various influences that could transform them into weapons of mass deception.

The very concept of critical thinking that underpins media literacy seems alien to young people weaned on a steady diet of rote learning and passive intake. This is particularly evident in schools following the French and Arabic educational systems where the very idea of questioning authority has, traditionally, been anathema. Even British and American systems have sometimes fallen short of their stated goals of effective learning and questioning.

Raja Kamal, an associate dean for resource development at the Harris School for Public Policy Studies at the University of Chicago, said higher education in the Arab world had performed inadequately and produced graduates who were having a difficult time integrating and assimilating into the global economy. 'The vast majority of Arab universities teach their students what to think instead of how to think,' he said. 'Unless this mentality changes fast, little hope of progress will be seen on the horizon' (Kamal, 2007). Kamal urged Arab countries to incorporate higher education into their strategic planning and create a partnership between the private sector and educators.[12]

In January 2008, this writer presented a paper at a UNESCO conference on cultural diversity and education entitled *Fostering Critical Capacities and Fighting Against Unilateral Points of View: Finding Common Ground and the Subject Matters Amenable to Cultural Diversity Learning – The Journalism Education & Training Dimension:*

> Stereotypical images and misunderstandings arise when there is lack of information, when information is distorted and mis-communicated and sometimes when there is ill intent. So we need a solid media education, proper media literacy, adequate research, perseverance, patience, an enterprising spirit and willingness to see and think outside the box.

A major report grew from the initial event in Barcelona, Spain and was launched at the UN's Alliance of Civilizations in Rio de Janeiro, Brazil in May 2010. The author's recommendations in the first conference paper were included in the report.[13] Since then, I have lectured on the topic and conducted workshops on media and information literacy in Lebanon, Qatar, Morocco, Tunisia and Yemen. Elsewhere in Lebanon, others seem to have picked up the mantle. The American University of Beirut established the Media & Digital Literacy Academy of Beirut[14] grouping participants and speakers from across the Arab world and beyond. Its efforts have yet to translate into implementation of a viable and sustainable program involving all educational institutions in the country and in all three major languages of instruction. International College[15] (IC), a private K-12 school with two campuses in Beirut and Ain Aar, Lebanon, has been a keen adopter of media and information literacy concepts and practices. Its teachers, coordinators and section heads have undergone some initial training in media and information literacy but still need further immersion in the subject. On the student front, IC has devised what it calls a *Responsible Digital Citizenship Contract* for pupils at the elementary, mid- and secondary levels focused on respecting, educating and protecting themselves and others.[16] Students are expected to sign this agreement of rules for Internet safety and digital citizenship with their parents in a bid to create awareness and foster responsibility online. A similar arrangement needs to be adopted nation-wide.

Elsewhere, the Greek Orthodox Archdiocese of Beirut introduced e-books in the classroom to replace heavy texts students carry as part of the 'EDUVATION' school network[17] grouping three institutions under its jurisdiction.[18] The 'eBok Book Series' developed by the school system educators of the Ecole des Trois Docteurs, Beirut Annunciation Orthodox College and Saint Mary's Orthodox College cover Arabic, Social Studies, English, French, Mathematics and Science for grades 1-3.[19] Students are required to provide their own tablets (iPads, etc.), but there's little indication the critical thinking skills they're trained to use include deciphering media messages. The 'eBok Book

Series' seems more focused on developing ICT skills to complement the learning process than delving into the realm of digital messages and multimedia. The daily newspaper *Annahar*[20] went through several phases of producing children's and youth supplements – as have other print media – and was briefly involved in a modest experiment with the World Association of Newspapers and News Publishers' (WAN-IFRA) *Newspapers in Education* program [21]. However, the plan did not go far and was unsustainable.

In May 2012, Lebanon's then education and higher education minister Hassan Diab and former telecommunications minister Nicolas Sehnaoui announced the provision of tablets to public school students at grades 10 and 11 to improve curricula and advance the country's educational system. The Ministry of Education and Higher Education had received an initial gift of 1,500 tablets to use as testing samples in public and private schools. The ministry also set up a media and information literacy program aimed at establishing a network to serve schools across the country (Ministry of Education & Higher Education 2012). But little else has emerged about the scheme. That particular Lebanese cabinet (and the ministry) changed hands, political life in Lebanon has gone through several stumbling blocks, security has been adversely affected, and the school educational system has since been riding on a public and private teachers' syndicate-led roller coaster of strikes and school disruptions, thereby paying scant attention to what might be considered of secondary importance.

Moreover, the ambitious plan to promote MIL has had to contend with absurd recurring inconveniences like chronic power cuts and shortages and slow Internet connectivity despite official claims of providing ADSL service. Sadly, a culture of media and information literacy has not yet permeated Lebanon's academic institutions at the elementary, middle, secondary and university levels. Parents have not yet been fully engaged in the process. The government has not yet allocated adequate resources to provide MIL programs in all public schools. Most of all, content and materials for MIL have not been made widely available in Arabic (the country's official language) as well as French and English for schools where those are the languages of instruction, and, to a lesser extent, Armenian, the language of the largest national minority in the country.

Conclusion

How do we contribute to media and information literacy in Lebanon? Gaming is one way to channel young people's energy and is a booming industry that caters to multiple tastes. Games, particularly the electronic and virtual varieties, are used in education to teach life skills, mathematics, science, languages and a host of topics, both as standalone software and as applications. Want 'better adjusted' children? An hour of video gaming a day (and no more) might help, advise experts:

> Playing video games might actually be good for child development according to a new study from the University of Oxford, but only if kids play for less than an hour a day.

Research undertaken by experimental psychologist Dr Andrew Przybylski suggested that young people who played video games for just a few hours a week were better adjusted, more likely to care about the welfare of their peers and presented fewer behavioural problems over all.[22]

But games and 'apps' also come in sinister forms with a heavy emphasis on violence, wars, and deviant behavior. With wars raging in various Arab countries and instability ruling the day in Lebanon, it's important to demonstrate to impressionable young people that games based on conflicts are not necessarily good examples to follow. Animated cartoons, another form dear to young and old, can be instrumental in promoting and perpetuating stereotypes, reflecting positive and negative images, and in prompting actions and reactions. The trick is to capitalize on the positive.

Their predecessors, comic books, have also had a similar effect on readers who sometimes mixed myth with reality. They are still a popular form of media and can be used to good effect in teaching and learning. In Lebanon, comic books are available mostly in Arabic, French and English, although these publications can also be found in other languages. Tie in the lure of advertising across various platforms and its power of influencing behavior, and the mix can swing either way – positive and negative messages. Throw in posters and street signs for good measure and you're starting to get inundated. Newspapers and magazines are not as dominant as digital and mobile media and radio plays a secondary role to online audio and video content. Television was once termed a 'babysitter' when parents sought to pacify their children. It has since taken a back seat to all things mobile and online and in which user-generated content is ubiquitous. In an environment of mash-ups and media mixes, it's easy to lose sight of ethics, copyrights and violations of privacy. The Lebanese have had a longstanding struggle with copyright laws and registered trademarks. They flout them. Understanding all these concepts and practices and how to navigate the choppy waters is imperative in a globalized 21st Century world.

In Lebanon, MIL is tied to education, pedagogy, religion, and media in the general sense. Information is often brought in as an adjunct, with technology playing a supportive role. Implementation of programs that promote digital knowledge along with media literacy is where the heavy work is needed and given the country's geographic location, there's an urgent requirement to provide more practical content in Arabic, while producing materials in French and English to cater to the different sub-groups. Meanwhile, Dennis Hayes, a professor of education at the University of Derby in Britain, offers a contrarian view to what we've been hearing and preaching lo these many years. In a blog post entitled *Let's Stop Trying to Teach Students Critical Thinking*, Hayes suggests that concept is not a skill. It means indoctrination and critical theories are uncritical:[23]

The truth is that you can't teach people to be critical unless you are critical yourself. This involves more than asking young people to "look critically" at something, as if criticism was a mechanical task.

As a teacher, you have to have a critical spirit. This does not mean moaning endlessly about education policies you dislike or telling students what they should think. It means first and foremost that you are capable of engaging in deep conversation. This means debate and discussion based on considerable knowledge – something that is almost entirely absent in the educational world. It also has to take place in public, with parents and others who are not teachers, not just in the classroom or staffroom.

On that note, this author would ask readers to think about the issue, engage in deep conversation, debate and discuss in public, and involve others in a bid to better serve media and information literacy.

Notes

1. http://www.businessinsider.com/robin-williams-internet-prophet-2014-8
2. http://www.themediablog.co.uk/the-media-blog/2014/08/robin-williams-newspaper-coverage.html
3. http://www.futuretvnetwork.com/node/106731
4. http://antiviral.gawker.com/stop-sharing-that-fake-robin-williams-death-photo-1620835563/ +leahfinnegan?utm_campaign=socialflow_gawker_twitter&utm_source=gawker_twitter&utm_medium=socialflow.
5. http://ipj.lau.edu.lb/outreach/1999/ausace/ausace1.php.
6. http://ipj.lau.edu.lb/outreach/2002/03_ljr/ljrspring2002.php
7. ibid
8. http://ipj.lau.edu.lb/outreach/2004/05_youth/media_literacy.pdf
9. ibid
10. Abu-Fadil, M. (2006).
11. http://unesdoc.unesco.org/images/0016/001611/161157e.pdf
12. ibid
13. Abu-Fadil, M. (2009).
14. https://www.facebook.com/mdlab.aub
15. www.ic.edu.lb
16. http://cld.bz/bookdata/uFKqVZt/basic-html/page40.html
    http://cld.bz/bookdata/SOIKqHt/basic-html/page50.html
17. http://www.eduvation.edu.lb
18. http://www.dailystar.com.lb/News/Lebanon-News/2015/Apr-10/293984-textbooks-at-eduvation-school-network-go-high-tech.ashx
19. http://www.lorientlejour.com/article/929878/le-cursus-scolaire-libanais-adapte-sur-support-numerique.html
20. www.annahar.com
21. http://www.wan-ifra.org/microsites/youth-engagement-news-literacy
22. http://www.independent.co.uk/life-style/gadgets-and-tech/gaming/want-better-adjusted-children-an-hour-of-video-gaming-a-day-and-no-more-might-help-9645834.html
23. http://theconversation.com/lets-stop-trying-to-teach-students-critical-thinking-30321

References and Resources

Abu-Fadil, M. and Gafke, R. (1999) "Internationalizing a Journalism Curriculum Using Distance Education Technology: A Pilot Project Between Lebanese American University and the University of Missouri – Columbia (Missouri School of Journalism). Prepared for the 4th Annual Conference of the Arab-U.S. Association for Communication Educators (AUSACE), Beirut, Lebanon, October 26-29, 1999." http://ipj.lau.edu.lb/outreach/1999/ausace/ausace1.php.

Abu-Fadil, M. "Keep Kids in Mind When Writing that Story: Are Detailed Graphics Really Worth It?" *Lebanon Journalism Review*, Spring 2002. http://ipj.lau.edu.lb/outreach/2002/03_ljr/ljrspring2002.php

Abu-Fadil, M. "Media Literacy: Awareness vs. Ignorance" Paper at *seminar* "Young People & the Media" organized by the Swedish Institute, Alexandria, Egypt, May 2004. http://ipj.lau.edu.lb/outreach/2004/05_youth/media_literacy.pdf

Abu-Fadil, M. (2006) "Lebanese Youth and the Media: Social and Political Influences," In Carlsson, U., and von Feilitzen, C. (Eds) *In The Service of Young People? Studies and Reflections on Media in the Digital Age. Yearbook 2005/2006.* The International Clearinghouse on Children, Youth and Media, Nordicom, University of Gothenburg, Sweden. Available at: www.nordicom.gu.se

Abu-Fadil, M. "Media Literacy: A Tool to Combat Stereotypes and Promote Cultural Understanding." Research paper prepared for the UNESCO Regional Conferences in Support of Global Literacy, Doha, Qatar, March 2007. http://unesdoc.unesco.org/images/0016/001611/161157e.pdf

Abu-Fadil, M. (2009). "Implementing Media Literacy Programmes," *UNESCO World Report: Investing in Cultural Diversity and Intercultural Dialogue*, UNESCO, Paris, France. Available at:e http://unesdoc.unesco.org/images/0018/001852/185202e.pdf

Ministry of Education & Higher Education in Lebanon. (2013): "Book Documenting the Administration of Minister Professor Hassan Diab at the Ministry of Education & Higher Education," First Edition, pp. 124-127. https://www.linkedin.com/profile/view?trk=nmp_pymk_name&authToken=ME-V&authType=name&id=325913617

Gell, A. "Robin Williams Was An Unwitting Prophet of the Internet Era," *Business Insider*, August 12, 2014. http://www.businessinsider.com/robin-williams-internet-prophet-2014-8

Hayes, Dennis."Let's Stop Trying to Teach Students Critical Thinking," *The Conversation.* August 9, 2014. http://theconversation.com/lets-stop-trying-to-teach-students-critical-thinking-30321

Hongo, H. "Stop Sharing That Fake Robin Williams Death Photo," Antiviral Gawker, August 13, 2013.http://antiviral.gawker.com/stop-sharing-that-fake-robin-williams-death-photo-1620835563/+leahfinnegan?utm_campaign=socialflow_gawker_twitter&utm_source=gawker_twitter&utm_medium=socialflow

International College, Lebanon."Responsible Digital Citizenship Contract." http://cld.bz/bookdata/uFKqVZt/basic-html/page40.html and http://cld.bz/bookdata/SOIKqHt/basic-html/page50.html

Weatherbee, Sarah, "Textbooks at Eduvation school network go high-tech," *The Daily Star*, April 10, 2015. http://www.dailystar.com.lb/News/Lebanon-News/2015/Apr-10/293984-textbooks-at-eduvation-school-network-go-high-tech.ashx

Carlier, Rémi. "Le cursus scolaire libanais adapté sur support numérique," *L'Orient-Le Jour*, June 16, 2015. http://www.lorientlejour.com/article/929878/le-cursus-scolaire-libanais-adapte-sur-support-numerique.html

"Robin Williams: Media Flout Suicide Guidelines," The Media Blog, August 13, 2014. http://www.themedia-blog.co.uk/the-media-blog/2014/08/robin-williams-newspaper-coverage.html

"The First Picture After Robin Williams' Suicide," Arabic blogpost and two photos on Lebanon's Future TV website, August 13, 2014. http://www.futuretvnetwork.com/node/106731

Vincent, James. "Want 'better adjusted' children? An hour of video gaming a day (and no more) might help," *The Independent*, August 4, 2014. http://www.independent.co.uk/life-style/gadgets-and-tech/gaming/want-better-adjusted-children-an-hour-of-video-gaming-a-day-and-no-more-might-help-9645834.html

World Association of Newspapers and News Publishers (WAN-IFRA), "Newspapers in Education (NIE) http://www.wan-ifra.org/microsites/youth-engagement-news-literacy

13. Empowering Children and Youth in Tunisia

Carmilla Floyd & Gabriella Thinz

Tunis, early morning February 2014. The first rays of sun were trying to break through the haze, the air was cold. Every news channel highlighted the anniversary of the murder of Chokri Belaïd, the secular politician who was killed in the street outside his home in Tunis a year earlier, on 5 February 5, 2013. There was tension in the air – or was that our imagination? Because we knew that Tunisia and Tunis – a vibrant city of millions, a mix of new and old worlds, tradition and modernity – had gone through more than one would think possible in only a few years. We were a small team of media trainers on our way to Beni Khaled, a small town an hour's drive from Tunis, to hold the first of a series of media and information literacy workshops. Our project, *Empowering Children and Youth Through Media and Information Literacy: Fusing Education and Media* had existed on paper since 2011. Now, in February 2014, we were about to hit the ground to try to transform ideas and concepts into practice for the first time.

In the afternoon we would meet children and young people frequenting a local youth center, to give them a crash course in Media and Information Literacy (MIL). Before that, a morning session was set up with a group of youth leaders working at the center. But our car was still moving at a crawling pace through the rush hour of Tunis city center as sidewalks filled with people on the move. We spotted soldiers and police officers in riot gear, and passed a government building surrounded by barbed wire and tanks. What we did not know was that only hours earlier, a few kilometers away, a terrorist cell was blown up – literally. So, the tension was not imaginary. We finally made it out of the crammed city center and drove on narrow, winding streets. While central Tunis bears the marks of modern city landscaping, there are huge contrasts between the city center, suburbs and countryside. After an hour on a bumpy highway we finally reached Beni Khaled and parked outside a graffiti covered building in the midst of busy streets. We were nervous and excited to get started. But first a word about Tunisia and the background to this project.

Why Tunisia?

It was here in Tunisia that the Arab Spring began. In December 2010 a street vendor named Mohamed Bouazizi set himself on fire in Sidi Bouzid, a small town in central Tunisia. This became the spark that ignited the uprisings in Tunisia, then in Egypt and Libya. The consequences of the revolution from a media perspective are almost impossible to grasp.

Picture this: A regime that unscrupulously controlled the media was forced to give up power. Before the revolution, censorship was commonplace. Journalists were often subjected to harassment.[1] For the first time, during the revolution Tunisian journalists went out on the streets and reported live – letting the public voice their opinion without any censorship. With the fall of the regime, the Ministry of Information, a once-feared instrument of media control, was abolished. Suddenly there was free speech. An explosion of new radio stations, TV channels and online news sites followed, while state broadcasters re-organized, and an endless stream of information and news was shared through online news services and social networks. After the first euphoric sense of freedom, people became weary. State-owned media that turned into public service broadcasters were desperately trying to convince audiences they had changed, but were still considered by many to be part of the old regime. And since virtually all mainstream Tunisian media were once connected, to a greater or lesser degree, to the deposed Ben Ali regime, people remained cautious. The media were flooded with rumors, all sides wanting to give their own versions of the past and present. At the center of the turmoil one found a young population – at least half of all Tunisians are below the age of 20[2]. They grew up being told certain rules applied, only to find they had to learn quickly it was no longer important. Who should one listen to, who could one trust?

According to a 2013 study from the Gerhart Center for Philanthropy and Civic Engagement and the British Council, media in post-revolutionary Tunisia are still largely viewed by young people as "commercial and manipulative, and agenda-driven rather than truth-driven," unprofessional and responsible for spreading bogus news. While the role that social media played in the revolution is undeniably positive, the research shows that perception among youth is that its influence has shifted from a positive to a negative one: "Though social media previously contributed towards mounting awareness, many now fear it as an unwieldy tool for fostering division and spreading rumors. Social media's current use for political mobilization has further led to stereotyping and manipulation that have made many of the study participants consider its revolutionary role to be over." However, in spite of these fears, there is an overall positive but cautious attitude amongst young respondents in the study towards media and the newly experienced freedom of expression. These changes are considered important and positive by youth and there remains a persistent conviction that media can be used as a tool for democracy[3]. This makes for fertile soil for an MIL project. The project Tunisian and Swedish partners were about to embark on in February 2014 had a broad approach. Early on, we had decided to involve capacity building not only for youngsters and educators but also for media producers. The ultimate project goal is for children and young people to become active and have a voice in matters of human rights and a democratic Tunisia. To achieve this, we believe that adults also need to become media and information literate – teachers, youth leaders and parents. In addition we were determined to reach out to those who produce the media: journalists, editors, newsroom managers, TV producers and bloggers. These worlds must meet to promote inclusion and cross-fertilization of knowledge, ideas and insights. We believe media producers must listen to children and youth and include them in their creative processes. In this way, media can become more relevant for young people and contribute to their participation in a democratic society. Put simply, if the media disseminate a biased message without checking sources – instead reinforcing stereotypes, with no concern for their audience – does it really matter if young people become media literate? The opposite is also true: How can the media evolve if young people from all walks of life don't have the skills to 'read' the media and their subtexts?

Meeting reality

Back to Beni Khaled, where we were standing on a street corner looking for the entrance to the youth center with an interpreter who would translate English and French into the local Arabic dialect, Darija used by most teenagers here. A group of young people called out to us and pointed to a doorway. One of them said: "You must be from Sweden, right? Welcome!" A group of youth leaders were waiting for us, offering tea, sweet cookies and many questions. We answered and asked our own, slowly forming a picture of their views, knowledge and awareness on media in general and MIL in particular.

The center in Beni Khaled is one of over 300 similar locales around the country[4] that were established during the Ben Ali regime and sometimes used as hubs for propaganda by the ruling party. Since May 2011 they have been legally governed by Revolutionary Decree that give the centers more freedom vis-à-vis the government. The youth leaders described their area as 'socially vulnerable,' an industrial and rural region with high unemployment numbers. The Director said that many, perhaps a majority, of the children and youth that use the center come from poor families and face many problems including poverty, drugs and domestic violence. Together we discussed how their young charges used the media and were affected by them. We talked about social media, gender stereotypes and politicization. The youth leaders were open minded, and very sharp. All were passionate about supporting the young people at the center, but felt that children and youth had no voice in the mainstream media. Due to financial constraints, they said, young people in Beni Khaled had limited access to social media, otherwise an arena where many young Tunisians have taken an active role. All of the youth leaders felt issues concerning the media were very important in today's Tunisia, but also said the MIL concept was virtually unknown in schools and at youth centers, and at the Bir El Bey Advanced Institute for Youth and Culture, where practically all youth leaders in Tunisia get their degrees in youth recreation pedagogy and leadership. Shortly before lunch we toured the small center and its bare but brightly painted rooms. With pride the youth leaders told us about their latest project: a simple web radio station that would broadcast from the youth center with content produced and presented by young people. We visited the small, makeshift studio and they asked our opinions.

This was our first visit to a Tunisian youth center and we did not realize how far they had come in Beni Khaled compared to many other centers around the country. We did not know how many barriers existed for a non-commercial, secular and apolitical venture to be heard on the air, notably one involving young people. This we realized much later, after traveling to other parts of the country, meeting many more people and visiting other youth centers that had barely any equipment or space. The passion for change and youth empowerment was evident everywhere. But to actually, in practice, be able to offer children and young people the opportunity to make their voices heard on the air was rare. In the afternoon we met the young people for the first time.

We had asked for a group of about 15, but at least 30 eager girls and boys between the ages of 12–20 were waiting for us in a large room otherwise used for everything from after-school tutoring to dance practice and rap music performances. Kids continued to drop in all afternoon to participate in the workshop, as schools closed and the rumor spread that something was happening at the center. We started with the basics. Using simple, interactive learning activities we explored how the youngsters defined media and what they meant to them. Some of the older teens had cheap and simple mobile phones, but they managed to use them to access Facebook and Google. To watch YouTube clips they used the few computers at the youth center, or went to one of the local Internet cafés. Very few had access to computers at home. The workshop was to continue the next morning and when we returned to the center we were surprised to see young people already waiting in line outside.

More than 60 youngsters, an equal number of boys and girls, crammed into the room, sitting around tables, along the walls and on the floor. "They are hungry for knowledge, anything that is new," explained one of the youth leaders. It was slightly daunting – the largest group any of us had ever worked with using interactive classroom activities. We began with a classic counting heads activity, dividing the youngsters into smaller groups and asking them to count women and men, but also children and youth in photos in a week's batch of local and national newspapers. Not surprisingly, we found that women and children were practically non-existent in the news. Teenagers were slightly more visible, but only as victims or delinquents. We trainers were expecting this, after many studies over the years have shown that this ratio repeats itself in nearly all forms of media around the world.[5] But the young participants in the room were surprised, then angry. "Why is there nothing about me? About us?" asked a young girl who for the first time had discovered that she and her peers, especially the girls, were nearly invisible in the media. During the rest day, we focused on turning anger and frustration into action. We tried many different activities; writing headlines and captions; analyzing social media posts and short videos; forming a mock editorial room, letting the teenagers plan their own news show. Afterwards, we were exhausted but filled with enthusiasm and new knowledge. We felt we were on the right track.

A joint effort

The idea for launching an MIL project in Tunisia came from *Le Centre Africain de Perfectionnement des Journalistes et Communicateurs (CAPJC)*, the African Center for Training Journalists and Communicators. CAPJC, that celebrated its 30th anniversary in 2013, underwent a complete overhaul after the revolution. A new leadership was appointed after the ousting of the president in 2011, to restructure and upgrade the organization and its services to be able to respond to existing and emerging needs and challenges faced by Tunisian media. Early on, CAPJC identified the need for empowering young Tunisian media consumers through MIL education and sought a partnership with Swedish Radio's Media Development Office[6] (SR MDO). SR MDO runs as part of Swedish Radio[7] (SR), a Public Service Broadcaster that has for several consecutive years been the most trusted institution in the eyes of the Swedish public.[8] SR MDO has 20 years of experience of development cooperation in Asia and Africa, and can provide competencies and expertise for journalist training and media development from all of the public service institutions in Sweden: SR, Swedish Television[9] (SVT) and the Swedish Educational Broadcasting Corporation[10] (UR). UR has a special mission to work actively to promote Media and Information Literacy. Annually it produces numerous educational and general knowledge programs and educational multimedia packages for the educational sector, from pre-school to high school. It has been especially successful in building bridges between the media and schools. UR is also part of a national network[11] working to implement MIL in the educational system.

Collaborating with international partners is an important part of CAPJC's re-structuring. It also works with International Media Support (IMS), Denmark, a non-profit organization aimed at strengthening the capacity of media to reduce conflict, strengthen democracy and facilitate dialogue; Deutsche Welle Akademie (DW), Germany's leading organization for international media development; and the Friedrich Naumann Foundation (FNF), a German institution that supports projects for human rights, rule of law and democracy. Additionally, CAPJC is in charge of a European Union (EU) assistance program to Tunisian media[12], along with the European Center of Journalism at Maastricht and other Tunisian partners.

Covering a three-year period, the program aims at strengthening the role and professional capacities of Tunisia's journalists and media through deepening ties among the media, socio-economic development entities and civil society. Here, MIL can also play an important role. CAPJC and SR MDO designed the MIL project together as a tool for democratization and empowering youth, drawing on our different experiences and expertise. Key people involved in the project had previously developed and run other international MIL projects in, for example, Palestine and Belarus. Inspiration also came from different Swedish national and international MIL projects, including a successful national campaign that combatted gender stereotypes and promoted civic engagement for adolescent girls across Sweden in 2005. Run jointly by Sweden's Ministry of Social Affairs and a network of NGOs and media outlets, it targeted teachers, middle and high school students, and the media, conducting workshops and launching a public awareness campaign. The CAPJC and SR MDO MIL project in Tunisia is funded by the Swedish International Development Cooperation Agency[13] (Sida), in line with the Swedish Government's strategy for development cooperation with the Middle East and North Africa[14]: to foster stronger democracy and greater respect for human rights; and, sustainable development that improves conditions for peace, stability and freedom in the region. In the MENA region Sida provides support to groups in civil society that promote democratization and human rights by means of lobbying, opinion building and through independent media and journalism.

Fusion of media and education

After the training in Beni Khaled, several workshops were held at other youth centers. Several seminars and meetings were also organized in and around Tunis to establish an MIL network with different actors who were passionate about empowering youth in the media, including bloggers and policy makers, social activists and university professors, film producers, journalists, teachers and artists. Meetings were also held with international and local institutions and organizations working in Tunisia.

In April 2014 SR MDO and CAPJC organized a second series of MIL workshops. This time, the objective was to include media professionals, primarily TV and radio producers as active participants. When the team members from Sweden arrived in Tunis in April, the political climate had calmed down. Street cafés were filled with people of all ages, women and men, girls and boys, talking, arguing and smiling. A new constitution was finally in place, being applauded worldwide as unique, forward thinking and progressive. Parts of the country that we had previously been dissuaded from visiting only two months earlier were now opening up.

In this series of workshops, producers and journalists were asked to create a series of short videos focusing on youth and the media in Tunisia, through a participatory learning process. Workshops were held in Tunis and Sfax, and the media professionals had to work closely with youth leaders, children and teenagers. The key words were inclusion, cooperation and innovation.

The first workshop was held in Tunis at the CAPJC training center. Before we let the journalists loose on the stories, we gave them the basics of media and information literacy, using the same learning activities that we had run in February 2014 with youth leaders and youngsters at the youth centers in Beni Khaled and beyond. When the journalists performed the counting heads activity, counting males and females, children and adults in the media, they were just as surprised and provoked as the 15-year-old girl who was sitting on the floor of the youth center in Beni Khaled. "What is this?" asked one of the journalists, pointing to the results on the board. "Are only middle-aged men allowed to be seen?" We had invited youth and youth leaders who had participated in the February workshops in Beni Khaled to meet the media producers in Tunis. And it was at this very moment that the practical aspect of MIL became visible to all of us in the project team: When a media producer includes her or his young audience in the creative process, it affects the finished media product in a very positive way. Suddenly children and youth had leading roles in telling the stories. The participating journalists remarked that it was the first time they were talking *with* young people instead of *about* them. A reference group was formed with young people that later were invited back to evaluate the short videos produced by adult workshop participants. All the important questions were asked: How are the subjects portrayed? What is being said and what is not being said? Are there any hidden messages? The youth's presence and feedback made the journalists question their work more and in a new way.

After the workshops in Tunis we traveled to the south and Sfax, Tunisia's second largest city. Sfax is more polarized than Tunis, with a strong leftist movement as well as many influential conservative and Islamist groups. Again we worked with local journalists, primarily from radio and local newspapers, youth leaders and young people. We more or less replicated what we did in Tunis but here everything became sharper and clearer. The yoke of decades of censorship and exercise of power could still be felt at the media organizations and youth centers. The journalists with whom we worked said they had practically never interviewed a child or a young person before, but that they were ready for a change. What they said mirrored an interview[15] with the head of DW Akiademe's Tunis, Rüdiger Maack: "For 25 years journalism didn't really exist (in Tunisia). They (journalists) simply held out a microphone to those in power and recorded them, but never in a journalistic sense with viewers or listeners in mind."

Looking to the future

The April workshops resulted in several short videos about current topics seen from the perspective of Sfax youth. The participating media felt they had learned new important skills, not least through interacting with the youth. The youth said they felt more confident in sharing their views and ideas with the media. Actually, none of the participants wanted to leave when the workshops were over, irrespective of age, experience or gender. One young female radio journalist said: "We used to do things because we were told to do them. Now, we want to meet and have a dialogue about what we do and why. We have to listen to each other."

To us in the team, the workshops and resulting videos provided important input to the continuation of the project, since one of our key objectives was to develop a locally adapted approach and MIL toolkit containing training methods and materials, through a participatory process. Thus, the first year of activities – workshops, seminars, network meetings and trainings for journalists – all had a common goal: to map local needs and try out different learning activities that could be included in the locally adapted educational package. And as the first project year drew to a close in August 2014, we felt we had reached further than we had even hoped. We had met with hundreds of young people, youth leaders and media professionals who helped us shape the design for the next phase, that started in 2015. Together, we had drafted an outline for our toolkit and media guidelines suited to the specific circumstances and needs of Tunisia and its fast changing media landscape. Young people, youth leaders and media producers had been actively involved in the creative process, while, at the same time, improving their own capacity and skills.

As we look to the future, we are happy to also have a wide network in place, including representatives from international and national organizations and institutions such as UNESCO[16], UNICEF[17], OHCHR[18], The Institute of Press and Sciences Information[19] (IPSI), Association Tunisienne de Défense de Droits des Enfants[20] (ATDDE), or the Tunisian Association for Defending the Rights of the Child, The Tunisian Department of Youth and Culture, Centre National d'Innovation Pédagogique et de Recherches en Education (CNIPRE), or the Center for Pedagogical Innovation and Education Research. Although few other MIL projects are up and running in Tunisia, a multitude of media development initiatives and activities were implemented in the country after the revolution. Many touch on, or include, MIL aspects. For example, international non-profit organization Internews has trained young journalists and bloggers through a series of workshops on political talk shows, covering human rights issues through radio reporting, and investigative journalism in dealing with corruption[21]. The Institute for War and Peace Reporting (IWPR) has supported the Tunisia Youth Media Network (TYMN), a two-year project that started in 2011 and involved the training of young journalists and bloggers in best practices, as well as establishing Internet centers as publication and training hubs, and community radio stations[22]. A pilot project to strengthen citizenship and human rights education was launched in 2012 under the coordination of UNESCO, grouping six UN agencies (OHCHR, UNDP, UNESCO, UNFPA, UNHCR and UNICEF), the Tunisian government, the Arab Institute for Human Rights (AIHR) and local NGOs. Its aim is to create citizenship and human rights school clubs in seven regions of Tunisia.

Although there are no national MIL policies or strategies in development yet, there has been overwhelming consensus during all our meetings and activities regarding the need for MIL education in the dramatically transformed media landscape of post-revolution Tunisia. Government officials have also expressed a strong interest, not least since they recognize that strengthening democratic values lies at the very core of MIL. The need for MIL was also stressed in meetings with La Haute Autorité Indépendante de la Communication Audiovisuelle[23] (HAICA), the Independent High Authority for Audiovisual Communication – Tunisia's principal organization set up in May 2013 to regulate the audiovisual sector in the country. The Authority clearly stated, as have all our other network partners in Tunisia, that all Tunisians and especially children and young people are in desperate need of skills to filter, analyze and process a never-ending flow of messages that fill their daily lives. In this project, we feel that we have taken a big step forward through enabling, in practice, a qualitative encounter between media producer and media consumer that results in new ways of thinking and acting.

Notes and references

1. http://en.rsf.org/
2. http:// ww.unicef.org/infobycountry/Tunisia_statistics.htmlw
3. Research study: The Revolutionary Promise: Youth Perceptions in Egypt, Libya and Tunisia. The Gerhart Center for Philanthropy and Civic Engagement and the British Council, 2013 http://www.britishcouncil.org/sites/britishcouncil.uk2/files/revolutionary-promise-summary_0.pdf
4. Erik Churchill: Report: Youth work in Tunisia after the revolution (2013), EUROMED. http://euromedyouth.net/IMG/pdf/youth_work_in_tunisia.pdf
5. http://whomakesthenews.org/
6. http://www.srmdo.se/
7. http://www.sverigesradio.se
8. Gothenburg University/SIFO: Förtroendebarometern (2014), a survey published annually Medieakademin and Gothenburg University, Sweden, measuring the public's confidence in different media, private companies and institutions, since 1997.
9. http://svt.se
10. http://www.ur.se/
11. http://mik.statensmedierad.se/
12. http://www.capjc.nat.tn/index.asp?pId=75
13. http://www.sida.se/
14. Sida's Regional Strategy for Development Cooperation with the Middle East and North Africa (2010-2015). http://www.government.se/sb/d/574/a/156049
15. http://www.dw.de/interview-r%C3%BCdiger-maack-head-of-dw-akademies-tunis-office/a-17017431
16. http://www.unesco.org/new/en/unesco/worldwide/unesco-regions/arab-states/tunisia/
17. http://www.unicef.org.tn/
18. http://www.ohchr.org/EN/countries/MENARegion/Pages/TNIndex.aspx
19. http://www.ipsi.rnu.tn/
20. http://www.enfant.tn/
21. Media Literacy 2.0: A Sampling of Programs Around the World. An Update for the Center for International Media Assistance. November 2013. Internews Report. https://internews.org/sites/default/files/resources/CIMA-MediaLiteracy_2_0-11-21-2013.pdf
22. ibid
23. http://haica.tn/

فرص جديدة للتربية الإعلامية والمعلوماتية في منطقة الشرق الأوسط وشمال أفريقيا

المحررون:

ماجدة أبو فاضل (المحرر الرئيسي)، جوردي تورنت وآلتون غريزل

The International Clearinghouse on
CHILDREN, YOUTH & MEDIA
at NORDICOM, University of Gothenburg

فرص جديدة للتربية الإعلامية والمعلوماتية
في منطقة الشرق الأوسط وشمال أفريقيا

المحررون: ماجدة أبو فاضل (المحرر الرئيسي)، جوردي تورنت وآلتون غريزل

عمـل تـم إنجـازه بالتعـاون بيـن برنامـج الأمـم المتحـدة لتحالـف الحضـارات (UNAOC) واليونسـكو (UNESCO) مـع المركـز الـدولي لتبـادل المعلومـات حـول الأطفـال والشـباب والإعـلام التابـع لمركـز «نورديكـوم»، جامعـة غوتنـبرغ.

© مسائل التحرير والاختيار، والمحررين؛ والمقالات والأفراد المساهمين

إن التسـميات المسـتخدمة والمـواد المقدّمـة في إطـار هـذا الكتيّـب لا تمثّـل تعبيـراً عـن أي رأي كان مـن جانـب برنامـج الأمـم المتحـدة لتحالـف الحضـارات (UNAOC) أو اليونسـكو (UNESCO) بشـأن الوضـع القانـوني لأي بلـد أو إقليـم أو مدينـة أو منطقـة أو لسـلطات أي منهـا، أو بشـأن ترسـيم حدودهـا أو تخومهـا. إن كافـة الأفـكار والآراء الـواردة في هـذا الكتيّـب تمثّـل الآراء الشـخصية للمؤلفيـن، وليسـت بالضـرورة آراء برنامـج الأمـم المتحـدة لتحالـف الحضـارات (UNAOC) أو اليونسـكو (UNESCO) كمـا أنهـا ليسـت ملزمـة بـأي شـكل للمنظمة.

ISBN 978-91-87957-33-8
Published by:
The International Clearinghouse on Children, Youth and Media
Series editor: Ingela Wadbring
Nordicom
University of Gothenburg
Box 713
SE 405 30 Göteborg
Sweden
Cover by: Karin Persson
Printed by: Billes Tryckeri AB, Mölndal, Sweden 2016

يسعدنا أن نقدّم هـذا الإصـدار الـذي يحمـل عنـوان «فـرص انتشـار التربيـة الإعلاميـة والمعلوماتيـة في منطقة الـشرق الأوسـط وشـمال أفريقيـا» بمثابـة الكتـاب السنوي للعـام 2016 مـن «إنترناشـيونال كليرينج هـاوس» التابع لمؤسسة بلدان الشمال الأوروبي للبحوث في ميدان وسائط الإعلام والاتصالات (نورديكوم). وقد نشر هـذا الكتاب السنوي بالتعاون بيـن اليونسكو (UNESCO) وبرنامج الأمـم المتحدة لتحالف الحضارات (UNAOC).

يتمثّـل هـدف مركز «إنترناشـيونال كليرينج هـاوس» في تعزيـز الوعـي والمعرفة حول الأطفال والشباب والإعلام. ونأمل في أن يساهم توفير المعلومات والمعرفة حول نتائج البحوث الجديـدة والأمثلـة الإيجابيـة في تقديـم أسـاس متيـن لوضـع السياسـات ذات الصلـة، وأن يُسـهم في إطلاق مناقشـة عامة بناءة، وتعزيـز التربيـة الإعلاميـة والمهارات الإعلاميـة لـدى فئـتي الأطفـال والشباب.

ساهـم التقدم السريع الحاصل في مجال في تكنولوجيا المعلومات والاتصالات، بالإضافة الى فـرص المشـاركة الـتي، على سبيل المثال، توفرهـا وسـائل التواصل الاجتماعي للمواطنيـن، في تغيير كيفية انتشار المعلومـات ووتيرة انتقالهـا بيـن الأشـخاص. في وقت يمكن للجميع تقريبـاً أن يقومـوا بـدور النـاشر، تـؤدي وفـرة المحتوى الإعلامي بمنحنا فرصـاً متزايـدة للعثور عـلى المعلومات، لكن أيضـاً عـلى المعلومات الخاطئة والمضلّلة. بالتـالي، أدى هـذا التطور إلى إبراز تحديـات جديـدة. فقد أصبحت الحاجـة إلى المعلومات والتعليم المرتبط بالإعلام والتربيـة الإعلاميـة أكـثر فأكـثر إلحاحـاً. بفضل امتلاكهـم للمهارات الإعلاميـة والمعلوماتيـة، يصبـح المواطنون مخوّليـن وقادريـن عـلى ممارسة الحقـوق الإنسـانية الأساسية بالكامـل، مثل حرية الإعلام وحرية التعبير، كما يتمكنون مـن إمعان النظـر في المحتوى الإعلامي بعين ناقدة.

7

يشكّل هـذا الإصدار، الـذي يحمل عنـوان «فرص انتشـار التربيـة الإعلاميـة والمعلوماتيـة في منطقـة الـشرق الأوسـط وشمال أفريقيـا»، الكتـاب السنوي السـابع عـشر الـذي يصدره مركز «إنترناشـيونال كليرينـج هـاوس»؛ وهـو يسدّ الثغـرة في مجموعـة الكتابـات حول التقـدم المحـرز في مجـال التربيـة الإعلاميـة والمعلوماتيـة في أجـزاء مختلفـة حول العالم. نحـن نعتبر أنـه مـن الأهميـة بمكان أن نسلّط الضـوء علـى منطقـة، هـي منطقـة الـشرق الأوسـط وشمال أفريقيـا، حيـث تركـز التقاريـر الإخباريـة في كافـة أنحـاء العالـم في السـنوات الأخيـرة علـى مشـاركة شريحـة المواطنيـن الشبـاب في الإعـلام، كمـا يشـهد الوعـي بشـأن مهارات التربيـة الإعلاميـة والمعلوماتيـة تقدمـاً متزايـداً. إن كافـة الكتـب التـي نشـرها مركـز «إنترناشـيونال كليرينـج هـاوس» تهـدف إلى تحفيـز المزيـد مـن البحـوث حـول الأطفـال والشبـاب والإعـلام. وتستهدف تلـك الكتـب مجموعـات مختلفـة مـن المستخدميـن، مثـل الباحثيـن وصناع القـرار والإعلاميـين المحترفيـن والمنظمـات التطوعيـة والمعلميـن والطـلاب والمهتميـن. ونحـن نأمـل في أن يوفّـر هـذا الكتـاب السنوي رؤى تحليليـة جديـدة لهـذه الفئـات المستهدفة في كافـة أنحـاء العالـم.

إنجيلا وادبرينغ

مديـرة، مركـز «إنترناشـيونال كليرينـج هـاوس» التابع لمؤسسـة بلـدان الشمال الأوروبي للبحـوث في ميـدان وسـائط الإعـلام والاتصـالات (نورديكـوم).

مقدمة:

يشكّل هـذا الكتـاب ثمـرة مـن ثمـار سلسـلة ورش العمـل لتدريـب المدرّسين في مجـال التربيـة الإعلاميـة والمعلوماتيـة الـتي شـارك برنامـج الأمـم المتحـدة لتحالـف الحضـارات بتنظيمهـا خـلال عـام 2013 و 2014 في فـاس بالمغـرب والقاهـرة بمصر. (1)

وقـد أدرك برنامـج الأمـم المتحـدة لتحالـف الحضـارات منـذ وقـت مبكر الأهميـة القصـوى للتربيـة الإعلاميـة والمعلوماتيـة في بنـاء مجتمعـات سـلمية، يتعايـش فيهـا الأفـراد مـن خلفيـات ثقافيـة ودينيـة مختلفـة في وئـام تـام جنبـاً إلى جنـب؛ باعتـراف تقريـر المجموعـة رفيعـة المسـتوى التابعـة لـ «برنامـج الأمـم المتحـدة لتحالـف الحضـارات».

شكّل التعـرض المسـتمر لمجموعـات السـكان لوسـائل الإعلام تحديـاً تعليميـاً، إزداد تعقيـداً في العصـر الإلكـتروني والرقمـي. إن تقييـم مصـادر المعلومـات يتطلب المهـارات والتفكيـر الناقـد، كمـا أنه يشكّل مسـؤولية تعليميـة، يتم الاستخفاف بأهميتهـا في كثير مـن الأحيـان. إن فصـل الواقـع عـن الـرأي، وتقييـم النـص والصـورة مـن دون تحيـز، بالإضافـة الى بنـاء وتفكيـك النـص بالارتكاز علـى مبـادئ المنطـق هي مهـارات قابلـة للتعليـم. كمـا أن تعليـم التربيـة الإعلاميـة والمعلوماتيـة ليـس معروفـاً علـى نطـاق واسـع لأهميته كأحـد جوانـب التعليـم المدنـي والتعليـم مـن أجـل السـلام؛ وبالتالـي لـم يتـم تطويـر سـوى عـدد قليل مـن البرامـج التعليميـة كجـزء مـن التعليـم الأساسـي الحديـث.» ويوصـي التقريـر «بضـرورة تنفيـذ برامـج التربيـة الإعلاميـة في المـدارس، وخاصـة في المرحلـة الثانويـة، للمسـاعدة في تطويـر مقاربـة واعيـة ونقديـة لتغطيـة الأخبـار مـن قبـل مستهلكي الإعلام، وتعزيـز الوعي الإعلامـي وتطويـر التثقيـف علـى الإنترنت لمكافحـة سـوء الفهـم والتعصـب وخطـاب الكراهيـة.» (2)

وقـد إزدادت الحاجـة اليـوم إلى تنفيـذ التربيـة الإعلاميـة والمعلوماتيـة في المـدارس بنسـب اسـتثنائية. فقـد اسـتقطبت السـلطة المتناميـة والسـريعة الانتشـار لوسـائل التواصـل الإجتماعـي إهتمـام الكثيريـن، ليـس فقـط المعلنين في مجـال السـلع الاسـتهلاكية، بـل ايضـاً، وبشـكل مأسـوي، كافـة محـركات الدعايـة الرقميـة للمجموعـات الـتي تنشـر الكراهيـة والتباعـد والعنـف الشـديد في كافـة أنحـاء العالـم. ينبغـي أن يتم فهـم التربيـة الإعلاميـة

9

والمعلوماتيـة كعنصـر أساسـي فـي الجهـود الراميـة إلـى تعزيـز المرونـة والصمـود فـي وجـه رسـائل المتطرفين المشهود لهم بالعنف. يجب ان تشكل التربية الإعلامية والمعلوماتيـة، ليـس أداة رقابـة، بـل كمنصـة لتطويـر مهـارات التفكيـر النقـدي، وخلـق رسـائل مضـادة للخطـاب الـذي يمجـد المـوت والعنـف.

نأمـل أن يصبـح هـذا الكتـاب مصـدر إلهـام ومـورداً هامـاً للمدرّسـين فـي منطقـة الشـرق الأوسـط وشمـال أفريقيـا الذيـن يبحثـون عـن فـرص لإدخـال عناصـر تعليـم التربيـة الإعلاميـة والمعلوماتيـة الـى صفوفهـم؛ أمـلاً فـي أن يسـهّل ذلـك تطويـر تفاهـم أفضـل بيـن الأفـراد مـن مختلـف الأديـان و الخلفيـات الثقافيـة.

ونرغـب فـي توجيـه الشـكر الـى الحكومـة الإسبانيـة لتوفيرهـا التمويـل اللازم لـورش العمـل المذكـورة أعـلاه وتسـهيل عمليـة نشـر هـذا الكتـاب. كمـا نـود أن نشـكر جميـع المسـاهمين فـي هـذا الكتـاب، لا سيما السيدة ماجدة أبـو فاضل التـي تولت مهمة مزدوجة مـن خـلال عملهـا كالمحـررة الرئيسـية للنصـوص كافـة باللغتيـن الإنجليزيـة والعربيـة. نحـن ايضـاً ممتنـون لـكل مـن السـيد آلتـون غريـزل واليونسـكو، لضـم جهودهـم الـى برنامـج الأمـم المتحـدة لتحالـف الحضـارات، لجعـل نشـر هـذا الكتـاب ممكنـاً.

أود أن أتوجـه بشـكر خـاص الـى «نورديكـوم»، تقديـراً لدعمهـم مـن أجـل نشـر هـذا الكتـاب، وضمـان توزيعـه علـى الصعيـد العالمـي.

جـوردي تورنت
مدير المشروع
مبادرات التربية الإعلامية والمعلوماتية
برنامج الأمم المتحدة لتحالف الحضارات

(1) اختـبرت ورش العمـل المذكـورة أعـلاه وناقشت مـع مدرّسـين مـن المراحـل الثانويـة الفـرص والتحديـات التـي تواجـه عمليـة تنفيـذ مناهـج التربيـة الإعلاميـة والمعلوماتيـة للمدرّسـين» الخاصـة باليونسـكو. يرجـى زيـارة الرابـط التالـي:http://unesco.mil-for-teachers.unaoc.org

(2) يرجى زيارة الرابط التالي: http://www.unaoc.org/who-we-are/high-level-group

مقدمة:

لا يوجـد وقـت ملائـم أكـثر مـن الآمـن اجـل تعزيـز، وتعليـم، واسـتخدام التربيـة الإعلاميـة والمعلوماتيـة بكافـة تعديلاتهـا في كافـة أنحـاء منطقـة الـشرق الأوسـط وشـمال أفريقيـا، ولا سـيما في الـدول العربيـة الـتي تشـهد تغـيرات جذريـة هامـة. إن فكـرة التربيـة الإعلاميـة والمعلوماتيـة حديثـة الوجـود في معظـم البلـدان الـتي شـملتها هـذه الدراسـة، وتطبيـق البرامـج الـتي تـدرج تحـت مظلـة التربيـة الإعلاميـة والمعلوماتيـة تختلـف مـن شـبه معدومـة إلى حيويـة نسـبياً، وإن كان ذلـك عـلى نطـاق محـدود.

يعـود ذلـك إلى حـد كبـير الى أنظمـة التعليـم المختلفـة في أنحـاء العالـم العربـي؛ عـلى الرغـم مـن وجـود نقـاط مشـتركة تتمثـّل في أن عمليـة نقـل المعلومـات مـن أعـلى إلى أسـفل (وليـس دائمـا المعرفـة) تشـكّل القاعـدة وليسـت الاسـتثناء ولا تـزال موجـودة في المـدارس والجامعـات. كمـا أن التفكـير النقـدي لا يـزال ينتظـر أن يتجـذر في كافـة المجـالات. ووتوجـد أمثلـة عـلى بعـض المؤسسـات التعليميـة الـتي تشـجّع ذلـك، ولكـن هنـاك عـدة عوامـل هامـة تدخـل حـيز التنفيـذ عنـد التطبيـق.

سـاهمت التقاليـد الدينيـة والاجتماعيـة السـائدة في المنطقـة بفـرض المعايـير، حيـث يحظـى بعـض الشـخصيات مثـل الآبـاء والأمهـات والمعلمـين بالاحـترام والتقديـر الكبـير، لدرجـة انـه لا ينبغـي التشـكيك في وجهـات نظرهـم ومعرفتهـم. وتقـوم بعـض الشـخصيات الدينيـة أحيانـاً بمهمـة المعلمـين ومـن المفـترض ان تـتم معاملتهـم بتقديـر عـال، بالتـالي، فمـن المرجـح أن تكـون مقاربتهـم في مجـال التربيـة الإعلاميـة والمعلوماتيـة متشـرّبة مـن وجهـة نظرهـم الأخلاقيـة والأكـثر تحفظـاً عـلى الموضـوع.

توجـد ايضـاً مسـألة النظـم التعليميـة المختلفـة المنتـشرة في المنطقـة. إذ توجـد مـدارس عامـة وخاصـة، ومـدارس دينيـة (الـتي يمكـن أن تكـون إمـا ممولـة مـن القطـاع العـام أو مدعومـة مـن القطـاع الخـاص) ويوفـر التعليـم في تلـك المـدارس في معظمـه باللغـة العربيـة (اللغـة المشـتركة في البلـدان العربيـة)، والفرنسـية (في الـدول الـتي كانـت مسـتعمرات فرنسـية،

والإنكليزية (حيث امتد نفوذ الإمبراطورية البريطانية). يُضاف الى ذلك تأثير الدخول الأميركي في المشهد التربوي والديني من خلال المبشرين الذين أسسوا لهم موطئ قدم في الكثير من البلدان، وكذلك من خلال التدريس باللغات المحلية و / أو العرقية مثل لغة الأمازيغ في دول شمال أفريقيا واللغة الكردية في بعض مناطق الشرق الأوسط، والأرمنية في لبنان وسوريا حيث عاشت أقلية أرمينية طوال أكثر من قرن. أصبحت كل هذه العناصر جزءاً من محتوى الوسائط المتعددة المتشابك والمتكامل، والتفاعل، والجماهير / المنتجين في المنطقة.

بما أن التربية الإعلامية والمعلوماتية كمجال دراسي هي جديدة نسبياً، لا تزال تخضع للاستكشاف ويتم الارتكاز عليها في مختلف أنحاء العالم، ولا تزال تتقدم بخطوات بطيئة في منطقة الشرق الأوسط وشمال أفريقيا. يتم في كثير من الأحيان استخدام كلّ من التربية الإعلامية والتربية المعلوماتية بشكل مطابق. إلا أن ذوي الخلفيات الأكاديمية المتطورة، فإن التربية المعلوماتية تحظى بالأسبقية، في حين تأتي التربية الإعلامية كملحق. أما الأشخاص الأكثر انسجاماً مع المشهد الإعلامي، فيميلون إلى التركيز على ذلك الجانب من الطيف التربوي. التعريف الأمثل، يأتي من الأشخاص الذين عملوا في مجال الإعلام وشاركوا في المجال الأكاديمي وهم على دراية ببنية هذا الأخير. فهم يميلون إلى تأييد كلا الثقافتين بشكل أفضل من خلال فهمهم لما هو موجود وما ينبغي القيام به، شرط أن يقوموا، هم أيضاً، بمواكبة التقنيات والأولويات المتغيرة بسرعة.

يسلّط المؤلفون المشاركون في إعداد هذا الكتاب الضوء على هذا المشهد الواعد، على أمل أن يقدم عملهم المبتكر الأساس لبناء هيكل متين ومرن في الوقت عينه. يساهم هذا العمل المشترك في تسليط الضوء على الجهود الوطنية والمحلية والفردية المختلفة لخلق المزيد من الوعي، وإظهار أوجه القصور القائمة، وتوسيع دائرة أصحاب المصلحة المعنيين في مجال التربية الإعلامية والمعلوماتية.

في الفصل الذي وضعه ضمن الكتاب، بعنوان: «تحليل أولي مقارن للتربية الإعلامية والمعلوماتية في منطقة الشرق الأوسط»، استكشف آلتون غريزل، من شعبة تنمية وسائل الإعلام والمجتمع، اليونسكو، ما يحدث في الشرق الأوسط وشمال أفريقيا.

وقدم غريزل خارطة طريق للمنطقة، تتضمن لمحة عامة عن تركيبتها السكانية وبيئات المعلومات والإعلام فيها، في ظل وجود عدد كبير من المواطنين الشباب في

الـدول العربيـة. كمـا أكـد غريـزيل أن مفهـوم التربيـة الإعلاميـة والمعلوماتيـة بحـد ذاتـه يملـك تأثيـراً مباشـراً عـلى كيفيـة تصميـم برامـج التربيـة الإعلاميـة والمعلوماتيـة وتنفيذهـا ورصدهـا وتأثيرهـا عـلى حيـاة الشـباب بشـكل خـاص، والمواطنيـن بشـكل عـام. أمـا المنطـق الـذي تحـدث عنـه المؤلـف فهـو أن التربيـة الإعلاميـة والمعلوماتيـة في الـدول العربيـة تعتـبر وسيلـة لتحقيـق طيـف واسـع مـن أهـداف التطويـر الاجتماعـي، والسـياسي، والاقتصـادي. وقال : «مـن جهـة أخـرى، تشـكل التربيـة الإعلاميـة والمعلوماتيـة غايـة في حـد ذاتهـا، لأنهـا تمكّـن النـاس مـن اكتسـاب المهـارات الشخصيـة، والوعـي الـذاتي والإبـداع وتحقيـق الـذات.»

في هـذه الأثنـاء، في لبنـان، قـام كلّ مـن جـاد ملـكي، وهـو أسـتاذ مشـارك في دراسـات الصحافـة والإعـلام في الجامعـة الأميركيـة في بيـروت، ولبنـى معاليقـي، وهـي مديـرة أكاديميـة التربيـة الإعلاميـة والرقميـة في بيـروت (MDLAB) بتسـليط الضـوء عـلى الأكاديميـة ونشـاطاتها، وتطورهـا. أنطلقـت أكاديميـة التربيـة الإعلاميـة والرقميـة في بيـروتMDLAB في عـام 2013 عـلى يـد مجموعـة مـن الأكاديميـين العـرب والدوليـين «بهـدف تطويـر التربيـة الرقميـة والإعلاميـة في المنطقـة مـن خـلال تدريـب مـدرسي الإعـلام العـرب وتطويـر المناهـج الدراسيـة في مجـال التربيـة الرقميـة والإعلاميـة، ليـس فقـط باللغـة العربيـة، بـل وتطويـر المناهـج الدراسيـة في مجـال التربيـة الرقميـة والإعلاميـة، ليـس فقـط باللغـة العربيـة، بـل ايضـاً مـن خـلال التعمّـق في الثقافـات والاهتمامـات العربيـة.» ومذاك الحيـن، تعقـد الأكاديميـة دورات في الصيـف لاستضافة أكاديميـين وطـلاب الدراسـات العليـا والإعلاميـين مـن مختلـف الـدول العربيـة الذيـن يرغبـون في صقـل مهاراتهـم الرقميـة واكتسـاب فهـم أفضـل لكيفيـة ارتبـاط تلـك المهـارات مـع فهـم التربيـة الإعلاميـة والمعلوماتيـة. وبحسـب ملـكي: «تعتـبر التربيـة الرقميـة والاعلاميـة نوعـاً مـن الثقافـة الإعلاميـة للجماهيـر. إنهـا الثـورة الصامتـة التـي يمكنهـا مواجهـة أيديولوجيـات الجشـع والكراهيـة والمـوت والكفـاح مـن أجـل تعميـم العدالـة الاجتماعيـة ونظـم المسـاواة وعولمتهـا.» واختتـم الباحثـان فصلهمـا مـن الكتـاب بالتأكيـد عـلى أنـه لا يمكـن أن تكـون التربيـة الرقميـة والإعلاميـة متوفـرة فقـط لمجموعـة صغيـرة مـن الطـلاب الذيـن يسـتطيعون الحصـول عـلى تعليـم جامعـي. «نحـن بحاجـة إلى توفيـر دورات متصلـة بالانترنـت وغـير متصلـة وورش عمـل سـهلة المنـال باللغـة العربيـة للوصـول إلى جمهـور أوسـع. أكثـر مـن ذلـك، تحتـاج التربيـة الرقميـة والإعلاميـة إلى الانتقـال إلى المـدارس، وصـولاً الى التعليـم الابتـدائي ومـا بعـده. نحـن بحاجـة إلى تطويـر مجموعـة مترابطـة مـن المعلميـن والأكاديميـين والباحثيـن القادريـن عـلى نقـل التعليـم والأبحـاث في مجـال التربيـة الرقميـة والإعلاميـة إلى المسـتوى التـالي.»

مشـروع التربيـة الإعلاميـة والمعلوماتيـة في برنامـج الأممالمتحـدة لتحالـف الحضـارات (UNAOC)، اهتمامـه الى الشـباب والإعـلام الرقمـي، مـع تركيـز خـاص عـلى ورش العمـل الـتي تشـمل المدرّسين في المـدارس المتوسـطة والثانويـة في كلّ مـن مصر والمغرب. وقال: «شـكّلت حلقـات العمـل فرصـة لمعظم المدرّسين لـكي يناقشـوا لأول مـرة المفاهيـم الرئيسـية والركائـز الأساسـية لتعليـم التربيـة الإعلاميـة والمعلوماتيـة، وليفهمـوا أن المفاهيـم التقليديـة لمعرفـة القـراءة والكتابـة (كتابـة وقـراءة النصـوص المطبوعـة) لـم تعـد تعتبر مهـارات كافيـة للأفـراد لـكي يكونـوا مواطنين مشـاركين ونشـطين في المجتمعـات المعاصرة.» وفي حين تشـكّل مهـارات التكنولوجيـا الرقميـة شـرطاً أساسـياً هامـاً لتحقيـق النجـاح في عالـم اليـوم، أكـدت تورنـت أن التربيـة الإعلاميـة والمعلوماتيـة تجسـد بأشـكال عـدة «العلـوم الإنسـانية» أكـثر مـن «التكنولوجيـا». وقـد أجـرى المدرسـون في القاهـرة وفاس اسـتطلاعاً بسـيطاً للتعـرف الى العـادات الإعلاميةلطلابهـم واكتشـفوا أن التلفزيون كان الوسـيلة المفضّلة لـدى المسـتطلعين الشـباب. وأضاف تورنـت: أضـع عبـارة «مشـاهدة التلفزيـون» بين علامتي اقتبـاس لأن الشـباب اليـوم لا يشـاهدون التلفزيـون فقـط (لـم يعـد هـذا الجمهـور المأسـور والمفتـون بالشاشـة الـذي كان عليـه في عـصر مـا قبـل الإنترنت)، فهـو يسـتهلك أشـكالاً أخـرى مـن وسـائل الإعـلام أثنـاء مشـاهدة التلفزيـون. هـذا يشـمل تحميـل الصـور ومقاطـع الفيديـو عـلى مواقـع التواصـل الاجتماعـي، وإرسـال الرسـائل النصيـة، واسـتخدام منصـات متعـددة لأغـراض متعـددة.

حمـد أبـو عرقـوب حـول مفهـوم التربيـة الإعلاميـة والمعلوماتيـة في الأراضي الفلسـطينية المحتلـة، والضفـة الغربيـة والقـدس الشـرقية وقطـاع غـزة، والسـبب الـذي يجعلهمموضوعـاً معقـداً، ولـم ينبغي تمكينه . وقال المؤلفـان إن مفهـوم «التربيـة المعلوماتيـة» أكـثر انتشـاراً مـن «التربيـة الإعلاميـة».

الأمـر الملفـت بشـكل خـاص هـو أن الفلسـطينيين اضطروا إلى العيـش في تلـك الأراضي تحت سـيطرة الأردن ومـصر في إحـدى الفـترات، ثـم تحـت الاحتـلال العسـكري الإسرائيـلي، ثـم تحـت سـيطرة حكومتهـم الخاصـة الـتي انقسـمت مـا بين أنصـار منظمـة التحريـر الفلسـطينية (أو فتح باللغـة العربيـة) بشـكل خـاص في الضفـة الغربيـة لنهر الأردن والقـدس الشـرقية، وبين أنصـار حمـاس في قطـاع غـزة. وقـد أدت الانقسـامات الى خلـق مجموعتهـا الخاصـة مـن التحديـات، أقلهـا القيـود عـلى حركـة الفلسـطينيين، والعقـاب الفـردي والجماعـي ضـد أولئـك الذيـن يعارضـون الاحتـلال، والنقـص في الاحتياجـات الأساسـية مثـل الميـاه، والمشـهد الإعلامـي الفوضـوي حيـث يؤثـر التضـارب في سـلطات الـوزارات عـلى السـيطرة، والترخيـص،

واستئجار موجـات البـث ورسـوم الإعـلام، بالإضافـة الى حملـة مـن عمليـات القمـع ضـد وسـائل الإعـلام. في ظـل هـذه الظـروف مجتمعـة، أوضـح كلّ مـن نسـيبة وأبـو عرقـوب أن التربيـة الإعلاميـة والمعلوماتيـة لا تـزال مفهومـاً جديـداً نسـبياً في فلسـطين، سـواء في نظـام التعليـم أو في المجتمـع المـدني. وقـالا في معـرض تعليقهمـا عـلى الموضـوع: «هنـاك أيضـا إدراك متزايدلي الحاجـة لرفـع مسـتوى الوعـي لـدى النـاس حـول كيفيـة التفاعـل مـع وسـائل الإعـلام والتعامـل معهـا. ويتـمّ تنظيـم هـذه الأنشـطة في كافـة انحـاء قطاعـات المجتمـع، اي المجتمـع المـدني والأوسـاط الأكاديميـة والحكوميـة والقطـاع الخـاص.» وأضافـا: «عـدا التطـورات في مجـال التكنولوجيـا، كان للصـراع العـربي الإسرائيـلي المتواصـل ولا يـزال التأثيـر الأكـبر عـلى كل مـا لـه علاقـة بالإعـلام، بمـا في ذلـك التربيـة الإعلاميـة بالنسـبة للفلسـطينيين.»

في إطـار معالجتـه للاحتمـالات المختلفـة، أشـار الدكتـور عبـد الأمـير الفيصـل أن المـرء قـد لا يتمكـن مـن تحديـد اطـار محـدد لوضـع مشـهد المعلومـات في العـراق، لأنـه يتطـور باسـتمرار في بلـد يتوسـع في اسـتخدام المعلومـات في كافـة المسـتويات مـن خـلال إتصـال غـير مقيـد بالإنترنت.

وقـال: «واكبـت العـراق الطفـرة الحاليـة مـن حيـث تطـور وانتشـار المعلومـات الـتي يسـتخدمها الأفـراد والمنظمـات، لتعزيـز التطـورات التكنولوجيـة المتقدمـة لرصـد وجمـع ومعالجـة وتخزيـن واسـترجاع ونقـل واسـتخدام المعلومـات عـبر أجهـزة الكمبيوتـر، وتقنيـات الميكروفيلـم، والاتصـالات عـلى سـبيل المثـال لا الحـصر، واقترانهـا لتشـكيل مـا نسـميه 'تكنولوجيـا المعلومـات'». ثمـة تركيـز أكـبر عـلى تكنولوجيـا المعلومـات والاتصـالات ممـا يوجـد عـلى آليـة التربيـة الإعلاميـة والمعلوماتيـة الفعليـة، عـلى الرغـم مـن بـروز سياسـة إعلاميـة وطنيـة في العـراق. ركـز الدكتـور الفيصـل عـلى دور المكتبـات في العـراق لأنهـا تطـورت عـلى مـر السـنوات، في حيـن تشـكل التكنولوجيـا مصـدر الاهتمـام السـائد في معادلـة التربيـة الإعلاميـة والمعلوماتيـة هـذه. وكتـب الفيصـل: «باختصـار، بـدأت بصمـة تكنولوجيـا المعلومـات تظهـر في العـراق في عـام 2003، وشـهدت قفـزات نوعيـة. كمـا نجحـت في إجـراء تغيـرات واضحـة في الأداء العـام لتكنولوجيـا المعلومـات.»

في الجانـب الآخـر مـن العالـم العـربي، تنـاول الدكتـور رضـوان بوجمعـة، أسـتاذ وباحـث في جامعـة الجزائـر، قضيـة التربيـة الاعلاميـة في الجزائـر، وعلاقتهـا بالتطـورات التاريخيـة الـتي عرفتهـا منظومتهـا التربويـة، منـذ الاسـتقلال إلى اليـوم. اعـترف بوجمعـة أن الجزائـر عانـت مـن ارتفـاع معـدلات الأميـة في الجانـب الآخـر مـن العالـم العـربي،

تنـاول الدكتـور رضـوان بوجمعـة، أسـتاذ وباحـث في جامعـة الجزائـر، قضيـة التربيـة الاعلاميـة في الجزائـر، وعلاقتهـا بالتطـورات التاريخيـة التـي عرفتهـا منظومتهـا التربويـة، منـذ الاستقـلال إلى اليـوم. اعتـرف بوجمعـة أن الجزائـر عانـت مـن ارتفـاع معدلات الأميـة بسـبب الاستعمـار وآثـاره السـلبية وأنـه عنـد استقـلال البـلاد في عـام 1962،كانت نسبة الأميـة تفوق 86 بالمائـة، ومذاك الحين، لـم تحقـق البـلاد بعـد هـدف دمـج الإعـلام والاتصـالات في نظـام التعليـم باستخـدام تكنولوجيـا المعلومـات والاتصـالات. كمـا شهـدت الجزائـر أيضـاً مرحلـة مـن تحديـد الـذات، حيـث كان العـدد القليـل مـن المثقفين يسـتخدمون اللغـة الفرنسـية، لغـة المستعمريـن السـابقين، وحيـث الحاجـة إلى الاعتـراف بالجـذور العربيـة والأفريقيـة كان يتطلـب إعـادة النظـر في النظـام التعليمـي، وبالتـالي، المشهـد الإعلامـي. في هـذا الفصـل، ركـز المؤلـف علـى إدخـال وتعزيـز تكنولوجيـا المعلومـات والاتصـالات، في مقابـل التربيـة الإعلاميـة والمعلوماتيـة بمـا أن المفهـوم لـم يتـرسخ بعـد في الجزائـر، حيـث يتطلـب المدرّسـون والطـلاب تدريبـاً مكثفـاً وانغماسـاً في طبقاتهـا المتعـددة. وختـم المؤلـف قائـلاً: «غيـر أن إدخـال التكنولوجيـات لـن يكـون لـه أثـراً كبيـراً لوحـده، إذا لـم يرفـق بممارسـة تربويـة جديـدة، وبخلـق نشاطـات تربويـة أخـرى، مصحوبـة بديناميكيـة جديـدة؛ ديناميكيةيجـب أن تعبـد طريـق ايجـاد مسـار جماعـي لبنـاء المعـارف الجماعيـة.»

البروفسـور عبـد الحميـد النفيسـي مـن جامعـة سيـدي محمـد بـن عبداللـه في فـاس، بالمغـرب، وإدريسـية شـويت مـن جامعـة مولاي (المولى) إسماعيـل في مكنـاس، المغـرب، قامـا بدراسـة حالـة التربيـة الإعلاميـة والمعلوماتيـة في بلدهمـا. المؤلفـان قدمـا في دراستهمـا لمحـة عـن الطريقـة التـي أُدخلـت فيهـا التربيـة الإعلاميـة والمعلوماتيـة الى المغـرب، والإجـراءات التـي اتخـذت لتعزيزهابهـدف إعـداد المواطنيـن بصـورة أفضـل لعصـر المعلومـات، وأهـم خطـط العمـل والمبـادرات التـي ستنفـذ في المستقبـل. وبحسـب كلّ مـن النفيسـي وشـويت: «لا تـزال التربيـة الإعلاميـة والمعلوماتيـة في بداياتهـا في المغـرب. لـم يتـم تضمينهـا في النظـام التعليمـي، وليسـت علـى جـدول أعمـال النشطـاء وصانعـي السياسـات والمربيـن. كمـا أن النـاس ليسـوا علـى علـم بهـا لـي يفكـروا بهـا. بالنسبـة الى العديـد مـن المغاربـة، كلمـة «التثقيـف» (او التربيـة) تعنـي القـدرة علـى القـراءة والكتابـة، وتفسير الرسـائل المطبوعـة.» وأضـاف المؤلفـان، ان التربيـة الإعلاميـة والمعلوماتيـةأُدمجت في دورات الدراسـات الإعلاميـة المغربيـة، لكـن التربيـة المعلوماتيـة بحـد ذاتهـا لـم تدمـج في المناهـج الجامعيـة. لـذا كان هنـاك عنصـر مفقـود. قـالا: «بعـد تدريـس التربيـة الإعلاميـة والتربيـة المعلوماتيـة كلّ علـى حـدة في الفصـل الثانـي، اشتملـت الـدروس حـول الدراسـات الإعلاميـة والثقافـة

المعلوماتيـة التـي تـدرس في الفصـل الـدراسي الرابـع عـلى مزيـج مـن التربيـة الإعلاميـة والتربيـة المعلوماتيـة بمـا أنهـا تضمنـت كلاً مـن«الدراسـات الإعلاميـة»و«الثقافـة المعلوماتيـة». بمـا ان التربيـة الإعلاميـة والمعلوماتيـة لـم تكـن ضمـن اهتمامـات أي شـخص في المغـرب، وإيمانـاً منهـما بأهميتهـا لـكل مـن الشـباب والآبـاء وكل مواطـن، قررالمؤلفـان تنظيـم مؤتمـر دولي حـول هـذا الموضـوع لتعريـف الأكاديميين المغاربـة بـه وتوعيـة الأفـراد بأهميتـه في حياتهـم. مـذاك الوقـت، اشـتركا في أنشـطة أخـرى، تجدونهـا بالتفصيـل في فصلهـما مـن الكتـاب، وهمـا في طريقهـما إلى تعميـق فهـم التربيـة الإعلاميـة والمعلوماتيـة وتطبيقهـما.

مـصر، الـتي تقـع في قلـب الـدول العربيـة، تتمتعبأعـلى كثافـة سـكانية في المنطقـة. وتشـير التقديـرات إلى أن 95 في المائـة مـن السـكان يعيشـون ضمـن مسـاحة 3 بالمائـة فقـط مـن الأرض. الازدحـام الحـضري في معظـم المـدن، المترافـق مـع نظـام المـدارس العامـة المجانـي المكتـظ والمدرّسين الذيـن يتقاضـون أجـوراً يـرثى لهـا، وشـبكة المـدارس الخاصـة الـتي تتطلـب تكاليـف باهظـة لا يمكـن لمتوسـط المصرييـن تحملهـا، ومزيـج بيـن وسـائل الإعـلام المطبوعـة والمسـموعة والمرئيـة وعـلى الانترنـت الخاضعـة لسـيطرة الدولـة المختلفـة النزعـات والتوجهـات، كلهـا تحتـاج الى مترجميـن إعلاميـين فوريين مؤهلين للحـرص عـلى أن يفهـم المواطنـون مـا يسـتهلكونه. سـامي طايـع، رئيـس قسـم الصحافـة بكليـة الإعـلام في جامعـة القاهـرة، يعـترف أن بـلاده وصلـت متأخـرة الى عالـم التربيـة الإعلاميـة والمعلوماتيـة عـلى الرغـم مـن انتشـار وسـائل الأخبـار والترفيـه الـتي ظهـرت بعـد السـنوات التحويليـة وبعـد الثـورات الأخيـرة الـتي ولّدهـا «الربيـع العـربي «والعديـد مـن التغيـرات في الحكومـات في مـصر. وقـال طايـع أن الكليـة الـتي يعلـم فيهـا قدمـت مـادة التربيـة الإعلاميـة والمعلوماتيـة لطـلاب المرحلـة الجامعيـة في عـام 2005 وأن الجامعـات الحكوميـة والخاصـة الأخـرى حـذت حذوهـا. عـلاوة عـلى ذلـك، شـملت جهـوده ورش العمـل والمؤتمـرات وابتـكار الأدوات المناسـبة الـتي تهـدف إلى توفيـر المـوارد لأسـاتذة الجامعـات لاسـتخدامها في تدريـس التربيـة الإعلاميـة والمعلوماتيـة في المؤسسـات العامـة والخاصـة المختلفـة. لكنـه أوضـح ان العقبـات تزايـدت. وقـال: «يقـع التحـدي الرئيـس للتربيـة الإعلاميـة والمعلوماتيـة في مـصر عـلى عاتـق صانعـي السياسـات. لا توجـد سياسـة بهـذه المسـألة. حـاول بعـض العلمـاء والخبـراء أن يضمـوا ممثليـن عـن وزارة التربيـة والتعليـم ووزارة التعليـم العـالي في معظـم هـذه الأنشـطة؛ لكـن المشـاكل والعقبـات جـاءت عـادة مـن واضعـي السياسـات والعامليـن في وزارة التربيـة والتعليـم «.

واعترف يسار الـدرة مـن معهد الاعلام الاردني انه تعرف لأول مرة على مصطلح «التربية الإعلامية والمعلوماتيـة» خـلال مشـاركته في احـدى جلسات المناقشة مـع اليونسكو عـام 2012، وأنهاكانت قبـل ذلـك مجـرد سلسـلة مـن القيـم والأهـداف الـتي يتـم تدريسـها في مختلـف المناهـج الإعلاميـة التدريبيـة ولا تشـمل صغـار طـلاب المـدارس. وقـال الـدرة انه في السنوات الثلاث الماضية، اصبح هذا التعبير جـزءاً من المصطلحـات المستخدمة مـن قبـل الموظفيـن والطـلاب في معهـد الإعـلام الأردني(JMI)وقـد اكتسـب مزيـداً مـن الزخـم، مـع تلقـي الطـلاب الدعـوة بشـكل منتظـم للمشـاركة في ورش عمـل حـول موضـوع التربيـة الإعلامية والمعلوماتية.

وقـال الـدرة أن برنامـج التدريب الأكـثر شمـولاً والأطـول مـدة في الأردن والـذي يتمحـور حـول التربية الإعلامية والمعلوماتيـة ، حصـل عـام 2006 في إطـار مشـروع تطويـر «التعليـم عـبر الصحافـة» (NIE)، بمبـادرة مـن الاتحـاد العالمـي للصحـف وناشـري الأبـاء (WAN-IFRA). في حـين كانـت المـدارس في المناطـق الحضريـة أوفـر حظّـاً في تلقـي الانتبـاه والتمويـل مـن واضعـي السياسـات، فإنتلـك الموجـودة في المناطـق النائيـة في الأردن، التي اضطرت لاستقبال التدفـق المسـتمر للاجئيـن السـوريين الهاربيـن مـن بلدهـم الـذي مزقتـه الحـرب، تفتقـر إلى المـوارد اللازمـة للمسـاعدة في تحسـين وصـول البـلاد الى التربيـة الإعلاميـة والمعلوماتيـة.

وختـم قائـلاً: «في ظـل المنـاخ الحالـي البغيضالسـائد في المنطقـة، والـذي يتـم فيـه القـاء اللـوم عـلى فشـل نظـم التعليـم في معالجـة قضايـا التعدديـة، وحريـة التعبـير، وحـق الوصـول الى المعلومـات، يتحتـم عـلى وزارة التربيـة والتعليـم دمـج برامـج التربيـة الإعلاميـة والمعلوماتيـة في المناهـج التربويـة عـلى سـبيل الأولويـة.»وأوصـى الـدرة بتقديـم خطـة عمـل لوضـع الأردن عـلى خريطـة التربيـة الإعلاميـة والمعلوماتيةالدوليـة.

في سـلطنة عمـان، وجـدت الدكتـورة نايفـة عيـد سـليم، وهـي أسـتاذة مسـاعدة في قسـم دراسـات المعلومـات، أن تطويـر تكنولوجيـا المعلومـات والاتصـالات والتدفـق الهائـل في المعلومـات قـد سـاهما في تسـهيل عمليـة تبـادل المعلومـات بـين الجهـات الفاعلـة في المجتمـع المـدني، والـتي تناولهـا زعيـم البـلاد السـلطان قابوسـفي خطابـه في نوفمـبر مـن عـام 2008. وقـد تحدثـت الدكتـورة سـليم عـن دور وزارة الاعـلام العمانيةووزارة التـراث والثقافـة، بالإضافـة إلى هيئـة تكنولوجيـا المعلومـات الـتي تهـدف إلى تحويـل السـلطنة إلى مجتمـع معـرفي مسـتدام مـن خـلال تكنولوجيـا المعلومـات والاتصـالات، وأضافـت أن تلـك الكيانـات تهـدف إلى تزويـد المواطنـين والسـكان بمعلومـات دقيقـة، بالإضافـة إلى

18

مساعدة النـاس علـى معالجـة المعلومـات وتطويـر التفكيـر النقـدي والتحليلـي. ودعـت أيضا إلى إدخـال منهـج حـول التربيـة الإعلاميـة والمعلوماتيـة الى المـدارس، وحثت وزارة التربيـة والتعليـم الى تطبيـق مثـل تلـك المناهـج، نظـراً لتجربـة الـوزارة مـع مراكـز مصـادر التعلـم التـي تعـادل المكتبـات المدرسـية. وكتبـت فـي معـرض تعليقهـا علـى الامـر: «إذا كان محتـوى المـادة حـول التربيـة الإعلاميـة والمعلوماتيـة المقتـرح لا يتوافـق مـع المبـادئ التوجيهيـة والمعاييـر المحـددة لـوزارة التربيـة والتعليـم، مـن المتوقـع أن يتولـى مركـز مصـادر التعلـم توفيـر تلـك الـدورات، لأنـه مرتبـط بشـكل مباشـر ببرامـج الصحافـة والإعـلام بعـد موافقـة الـوزارة. » واقترحـت الدكتـورة سـليم البدائـل لتلـك المراكـز، مشـيرة الى أنـه فـي حـال عـدم تقديمهـا لمـواد التربيـة الإعلاميـة والمعلوماتيـة، ينبغـي علـى كلّ مـن الجامعـات الخاصـة والعامـة دمجهـا ضمـن خطـط التعليـم الخاصـة بهـا وجعلهـا شـرطاً أساسـياً لجميـع الطـلاب.

كانـت السـيدة ماجـدة أبـو فاضـل، وهـي صحفيـة دوليـة مخضرمـة، وأكاديميـة ومدونـة، مـن بيـن أول مـن تبنـى مفاهيـم التربيـة الإعلاميـة والمعلوماتيةوأيّدهـا. فـي عـام 1999، وبصفتهـا منسـقة برنامـج الصحافـة فـي إحـدى الجامعـات فـي لبنـان، شـاركت ابـو فاضـل مـع طلابهـا فـي مشـروع تبـادل إعلامـي إفتراضـي مـع أسـتاذ وطـلاب كليـة الصحافـة فـي جامعـة ميسـوري. مـن خـلال ذلـك المشـروع، شـكلوا جميعـاً جـزءاً مـن تجربـة فـي مجـال التواصـل بيـن الثقافـات، والقيـم، والأخبـار الهامـة، واسـتخدام التكنولوجيـا الناشـئة (لا سـيما الإنترنـت فـي لبنـان)، ومعرفـة مـا يهـم النـاس فعـلاً فـي بيئـة الإعـلام علـى قارتيـن مختلفتيـن. بصفتهـا مراسـلة أجنبيـة متعـددة اللغـات عملـتْ علـى تغطيـة الاخبـار مـن عواصـم مختلفـة فـي كافـة أنحـاء العالـم، كانـت أبـو فاضـل تـدرك جيـداً تأثيـر وسـائل الإعـلام علـى الجماهيـر وكانـت تعـي بشـكل خـاص آثارهـا الضـارة فـي كثيـر مـن الأحيـان علـى الأطفـال والشـباب. مـع انتشـار وسـائل الاعـلام علـى الانترنـت، ووسـائل الإعـلام الرقميـة ووسـائل التواصـل الاجتماعـي عبـر مختلـف المنصـات، أصبحـت أبـو فاضـل مـن أبـرز المؤيديـن لأخلاقيـات الإعـلام والمناديـن بالحاجـة الى خلـق الوعـي حـول تفكيـك الرسـائل والعمليـات والنتائـج وانعكاسـات التفاعـل والتكامـل والتقـارب، والتدفـق الهائـل للاتصـالات التـي تتحـول باسـتمرار وبسـرعة مذهلـة إلـى أشـكال جديـدة. ممـا كتبـت أبـو فاضـل: «إن الرسـائل المموهـة التـي يتـم إدراجهـا فـي البرامـج قـد تؤثـر علـى أنمـاط الشـراء. الحلقـات المليئـة بالصراعـات أو ألعـاب الفيديـو يمكـن أن تحـرض علـى العنـف وتـؤدي إلى السـلوك العـدواني حتـى المسلسـلات التـي تبـدو بريئـة فـي الظاهـر قـد تدفـع الشـباب الى الخلـط بيـن الخيـال والواقـع.. بالنتيجـة، فـإن الاسـتهلاك السـاذج للأخبـار ومـواد الترفيـه، وحتـى «التعليـم الترفيهـي» الأكثـر شـعبية

يمكـن أن تسـهم في خلـق مجتمعـات مفككـة وأفـراد مضطربيـن، أو، عـلى أقـل تقديـر، الى خلـق ارتبـاك حـول كيفيـة التفاعـل مـع الرسـائل المتنافـرة التـي تكتسـح مشـاعرنا الحسـية.» مـذاك الحيـن، تقـوم أبـو فاضـل بالكتابـة عـن هـذا الموضـوع بشـكل واسـع، وتتحـدث في المؤتمـرات عـن ضرورة تبنّي برامـج وطنيـة في مجـال التربيـة الإعلاميـة والمعلوماتيـة، وتدريـب المدرّسـين والطـلاب والعامليـن في وسـائل الإعـلام عـلى إيجابيـات وسـائل الإعـلام وسـلبياتها.

قدمـت كـلّ مـن كارميـلا فلويـد وغابرييـلا ثيـنز مقاربـة عمليةممتعـة في فصلهمـا مـن الكتـاب، والـذي يتنـاول تمكيـن الأطفـال والشـباب في تونـس عـن طريـق دمـج الإعـلام والتعليـم. وقـد أخـذا عـلى عاتقهمـا مهمـة تدريـب الطـلاب والمعلميـن عـلى كيفيـة مسـاهمة التربيـة الإعلاميـة والمعلوماتيـة في مسـاعدتهم عـلى إيجـاد معنـى في حياتهـم، لا سـيما في تونـس مـا بعـد الثـورة، وبعـد التضحيـة التـي قدمهـا محمـد البوعزيـزي، البائـع المتجـول الـذي أضرم النـار بنفسـه في ديسـمبر 2010،وهـو حـدث أطلقـت عليـه وسـائل الإعـلام اسـم «الربيـع العـربي». وكتبـت فلويـد وثيـنز مـا يـلي:

«تصوروا هـذا: اضطـر النظـام الـذي يسـيطر مـن دون وازع أو رادع عـلى الإعـلام الى التخلي عـن السـلطة. قبـل الثـورة، كانـت الرقابـة شـائعة. وكثيراًمـا كان الصحفيـون يتعرضـون للمضايقـات. لأول مـرة، أثنـاء الثـورة،خـرج الصحفيـون التونسـيون إلى الشـوارع ونقلـوا الأحـداث مبـاشرة وسـمحوا للـرأي العـام بالتعبيـر عـن رأيـه مـن دون أي رقابـة.»

مـع سـقوط النظـام، ألغيـت وزارة الإعـلام، التـي كانـت فيمـا مـضى أداةالسـيطرة الإعلاميـة الاكـثر اثـارة للرعـب. فجـأة، سـادت حريـة التعبيـر. وشـهددت تلـك الفـترة ارتفاعـاً سريعـاً في عـدد المحطـات الإذاعيـة الجديـدة، تبعتهـا محطـات التلفـاز والمواقـع الاخباريـة عـلى الانترنـت، في حيـن أعـاد مذيعـو الدولـة تنظيـم أنفسـهم، وتـمّ تشـارك كميـات لامتناهيـة مـن المعلومـات والأخبـار مـن خـلال الخدمـات الاخباريـة عـلى الانترنـت والشـبكات الاجتماعيـة.»

هنـا يـأتي دور المؤلفتيـن، اللتيـن تتمتعـان بخـبرة واسـعة بالعمـل مـع الشـباب في السـويد وغيرهـا، لبنـاء القـدرات مـن خـلال سلسـلة مـن ورش العمـل للشـباب والمربيـن ووسـائل الإعـلام والمخرجيـن الاعلاميـين في أجـزاء مختلفـة مـن البـلاد، بهـدف مسـاعدة الأطفـال والشـباب ليصبحـوا ناشـطين و يكـون لهـم صـوت في مسـائل حقـوق الإنسـان وانتشـار الديمقراطيـة في تونـس. وكتبـت المؤلفتيـن: «لتحقيـق تلـك الغايـة، فإننـا نعتقـد أن عـلى البالغيـن أيضـاً أن يكتسـبوا المهـارات في مجـال التربيـة الإعلاميـة والمعلوماتيـة، سـواء كانـوا مـن المدرّسـين أوقـادة الشـباب أوأوليـاء الأمـور. بالإضافـة إلى ذلـك، كنـا مصممتيـن عـلى

الوصول إلى أولئك الذين ينتجون المواد الإعلامية: الصحفيون ورؤساء التحرير ومديرو غرف الأخبار والمنتجين التلفزيونيين والمدونين.»

تقوم بعض الدول العربية بشق طريقها بسرعة وتهدف إلى الإنتقال إلى المستويات التالية. وتملك هذه الدول الموارد الاقتصادية و / أو قدراً معيناً من الحرية، حيث يتم تشجيع الإبداع والرؤية.

في دولة الإمارات العربية المتحدة، شاركت مؤسسة دبي لرعاية النساء والأطفال بشكل ناشط في الدعوة إلى إدراج التربية الإعلامية في المناهج الدراسية في محاولة للتخفيف من الآثار السلبية للتلفزيون والإنترنت على الشباب والحد من آثار العنف الذي يمكن لوسائل الإعلام المختلفة تعزيزه. كما أن برنامج محمد بن راشد للتعلم الذكي، الذي أطلق في عام 2012 وسمي تيمناً بنائب رئيس دولة الإمارات العربية المتحدة وحاكم دبي، كان ايضاً سباقاً في الترويج لأحدث الأدوات التكنولوجية وفي تجهيز الصفوف بالحواسيب اللوحية الرقمية بدلاً من الكتب المدرسية التقليدية، في خفض استخدام الورق، وتعزيز الوعي بشأن الحاجة إلى حماية البيئة. وقد قام رسام إماراتي شاب بإنشاء تطبيق كتاب للأطفال على الآيباد. وقد ساهم برنامج التعلم الذكي بمساعدة طلاب المدارس على التمتع، والانخراط في العملية التعليمية، والتفاعل بشكل أفضل مع معلميهم وزملائهم في الصف، وأينما كانوا، بفضل الاتصالات المتنقلة عالية السرعة. كما ساعدهم على تطوير فضولهم للبحث عن المعلومات عبر شبكة الإنترنت وغيرها من القنوات المتصلة. يشكّل البرنامج جزءاً من مشروع «رؤية الإمارات 2021». وقد منح البرنامج جائزة مؤتمر القمة العالمية لمجتمع المعلومات (WSIS) عن فئة «بناء القدرات» في جنيف، سويسرا في عام 2014. المنطقة الإعلامية والترفيهية الخالية من الضرائب «تو فور 54»، (TwoFour54) في أبو ظبي، التي توفر خدمات التلفزيون والسينما، هي أيضاً موطن لمختبر إبداعي ومركز تدريب متوفرين للطلاب والمهنيين. في عام 2014، بدأت المنطقة التعاون مع المنظمات الإعلامية العربية والترفيهية الرئيسية لدعم المنتجين الإعلاميين الشباب، ومطوري الألعاب والبرامج التي تتوافق مع الأعراف والتقاليد السائدة في البلاد.

في المملكة العربية السعودية، كان التقدم في مجال التربية الإعلامية والمعلوماتية بطيئاً. وعلى الرغم من الثروات الهائلة، كان نظام التعليم في البلاد أكثر تقليدية وكان المعلمون أقل انسجاماً مع مجتمع المعرفة الرقمية. كما أن التعلم الذي لقي بعض الاهمال

لصالح منهجيات أكثر كلاسيكية، لكن المملكة الصحراوية تمضي قدماً في محاولة اللحاق بركب الدول الأخرى في المنطقة. وقد بدأ التعلم عن بعد يحظى بإقبال كبير ويتم تشجيع المعلمين على تبنيه كواحد من طرق التدريس / التعليم المختلفة. وفي حين أثبت الإلمام باللغات الأجنبية أنه مفتاح التفاهم والتفاعل بشكل أفضل مع وسائل الإعلام والمعلومات؛ فشل النظام التعليمي السعودي العام في وضع مناهج تعليمية عصرية باللغة الإنجليزية وتوفير مدرسين مؤهلين يستخدمون أساليب التدريس الإبداعي، بدلاً من إخضاع طلابهم لطريقة التعلم عن ظهر قلب. لكن الوضع ليس ميؤساً منه ويمكن التعويض عن هذا الأمر. إذ أن هناك جهود جارية لتغيير مسار الأمور، ولو تدريجياً، بموجب التقاليد الدينية والثقافية. في النهاية، لا يزال هناك الكثير من المسائل التي تحتاج الى المعالجة، وتبقى التربية الإعلامية والمعلوماتية في الشرق الأوسط ومنطقة شمال أفريقيا عملاً في طور الإنجاز.

ماجدة ابو فاضل ـ المحررة الرئيسة

تحليل أولي مقارن حول التربية الإعلامية والمعلوماتية في منطقة الشرق الأوسط

آلتون غريزل

لقـد بلغـت التربيـة الاعلاميـة والمعلوماتيـة سـن الرشـد. بالتـالي، لا يجـدر بالحكومـات وصانعـي السياسـات في العالـم تجاهلهـا، نظـراً للمجموعـة الهائلـة مـن المؤلفـات الأكاديميـة التـي تدعـم أهميـة التربيـة الإعلاميـة والمعلوماتيـة. إن التربيـة الإعلاميـة والمعلوماتيـة هـي موضـوع ضـروري للتعلـم، وسـيلة للتعلـم والوعـي الـذاتي، والتنشـئة الاجتماعيـة الموجهـة ذاتيـاً أو التنظيـم الـذاتي. إنهـا أداة يمكـن تطبيقهـا علـى كافـة أشـكال قضايـا وسـياقات التنميـة. وأخيـراً، إن التربيـة الإعلاميـة والمعلوماتيـة هـي عبـارة عـن مجموعـة مـن الكفـاءات الخاصـة بالقـرن الحـادي والعشـرين يمكـن أن تـؤدي في نهايـة الامـر إلى تمكيـن المواطنيـن، والتعبيـر عـن الـذات والحـوار بيـن الثقافـات والأديـان.

في تشـابه ملحـوظ، يقـوم التقريـر العالمـي عـن رصـد التعليـم للجميـع (2006) الصـادر عـن اليونسـكو، بالارتـكاز إلى عمـل سـنوات لكثيـر مـن العلمـاء الأكاديميـين، باقتـراح أربـع طـرق لفهـم مسـألة التثقيـف؛ وقـد تطـور بالارتـكاز علـى التقاليـد التأديبيـة. أولاً، يعتبـر التثقيـف مجموعـة منفصلـة مـن المهـارات الملموسـة مثـل القـراءة والكتابـة والحسـاب، مسـتقلة عـن السـياق والتـي تمتـد إلى المهـارات اللازمـة للوصـول إلى المعلومـات والمعـارف. ثانيـاً، يُنظـر الى التثقيـف علـى انـه موضـوع يعتمـد علـى السـياق، ويتجـاوز مجـرد اكتسـاب المهـارات اللازمـة مـن اجـل تعزيـز وإبـراز اسـتخدام وتطبيـق هـذه المهـارات في مواقـف الحيـاة الحقيقيـة. ثالثـاً، يُنظـر الى التثقيـف باعتبـاره عمليـة تعلـم. فكلمـا تعلـم الأشـخاص، يكتسـبون تدريجيـاً وبشـكل فاعـل مهـارات القـراءة والكتابـة. بهـذا المعنـى، يعتبـر التثقيـف الوسـيلة والغايـة علـى حـد سـواء. وأخيـراً، يعتبـر التثقيـف «نصـاً» أو «موضوعـاً» - يقـع في مجـال الاتصـالات،

السياسة والسلطة ويمكن أن يتخذ أشكالاً عدة. اللغة المكتوبة هي أحد أشكال النص التي يتم من خلالها إيصال التعلم. لكن هناك نصوص أخرى، مثل الاتصال الشفهي، وسائل الإعلام (الإذاعة والتلفزيون والصحف) والنصوص التكنولوجية والفنية والتحف.

ترتبط وسائل الاعلام والتكنولوجيا بالتقاليد الأربعة لعملية التثقيف. في القرن الحادي والعشرين، أكثر من أي فترة أخرى في التاريخ، يتم تحقيق التعلم، والتنشئة الاجتماعية، والتبادل الثقافي والسياسي والنشاط الاجتماعي بوساطة وسائل الإعلام، والتكنولوجيا والإنترنت والفيض الهائل من المعلومات التي تجلبها. يمكن أن تساهم التربية الإعلامية والمعلوماتية بتمكين جميع المواطنين لكي يفهموا ما تجلبه وسائل الإعلام والتكنولوجيا من ابعاد جديدة الى خبراتهم. في القرن الحادي والعشرين، أكثر من أي وقت مضى، يتعلم المواطنون المزيد عن أنفسهم وعن العالم من حولهم خارج الفصول الدراسية (وات، 2012؛ انظروا ايضاً ماسيدو، 2007. 1.

إن التربية الإعلامية والمعلوماتية هي ذلك الجسر بين التعلم في الفصول الدراسية والتعلم الذي يحدث خارج الفصول الدراسية ويسمح لكلّ منهما بإثراء الآخر. هذا يستدعي بيداغوجيا تعليمية جديدة وتركيز أكبر على مهارات التثقيف غير التقليدية. إن التربية الإعلامية والمعلوماتية هي ذات صلة لمنطقة الشرق الأوسط وشمال أفريقيا كما هي الحال في كل منطقة أخرى من العالم.

مما كتبت السيدة أبو فاضل (2007): «لقد شهدت التربية الإعلامية والتوعية إهمالاً طويل الأمد في العالم العربي... كما أن موضوع التربية الإعلامية كمادة تدريس منظّمة نادراً ما كان يُدرّس في المدارس، وغالباً ما كانت تتم الاشارة اليها بواسطة مصطلحات غامضة في إطار مواد التدريس الجامعية التي تعجز عن معالجة سبب وجود وسائل الاتصال الجماهيري...» (P.1) بعد ست سنوات، باستخدام لبنان وقطر كدراسة حالة، اعترفت أبو فاضل بأن هناك تقدماً بطيئاً فيما يتعلق بوجود وتطوير برامج التربية الإعلامية والمعلوماتية في منطقة الشرق الأوسط وشمال أفريقيا، وأن «التفكير النقدي ليس مدمجاً في نظم التعليم في الكثير من الدول [على الرغم من أن العديد من الخبراء قد يتفقون بأن هذه ظاهرة شائعة في كافة مناطق العالم]...» لكن الكثير من المدرّسين المبتكرين وغيرهم من الجهات الفاعلة يقومون بتنفيذ المشاريع التي تمكن الطلاب من التفكير النقدي واستكشاف التعلم المتعدد الوسائط من خلال المنصات الإعلامية المتعددة. (أبو فاضل، 2013.) واط (2012) استشهد بميهايليديس (2009)،

بالقول «أنه لا يكفي التركيز على المحتوى الإعلامي وحده، لكن أيضاً على المواطنين باعتبارهم همزة الوصل في عالم المعلومات (P.65) ».

إن التعبير عن التربية الإعلامية والمعلوماتية باعتبارها المجال الذي يستحق اهتمام مجتمع التنمية والحكومات الوطنية، وعمق الوعي وتنفيذ مبادرات التربية الإعلامية والمعلوماتية هي مسائل تختلف من منطقة إلى أخرى. إن عمق واتساع ما تغير في مجال تعزيز الوعي بشأن التربية الإعلامية والمعلوماتية الوعي وتطبيقها في منطقة الشرق الأوسط وشمال أفريقيا منذ أول اجتماع دولي حول التربية الإعلامية في المنطقة - المؤتمر الدولي الأول للتربية الإعلامية في الرياض في مارس 2007 - هو موضوع هذا الفصل، وكامل هذا الكتاب بالواقع. سأعطي أولاً صورة عن البيئة الإعلامية والمعلوماتية في المنطقة. ثم انتقل بعدها لأعطي إطاراً أساسياً لتحليل نقدي أولي مقارن للتربية الإعلامية والمعلوماتية في المنطقة باستخدام أربعة أسئلة:

• كيف يتصوّر الخبراء في منطقة الشرق الأوسط وشمال إفريقيا التربية الإعلامية والمعلوماتية ؟

• ما هو المنطق الأساسي للتربية الإعلامية والمعلوماتية في الدول العربية؟

• هل تقوم هذه الدول بالتوفيق في هذا المجال؟

• هل تملك تلك الدول سياسات واستراتيجيات وطنية حول التربية الإعلامية والمعلوماتية ؟

نظرة عامة - التركيبة السكانية والمعلومات والبيئات الإعلامية:

إن منطقة الشرق الأوسط وشمال أفريقيا، والتي في كثير من الأحيان يُذكر أنها بشكل خاطىء انها تضم الدول العربية، تغطي المنطقة التي تشمل الدول الواقعة من شمال وشمال شرق أفريقيا وجنوب غرب آسيا 2 . في حين تشمل منطقة الشرق الأوسط إيران وتركيا، وهما دولتان غير عربيتين. إن الدول الـ 22 التي تقع في منطقة الشرق الأوسط وشما إفريقيا، بحسب جامعة الدول العربية، هي التالية، بالترتيب الأبجدي: الجزائر، البحرين، جزر القمر، جيبوتي، مصر، العراق، الأردن، الكويت، لبنان، ليبيا، موريتانيا، المغرب، عمان، قطر، المملكة العربية السعودية، الصومال، دولة فلسطين، السودان، سوريا، تونس، الإمارات العربية المتحدة، واليمن. ويختلف هذا الترتيب من مصدر الى آخر. على سبيل المثال، يذكر البنك الدولي تركيبة مكونة من 14 دولة بما فيها إسرائيل 3. أما مكتب الأمم المتحدة لحقوق الإنسان / مكتب المفوض السامي لحقوق الإنسان فيتحدث عن 19 دولة كجزء من منطقة الشرق الأوسط وشمال إفريقيا 4. ويشمل هذا

الترتيب أيضاً إسرائيل، لكنه لا يشمل جزر القمر والصومال والسودان وجيبوتي.

يقدر عدد سكان هذه المنطقة بنحو 416 مليون نسمة تقريباً 5. كما ان ما يقرب من 20 بالمائة من سكان منطقة الشرق الأوسط وشمال إفريقيا، بمعدل واحد من أصل خمسة أشخاص، هم من فئة الشباب الذين تتراوح أعمارهم ما بين 15 و 24 عاماً (أسعد ورودي- فهيمي، 2007). وقد بلغ عدد الشباب في المنطقة حوالى 95 مليون في عام 2005. (المصدر نفسه) كما ان فئة السكان الشباب موزّعة بالتساوي تقريباً بين البلدان العربية، وتتراوح نسبتها ما بين 15 بالمائة و23 بالمائة، في حين ان أربعة بلدان فقط لديها أقل من 18 بالمائة من الشباب كنسبة مئوية من عدد السكان. «إن نسبة تحوّل هذه المجموعة الكبيرة من الشباب الى أعضاء صحيحي البنية ومنتجين في مجتمعاتهم يعتمد على مدى قدرة الحكومات والمجتمعات المدنية على الاستثمار في المؤسسات الاجتماعية والاقتصادية والسياسية التي تلبي الاحتياجات الحالية للشباب». (المرجع نفسه).

يملك سبعة وثلاثون في المائة من سكان منطقة الشرق الأوسط وشمال إفريقيا يتمتعون بإمكانية الوصول إلى الإنترنت 6. (الاتحاد الدولي للاتصالات). وعند كتابة هذا الفصل، لم يتمكن المؤلف من ايجاد مصادر توفر عدد المحفوظات في المنطقة ككل أو البلد. بلغ عدد المكتبات العامة والأكاديمية والخاصة نحو 364،47. في حين بلغ عدد محطات الإذاعة والتلفزيون والصحف حوالى 584 و420 و201 على التوالي في منطقة الشرق الأوسط وشمال إفريقيا. (انظروا التفاصيل والمصادر في الجدول 1 أدناه).

الجدول 1: التعداد السكاني ونسبة الإلمام بالقراءة والكتابة في المنطقة العربية والشرق الأوسط

الدولة	عدد السكان 8	نسبة السكان الفقيرة 9	السكان 10	الأمية والتعليم 11	الأمية (المجلات) 11	نسبة الأمية لدى الذكور 12 (%)	نسبة أمية السكان الأكبر سناً (5) 13	الفصل 13
الجزائر	39,667.000	16.70	760	34	46	(2009) 59.60	...	17
البحرين	1,377.000	96.53	209	5	4	(2013) 31.8	(2013) 99.2	6
جزر القمر	788.000	6.55	3	6	...	...	...	1
جيبوتي	888.000	9.07	4	3	1	(2004) 50.00	...	...
مصر	91,508.000	48.34	11,048	65	64	(2013) 20.5	(2013) 96.9	...
العراق	36,423.000	7.79	11,395	55	28	...	...	...
الأردن	7,595.000	44.98	5,687	29	4	...	...	4
الكويت	3,892.000	86.86	132	18	13	...	...	8
لبنان	5,851.000	67.19	642	54	12	...	...	15
ليبيا	6,278.000	21.79	41	22	12	...	...	4
موريتانيا	4,068.000	11.43	38	16	1	...	...	3
المغرب	34,378.000	60.33	735	15	8	(2009) 67.48	(2011) 99.9	24

6	(2011) 93.9	13	(2010) 35.7	14	1.121	65.82	4.491.000	العنب
5	(2013) 94.8	1	(2013) 24.6	12	208	96.65	2.235.000	قطن
12	...	117	...	76	5.317	59.24	31.540.000	المحاصيل الزيتية
3	...	4	...	12	4	1.51	10.787.000	الحبوب
					1.086		4.668.000	
22	...	4	...	14	4.851	24.01	40.235.000	فواكه
	...	44	...	55	1.760	26.66	18.502.000	سيراميك
10	(2012) 97.7	26	(2012) 66.6	47	947	45.46	11.254.000	نزيف
55	(2012) 94.6		(2012) 52.9	23	1.364	93.24	9.157.000	العباءات
	...	...	...	...	...	...	...	العباءة المصنعة
6	...	3	...	9	12	19.14	26.832.000	المجموع

ويلاحظ، في ضوء هذه البيانات، أنّ السلطات تعمل على تحفيز إلى أخرى عند تحليل هذه البيانات، أنّ المحاصيل... على نحو تحفيز زراعة أخرى من محصول...

28

التربيــة الإعلاميــة والمعلوماتيــة بحسـب الخبــراء في منطقــة الـشـرق الأوسـط وشمال إفريقيا:

يمكن للأشخاص الذيـن يتابعـون كتابـاتي حـول التربيـة المعلوماتيـة والتربيـة الإعلاميـة والتربيــة الرقميــة أو التربيــة الإعلاميــة والمعلوماتيــة أن يعرفـوا أنـي أعانـي الكثيـر للتشـديد علـى ضـرورة اتبـاع نهـج متماسـك، مـع التركيـز علـى القواسـم الرئيسـية المشـتركة والمهـارات المترابطـة، بـدلاً مـن اعتمـاد نهـج تعريفـي مفكـك. لا أحـاول الاستفاضة بالشـرح حـول هـذه النقطـة، لكـن تصـور التربيـة الإعلاميـة والمعلوماتيـة يتمتـع بتأثيـر مباشـر علـى كيفيـة تصميم، وتنفيـذ ورصـد برامـج التربيـة الإعلاميـة والمعلوماتيـة، وبالتالـي تأثيرهـا علـى حيـاة الشـباب، والمواطنيـن بشـكل عـام. في اجتمـاع جمعنـا في سـبتمبر مـن عـام 2015، ذكّرنـي الدكتـور فهد بـن سـلطان السـلطان، نائـب الأميـن العـام لمركـز الملـك عبـد العزيـز للحـوار الوطنـي، إمكانيـات التغييـر مـن خـلال خلـق المعرفـة باللغـة المحليـة (في هـذه الحالـة - اللغـة العربيـة) بـدلاً مـن مجـرد ترجمـة المعرفـة أو المفاهيـم مـن لغـة إلـى أخـرى. الدكتـور السـلطان هـو ممثـل المسـتوى رفيـع المسـتوى مـن المملكـة العربيـة السـعودية، التـي تعـدّ واحـدة مـن أبـرز الشـركاء والداعميـن لحركـة تعزيـز التربيـة الإعلاميـة والمعلوماتيـة الخاصـة باليونيسكـو في منطقـة الشـرق الأوسـط وشمال إفريقيا. وكان علـى حـق. وقـد اعتـرف أيضاً أنـه عنـد حصـول ترجمـة المعـارف مـن لغـة إلـى أخـرى، ينبغـي أن يـدرج التغييـر في هـذا المزيـج. وأضـاف، بقولـه هـذا، أنـه وبهـدف خلـق المعرفـة الجديـدة، مـن الـضروري في كثيـر مـن الأحيـان الاستعارة والتعديـل نقلاً عـن مصـادر ولغـات اخـرى. وكمـا يفتـرض جنكيـنز (جنكيـنز وغيـره 2009)، «فـإن معظـم المـواد الكلاسـيكية الـتي ندرّسـها في المـدارس هـي نفسـها نتيجـة الاعتمـاد والتحويـل، أو مـا يمكـن أن نسـميه أخـذ العينـات والتعديـل.» (ص. 32). كمـا قال الأسـتاذ رضـوان بوجمعـة في فصلـه مـن الكتـاب عنـد التحـدث عـن واقـع تكنولوجيـا المعلومـات والاتصـالات والتربيـة الإعلاميـة في الجزائـر: «تقليديـا، كانـت كلّ مـن المعرفـة والثقافـة في صميـم الكثيـر مـن المناقشـات الفلسـفية والصراعـات الاجتماعيـة والسياسـية والأيديولوجيـة المختلفـة. كمـا أن نظـم التعليـم الحاليـة والمؤسـسات لا تشـكل اسـتثناء. منذ العقـد الثانـي مـن القـرن الماضـي، لعبـت وسـائل الاتصـال الجماهيـري دوراً محوريـاً سـواء في المبالغـة أو التقليـل مـن أهميـة التعليـم.» وقـد اسـتخدم جميـع مؤلفـي هـذا الكتـاب هـذا النهـج، سـواء هنـا أو في غيرهـا مـن التقاريـر الـتي كتبوهـا. وقـد قامـوا بشـكل مباشـر أو غيـر مباشـر بجمـع العينـات وتعديـل مفاهيـم كلّ مـن التربيـة المعلوماتيـة، الثقافـة الرقميـة أو التربيـة الإعلاميـة والمعلوماتيـة في مناقشـاتهم.

جاد ملكي ولبنى معاليقي، لبنان: في هـذا الكتـاب وفي غيـره مـن الكتابـات الأكاديميـة الأخـرى، يوجـد ميـل قـوي إلى الكفـاءات الرقميـة الحرجـة «التربيـة الإعلاميـة الرقميـة.» (انظـر ملكـي، (2013

جـوردي تورنـت، المغـرب ومصـر: يعـرّف التربيـة الإعلاميـة والمعلوماتيـة عـلى أنهـا مفهـوم مشـترك بالارتكاز عـلى نمـوذج اليونيسـكو.

لـوسي نسـيبة ومحمـد أبـو عرقـوب، فلسـطين: في هـذا الفصـل، يركـز المؤلفـان بالدرجـة الأولى عـلى التربيـة الإعلاميـة. وهمـا يقترحـان أن التربيـة الاعلاميـة هـي تعليـم كيفيـة عمـل وسـائل الإعـلام وكيـف يمكـن للمواطنـين الانخـراط بشـكل فعـال مـع وسـائل الإعـلام. إنـه «وقائيـة واستباقية في الوقـت عينه». وقائيـة عـلى صلة بتمكيـن الافراد مـن «تحليـل المحتـوى الإعلامـي، وقـراءة مـا بـين السـطور، وفهـم الرسـائل وراء الصـور، وبالتالي ليصبحوا أقـل تأثـراً»؛ واستباقية بمعنـى أنهـا تمكّـن الأفـراد مـن «العمـل بشـكل مبـدع وخـلاق - ليـس كفنيـين، لكـن مجـدداً فيمـا يتعلـق بالمحتـوى، لـكي يتمكنـوا مـن إنتـاج الرسـائل الإعلاميـة الخاصـة بهـم». في تصـور المؤلفـين، إن تعزيـز ثقافـة الانترنـت، وصحافـة المواطـن بالإضافـة الى الماجسـتير في الإعـلام والبكالوريـوس في الإعـلام كلهـا مرتبطـة بالتربيـة الإعلاميـة.

عبـد العامـر الفيصـل، العـراق: ركـز عبـد العامـر الفيصـل في فصلـه مـن الكتـاب عـلى المعلومـات وعـلى فهـم كيفيـة خلـق المعلومـات ونشـرها باعتبارهـا الركيـزة الأساسـية للتنميـة في العـراق. واسـتخدم المؤلـف كلمـة «المعلومـات» 41 مـرة و«تكنولوجيـا المعلومـات» 9 مـرات. كما ذكـر «التربيـة المعلوماتيـة» مـرة واحـدة فقـط في اشـارة الى أهـداف الاسـتراتيجية الوطنيـة لتكنولوجيـا المعلومـات في العـراق. في حـين سـلط الضـوء عـلى التأثـير الثـوري للتكنولوجيـات الجديـدة عـلى وسـائل الإعـلام وحريـة التعبـير في العـراق ومركزيـة المكتبـات ومراكـز التوثيـق - إلا أنـه لـم يذكـر التربيـة الإعلاميـة أو المعلوماتيـة أو التربيـة الإعلاميـة والمعلوماتيـة كمفاهيـم، عـلى الرغـم مـن كونـه ألمـح اليهـا بشـكل واضـح في حجمـه.

رضـوان بوجمعـة، الجزائـر: يوحـي عنـوان هـذا الفصـل بحـد ذاتـه إلى وجـود تركيـز خـاص. ويقـوم المؤلـف بمـزج تكنولوجيـا المعلومـات والاتصـالات في التعليـم والتربيـة الإعلاميـة والتعليـم والاتصـالات. كما يعـرّف التربيـة الإعلاميـة عـلى أنهـا «عمليـة الاسـتخدام الأمثـل لوسـائل الاتصـال مـن أجـل تحقيـق الأهـداف المنصـوص عليهـا في سياسـة التعليـم والاتصـالات في الدولـة. أمـا التعريـف الآخـر، فهـو أن العمليـة تتضمـن تعليـم الطـلاب والمدرّسـين وتدريبهـم عـلى كيفيـة التعامـل بشـكل انتقـائي وبوعـي مـع المحتـوى الإعلامـي

مـن أجـل تجنـب تأثيرهـا السـلبي، ممـا يـؤدي إلى تعزيـز الوعـي في التعامـل مـع الرسـائل والصـور الإعلاميـة.»

عبـد الحميـد النفيسـي وإدريسـية شـويت، المغـرب: يلحـظ المؤلفـان مـا يـلي: «لا يمكـن لإمكانـات التربيـة الإعلاميـة والمعلوماتيـة أن تتحقـق إذا لـم يتمتـع النـاس بالقـدرة عـلى الوصـول الى المحتـوى الإعلامـي ، وتحليلـه وتقييمـه وخلقـه». كما يفترضـان أيضاً أن التربيـة الإعلاميـة والمعلوماتيـة هـي «تزويـد الأفـراد بالمهـارات والأدوات اللازمـة لتقيـم ومعالجـة وتفسـير محتـوى الرسـائل والأصـوات والصـور القويـة في إطـار ثقافـة الوسـائط المتعـددة الخاصـة بنـا بشـكل نقـدي.» برأيهمـا، إن التربيـة المعلوماتيـة والتربيـة الإعلاميـة تمثـل عمليـة الانتقـال الطبيعـي مـن الثقافـة الأساسـية، نظـراً لانتشـار وسـائل الإعـلام والتكنولوجيـا. ويحسـب تحليلهمـا، إن التربيـة المعلوماتيـة هـي القـدرة عـلى تقييـم السـلطة، والمصداقيـة، وموثوقيـة المعلومـات، وتحديـد الاحتياجـات مـن المعلومـات في الفضـاء الإلكـتروني، وكيفيـة زيـارة المواقـع ذات الصلـة واسـتخدام تكنولوجيـا المعلومـات والاتصـالات عـلى نحـو فعـال. بالاسـتناد إلى تجربتهمـا في تدريـس الدراسـات الإعلاميـة والثقافـة الإلكترونيـة في قسـم اللغـة الإنجليزيـة، يـرى المؤلفـان مـن الـضروري المـزج بـين التربيـة المعلوماتيـة والتربيـة الإعلاميـة لتصبـح التربيـة الإعلاميـة والمعلوماتيـة. (انظـروا ايضـاً النفيـسي، 2014 والنفيـسي، 2013).

سـامي طايـع، مـصر: في حـين لـم تـرد إشـارة خاصـة إلى تصـور التربيـة الإعلاميـة والمعلوماتيـة في هـذا الفصـل، قـام المؤلـف، مـن خـلال وصفـه لأنشـطة التربيـة الإعلاميـة والمعلوماتيـة في مـصر، بالتلميـح إلى ضرورة أن يفهـم الشـباب الإعـلام وأن يسـتخدموا وسـائل التواصـل الاجتماعـي بفعاليـة.

يـاسر الـدرّة، الأردن: لـم يقـدم المؤلـف أي إشـارة إلى مـا تسـتلزمه التربيـة الإعلاميـة والمعلوماتيـة. بعدمـا تعـرّف للمـرة الأولى الى المفهـوم مـن خـلال مناهـج التربيـة الإعلاميـة والمعلوماتيـة الـتي تقدمهـا اليونسـكو، سرعـان مـا أصبـح المفهـوم أساسـاً لعمـل معهـد الإعـلام الأردني. بالتـالي، اسـتخدم هـذا المفهـوم بجـدارة لوصـف سلسـلة مـن الأنشـطة ذات الصلـة بعمليـة إشراك الشـباب في المسـاءلة السياسـية، وروايـة القصـص، وتماريـن المحـاكاة للشـباب كمنصـة للتعبـير عـن الـرأي والأخبـار في مجـال التعليـم، و«التوجيـه وتدريـب الصحفيـين وطـلاب الصحافـة و ممثلـي منظمـات المجتمـع المدنـي عـلى مـا يمكـن لقـوة البيانـات ان تفعلـه للمسـاعدة في جعـل هـذا الحـوار أكـثر فعاليـة وإطلاعـاً.»

نايفـة عيـد سـالم، عمـان: تقـوم البروفسـور سـالم، بالإرتـكاز الى خلفيتهـا في مجـال علـوم

المعلومات، بالتركيز على جوانب البيانات والمعلومات في التربية الإعلامية والمعلوماتية. وقالت في كتاباتها ان هناك حاجة «لتزويد المواطنين بالمهارات المناسبة والمعلومات أو ما يسمى بـ» الثقافة الإعلامية والمعلوماتية» التي تغطي المعرفة وكذلك المواقف. الوصول إلى المعرفة مرتبط بالبيانات اللازمة، وتوقيتها وكيفية الحصول عليها ومن اين، وكيفية تحليلها، وانتقادها، وترتيبها، والأهم من ذلك، كيفية استخدامها بشكل أخلاقي.» وهي تحدد التربية الإعلامية والمعلوماتية كما وصفتها منظمة اليونسكو وتبنى التربية الإعلامية والمعلوماتية كمفهوم مركب.

ماجدة أبو فاضل، لبنان: إستخدمت ماجدة أبو فاضل تعبير «التربية الإعلامية والمعلوماتية» في كلامها عن الموضوع على الرغم من انها سبق ان استخدمت تعبير التثقيف الإعلامي والتربية الإعلامية في مقالات أخرى (أبو فاضل 2013). وهي تربط التربية الإعلامية والمعلوماتية بشكل وثيق بتعليم الصحافة وأخلاقيات الإعلام. وهي تلقي الضوء على البيئة الإعلامية المختلطة السائدة في لبنان، والألعاب، والتطبيقات، والرسوم المتحركة، والكتب المصورة والملصقات واللافتات في الشوارع والصحف والتلفزيون ووسائل الإعلام الرقمية والمحمولة، والإذاعة، والوسائط المتعددة على الانترنت وغير المتصلة بالانترنت. وكتبت ماجدة أبو فاضل: « في لبنان، ترتبط التربية الإعلامية والمعلوماتية بالتعليم والتربية والدين والإعلام بالمعنى العام. وغالباً ما يتمّ إدخال المعلومات كعامل مساعد، فيما تلعب التكنولوجيا دوراً داعماً.»

كارميلا فلويد وغابرييلا ثينز، تونس: من خلال استخدامهما لتعبير «التربية الإعلامية والمعلوماتية»، لم تقدم المؤلفتان تعريفاً محدداً أو صريحاً. إلا أنهما إعتبرتا التربية الإعلامية والمعلوماتية هي أداة لتمكين الشباب والمشاركة المدنية. وأشارتا إلى أن المبادرات في مجال التربية الإعلامية والمعلوماتية في الجزائر إستمدت الإلهام من مشاريع مشابهة في فلسطين وروسيا البيضاء والسويد حيث تستخدم التربية الإعلامية والمعلوماتية لمكافحة الصور النمطية بين الجنسين، وتعزيز احترام حقوق الإنسان ومن أجل تعزيز «التنمية المستدامة التي تعمل على تحسين ظروف السلام والاستقرار...»

كما تولى عدد من الخبراء الآخرين في المنطقة أيضاً تقديم وجهات نظر هامة حول التربية الإعلامية والمعلوماتية. لم نذكر منهم سوى اثنين في هذا الكتاب من أجل الإيجاز. صالح (2011) يقول إن التثقيف الإعلامي (التربية الإعلامية أو التربية الإعلامية والمعلوماتية) يجب أن يبدأ في المدرسة الابتدائية حين تتم تنمية وتشكيل مهارات

المعرفة الأساسية والعادات. «يجب أن يتعلم الأطفال كيفية التشكيك في صدق وصحة القرارات وتقديم النقد والبدائل، وأن يفهموا ان هناك وجهات نظر ، وحلول أو وجهات نظر أخرى غير آرائهم وحلولهم.» (ص. 35). بالنسبة الى جمعة (2014)، فإن التربية الإعلامية والمعلوماتية تشمل القدرة على التفكير بشكل نقدي، وأن يكون المرء خلاقاً، بالإضافة الى «ممارسة المرء لواجباته وحقوقه كمواطن ناشط وفاعل بدلا من أن يكون [موضوعاً] من مواضيع الدولة.» (ص 33). ويقول كلّ من مختار، مجيد وآخرون، (2008) «... إن تدريس التربية المعلوماتية لا يشمل فقط التعليمات المكتبية والببليوغرافية أو القدرة على استخدام مصادر المعلومات المختلفة بشكل فعال. بل يشمل أيضاً تعليم مهارات التفكير النقدي والتحليل فيما يتعلق بالمعلومات، بالإضافة إلى القدرة على توليد أفكار جديدة من المعلومات الحالية والمعرفة السابقة. والأهم من ذلك، فهو يشمل ما سيتمكن الطلاب من معرفته، وتفكيره او القيام به نتيجة لذلك...» (ص 196).

إن ما يبدو واضحاً في التحليل أعلاه، هو أن هناك مجموعة متنوعة من الآراء حول الطريقة المناسبة لتصوّر التربية الإعلامية والمعلوماتية في منطقة الشرق الأوسط وشمال إفريقيا. ومع ذلك، لا يمكن للمرء سوى أن يلاحظ التقارب والتكامل بين وجهات النظر المقدمة. إن منطقة الشرق الأوسط وشمال إفريقيا لا تختلف عن بقية العالم في النضال من اجل الحرص على تقديم الوضوح في مجال ترسيم الميدان وعملية التربية الإعلامية والمعلوماتية.

الأساس المنطقي للتربية الإعلامية والمعلوماتية في الدول العربية:

إن الغرض أو الأساس المنطقي للتربية الإعلامية والمعلوماتية ضمني إلى حد ما، أو على أقل تقدير، يتطور بالاستناد الى التصورات العديدة في هذا المجال. بالارتكاز الى مساهمة المؤلفين في هذا الكتاب، ومصادر أخرى، والتحاليل الأولية لنتائج البحث الذي أقوم به، يتم التعاطي مع التربية الإعلامية والمعلوماتية على أنها وسيلة لتحقيق طيف واسع من أهداف التنمية الاجتماعية، والسياسية، والاقتصادية. وهي من ناحية أخرى، تشكّل غاية في حد ذاتها، لأن التربية الإعلامية والمعلوماتية تمكّن الناس من اكتساب المهارات الشخصية، والوعي الذاتي والإبداع وتحقيق الذات. (غريزل، 2013) 14. هذا ويشكك بعض الخبراء بالتشديد المفرط على استخدام التربية الإعلامية والمعلوماتية كأداة تسمح للمواطنين باكتساب هذه المهارات للاستخدام الشخصي والمتعة الشخصية والإبداع. (انظر مادريناس، 2014). وتقول ديفينا فراو- مايغز (2011)؛ «في الوقت الحاضر،

تعتبر التربية الإعلامية [التربية الإعلامية والمعلوماتية] على أنها نوع من العلاج العالمي الشافي لجميع الشركاء (القطاع العام والخاص والمجتمع المدني) ولكن من نواح عدة، يتم استخدامها كأداة تمويه لإخفاء السياسات الليبرالية الجديدة...» (ص 334).

وتشمل هذه الأسباب:

• مكافحة الصور النمطية وتعزيز التفاهم بين الثقافات (المملكة العربية السعودية وقطر والكثير من الدول العربية) (انظر أبو فاضل، 2007).

• تعزيز حرية الصحافة وفهم الأخبار.

• زيادة فرص الوصول إلى المعلومات وتسهيل تدفق الأفكار الحر (قطر، لبنان) (المرجع السابق).

• مكافحة تأثير وسائل الإعلام في حياة الشباب (مصر) [انظر طايع، 2011، 15، 2013 و 2014. انظر أيضاً صالح، 2009]

• الصحفيون الذين يحتاجون إلى المهارات الرقمية للتنافس مع تدفق الأخبار من خارج وداخل البلد (لبنان)

• تمكين الشباب من استخدام الشبكات الاجتماعية لأغراض إنتاجية وإنمائية غير الترفيه (لبنان، مصر).

• تأييد الأخلاقيات الإعلامية (لبنان).

• بالنسبة إلى الشباب، تحدي وجهات النظر العالمية في وسائل الإعلام وانتقاد التوجه الى الإعلام المتجانس والعلماني والديني في الشرق الأوسط (لبنان، مصر، المغرب، فلسطين).

• حماية والحفاظ على الثقافات المحلية والحوار بين الثقافات (المغرب، المملكة العربية السعودية، ومصر) (النفيسي، 2013 و 2014).

• وضع الأساس لصحافة المواطن (تونس، مصر، الأردن، لبنان، وقطر).

• تعزيز جودة التعليم (الجزائر وسلطنة عمان).

• تحسين نوعية البحوث وصنع القرار (المغرب، الجزائر، عمان).

• تعزيز السلم واللاعنف (فلسطين، ومصر، وتونس).

الاتجاهات نحو وضع سياسات وطنية حول التربية الإعلامية والمعلوماتية في منطقة الشرق الأوسط وشمال إفريقيا:

لا توجد أي سياسات وطنية حول التربية الإعلامية والمعلوماتية في أي بلد من بلدان منطقة الدول العربية. ربما تكون بعض الدول، مثل المغرب وقطر تسير في هذا الاتجاه، نظراً الى القرارات ذات الصلة التي اتخذتها حكومات تلك الجول والمبادرات الوطنية التي تدعمها. بيد أن معظم الدول العربية تملك سياسات وقوانين ذات صلة، ترتكز الى الدستور وبالإضافة الى قوانين بشأن المعلومات والبث. وتشمل تلك القوانين سياسات واستراتيجيات تكنولوجيا المعلومات والاتصالات، وقوانين الوصول الى المعلومات، وسياسات التعليم والسياسات الثقافية (كل البلدان في منطقة الشرق الأوسط وشمال إفريقيا)، وسياسات الإعلام والاتصال وسياسات وطنية خاصة بالشباب. انظر الجدول 2 أدناه.

الجدول 2: استراتيجيات مرتبطة بالمعلومات وتكنولوجيا المعلومات والاتصالات والسياسات الإعلامية في منطقة الشرق الأوسط وشمال أفريقيا:

البلد	سياسات/ استراتيجية المعلومات الوطنية	سياسات/استراتيجية تكنولوجيا المعلومات والاتصالات	الاتصالات الوطنية/ السياسات الإعلامية/ القوانين
الجزائر	نعم	نعم	نعم
البحرين	نعم	نعم 16	نعم 17
جزر القمر	غير متوفر	غير متوفر	غير متوفر
جيبوتي	غير متوفر	نعم 18 (يوجد دليل على ذلك عبر الانترنت لكن ليس النسخة الكاملة)	غير متوفر
مصر	نعم	نعم 19	نعم
العراق	غير متوفر	قيد الإعداد او التحضير	نعم
الاردن	نعم 20	نعم	نعم
الكويت	نعم	نعم	نعم
لبنان	غير متوفر	نعم 21	نعم
ليبيا	غير متوفر	غير متوفر	غير متوفر

غير متوفر	نعم 22	غير متوفر	موريتانيا
نعم	نعم 23	نعم	المغرب
غير متوفر	نعم 24	نعم	عمان
نعم	نعم 25	نعم	قطر
غير متوفر	نعم 27	نعم 26	المملكة العربية السعودية
غير متوفر	كلا 28	غير متوفر	الصومال
غير متوفر	نعم	غير متوفر	دولة فلسطين
غير متوفر	نعم 29	غير متوفر	السودان
غير متوفر	نعم	قيد الإعداد	سوريا
غير متوفر	نعم 30	نعم	تونس
غير متوفر	نعم	كلا	الامارات العربية المتحدة
غير متوفر	نعم	نعم	اليمن

* المصدر (إن لم يكن محدداً): الملامح الوطنية لمجتمع المعلومات
http://www.escwa.un.org/wsis/profiles.html

وقد تولى مركز الدوحة لحرية الإعلام وضع ملخص وتحليل، بالإضافة الى توصيات بشأن القوانين الإعلامية في كلّ من البحرين، والكويت والمملكة العربية السعودية، والامارات العربية المتحدة، وقطر، وسلطنة عمان، كتبه الدكتور مات جي. دافي 31. وهناك حاجة إلى تحليل واسع النطاق لهذه السياسات والاستراتيجيات أو القوانين القائمة للتأكد من مدى قدرتها على تغطية العناصر الملائمة لضمان وصول التربية الإعلامية والمعلوماتية الى الجميع. على سبيل المثال، هل توجد أي بنود في تلك السياسات تساهم بتعزيز وتوجيه وإرشاد المحاولات لتصميم وتنفيذ البرامج لتمكين المواطنين من اكتساب مهارات التفكير النقدي بشأن المعلومات والإعلام وتكنولوجيا المعلومات والاتصالات؟ يشكّل هذا السؤال موضوع ورقة عمل أخرى وبحوثاً شاملة. مع ذلك، فإن اقتراح تلك السياسات له آثار على العملية المستقبلية لصياغة سياسات التربية الإعلامية والمعلوماتية الوطنية في منطقة الشرق الأوسط وشمال إفريقيا وأماكن أخرى. من تلك الآثار هو ما إذا كانت تلك السياسات والاستراتيجيات والقوانين موجهة نحو تمكين المواطنين في مقابل التركيز على المؤسسات والعمليات التجارية أو الحكومية، ويفتح المجال لإمكانية التعبير عن سياسات التربية الإعلامية والمعلوماتية. على سبيل

ويفتح المجال لإمكانية التعبير عن سياسات التربية الإعلامية والمعلوماتية. على سبيل المثال، يعطي مينو (2002) تحليلاً دقيقاً حول كيفية دمج التربية المعلوماتية (التربية الإعلامية والمعلوماتية) في سياسات تكنولوجيا المعلومات والاتصالات الوطنية، مشيراً الى عدد من الحالات من أمريكا اللاتينية.

في حين يبدو من الواضح أن يمكن الوصول الى المواطنين، وغالباً ما تكون هذه هي الحال، من خلال المؤسسات، فإن السياسات التي تخدم المؤسسات قد لا تخدم بالضرورة المواطنين. لا ينبغي أن يتم تطوير سياسات التربية الإعلامية والمعلوماتية في عزلة من المواطنين. بل ينبغي وضعها في إطار أوسع وأن يُنظر إليها باعتبارها محفزاً لفعالية السياسات الأخرى ذات الصلة التي قد تشمل الشباب، والسياسات الثقافية والتعليمية (غريزل، مور وآخرون 2013).

ويبين الرسم 1 أدناه الترابط بين السياسات الوطنية المختلفة. كما ان التعاون الهادف بين الوزارات أو الجهات الحكومية ضروري من أجل تطوير السياسات المتعددة الأطراف، وهو نوع من التقاطع بين السياسات يدمج التربية الإعلامية والمعلوماتية في كافة الجوانب ذات الصلة للسياسات العامة (راجع المصدر نفسه). ومن الضروري أن نلحظ هنا أن السياسات والاستراتيجيات الوطنية المرتبطة بالتربية الإعلامية والمعلوماتية ليست فقط من اختصاص الحكومات الوطنية. ينبغي على جميع مزودي المعلومات مثل المكتبات والأرشيف والمؤسسات الإعلامية ومنظمات الاتصالات، والناشرين، ومقدمي خدمة الإنترنت، والمتاحف... أن يشاركوا في صياغة سياسات التربية الإعلامية والمعلوماتية الداخلية واستراتيجيات التوعية لصالح جمهورهم والمستخدمين.

الرسم 1: اليونسكو- المبادئ التوجيهية لسياسة واستراتيجية التربية الإعلامية والمعلوماتية

المصدر: غريزل، مور وآخرون. 2013

ينبغـي عـلى صياغـة وتطبيـق السياسـات الوطنيـة / الإقليميـة والاستراتيجيـات في مجـال التربيـة الإعلاميـة والمعلوماتيـة أن تأخـذ في الاعتبـار خمـس مقاربـات متشـابكة عـلى الشـكل التـالي:

1) التقارب – مقاربة متصلة كما هو موضح في الرسـم رقم 1 أعلاه؛

2) مقاربـة قائمـة عـلى الحقـوق - الاعـتراف بـأن التربيـة الإعلاميـة والمعلوماتيـة هـي نتيجـة مبـاشرة للحـق في التعليـم الجيـد، والحـق في الوصـول إلى المعلومـات، والحـق في حريـة التعبيـر، والحـق في السـلام والأمـن؛

3) التحـول مـن التركيـز فقـط عـلى حمايـة المواطنيـن مـن الجوانـب السـلبية المحتملـة للمعلومـات والإعـلام والتكنولوجيـا الى تمكينهـم مـن التنظيـم الـذاتي وكذلـك مـن امتـلاك فوائـد المعلومـات والتكنولوجيـا العـصر القائـم عـلى الاعـلام (ميهايليديـس، 2008)؛

4) بنـاء مجتمـع معـرفي شـامل / الاتصـالات والمعلومـات مـن أجـل التنميـة، بمـا في ذلـك مقاربـة الثقافـة والتنـوع اللغـوي.

5) مقاربـة قائمـة عـلى الجنـس – التأكيـد عـلى المسـاواة في الوصـول والمشـاركة وريـادة النسـاء والرجـال في دورة حيـاة المعلومـات، ووسـائل الإعـلام وتطويـر التكنولوجيـا، وتزويـد الرجـال والنسـاء بالوصـول المتسـاوي الى التربيـة الإعلاميـة والمعلوماتيـة (انظـر التحليـل بالتفصيـل في المرجـع نفسـه).

الاستراتيجيات الوطنية بشأن التربية الإعلامية والمعلوماتية وتطبيقها:

لا توجـد اسـتراتيجيات وطنيـة منهجيـة في التربيـة الإعلاميـة والمعلوماتيـة. في الأسـاس، يوجـد العديـد مـن ورش العمـل والمحـاضرات الهامـة، ولكـن المجـزأة في كثيـر مـن الأحيـان. ويتـم تسـليط الضـوء عـلى جيـوب النجـاح، وهـي في الغالـب بقيـادة الجامعـات والمكتبـات، وفي بعـض الحـالات، المنظمـات غـير الحكوميـة، في هـذه الأماكـن:

• مشروع «مينتور»، جامعة القاهرة، مصر - جمعية «مينتور» الدولية لتربية الإعلامية.

• مكتبـة الإسـكندرية، نـدوة رفيعـة المسـتوى حـول التربيـة المعلوماتيـة والتعلـم مـدى الحيـاة، الإسـكندرية، مـصر.

• الجامعة الأمريكية في القاهرة، مختبرات التربية الإعلامية والمعلوماتية 32 .

• جامعـة سـيدي محمـد بـن عبـد اللـه، المغـرب - المعهـد الـدولي للتربيـة الإعلاميـة والمعلوماتيـة .

• مركـز تطويـر الإعـلام، جامعـة بيرزيـت، فلسـطين - برنامـج التربيـة الإعلاميـة (التربيـة الإعلاميـة والمعلوماتيـة) - تعـاون مـع وزارة التربيـة والتعليـم وتطويـر المـواد للمدرّسـين والطـلاب 33.

• مركـز الدوحـة لحريـة الإعـلام - برنامـج التربيـة الإعلاميـة والمعلوماتيـة يشـمل 10 بالمائـة مـن المـدارس الابتدائيـة العامـة والخاصـة في قطـر، مـع توقعـات بتنفيـذ البرنامـج في كافـة المـدارس الابتدائيـة البالـغ عددهـا 150 مدرسـة.

• مكتبـة جامعـة قطـر، برنامـج التربيـة المعلوماتيـة والفصـل المتعلـق بدولـة قطـر في شـبكة التربيـة المعلوماتيـة في منطقـة الخليـج 34.

• مشـروع «مينتـور» / جامعـة القاهـرة: اتخـاذ الخطـوات اللازمـة لانشـاء برنامـج الماجسـتير في التربيـة الإعلاميـة والمعلوماتيـة .

• أدوات التربيـة الإعلاميـة والمعلوماتيـة للـدول العربيـة بدعـم من اليونسـكو.

• وزارة التربيـة والتعليـم في المغـرب تقـود عمليـة الدمـج الوطنيـة للتربيـة الإعلاميـة والمعلوماتيـة في مجـال تدريـب المدرّسـين بدعـم مـن اليونسـكو.

• تولـت ماجـدة أبـو فاضـل تنظيـم ورش عمـل في مدرسـة القلبيـن الاقدسـين وطـلاب الثانويـة العليـا في مدرسـة «انترناشـيونال كولـدج» (لبنـان)، وكذلـك للمعلميـن والمنسـقين في مدرسـة «انترناشـونال كولـدج» (لبنـان)، للمدرّسـين والمنسـقين في عشـرات المـدارس في قطـر، والصحفييـن في المغـرب وتونـس وموريتانيـا، وفي برنامـج للتربيـة الإعلاميـة عـن بعـد مـع كليـة الصحافـة بجامعـة ميسـوري، علـى سـبيل المثـال لا الحصـر.

• برنامـج التربيـة المعلوماتيـة في مدرسـة خاصـة في لبنـان 35.

• يعمـل فريـق البحـث في مجـال الثقافـات التفاعليـة في شـراكة مـع شـركة «ميـدان» للتكنولوجيا في الولايـات المتحـدة بهـدف «تطويـر المواطنيـن الصحفيـن في المنطقـة العربيـة»، (تونـس، مـصر، الأردن، لبنـان).

• شـبكة المغـرب العربـي لخبـراء التربيـة الإعلاميـة والمعلوماتيـة التـي أطلقتهـا اليونسـكو 36.

حيـث الحكومـات تتـولى الأمـور، توجـد أدلـة علـى برامـج أكـثر اسـتدامة في مجـال التربيـة الإعلاميـة والمعلوماتيـة أو ربمـا أطـول وقتـاً وأكـثر شـمولاً. ويظهـر هـذا الأمـر واضحـاً في قطـر، مـن خـلال برنامـج التربيـة الإعلاميـة والمعلوماتيـة الـذي تنفـذه الحكومـة في مركـز الدوحـة لحريـة الإعـلام 37.

هـل تسـاهم برامـج التربيـة الإعلاميـة والمعلوماتيـة في هـذه البلـدان بتعزيـز الإنسـجام في هـذا المجـال؟

- الأنشطة بشكل عام هي ذات صلة إما بالتربية الإعلامية أو بالتربية المعلوماتية.
- في بعض الحالات، تشتمل التربية الإعلامية أو التربية المعلوماتية على المهارات الرقمية / تكنولوجيا المعلومات والاتصالات.
- في حالات قليلة، تُعتبر التربية الإعلامية والمعلوماتية (استخدام منهج اليونسكو للتربية الإعلامية والمعلوماتية الخاص بالمدرّسين) في البلدان التي بدأت في الآونة الأخيرة باتخاذ إجراءات منهجية لتعزيز التربية الإعلامية والمعلوماتية. وتشمل هذه الدول المغرب، مصر، قطر، لبنان، تونس، والأردن.

هل يقيم ويعمل العديد من خبراء / ممارسي التربية الإعلامية والمعلوماتية في المناطق؟

في وقت كتابة هـذا التقريـر، كنـت وسـط إجراء تحليـل أولي للبحـوث، الـتي مـن مكوناتهـا، التأكـد مـن وجـود خبـراء التربيـة الإعلاميـة والمعلوماتيـة عـلى الصعيـد العالمـي ومسـتواهم. وينظـر البحـث في معاييـر مثـل هـذا المسـتوى ومجـال التأهيـل، ومسـتوى وفـترة الانخـراط في التربيـة الإعلاميـة والمعلوماتيـة والكتابـات الأكاديميـة في التربيـة الإعلاميـة والمعلوماتيـة، ومـا إلى ذلـك، في منطقـة الـشرق الأوسـط وشـمال إفريقيـا. وقـد دعـي أكـثر مـن 150 خبـيراً مـن مختلـف التخصصـات مثـل المعلومـات والإعـلام والاتصـالات والتعليـم وغيرهـم مـن الممارسـين، لاستكمال الاسـتبيان. وأشـار التحليـل الأولي أن المتخصصـين في مجـال المكتبـات والمعلومـات، والمتخصصـين في مجـال الإعـلام والاتصـالات، والصحفيـن كاوا المحركيـن الأساسـيين للتربيـة الإعلاميـة والمعلوماتيـة. في مـا يتعلـق بالخبـراء الذيـن يقضـون أكـثر مـن نصـف وقتهـم في الأنشـطة المتعلقـة بالتربيـة الإعلاميـة والمعلوماتيـة، يبيّـن الجـدول 3 مقارنـة بـين منطقـة الـشرق الأوسـط وشـمال إفريقيـا وبقيـة العالـم.

الجـدول 3: الـدول العربيـة مقارنـة بالمناطـق الأخـرى فيمـا يتعلـق بخـبراء التربيـة الإعلاميـة والمعلوماتيـة.

المناطق الأخرى في العالم	منطقة الشرق الأوسط وشمال إفريقيا
منطقة إفريقيا جنوب الصحراء الكبرى	أقل من أو مساو لها
أمريكا اللاتينية	أقل من
منطقة آسيا المحيط الهادىء	أقل من
الكاراييب	أقل من
أوروبا	أقل من
أمريكا الشمالية	أقل من

باستخدام المبادئ التوجيهيـة لسياسـة واستراتيجية التربيـة الإعلاميـة والمعلوماتيـة والإطار المرجعـي لتقيـيم التربيـة الإعلاميـة والمعلوماتيـة الخاصـة باليونسكو كأسـاس، بالاضافـة الى المراجعـات الأدبيـة حـول التربيـة الإعلاميـة والمعلوماتيـة في منطقـة الـشرق الأوسـط وشمال إفريقيا، بما في ذلك الفصول التـي يتضمنهـا هذا الكتاب، والتحليـل الأولي للبحث الأساسـي الـذي أقوم بـه، يقدم الجـدول رقم 4 تصنيفـاً أوليـاً لاعتماد التربيـة الإعلاميـة والمعلوماتيـة في بلـدان الـشرق الأوسـط وشمال إفريقيا عـبر أربعـة سيناريوهات محتملـة.

الجـدول رقـم 4: التصنيـف الأولي لاعتمـاد التربيـة الإعلاميـة والمعلوماتيـة في منطقـة الـشرق الأوسـط وشـمال أفريقيـا:

البلدان	السيناريو
البحرين، ليبيا، العراق، الكويت، الصومال، السودان، سوريا وجزر القمر واليمن وموريتانيا وفلسطين وسلطنة عمان.	التربية الإعلامية والمعلوماتية غير معروفة على نطاق واسع وغير متطورة
جيبوتي والجزائر والإمارات العربية المتحدة.	التربية الإعلامية والمعلوماتية حديثة العهد وجديدة كمفهوم
قطر، الأردن، لبنان، المغرب، المملكة العربية السعودية، تونس ومصر.	التربية الإعلامية والمعلوماتية مدمجة نوعاً ما ضمن البرامج والمؤسسات المتخصصة ويستفيد بعض المواطنين من الوصول الى تلك المبادرات
	التربية الإعلامية والمعلوماتية مفهومة على نطاق واسع، وتوجد برامج للتربية الإعلامية والمعلوماتية متوفرة لمعظم المواطنين.

الترتيب المنهجي للتربية الإعلامية والمعلوماتية في منطقة الشرق الأوسط وشمال إفريقيا والتضامن من خلال التحالفات الإقليمية والدولية:

يعتمد مستقبل التربية الإعلامية والمعلوماتية في منطقة الشرق الأوسط وشمال إفريقيا على جميع أصحاب المصلحة من أفراد ومنظمات خاصة وعامة أو المؤسسات والمنظمات الإنمائية الدولية، والمجتمع المدني بشكل عام. حاولنا من خلال هذا التحليل الأولي أن نسلط الضوء على بعض الخطوات الأولى التي ينبغي النظر فيها، مثل المقاربة المنسقة في تصور المهارات في مجال التربية الإعلامية والمعلوماتية وصياغتها، والاعتراف في الوقت عينه بأن هناك سياسات عامة ذات الصلة قائمة بالفعل في منطقة الشرق الأوسط وشمال إفريقيا، والتي يمكن الاعتماد عليها لبناء سياسات التربية الإعلامية والمعلوماتية، بالإضافة الى الحاجة لإيجاد إجماع حول ضرورة نشر التربية الإعلامية والمعلوماتية. مما لا شك فيه أن هناك تجربة هامة في المنطقة يمكن الارتكاز عليها لهذا الغرض. ويتمثل التحدي الرئيسي بالنسبة الى المنطقة، أي غياب اي سياسة واضحة، كما لحظ ذلك سامي طايع، وهو خبير رائد في خلال المؤتمرات الإقليمية والدولية المختلفة. وبالتالي، فإن نقطة الانطلاق الأساسية تكون بتعزيز الوعي حول التربية الإعلامية والمعلوماتية بين واضعي السياسات والمدرسين وتعزيز الشراكات الملموسة بين الأطراف الفاعلة في المنطقة لتسريع إيصال التربية الإعلامية والمعلوماتية للجميع. كان هذا هو موضوع «المنتدى الإقليمي حول التربية الإعلامية والمعلوماتية في الدول العربية» الذي عُقد في القاهرة بمصر، في 22-23 أبريل عام 2015 والذي نظمته اليونسكو بالتعاون مع جامعة الدول العربية، والوكالة الدولية للتنمية السويدية (SIDA)، جامعة الأهرام الكندية، واللجنة الوطنية المصرية لليونسكو.

جمع المنتدى نحو 140 مشاركاً من الجزائر، والبحرين، ومصر، والأردن، والكويت، ولبنان، وليبيا، والمغرب، وعمان، وفلسطين، والسودان، وتونس، واليمن، والإمارات العربية المتحدة. واشتمل المشاركون واضعي السياسات وخبراء وضع المناهج والمدرّسين وخبراء الإعلام والمعلومات. السيدة زينب الوكيل، مساعد الأمين العام للجنة الوطنية المصرية لليونسكو، ممثّلة الأستاذ السيد عبد الخالق، وزير التعليم العالي في مصر، الدكتورة هيفاء أبو غزالة، الأمين العام المساعد لجامعة الدول العربية، والدكتور فاروق إسماعيل، رئيس جامعة الأهرام الكندية، أكدوا جميعهم أهمية التربية الإعلامية والمعلوماتية في الدول العربية في السياق الاجتماعي والسياسي الحالي. كما شددوا على ضرورة إدخال هذه المهارات في مرحلة مبكرة من حياة الطلاب والمواطنين بشكل عام،

في المدارس والنوادي، والعمل، وعلى شبكة الإنترنت أو وسائل التواصل الاجتماعي، وغيرها من الأماكن (المرجع 38).

وبهدف تعزيز الشراكات بين الجهات الفاعلة في مجال التربية الإعلامية والمعلوماتية في المنطقة، قامت اليونسكو في عام 2013 بإطلاق التحالف العالمي من أجل الشراكات في مجال التربية الإعلامية والمعلوماتية (GAPMIL) مع ثلاثة أهداف هي على الشكل التالي: 1) صياغة شراكات ملموسة لتطوير التربية الإعلامية والمعلوماتية وتعزيز تأثيرها؛ 2) تمكين مجتمع التربية الإعلامية والمعلوماتية من التحدث بصوت واحد بشأن بعض المسائل الهامة، لا سيما تلك التي تتعلق بالسياسات؛ و3) الاستمرار بتعميق استراتيجية التربية الإعلامية والمعلوماتية من خلال توفير منصة موحدة للشبكات والجمعيات ذات الصلة بالتربية الإعلامية والمعلوماتية. وقد أطلقت دعوة رسمية لجذب العضوية الى التحالف من خلال استفتاء مستمر باللغة الإنجليزية والفرنسية والإسبانية. وقد يكون هذا الأمر طريفاً، إلا أنه منذ ذلك الحين، لم تنضم سوى 13 منظمة من منطقة الشرق الأوسط وشمال إفريقيا إلى التحالف، الذي يضمّ حالياً أكثر من 600 عضو (انظروا الجدول رقم 5).

الجدول رقم 5: أعضاء التحالف العالمي من أجل الشراكات في مجال التربية الإعلامية والمعلوماتية من منطقة الشرق الأوسط وشمال أفريقيا:

اسم المنظمة	المدينة	البلد
مركز الدوحة لحرية الاعلام	الدوحة	قطر
جامعة الدلتا للعلوم والتكنولوجيا	المنصورة	مصر
منظمة البحث عن ارضية مشتركة	الرباط	المغرب
جامعة زايد	ابوظبي	الامارات العربية المتحدة
المجلس الأعلى للاتصالات وتكنولوجيا المعلومات (آي سي تي قطر)	الدوحة	قطر
"ايديتوري ليبري اي كومونيكاسيون" (ناشر كتب)	مصر	القاهرة
مقر المركز الدولي لأفلام للأطفال والنشء	طهران	ايران

جامعة البتراء	عمان	الأردن
جامعة الحسين بن طلال	معن	الأردن
الجامعة الهاشمية	الزرقاء	الأردن
المركز الإقليمي للتربية الإعلامية والمعلوماتية والحوار بين الثقافات	فاس	المغرب
معهد الإعلام الأردني	عمان	الأردن
قطر	الدوحة	المجلس الأعلى للاتصالات وتكنولوجيا المعلومات (آي سي تي قطر)
القاهرة	مصر	"ايديتوري ليبري اي كومونيكاسيون" (ناشر كتب)
ايران	طهران	مقر المركز الدولي لأفلام للأطفال والنشء

أطلـق الفصـل الخـاص بالـدول العربيـة حـول التحالـف العالمـي للشـراكات في مجـال التربيـة الإعلاميـة والمعلوماتيـة خـلال المنتـدى. وقـد تـم وضـع اللمسـات الأخيـرة عـلى خطـة عمـل مفصلـة لفصـل التحالـف العالمـي مـن أجـل الشـراكات في مجـال التربيـة الإعلاميـة والمعلوماتيـة (GAPMIL) الخـاص بالـدول العربيـة مـن قبـل أعضـاء اللجنـة مـن 14 بلـداً.

كما قامـت اليونسـكو بتطويـر أربـع مـوارد دوليـة أساسـية بهـدف المسـاهمة، مـن خـلال التكيـف والتعديـل، في وضـع منهجيـة لسياسـات وبرامـج التربيـة الإعلاميـة والمعلوماتيـة الوطنيـة في منطقـة الشـرق الأوسـط وشـمال إفريقيـا. وفي مجـال المناهـج الدراسـية، يوجـد منهـج التربيـة الإعلاميـة والمعلوماتيـة للمدرّسـين. وهـو قابـل للتكيـف مـع كافـة مسـتويات المجتمـع، وهـو متوفـر باللغـة العربيـة 39. في مجـال السياسـة والاسـتراتيجية، يمكـن للبلـدان الوصـول إلى نمـوذج المصـدر 40 المتعلـق بسياسـة واسـتراتيجية التربيـة الإعلاميـة والمعلوماتيـة الـذي سـيكون متاحـة باللغـة العربيـة في الربـع الأول مـن عـام 2016 مـن خـلال مشروع ثقافـة السـلام الخـاص بمنظمـة اليونسـكو والمملكـة العربيـة السـعودية. في مجـال الرصـد والتقييـم، أصـدرت منظمـة اليونسـكو الإطـار المرجعـي لتقييـم التربيـة الإعلاميـة والمعلوماتيـة: جاهزيـة البلـد والمهـارات 41. في مجـال المـوارد التعليميـة، وبهـدف جعـل هـذه المـوارد أكـثر توفـراً للمدرّسـين والمدربـين، دخلـت اليونسـكو في شراكـة مـع برنامـج الأمـم المتحـدة لتحالـف الحضـارات (UNAOC)، بشـكل مرتبـط مـع مشروع ثقافـة السـلام

الخاص باليونسكو والمملكة العربية السعودية، من اجل انشاء أداة دولية متعددة الوسائط عبر الإنترنت، بين الثقافات في مجال موارد تعليم التربية الإعلامية والمعلوماتية. هذه المنصة على الانترنت، في حين انها متوفرة للجمهور، لا تزال قيد التطوير وتتضمن مكونات باللغات العربية والفرنسية وغيرها من اللغات.

وأخيراً، يتطلب وضع منهجية للسياسات والاستراتيجيات الوطنية في مجال التربية الإعلامية والمعلوماتية الاستفادة من الأشكال والأساليب الجديدة لتثقيف المواطنين. ومن أجل تعزيز إمكانية وصول الشباب إلى التربية الإعلامية والمعلوماتية في الدول العربية، دخلت اليونسكو في شراكة مع الجامعة الأميركية في بيروت وهي تقوم بإعداد أول «دورة تعليمية مفتوحة على الإنترنت (MOOC) في التربية الإعلامية والمعلوماتية باللغة العربية. وهو نموذج مكيّف ومعدل لبرنامج التربية الإعلامية والمعلوماتية الدولي بين الثقافات عبر الانترنت الذي قامت اليونسكو بتطويره. وستشمل النسخة العربية تعاوناً بين الكثير من الجامعات الأخرى في منطقة الشرق الأوسط وشمال إفريقيا. ينبغي على قارئ هذا الفصل أن يعترف بأن الجزء التقليدي من التربية المعلوماتية ليس غنياً مثل البرنامج التقليدي للتربية الإعلامية. يرجع ذلك إلى الغياب العام للمواد الأدبية ذات الصلة. وسيتم بذل المحاولات لمعالجة هذا النقص في مقال مستقبلي. ويحاول هذا الفصل، لا بل هذا الكتاب، أن يعزز معرفة أصحاب المصلحة بشأن التربية الإعلامية والمعلوماتية في منطقة الشرق الأوسط وشمال إفريقيا. عندما يجهل المرء امراً وبالتالي لا يفعل شيئاً، يكون لا بد من اتخاذ اجراءات معينة. وعندما يكون المرء مدركاً للأمر ومع ذلك لا يفعل شيئاً، فإن هذا الأمر يثير أسئلة أخرى. في يونيو 2016، كنت أتصفح الكتاب الاخير للخبير الشهير بول زوركوسي، الذي اخترع مفهوم «التربية المعلوماتية». أثناء قراءتي للكتاب، الذي يحمل عنوان، «العمل من اجل تعزيز محو الأمية - تمكين «نحن الشعب» في عصر المعلومات»، تعلمت شكلاً جديداً من المعرفة ويسمى «العمل من اجل تعزيز محو الأمية». وبحسب بول زوركوسي، العمل من اجل تعزيز محو الأمية يعني «القدرة على تحويل المعلومات الجيدة الى عمل أخلاقي. أن يعمل المرء من أجل تعزيز محو الأمية يعني أن أعمال المرء الأخلاقية مترسخة بشكل قوي في المعلومات الجيدة». ويضيف الكاتب: «الأعمال مفيدة، الأعمال جيدة. ويتم القيام بالأعمال الصحيحة حتى عندما تكون صعبة. » يوجد الكثير من الاستدلالات التي يمكن أن نستخلصها من هذا التعريف حول «العمل من اجل تعزيز محو الأمية».

في هذا الصدد، اقترح أنا واليونسكو نقطتين للتفكير:

اولاً: العمل مـن اجـل تعزيـز محـو الأميـة هـو جـزء مـن التربيـة الإعلاميـة والمعلوماتيـة. عندمـا نتمتـع بمهـارات التربيـة الإعلاميـة والمعلوماتيـة بشـكل كامـل، يتعيـن علينـا القيـام بأعمـال إيجابيـة وهادفـة بشـأن كيفيـة اسـتخدام، والانخـراط فـي، والتعامـل مـع الآثـار الإيجابيـة والسـلبية للمعلومـات والإعـلام والتكنولوجيـا فـي حياتـا الشـخصية والاقتصاديـة والاجتماعيـة.

ثانياً: تقـوم اليونسـكو، متسـلحة بالمعلومـات حـول التربيـة الإعلاميـة والمعلوماتيـة فـي منطقـة الـشرق الأوسـط وشـمال إفريقيـا، بتشـجيع جميـع الاطـراف المعنيـة لمعاينـة التحديـات الـتي تواجـه المنطقـة. نحتـاج اولاً إلى الـتزام جميـع اللاعبيـن. يمكننـا القيـام بذلـك مجتمعيـن، لكـن ينبغـي اولاً أن تلـتزم وتتخـذ الإجـراءات اللازمـة.

تمامـاً كتلـك الفتـاة الـتي تبلـغ مـن العمـر 13 عامـاً، والـتي كانـت عازمـة عـلى مواجهـة التنمـر الالكـتروني، مـن خـلال ابتـكار البرنامـج الابتـكاري، (إعـادة التفكـير) «ريثينـك» 42، يجـب علينـا أن نعيـد التفكـير فـي أهميـة التربيـة الإعلاميـة والمعلوماتيـة فـي منطقـة الـشرق الأوسـط وشـمال إفريقيـا وفـي العالـم اجمـع. كمـا ينبغـي أن نتخـذ إجـراءات سريعـة ومبتكـرة لدعـم عمليـة التغيـير.

المراجع:

•أبـو فاضـل، م. (2013). يتعلـم المدرّسـون فـي قطـر كيفيـة دمـج التربيـة الإعلاميـة فـي المناهـج الدراسيـة، ص. 381-386، فـي «التربيـة الإعلاميـة والمعلوماتيـة والحـوار بـين الثقافـات». أ. كارلسـون وش. ه. كالفـر (محررتـا نصـوص). الكتـاب السـنوي للشـبكة الجامعيـة للتربيـة الإعلاميـة والمعلوماتيـة والحـوار بـين الثقافـات (2013، MILID، «نورديكـوم»، جامعـة غوتنـبرغ، السـويد. متوفـر عـبر شـبكة الانترنـت عـلى الرابـط التـالي: www.nordicom.gu.se/clearinghouse

•أبـو فاضـل، م. (2007). التربيـة الإعلاميـة، أداة لمكافحـة القوالـب النمطيـة وتعزيـز الحـوار بـين الثقافـات. ورقـة بحثيـة أعـدت لصالـح مؤتمـرات اليونسـكو الإقليميـة لدعـم محـو الأميـة فـي العالـم. الدوحـة، 12-14 مـارس 2007.

•م. أبـو فاضـل (2006). الشـباب اللبنـاني والإعـلام - التأثيـرات الاجتماعيـة والسياسيـة، ص 183-195، فـي «فـي خدمـة الشـباب؟ دراسـات وتأمـلات فـي وسـائل الإعـلام فـي العـصر

الرقمي. أ. كارلسون وس. فون فيليتزن (محررتا نصوص). «نورديكوم»، جامعة غوتنبرغ، السويد.

•ر. أسعد، ، والدكتورة ف. رودي فهيمي (2007). الشباب في منطقة الشرق الأوسط وشمال أفريقيا: فرصة ديموغرافية أو تحدّ؟ -http://www.prb.org/pdf07/youthinme na.pdf تمّت مراجعته في 7 سبتمبر 2015.

•أ. ديجـاني و ر. ديجـاني (2015). استطلاع لتصورات ومواقف الشباب بشأن التغطية الإعلامية في إسرائيل. تمّ إجراء البحث بتكليف من اليونسكو الى مجموعة «جيوكارتوغرافي».

•أ. إ. فهمـي، ون. م. رفعـت (2010). الوعـي حـول التربيـة الإعلاميـة في الشـرق الأوسـط وتحديـات المحتـوى العـربي الأصـلي، ص. 123-111. دوريـة المعلومـات والمكتبـات الدوليـة، المجلـد 42 (2).

•د. فـراو- ميغـز (2011). الشـؤون الإعلاميـة في التناقضـات الثقافيـة لمجتمـع المعلومـات – نحـو الحوكمـة القائمـة عـلى حقـوق الإنسـان، ص.334. مجلـس أوروبـا، ستراسـبورغ، فرنسـا.

•أ. ه. جمعـة.(2014). إنتـاج الفيديـو كأداة لتعزيـز التربيـة الإعلاميـة والمواطنـة في مـصر، ص. 43-33، في «المواطنـة العالميـة في العـالم الرقمـي». ش. ه. كالفـر وب. كـير (محررتـا نصـوص). الكتـاب السـنوي للشـبكة الجامعيـة للتربيـة الإعلاميـة والمعلوماتيـة والحـوار بـين الثقافـات (MILID) جامعـة غوتنبرغ، السـويد. متوفـر عـبر شـبكة الانترنـت عـلى الرابـط التـالي: www.nordicom.gu.se/clearinghouse

•آ. غريـزل (2015). قيـاس التربيـة الإعلاميـة والمعلوماتيـة: الانعكاسـات عـلى أهـداف التنميـة المستدامة، ص. 129-107، في «التربيـة الإعلاميـة والمعلوماتيـة مـن أجـل تحقيـق أهـداف التنميـة المسـتدامة». ج. سـينغ، آ. غريـزل، س. ج. ي وش. ه. كالفـر (محـررو نصـوص). الكتـاب السـنوي للشـبكة الجامعيـة للتربيـة الإعلاميـة والمعلوماتيـة والحـوار بـين الثقافـات (2015، MILID «نورديكـوم»، جامعـة غوتنبرغ، السـويد. متوفـر عـبر شـبكة الانترنـت عـلى الرابـط التـالي: www.nordicom.gu.se/clearinghouse

•آ. غريـزل (2009). «التربيـة الإعلاميـة – المنظـور العالمـي. عـرض رئـيسي تـمّ تقديمـه في نـدوة «أوروميـدوك» حـول التربيـة الإعلاميـة وتملّـك الإنترنـت مـن قبـل الشـباب. فـارو، البرتغـال.

•آ. غريـزل، وب. مـور، وم. ديزوانـي وم. أسـتانة وس. يلسـون، وف. بانـدا وس. أونومـا (2013) المبـادئ التوجيهيـة لسياسـة واسـتراتيجية التربيـة الإعلاميـة والمعلوماتيـة. اليونسـكو، باريـس، فرنسـا. متوفـر عبـر شـبكة الانترنـت علـى الرابـط التالـي: www.unesco.org

•ف. و. هورتـون. (2013). نظـرة عامـة علـى مـوارد التربيـة المعلوماتيـة فـي كافـة أنحـاء العالـم. اليونسـكو، باريـس، فرنسـا.

•م. ايتـو (2013). دمـج التربيـة الإعلاميـة والمعلوماتيـة فـي المناهـج الوطنيـة لتدريـب المعلميـن فـي المغـرب، ص. 276-275، فـي «التربيـة الإعلاميـة والمعلوماتيـة والحـوار بيـن الثقافـات. أ. كارلسـون وش. ه. كالفـر (محـررتا نصـوص). الكتـاب السـنوي للشـبكة الجامعيـة للتربيـة الإعلاميـة والمعلوماتيـة والحـوار بيـن الثقافـات (MILID) جامعـة غوتنبـرغ، السـويد. متوفـر عبـر شـبكة الانترنـت علـى الرابـط التالـي: www.nordicom.gu.se/clearinghouse

•ه. جنكيـنز، ك. كلينتـون، ور. بوروشـوتما، أ. ج. روبيسـون، وم. فيغـل (2009). مواجهـة تحديـات ثقافـة المشـاركة: التربيـة الإعلاميـة فـي القـرن الحـادي والعشـرين. دار النشـر «إم أي تـي بـرس «، لنـدن، إنجلتـرا.

•د. كاميريـر. (2013). التربيـة الإعلاميـة. اتجاهـات البحـوث فـي مجـال الاتصـالات - مركـز لدراسـة الاتصـالات والثقافـة، المجلـد 32 (1).

•د. كيلنـر، وج. شـير. (2007). التربيـة الإعلاميـة الحرجـة، الديمقراطيـة، وإعـادة بنـاء التعليـم، ص 23-3 فـي «التربيـة الإعلاميـة: قـارئ. د. ماسـيدو وس.ر شـتاينبرغ (محـرران). دار «بيـتر لانـج» للنشـر، نيويـورك، الولايـات المتحـدة الأمريكيـة.

•ك. ر. مادرينـاس، «التربيـة الإعلاميـة واللغـة الإنجليزيـة كمنهـج لغـة ثانيـة: نقـد المناهـج الدراسـية وأحـلام للمسـتقبل» (2014). مخـزن الرسـائل والاطروحـات الإلكـتروني. الورقـة البحثيـة رقـم 2529.

•م. المصمـودي (2006). الطفـل العـربي ومجتمـع المعلومـات، ص. 100-77، فـي «فـي خدمـة الشـباب؟ دراسـات وتأمـلات فـي وسـائل الإعـلام فـي العصـر الرقمـي. أولـلا كارلسـون وسيسـيليا فـون فيليتـزن (محـررتا نصـوص). «نورديكـوم»، جامعـة غوتنبـرغ، السـويد.

•ج. ملـكي (2013). بـذر بـذور التربيـة الرقميـة والإعلاميـة فـي لبنـان والعالـم العـربي، ص 86-77، فـي «آليـة التربيـة الإعلاميـة:

وجهـات نظـر نظريـة وتربويـة. ب. س. دي أبـرو وب. ميهايليـدس (محـرران). روتليـدج، نيويـورك، الولايـات المتحدة.

•م. مينـو (2002). التربيـة المعلوماتيـة فـي سياسـات تكنولوجيـا الاتصـالات والمعلومـات الوطنيـة: البعـد المفقـود وثقافة المعلومـات. ورقة بيضـاء تـم إعدادهـا لصالح اليونسكو، واللجنـة الوطنيـة الامريكيـة حـول يـوم المكتبـات وعلـم المعلومـات، والمنتـدى الوطـني للتربيـة المعلوماتيـة، لاستخدامها فـي اجتمـاع خبـراء التربيـة المعلوماتيـة، فـي بـراغ، جمهوريـة التشيـك. متوفـرة عـلى الرابـط التـالي:

. http://www.nclis.gov/libinter/infolitconf&meet/papers/menou-fullpaper.pdf

•ب. ميهايليـدس، (2008). مـا بعـد التهكّـم : كيـف يمكـن للتربيـة الإعلاميـة والمعلوماتيـة أن تجعـل مـن الطـلاب مواطنـين أكـثر انخراطـاً. أطروحـة مقدمـة إلى كليـة الدراسـات العليـا فـي جامعـة ماريـلاند، الولايـات المتحـدة الأمريكيـة.

•أ. إ. مختـار، وس. ماجـد، وس. فـو (2008). تعليـم التربيـة المعلوماتيـة: تطبيقـات التعلـم غـير المبـاشر والذكـاءات المتعـددة. بحـوث المكتبـات وعلـم المعلومـات. المجلـد رقـم 30 ص. 195 206-.

•م. محمـد، ون.أ. المنعـم، (2013). تقييـم تأثـير الإعلانـات الخارجيـة عـلى التنسـيق الحضـري فـي المواقـع التاريخيـة فـي مصـر، ص. 123-115، فـي: التربيـة الإعلاميـة والمعلوماتيـة والحـوار بـين الثقافـات. أولا كارلسـون وشيري هـوب كالفر (محررتان)، الكتـاب السنـوي للشبكـة الجامعيـة للتربيـة الإعلاميـة والمعلوماتيـة والحـوار بـين الثقافـات (MILID)، جامعة غوتنبـرغ، السـويد. متوفـر عـبر شبكـة الانترنـت عـلى الرابـط التـالي:

www.nordicom.gu.se/clearinghouse

•أ. النفيـسي (2014). التربيـة المعلوماتيـة فـي العصـر الرقمـي: المغـرب كدراسـة حالـة، ص 399-389، فـي: المواطنـة العالميـة فـي العالـم الرقمـي. شـيري هـوب كالفر وبوليـت كـير (محررتان). الكتـاب السنـوي للشبكـة الجامعيـة للتربيـة الإعلاميـة والمعلوماتيـة والحـوار بـين الثقافـات (MILID) 2014، جامعـة غوتنبـرغ، السـويد. متوفـر عـبر شبكـة الانترنـت عـلى الرابـط التـالي: www.nordicom.gu.se/clearinghouse

•أ. النفيـسي (2013). تطـورات التربيـة الاعلاميـة والمعلوماتيـة فـي المغـرب، ص. 96-87، فـي: التربيـة الإعلاميـة والمعلوماتيـة والحـوار بـين الثقافـات. أولـلا كارلسـون وش. ه. كالفـر

(محررتان)، الكتاب السنوي للشبكة الجامعية للتربية الإعلامية والمعلوماتية والحوار بين الثقافات (MILID) 2013، جامعة غوتنبرغ، السويد. متوفر عبر شبكة الانترنت على الرابط التالي: www.nordicom.gu.se/clearinghouse

• إ. ن. أورهون (2009). التربية الإعلامية في تركيا: نحو إطار عمل شامل لأصحاب المصلحة المتعددين، ص 211-224، في: وضع خارطة سياسات التثقيف الإعلامي في العالم - الرؤى والبرامج والتحديات. د. فراو-ميغز وج. تورنت (محرران). برنامج الأمم المتحدة لتحالف الحضارات، الولايات المتحدة الأمريكية.

• ر. صقر، وم. النبهاني، وإ. أوسطا (2009). وصف وتقييم برنامج التربية المعلوماتية في مدرسة خاصة في لبنان: دراسة حالة، ص 28-44. مكتبات المدارس حول العالم. المجلد رقم 15 (1).

• إ. صالح (2015). من غرف الجلوس إلى الصفوف: «أضيئوا أنوار» التعلم المتنقل في منطقة الشرق الأوسط وشمال إفريقيا، ص 83-89، في: «التربية الإعلامية والمعلوماتية من أجل تحقيق أهداف التنمية المستدامة». ج. سينغ، آ. غريزل، س. ج. بي وش. ﻩ. كالفر (محررو نصوص). الكتاب السنوي للشبكة الجامعية للتربية الإعلامية والمعلوماتية والحوار بين الثقافات (MILID)، «نورديكوم»، جامعة غوتنبرغ، السويد. متوفر عبر شبكة الانترنت على الرابط التالي: www.nordicom.gu.se/clearinghouse

• إ. صالح (2013). التقارب بين الشباب والنشاط الشبابي في مصر - الحركات الاجتماعية الجديدة، ص 201-214، في: التربية الإعلامية والمعلوماتية والحوار بين الثقافات. أ. كارلسون وش. ﻩ. كالفر (محررتان)، الكتاب السنوي للشبكة الجامعية للتربية الإعلامية والمعلوماتية والحوار بين الثقافات (MILID)، جامعة غوتنبرغ، السويد.

• إ. صالح (2011). ما يأتي وراء الأطفال، ووسائل الإعلام والديمقراطية في منطقة الشرق الأوسط وشمال أفريقيا؟ ص. 29-37، في: أسئلة جديدة، ورؤى جديدة، ومقاربات جديدة. أولا كارلسون وسيسيليا فون فيليتزن وكاثرين بوكت (محررات). الكتاب السنوي، جامعة غوتنبرغ، السويد.

• إ. صالح (2009). التربية الإعلامية في منطقة الشرق الأوسط وشمال إفريقيا: الانتقال ما وراء الحلقة المفرغة للتناقض اللفظي، ص. 155-174، في: وضع خارطة سياسات التثقيف الإعلامي في العالم - الرؤى والبرامج والتحديات. ديفينا فراو-ميغز وجوردي

تورنـت (محـرران). برنامـج الأمـم المتحـدة لتحالـف الحضـارات، الولايـات المتحـدة الأمريكيـة.

•س. طايـع (2014). نحو وعـي متزايد حول التربية الإعلاميـة والمعلوماتيـة في مصـر، ص. 347-354، فـي: المواطنـة العالميـة في العالـم الرقمـي. ش. ه. كالفـر وب. كيـر (محررتـان). الكتـاب السنوي للشبكة الجامعيـة للتربية الإعلاميـة والمعلوماتيـة والحوار بيـن الثقافات (MILID) 2014، جامعـة غوتنبرغ، السـويد. متوفر عـبر شبكة الانترنت على الرابط التالي: www.nordicom.gu.se/clearinghouse

•س. طايـع (2015). تأثير وسـائل التواصـل الاجتماعـي علـى المشـاركة السياسـية للشباب المصـري، ص. 169-178، فـي: «التربيـة الإعلاميـة والمعلوماتيـة مـن أجـل تحقيـق أهداف التنميـة المسـتدامة». ج. سـينغ، آ. غريـزل، س. ج. يي وش. ه. كالفـر (محررو نصـوص). الكتـاب السنوي للشبكة الجامعيـة للتربية الإعلاميـة والمعلوماتيـة والحوار بيـن الثقافات (MILID) 2015، «نورديكـوم»، جامعـة غوتنبرغ، السـويد. متوفـر عـبر شبكة الانترنت على الرابـط التالـي: www.nordicom.gu.se/clearinghouse

•اليونسـكو (2013). الإطار المرجعـي لتقييـم التربيـة الإعلاميـة والمعلوماتيـة: جاهزيـة البلـد والمهـارات. اليونسـكو، باريـس، فرنسـا. متوفـر عـبر شبكة الانترنـت علـى الرابـط التـالي: www.unesco.org

•اليونسـكو (1998). إحصـاءات عـن الأطفـال في العالـم، ص. 289-299، فـي: الأطفـال والعنـف الإعلامـي. أ. كارلسـون وس. فـون فيليتـزن (محررتـان)، «نورديكـوم»، جامعـة غوتنـبرغ، السـويد.

•اليونسـكو (1998). إحصـاءات عـن وسـائل الإعـلام في العالـم، ص. 261-285، فـي: الأطفـال والعنـف الإعلامـي. أولـا كارلسـون وسيسـيليا فـون فيليتـزن (محررتـان)، «نورديكـوم»، جامعـة غوتنـبرغ، السـويد.

•اليونسـكو (2006). محـو الأميـة مـن أجـل الحيـاة. التقريـر العالمـي لرصـد التعليـم للجميـع. اليونسـكو، باريـس، فرنسـا.

•د. واط (2012). الحاجـة الملحـة للتربيـة الاعلاميـة المرئيـة في العالـم مـا بعـد الحـادي عـشر مـن ايلـول: قـراءة صـور النسـاء المسـلمات في وسـائل الإعـلام المطبوعـة. مجلـة تعليـم التربيـة الاعلاميـة. المجلـد رقـم 4 (1) ص. 32-43.

•س. ويلسون، آ. غريزل، ر. تـوازون، وك. أكيمبونـغ، وس. تشـونغ (2011). منهـج التربيـة الإعلاميـة والمعلوماتيـة للمدرّسـين. اليونسكو، باريـس، فرنسـا. متوفـر عبـر شبكة الانترنت علـى الرابـط التالـي: www.unesco.org

•مر. ن. يلديـز (2014). ثقافـات مختلفـة، تحديـات مماثلـة - دمـج الوسـائط المتعـددة اللغـات والثقافـات في تعليـم التربيـة الإعلاميـة، ص 259-270، في: المواطنـة العالميـة في العالـم الرقمـي. ش. ه. كالفـر وب. كيـر (محررتـان). الكتـاب السـنوي للشـبكة الجامعيـة للتربيـة الإعلاميـة والمعلوماتيـة والحـوار بيـن الثقافـات (MILID) 2014) جامعـة غوتنـبرغ، السـويد. متوفـر عـبر شبكة الانترنت علـى الرابـط التالـي: -www.nordicom.gu.se/clearin ghouse

•ب. زوركوسـكي (2014. العمـل مـن اجـل تعزيـز محـو الأميـة - تمكيـن «نحـن الشـعب» في عـصر المعلومـات». الناشـر: «أول غـود ليتراسـيز بريـس»، لوريـل، ماريلانـد، الولايـات المتحـدة الأمريكيـة.

هـذا النـص مرتبـط بدراسـة بحثيـة عـن تحليـلات في مجـال التربيـة الإعلاميـة والمعلوماتيـة حـول العالـم واسـتجابة المواطنيـن لمهـارات التلريـة الإعلاميـة والمعلوماتيـة فيمـا يتعلـق بالتحديـات الشـخصية والاجتماعيـة والاقتصاديـة والسياسـية والثقافيـة والدينيـة والفـرص المتصلـة بالانترنت أو غـير المتصلـة بالانترنت بعـد اكتسـاب مهـارات التربيـة الإعلاميـة والمعلوماتيـة ذات الصلـة مـن خـلال أنـواع مختلفـة مـن الـدورات عـبر الانترنت. يتـم إجـراء هـذا البحـث في جامعـة برشـلونة المسـتقلة تحـت إشراف البروفيسـور خوسـيه مانويـل بيريـز تورنيـرو 43.

---

1   ملاحظة للمحررين: غير متوفر في لائحة المراجع

2   رأي مسـتقل مـن موقـع العالـم العربـي: http://www.arableagueonline.org تمّت زيـارة الرابـط في 7 سـبتمبر 2015. (ملاحظـة: هـذا ليـس الموقـع الرسـمي لجامعـة الـدول العربيـة. رؤيـة: http://www.arableagueonline.org/remark. الموقـع الرسـمي: // http www.lasportal.org/ar/Pages/default.aspx . ولا يوجـد مـرادف لـه بالانكليزيـة.)

3   http://www.worldbank.org/en/region/mena تمت زيارة الرابط في 26 أكتوبر 2015.

4   http://www.ohchr.org/EN/Countries/MenaRegion/Pages/MenaRegionIn- dex.aspx تمـت زيـارة الرابـط في 26 أكتوبـر 2015.

5   بالارتكاز الى ترتيب جامعة الدول العربية.

6   الاتحـاد الـدولي للاتصـالات: تكنولوجيـا المعلومـات والاتصـالات. حقائـق وأرقـام - العالـم في عـام 2015. جنيـف: الاتحـاد الـدولي للاتصـالات: http://www.itu.int/en/ITU-D/ Statistics/Pages/facts/default.aspx تمـت زيارتـه في 16 سـبتمبر 2015.

7   يتعيّـن علـى القـراء اسـتخدام هـذا الجـدول بعنايـة عنـد إجـراء المقارنـة نظـراً لعـدم توفـر بيانـات كاملـة مـن مصـدر واحـد، وفي بعـض الحـالات، البيانـات ليسـت متوفـرة لنفـس مجموعـة التواريـخ.

8   الأمـم المتحـدة، إدارة الشـؤون الاقتصاديـة والاجتماعيـة، شـعبة السـكان (2015). التوقعـات السـكانية في العالـم: تنقيـح 2015. http://esa.un.org/unpd/wpp /أو مباشرة علـى الرابـط التـالي: _http://esa.un.org/unpd/wpp/publications/files/key_findings wpp_2015.pdf تمـت زيـارة الرابـط في 16 سـبتمبر 2015.

9   Internetlivestats.com، «مسـتخدمي الانترنت بحسـب البلد (2014) - إحصائيـات الانترنت الحيـة». http://www.internetlivestats.com/ . تمـت زيـارة الرابـط في 16 سبتمبر 2015.

10   oclc.org . مكتبـة الاحصائيـات العالميـة. -www.oclc.org/content/dam/oclc/glo ballibrarystats/globalstats_countrydataset_oclcweb.xlsx . تمـت زيـارة الرابـط في 16 سـبتمبر 2015.

11   Cia.gov . كتـاب حقائـق العالـم. /https://www.cia.gov/library/publications the-world-factbook/ تمـت زيـارة الرابـط في 16 سـبتمبر 2015.

12   https://www.quandl.com/collections/society/households-with-a-radio-by-country. Accessed on 7 November, 2015

13   Data.uis.unesco.org . «الاتصـالات والمعلومـات: الصحـف». http://data.uis. unesco.org/ تمـت زيـارة الرابـط في 16 سـبتمبر 2015.

14   ملاحظة للمحررين: المرجع غير متوفر

15   ملاحظة للمحررين: المرجع غير متوفر

16   برنامـج الحكومـة الالكترونيـة للبحريـن، «النظـر مـا بعـد مـا هـو واضـح» 2009، http://www.ega.gov.bh/. تمـت زيـارة الرابـط في 7 نوفمـبر 2015.

17   الخطـة الاسـتراتيجية الخمسـية (2013- 2018) وتسـعى لدعـم الاحـتراف في الممارسـة الإعلاميـة والإنتـاج والمسـاهمة في نشـر الوعـي والمعرفـة في جميـع أنحـاء المجتمـع. الملامـح الوطنيـة لمجتمـع المعلومـات في المجتمـع. الملامـح الوطنيـة لمجتمـع المعلومـات في البحريـن (2013)، ص. 31.

18 اسـتراتيجية تكنولوجيـا المعلومـات والاتصالات الوطنيـة في جيبـوتي وخطـة العمـل المرفقـة. اختفـى مـن الموقـع. وهـو مذكـور عـلى الرابـط التالي الـذي قـد لا يكـون حسـن السـمعة نظـراً للتنويـه. http://www.hartford-hwp.com/archives/33/index-bc.html 1

19 اسـتراتيجية تكنولوجيـا المعلومـات والاتصالات الوطنيـة: 2005 – حـتى الوقـت الحاضـر، خطـة مفصّلة تركـز عـلى البنيـة التحتيـة وحوكمـة شبكات تكنولوجيا المعلومـات والاتصالات. http://www.mcit.gov.eg/ict_sector

20 حرية الوصول الى قانون المعلومات رقم 2007/47.

21 الاسـتراتيجية الإلكترونيـة الوطنيـة في لبنان، وثيقـة رقـم 4: سياسـات تكنولوجيـا المعلومـات والاتصالات والمبـادرات السـبع (2003)، http://siteresources.worldbank.
org/EDUCATION/Resources/WorldBankMasterICT-EdPolicyDocumentList-Draft_
June2011_for-external-site.pdf . تمـت زيـارة الرابـط في 7 نوفمـبر 2015

22 خطـة تطويـر البنيـة التحتيـة الوطنيـة للمعلومـات والاتصالات 1999-2002 (متوفر باللغـة الفرنسـية، 2000) – http://www.uneca.org/AISI/NICI/Documents/Mauritanie_
NICI_PLan.html اختفـى عـن الموقـع.

23 تعميـم إدمـاج تكنولوجيـا المعلومـات والاتصالات في التعليـم (برنامـج «جيـني» – الفرنسـية / العربيـة)؛ الاسـتراتيجية الوطنيـة لمجتمـع المعلومـات والاقتصـاد الرقمـي «المغـرب الرقمـي» 2013. http://www.men.gov.ma/sites/fr/SiteCollectionDocu-
ments/G%C3%A9n%C3%A9ralisation_TICEnseignement_Vf2.pdf . تمـت زيـارة الرابـط في 7 نوفمـبر 2015.

24 اسـتراتيجية تكنولوجيـا المعلومـات الوطنيـة تحـت عنـوان اسـتراتيجية «عمـان الرقميـة» 2002. http://www.ita.gov.om (متوفـرة باللغـة العربيـة هنـا).

25 وضع المجلس الأعلى للاتصالات وتكنولوجيا المعلومـات (آي سي تي قطـر) خطـة تكنولوجيـا المعلومـات والاتصالات الاسـتراتيجية الشـاملة في عـام 2010. http://www.ictqatar.qa/en/news-events/news/ictqatar-releases-2010-annual-re-
port تمـت زيـارة الرابـط في 8 نوفمـبر 2015.

26 سياسـة الوصـول العالمـي والخدمـة الشـاملة. siteresources.worldbank.
org/.../2012-02-29-AndrewDymond.pptx . تمـت زيـارة الرابـط في 8 نوفمـبر 2015.

27 الخطـة الوطنيـة لتكنولوجيا المعلومـات والاتصالات. www.kacst.edu.sa/en/re-
search/Documents/InformationTechnology.pdf و www.mcit.gov.sa.
تمت زيارة الرابط في 8 نوفمبر 2015.

28 دراسـة تكنولوجيـا المعلومـات والاتصـالات والتعليـم في أفريقيـا: تقريـر عـن الصومال. https://www.infodev.org/infodev-files/resource/InfodevDocuments_428.pdf

29 دراسـة تكنولوجيـا المعلومـات والاتصـالات والتعليـم في أفريقيـا: تقريـر عـن السـودان. https://openknowledge.worldbank.org/handle/10986/10660

30 تونـس – مسـاهمة تكنولوجيـا المعلومـات والاتصـالات في التنميـة وتوليـد فـرص التوظيـف (المجلـد 2)، تقريـر تقـني، http://documents.banquemondiale.org/. تمـت زيـارة الرابـط في 8 نوفمـبر 2015.

31 قوانين الإعـلام والأنظمـة المعمـول بهـا في دول مجلـس التعـاون الخليجـي: ملخـص وتحليـل وتوصيـات بواسـطة الدكتـور مـات جـي. دافي. http://www.dc4mf.org/sites/de-fault/files/gcc_media_law_en_0.pdf تمـت زيـارة الرابـط في 7 نوفمـبر 2015.

32 http://library.aucegypt.edu/dept/infoliteracy/index.htm تمـت زيـارة الرابـط في 7 نوفمـبر 2015.

33 http://mdc.birzeit.edu/en تمت زيارة الرابط في 4 أكتوبر 2015.

34 الاتحـاد الـدولي لجمعيـات ومؤسسـات المكتبـات http://blogs.ifla.org/literacy-2014/03/16/qatar-information-literacy-network-meeting/، وجامعـة قطـر، http://library.qu.edu.qa/index.php/services/faculty/information-literacy-program تمـت زيـارة الرابـط في 7 نوفمـبر 2015.

35 مراجعـة مقتطفـات مـن المقـال الأكاديمـي «وصـف وتقييـم برنامـج التربيـة المعلوماتيـة في مدرسـة خاصـة في لبنان: دراسـة حالـة، https://www.questia.com/libra-ry/journal/1P3-1741798951/description-and-evaluation-of-the-information-litera-cy، تمـت زيـارة الرابـط في 7 نوفمـبر 2015.

36 الموقـع الالكـتروني لليونسـكو، http://www.unesco.org/new/en/media-services/single-view/news/unesco_launches_maghreb_network_of_media_and_information_literacy/#.Vj-UXfxdHIU تمـت زيـارة الرابـط في 7 نوفمـبر 2015.

37 http://www.dc4mf.org/en/content/media-literacy-another-vision-teaching تمـت زيـارة الرابـط في 4 أكتوبـر 2015.

38 الرجـاء الاطلاع عـلى المقـالات الإعلاميـة الـتي نُـشرت عـلى الموقـع الالكـتروني لليونسـكو مـن تأليـف وكتبـه الحـارة Padhy، مستشـار الاتصـالات والمعلومـات، مكتـب اليونسـكو في القاهـرة، وألتـون غريـزل، اليونسـكو، باريـس، http://www.unesco.org/new/en/communication-and-information/resources/news-and-in-focus-articles/all-news/news/unesco_gave_boost_to_media_and_information_literacy_for_arab_states/#.VhCtj_yhflU تمـت زيـارة الرابـط في 4 أكتوبـر 2015. ربمـا تكـون صفـة ومركـز بعـض هـؤلاء المسـؤولين قـد تغـيرت وقـت نـشر هـذا الكتـاب.

39   ويلسون وغيره (2011).

40   غريزل وغيره (2013)

41   اليونيسكو 2013

42   http://rethinkwords.com/ تمت زيارة الرابط في 4 أكتوبر 2015

مساعدة التربية الإعلامية والرقمية العربي والإعلامية على الازدهار: ثلاث سنوات على إطلاق أكاديمية التربية الإعلامية والرقمية في بيروت (MDLAB)

جاد ملكي، ولبنى معاليقي

إدراكا منها لأهميـة تثقيـف الشـباب حـول أنظمـة وسـائل الإعـلام المنتشـرة في كل مـكان والرسـائل الـتي تحيـط بـكل جانـب مـن جوانـب حياتهـم، تبـنى الكثـير مـن البلـدان حـول العالـم التربيـة الإعلاميـة والمعلوماتيـة كواحـد مـن المكونـات الأساسـية للمناهـج الجامعيـة، وفي بعـض الحـالات، مـن مناهـج المـدارس المتوسـطة والثانويـة. لكـن، لسـوء الحـظ، تأخـرت المنطقـة العربيـة في التوصـل الى ذلـك الإدراك (ملـكي، 2009؛ 2011).

وفي الوقـت الـذي تسـاهم فيـه وسـائل التواصـل الاجتماعـي في دعـم الانتفاضـات العربيـة، لا تـزال معظـم أنظمـة التعليـم العـالي العربيـة غـير مدركـة لفوائـد دمـج التربيـة الرقميـة والإعلاميـة ضمـن متطلبـات التعليـم الأساسـية. وبالتـالي، تبـقى الكفـاءات المرتبطـة بالتربيـة الإعلاميـة الأساسـية غائبـة في معظـم الحـالات حـتى عـن برامـج الصحافـة والاعـلام. في الواقـع، حـتى وقـت قريـب، كانـت معظـم المبـادرات في مجـال التربيـة الرقميـة والإعلاميـة في المنطقـة العربيـة مدفوعـة بشـكل فـردي أو تحظـى بالترويـج العابـر مـن قبـل عـدد قليـل مـن منظمـات المجتمـع المـدني مـن خـلال حلقـات العمـل التدريبيـة وحمـلات التوعيـة (ملـكي 2013 ب، 2015 ب). ولكـن حـتى المبـادرات الأكاديميـة الفرديـة - بشـكل خـاص في نخبـة الجامعـات العربيـة الخاصـة – قـد واجهـت المعارضـة وعـدم التشـجيع بسـبب المصالـح المترسـخة للأكاديميـين الإعلاميـين العـرب التقليديـين الذيـن قاومـوا الإبداعـات الـتي تهـدد مجـال عملهـم وتشـبثوا بالنظريـات الإعلاميـة القديمـة الطـراز الـتي تعتـبر ثـورة الإعـلام الرقمـي مسـألة تافهـة. بالإضافـة إلى ذلـك، واجـه عـدد كبـير مـن الأكاديميـين العـرب الذيـن كان يمكـن ان يناصـروا التربيـة الرقميـة والإعلاميـة في جامعاتهـم نـدرة في مـواد المناهـج

57

الدراسية العربية، وغياب المرافق والتجهيزات اللازمة. وكان العديد منهم غير واثقين من مهاراتهم ومعارفهم ليتمكنوا من تنمية التربية الرقمية والإعلامية وتعليمها. في السنوات القليلة الماضية، أطلقت جهود متعددة لتعزيز التربية الرقمية والإعلامية في العالم العربي من قبل التحالفات الأكاديمية والمؤسسات الدولية، مثل الشبكة الجامعية للتربية الإعلامية والمعلوماتية والحوار بين الثقافات (MILID)، ومركز الدوحة لحرية الإعلام (DCMF)، وجمعية المعلمين الكويتية والمركز الكويتي للتربية الإعلامية (KCML). وقد كان لهذه الجهود الرائعة حتى الآن نتائج متفاوتة. إذ يبدو أن كلاً من مركز الدوحة لحرية الإعلام (DCMF)، والمركز الكويتي للتربية الإعلامية (KCML) هما ذات تركيز وطني إلا أنهما لم يحققا نتائج هامة، ملموسة وطويلة الأمد حتى الآن (أقام مركز الدوحة لحرية الإعلام DCMF برنامج توعية إشتمل على ورش عمل في الأردن والمغرب وغيرها من الدول). إلا أن الشبكة الجامعية للتربية الإعلامية والمعلوماتية والحوار بين الثقافات (MILID) تبقى المبادرة الدولية الواعدة التي نأمل أن تعطي ثمارها قريباً في المنطقة العربية.

انطلاق أكاديمية التربية الإعلامية والرقمية في بيروت (MDLAB)

من المبادرات المؤسسية الأخرى التي حاولت معالجة هذا الوضع وملء الفجوة هي المبادرة التي قامت بها أكاديمية التربية الإعلامية والرقمية في بيروت (MDLAB). وقد انطلقت أكاديمية التربية الإعلامية والرقمية في بيروت في عام 2013، برعاية مؤسسة المجتمع المفتوح (OSF)، وموقع «المونيتور» الإلكتروني، والجمعية العربية الأوروبية لباحثي الإعلام والاتصال (AREACORE) من خلال الهيئة الألمانية للتبادل العلمي، على يد مجموعة من الأكاديميين العرب والدوليين بهدف تطوير التربية الرقمية والإعلامية في المنطقة من خلال تدريب مدرسي الإعلام العرب وتطوير المناهج الدراسية في مجال التربية الرقمية والإعلامية، ليس فقط باللغة العربية، بل ايضاً من خلال التعمّق في الثقافات والاهتمامات العربية. إستناداً إلى نموذج أكاديمية سالزبورغ للإعلام والتغيير العالمي، وهي شراكة دولية من أكثر من اثني عشرة جامعة من مختلف أنحاء العالم، تنظم أكاديمية التربية الإعلامية والرقمية في بيروت أكاديمية صيفية سنوية تجمع 50 طالب دراسات عليا ومدرساً إعلامياً عربياً، بالإضافة إلى مدرّبين عرب ودوليين وخبراء في مجال التربية الإعلامية، لا سيما من شبكة أكاديمية سالزبورغ. كما تعمل الأكاديمية على مدار العام على تطوير المناهج، ودعم مبادرات التربية الإعلامية في المنطقة، وتعمل بمثابة مركز لشبكة من المدرّسين في مجال التربية الإعلامية العربية. وتشمل

مهام أكاديمية التربية الإعلامية والرقمية في بيروت خمسة أهداف على الشكل التالي:

(1) نشر المعرفة وتعليم التربية الرقمية والإعلامية وتعزيز أهميتها بين الجامعات العربية.

(2) تدريب المدربين الجامعيين العرب الشباب كل عام وتخريج طلاب الدراسات العليا الذين اكتسبوا المعارف في مفاهيم وكفاءات التربية الرقمية والإعلامية.

(3) تطوير مناهج جامعية سنوياً تشمل الخطط الدراسية، وحدات المناهج الدراسية، وكتيبات التدريب، ودراسة الحالات، ومحتوى الوسائط المتعددة.

(4) إنشاء مركز لشبكة من الجامعات الإقليمية ومدرّسي الإعلام تركز على تطوير التربية الرقمية والإعلامية وتعزيزها.

(5) إنشاء والحرص على استمرار فضاء مفتوح عبر الإنترنت بهدف نشر المواد الدراسية وربط خريجي الأكاديمية والمساهمين والمتعاونين المحتملين.

الأكاديمية

ظهرت فكرة أكاديمية التربية الإعلامية والرقمية في بيروت (MDLAB) أولاً كتوصية من المؤتمر السنوي للجمعية العربية الأمريكية لأساتذة الاتصال لعام 2011 (AUSACE) تحت عنوان «التربية الرقمية والإعلامية: الاتجاهات الجديدة» والدراسة العالمية لرسم الخرائط الرقمية التي ترعاها مؤسسة المجتمع المفتوح (ملكي،2012). أوصى المشروعان بتوسيع وتعميم التربية الرقمية والإعلامية في المنطقة العربية. من خلال توفير التدريب اللازم والموارد والمواد الدراسية، وتحفيز أعضاء هيئة التدريس لنقل ما تعلموه إلى مؤسساتهم، تهدف الأكاديمية الى نشر مثل هذه المعرفة في كافة الجامعات العربية، وخلق تأثير مضاعف. تركز أكاديمية التربية الإعلامية والرقمية في بيروت MDLAB بشكل أساسي على المعلمين المبتدئين وطلاب الدراسات العليا الذين يتمتعون بأعلى درجة من الإمكانات والمرونة لتعلم المهارات الرقمية المتقدمة، وتقبّل الأفكار المبتكرة، بالإضافة إلى كونها على اتصال وثيق مع أكبر مجموعة من السكان العرب الذين يقودون التغيير حالياً في المنطقة.

بعد ثلاث سنوات على إطلاق أكاديمية التربية الإعلامية والرقمية في بيروت MDLAB، بدأت نحو 24 جامعة عربية بتدريس التربية الرقمية والإعلامية في مجموعة متنوعة

مـن الأشـكال بنـاء عـلى مناهـج تـمّ تطويرهـا في الأكاديميـة. بعضهـا قـام بإدخـال دورات كاملـة. والبعـض الآخـر اسـتخدم النمـاذج لدمـج المفاهيـم والكفـاءات الرقميـة والإعلاميـة في الـدورات الإعلاميـة التقليديـة التـي يقدمهـا، فيمـا يواصـل المعركـة مـع الحكومـة والمؤسسـات البيروقراطيـة والعقبـات المضجـرة التـي أخـرت الموافقـة عـلى دورات التربيـة الرقميـة والإعلاميـة المسـتقلة. مـع ذلـك، تمكنـت اليـوم تسـع جامعـات عربيـة مـن تقديـم دورات كاملـة في مجـال التربيـة الرقميـة والاعلاميـة وهـي: جامعـة دمشـق، والجامعـة الأمريكيـة في الشـارقة، والجامعـة الأمريكيـة في بـيروت، وجامعـة الأهـرام الكنديـة، والجامعـة اللبنانيـة الأمريكيـة، وجامعـة رفيـق الحريـري، وجامعـة سـيدة اللويـزة، وجامعـة بيرزيـت، وجامعـة العـزم. ومـن المتوقـع أن يتضاعـف هـذا العـدد في العـام المقبـل، خصوصـاً بعـد موافقـة وزارة التربيـة العراقيـة عـلى منهـاج وطنـي مقـترح يتضمـن دورة إلزاميـة في التربيـة الرقميـة والإعلاميـة.

عـلى الرغـم مـن أن الأكاديميـة ركـزت في السـنتين الأوليـن عـلى البلـدان العربيـة الشرقيـة وبالتحديـد لبنـان وسـوريا وفلسـطين والأردن والعـراق، فقـد تضمنـت الأكاديميـة عـام 2015 مشـاركين مـن مـصر وعـمان واليمـن وقطـر والسـودان والإمـارات العربيـة المتحـدة وإيـران. وفي العـام نفسـه، شـملت أكاديميـة التربيـة الإعلاميـة والرقميـة في بـيروت MDLAB ثلاثـة مدرسـين مـن مدرسـة «إنترناشـونال كولـدج» في لبنـان، وهـي أول مدرسـة عربيـة تضـع التربيـة الإعلاميـة كواحـدة مـن أولوياتهـا الاسـتراتيجية. وتشـمل الخطـط المسـتقبلية التوسـع إلى بـاقي دول المنطقـة العربيـة، إضافـة المزيـد مـن المدرّسـين، والمشـاركين الدوليـن الآخريـن. ومـن أبـرز قـرارات أكاديميـة التربيـة الإعلاميـة والرقميـة في بـيروت MDLAB هـو التوصـل بحلـول نهايـة هـذا العقـد، إلى إقنـاع كل بلـد عـربي بأهميـة أن يتضمـن مدرسـة واحـدة أو جامعـة واحـدة عـلى الأقـل، تقـدم التربيـة الرقميـة والإعلاميـة كأحـد المناهـج الدراسـية الأساسـية.

المناهج الدراسية والوسائل المستخدمة

فيمـا يتعلـق بالمناهـج الدراسـية، وأسـاليب التدريـس والتعلـم، سـعت أكاديميـة التربيـة الإعلاميـة والرقميـة في بـيروت MDLAB لتخطـي التعريـف التقليـدي للتربيـة الإعلاميـة الـذي يعرّفهـا بأنهـا «القـدرة عـلى الوصـول الى وتحليـل وتقييـم وخلـق المـواد الإعلاميـة في مجموعـة متنوعـة مـن الأشـكال» (مركـز الثقافـة الإعلاميـة، 1992). مـن هـذا المنطلـق، تتخطـى التربيـة الرقميـة والإعلاميـة مهمـة تدريـب الطـلاب ليصبحـوا مسـتهلكين ناقديـن للاعـلام. وفي عـصر يتميـز بوفـرة إمكانـات الإعـلام الرقمـي والاتصـالات المعولمـة، تصبـح

التربيـة الرقميـة والإعلاميـة أساسـية للاسـتمرار في عصـر المعلومـات وأكـثر أهميـة لثقافاتنـا المعولمـة وأنظمتنـا الاقتصاديـة. وبالتالي، فـإن التربيـة الرقميـة والاعلاميـة تقـدم، ليـس فقـط الكفـاءات الضروريـة لقـراءة، وسـماع ومشـاهدة محتـوى الوسـائط المتنوعـة وتفسـير عقائدهـا الكامنـة، وتقييـم نواياهـا التسـويقية والدعائيـة المضمنـة، ونتائجهـا الضـارة الخفيـة؛ بـل إن التربيـة الرقميـة والاعلاميـة تسـمح ايضـاً بتمكيـن الأفـراد والمجتمعـات. وهي تسـاعد النـاس عـلى إدارة اسـتخداماتهم الإعلاميـة الخاصـة بـذكاء واسـتخدام أدوات الإعـلام الرقمـي والاجتماعـي بفعاليـة بهـدف التطويـر الشـخصي والمجتمعـي المشـترك، والانخـراط عـلى نحـو اسـتباق في المناقشـات العالميـة التعاونيـة والعمـل المـدني. كما تقـدم التربيـة الرقميـة والاعلاميـة المعرفـة والكفـاءات الضروريـة للأفـراد المهمشـين والمجتمعـات المحرومـة لتسـمح لهـا باسـتعادة المبـادرة وتحقيـق التـوازن بيـن صلاحيـات الأعمـال التجاريـة الكبيرة، والثـروة المركـزة، والأنظمـة السـلطوية السـائبة. «تعتبر التربيـة الرقميـة والاعلاميـة نوعـاً مـن الثقافـة الإعلاميـة للجماهير. إنهـا الثورة الصامتـة الـتي يمكنهـا مواجهـة أيديولوجيـات الجشـع والكراهيـة والمـوت والكفـاح مـن أجـل تعميـم العدالـة الاجتماعيـة ونظـم المسـاواة وعولمتهـا.» (ملـكي، 2015 ب). ويتنـاول منهـج أكاديميـة التربيـة الإعلاميـة والرقميـة في بـيروت MDLAB المواضيـع الاجتماعيـة والسياسـية والاقتصاديـة المتنوعـة، المتكاملـة مـع الكفـاءات الرقميـة الأساسـية والمهـارات البحثيـة، وكلهـا تسـترشد بالدراسـات الـتي تنظـر في الاسـتخدامات الإعلاميـة والنشـاط الرقمـي للشـباب العربـي والاضطرابـات ذات الصلـة بالإعـلام والاتجاهـات السـائدة في المنطقـة (حـتي، ملـكي، ومفـرج، 2014؛ ملـكي، 2013 أ، 2015 أ؛ ملـكي وملـاط، 2014 أ، 2014 ب، ملـكي، حـتي، أوغليـا، ومفـرج، 2014). وتشـمل النمـاذج المفاهيميـة الأساسـية تأثـيرات ملكيـة الـشركات والممارسـات التجاريـة عـلى الإنتـاج الإعلامـي، وسياسـة بنـاء الأخبـار والتحكـم بهـا، وقـدرة الصـور عـلى الإقنـاع، والدعايـة وآثارهـا المدمـرة عـلى صـورة الجسـم وتقديـر الـذات، والتمثيـل الإعلامـي للجنـس أو العـرق، والنشـاط الجنـسي، وتفسـير رسـائل ومؤسسـات الدعايـة.

يسـعى المنهـج إلى دمـج التحليـل الاعلامـي النقـدي مـع كفـاءات الانتـاج الرقمـي والمهـارات البحثيـة العلميـة بطريقـة سـهلة ومتماسـكة (ملـكي، 2013 أ). وتتضمـن المحـاضرات النظريـة في صميمهـا مجموعـة مـن الأسـاليب البحثيـة وورش عمـل في مجـال التكويـن الرقمـي تجسّـد كـلّ منهـا نظريـات التربيـة الإعلاميـة وتقـدم للطلاب مجموعـة واسـعة مـن التقنيـات المثـيرة للتعلـم والاسـتخدام بشـكل خـلاق. وتشـمل الكفـاءات الرقميـة والبحثيـة الأساسـية كلاً مـن المدونـات، والتلاعـب بالصـور والصـوت وتحريـر الفيديـو، والأرشـفة الرقميـة، والتحليـل

الاعلامـي المقـارن، وتحليـل الشـبكات الاجتماعيـة، والاسـتخدام الفعـال لأدوات البحـث الرقميـة. ويسـعى المنهـج جاهـداً لربـط كلّ مـن هـذه الكفـاءات الرقميـة والبحثيـة بمفاهيـم التربيـة الإعلاميـة النظريـة والنقديـة المطابقـة. علـى سـبيل المثـال، إن تعليـم خاصيـة التلاعـب بالصـور باسـتخدام التطبيقـات المجانيـة مثـل تطبيـق «بيكسـلر» لمعالجـة الصـور يرتبـط ارتباطـاً وثيقـاً بالمحاضـرات المتعلّقـة بقـوة الصـور فـي الأخبـار وتمثيـل الجسـم فـي مجـال الإعلانـات، فـي حيـن ان تعلـم الأرشـفة الرقميـة والحفـظ والتحليـل المقـارن بواسـطة تطبيقـات مثـل «سـتوريفاي» و«ميوغـراف» يرتبـط بالـدروس المتعلّقـة ببنـاء الأخبـار ودور الإعـلام فـي الحـرب. وفـي حيـن يتـمّ تعليـم مفاهيـم التربيـة الإعلاميـة النظريـة والنقديـة مـن خـلال سلسـلة مـن المحاضـرات والمناقشـات التـي يديرهـا عـدد مـن الأكاديميين المشـهورين فـي مجـال التربيـة الرقميـة والإعلاميـة، قـام فريـق مـن خبـراء إنتـاج الإعـلام الرقمـي ويطلـق عليهـا اسـم «الفرقـة الرقميـة» بـإدارة ورش العمـل الإعلاميـة الرقميـة. وتعتمـد ورش العمـل الرقميـة علـى نهـج تعلـم مصمّـم بعنايـة ويرتكـز علـى أربعـة مبـادئ توجيهيـة: العـروض السـمعية؛ التوجيـه المباشـر، التماريـن غيـر الخطيـة، وتقنيـات دعـم التعلّـم (ملكـي، 2013 أ). وتسـمح طريقـة التعليـم غيـر الخطيـة للمشـاركين الذيـن يتمتعـون بمسـتوى أعلـى مـن المهـارات التقنيـة اللازمـة بالانتقـال إلـى مهمـة مختلفـة فيمـا ينتظـرون مسـاعدة المعلـم، الأمـر الـذي يوفـر الوقـت ويقلـل مـن مسـتويات الإحبـاط. بالإضافـة إلـى ذلـك، يمكـن لهـؤلاء المشـاركين المتقدميـن تقديـم مسـاعدة كبيـرة خـلال ورشـة العمـل. كلمـا انجـز أحـد المشـاركين التمريـن بسـرعة، نقـوم بتوكيلـه / او توكيلهـا لمسـاعدة المشـاركين الآخريـن خـلال التمريـن، الامـر الـذي يتيـح أيضـاً للمشـاركين فرصـة اختبـار مهاراتـه / مهاراتهـا فـي التعليـم. تبـدأ ورشـة العمـل الرقميـة عـادة بمحاضـرة تسـتغرق 15 دقيقـة حـول تنسـيقات الصـوت الرقميـة ومفهـوم تقنيـة تدفـق البيانـات التـي تسـتخدمها تطبيقـات البـث. بعدهـا، تقـدم الفرقـة الرقميـة عرضـاً قصيـراً عـن كيفيـة اسـتخدام تطبيقـات تسـجيل الصـوت الرقميـة، مثـل تطبيـق «أوداسـيتي»، لتسـجيل وتحريـر واصـدار الملفـات الصوتيـة. بعـد ذلـك مباشـرة، يقـوم المشـاركون بتمريـن خطـي يرشـدهم خطـوة بخطـوة الـى كيفيـة انجـاز مهمـة محـددة، مثـل اعـداد مقابلـة صوتيـة مدتهـا 60 ثانيـة مرفـق بتصريـح مسـجّل واحـد. يتـم نشـر التعليمـات المكتوبـة بالتفصيـل علـى الانترنـت مـع كافـة المناهـج الدراسـية والمحاضـرات والتدريبـات التـي تـم إعدادهـا فـي الأكاديميـة للاسـتخدام مـن قبـل المشـاركين فـي المسـتقبل عندمـا يخططـون لتعليـم التربيـة الرقميـة والإعلاميـة فـي جامعاتهـم. وقـد تـم تطويـر نهـج التدريـس والتعليـم التكاملـي هـذا واختبـاره علـى مـدى

عـدة سنوات، بالتعـاون مـع أكاديميـين دوليـين ضمـن دائـرة أكاديميـة سـالزبورغ (بـول ميهايليديـس، 2011، 2014؛ موسى شوماو، 2014). ولطالما أثبتت هـذه الطـرق أنها واعـدة:

يستند الدمج الفعال للمهـارات الرقميـة والبحثيـة في الإعـلام وتعليـم النقـد الإعلامـي عـلى مهارات القراءة النقديـة الـتي تنتجهـا فصـول التربيـة الإعلاميـة التقليديـة، وتساعد الطـلاب عـلى الانتقـال مـن مجـرد مستهلكين للإعـلام الى منتجـين بارعـين ودقيقـين للمعلومـات والمعرفة بغيـة تحويلهـم الى مواطنـين عالميـين نافذيـن، يشـاركون في مناقشـات هامـة وقادريـن عـلى الانتظـام ضمـن شبكات تتمتـع بوضـع ملائم لتغيـير المجتمعـات والمناطـق وتعزيـز أوضاع الأفـراد المهمشـين والجماعـات المحرومـة مـن حقوقهـا. (ملـي، 2013 أ)

الاستناد الى التجارب

ساهم العمل الجاد الـذي قام بـه المشاركون في أكاديميـة التربيـة الإعلاميـة والرقميـة في بـيروت MDLAB بمساعدتنا عـلى إعـادة تركيـز المناهـج والتعامـل بشـكل أفضـل مـع أولويـات المجتمعـات العربيـة. وبفضـل ردود الفعـل الواسعـة مـن المشاركين خـلال جلسـات النقـاش ومجموعـات التركيـز، يتضمـن المنهـج الأساسي حاليـاً موضوعـات مثـل الإعـلام والإرهـاب، والطائفيـة والتطـرف والحـرب؛ ويشـدد عـلى حقـوق الإنسـان والتسامـح والنشـاط المـدني والمواطنـة العالميـة. وتشمل التوصيـات الأخـرى تعزيـز عناصـر التدريـب عـلى تحليـل الشبكات الاجتماعيـة، والبحـوث في مجـال الإعـلام الرقمـي، وكفـاءات التعامـل مـع البيانـات، بالاضافـة الى فـرص التواصـل والأنشطـة المستمـرة عـلى مـدار السنـة، مثـل المؤتمـرات وورش العمـل القصـيرة الـتي تنفـذ في حـرم كل جامعـة مشـاركة. علاوة عـلى ذلـك، توفـر الأكاديميـة أنشطـة مدروسـة في مجـال الدمـج الاجتماعـي، بالاضافـة الى رحـلات ثقافيـة وفعاليـات للتواصـل لمساعـدة المشاركين مـن مختلـف البلـدان والثقافـات عـلى فهـم وبنـاء علاقـات طويلـة الأمـد. قمنـا بتعزيـز مثـل هـذه النشاطـات بعـد الأكاديميـة الاولى، عندمـا لاحظنـا المشاركين يتجمعـون في مجموعـات وطنيـة وحتـى طائفيـة، في حيـن لـم تشهـد المجموعـات سـوى القليـل مـن التفاعـل.

خـلال تلـك السنـة الأولى، سجّلت حالـة واحـدة عـلى الأقـل لتعـرض بعـض المشاركين الى السخريـة مـن قبـل أفـراد ينتمـون الى جماعـة وطنيـة أخـرى. وقـد تمّت معالجـة تلـك المسألـة بشـكل فعـال في الأكاديميـة التاليـة مـن خـلال الحـرص عـلى أن يتضمـن كل فريـق عمـل - وكذلـك الزمـلاء في غـرف الفنـدق - مشـاركين مـن مختلـف البلـدان ومـن خـلال تنظيـم عـدة «لقـاءات تعـارف سريعـة»، حيـث يمضي المشاركون بعـض الوقـت للقـاء أشخـاص آخريـن للاستفسـار عـن حياتهـم وخلفياتهـم المهنيـة. كمـا أصبحـت عمليـة اختيـار مقدمـي

الطلبات أشد صرامة في السنتين الثانية والثالثة، بما في ذلك المقابلات الهاتفية التي تطرح الأسئلة حول الانفتاح على الثقافات الأخرى والتسامح وتقبل الفوارق. من الأمور التي ساهمت أيضاً في تحسين نوعية المشاركين بشكل كبير، كانت الزيادة في مجموع الطلبات المقدمة من أقل من 70 في السنة الأولى (معدل القبول 70 بالمائة) إلى أكثر من 200 في السنة الثالثة (معدل القبول 25 بالمائة). ونتوقع مزيداً من التحسن في هذا المجال، كما نتوقع أن يتخطى عدد مقدمي الطلبات الـ250 في السنة الرابعة، مع مواصلة الأكاديمية بناء سمعة قوية إقليمياً ودولياً ومع إزدياد نسبة دورات التربية الرقمية والإعلامية في الجامعات العربية. لكن أهداف أكاديمية التربية الإعلامية والرقمية في بيروت MDLAB على المدى الطويل في المنطقة لا تزال بعيدة المنال. ومع أن تعزيز تدريس دورات التربية الرقميو والإعلامية في الجامعات العربية يشكّل خطوة إيجابية في الاتجاه الصحيح إلا أنها لا تزال غير كافية. وينبغي ان تكون مناهج الصحافة والاعلام العربية والمناهج الاتصالات - بغض النظر عن الاختصاص - متجذرة في النظريات والمفاهيم ومهارات التربية الرقمية والإعلامية. سواء كان التخصص هو الصحافة أو الإعلان أو العلاقات العامة، أو العلوم السياسية أو العلوم الصحية أو أي من التخصصات الفرعية الأخرى في هذا المجال، ينبغي أن تضمّ كافة الدورات والمناهج مفاهيم التربية الإعلامية الأساسية ومهارات التربية الرقمية التطبيقية. على سبيل المثال، ينبغي ألا يكون تدريس الإعلان خالياً من التدريس النقدي حول الآثار السلبية للإعلان والنزعة الاستهلاكية على المجتمع. ويجب على التدريب الصحفي أن يشتمل على مهارات صحافة المواطن الرائعة وصحافة البيانات، والنشاط الرقمي، فضلاً عن أحدث المعارف بشأن استراتيجيات وتكتيكات الدعاية، خاصة تلك المستخدمة في الحروب والنزاعات من قبل المتطرفين والإرهابيين. وينبغي ان تكون الأسئلة المرتبطة بالنوع والجنس والعرق والدين جزءاً لا يتجزأ من أي تدريب على التواصل والأبحاث، في حين ينبغي على المشاركة المدنية والمواطنة العالمية، والعدالة الاجتماعية والتسامح أن تكون مرشداً للأهداف. بالإضافة إلى ذلك، لا يمكن أن تكون التربية الرقمية والإعلامية متوفرة لمجموعة صغيرة من الطلاب الذين يستطيعون الحصول على تعليم جامعي. نحن بحاجة إلى توفير دورات متصلة بالانترنت وغير متصلة وورش عمل سهلة المنال باللغة العربية للوصول إلى جمهور أوسع. أكثر من ذلك، تحتاج التربية الرقمية والإعلامية إلى الانتقال إلى المدارس، وصولاً الى التعليم الابتدائي وما بعده. نحن بحاجة إلى تطوير مجموعة مترابطة من المعلمين والأكاديميين والباحثين القادرين على نقل التعليم والأبحاث في مجال التربية الرقمية والإعلامية إلى المستوى التالي.

المراجع

- مركز الثقافة الإعلامية. (1992). تقرير أسبن حول مؤتمر التربية الإعلامية. متوفر على الرابط التالي: http://www.medialit.org/reading-room/what-media-literacy- definitionand-more

- إ. حتي؛ ج. ملكي؛ ع. مفرج. (2014). انتشار ومحددات استخدام المنشطات بين مرتادي مراكز اللياقة البدنية في لبنان. مجلة «سبورت ميد» الدولية، 15 (4)، 391-401.

- آر. هوبز (1998). سبعة مناقشات كبيرة في حركة التربية الإعلامية. مجلة الاتصالات، 48 (1)، 16-32.

- بي. آر. جونز كافالييه؛ وإس. إل فلانيغان (2006). الربط بين النقاط الرقمية: الثقافة في القرن الحادي والعشرين. منشورة منظمة «إديوكوس» الفصلية، 2.

- إس. ليفينغستون (2004). التربية الإعلامية وتحدي تكنولوجيا المعلومات والاتصالات الجديدة. مجلة «كوميونيكايشن ريفيو»، 7، 3/14.

- ج. ملكي (2009). الصحافة والدراسات الإعلامية في لبنان. دراسات الصحافة، 10 (5)، 672-690.

- ج. ملكي (2011). محنة التربية الإعلامية والبحوث في مجال التعليم العالي العربي. في تقرير الدكتور شي كيم شونغ، بحوث في التربية الإعلامية (ص 83-108). نيويورك: نوفا ساينس.

- جاد ملكي (2013 أ). دمج منهجيات البحوث المعمّقة والمهارات الرقمية مع مناهد التربي الإعلامية التربوية. في تقرير بول ميهاليديس، التربية الإعلامية: وجهات نظر عالمية لغرفة الأخبار والصفوف (ص 139-160). سلسلة الاعلام ووسائل الاتصال الجماهيري، نيويورك، دار بيتر لانج للنشر.

- ج. ملكي (2013 ب). نشر بذور التربية الرقمية والإعلامية في لبنان والعالم العربي: أهمية المنهج المحلي والمستدام. تقرير ب. دي أبرو و ب. ميهاليديس، التربية الإعلامية في العمل: وجهات النظر النظرية والتربوية. روتليدج.

- ج. ملكي (2015 أ). توجيه تطوير التربية الرقمية والإعلامية في المناهج العربية من خلال فهم استخدامات الإعلام من الشباب العربي. مجلة التربية الإعلامية، 6 (3)، 14-28.

- ج. ملكي (2015 أ). التربية الإعلامية تقدم للعالم العربي سبيلاً للمضي قدماً. الفنار.

- http://www.al-fanarmedia.org/2015/07/media-literacy-offers-the-arab-world-a-way-forward/

- ج. ملكي؛ ي. ي. الدبوس؛ ن. خالد، وسارة ملاط (2012). رسم خريطة الإعلام الرقمي: لبنان. في رسم خريطة الإعلام الرقمي، دراسة قطرية متعددة، تقرير ببرنامج مؤسسة المجتمع المفتوح الإعلامي. متوفر على الرابط التالي: -www.opensocietyfoun dations.org

- ج. ملكي؛ إ. حتي؛ م. أوغيا؛ وع. مفرج (2014). التعرض الإعلامي، مقارنة اجتماعية مؤثرة مع الصور المثالية لقوة العضلات، واستخدام المنشطات. «هيلث كوميونيكايشن»، 30 (5)، 473-84

- ج. ملكي؛ وس. ملاط (2014 أ). إمنعوا دخولها، وأعيقوا تطورها، وادفعوها للخروج: التمييز بين الجنسين والتحرش الجنسي، والبيئة القانونية والاجتماعية المعطلة التي تواجه الصحفيات في العالم العربي. دراسات في الصحافة، 17 (1).

- ج. ملكي؛ وس. ملاط (2014 ب). النشاط الرقمي: كفاءات وأعباء الإعلام الرقمي والاجتماعي على النشاط المدني. وسائل الإعلام العربية والمجتمع (طبعة خاصة)، 19 (الخريف).

- ب. ميهايليديس (2009). ما وراء السخرية: التربية الإعلامية ونتائج التعليم المدني في الجامعة. المجلة الدولية للإعلام والتعليم 1، (3).

- ب. ميهايليديس (2011). إتقان فن الأخبار: وجهات نظر عالمية لغرفة الأخبار والصفوف الدراسية. نيويورك: دار بيتر لانج للنشر.

- بول ميهايليديس (2014). التربية الإعلامية والمواطن الناشئ: إشراك الشباب والمشاركة في الثقافة الرقمية. نيويورك: دار بيتر لانج للنشر.

- موسى شوماو (2014). المجتمعات الإعلامية: الأصوات المدنية والتمكين والتربية الإعلامية في العصر الرقمي. نيويورك: دار بيتر لانج للنشر

لمحة عامة عن التربية الإعلامية والمعلوماتية في الأراضي الفلسطينية المحتلة

لوسي نسيبة ومحمد أبو عرقوب

مقدمة:

يعطي هـذا المقال لمحـة موجـزة عـن حالـة التربيـة الإعلاميـة والمعلوماتيـة في الأراضي الفلسطينية المحتلـة، ويلقي في البدايـة نظـرة سـريعة عـلى هـذا المفهـوم، بمـا في ذلـك السـبب الـذي يجعـل مـن الضروري أن يكـون مركبـاً، ولـم ينبغي أن يكـون التركيـز عـلى التمكيـن. كما يركـز هـذا الفصل عـلى التربيـة الإعلاميـة والمعلوماتيـة بـين السـكان الفلسـطينيين في كلّ مـن الضفـة الغربيـة وقطـاع غـزة (الأراضي الفلسطينية المحتلـة)، بما في ذلك القدس الشرقية، وبـين طلاب المـدارس والجامعـات، وبين الناس بشكل عـام. كما ينظـر هـذا الفصل أيضاً بشـكل وجيز الى السـياق الإعلامي العـام والوضـع، وأنشطة التربيـة الإعلاميـة والمعلوماتيـة المختلفـة، والاحتياجـات الأكـثر إلحاحـاً بالنسـبة للسـكان الفلسـطينيين فيمـا يتعلـق بالتربيـة الإعلاميـة والمعلوماتيـة.

التربية الإعلامية والمعلوماتية كمفهوم

التربيـة الإعلاميـة والمعلوماتيـة مفهـوم ذو اتجاهـين. وهـو يتضمـن التثقيـف حول كيفيـة العمـل الإعلامي، وكيـف يمكـن التلاعـب بالعواطـف والصـور، وكيـف يمكـن العمـل بنشـاط مـع وسـائل الأعـلام وبشـكل خـاص الإعـلام الجديـد والتكنولوجيـا. بالإضافة الى ذلـك، إن التربيـة الإعلاميـة والمعلوماتيـة تعتـبر موضوعـاً لا يـزال في طـور التسـوية، ولا يـزال تعريفـه ونطاقـه يشـكلان محـور نقاشـات سـاخنة. لكن إن نظرنـا اليهـا كمفهـوم مركـب، يضـم التكنولوجيـا (التربيـة المعلوماتيـة أو التثقيـف المعلومـاتي) جنبـاً إلى جنب مـع المهـارات التحليليـة (التربيـة الإعلاميـة أو التثقيـف الإعلامي)، فهـي تجمـع مـا هـو ضروري للمشـاركة الكاملـة في عالـم اليـوم. مـن حيـث المبـادىء التوجيهيـة للسياسـة والاسـتراتيجية ا المعتمـدة مـن قبـل منظمـة الأمـم المتحـدة للتربيـة والعلـم والثقافـة (اليونسكو)، فـإن

التربية الإعلامية والمعلوماتية، «هي الأساس لتعزيز الوصول إلى المعلومات والمعرفة، وحرية التعبير، وجودة التعليم. وهي تصف المهارات والمواقف اللازمة لتقييم وظائف مقدمي المواد الإعلامية وغيرها من المعلومات، بما في ذلك تلك المتوفرة على شبكة الإنترنت، وفي المجتمعات؛ وإيجاد وتقييم المعلومات والمحتوى الإعلامي وإنتاجها. بتعبير آخر، تشمل التربية الإعلامية والمعلوماتية الكفاءات الحيوية للناس التي تخوّل الناس المشاركة بفعالية في كافة جوانب التنمية.»

ومع انتشار وسائل الإعلام المختلفة خلال السنوات العشرين الماضية، كذلك انتشرت تسميات وأشكال مختلفة من التثقيف، مثل تعليم الإعلام الرقمي والتثقيف في مجال الإنترنت، والتثقيف في كجال شبكات التواصل الاجتماعي؛ وتترافق التعابير الجديدة مع التطورات الجديدة في مجال التكنولوجيا. ويمكن أن تُعتبر كل هذه المجالات جزءاً من المظلة الشاملة للتربية الإعلامية والمعلوماتية ii. وفي حين تتعارض التربية الإعلامية أحياناً مع التربية المعلوماتية أو تعليم الإعلام الرقمي، والتي تتركز بشكل خاص على المهارات والملاحة عبر الإنترنت، فإنها مزيج هذين النوعين هو الذي يحتوي على معظم القوة. وتوفر ورقة اليونسكو الخاصة بسياسة واستراتيجية التربية الإعلامية والمعلوماتية تفاصيل واضحة عن كيفية الدمج بين المفهومين المنفصلين: «تركز التربية المعلوماتية على أغراض التعامل مع المعلومات وعملية الإطلاع iii.

«في حين يركز مفهوم التربية المعلوماتية على مستخدم المعلومات بوصفه صانع قرار مستقل، ومواطن ومتعلم، فإن التربية الإعلامية تنظر في السبل التي بواسطتها تساهم البيئة الإعلامية بتسهيل وتغيير وتمكين التعامل مع المعلومات وعملية الاتصال أو تقييدها احياناً؛ سواء كان ذلك لصالح التعلم المتعمد أو غير المباشر، المشاركة الاجتماعية أو لمجرد التسلية » iv.

في حالة الأراضي الفلسطينية المحتلة، «التربية المعلوماتية» أكثر حضوراً كما أنها معروفة أكثر من «التربية الإعلامية» أو من المفهوم المركب أي «التربية الإعلامية والمعلوماتية». على سبيل المثال، في حالة المكتبات، فإن التدريب يجري على التربية المعلوماتية: «التغيرات في التكنولوجيا تترك تأثيراً كبيراً على المكتبات وبرامج التعليم الخاصة بها. هذه التغييرات تفرض ان تصبح برامج التربية المعلوماتية للمستخدمين أكثر فعالية وكفاءة ومستقلة في بحثها عن المعلومات.» ثمة تقدير عام لأهمية التربية المعلوماتية: تقدم كافة الجامعات الفلسطينية والبالغ عددها 13 جامعة دورات في مجال تكنولوجيا المعلومات والاتصالات، كما يفعل العديد من كليات المجتمع الأصغر، و في المناهج

الدراسة الفلسطينية المعدلة، يُفترض أن تتضمن الصفوف الممتدة من الصف الخامس الى العاشر تعليم التكنولوجيا كجزء من منهج تعليم مجالات العلوم والتكنولوجيا والهندسة والرياضيات الشامل «STEM».

إلا أن المفهوم المركب للتربية الإعلامية والمعلوماتية، مع التركيز على عنصر المعلوماتية، هو الأكثر ملاءمة للأراضي الفلسطينية المحتلة، الأمة التي، بغض النظر عن وضع الاحتلال الطويل والمحبط (وأيضاً بسببه في الواقع) ، تحتاج إلى المضي قدماً نحو التحول إلى مجتمع التعلم، يتمتع بقاعدة معرفة، من أجل بناء ديمقراطية قابلة للحياة. «عندما يتم جمعهما، من الملاحظ ان التربية الإعلامية والمعلوماتية لا تتفاعلان فحسب، بل تضيفان القيمة في تعزيز المشاركة في مجتمعات المعرفة المستقبلية.»

بالإضافة إلى النقاش حول التعبير الفعلي، (أي نوع من التثقيف؟)، حصل جدل كبير حول ما إذا كانت التربية الإعلامية والمعلوماتية وقائية أو عامل تمكين (استباقية). ويمكن أن ينظر إليها على أنها وقائية حيث يتعلم الناس من خلالها تحليل المحتوى الإعلامي وقراءة ما بين السطور، وفهم الرسائل وراء الصور، ليصبحوا بالتالي أقل تأثراً ولا يتحولوا الى فريسة سهلة. هذا يتعلق بشكل خاص بالأطفال والإعلام، حيث تميل الأبحاث إلى التركيز على التأثيرات السلبية المحتملة، او حتى على مخاطر الإعلام غير المعالج والمعدّل. لكن عنصر التمكين الاستباقيالذي يميز التربية الإعلامية والمعلوماتية هو ما يجعله ضرورياً لكافة قطاعات المجتمع. على سبيل المثال، تصف رينيه هوبس من جامعة رود آيلاند كيف: «نتطلع إلى التربية الإعلامية والرقمية لمساعدتنا على التعاطي بشكل أعمق مع الأفكار والمعلومات لاتخاذ القرارات والمشاركة في الحياة الثقافية.»

تعتبر التربية الإعلامية والمعلوماتية عنصر تمكين استباقي حيث تعلم الناس على القراءة، والاستماع، والمشاهدة، وربما التفاعل، باستخدام مقاربة نقدية نشطة، وليس مجرد التقبل السلبي. كما تعتبر ايضاً استباقية بحيث تعلم الناس العمل بشكل خلاق - ليس كفنين، لكن مرة أخرى فيما يتعلق بالمحتوى، لكي يتمكنوا من اختيار وتطوير وإنتاج الرسائل الإعلامية الخاصة بهم.

مرة أخرى، تلخص اليونسكو الموضوع بشكل جيد:

«إن 'الوجود الكلي والشامل' للمعلومات والإعلام، والإنترنت ومقدمي المعلومات الآخرين، يتطلب تركيزاً أكبر لتمكين المواطنين من خلال الحرص على امتلاكهم المهارات

والمواقف والمعارف التي تمكنهم من التفاعل بشكل انتقادي وفعال مع المحتوى في كافة أشكال وسائل الإعلام ومع جميع مزودي المعلومات. بالتالي، يشترط العصر الرقمي التحول من نهج «الحماية فقط» إلى التركيز على تمكين المواطن. هذا لا يوحي بالضرورة أنه ينبغي التخلي كلياً عن الحماية، مثل سلامة استخدام الإنترنت؛ بل ينبغي التركيز على التمكين بشكل خاص. التركيز على الحماية فقط قد يؤدي إلى فرض قيود مفرطة على وسائل الإعلام وغيرها من مقدمي المعلومات. وعلاوة على ذلك، فإن الأطفال الذين لا يكتسبون الكفاءات التي تسمح لهم بانتقاد وسائل الإعلام والمعلومات سيكونون أكثر عرضة للتأثيرات السلبية المحتملة للمعلومات والمحتوى الإعلامي وأقل استعداداً للاستفادة من الفرص عندما يصبحون بالغين.» viii

من خلال تشجيع زيادة وعي القوى المجتمعية المختلفة، مثل مالكي وسائل الإعلام، والأعمال التجارية، والمصالح الخاصة، تساهم برامج التربية الإعلامية والمعلوماتية بتشجيع المشاركة المدنية.

«المواطن هو نقطة الانطلاق في برامج التربية الإعلامية والمعلوماتية. من خلال معالجة وضع المواطن، تحظى التربية الإعلامية والمعلوماتية بالدعم من حقوق الإنسان.» مع ذلك، لا ينظر الى الناس على انهم غير نشطين من منظور التربية الإعلامية والمعلوماتية، بل إنهم يشاركون بشكل نشط في بناء واقعهم الخاص. وبالتالي، يصبح الغرض من التربية الإعلامية والمعلوماتية هو تمكين الناس من المشاركة الفعالة في تحديد الظروف التي يعيشون فيها.» ix

أكثر من ذلك، تصبح التربية الإعلامية والمعلوماتية محركاً للتمكين بحد ذاتها. «ثمة أدلة قوية تدعم فرضية أنه في حال حصلت فئة الشباب على تثقيف إعلامي أكبر وإمكانية الوصول إلى شبكة الإنترنت، سوف تستخدم هذه الوسائل للحصول على معلومات عن المواضيع السياسية والعامة والتعبير عن وجهات نظرهم بشأنها.» x

شكّل الأمثلة على مشاريع التربية الإعلامية (التثقيف الإعلامي) في الأراضي الفلسطينية المحتلة، مثل تلك التي تعلّم الأطفال أن يكتسبوا «الذكاء الإعلامي» أو تعزيز سيادة القانون، أو الفيديو التشاري، كلها أمثلة على التربية الإعلامية والمعلوماتية كأداة تمكين. إن التربية الإعلامية والمعلوماتية كعنصر حماية يمكن أن تسهم في التوعية بشأن التلاعب بالكلمات والصور والدعاية العامة، مما يوفر بعض الحماية ضد التلاعب، وضد سياسة الترويع ونشر الانقسام؛ على الرغم من أن هذه الأمور تشكّل أيضاً نوعاً من التمكين. إلا ان المبالغة في إعتماد النهج الوقائي قد يشكّل قيداً آخر على الحياة المقيدة بالفعل،

التي تفتقر إلى حقوق الإنسان.

إن عنصري الحماية والتمكين هي ذات صلة في سياق النزاع. وتتيح التربية الإعلامية والمعلوماتية «التنوع والحوار والتسامح». xi بالإضافة الى ذلك، يمكن أيضاً إعتبار التربية الإعلامية والمعلوماتية عنصراً هاماً لبناء السلام لأنها تساهم بتشكيل الوعي الذاتي ووعي الآخرين والوعي بشأن التحيز والتنميط، وبالتالي بناء مقاومة لها، وعموما للدعاية. xii

لمحة موجزة عن الوضع السياسي والمشهد الإعلامي:

تطلق تسمية الأراضي الفلسطينية المحتلة على القدس الشرقية والضفة الغربية وقطاع غزة)، التي تبلغ مساحتها نحو 6.220 كيلومتر مربع، وعدد سكانها أكثر من 4.5 مليون نسمة في عام 2014 (منهم 2.790.000 في الضفة الغربية، بما في ذلك القدس الشرقية، و1.760.000 في قطاع غزة) منهم ما يقرب من 70 بالمائة تقل أعمارهم عن 30 عاماً. xiii منذ حزيران 1967، وطوال نحو 50 عاماً، يعيش الفلسطينيون في الضفة الغربية وقطاع غزة تحت نير الاحتلال العسكري الإسرائيلي، وفي القدس الشرقية، التي ضمتها اسرائيل، يخضع الفلسطينيون أيضاً مباشرة للقوانين الإسرائيلية. تحتفظ إسرائيل بالسيطرة على كل جانب من جوانب حياة الفلسطينيين.

يلخص مكتب الأمم المتحدة لتنسيق الشؤون الإنسانية (أوتشا) الوضع الحالي للشؤون للفلسطينيين في الأراضي الفلسطينية المحتلة بما يلي: xiv

يستمر «المدنيون الفلسطينيون الذين يعيشون في الأراضي الفلسطينية المحتلة في تحمل وطأة الصراع الدائر والاحتلال الإسرائيلي. وقد أدى عدم احترام القانون الدولي الإنساني وحقوق الإنسان الى أزمة حماية ذات عواقب إنسانية وخيمة وسلبية. في قطاع غزة، تواصل إسرائيل فرض حصار بري وبحري وجوي، تسبّب في تقويض سبل العيش إلى حد كبير، وأدى الى تضاؤل نوعية، وإمكانية الوصول إلى الخدمات الأساسية بشكل خطير؛ الأمر الذي يمثل عقاباً جماعياً لسكان قطاع غزة. أما في الضفة الغربية، فإن القدس الشرقية معزولة عن باقي الضفة الغربية. ويواجه سكان المناطق المصنّفة (ج) مجموعة من الضغوط، بما في ذلك أعمال الهدم، والعنف من قبل المستوطنين، والقيود المفروضة على حرية الحركة والتنقل، التي تجعل تلبية الاحتياجات الأساسية أكثر فأكثر صعوبة وتهدد الوجود الفلسطيني في المنطقة. أما البدو المزارعين والرعاة، فهم عاجزون ومغلوب على أمرهم بشكل خاص. ويشكل نشاط الاستيطان الإسرائيلي

غير المشروع أساس الكثير من الصعوبات الإنسانية التي تواجه الفلسطينيين في الضفة الغربية. بشكل عام، أدى انتشار عدم المساءلة عن انتهاكات حقوق الإنسان والقانون الإنساني، إلى جانب الفشل في تطبيق سيادة القانون بشكل فعال عندما يتعلق الأمر بالهجمات على الفلسطينيين وممتلكاتهم من قبل القوات العسكرية الإسرائيلية أو المستوطنين الإسرائيليين، أدى الى خلق جو من الإفلات من العقاب الذي يسهم في مزيد من العنف ».

أ) تاريخ :

صدرت اول صحيفة فلسطينية في 18 سبتمبر 1908، xv بعد الحصول على ترخيص من الحكام العثمانيين، تبعتها سريعاً تراخيص لصالح 15 صحيفة ومجلة أخرى. عدا التوقف الوجيز خلال الحرب العالمية الأولى، واصلت وسائل الإعلام التطور والازدهار أولاً تحت حكم العثمانيين ثم تحت الانتداب البريطاني (1922-1948). وفي مارس 1936، تم إطلاق أول محطة إذاعية، حملت اسم «هنا القدس» (This is Jerusalem Calling). من عام 1948 إلى عام 1967، كان قطاع غزة تحت سيطرة مصر، وكانت الضفة الغربية لنهر الأردن تحت سيطرة الأردن، واستمرت وسائل الإعلام بالعمل تحت رعاية كل منهما، فيما شكّلت بقية المناطق الفلسطينية التي كانت تحت الانتداب البريطاني الدولة الإسرائيلية.

انتهت حرب الأيام الستة في يونيو 1967، بانتصار إسرائيل واستيلائها على الضفة الغربية وقطاع غزة، وكذلك شبه جزيرة سيناء المصرية ومرتفعات الجولان السورية. وفرضت اسرائيل الاحتلال العسكري على الضفة الغربية وقطاع غزة وضمت القدس الشرقية، وقامت بتضييق الخناق على وسائل الإعلام الفلسطينية. في عام 1968، سمح بالصدور لعدد من الصحف، مثل صحيفة القدس، والشعب، والنهار والفجر، المطبوعة في القدس وتمثل مختلف الفصائل الفلسطينية، لكن بعد خضوعها لرقابة شديدة، ما كان يؤدي الى صدور تلك الصحف مع فراغات كبيرة على صفحاتها. xvi ولم يُسمح لمحطات التلفزيون والاذاعة الفلسطينية بالعمل. بالتالي، وقبل إنتشار إمكانية الوصول الى الأقمار الصناعية على نطاق واسع، كان الفلسطينيون الرازحين تحت الاحتلال يشاهدون التلفزيون الأردني أو الاسرائيلي بشكل عام. إلا أنهم كانوا يتمتعون بالوصول إلى مجموعة واسعة من الإذاعات العالمية، والكثير من المجلات الشهرية، بما في ذلك تلك التي تنشر في إسرائيل. xvii

بالإضافة الى ذلك، كانت وسائل الإعلام الأقل تقليدية بارزة أيضاً. خلال «الانتفاضة» الفلسطينية ضد الاحتلال الاسرائيلي في عام 1987، كانت الوسيلة الإعلامية الرئيسة التي تعطي تعليماتها لأشكال المقاومة غير العنيفة (مثل أفضل يوم للإضراب، أي ساعة ينبغي أن تغلق المتاجر...) وتقود الانتفاضة، هي المنشورات التي كانت توزع باسم «القيادة الوطنية الموحدة للانتفاضة». كما استخدمت الكتابة على الجدران أيضاً في تلك المرحلة، ولا تزال جزءاً من المشهد الإعلامي الفلسطيني الى حد كبير، وتعبّر بشكل عام عن الانتماء السياسي.

كان لا بد من الانتظار حتى ما بعد اتفاقات أوسلو للسلام عام 1993 و 1995، لتنال محطات الإذاعة والتلفزيون الفلسطينية الحق بالعمل. هذه المرة، وبمعزل عن الصحف الأصلية، سمح لها بالعمل فقط في الضفة الغربية وقطاع غزة وليس في القدس، كما لم يسمح للسلطة الفلسطينية بالعمل في القدس. على الرغم من الانتشار السريع لوسائل الإعلام، لا يزال الوضع معقداً فيما يتعلق بحرية التعبير، والترددات، وغيرها من المسائل الأساسية الأخرى، ولا يزال بشكل أساسي تحت السيطرة الإسرائيلية.

ب) المشهد الإعلامي:

«إن البيئة الإعلامية في الضفة الغربية وغزة مربكة إذا صحّ التعبير. ثمة ثلاث وزارات تتحكم بالترخيص وتأجير الموجات الهوائية، والرسوم المالية، وكانت في حال من الصراع حتى أواخر عام 2005. كما أن قانون الإعلام على خلاف مع القانون الأساسي. وتجري حالياً إعادة صياغة قانون الصحافة والمطبوعات فيما يقول كثيرون ان هناك عدد كبير من وسائل الإعلام. xviii

تعتبر هيئة الإذاعة والتلفزيون الفلسطينية وسيلة الإعلام الرئيسة، وقد أنشئت عام 1995 مع «تلفزيون فلسطين»، كالتلفزيون الفضائي الوطني (والأرضي أيضاً في الاساس)، ومع إذاعة «صوت فلسطين»، محطة الإذاعة الوطنية، ووكالة الأنباء الوطنية «وفا» (باللغات العربية والإنجليزية والفرنسية والعبرية). بعدما كانت تبث أصلاً من غزة، انتقلت هيئة الإذاعة والتلفزيون الفلسطينية إلى رام الله في عام 2007، عند حصول الانقسام بين الفصيلين الفلسطينيين الرئيسيين، فتح وحماس، ما أدى إلى فصل الحكومات في الضفة الغربية وقطاع غزة.

في استطلاع نشرته شبكة «إنترنيوز» في عام 2014، xix «توجد في الضفة الغربية وحدها، 17 محطة تلفزيون أرضية و 72 محطة إذاعية؛ غالبيتها موجودة في المدن الرئيسة (الخليل نابلس ورام الله).»

وفقا للتقرير الـذي أعدتـه اليونسكو بشـأن تنميـة وسائل الإعـلام في فلسطين اسـتنادا لمـؤشرات اليونسكو، والـذي نُشـر في عـام 2014، توجـد: «85 محطـة إذاعيـة - 70 منهـا في الضفة الغربية و 15 في قطاع غـزة - و17 محطة تلفزيون محلية تبث من الضفة الغربية. توجـد أيضـاً أربعة محطـات فضائيـة: «معـاً و»فلسطينيات» في الضفـة الغربيـة والأقصى و «قناة الكتاب الفضائيـة» «من غزة». xx بالإضافة إلى وسائل الإعلام المحلية، يشـاهد الفلسطينيون قنـاة «الجزيـرة» (الـتي أنشـئت في عـام 1996) و «العربيـة» (الـتي تأسسـت في عـام 2003)، وأي مـن مجموعـة واسـعة مـن القنـوات الفضائيـة المتاحـة. xxi

توجـد ايضـاً ثـلاث صحـف رئيسـية في الضفـة الغربيـة، وهـي: «القـدس» (وتصـدر في القـدس)، «الأيام» (وتصدر في رام الله) و «الحيـاة الجديـدة» (تصدر ايضـاً في رام الله). هناك صحيفة واحدة تصدر في غزة وتدعى «الرسالة». «توجـد نحو 18 وكالة أنبـاء محلية موزعة في مناطق مختلفة في غـزة والضفة الغربية.» xxii كما تملك الصحف نسخة تصدر عـبر شـبكة الانترنت.

بحسب الجهاز المركزي للإحصاء الفلسطيني، فـإن واحـدة مـن كل خمس أسـر فلسطينية تبتاع صحيفة يوميـة وأكـثر مـن النصف تفضـل الاستماع إلى الأخبار:

«بلغت نسبة الأسـر في فلسطين الـتي تبتاع صحيفة يوميـة 20.4 بالمائة موزعـة عـلى النحو التالي: 23.7 بالمائة في الضفـة الغربية و 14.1 بالمائة في قطاع غزة مقارنة مـع 32.1 بالمائة في عـام 2009. بالإضافة الى ذلك، فـأن 22.6 بالمائة مـن الأشـخاص الذيـن تتراوح أعمارهـم بـين 10 سنوات وما فوق في المجتمع الفلسطيني يقرأ الصحف: 26.9 بالمائة مـن الذكور و 18.2 بالمائة مـن الإنـاث ».

بلغت نسبة الأسـر الـتي تسـتمع إلى المحطـات الإذاعيـة 60.8 بالمائـة، بما في ذلك 57.3 بالمائـة في الضفـة الغربيـة و 67.6 بالمائـة في قطـاع غـزة. أمـا الخيـار الأول بالنسـبة الى الأسـر مـن حيـث البرامج، احتلـت الأخبـار المرتبـة الأولى، تليهـا البرامـج الدينيـة والموسـيقى والأغـاني. xxiii

ذلك، تشـهد وسـائل الإعـلام الجديـدة تطوراً سريعاً. في العقد الـذي يسـبق عـام 2014، تضاعـف عـدد الشـباب الذيـن يتمتعـون بالوصـول إلى الهواتـف الجوّالـة: 75.2 بالمائـة مـن الشـباب يمتلكون هاتفـاً محمولاً (79.4 بالمائـة في الضفـة الغربيـة مقابـل 68.5 بالمائـة في قطـاع غـزة) مقابـل 34.9 بالمائـة في عـام 2004.

بالنسبة الى 28 بالمائة من الشباب الذين تتراوح أعمارهم بين 35-18 عاماً، أصبحت شبكة الإنترنت الآن المصدر الرئيسي للمعلومات؛ في حين أن 25 بالمائة من الناس يستخدمون الإنترنت يومياً. كما أن نحو 49.9 بالمائة من الشباب الذين تتراوح أعمارهم بين 29-15 عاماً في الأراضي الفلسطينية لا يقرأون الصحف أو المجلات على الإطلاق - 40.4 بالمائة في الضفة الغربية و 65.1 بالمائة في قطاع غزة (بحسب الجهاز المركزي للإحصاء الفلسطيني، 2013).

في عام 2013، استخدمت 67.5 بالمائة من الشباب الذين تتراوح أعمارهم بين 29-15 عاماً جهاز كمبيوتر (70.4 بالمائة في الضفة الغربية و 62.7 بالمائة في قطاع غزة)، و43.0 بالمائة استخدموا البريد الإلكتروني (بحسب الجهاز المركزي للإحصاء، 2013).

المشهد يتغير وينتقل الى المستخدمين الأصغر، كما يتضح من الأرقام الصادرة عن الجهاز المركزي للإحصاء الفلسطيني، والتي تشير الى أنه في عام 2014، 60.2 بالمائة من السكان الذين تتراوح أعمارهم بين 10 أو أكثر استخدموا جهاز الكمبيوتر و53.7 بالمائة استخدموا الإنترنت. (بحسب الجهاز المركزي للإحصاء الفلسطيني، 2014). xxiv بالتالي، لا بد أن يساهم كل ذلك هذا في تسهيل برامج التربية الإعلامية والمعلوماتية في المدارس.

حتى في عام 2012، ذكرت اليونسكو أن نسبة مستخدمي الإنترنت في الأراضي الفلسطينية المحتلة بلغت 58 بالمائة، وكانت أعلى بنحو 20 بالمائة من المعدل (40 بالمائة) لمنطقة الشرق الأوسط.

تلفت اليونسكو الانتباه إلى تطوير المؤسسات الإعلامية المجتمعية، مشيرة إلى أنه «على الرغم من محدودية الوصول إلى شبكة الإنترنت، تستخدم وسائل الإعلام المجتمعية تكنولوجيا المعلومات والاتصالات المتوفرة لنقل رسالتها الى المجتمع وتشجيع التفاعل العام من خلال وسائل الاتصال القائمة، مثل الهواتف الجوالة وخطوط الهاتف الأرضية.» xxv وقد قامت محطتان إذاعيتان (وهما «أجيال» و«راية») بتطوير تطبيقات لبث برامجها على الهواتف الذكية في المناطق التي تقع خارج نطاق الترددات. كما تذكر اليونسكو مثالاً آخر على وسائل الاعلام المجتمعية، وهي «هنا القدس» وإذاعة مجتمعية ووكالة انباء في مدينة القدس القديمة الموجهة الى المجتمع المقدسي وتبث عبر شبكة الإنترنت. xxvi

إلا أن وسائل التواصل الاجتماعي تبقى أسلوب التواصل الأكثر شعبية بين الفلسطينيين،

ويشكّل موقع فيسبوك الى حد كبير، الشكل الأكثر انتشاراً (يُستخدم في المقام الأول للدردشة ومن قبل ما يقرب من نصف السكان، xxvii بحسب شركة «سوشيال بايكرز» (الرائدة في مراقبة بيانات وسائل التواصل الاجتماعي وشركة اعلانات لصالح فيسبوك»).

«إن عدد مستخدمي الفيسبوك هو ثالث أعلى عدد مستخدمين في المنطقة، مع أكثر من 1.987.000 مستخدم، ما يجعله يحتل المرتبة 81 في ترتيب كافة إحصاءات فيسبوك بحسب البلد في منطقة يبلغ عدد سكانها نحو 4 ملايين نسمة.» مرة أخرى، وفقاً لشركة «سوشيال بايكرز»، «على الرغم من أن تويتر كان بطيئاً في الاستئثار باهتمام الفلسطينيين، ازداد الاهتمام والاستخدام في السنوات الثلاث منذ الانتفاضة العربية. وفي عام 2013، بلغ عدد مستخدمي تويتر النشطين 36.800 مستخدم.»

ج) الترددات -

تلخص اليونسكو الموضوع بما يلي: «تقررت شروط استخدام فلسطين لترددات البث في اتفاقات أوسلو لعام 1993 وعام 1995. وقد مُنحت الترددات لمحطات الإذاعة والتلفزيون الحكومية الفلسطينية فقط وليس بشكل رسمي الى وسائل الاعلام الخاصة أو المجتمعية. ولم تقم السلطة الفلسطينية حتى الآن، بوضع خطة لتخصيص الطيف وإدارته. وتسعى السلطة الفلسطينية حالياً لوضع خطة للانتقال الرقمي، من المقرر ان يتم تنفيذها منتصف عام 2015، وفقا لخارطة الطريق التي وضعها الاتحاد الدولي للاتصالات (ITU). إن غياب اي أساس قانوني سليم يجعل إدارة الطيف الفلسطينية مسألة غير واضحة وغير مستقرة.» xxix غير واضحة وغير مستقرة، تعني أنه يمكن لإسرائيل اقفال المحطات الفلسطينية متى شاءت، بحجة أنها تشوّش على اتصالاتها.

إلا أن من شأن ذلك أن يتغير قريباً. إذ أنه وفي ما يتعلق بوسائل الإعلام التقليدية، لا سيما الإذاعة والتلفزيون، من المتوقع أن يتغير المشهد الإعلامي بين عامي 2015 و 2020، مع بدء انتقال ترددات الاذاعة والتلفزيون في كافة أنحاء العالم العربي من البث التماثلي إلى البث الرقمي. xxx

ويقول مأمون مطر، الخبير الفلسطيني الذي يعمل على هذا الموضوع، في معرض تعليقه على الأمر: «من أبرز ميزات التحول الرقمي هو أن الطيف الحالي سيخلو من الترددات التي يمكن أن تحظى باستخدامات أخرى. سوف يسمح ذلك لشركات الهاتف المحمول المحلية باستخدام تكنولوجيات الجيل الرابع '4 جي'، ويسمح لنا بالتالي ان

نتخطى المشاكل حول الجيل الثالث '3 جي'، التي ترفض إسرائيل منحها لشركات الهاتف المحمول الفلسطينية، بحجة أن طيف التردد الخاص بالجيل الثالث ملء بالفعل.» xxxi

ويشكل هذا الارتباك بشأن الترددات جزءاً من المشهد الإعلامي الفلسطيني، الذي يتضمن هجمات على كلّ من البنية التحتية وعلى الصحفيين أنفسهم. xxxii

د) انعدام الأمان بالنسبة للصحفيين الفلسطينيين، ومشاكل بشأن حرية التعبير -

في حين أن مشاكل السلامة وحرية التعبير التي تواجه الصحفيين ليست مرتبطة مباشرة بالتربية الإعلامية والمعلوماتية، لا تزال لهذه المشاكل تأثيرها على المجال الإعلامي الشامل في فلسطين. فالاحتلال الإسرائيلي يتغلغل في المشهد الإعلامي كما هي الحال بالنسبة الى المشهد السياسي، و «حيث يوجد جو من الخوف، لا يمكن لوسائل الإعلام أن تؤدي دورها بفعالية في نشر المعلومات الى الجمهور وتعزيز الديموقراطية. كما أن معايير السلامة للصحفيين في فلسطين رديئة. وقد سجلت المؤسسات الدولية والمحلية التي ترصد الانتهاكات اعتداءات عدة ضد الصحفيين الفلسطينيين.» xxxiii

غالباً ما يتأثر الصحفيين بسبب تقييد الإسرائيليين لحرية تحركهم (بما في ذلك حرمانهم من دخول القدس) شأنهم شأن بقية السكان. كما يتعمّد الجيش الإسرائيلي أحياناً التعرض للصحفيين، لكي يثنوهم من التنقل بشكل عام.

بحسب ما أورده تقرير نُشر عام 2014 من قبل المركز الفلسطيني للتنمية والحريات الإعلامية (مدى)، فإن الانتهاكات ضد الصحافيين الفلسطينيين تتصاعد. xxxiv «إن الانتهاكات التي رصدها مركز 'مدى' قد تزايدت في الضفة الغربية بما في ذلك في القدس الشرقية، وقطاع غزة في عام 2014، مقارنة مع الانتهاكات ضد الصحفيين والحريات الإعلامية في فلسطين التي رُصدت في السنوات السابقة. بلغ العدد الإجمالي للجرائم والانتهاكات في الضفة الغربية وقطاع غزة والقدس 465 في عام 2014. وقد ارتكبت قوات الاحتلال الإسرائيلي أخطر الإنتهاكات: 351 حالة، أي 75 بالمائة من إجمالي الانتهاكات. أما الإنتهاكات من الجانب الفلسطيني فقد بلغت 114 انتهاكاً، أي 25 بالمائة من مجموع الإنتهاكات. وشكّلت الانتهاكات الإسرائيلية ضعف عدد الانتهاكات التي ارتكبت في عام 2013، وارتفع عدد الانتهاكات الإسرائيلية من 151 في عام 2013 الى 351 اعتداءً في عام 2014، ما يعني تصعيداً بنسبة 132 بالمائة «. وأشار مركز 'مدى' أيضاً أن نصف الهجمات الإسرائيلية تهدد مباشرة حياة الصحفيين. وعلاوة على ذلك، قُتل 17 صحفياً

وموظفاً إعلامياً فلسطينياً في صيف عام 2014 وحده، في العملية الاسرائيلية التي أطلق عليها اسم «الجرف الصامد». xxxv

بالتالي، يمكن القول ان تأثير الصراع على الإعلام بالنسبة للفلسطينيين، تماماً مثل الجوانب الأخرى للاحتلال، ظالم ومقيّد للحريات. كما تسبب بتأخير انتشار التربية الإعلامية والمعلوماتية إلى جانب كافة التطورات الأخرى التي يمكن أن تحدث في بيئة مواتية أكثر. في جو من الخوف وانعدام الأمن، من الضروري التمكن من التمييز بين الحق والباطل وبين الحقيقية والوهم، أكثر ما هو ضروري في جو من السلام والأمان، والتمكن من الانخراط في العمل، بما في العمل الإعلام ، التي يمكن ان تحسّن الوضع.

بيد أن الاحتلال الإسرائيلي ليس وحده ما يترك تأثيراً سلبياً على المشهد الإعلامي الفلسطيني. فقد تأثر المشهد الإعلامي الفلسطيني سلباً وبشكل خطير من جراء الصدع في العلاقات بين الفصيلين الرئيسيين، فتح وحماس الذي بدأ في مايو 2007. xxxvi

على الرغم من حصول مصالحة رسمية وإنشاء «حكومة وحدة وطنية» تتكون من أعضاء من فتح وحماس منذ عام 2014، فإنه ليس من الواضح كم سيستمر هذا الأمر، وبالتالي، يبقى الوضع متوتراً. وبما أن التحزب المتطرف والانقسامات العدوانية تشجّع استخدام وسائل الإعلام والنظر إليها على أنها دعاية وأدوات هجوم بدلاً من كونها مصادر موثوقة للمعلومات، فإن البيئة الإعلامية الفلسطينية تميل إلى أن تترك تأثيراً سلبياً على وسائل الاعلام وعلى التربية الإعلامية. وبدلاً من تشجيع التعددية واحترام حقوق الإنسان، يساهم المناخ الإعلامي بتشجيع الانقسامات والتحيز وحتى العنف، ويدفع الناس بعيداً من التفاهم المتبادل.

فيما يتعلق بالتربية الإعلامية والمعلوماتية، يشاهد الفلسطينيون تلفزيون فلسطين (فتح) أو تلفزيون الأقصى (حماس) بشكل أساسي، ويتمتعون بمستويات متفاوتة من قابلية التصديق. كما ان هناك انتقاد قليل أو تحليل، الى جانب القليل من التسامح لوجهات النظر المناقضة. تجدر الإشارة الى أن اللمحة السابقة عن المشهد الإعلامي في فلسطين هي ذات صلة خاصة بالتربية الإعلامية المحلية حيث ان التحيز في تغطية الأخبار قد إزداد تطرفاً.

عنوان، مراسل وكالة فرانس برس في غزة: «مما لا شك فيه أن الانقسام الفلسطيني الداخلي قد أثر سلباً على الإعلام الفلسطيني. ويتمثّل التأثير الأهم في الابتعاد

التدريجي بين الصحفيين عن القيم والمعايير الأخلاقية والمهنية والموضوعية لصالح الأجندات السياسية، وما ينتج عن ذلك من استغلال وكالات الأنباء في المجالات ذات الصلة. بالتالي، فقد ساهم العديد من وكالات الأنباء في تعزيز الانقسام نفسه، من خلال الموافقة على أن يكون أداة للتقسيم.» xxxvii

الزيادة في المواقف الحزبية التي تمّ التعبير عنها في وسائل الإعلام الفلسطينية لم تقتصر عليهم، بل تجلّت أيضاً في الهجمات على الصحافة، وعلى الصحفيين والمدوّنين. وتبيّن الأرقام التي نشرها مركز «مدى» (أعلاه) دليلاً على ذلك. xxxviii

كما ترتبط مشكلة النزاع بين فتح وحماس والتراجع في الأخلاقيات الإعلامية بحرية التعبير ومسألة التعددية والتنوع في الإعلام xxxix - ويؤثر الصدع على القوانين لانه لا يمكن أن تكون هناك انتخابات، وبالتالي، يكون النظام بكامله مشلولاً.

حرية التعبير هي جزء من الدستور الفلسطيني، بحيث تنصّ المادة 19 على أنه «لا مساس بحرية الرأي. ولكل إنسان الحق في التعبير عن رأيه ونشره بالقول أو الكتابة أو غير ذلك من وسائل التعبير أو الفن، مع مراعاة أحكام القانون.» xl

ولكن المسألة ليست بهذه البساطة، إذ توجد في الواقع عدة قوانين متناقضة. ثمة قوانين مختلفة لتنظيم الصحافة تكفل حرية الرأي والتعبير لكل فلسطيني وحرية الصحافة، مثل المادة 4 من قانون المطبوعات والنشر الفلسطيني، في حين تنص المادة 7 أنه «من غير شرعي نشر أي شيء يخالف النظام العام»، من دون تحديد ما يعنيه ذلك.»

بالفعل، يفرض القانون عدداً من القيود واسعة النطاق على المحتوى الذي يمكن نشره، وغالباً ما يكون كثير منها شامل أو مبهم بشكل غير مقبول. xli في الواقع، الوضع القانوني غير واضح للغاية، والقوانين الموجودة لا تزال سارية المفعول منذ العصر العثماني، من عهد الانتداب البريطاني ومن الأردن. xlii

على سبيل المثال، قانون العقوبات الأردني رقم 16 لسنة 1960 المطبق في الضفة الغربية يعرّف الذم على النحو التالي: «الذم : هو إسناد مادة معينة إلى شخص - ولو في معرض الشك والاستفهام - من شأنها أن تنال من شرفه وكرامته أو تعرضه إلى بعض الناس واحتقارهم سواء أآنت تلك المادة جريمة تستلزم العقاب أم لا.» xliii وهذا يسمح بأي عدد من القيود والاعتقالات على أساس الذمّ أو التشهير، وعلى غرار الجرائم الجنائية، هي أفعال يعاقب عليها بالسجن.

تقول اليونسكو إن «كل من السلطة الفلسطينية وسلطات الأمر الواقع في غزة تمارس رقابة مشددة على المعلومات التي تنشرها وسائل الإعلام. ففي بعض الأحيان، جرى اقتطاع بعض من المحتوى الإعلامي واحتجز الصحفيون واضطهدوا لأنهم قاموا بالتعبير عن الآراء السياسية وقاموا بالإبلاغ عن انتهاكات ضد حقوق الإنسان.» xliv

وتضيف اليونسكو أن «الهيئات الرسمية تحاكم في أغلب الأحيان رداً على المواد المنشورة التي يزعم أنها تشكل تشهيراً بحق الشخصيات السياسية أو تضرّ بالأمن القومي وتحرض على الكراهية أو تحتوي على معلومات غير دقيقة». xlv

بالإضافة إلى القيود الخارجية على حرية التعبير، توجد أيضاً مشكلة خطيرة مع الرقابة الذاتية.

في دراسة نشرت في ديسمبر كانون الاول عام 2014، تبين أن 80 بالمائة من الصحفيين الذين تمّ استطلاعهم يمارسون الرقابة الذاتية. وقد أشار المدير العام لمركز «مدى» موسى الريماوي إلى أن انتشار الرقابة الذاتية يؤثر بشكل خطير على نوعية الصحافة الفلسطينية، بالإضافة إلى إعاقة حرية التعبير و حق المواطنين في الحصول على المعلومات. وأوضح أن الرقابة الذاتية تعرقل الدور الذي يتوجب على الصحافة أن تؤديه في مجتمع ديمقراطي. xlvi

تظهر مسألة التعددية والتنوع في وسائل الإعلام واضحة من خلال المشاكل الناجمة عن الصدع بين فتح وحماس والتحيز الشديد في بعض وسائل الإعلام. ولكن، كما يظهر في الكمّ الهائل من وسائل الإعلام، هناك وصول مفتوح إلى تلك الآراء المتعارضة. بشكل عام، تعكس وسائل الإعلام تقليد الانفتاح والتسامح السائد في المجتمع الفلسطيني نحو مجموعات مختلفة.

لكن المشكلة بشكل خاص هي مع إدراك التحيز في وسائل الإعلام، وليس في وجود مجموعة واحدة تسيطر عليها. تقول اليونسكو إن «لا يبدو بالضرورة أن هناك الكثير من الثقة بوسائل الإعلام عموماً،» xlvii وأن «عدداً من وسائل الإعلام الفلسطينية يميل الى التحيز لصالح توجه سياسي واحد، ويُقال أنها تصمّم برامجها على أساس ميولها السياسية بدلاً من احتياجات جماهيرها». xlviii

وضع التربية الإعلامية والمعلوماتية

لا يـزال مفهـوم التربيـة الإعلاميـة والمعلوماتيـة جديـداً نسبيـاً في فلسطين، سـواء في نظـام التعليـم المـدني أو في المجتمـع المـدني. وقـد تعـرّف كاتـبا هـذا الفصـل علـى التربيـة الإعلاميـة والمعلوماتيـة خـارج سـياق فلسطين - خـلال عملهمـا علـى مسـائل اللاعنف والمسـاواة بيـن الجنسيـن، ومـع برنامـج الأمـم المتحـدة لتحالـف الحضـارات، والأنشـطة الإعلاميـة في الأردن.

منـذ عـام 2009، حصـل تقديرمتزايـد لأهميـة التربيـة الإعلاميـة والمعلوماتيـة. كمـا تزايـد عـدد الأنشـطة المتعلقـة بالتربيـة الإعلاميـة والمعلوماتيـة، وعـدد مـن المشـاريع، أي تطويـر المهـارات، وكيفيـة التنقـل في العالـم الرقمـي اليـوم.

انتشـر ايضـاً إدراك متزايـد الى الحاجـة لرفـع مسـتوى الوعـي لـدى النـاس حـول كيفيـة التفاعـل مـع وسـائل الإعـلام والتعامـل معهـا. ويتـمّ تنظيـم هـذه الأنشـطة في كافـة انحـاء قطاعـات المجتمـع، اي المجتمـع المـدني والأوسـاط الأكاديميـة والحكوميـة والقطـاع الخـاص.

علـى سـبيل المثـال، «وفيمـا يتعلـق المـدارس والتربيـة المعلوماتيـة، كان لـوزارة التربيـة والتعليـم عـدة مبـادرات متعلقـة بالتعلم الإلكترونـي منـذ عـام 1995، ونفذ الكثيـر مـن المشـاريع مثـل مبـادرة «إنتـل» التعليميـة التـي كانـت مرتبطـة بتدريـب المدرّسـين علـى اسـتخدام تكنولوجيـا المعلومـات والاتصـالات في التعليـم وتدريبهـم علـى مهـارات الكمبيوتر الأساسيـة، وشـملت أكثـر مـن 10 آلاف مـدرّس. مـن المشـاريع الكبـرى الأخـرى المتعلقـة باسـتخدام تكنولوجيـا المعلومـات والاتصـالات في التعليـم ، مبـادرة «وورلـد لينكـس» التـي يمولهـا الاتحـاد الأوروبـي؛ مبـادرة «سـيد» SEED بتمويـل مـن الوكالـة اليابانيـة للتعـاون الـدولي (JICA) ، بالإضافـة الى المشـاريع الصغيـرة.

عـدا التطـورات في مجـال التكنولوجيـا، كان للصـراع المتواصـل ولا يـزال التأثيـر الأكبـر علـى كل مـا لـع علاقـة بالإعـلام، بمـا في ذلـك التربيـة الإعلاميـة بالنسـبة للفلسطينيين. مـن الجوانـب المختلفـة للاحتـلال، علـى سـبيل المثـال، هـي القيـود الصارمـة علـى الحركـة المفروضـة في كثيـر مـن الأحيـان علـى السـكان الفلسطينيين. ويعتبـر الإعـلام واحـدة مـن الوسـائل التـي يمكـن أن تسـاعد في التغلـب علـى تلـك القيـود. مـن تعليـم الأطفـال بواسـطة الـدروس المتلفـزة، (في الخليـل)، الى الفيسـبوك، والاجتماعـات عـن طريـق الفيديـو الرقمـي بيـن الضفـة الغربيـة وقطـاع غـزة، علـى الرغـم مـن أنهـا غالبـاً مـا تكـون غيـر ممكنـة نظـرا لغيـاب التغذيـة الكهربائيـة الكافيـة. ا.

يسود حالياً وضع من الإحباط والتشردذم بين صفوف الفلسطينيين، مع استمرار الاحتلال الإسرائيلي، وترسخه على نحو متزايد، ومع تراجع مستوى الأمن البشري وتلاشي الأمل بالتوصل الى حل عادل. ويبقى الاحتلال الميزة المهيمنة في حياة جميع الفلسطينيين. كما يبقي الجزء الأكبر من السكان مركزين باستمرار على الإعلام من أجل مواكبة ما يحدث من حولهم.

تعتبر التربية الإعلامية أمراً مهماً بشكل خاص بالنسبة للفلسطينيين. ومع تنامي الوعي الإعلامي ومصادره ورسائله المختلفة، جنباً إلى جنب مع القدرة على تحليلها، قد يتمكن الفلسطينيون ربما من السيطرة بشكل أفضل على حياتهم وعلى عملية الصراع، «وبالتالي، تحديد الظروف التي يعيشون في ظلها بشكل فعال» Ii، والبدء في تحسين أمنهم الانساني.

ونظرا لشدة التركيز الدولي على الصراع الإسرائيلي-الفلسطيني، اعتاد الفلسطينيون على رؤية أنفسهم ممثلين في وسائل الإعلام. ويبلغ عدد الصحفيين الأجانب الذين يغطون النزاع المئات. لكن هذا التمثيل الفلسطينيين يكون في كثير من الأحيان سلبياً، سواء كضحايا أو كجهات فاعلة وعنيفة وإرهابيين، وبالتالي يغذون الصور النمطية القائمة. ما هو أكثر من ذلك، تؤثر هذه الصور السلبية على الصورة الذاتية وتؤدي إلى عدم التمكين والى نشر الإحباط بين الفلسطينيين.

التربية الإعلامية يمكن أن تساعد الفلسطينيين على الهروب من بعض هذه السلاسل، فيما يتواصلون بشكل أكثر وأفضل مع العالم الخارجي، وفيما يبنون الحرية الداخلية والديمقراطية في داخل المجتمع الفلسطيني، ويتأكدون أكثر من هويتهم المحطمة.

التربية الإعلامية من خلال الجامعات:

بدأ تنفيذ عدة مشاريع حول التربية الإعلامية، في مقابل التربية المعلوماتية فقط، من خلال الجامعات وبدأت تحقق تأثيراً مهماً. ويتخرّج نحو 300 طالب سنوياً من الجامعات الفلسطينية العشر الموجودة في الضفة الغربية والقدس الشرقية وقطاع غزة والتي تقدم حالياً درجة البكالوريوس في الأشكال المختلفة من الدراسات الإعلامية، في حين أن جامعتي «بيرزيت» و«القدس» فقط تقومان بعمل إضافي حول التربية الإعلامية.

الجامعة الإسلامية في غزة هي المؤسسة الفلسطينية الوحيدة حتى الآن التي تقدم درجة الماجستير في الصحافة والإعلام. ولا تشكّل التربية الإعلامية تخصصاً منفصلاً أو مجال

تركز تحت مظلة الدراسات الإعلامية، على الرغم من أنه يتم تضمينها بشكل عام في دورات تشمل كافة المجالات من المجالات النظري عبر «مقدمة إلى وسائل الإعلام» و«وسائل الإعلام الدولية،» الى مجموعة متنوعة من الدورات العملية حول التقنيات الإعلامية المختلفة.

جامعة القدس المفتوحة (التي تشكّل كياناً مختلفاً تماماً عن جامعة القدس في القدس، التي تملكها وتمولها السلطة الفلسطينية وتملك جسماً طلابياً افتراضياً كبيراً جداً، يبلغ عشرات الآلاف، ومكاتب في كافة المراكز السكانية الرئيسية)، ومن خلال تعاونها مع وزارة الاعلام الفلسطينية، قدمت تدريباً تثقيفياً في الإعلام لطلبة جامعة القدس المفتوحة. وشمل هذا التدريب زيارات ميدانية الى مؤسسات إعلامية فلسطينية أو غيرها من المؤسسات الإعلامية، بهدف لفت إنتباه الطلبة الى الإعلام كوسيلة يمكن من خلالها التأثير وإحداث التغيير في المجتمع. كما يوفر تعريفاً بالتربية الإعلامية كوسيلة للتمكين.

وأخيراً، وبشكل مرتبط بشكل عرضي فقط مع التربية الإعلامية، ومنذ عام 2013، وضعت جامعة القدس سلسلة من كتيبات التدريب حول الصحافة الاستقصائية، لصالح الصحفيين المحترفين، والمجتمع المدني (بما في ذلك تدريب 30 ممثلاً عن المنظمات غير الحكومية)، والطلاب الجامعيين. منذ فبراير 2014، تمت الموافقة على الدورة وأدرجت كشرط لجميع الطلاب الجامعيين. هذا جزء من مشروع ممول من قبل صندوق الأمم المتحدة للديمقراطية (UNDEF)، شمل أيضاً إنتاج 36 تقريراً استقصائياً، بهدف رفع مستوى التوقعات من جانب الجمهور بشأن وسائل الإعلام الفلسطينية.

في حين أن ما سبق لا يُعتبر تربية إعلامية ومعلوماتية على وجه التحديد، من خلال رفع التوقعات بشأن التقرير، فهو يشجع التربية الإعلامية بشكل غير مباشر، في وقت بدأت فيه الجماهير البحث عن المزيد من العمق والدقة وبشكل عام تنظر الى التقارير الإخبارية بمزيد من الانتقاد.

مشاريع التربية الإعلامية

عملت كل من جامعة القدس وجامعة بيرزيت بشكل محدد على مشاريع التربية الإعلامية والمعلوماتية. وتولت جامعة بيرزيت، بالاشتراك مع معهد «فوجو» السويد، قيادة مشروع حول التربية الإعلامية والمعلوماتية في المدارس الثانوية.

وقد دمجت جامعة القدس برامج التربية الإعلامية والمعلوماتية من خلال المشاريع

المدرسـية المجتمعيـة والمحليـة، مثل تدريـب الناشطين السـلميين التابعين «للمقاومـة الشـعبية»، (مجموعـات مـن الفلسطينيين الذيـن ينظمـون اسـبوعياً ومنـذ عـام 2005، المظاهـرات السـلمية في قراهـم، في محاولـة لتغييـر مسـار جدار الفصـل الإسرائيلي) حـول كيفيـة اسـتخدام وسـائل الإعـلام وتحليلهـا.

أطلـق مركـز تطويـر الإعـلام في جامعـة بيرزيت أول مـشروع في مجال التربيـة الإعلاميـة والمعلوماتيـة تحت عنـوان «مسـاعدة الأطفال الفلسطينيين عـلى أن يصبحوا ماهريـن في مجال الإعـلام» في عام 2007. ويتمثل الهدف مـن هـذا المـشروع في تعميـق فهـم الأطفال والمراهقيـن للإعـلام؛ وتزويدهـم بالأدوات اللازمة للتحليل والنقد للرسـائل الإعلاميـة عـلى اختـلاف أنواعهـا. ويهـدف ايضـاً الى تشجيعهم عـلى القيـام بانتاجهـم الإعلامي الخـاص.liii

«واشـتمل المـشروع عـلى مجموعـة أدوات جديـدة في مجال التربيـة الإعلاميـة والمعلوماتيـة لصالح المـدارس الفلسطينية ولمسـاعدة الأطفال لكي يصبحوا «ماهرين في مجال الإعـلام». كانـت تلـك الأدوات ثمـرة مـشروع مشـترك بيـن كلّ مـن مركـز تطويـر الإعـلام التابع لجامعـة بيرزيت في رام الله، ومعهـد التعليـم الإضـافي للصحافيـن السـويدي «فوجـو». وقد تـم اختبـار بعـض الأنشـطة في إطار ورشـة عمـل تجريبيـة لطـلاب المـدارس الفلسطينية في منطقـة رام الله - 21 طفلاً تـتراوح أعمارهـم بيـن 9 و14 عامـاً. وقد أمضى ثلاثة مدرّسـين يومـاً كامـلاً في المركـز الإعلامي لجامعـة بيرزيت، في مناقشـة مـا يحفـز وسـائل الإعـلام، وكيفيـة تأثيرهـا عـلى حياتـا. وتـولى الأطفال تحليـل كافة أنـواع وسـائل الإعـلام، مـن الصحـف إلى الإنترنت والكتابـات الجداريـة. وبعـد مناقشـة مسهبة، انهى الأطفال ورشـة العمـل بانتاج «مجلـة متخصصة» خاصة بهـم. وكانـت تصريحـات الأطفال المشاركين في الورشـة تعبر عـن حماسـة شـديدة:

* «تعلمـت في خـلال ورشـة العمـل كيفيـة التفريـق بيـن الأخبار الهامة والأخبار غـير الهامة التي لا تمـس حياتـا أو اهتماماتـا، لكنها للأسـف تملأ الصحـف. انا أحلم بصحيفة فلسطينية متكاملـة أو مجلة تلـبي بشـكل علـم أذواق الأطفال والمراهقيـن والأسـرة واحتياجاتهـم.» آيـة الجيـوسي - الصف السـادس، 12 عامـاً.

المرحلـة الأولى مـن هـذا المـشروع، الـتي نفـذت خـلال عـام 2008/2009، تضمنـت إنتـاج دليـلين: أول دليـل للتثقيـف الإعلامـي لطلبة الصـف السـابع، ودليـل آخـر اسـتهدف المعلمـين. وجاء إعـداد الدليـلين بعـد العـشرات مـن المقابـلات والاجتماعـات وورش العمـل مـع مؤسسـات متخصصة بإعـلام الطفل، وإعلاميـين، ومعلميـن، وأدبـاء ومثقفيـن، وأطفـال

ومراهقين وأولياء أمور.

في الإجمال، تم نشر نحو 2000 نسخة ورقية من هذين الدليلين. وهما غير متوفرين على شبكة الإنترنت. أما في عام 2009 فتم إختبار الدليل في ثماني مدارس حكومية، وخاصة، وأخرى تابعة لوكالة الأمم المتحدة لغوث وتشغيل اللاجئين الفلسطينيين (الاونروا). . وأثمرت مرحلة التقييم والمزيد من المشاورات عن فصل إضافي حول فنون الكتابة الصحافية، وتمارين عملية في الإعلام، أضيفت للدليلين. وقد بُني الدليلان على خبرات وطنية، وباستخدام مواد إعلامية ونماذج فلسطينية، ورُفدا بعشرات من أوراق العمل التدريبية في التربية الإعلامية، ليكون المضمون بذلك شاملاً لمقابلات متخصصة وأخرى متنوعة، ومواد نظرية عن الإعلام، وأوراق عمل تدريبية.

استمر المشروع لمدة عامين وتضمن تطوير الدليلين وتوزيع الكتيبات، بمشاركة 17 مدرسة. وكان المشروع تشاركياً جداً في طبيعته، وتواصل العمل بشكل مستمر على الدليلين بصفتهما مسودة للعمل، وشهد عملية استقاء ودمج منتظمة لردود الفعل. وعلى الرغم من وجود مخطط للاستمرار في المشروع، فقد عُقد آخر اجتماع في فبراير من عام 2011.

وتكمن أهمية هذا المشروع، على الرغم من مستوى التعليم الرسمي في المدارس، أن هناك دائماً معوقات بسبب الضغط المستمر من اجل التركيز على المناهج الدراسية الرسمية كل عام، واستكماله في الوقت المخصص له.

في الأراضي الفلسطينية المحتلة، قد يشكّل هذا الأمر تحدياً كبيراً بحيث يشهد العام الدراسي اضطرابات وتوقف طوال العام الدراسي، وذلك بسبب التدخل «العادي» من قبل الاحتلال الإسرائيلي، مثل إغلاق الطرق والتوغلات، وتفاقم الصراع الشامل.

توجد رسمياً حصة واحدة في الأسبوع مخصصة «للأنشطة» مثل التربية الإعلامية والمعلوماتية والتربية المدنية، أو الدراما، لكن من أجل العمل بفعالية مع نظام التعليم الرسمي، سيكون من الضروري دمج التثقيف الإعلامي (التربية الإعلامية) في المناهج الدراسية الرسمية عن طريق وزارة التربية والتعليم، وخصوصاً إدراج التربية الإعلامية كمادة في الامتحانات المدرسية النهائية.

هذا يعني أن الكثير من العمل الحالي على برامج التثقيف الإعلامي (التربية الإعلامية) مع طلاب المدارس ينبغي أن يتمّ عن طريق التعليم غير الرسمي، من خلال المشاريع

مع المؤسسات الإعلامية والمنظمات غير الحكومية.

لا بد من الاشارة الى أن الجزء الأكبر من برامج التربية الإعلامية والمعلوماتية يتمّ من خلال المجتمع المدني. هناك العشرات من المشاريع (توجد أكـثر مـن 2400 منظمة غير حكومية في الأراضي الفلسطينية المحتلة، بحسب التقديرات من عام 2010 liv) والتي تشمل بعض عناصر التدريب الإعلامي والتمكين، مثل المناقشة الإذاعية أو فيلم سينمائي، بالإضافة الى المدوّنات أو عناصر خاصة بمواقع التواصل الاجتماعي. إلا أن قلة منها تدمج عنصراً محدداً من التربية الإعلامية مثل التوعية الاعلامية، إلا أنها موجودة أيضاً.

كما تنفذ المنظمات الشبابية احياناً كثيرة المشاريع التي تموّلها أساساً الوكالة الأمريكية للتنمية الدولية (USAID) والاتحاد الأوروبي، والتي تشمل التدريب الإعلامي والإنتاج.

وكمثال على مشروع تمكين الشباب، قامت جامعة القدس في عـام 2013- 2014 بتنفيذ مشروع ممول مـن خلال مبادرة الشراكة الأمريكية الـشرق أوسطية للتعليم (MEPI)) التي شملت تدريب 30 شاباً مهمشاً من القدس الشرقية، وكثير منهم لـم يكملوا دراستهم، ليصبحوا «صحفيين مواطنين».

نتيجة لذلك، بـرزت مجموعة مـن الشباب الواثقين والمتمكنين، استطاع الكثير منهم العثور على عمل، وجميعهم قادر الان على التعبير عن نفسه امام الكاميرا وعبر كافة أشكال الإعلام العصري. وركز التدريب الـذي خضعوا لـه على التربية الإعلامية وكذلك على المهارات والكفاءات المحددة.

من المشاريع الواسعة الامتداد والتي تتمحور حول الشباب والممول مـن الوكالة الأمريكية للتنمية الدولية (USAID)، هو المشروع الـذي بـدأ في عـام 2009 بتدريب ثلاث مجموعـات مـن الشباب على المهارات الإعلامية وإنشاء مراكز إعلامية للشباب في ثلاثة مدن رئيسية. مرة أخرى، هـذا مرتبط بالمهارات الإعلامية والتربية المعلوماتية، وليس بالتربية الإعلامية بشكل محدد. مع ذلك، أعيد إطلاق المشروع في عـام 2015 مـن قبل مجلس الأبحاث والتبادل الـدولي «IREX» بإسم «الشراكة مـع الشباب». وفي إطار المشروع، يتم تدريب الشباب في الضفة الغربية على تطوير مهارات مـا قبل التوظيف ومهارات قابلية التوظيف مـن خـلال المشاركة الفعالة في الأنشطة الإعلامية وبرامج تكنولوجيا المعلومات والاتصالات ومجالات أخرى مثل اللغة الإنجليزية، والرياضة،

والدراما، والبيئة. وهذا يشمل التدريب العملي شاملاً في تقنيات الإعلام العصري، كما تضمن المشروع إنتاج دليل التدريب الإعلامي للشباب، مع بعض مكونات التربية الإعلامية (التثقيف الإعلامي).

من مشاريع التربية الإعلامية والمعلوماتية المهمة الأخرى والتي تركز فعلاً على التثقيف بقدر تركيزها على المهارات، مزج بين التعلم عن القانون مع التعلم عن الإعلام. في يناير 2012، باشر معهد الإعلام العصري التابع لجامعة القدس التثقيف الإعلامي والمعلوماتي من خلال سلسلة من المشاريع الرامية إلى تعزيز العدالة وسيادة القانون من خلال استخدام وسائل الإعلام.

وقد تم تمويل هذه المشاريع من قبل برنامج تعزيز العدالة الفلسطينية (PEJP) الممول من الوكالة الأمريكية للتنمية الدولية «USAID» بهدف رفع مستويات المعرفة والوعي بشأن مبادئ سيادة القانون بين طلاب المدارس والمدرّسين في المحافظات الفلسطينية؛ وكوسيلة لمكافحة العنف المجتمعي الداخلي (20 طالباً و10 مدرّسين). lvi كما شارك الطلاب والمدرّسون في ورش عمل تناولت كيفية إعداد الرسائل الإعلامية وتحليلها. وقد تلقوا أيضاً التدريب على استخدام ومساءلة وسائل الاعلام فيما يتعلق بالكثير من القضايا التي تهم كل من المجتمع والأفراد في المجتمع الفلسطيني. وقد أنتجوا ثلاثة أفلام وثائقية، وأربعة برامج حوارية، خمسة تقارير إذاعية، و 20 تقريراً مكتوباً.

تضمن التدريب سلسلة من الأساليب التربوية المختلفة لضمان الحصول على انتباه الأطفال وتفاعلهم مع المدرب والمواد التي يتم تدريسها. كانت ردود فعل المدرب على تدريب المدرّسين إيجابية للغاية؛ فقد قال إن دورة تدريب المدرّسين تضمنت مناقشة مثيرة للاهتمام وحيوية تناولت الغياب الحالي لجهود إنفاذ القانون، والعقبات والفرص المتوفرة للتغلب عليها.

جنى حمارشة، طالبة في الـ 15 من العمر من مدينة جنين كانت إحدى المشاركات في ورشة العمل. وفي المقابلة التي اجريت معها، قالت جنى إنها كانت سعيدة جداً خلال مشاركتها في التدريب، وكانت تجربة مميزة جداً بالنسبة لها وساهمت بتعزيز فهمها للقانون، وقطاع القضاء ودور الإعلام كأداة لإطلاع المجتمع، يمكن يمكن استخدامها لتعزيز سيادة القانون.

وأضافت جنى أنها استمتعت شخصيا بالجزء الـذي يتـم فيه تدريـب المشاركين عـلى كيفية إعـداد التقاريـر التلفزيونيـة والإذاعيـة. وأضافت أن المدربيـن طلبـوا مـن طـلاب المـدارس إعطاء أمثلـة مـن حياتهـم اليوميـة، مثـل مشكلـة تغيـب الطـلاب عـن المدرسـة أو الحـق في التصويـت، واستخدمـوا هـذا المثـال لتوضيـح كيـف يمكـن لسـيادة القانـون المسـاعدة في حل هـذه المشكلـة وكيـف يمكـن إسـتخدام الإعـلام لنشـر المعلومـات والوعـي حـول هـذا الموضوع. وقالت جنى انها تخطط لمشاركة الخبرة التـي اكتسـبتها في ورشـة العمـل هـذه مـع زملائهـا.

وكمثـال عـلى التمكيـن مـن خـلال النربيـة الإعلاميـة والمعلوماتيـة، سـاهم مـشروع آخـر نفذته جامعة القدس عـام 2008، تحت عنـوان «جميع الأطفال معـا» (ACT) بتمويـل مـن الوكالـة الكنديـة للتنميـة الدوليـة (CIDA)، بتعليـم الأطفـال ذوي الاحتياجـات الخاصة تـدرس كيفية اسـتخدام الاعـلام للخلـق وإعـداد التقاريـر مـن خـلال برامـج تلبـي احتياجاتهـم. فقـد مكنهـم ذلـك مـن التعبيـر عـن حاجتهـم لأن يتـم إدراجهـم في نظـام التعليـم العـام الـذي كثيراً مـا يسـتبعدون منه.

مؤسسات المجتمع المدني والاعلام

عـلى صعيـد المجتمـع المـدني، وعـلى عكـس الجامعـات، كان لمؤسسـة المسـتقبل إهتمـام بتدريـب أفـراد المجتمـع الفلسـطيني عـلى المسـاءلة المجتمعيـة عـبر الاعـلام. وقـد نفـذت المؤسسـة في هـذا الاطـار برنامجـاً تدريبيـاً بالشراكـة مـع شـبكة معـا الاخباريـة في بيـت لحـم بـدأ عـام 2011، تـدرب المشـاركون خلالـه عـلى كيفيـة اسـتخدام الاعـلام في مراقبـة اداء مختلـف المؤسسـات العاملـة في المجتمـع ومحاسـبة المسـؤولين عـن الاخطـاء وقضايـا الفساد.

حمـل المـشروع عنـوان «تمكيـن المواطنيـن والمجتمـع المـدني والإعـلام مـن طلـب المسـاءلة والحكـم الرشـيد في الأراضي الفلسـطينية المحتلـة». وركـز المـشروع بشـكل أسـاسي عـلى تدريـب 10 صحفييـن فلسـطينيين وممثليـن فاعليـن مـن المجتمـع المـدني عـلى كيفيـة التـصرف كمحاوريـن أقويـاء ومسـتقلين بيـن السـكان الفلسـطينيين والذيـن في مواقـع السـلطة في السـلطة الوطنيـة الفلسـطينية. وقـد صمـم التدريـب عـلى وجـه التحديـد للتركيـز عـلى اسـتخدام الأنشـطة الإعلاميـة المبتكـرة وتعزيـز الوعـي بأفضـل الممارسـات.

مـن المقاربـات الاخـرى للمجتمـع المـدني هـو «الفيديـو التشـاركي»، وهـو شـكل مـن أشـكال

التمكين مـن خـلال تدريـس تقنيـات الفيديـو / وتصويـر الافـلام لمجموعـات صغيـرة مـن الاشخاص العاديين - غالباً مـا يكونـون مـن الجماعـات المهمشـة، مثـل النسـاء والشـباب - حيـث يتعلمـون التصويـر والمشـاركة بالتصويـر وكيـف يدركـون صورتهـم الخاصـة.

وقـد استخدمـت هـذه الطريقـة بشـكل خـاص في مركـز الـشرق الأوسـط للاعنـف والديمقراطيـة (MEND) في المشـاريع الـتي يدعمهـا برنامـج الأمـم المتحـدة الإنمائـي (UNDP)، وصنـدوق الأمـم المتحـدة الإنمائـي للمـرأة (اليونيفيـم)، ومؤخـرا في معهـد دراسـات التنميـة (IDS) في جامعـة ساسـكس. lvii.

وقـد أجـري مـشروع مركـز الـشرق الأوسـف للاعنـف والديمقراطيـة (MEND) الـذي أقيـم بالتعـاون مـع جامعـة ساسـكس في سـياق البحـوث عـن التغييـر، وأهميـة المشـاركة كعنـصر في إحـداث التغييـر، وذلـك بهـدف إثبـات مـدى أهميـة النهـج التشـاركي لصياغـة المجموعـة التاليـة مـن أهـداف التنميـة المسـتدامة.

وقـد عرضـت الأفـلام في صنـدوق الأمـم المتحـدة للطفولـة (اليونيسـيف) في سبتمبر عـام 2013، كجـزء مـن حملـة للتأثيـر عـلى صانعـي السياسـات لاعتمـاد نهـج تشـاركي بشـأن أهـداف التنميـة المسـتدامة. وقـد تـم تصميـم الأفـلام القصيـرة والـتي أنتجتهـا مجموعتيـن مـن النسـاء الريفيـات مـن القـرى الواقعـة عـلى مشـارف القـدس والـتي انقطعـت تمامـاً عـن المدينـة بسـبب جـدار الفصـل الإسـرائيلي. ورغـم عـدم تمتعهـنّ بـأي خبـرة إعلاميـة مسـبقة، وبعـد 52 سـاعة مـن التدريـب، كانـت النسـاء مسـؤولات بشـكل مبـاشر عـن كل مرحلـة مـن مراحـل كل فيلـم؛ إذ اخـترن مواضيعهـن الخاصـة، وكتـبن السـيناريو الخـاص بهـن، وتولّـن عمليـة التصويـر بأنفسـهن. كل شيء مـا عـدا المونتـاج. لكنهـن عملـن ايضـاً مـع المحـرر (منفـذ المونتـاج) في اليـوم الـذي أعطـي لـكل فيلـم.

الأمثلـة المذكـورة أعـلاه مسـتمدة مـن الضفـة الغربيـة والقـدس الشرقيـة، حيـث عـلى الرغـم مـن المشـاكل الكثيـرة والقيـود المفروضـة عـلى حقـوق الإنسـان بسـبب الاحتـلال، لا يـزال هنـاك قـدر مـن حريـة الإعـلام.

يمكـن القـول أن الجهـود المتعلقـة بالتثقيـف الاعلامـي ومحـو اميـة الاعـلام في قطـاع غـزة كانـت أقـل وتيـرة نظـرا للظـروف الامنيـة وظـروف الحصـار الـتي يعيشـها قطـاع غـزة منـذ عـام 2007. لكـن جهـودا بذلـك وإن كانـت قليلـة هدفـت الى تثقيـف طلبـة المـدراس والاطفـال بهـذا بكيفيـة التعامـل والتعاطـي مـع الاعـلام. فقـد نفـذت وزارة الشـباب والرياضـة في غـزة

عـام 2010 دورة التثقيـف الإعلامـي للأطفـال، في مقر الـوزارة، بمشاركة 20 فتـى وفتـاة، بعضهـم يافـع جـداً، لدرجـة أن احدهـم كان يُقـال عنـه انـه «طفل».

كما نظمـت الـوزارة ورشـة عمـل إضافيـة بمشاركة المختصين لمناقشة وضـع تصـور لتفعيل الرياضـة المدرسيـة. وقـد نفـذت الـدورة بواقـع 12 سـاعة تدريبيـة، وشـملت تعريفـاً مبسـطاً لمفاهيـم الصحافـة والخبـر والتقريـر والمقابلـة، بالإضافـة لطبيعـة عمـل المواقـع الإلكترونيـة الإخباريـة، وكيفيـة تحليـل المضاميـن والتعامـل معهـا والتفاعـل الجيـد مـع وسـائل الاعـلام.

للأسـف، ومـع تدهـور الأوضـاع في غـزة، لا سـيما خـلال الحـرب التـي اندلعـت صيـف عـام 2014، تحـول التركيـز إلى الاحتياجـات الأساسـية العاجلـة. lix.

التربية الإعلامية (التثقيف الإعلامي) في سياق بناء السلام:

إن العيـش تحت نيـر الاحتـلال غالبـاً مـا يكون مهينـاً، سـواء بشـكل مباشـر أو غيـر مباشـر. هـذا الاذى الـذي يلحـق بالكرامـة واحتـرام الـذات يشـكل ايضـاً ضـرراً عـلى الإحسـاس بالـذات. يمكـن لعمليـة التربيـة الإعلاميـة والمعلوماتيـة (التثقيـف الإعلامـي والمعلومـاتي) مـن خـلال مـا تسـمح بـه مـن تمكيـن، أن تسـاعد في إعـادة بنـاء احتـرام الـذات والإحسـاس القـوي بالهويـة. وهـي تشـكل أيضـاً قاعـدة أساسـية للقـدرة عـلى الانخـراط في الحـوار بيـن الثقافـات وبنـاء السـلام.

إن عمليـة تشـكيل الهويـة الذاتيـة هـي مـن المقومـات الأساسـية للحـوار بيـن الثقافـات، وهـي تسـمح للنـاس بفهـم نقـاط الانطـلاق الثقافيـة الخاصـة بهـم، وبالتـالي الدخـول في حـوار عـلى أسـاس «التواصـل الأصيـل» الـذي مـن خلالـه «يصبحـون اكـثر ادراكـاً بالطـرق التـي قـد يتعرضـون بواسـطتها للتلاعـب أو الإكـراه وإدراكـاً بالطـرق التـي تؤثـر فيهـا السـلطة التفاضليـة في المجتمـع». lx

أضـف الى ذلـك، يمكـن أيضـاً إعتبـار التربيـة الإعلاميـة والمعلوماتيـة مـن المقومـات الهامـة لبنـاء السـلام باعتبارهـا تشـكل الوعـي الـذاتي والوعـي بالآخريـن والوعـي بشـأن التحيـز والتنميـط، وبالتـالي بنـاء مقاومـة لهـا، وعمومـا للدعايـة السياسـية. lxi.

يمكـن ان تكـون للمشـاريع التـي تسـتخدم التثقيـف الإعلامـي والمعلومـاتي كأداة لبنـاء السـلام الكثيـر مـن الإمكانيـات، ويمكـن أن تكـون وسـيلة لتغييـر بعـض الصـور النمطيـة السـلبية التـي تسـاهم (مباشـرة أو غيـر مباشـرة) باسـتمرار الاحتـلال، والعمـل عـلى التغلـب عـلى بعـض العقبـات النفسـية امـام السـلام.

قد سُجّلت محاولة واحدة للعمل مع الثقيف الإعلامي كنهج لصنع السلام، بتمويل من الاتحاد الأوروبي تولّت تنفيذها من الجانب الفلسطيني مجلة فلسطين-إسرائيل الفصلية للسياسة والاقتصاد والثقافة، والتي تملك هيئة تحرير إسرائيلية فلسطينية مشتركة وفريق عمل مشترك. كونه مشروعاً مشتركاً، يركز على الوصول إلى الجانب الإسرائيلي، فهو يكاد يطال نطاق هذا الفصل، لكنه نجح مع بعض الشبان الفلسطينيين وركز بشكل خاص على الإعلام «بهدف تشجيع الطلاب على تطبيق التفكير النقدي لدى تحليل عمل الإعلام القديم والحديث، ولتقديم أساليب بديلة، ورسائل حول تغطية الصراعات.

«تضمن المشروع، المموّل من الإتحاد الأوروبي في إطار مشروعه «تعليم السلام من خلال الإعلام»، ثلاث جلسات نقاش حوارية بين الخبراء (15 20- مشاركاً) وعقد في القدس في عام 2010 وعام 2011. تضمن ايضاً وثيقة توجيهية مفصلة عن «المبادئ الإعلامية التوجيهية لتغطية النزاع في الشرق الأوسط»lxii، تم تصميمها على غرار الأسس النظرية للتثقيف الإعلامي النقدي لغرض تطوير التحليل النقدي لدى الطلاب وتقييم الأطر الإعلامية للصراع الإسرائيلي الفلسطيني. وهو يقوم على الموارد تجريبية لثلاث كليات الأكاديمية في إسرائيل (اثنان منهم مؤسسات تدريب المعلمين)، التي تشجع الطلاب على تطبيق التفكير النقدي لعمل وسائل الإعلام القديمة والجديدة، وتقديم أساليب بديلة ورسائل حول تغطية الصراع. بهذه الطريقة، يساهم بتزويد الطلاب بالخبرة، كمستهلكين ومنتجين على حد سواء، ليكونوا مواطنين ناقدين للإعلام الرقمي الحالي الجديد.»lxiii

المشروع المشترك الآخر: يركز مركز رجال أعمال الغد في الشرق الأوسط «MEET» يركز على التربية المعلوماتية (التثقيف المعلوماتي). المركز، الذي أنشىء في عام 2005 تحت رعاية معهد ماساتشوستس للتكنولوجيا، يعمل مع طلاب المدارس الثانوية الفلسطينيين والإسرائيليين في إطار برنامج مدته ثلاث سنوات «يسمح للمشاركين باكتساب الأدوات التكنولوجية والقيادية المتقدمة، ويمكنهم في الوقت نفسه من إحداث تغيير اجتماعي إيجابي داخل مجتمعاتهم». lxiv يتم التدريس في الجامعة العبرية. وكما هي الحال في القدس الشرقية، وبسبب القيود الإسرائيلية المفروضة على وصول الفلسطينيين، فالتدريس مفتوح فقط للأولاد الفلسطينيين من القدس.

الاحتياجات التعليمية:

التعليـم هـو أحـد الجوانـب التـي تعانـي باستمرار مـن الآثار السـلبية للاحتلال الإسـرائيلي، وذلـك بسـبب إغـلاق المـدارس والطـرق، أو بسـبب عنـف المسـتوطنين، وكذلـك تفجـر الـصـراع. lxv

المطبوعـة الوحيـدة المنتجـة محليـاً بشـكل محـدد عـن التربيـة الإعلاميـة (التثقيـف الإعلامـي) هـو عبـر مشـروع معهـد فوجـو / جامعـة بيـر زيـت. ويشـمل المشـروع الممـول مـن مجلـس الأبحـاث والتبـادل الـدولي «IREX» يتضمـن دليـلاً تدريبيـاً باللغـة العربيـة، لكنـه يركـز بشـكل محـدد عـلى المهـارات الإعلاميـة العمليـة بـدلاً مـن التركيـز عـلى المنهـج التحليـلي للتربيـة الإعلاميـة والمعلوماتيـة (التثقيـف الإعلامـي والمعلومـاتي). وفي حيـن انـه يوجـد دليـل ممتـاز لتدريـب المدرّسـين، مـن إنتـاج اليونسكـو باللغـة العربيـة، lxvi للأسـف، ليـس هـذا الأمـر معروفـاً عـلى نطـاق واسـع، مقارنـة مـع العديـد مـن المـوارد حـول الموضـوع باللغـة الإنجليزيـة.

يعكـس هـذا الأمـر مشـكلة حقيقيـة، إذ يرغـب العديـد مـن المؤسسـات التعليميـة في تقديـم التربيـة الإعلاميـة، إلا أنهـا تجـد صعوبـة في العثـور عـلى المـواد التعليميـة والتدريبيـة لتنفيـذ برامجهـا بشـكل موثـوق. عـلى سـبيل المثـال، تـم التعريـف بكاتـي هـذا الفصـل عـبر المـواد المقدمـة بواسـطة الترجمـة وعـبر مشـاريع أخـرى.

إذاً، وبشـكل عـام ، يمكـن القـول أن البيئـة التعليميـة الفلسطينيـة تعيـق التربيـة الاعلاميـة (التثقيـف الإعلامـي) مـن خـلال اعاقـة كل أشـكال التفكيـر النقـدي والاستعلام. ويستنـد امتحـان المدرسـة الثانويـة النهائـي، الـذي يُعـرف بالامتحـان التوجيهـي، عـلى التعلـم عـن ظهـر قلـب في كافـة المـواد الدراسيـة. lxvii حـتى في العلـوم ، مـن الممكـن نيـل درجـة 99 بالمائـة مـن دون أجـراء أن يكـون الطالـب قـد أجـرى تجربـة علميـة مـن قبـل. lxviii بالمقابـل، تسـمح التربيـة الإعلاميـة (التثقيـف الإعلامـي) كمهـارة بتطويـر نهـج غريـب، نقـدي وتحليـلي، يمكـن وينبغـي أن تـدرّس حـتى في المـدارس الابتدائيـة. lxix

ويشـمل ذلـك التعريـف والتثقيـف بالانترنت. لكـن في حيـن يبـدو أن التثقيـف في مجـال الإنترنت يوفـر نقطـة دخـول محتملـة، للأسـف الغالبيـة العظمـى مـن الحكومـة والأونـروا، عـلى الرغـم مـن إدخـال التكنولوجيـا كمـادة إلزاميـة مـن الصـف الخامـس الى العاشـر، لا يملـك الكثيـر مـن المـدارس الحكوميـة مـا يكفـي مـن أجهـزة الكمبيوتـر أو عـرض النطـاق التـرددي الإنترنت.

وغالباً ما تملك تلك المدارس جهاز كمبيوتر واحد على الأكثر، لمدير المدرسة وليس للطلاب. كما أن بعض المدارس يعجز عن الحصول على الاتصال بالإنترنت بشكل مستمر في كثير من الأحيان (بتكلفة نحو 40 دولاراً في الشهر).

وعلى الرغم من التقدم الكبير في توفير المواد والمعدات وتكنولوجيا المعلومات والاتصالات، يبقى التحدي الأبرز هو الحصول على دليل على استخدامها الفعلي في المدارس والصفوف. lxxx هذا يعني الاستعلام عن مدى استخدامها، وكثافة استخدامها وفي اية مواضيع، ومستوى التكامل مع المنهج؛ والأهم من ذلك، الأثر على نتائج أداء الطالب وقدرته على التعلم. كلها عناصر رئيسية لجدول الأعمال المستقبلي لتحسين نوعية وملاءمة التعليم في الضفة الغربية وقطاع غزة.

ان موضوع التثقيف الاعلامي (التربية الإعلامية) في المناهج الفلسطيني يمكن أن يقال عنه انه ضعيف جداً أو غير موجود. ولم تكن هناك مناقشات بشأن التربية الإعلامية والمعلوماتية (التثقيف الإعلامي والمعلوماتي) على المستوى الوطني، ولم يتخذ قرار بعد بإدارج هذا الموضوع ضمن المنهاج الفلسطيني بشكل بارز، على الرغم من التطور الكبير والمتسارع في الاعلام ووجود وسائل التواصل الاجتماعي واتساع تأثيرها على الطلاب والمدارس.

كما توجد حاجة ملحة لتحديد مقاربات سليمة وأدوات تعليمية للتعامل مع هذه التطورات الجديدة وتعليم الشباب كيفية تحليل الكم الهائل من المعلومات في وسائل الإعلام المختلفة. وفي حين ان الحاجة شديدة الى التربية الإعلامية (التثقيف الإعلامي)، وهي ذات أهمية كبيرة في عالم اليوم بالنسبة للفلسطينيين والجميع في منطقة الشرق الأوسط، لا بد من تكريس الوقت الطويل والعمل المتفاني مع وزارة التربية والتعليم لإقناع صانعي السياسات بمدى أهميتها كموضوع تركيز منفصل في المناهج الدراسية قبل أن يتم تعميمها.

التوصيات:

إن التربية الإعلامية والمعلوماتية، بما تعنيه من فهم للإعلام والقدرة على التحليل والانتقاد، ومعرفة كيفية استخدام الاعلام والمشاركة، لا سيما من خلال استخدام الأدوات الرقمية، تشكل جانباً أساسياً لتنمية وتمكين كلّ من الأفراد والمجتمعات. lxxi ويعتبر المؤلفون أنه من الضروري إدراجها في نظام التعليم الرسمي في الأراضي الفلسطينية المحتلة، من المدارس الابتدائية وصولاً الى الجامعات.

يمكن تعميم التربية الإعلامية والمعلوماتية بشكل أكثر فعالية باستخدام استراتيجية من أسفل لأعلى ومن أعلى لأسفل. من أسفل لأعلى للتأكد من إلقاء الضوء على احتياجات الجمهور، وخاصة النساء والشباب والفئات المهمّشة، وتلبية تلك الإحتياجات من خلال أي برنامج. من أعلى لأسفل، للتأكد من أن إمكان تطبيق العملية في كافة الأنظمة التعليمية - التعليم الابتدائي والثانوي والعالي، والرسمي وغير الرسمي.

وبالتالي يمكننا أن نطلق التوصيات المحددة التالية:

1. تشاور رفيع المستوى بين أصحاب المصلحة المتعددين:

إن أفضل السبل للمباشرة ببرامج التربية الإعلامية والمعلوماتية ومنحها الزخم الفوري سيكون بتنظيم مشاورات رفيعة المستوى مع ممثلين عن كلّ من برنامج الأمم المتحدة لتحالف الحضارات، واليونسكو، وغيرها من وكالات التنمية التي تتمتع بالخبرة في مجال التربية الإعلامية والمعلوماتية والتي يمكن أن تقوم بإشراك مسؤولين رفيعي المستوى من السلطة الفلسطينية والمجتمع التعليمي في تقدير أهمية التربية الإعلامية والمعلوماتية وصياغة استراتيجية وطنية.

كما سيكون من المهم إدراج الرصد والتقييم منذ البداية للتأكد من تنفيذ المشروع في موعده المقرر وألا يقوم كلّ من المدارس والمدرّسين بوضعه جانباً. من الأفضل البدء بخطوات صغيرة وإثبات فعالية التربية الإعلامية والمعلوماتية.

2. إعادة: التعليم الابتدائي والثانوي:

لا بد من إدراج التربية الإعلامية والمعلوماتية إلى المنهج الرئيسي (الإلزامي) للمدارس الابتدائية والثانوية، بدءا من الصف الأول. لا بد ايضاً من اعتبار هذا الموضوع شكلاً أساسياً من أشكال التثقيف في هذا العصر. وينبغي أن يكون التركيز على التمارين العملية، وليس على النظريات، وعلى تشجيع الأطفال على طرح الأسئلة، وليس الاكتفاء بالتعلم عن ظهر قلب.

لا يكفي إقتراح التربية الإعلامية والمعلوماتية كخيار. بل ينبغي إدراجها في المناهج بدءاً من المدرسة الابتدائية وصولا إلى الامتحان النهائي «التوجيهي» (المدرسة الثانوية).

يمكن أن تكون الخطوة الأولى ورشة عمل / أو جلسة تشاور تحت إشراف الأمم المتحدة، وخصوصاً بالتزامن مع التحالف الدولي للثقافة الإعلامية والمعلوماتية (GAPMIL) lxxii

لتعزيـز الوعـي بالنجـاح فـي سـياقات أخـرى، وتقاسـم الأدوات مثـل منهـج التربيـة الإعلاميـة والمعلوماتيـة للمدرّسـين، ونظـام التقييـم. بشـكل خـاص، مـن المناسـب أن يعطـى الفلسـطينيون مثـل الأرجنتيـن والعمـل مـع الأطفـال الصغـار فـي ذلـك البلـد. مثـل ورشـة العمـل هـذه سـتحتاج لأن تشـمل جميـع أصحـاب المصلحـة المحليـين، وخاصـة وكالـة الغـوث (الأونـروا)، وهـي المسـؤولة عـن مـا يقـرب مـن نصـف المـدارس الفلسـطينية. وبمـا أن الأونـروا تملـك برنامجـاً نفسـياً واجتماعيـاً شـاملاً، يمكـن أن يسـاهم ذلـك الى الطريقـة التـي يمكـن مـن خلالهـا ان تقـوم التربيـة الإعلاميـة والمعلوماتيـة بتلبيـة هـذه الاحتياجـات، سـواء فـي الأراضـي الفلسـطينية المحتلـة، او فـي بلـدان أخـرى فـي منطقـة الشـرق الأوسـط وافريقيـا.

لهـذا، لا بـد مـن خضـوع المدرّسـين والمسـؤولين للتدريـب، أو علـى الأقـل إعطاؤهـم مقدمة شـاملة عـن التربيـة الإعلاميـة والمعلوماتيـة.

بلإضافـة الى ذلـك، لا بـد مـن الإشـارة إلى أن الرصـد والتقييـم سـيكونان عنصريـن ضروريـن فـي كافـة مراحـل العمليـة.

3. إعادة: الجامعات / التعليم العالي:

ينبغـي أن تكـون التربيـة الإعلاميـة والمعلوماتيـة مطلبـاص أساسـياً لجميـع الطـلاب الجامعيـن (إلى جانـب الـدروس الأساسـية مثـل الثقافـة الإسـلامية، الـخ.)، ويجـب أن يكـون التركيـز علـى الجانـب العملـي وليـس النظـري.

يمكـن ان تكـون الخطـوة الأولـى نحـو دعـم التعليـم العالـي، بالإضافـة إلى المشـاورات الرفيعة المسـتوى، عقـد مؤتمـر كبيـر تحـت رعايـة الأمـم المتحـدة، يجمـع عـدداً مـن المتحدثـين الدوليـين وتأمـين التغطيـة الإعلاميـة لإدخـال الموضـوع فـي سـياق الحديـث. يمكـن أن يُعقـد يومـان للمؤتمـر ويـوم واحـد للمناقشـات العمليـة جـداً حـول بنـاء الـدورات لمسـاعدة كل جامعـة مشـاركة علـى ابتـكار دوراتهـا الخاصـة لهيئـة طلابهـا المحـددة.

مـرة أخـرى، يجـب أن يُدمـج الرصـد والتقييـم فـي الـدورات؛ علـى أن تجتمـع الجامعـات المشـاركة وغيرهـا مـن مؤسسـات التعليـم العالـي كل بضـع سـنوات لعقـد مؤتمـر متابعـة لتحليـل الآثـار والنتائـج.

4. إعادة: المجتمع المدني:

لا بـد مـن انتـاج دليـل - دليـل عملـي للمجتمـع المدنـي - حـول كيفيـة التعامـل مـع الإعـلام

المحلي والـدولي. يمكـن أن يصـدر هـذا الأمـر أيضاً عـن مؤتمـر للامـم المتحـدة، وينبغي أن يشـمل الأسـئلة التـي تظهـر خـلال المؤتمـر. وسيكون مـن المثالي إعـداد استبيان ودراسـة مقارنـة أساسـية أولاً. مـن شـأن ذلـك ان يساعد في تعزيـز الوعـي حـول الموضوع، ويسـاعد سـواء في المؤتمـر او في إنتـاج المـواد التعليميـة والتدريبيـة ذات الصلـة. كما يسـاهم الاستطلاع أيضاً بتوفير الأسـاس لعمليـات القيـاس والتقييـم لمختلـف البرامـج المقترحة.

ينبغي إعـداد برامـج تدريبيـة محـددة في مجـال التربيـة الإعلاميـة للمجتمـع المـدني وينبغي تنفيذهـا مـن قبـل المنظمـات غيـر الحكوميـة ولصالحهـا، اسـتناداً إلى الأجوبـة التـي جُمعـت في الاستطلاع.

ينبغي عـلى مجتمـع المانحين أن يدعـم هـذه التطـورات والتدريـب وغيرهـا مـن المشاريع ذات الصلـة، مـن اجـل تعزيـز الوعـي وخلـق مسـتوى أساسـي مـن الوعـي عـلى الأقـل بشـأن الإعـلام. سـيكون مـن المهـم أن تـدرج هـذه الامـور في المؤتمـر وفي عمليـة التدريـب لكـي يصبـح جهـداً لأصحـاب المصلحـة المتعددين.

5. إعادة: وسائل الإعلام:

لا بـد ايضاً مـن تدريـب وسائـل الإعـلام المختلفـة لتعلـم كيفيـة التعامـل مـع ردود الفعـل، لمشاركة إنتـاج المـواد الإعلاميـة، وتشجيع النـاس بواسـطة التوعيـة الإعلاميـة للعمـل معهـم نحـو مزيـد مـن الانفتاح وتشجيع المسـاءلة الإعلاميـة والأخلاقيـات الإعلاميـة. lxxiii ينبغي أن تعالـج إحـدى هيئـات المؤتمـر المشـاكل التـي تواجـه وسائـل الإعـلام في الأراضي الفلسطينية المحتلـة، وينبغـي أن تـدرج وسائـل الإعـلام في كافـة المراحـل كالمشاورات والمؤتمـر نفسـه.

بالإضافة إلى ذلـك، يمكـن أن تشـارك وسائـل الإعـلام في حملـة (حـتى عـلى مسـتوى منطقـة الـشرق الأوسـط وإفريقيـا) وطنيـة لتعزيـز التربيـة الإعلاميـة والمعلوماتيـة، مـن خـلال سلسـلة مـن الاعلانـات عـلى الراديـو والتلفزيـون، والتطبيقـات، والألعـاب، الـخ. ويمكـن مناقشـة ذلـك في البدايـة في إطار المشاورات والمؤتمـرات واسـتخدام نتائـج الاسـتبيانات لهـذه الغايـة. كذلـك، ربما تتمكـن إحـدى وسائـل الاعـلام مـن تطويـر شـخصية كرتونيـة (أو اثنتيـن - رجـل وامـرأة)، يقومـون بالتعلـم، وارتكـاب الأخطـاء، ويمكـن التعـرف اليهمـا بسـهولة، لابـراز أهميـة التربيـة الإعلاميـة والمعلوماتيـة وجدواها.

6. إعادة: المجتمع الفلسطيني ككل:

لا بـد مـن البـدء بوضـع نهـج أكـثر نقديـة بيـن المجتمـع المـدني والإعـلام، والجمهـور.

العـام، وتعزيـز مفهـوم المسـاءلة الإعلاميـة. يمكـن ان يسـاهم المؤتمـر مـن خـلال تعزيـز الوعـي وينبغـي أن يقـوم بإعـداد صفحـة تفاعليـة لإشـراك الجمهـور، يمكـن ربطهـا مـع مبـادرة التحالـف الـدولي للثقافـة الإعلاميـة والمعلوماتيـة (GAPMIL)، لمواكبـة المناقشـات الجاريـة.

بالنسـبة للشـباب، يمكـن للمخيمـات الصيفيـة في مجـال التربيـة الإعلاميـة والمعلوماتيـة أن تشـكّل خيـاراً جذابـاً، لا سـيما إذا كانـت دوليـة. ويصبـح الشـباب الذيـن تـم تدريبهـم في مجـال التربيـة الإعلاميـة والمعلوماتيـة أن يصبحـوا مدربيـن وربمـا يسـاعدون في تطويـر البرنامـج ونشـره بشـكل موسـع وسـريع في المـدارس الابتدائيـة والثانويـة.

---

i سياسة اليونيسكو في مجال التربية الإعلامية والمعلوماتية والمبادىء التوجيهية للاستراتيجية، اليونيسكو 2013، الصفحة 8:

http://unesdoc.unesco.org/images/0022/002256/225606e.pdf

ii	اليونيكسو – الموقع نفسه. الصفحة 53 - 54
iii	اليونيكسو – الموقع نفسه. الصفحة 47
iv	اليونيكسو – الموقع نفسه. الصفحة 48
v	الدكتور رشيد الجيوشي: مستشار التعلم الالكتروني لدى وزارة التربية والتعليم الفلسطينية
vi	اليونيكسو – الموقع نفسه. الصفحة 54

vii رينيه هوبس: التربية الإعلامية والرقمية: خطة عمل، معهد أسبن، 2010
http://www.knightcomm.org/wpcontent/uploads/2010/12/Digital_and_Media_
Literacy_A_Plan_of_Action.pdf

viii	اليونيكسو – الموقع نفسه. الصفحة 22
ix	اليونيكسو – الموقع نفسه. الصفحة 151

x منظمة «ميرسي كور» الدولية: المشاركة المدنية للشباب في منطقة الشرق الأوسط وشمال أفريقيا: تحليل العوامل الرئيسية والنتائج، مارس 2012، ص. 16
http://www.mercycorps.org/sites/default/files/mena_youth_civic_engagement_study_-_final.pdf

xi   اليونيكسو – الموقع نفسه. الصفحة 18

xii   اليونيكسو – الموقع نفسه.

xiii http://www.pcbs.gov.ps/site/881/default.aspx الارقام الصادرة عن الجهاز المركزي للإحصاء الفلسطيني، 2014.

xiv https://www.ochaopt.org/documents/ochaopt_atlas_opt_general_de-cember2011.pdf

مكتب تنسيق الشؤون الإنسانية يقدم تحديثات أسبوعية ممتازة عن الوضع كما يقوم بإعداد تقارير مفصلة وصحائف وقائع، على سبيل المثال حول مشاكل المنطقة «سي» (60 بالمائة من الضفة الغربية)

https://www.ochaopt.org/documents/ocha_opt_area_c_factsheet_august_2014_english.pdf

xv   ماري حنانيا، مجلة الدراسات الفلسطينية، 2007. العدد 32 الصفحة 51، جورجي حبيب حنانيا، تاريخ الصحافة في فلسطين 1908 - 1914

http://www.palestine-studies.org/jq/fulltext/77872

xvi   روبرت إي. فريدمان، مجلة الدراسات الفلسطينية، الرقابة الإسرائيلية على الصحافة الفلسطينية، المجلد 13، الرقم 1:

http://www.jstor.org/stable/2536927?seq=1#page_scan_tab_contents

xvii هذه ذكرى شخصية – لم اتمكن من العثور على مصدر مكتوب - يمكن محوها إذا شئت

xviii تقرير إنترنيوز عن الفلسطينيين والإعلام، الاستخدام، والثقة والفعالية:

http://www.internews.org/sites/default/files/resources/Palestinians%26Media070314.pdf

xix لمزيد من التفاصيل انظر:

http://www.internews.org/research-publications/media-landscape-west-bank-ga-za#sthash.Vug7lu3c.dpuf

ايضاً اليونسكو المذكور بالاسفل

xx   http://www.unesco.org/new/en/communication-and-information/resources/publications-and-communication-materials/publications/full-list/assessment-of-me-dia-development-in-palestine/

المرجع نفسه ص. 31

xxi «نبـذة عـن القنـاة الفضائيـة، 48 بالمائـة يشـاهدون قنـاة الجزيـرة، 15 بالمائـة يشـاهدون قنـاة العربيـة وتلفزيـون فلسـطين، 7 بالمائـة يشـاهدون القنـوات العربيـة الأخـرى، و 4 بالمائـة يشـاهدون قنـاة المنـار، 2 بالمائـة يشـتهدون الأقـصى، و«بي بي سي»، في حين أن 7 بالمائة يشـاهدونالقنوات الأخـرى.» (الشرق الأدنى للاستشارات، تقرير أبريل مايو عام 2010؛ /http://www.neareastconsulting.com/press

xxii إنترنيوز. المرجع نفسه

xxiii http://www.pcbs.gov.ps/site/512/default.aspx?tabID=512&lang=en&Ite-mID=1342&mid=3171&wversion=Staging

xxiv http://www.pcbs.gov.ps/site/881/default.aspx#InformationSociety

xxv اليونسكو، البرنامج الدولي لتنمية الاتصال(IPDC)، المرجع نفسه، ص. 103

xxvi المرجع نفسه

xxvii تقرير الإعلام الاجتماعي العربي عام 2015، الصفحة 24. www.wpp.com/govtpractice/~/.../arabsocialmediareport-2015.pdf.

xxviii إنترنيوز. المرجع نفسه و www.socialbakers.com

xxix http://www.unesco.org/new/en/communication-and-information/re-sources/publications-and-communication-materials/publications/full-list/assess-/ment-of-media-development-in-palestine ص. 12

xxx التحول إلى التلفزيون الرقمي يواجه طريقاً وعرة في فلسطين، داود كتّاب، 4 مايو 2015: http://www.al-monitor.com/pulse/originals/2015/05/palestinian-television-digi-tal-media-independent.html#ixzz3er6gyFzQ

«امعظم الفلسطينيين، 17 يوليو 2015، يعني القليل. لكن بالنسبة لأولئك الذين يعملون منذ فترة طويلة تجاه انتقال كافة ترددات البث التلفزيوني الفلسطيني من البث التماثلي إلى البث الرقمي، التاريخ محفور في الحجر. بتكليف من الاتحاد الدولي للاتصالات وبموافقة الجامعة العربية، وافقت كل الدول العربية في عام 2006

xxxi المونيتور. المرجع نفسه.

xxxii غموض الترددات يؤثر أيضاً على القدرة على بث كما في فبراير 2011، عندم تمّ الاستيلاء على أجهزة الإرسال الخاصة بتلفزيون القدس والوطن من قبل الإسرائيليين على أساس أنها تتداخل حركة الملاحة الجوية

xxxiii اليونسكو - المرجع نفسه. ص. 76

xxxiv مركز مدى: انتهاكات الحريات الإعلامية في فلسطين، التقرير السنوي لعام 2014، ص 5 و 6:
http://www.madacenter.org/images/text_editor/Study%20pdf.pdf

xxxv مركز مدى: المرجع نفسه.

xxxvii مقابلة: الدراسة الاستقصائية للاعلام الفلسطيني، الشرق الأدنى للاستشارات (2010) - لمزيد من التفاصيل عن هذا الموضوع بالعربية:
http://www.madacenter.org/images/text_editor/Study%20pdf.pdf

xxxviii http://www.madacenter.org/images/text_editor/Study%20pdf.pdf
والتقارير السنوية.

xxxix http://mdc.birzeit.edu/files/English_Report_for_wessed.pdf
ص. 85

xl القانون الأساسي الفلسطيني، المادة 19

xli http://www.med-media.eu/wp-content/uploads/2014/07/palestine-me-dia-framework.pdf

xlii كما نصّ عليه ياسر عرفات في عام 1994 يوم تأسيس السلطة الفلسطينية: «»يستمر العمل بالقوانين والأنظمة والأوامر التي كانت سارية المفعول قبل تاريخ 5/6/1967 في الضفة الغربية وقطاع غزة .» «الجريدة الفلسطينية: رقم 1 20/11/1994

xliii القانون الجنائي الاردني: الرقم 16 لعام 1960، المادة 188 (1) - وضع هذا القانون عندما كان الاردن يحكم الضفة الغربية، ويبدو أكثر ملاءمة للملكية منه الدولة الحديثة.

xliv اليونسكو - البرنامج الدولي لتنمية الاتصال(IPDC). المرجع نفسه، ص. 11

xlv اليونسكو - المرجع نفسه، ص 38

http://www.madacenter.org/news.php?lang=1&id=161   xlvi

xlvii   اليونسكو - المرجع نفسه الصفحة 75

xlviii   اليونسكو - المرجع نفسه، الصفحة 31

xlix   رشيد الجيوشي، الاتصال عبر البريد الالكتروني.

l   لمزيد من التفاصيل، وخاصة عن موضوع غزة، يرجى مراجعة تقارير مكتب تنسيق الشؤون الإنسانية المشار إليها أعلاه

li   اليونسكو – التربية الإعلامية والمعلوماتية - ص. 151 الثاني - ص. 107

http://milunesco.unaoc.org/helping-palestinian-children-become-me-   lii
/dia-smart

liii   الأونروا هي هيئة تابعة للأمم المتحدة مسؤولة عن الاحتياجات الأساسية، ولا سيما الصحية والتعليمية للاجئين الفلسطينيين. هذا يعني أنها مسؤولة عن ما يقرب من نصف المدارس في الأراضي المحتلة.

http://www.palestine.rosalux.org/fileadmin/ab_palestine/pdf/RLF_news-   liv
letters_EN/RLF_PAL_Gerster_PNGOs.pdf

https://www.irex.org/projects/partnerships-with-youth   lv

lvi   (تقرير المشروع – الملحق بي -6 تقرير الانجازات رقم 1)

lvii   نشرت جامعة «ساسكس» كتاباً عن هذا الموضوع، يتضمن فصلاً عن الفيديو التشاركي وآخر عن قوة رواية القصص الرقمية: «المعرفة من الهوامش: مختارات من شبكة عالمية على الممارسة القائمة على المشاركة والتأثير على السياسة». يمكن مشاهدة أو تحميل المنشور عبر الرابط التالي:
http://opendocs.ids.ac.uk/opendocs/handle/123456789/4199#.U8aGllGfj2s
https://www.irex.org/projects/partnerships-with-youth

viii   الروابط للافلام:

(عيد ميلاد تعيس) https://www.youtube.com/watch?v=nHs3otiFHfA

(الأرجوحة) https://www.youtube.com/watch?v=HZiFSBZfezw

(أحتاج الى عمل) https://www.youtube.com/watch?v=81pcETn6sxI

(الهوية الزرقاء والهوية الخضراء) https://www.youtube.com/watch?v=EWTFunqqicE

(النبي صموئيل) http://www.youtube.com/watch?v=48W2j1sN8Ag&feature=youtu.be

lix تعطي تقارير مكتب تنسيق الشؤون الإنسانية التفاصيل حول هذه - كيف أنه وحتى قبل عملية «الجرف الصامد» الاسرائيلية، كان هناك نقص بنسبة 200 مدرسة في قطاع غزة. https://www.ochaopt.org/documents/gaza_mira_report_9september.pdf

lx اليونسكو - المرجع نفسه، الصفحة 18

lxi اليونسكو - المرجع نفسه

lxii http://www.pij.org/policypapers/PETMed_PolicyPaper.pdf

lxiii المرحلة الثانية من هذا المشروع، الممول أيضاً من قبل الاتحاد الأوروبي، عملت فقط مع الإسرائيليين، وشملت وضع دليل تدريب المعلمين.

lxiv http://meet.mit.edu/

lxv خارج نطاق هذا الفصل، تقدم تقارير المنظمات غير الحكومية مثل منتدى شارك الشبابي على معلومات إضافية: www.youthpolicy.org/national/Palestine_2009_Youth_Study.pdf

lxvi http://unesdoc.unesdoc.org/images/0019/001929/192971a.pdf

lxvii شارك، الصفحة 23

lxviii لا يملك الكثير من المدارس المختبرات. «وعلى الرغم من النجاح الشامل الذي لا يمكن إنكاره لعملية تصميم وتطوير المنهاج الفلسطيني الجديد، فإن الأدلة التي تم جمعها خلال السنوات القليلة الأولى من التنفيذ تكشف عن مشكلة خطيرة هي «الحمولة الزائدة». ويتفق كلّ من مديري المدارس والمدرّسين وأولياء الأمور والطلاب والمشرفين ومدربي المدرسين على أن المنهج الجديد هو «طويل جداً» و «متطلب جداً». وتتعرض فرص التعلم للتقويض عندما يكون هناك وقت قليل مخصص لكثير من الموضوعات الرئيسية؛ كما ان حقيقة أن المدرسين والطلاب يمددون طوعاً وقت الدراسة في بعض المدارس ليتمكنوا من تغطية المنهاج.

إن النهج التقليدي الذي يلقي الضوء على الحقائق والمعرفة الوصفية والنظرية المجردة لا يترك مجالاً في المناهج أو وقتاً في الفصول الدراسية، لتنمية المهارات المعرفية والمواطنة المطلوبة من الخريجين في القرن الحادي والعشرين. لمزيد من المعلومات، بما في ذلك تفاصيل عن أعداد مختبرات العلوم وتكنولوجيا المعلومات والاتصالات،

يرجى الاطلاع على الرابط: http://unispal.un.org/pdfs/ESASept06.pdf

مجموعة البنك الدولي. تحليل قطاع التعليم 2006، الصفحة 28 و 29

xix

lxx   فشـل محاولـة للعمـل مـع «تويـغ»، وهـي مؤسسـة تعليميـة مبتكـرة ومقرهـا بريطانيـا تتـولى إنتـاج أفـلام تعليميـة مدتهـا ثـلاث دقائـق لتوضيـح واستكمال المناهـج الدراسـية الخاصـة بالمـدارس الثانويـة وتعزيـز بيئـة الصـف. وتأمـل «تويـغ» في العمـل مـن خـلال افلامهـا في المـدارس الفلسطينية، لكنهـا لـم تتمكـن مـن البـدء بذلـك حتـى، اذ اظهـرت الاختبـارات، ان المـدارس تفتقـر الى قـدرة الإنترنـت لعـرض الأفـلام خـلال الفصـول الدراسـية.

lxxi   استراتيجية اليونسكو في مجال التربية الإعلامية والمعلوماتية – كما هو مذكور سابقاً

lxxii   http://www.unesco.org/new/en/communication-and-information/
media-development/media-literacy/global-alliance-for-partnerships-on-me-
/dia-and-information-literacy

http://www.unesco.org/new/en/communication-and-information/media-deve-
lopment/media-literacy/global-alliance-for-partnerships-on-media-and-informa-
/tion-literacy

وبالنسبة للخطط:
http://www.unesco.org/new/fileadmin/MULTIMEDIA/HQ/CI/CI/pdf/Events/gap-
mil_framework_and_plan_of_action.pdf

lxxiii   كخطـوة هامـة نحـو إعـداد قواعـد السـلوك، مايـو ويونيـو عـام 2015، في قطـاع غـزة وفي الضفـة الغربيـة
http://www.unesco.org/new/en/member-states/single-view/news/introdu-
cing_best_practices_for_code_of_conduct_and_ethics_among_journalists/#.
VZrKR6bvs7A

lxxi   استراتيجية اليونسكو في مجال التربية الإعلامية والمعلوماتية – كما هو مذكور سابقاً

lxxii   http://www.unesco.org/new/en/communication-and-information/
media-development/media-literacy/global-alliance-for-partnerships-on-me-
/dia-and-information-literacy

وبالنسبة للخطط:
http://www.unesco.org/new/fileadmin/MULTIMEDIA/HQ/CI/CI/pdf/Events/gap-
mil_framework_and_plan_of_action.pdf

103

lxxiii   كخطوة هامة نحو إعداد قواعد السلوك، مايو ويونيو عام 2015، في قطاع غزة وفي الضفة الغربية

http://www.unesco.org/new/en/member-states/single-view/news/introdu-cing_best_practices_for_code_of_conduct_and_ethics_among_journalists/#.VZrKR6bvs7A

الشباب والإعلام الرقمي:
إعداد المشهد من فاس والقاهرة

جوردي تورنت

في نوفمبر 2013 وفبراير 2014، نظم برنامج الأمم المتحدة لتحالف الحضارات (UNAOC) حلقتي عمل حول التربية الإعلامية والمعلوماتية للمدرّسين في القاهرة، بمصر، وفاس، بالمغرب. كان المنظم المحلي في مصر هو جامعة القاهرة (i)، وفي المغرب، جامعة سيدي محمد بن عبد الله (ii). كانت الجامعتان شريكتين في الشبكة الجامعية للتربية الإعلامية والمعلوماتية والحوار بين الثقافات (MILID Network) وتحظى بدعم اليونيسكو وبرنامج الأمم المتحدة لتحالف الحضارات. (iii). وقد تمكنت الجامعتان من الحصول على دعم ومشاركة وزارة التربية والتعليم في بلدهما، الأمر الذي ساهم بتسهيل مشاركة المدرّسين من المدارس المتوسطة والثانوية في التدريب على التربية الإعلامية والمعلوماتية خلال حلقات العمل هذه (التي يمكن اعتبارها فرصة للتطوير المهني). ومن أبرز الشركاء الآخرين في حلقات العمل تلك، نذكر اليونسكو؛ ومركز الدوحة لحرية الإعلام، و، في ما يتعلق بحلقات العمل التي نظمت في فاس، منظمة البحث عن أرضية مشتركة (iv). وقد شارك ما مجموعه 36 مدرّساً في القاهرة و 27 مدرّساً في فاس؛ في حلقات العمل التي نُظمت باللغة العربية. وكان الغرض الرئيسي من حلقات العمل هذه إدخال مفاهيم التربية الإعلامية والمعلوماتية وإطار عمل للمدرّسين، باستخدام النسخة العربية من «منهج التربية الإعلامية والمعلوماتية للمدرّسين» الخاص باليونسكو (v)، بالإضافة الى الموارد التدريبية المتقدمة للمدرسين حول التربية الإعلامية والمعلوماتية التي يقدمها مركز الدوحة لحرية الإعلام(vi). وقد شكّلت حلقات العمل فرصة لمعظم المدرّسين لكي يناقشوا لأول مرة المفاهيم الرئيسية والركائز الأساسية لتعليم التربية الإعلامية والمعلوماتية، وليفهموا أن المفاهيم التقليدية لمعرفة القراءة والكتابة (كتابة وقراءة

النصوص المطبوعة) لـم تعد تعتبر مهارات كافية للأفراد لـكي يكونوا مواطنين مشاركين
ونشطين فـي المجتمعات المعاصرة. وخـلال حلقات العمل، تـم التأكيد أيضاً عـلى أن مجرد
تدريـس «مهارات التكنولوجيا الرقميـة» (كيفية استخدام جهاز كمبيوتر، إنشاء مدوّنة،
الترميـز الأساسي، وما إلى ذلك) لا يدخـل في إطار تعليـم التربية الإعلاميـة والمعلوماتيـة
بحد ذاته. إن تطويـر مهارات التفكير النقدي التـي تطبـق على الرسائل الإعلامية، وإدخال
تحليـل التمثيل الإعلامي للأحـداث التاريخيـة فـي الدراسات الاجتماعية، وتشجيع الطلاب
عـلى إنتاج الرسائـل الإعلاميـة الأخلاقيـة ذات الصلـة، الـخ... كـل مـا سبق يشكّل جزءاً مـن
تعليـم التربية الإعلامية والمعلوماتيـة.

لا بـد مـن التوضيـح أن التربيـة الإعلاميـة والمعلوماتيـة تجسـد بأشـكال عـدة «العلـوم
الإنسانية» أكـثر مـن «التكنولوجيا»، وأن تعليـم التربية الإعلاميـة والمعلوماتيـة هـو
منصة جيدة لإعادة تقديم الموضوعـات الإنسانية في إطار تعليمي، يميـل حاليـاً إلى
إعطـاء الأولويـة للعلوم والتكنولوجيا عـلى الفلسفة والتاريخ والدراسـات الاجتماعيـة في
أنحـاء العالـم. خـلال حلقـات العمل ايضـاً، تمت مناقشة مسائل مختلفة، مثـل سلطة
الدولـة، ومراقبـة وسائل الإعـلام، وحريـة التعبيـر، المسـؤوليات الأخلاقيـة للمواطنيـن
بصفتهم منتجين إعلاميين، والرقابة، وخطاب الكراهية في وسائل التواصل الاجتماعي،
ومـا إلى ذلك. نظـراً للحـركات السياسية والاجتماعيـة الصعبـة التـي تعرفهـا دول معينـة
في منطقة الـشرق الأوسـط وإفريقيـا، عبّر بعـض المدرّسين عـن مخاوفهـم مـن أن يتـمّ
تفسير قيامهم بتعليـم التربية الإعلامية والمعلوماتية في مدارسهم على أنه شكل مـن
أشـكال النشاط الاجتماعي ذات تداعيـات سياسية يمكن أن تعرض للخطر سلامة طلابهم
ومستقبلهم. وقال آخرون إنه عـلى الرغـم مـن أن التعليـم الحقيقـي للتربية الإعلاميـة
والمعلوماتيـة ينطوي عـلى بعض جوانب النقد الاجتماعي، فمن الصحيح أيضاً أن تعلم
القراءة والكتابة هـو بالفعل عمل سياسي. بهذا المعنـى، فإن تعليم التربية الإعلامية
والمعلوماتيـة ليس تعليمـاً مختلفـاً عـن «النشاط السياسي» ممـا هو عليه تعليـم القراءة
والكتابة – إلا أنه طريقة أفضل وأكـثر قابليـة للتطبيق، لتعليـم «مهارات القراءة والكتابة»
في العالـم الوثيـق الارتباط بالاعـلام الـذي نعيش فيـه.

استبيان حول استخدامات وسائل الاعلام

في نهاية حلقـات العمـل، طُلب مـن المدرّسين توزيع استبيان في صفوفهم، بهدف تقييم
العادات الإعلامية لطلابهم.

الجـدول 1: اسـتخدام وسـائل الاعـلام بـين فئـة الشـباب في مـصر والمغـرب 2014 – 15 (بالنسـبة المئوية)

فاس، المغرب	القاهرة، مصر	الشباب ما بين 10-20 سنة
62%	67%	مشاهدة التلفزيون من 1الى 3 ساعات في اليوم
11%	18%	مشاهدة التلفزيون من 4 إلى 6 ساعات في اليوم
4%	13%	تصفح الإنترنت من المدرسة
32%	65%	تصفح الإنترنت من المنزل
16%	39%	تصفح الإنترنت باستخدام الهاتف الخليوي
38%	45%	تصفح الإنترنت من ساعة الى 3 ساعات في اليوم
15%	16%	تصفح الإنترنت من 4 الى 6 ساعات في اليوم
36%	90%	استخدام الانترنت لتصفح وسائل التواصل الاجتماعي والتسلية
5%	15%	استخدام الانترنت للحصول على الأخبار
49%	78%	تحميل الصور وأشرطة الفيديو على وسائل التواصل الاجتماعي
7%	31%	تحميل الصور وأشرطة الفيديو على وسائل التواصل الاجتماعي، كل يوم
40%	42%	تحميل الصور وأشرطة الفيديو على وسائل التواصل الاجتماعي، مرة في الأسبوع
70%	92%	اقتناء هاتف خليوي
90%	80%	استخدام الهاتف الخليوي للصور

80%	39%	استخدام الهاتف المحمول لأشرطة الفيديو
30%	13%	استخدام الهاتف الخليوي للرسائل القصيرة - أكثر من 10 رسائل في اليوم
25%	21%	قراءة الكتب، كل يوم
34%	10%	قراءة الكتب، مرة واحدة في الشهر
9%	16%	الواجبات المدرسية، أقل من 15 دقيقة في اليوم
34%	25%	الواجبات المدرسية، نحو 30 دقيقة في اليوم
30%	57%	لقاء مع الأصدقاء بعد المدرسة، كل يوم
44%	8%	لقاء مع الأصدقاء بعد المدرسة، مرة واحدة في الاسبوع
16%	22%	التحادث مع الأسرة، ومرة واحدة في الأسبوع
12%	20%	التحادث مع الأسرة، مرة واحدة من حين الى آخر

ملاحظة: بلغ عدد المستطلعين في المغرب 201 طالباً و 233 طالباً آخراً من القاهرة. كان تمثيل الذكور والإناث متعادلاً، بنسبة 50/50، في حين تراوحت اعمار المستطلعين بين 10 و20 سنة.

عند تفحص نتائج البحث، نقرّ أن التلفزيون لا يزال الوسيلة المفضلة لدى هؤلاء الشباب، إذ أن أكثر من 60 بالمائة من الشباب (في القاهرة وفاس) يقضون ما بين ساعة الى 3 ساعات يومياً في مشاهدة التلفزيون. في حين أن 18 بالمائة منهم في القاهرة يقضون ما بين 4 الى 6 ساعات يومياً أمام شاشة التلفزيون. وهم لا يختلفون عن الشباب من نفس الفئة العمرية في بلدان أخرى. وأفادت دراسة نيلسن التي نشرت عام 2015 أن الشباب في أميركا الشمالية من نفس العمر يشاهدون التلفزيون بما معدله 2.8 ساعة في اليوم (viii). ونظراً لكون هذا الرقم حساباً تقريبياً، يمكننا أن نستنتج أن 18 بالمائة على الأقل، إن لم يكن أكثر، من المراهقين الأميركيين يقضون أيضاً 4 الى 6 ساعات يومياً في

«مشاهدة التلفزيون». أضع عبارة «مشاهدة التلفزيون» بين علامتي اقتباس لأن الشباب اليوم لا يشاهدون التلفزيون فقط (لم يعد هذا الجمهور المأسور والمفتون بالشاشة الذي كان عليه في عصر ما قبل الإنترنت)، فهو يستهلك أشكالاً أخرى من وسائل الإعلام أثناء مشاهدة التلفزيون. وجدنا أن نحو 16 بالمائة من الشباب في فاس والقاهرة ممن شاركوا في الاستبيان، يقضون ما بين 4 الى 6 ساعات يومياً في تصفح الانترنت. ويشاهد الشباب التلفاز أثناء تصفحهم الإنترنت ويرسلون الرسائل القصيرة من هواتفهم لأصدقائهم، والبعض منهم يستمع الى الموسيقى أيضاً في الوقت عينه. هذا ما يسمى بظاهرة تعدد المهام: الوسائط المتعددة (المنصات المتعددة، والشاشات المتعددة) التي تستخدم في وقت واحد. تجدر الإشارة إلى أن هذه الظاهرة تتكرر على الصعيد العالمي؛ إذ تشهد بلدان أخرى تفاعلات مماثلة للشباب مع وسائل الإعلام (ix). كما أظهرت الدراسة أن الشباب من فاس والقاهرة يقومون بتحميل الصور و / أو الفيديو على صفحتهم الخاصة عبر مواقع التواصل الإجتماعي التي يختارونها مرة واحدة على الأقل في الأسبوع، فيما يفعل نحو 31 بالمائة منهم ذلك بشكل يومي. في فاس، يقوم نحو 30 بالمائة من الشباب بإرسال أكثر من 10 رسائل قصيرة إلى أصدقائهم كل يوم. في المقابل، يقوم 16 بالمائة منهم بالتحادث مع أفراد أسرتهم مرة واحدة فقط في الأسبوع. كما يقضي نحو 40 بالمائة من الشباب في كلتا المدينتين حوالي 30 دقيقة أو أقل في اليوم في إنجاز فروضهم المدرسية؛ في حين أن ربع هذا العدد فقط يقرأ كتاباً كل يوم. من الواضح إذاً أن لدى وسائل الإعلام مصلحة كبيرة في تنمية الشباب من الناحية الاجتماعية وكذلك في تشكيل كلٍّ من هويتهم وشخصيتهم. إذ أنه من خلال استهلاك المواد الإعلامية وإنتاجها يمكن للشباب أن يبنوا شخصيتهم الاجتماعية، وأن يبنوا فهمهم لأنفسهم، ولمجتمعهم، والعالم بأسره، وفهمهم «للآخر».

لكل هذه الأسباب المذكورة أعلاه، لا بد من إدماج التربية الإعلامية والمعلوماتية في المناهج الدراسية الإلزامية في المدارس المتوسطة والثانوية. سررنا كثيراً لتمكن ممثلي وزارتي التربية والتعليم في المغرب ومصر الحاضرين أثناء حلقات العمل من فهم نطاق وأهمية التربية الإعلامية والمعلوماتية. ونأمل أن يكونوا قد نقلوا الى رؤسائهم المعلومات والمعرفة التي سيتم تطويرها قريباً وإدراجها في السياسات التعليمية الجديدة التي لا تكتفي بالاعتراف بالتربية الإعلامية والمعلوماتية فحسب، بل الأهم من ذلك، تقوم بإدراجها في المناهج الدراسية في بلدانهم. وإذ نقرّ بأهمية الحاجة الى تدريب الكثير من المدرّسين على مفاهيم التربية الإعلامية والمعلوماتية، نأمل أيضاً

أن تكون حلقات العمل هذه تمهيداً لبرنامج تدريب المدرّسين على التربية الإعلامية والمعلوماتية في المنطقة. نحن نرحب بجهود الكثير من المنظمات التي تعمل بنشاط على تعزيز التربية الإعلامية والمعلوماتية في منطقة الشرق الأوسط وإفريقيا، وقد ذكرنا الكثير منها في مقدمة هذا الإصدار والتقارير الواردة فيه. يفهم برنامج الأمم المتحدة لتحالف الحضارات جيداً أن الأفراد الذين يتمتعون بثقافة إعلامية هم أقل عرضة لأن يتم إبعادهم بشكل عنيف عند العثور في خياراتهم الإعلامية على رسائل قد تكون مهينة لعقيدته أو عقيدتها. المواطن الذي يتمتع بثقافة إعلامية قادر على خلق الفرص للدخول في محادثة، وليس في مواجهة عنيفة. لهذه الأسباب، قام برنامج الأمم المتحدة لتحالف الحضارات منذ نشأته، بتعريف التربية الإعلامية على أنها مبادرة تعليمية لا بد من دعمها وتشجيعها، كما هو مذكور بوضوح في التقرير الأولي لفريق برنامج تحالف الحضارات رفيع المستوى.(x)

ملاحظات:

i شكر خاص للبروفسور سامي طايع من جامعة القاهرة

ii شكر خاص للبروفسور عبد الحميد النفيسي من جامعة سيدي محمد بن عبدالله

iii الرجاء زيارة الرابط التالي: http://milunesco.unaoc.org/unitwin و www.unesco.org/new/en/gapmil

iv يتضمن المدربون الآخرون كلاً من: أيمن بردويل؛ يوسف عمر؛ فؤاد حلمي؛ عدلي رضا؛ حسن عماد؛ أمل الشافي؛ دريسيا شويت؛ خالد عطيل؛ راوية الحميدان؛ أحمد المهندي؛ محمد فوبار؛ صفيانا الحمدي؛ محمد عزمي؛ يوسف بن عبد الرزاق.

v الرجاء زيارة الرابط التالي: -http://www.unesco.org/new/en/communica tion-and-information/resources/publications-and-communication-materials/pu-blications/full-list/media-and-information-literacy-curriculum-for-teachers

vi الرجاء زيارة الرابط التالي: -http://www.dc4mf.org/en/content/media-litera cy-another-vision-teaching

vii شكر خاص الى محمد سامي عبد الرؤوف ونورا س. عبد الرؤوف محمد (القاهرة) ومحمد فوبار (فاس) لدعمهم هذا البحث

viii الرجاء زيارة الرابط التالي: http://www.adweek.com/news/television/infographic-look-kids-media-consump-tion-163087

110

ix   الرجاء الاطلاع على التقرير: «تقرير أوفكوم حول استخدام الإعلام والمواقف 2015»
http://stakeholders.ofcom.org.uk/binaries/research/media-literacy/media-lit-
10years/2015_Adults_media_use_and_attitudes_report.pdf

x   الرجاء زيارة الرابط التالي: http://www.unaoc.org/repository/report.htm

المشهد المعلوماتي في العراق

عبد الامير الفيصل

يشكل العلم والمعرفة ركيزة اساسية من ركائز النمو والتطور لاي بلد من البلدان حيث تعتبر المعلومات احدى الجوانب الرئيسية والمهمة في بناء العلم واثراء المعرفة، اضافة الى كونها اداة مهمة تساعد في عملية اتخاذ القرارات وعليه فان فشل وانجاح أي منظمة ادارية في تحقيق اهدافها يبقى مرهونا على صحة ومصداقية ودقة المعلومات التي تساهم في عملية صياغة واتخاذ القرارات من قبل الادارات العليا وهذا بدوره كان الدافع الاساسي للعديد من دول العالم في اعطاء الاهتمام المتزايد ورصد مبالغ لغرض تأمين حصولها على الملعومات.

والعراق لم يكن بمعزل عن دول العالم اذ يشهد تحولا جذريا على جميع الاصعدة والميادين وكان في مقدمة هذه التحولات هو التقدم العلمي والتكنولوجي الذي يشهده العراق وتعتبر المكتبات ومراكز البحوث واستطلاعات الرأي العام هي المعين الحيوي الذي لا ينضب والرافد المتدفق لامداد الحركة العلمية والتكنولوجية بكل مقومات التقدم والرقي.

وقد لا نستطيع الالمام باطراف المشهد المعلوماتي في العراق كونه مشهد يتشكل في بلد يتحول الى استخدام المعلومات في كل مفاصله بشكل سريع وعميق في ظل استخدام عام للتكنولوجيا باحدث اجيالها وبشبكة انترنت مفتوحة من دون قيود .

فكلما تطورت المجتمعات، وتعقدت أساليب الحياة تراكمت المعلومات، واتسع نطاق استخدامها، وبالتالي تزداد حاجاتنا الى المزيد من المعلومات التي تساعدنا في اتخاذ القرارات السليمة، فالمعلومات مورد لا ينضب، وعنصر لا غنى لأي مجتمع ولأي فرد. وقد تعرض مجال «المعلومات» لتطورات حيوية سريعة الإيقاع، أملتها احتياجات حضارية، وصاحبتها ثورة تكنولوجية أبرزت دور المعلومات كركيزة أساسية في مختلف أوجه النشاط الإنساني، ومورد أساسي فعال يشكل جزءاً لا يتجزأ من خطط وبرامج

113

التنمية الاجتماعية والاقتصادية، ومن ثم أطلق على العصر الحالي «عصر المعلومات» باعتبار ان المعلومات هي أبرز علاماته المميزة .

فالمجتمع الآن، كما يراه العديد من المراقبين هو «مجتمع المعلومات» وهو البديل الجديد «للمجتمع الصناعي» الذي عايشناه معظم القرن العشرين، والدليل على هذا الاستنتاج هو حقيقة ان العمل في مجال المعلومات information occupation قد زادت نسبته من 10٪، من حجم القوى العاملة الى حوالي 30٪، ومن ناحية أخرى تناقص حجم العمالة في المهن الزراعية الى اقل من 4٪ فقط.

وواكب العراق الطفرة المعاصرة في نمو وتكاثر المعلومات التي ينهل منها الفرد والمنظمة على حد سواء، ترويج تطورات تكنولوجية متقدمة للتحكم في المعلومات وتجميعها ومعالجتها واختزانها واسترجاعها ونقلها واستخدامها، ومن امثلة هذا الحاسبات الآلية او اجهزة الكمبيوتر بكل اجيالها، وتقنيات المصغرات الفيلمية، ووسائل الاتصالات عن بعد، وتزاوجها وارتباطها معا في اطار ما نطلق عليه «تكنولوجيا المعلومات».

شبكة الانترنت ووسائل الاعلام:

احدثت تكنولوجيا الانترنت تاثيرا في الأوساط الاعلامية كسابقاتها من الاكتشافات الجديدة في الميدان الاتصالي والمعلوماتي، وفي نهاية الامر حافظت كل وسيلة على شخصيتها وقوتها وشعبيتها ..

في الصناعة الاعلامية الانترنت احدثت ثورة عارمة في عالم الصحافة العراقية حيث ان غالبية الصحف لجأت لحجز موقع في الشبكة، وتقديم الصحيفة الى القراء عبر الانترنت وهذه التقنية الجديدة تحتم بطبيعة الحال على الصحف ضرورة الابداع والابتكار والخروج عن المألوف وتجنب التقليدي، هذا يعني ان الشبكة فرضت منطقا جديدا غير في العمق ميدان صناعة الاخبار وتبادلها، وللعلم فإن شبكة الانترنت تحتوي على اكثر من 134موقع لجرائد ورقية و 47 مجلة مطبوعة بالاضافة الى الالاف من المواقع الالكترونية المختلفة في مختلف انحاء العراق .

والصحافة العراقية اصبحت تهتم أكثر فاكثر بالتحليلات والدراسات والتعليقات الجادة وتعد الانترنت مصدراً ووسيلة مهمة في خدمة هذه الانواع الصحفية التي تتطلب تعمقاً في التحليل وغزارة في المعلومات، وقوة في الاقناع والتأثير، فشبكة الانترنت تحتوي على مئات الصحف والمجلات ومحطات الاذاعة والتلفزيون ووكالات الانباء، كل هذه الوسائط تعد روافد مهمة للمعلومات التي تبحث عنها الصحيفة لتقديمها للجمهور .

الاعلام وخدمة المشروع الوطني العراقي

تستدعي التحولات الكبيرة التي شهدها العراق على كافة الصعد السياسية والاقتصادية والاجتماعية والامنية بعد الاجتياح الامريكي في ابريل 2003 وجود حركة اعلامية وطنية نشطة قادرة على استيعاب تلك المتغيرات وفق اسس واليات مهنية عالية ، نستطيع من خلالها بناء عراق حر لكل العراقيين ويمتلك الوسائل والمؤهلات التي تمكنه من الصمود بوجه التحديات الجديدة بكافة انواعها وصورها ومفاصلها ومن اجل اداء مهامها ووظائفها المتعددة ،في ظل وجود حركة اعلامية عامرة في المحيطين الاقليمي والدولي ،اذ اضحت عملية مناقشتها امر صعب المنال بالنسبة للمؤسسات الاعلامية ووسائل الاعلام العراقية الفتية اذ شهدت الفترة ما بعد نيسان 2003 ، انتشار وسائل الاعلام والاتصال الجماهيري بشكل منقطع النظير حيث ازدادت في فضائها الواسع مئات الصحف والمطبوعات والفضائيات والاذاعات الالكترونية وقد ساعد ذلك تخصيص مليار دولار من قبل الحكومة الامريكية عام 2004 لدعم القطاع الاعلامي العراقي في اطلاق كم هائل من الفضائيات – الاذاعات – الصحف – المواقع الالكترونية وكان اهتمام الحكومات المتعاقبة لبناء مشروع اعلامي هدفه التغطية الاخبارية في وسائل الاعلام المرئية والمسموعة والمطبوعة وابراز القضايا الاجتماعية والاقتصادية والسياسية التي يمر بها البلد والاهتمام بالاعلام الهادف شريطة طرح الافكار وتوفير الموارد التي من شأنها ان تساعد وسائل الاعلام المحلية وتوفير التغطية المتعمقة للقضايا المحلية والالتزام بواقعية الحدث لكي يتفاعل المواطن مع الوسيلة الاعلامية .

فقد شهد تجربة اعلامية غير مسبوقة نتيجة لتغير فلسفة النظام السياسي الجديد القائم على حرية التعبير والممارسات الديمقراطية التي اقرها الدستور في المادة (2) من المبادئ الاساسية اولاً والفقرة ب- لايجوز سن قانون يتعارض مع مبادئ الديمقراطية اما المادة (36) من الدستور تكفل الدولة بما لا يخل بالنظام العام والاداب

اولا: حرية التعبير عن الرأي بكل الوسائل

ثانيا :حرية الصحافة والطباعة والاعلان والاعلام والنشر

ثالثا : حرية الاجتماع والتظاهر السلمي وتنظيم بقانون

الاستراتيجية الوطنية لتكنولوجيا المعلومات في العراق

تتضمـن الاسـتراتيجية الوطنيـة العامـة لتكنولوجيـا المعلومـات في العراق مجموعـة مـن الاهداف يمكن اجمالها بـالاتي :

1- الاسـتمرار في تطويـر البيئـة القانونيـة والتنظيميـة لضبـط وتنظيـم وحمايـة العمـل والتعامـل في هـذا المجال بما يتلائـم مـع التطورات في مجـال اسـتخدام تطبيقـات ونظـم المعلومـات التكنولوجيـة.

2- تاهيـل المـوارد البشريـة واكسـابها القـدرة عـلى التخطيـط ، والادارة ، والتشـغيل والاسـتخدام الامثـل لتطبيقـات تكنولوجيـا المعلومـات والاتصـالات.

3- تعميـم ثقافـة المعلوماتيـة وتعزيـز القـدرة عـلى امتـلاك واسـتخدام التقنيـات الحديثـة لـدى فئـات المجتمـع كافـة ومحـو الأميـة الحاسـوبية.

4- زيادة وتشجيع القدرات البحثية الاكاديمية ودعم الابتكار.

5- نـشر وتشـجيع ثقافـة اسـتخدام وتطويـر برمجيـات المصـادر المفتوحـة-(Open Sources)☒بخاصة تلـك التـي يمكن اسـتخدامها في عمليـات تطويـر حـزم برامجيـات جديـدة.

6- تسـهيل الوصول الى المعلومات واستخدام الانترنت لجميع شرائح المجتمع .

7- تبـني مفهـوم الشراكـة الحقيقيـة بـين القطاعـات الحكوميـة والخاصـة في مجـال وضـع وتنفيـذ الخطط المتعلقـة بنقـل وتوطين تطبيقـات تكنولوجيا المعلومـات ومصادر المعرفـة محليا.

8- حماية البيانات الفردية وقواعد البيانات المؤسسية.

9- حماية الملكية الفكرية للمصنفات الرقمية.

المعلومات واستراتيجية التنمية الوطنية في العراق

تعـد المعلومات المحـور الرئيـسي في كل عمل ،وعـلى فهمهـا وتنظيمهـا وكيفيـة إسـتخدامها يتوقـف النجـاح او الفشـل للوصـول الى الأهـداف والغايـات المهمـة ، فالمعلومـات احـد مصـادر الـثروة الإقتصاديـة ،لأنّ الخطـة الإسـتراتيجية لعمليـة التخطيـط تعتمـد بالدرجـة الأولى عـلى المعلومـات الصحيحـة التـي يتـم في ضوئهـا إتخـاذ القرار السـليم الـذي يحقـق النتائج الصحيحة .

وللمعلومـات أبعـاد إقتصاديـة وإجتماعيـة وثقافيـة وسياسـية مـن خـلال المكتبـات ومراكـز المعلومـات والنظـم فهـي القنـوات لتسـويق المعلومـات وتنميـة مصـادر المعلومـات وإيصالهـا الى المستفيدين مـن الباحثين والعاملين والدارسين في مجـال التنمية ،وإستخدام وسـائل التقنيـة المتاحـة ، وبالنسـبة للاستراتيجية الوطنيـة في العراق ، التي تضمنت برنامجاً تنمويـا إقتصاديـا وإجتماعيـا شـاملاً وتعتمـد عـلى معلومـات مفصلـة ودقيقـة أعـدت تلـك الدراسـة الأمـم المتحـدة والبنـك الـدولي بصـورة مشـتركة تحـت عنـوان تقويـم إحتياجـات العـراق وقدمـت الى مؤتمـر مدريـد .

وقد قـدرت كلفـة الإسـتثمارات لأغـراض إعـادة إعمـار العـراق بحـدود (136) مليـار دولار ، ومـن الممكـن ان نشـير ان عنـاصر الاستراتيجية الوطنيـة لـم تتطـرق الى وضـع اسـتراتيجية الى سياسـات المعلومـات في القطـر والاهتمـا م بالبنيـة الاساسـية لتكنولوجيـا المعلومـات والاتصالات ، وضعـف الدعـم الحكومـي لهـذا القطـاع ، وهـو مـن اختصـاص وزارة العلـوم والتكنولوجيـا في العراق الريـادة في عمليـة التحـول نحـو تطبيقـات تكنولوجيـا المعلومـات .

عناصر السياسة الوطنية للمعلومات

تؤكـد عنـاصر سياسـة المعلومـات الوطنيـة عـلى قيمـة المعلومـات وعـلى الإطار القانـوني والتنظيمـي لترويجهـا وأدارتهـا ، بمـا في ذلـك دور الحكومـة في هـذا المجـال . وتتنـاول هـذه العنـاصر أيضـا السياسـة المتعلقـة بالبنيـة التحتيـة للمعلومـات وتكنولوجيـا المعلومـات بهـدف تطويرهـا وتعـد الجوانـب الثقافيـة والعامـل الإنسـاني عنـاصر هامـة في سياسـات المعلومـات الوطنيـة ، فضلا عـن أهميـة التعـاون الإقليمـي والـدولي في هـذا المجـال الحيوي ، وتعـد الإطار العـام لسياسـة المعلومـات الوطنيـة في العـراق ، لـذا فـان الاطار العـام لسياسـة المعلومـات الوطنيـة يدعـم كل النشـاطات الهادفـة الى:

1 - تحديد واسـتخدام وتعزيـز المعاييـر المشـتركة التـي تشـمل التطـورات الحاصلـة في مجـال تكنولوجيـا المعلومـات.

2 - تجميـع مصـادر المعلومـات بهـدف اسـتغلالها مـن اجـل المسـاعدة في عمليـة صنـع القـرار وشـموليته.

3 - إزالـة الحواجـز التـي تمنـع تبـادل المعلومـات مـع احـترام مسـؤوليات الافـراد والمؤسسـات التـي تؤكـد خصوصيـة المعلومـات ووحدتهـا.

4 - تشجيع الأسلوب ألتشاركي ضمن آلية تنسيقية جيدة تتناول القضايا الاجتماعية والقطاعيـة والتنظيميـة.

5 - تشجيع الجهـود الراميـة لإنشـاء بنيـة تحتيـة للاتصالات المعلومـات والتـي تعد حاجـة ملحـة مـن اجـل الربـط بيـن المعلومـات وتبادلها.

6 - تشجيع الجهود الهادفة لجعل العراق مركز معلومات إقليمي .

لقد ادى التطور المذهـل في جميع الميادين العلمية والتقنية وما صاحبها مـن تطورات تقنيـة حديثـة ,الى زيادة هائلـة مـن حجـم المعلومـات المنشـورة ,وكان لذلـك التضخـم انعكاسـاته المباشرة عـلى التنميـة الاقتصاديـة والاجتماعيـة في كل دولـة مما ادى الى إنشـاء مؤسسات متخصصة في جمع المعلومات وتنظيمها وتخزينها واسترجاعها ومن ثم توصيلها الى طالبيها مـن باحثين ودارسـين وصانعـي قـرارات وعلمـاء وغيرهـم بالقـدر المناسب وفي الوقت المناسب ايضا.

البنية الأساسية لتكنولوجيا المعلومات والاتصالات في العراق

في بدايـة القرنيـن التاسـع عـشر والعشريـن وجدت كثير مـن المكتبـات في المسـاجد والجوامع والمكتبات الخاصة عند البيـوت والأشراف وسرعان مـا انتـشرت المكتبـات في المـدن الكبيرة إلى الاقضيـة والنواحـي , إن أول مكتبـة أنشـأت في بغداد عـام 1920 وهـي مكتبـة عامـة وسميت بـ(مكتبـة السـلام) ثم توالـت افتتاح مكتبـات أخـرى في الموصل والبصرة وغيرها مـن مـدن العـراق , وكانـت نواة مجاميع تلـك المكتبـات عـن طريق التبرع مـن الأهالي.

لقد فـرض الحصـار الثقـافي والعلمـي عـلى العـراق جـراء الحـروب الـتي مـرت بهـا.ولكـن عزيمـة مـن يعمـل في مجـال المعلومـات لـم تـثنِ عزيمتهـم عـن المواصلـة حيث عقدت المؤتمـرات والنـدوات والحلقـات والملتقيـات في العديد مـن التواريـخ منـذ عـام 1995 حيث عقـدت نـدوة في جامعـة الموصـل الـتي لـم تخـل مـن دور المعلومـات.كمـا أجـاز قسـم المعلومـات والمكتبـات /كليـة الآداب رسـائل بهـذا الخصوص هذا عـلى الصعيـد المحلي ,أما عـلى الصعيـد العـربي والعالمـي هـو التحضير للقمـة العالميـة لمجتمع المعلومـات الـذي انعقـد في مرحلتهـا الأولى في جنيـف خـلال شـهر كانـون الأول 2003 ، كـما عقـدت الاسكوا) لجنة الأمـم المتحـدة الاقتصاديـة والاجتماعيـة لغـربي آسـيا(اجتماعـا للخـبراء حـول تعزيـز المحتوى الرقمـي العربيـة وذلـك في الفـترة مـن 5-3 حزيـران 2005 في بيت الأمـم المتحـدة في بيروت ، وكان الهـدف مـن الاجتماع هـو بحـث أفضل السـبل لتمكين

البلـدان العربيـة عامـة وبلـدان آسـيا خاصـة مـن الارتقـاء بالمحتـوى العربـي عـلى الانترنت وعـلى الوسـائط الرقميـة المختلفـة ، وتحديـد الاستراتيجيات والآليـات الأكثـر ممـا عليـه في هـذا المضمـار.

مؤسسات المعلومات في العراق

انتـشرت المكتبـات العامـة في العراق في منتصـف الخمسـينات مـن القرن المـاضي عـلى اثـر تشريع قانون الإدارات المحلية للمحافظات في عـام 1945.وقـد دأبت تلـك الإدارات بدعـم المكتبـات وتزويدهـا بالكتـب والمجـلات وتعييـن الموظفيـن الفنييـن لإدارتهـا وتنظيمهـا ودعمهـا بالأمـوال ، ولكـن تبعيـة تلـك المكتبـات وتذبذبهـا مـا بيـن وزارة الحكـم المحـلي ووزارة الداخليـة ممـا جعلتهـا غـير فعالـة ولـم تـؤد خدماتهـا عـلى الوجـه المطلـوب عـدا المكتبـة الوطنيـة ودار الوثائـق والكتـب التـي تقـدم خدماتهـا للباحثيـن مـن الاساتذة والطلبة وغيرهـم .

بلـغ عـدد المكتبـات في محافظـة بغـداد 54 مكتبـة عامـة و(176) مكتبـة عامـة في محافظـات القطر.

وجـود مكتبـة مدرسـية في كل مدرسـة ينبغـي أن يكـون هـدف وزارة التربيـة وخاصـة في المدرس الثانويـة , إذ أن المكتبـة جـزء مكمـل للأهـداف والبرامـج التعليميـة والتربويـة التـي تطلـع إليهـا الدولة ولايمكن تعزيز المناهج الدراسـية دون أن يتـم التعـاون بيـن أميـن المكتبـة الـذي يكـون بالطبـع عضـوا في الهيئـة التدريسـية وبيـن المدرسـين وإدارة المدرسـة,وان يتـم التعـاون مـع مديريـة المكتبـات المدرسـية لاختيـار المصـادر وحسـب توجيهـات المدرسـة ومناهجهـا وتطلعـات الطلبـة بحيـث تسـمح للطالـب مجـال المقارنـة والإطـلاع الواسـع وربط الموضوعـات الدراسـية وذلـك لإعـداد الطالـب لمواجهـة الحيـاة وليصبـح مواطنـا صالحـا مـدركا لجميـع نواحـي حياتـه الاقتصاديـة والاجتماعيـة والسياسـية . أن تركـيز في أنشـطة المكتبـة المدرسـية عـلى توفـير الوسـائل وأوعيـة المعلومـات والأجهـزة والتكنولوجيـا الحديثـة يدفـع الطالـب إلى تفهـم أوضـاع بـلاده وتاريخهـا وواقعهـا

أدناه عدد المكتبات في المدارس بأنواعها وكما يلي:

الجدول رقم (1):
عدد المكتبات في المدارس في العراق، حسب السنوات (1971، 1988، 2005 و2013)

عدد مكتبات المدارس المهنية	عدد مكتبات المدارس الثانوية	عدد مكتبات المدارس الابتدائية	السنة
305	648	358	1971
-	1524	5692	1988
-	217	1783	2005
2156	7543	2371	2013

دلّ الجدول رقـم (1) ان عـدد المكتبـات المدرسـية لا يلـبي طموحـات اعضـاء الهيئـة التدريسـية كمـا يظهـر في الجـدول رقـم (2)

الجدول رقم (2)
عدد المدارس وطلابها وعدد اعضاء الهيئة التدريسية للمراحل كافة في العراق (السنة؟)

عدد أعضاء الهيئة التدريسية	عدد الطلاب	عدد المدارس	المراحل
165738	3507975	9115	التعليم الابتدائي
65681	1132106	3138	التعليم الثانوي (المتوسط والإعدادي)
6636	65377	234	التعليم المهني
1620	42669	151	معاهد إعداد المعلمين
369	6000	18	الكليات المفتوحة

أمـا بالنسـبة إلى وجـود المـواد السـمعية والبصريـة والتقنيـات الحديثـة مـن الحاسـبات والأقـراص الليزريـة والاتصـال عـن بعد أي الانترنـت والحصـول عـلى المعلومـات غـير الـو رقيـة فحالهـا مختلـف حيـث شـاع اسـتخدامها بشـكل واسـع وخاصـة بـين اوسـاط الشـباب والطلبـة. لكـن بالنظـر إلى أن في العـراق مـا يزيـد عـلى 12.600 مدرسـة ابتدائيـة ومهنيـة وثانويـة ، وحـوالي 4.75 مليـون طالبـاً ، ومـا يناهـز مـن ربـع مليـون عضـو هيئـة تدريسـي، فـان (13) مليـون مـن هـؤلاء بحاجـة إلى الإطـلاع والتثقيـف لتقديـم خدمـات للعـراق.

يبيّن الجـدول رقـم (3) عـدد المكتبـات الأكاديميـة والجامعـات والكليـات والمراكـز البحثيـة المرتبطـة بـوزارة التعليـم العـالي والبحـث العلمي حسـب الإحصائيـات. في حين بيّـن الجدول رقـم (4) عـدد الجامعـات العراقيـة في اقليـم كردسـتان.

الجدول رقم (3):
الجامعات العراقية

ت	الجامعات	عدد المراكز	عدد الكليات	عدد الاقسام	عدد التدريسين	عدد الطلبة في الدراسة الاولية	نسبة تدريسي الى طالب	عدد الطلبة في الدراسات العليا	سنة التأسيس
1	بغداد	11	24	100	4391	63289	15:1	1556	1956
2	البصرة	8	17	61	1728	32877	13:1	55	1963
3	الموصل	5	21	71	2548	26802	11:1	418	1964
4	المستنصرية	6	11	48	1788	39137	22:1	225	1965
5	التكنولوجيا	7	13	بمثابة كليات	832	13660	17:1	264	1975
6	الكوفة	2	10	29	549	10399	19:1	152	1987
7	تكريت	1	11	41	674	7728	12:1	248	1987
8	القادسية	1	12	31	492	11947	24:1	52	1987
9	الانبار	1	12	47	596	9343	16:1	89	1987
10	النهرين	3	6	13	324	1676	5:1	454	1988
11	العراقية	0	4	10	74	2315	31:1	83	1989
12	بابل	4	13	39	648	13625	21:1	198	1991
13	ديالى	2	9	33	374	12608	34:1	77	1999
14	كربلاء	2	6	13	223	4564	21:1	4	2001
15	ذي قار	1	6	14	245	4858	20:1	10	2001
16	كركوك	1	7	18	154	4502	29:1	11	2002
17	واسط	0	4	14	130	4901	38:1	18	2002
18	هيئة التعليم التقني المركزية	4	36	280	2300	13000	6:1	129	1969

سنة التأسيس	عدد الطلبة في الدراسات العليا	نسبة تدريسي الى طالب	عدد الطلبة في الدراسة الاولية	عدد التدريسين	عدد الاقسام	عدد الكليات	عدد المراكز	الجامعات	ت
-	438	-	-	16	-	-	-	المجلس العراقي للاختصاصات الطبية	19
-	12	-	-	47	-	-	-	الهيئة العراقية للحاسبات والمعلوماتية	20
1988-		-	24719	671	89	18	-	الكليات الأهلية	21
-	4493	-	291950	18804	1342	240	59	المجموع	

الجدول رقم (4): الجامعات العراقية في اقليم كردستان

سنة التأسيس	عدد الطلبة (بالآلاف)			عدد التدريسين	عدد الأقسام	عدد الكليات	عدد المراكز	الجامعات	ت
	عليا	مسائي	صباحي						
1968	-	-	12741	1023	49	19	-	صلاح الدين	1
1992	-	1795	8197	486	41	16	-	السليمانية	2
1992	-	408	4041	377	34	11	-	دهوك	3
2005	-	426	1522	122	23	10	-	كويه	4
-	-	-	-	-	45	8	-	هيئة التعليم التقني / اربيل	5
-	-	-	410	12	42	7	-	هيئة التعليم التقني / سليمانية	6
	2629	26911		2020	234	71		المجموع	

بحسب الجدولين (3) و(4)، هناك 59 مركز بحثي و240 كلية و1342 قسم تابع إلى وزارة التعليم العالي والبحث العلمي ،أما في اقليم كردستان هناك 71 كلية و234 قسم. إي وجود 1946 مكتبة في الجامعات العراقية الرسمية فضلا عن مكتبات الكليات الأهلية التي هي بحاجة إليها وتعد أكثر من خمسين مكتبة كلية بعضها منها تحتاج إلى رفدها بالمصادر الحديثة ولكونها حديثة التأسيس وتحتاج إلى وسائل الاتصال الحديثة من الانترنت والأجهزة والى تهيئة الكادر المتخصص والمؤهل على استخدام واستعمال التكنولوجيا والأجهزة المتطورة.

من المعلوم ان المكتبات المتخصصة تهتم بالنتاج الفكري المتخصص في مجال موضوعي معين فهناك أشكال من المكتبات المتخصصة وتختلف فيما بينها باختلاف أهداف ووظائف المؤسسة الام التي تعد المكتبة واحدة منها . فهناك المكتبات التي تخدم الشركات الصناعية او التجارية وغيرها من مكتبات الوزارات ، والمستشفيات والمساجد والمتاحف والسجون او مكتبات النقابات المتخصصة المهنية كالحقوق والطب ...الخ ومن أنواع المكتبات المتخصصة:

- مكتبات مراكز البحوث مثل مكتبة مركز دراسات وبحوث الوطن العربي/ الجامعة المستنصرية.
- مكتبات المؤسسات الصناعية والتجارية مثل مكتبة غرفة تجارة بغداد .
- مكتبات الوزارات والدوائر الحكومية التابعة لها
- مكتبات المنظمات المهنية والشعبية مثل مكتبة رابطة المرأة العراقية ، أو رابطة المهندسين العراقيين(وزارة الدولة)
- مكتبات المتاحف ودور الوثائق التاريخية .
- مكتبات الخاصة بالمعاقين وأصحاب العاهات.

مكتبة المجمع العلمي العراقي هي من أفضل المكتبات في العلوم الاجتماعية والإنسانية في البلاد وخصوصا في موضوعات اللغة العربية والكردية والسريانية وآدابها والتاريخ والجغرافية والرحلات والتراث العربي والإسلامي ، وهي ترفد الأساتذة والباحثين بالمعلومات .

المكتبة مقسمة الى خمسة أقسام اكبرها المكتبة العربية وتضم (160000) كتاب ومجلد للدوريات وهناك اربعة مكتبات وهي مكتبة المخطوطات والمكتبة الاجنبية والمكتبة الكردية والمكتبة السريانية . وتصل المجاميع اما عن طريق الشراء او الاهداء وتصل ما يزيد عن (30) مجلة شهريا الى المكتبة.

المكتبـات الخاصـة مثـل مكتبـات المسـاجد والجوامـع والحسـينيات والكنائـس والأديـرة والابريشيات منهلا للعلمـاء والباحثيـن وفي حفـظ التـراث العربـي والإسلامي والاديان الأخـرى منـذ القـدم وقد أولت الدولة بتعميرها والاهتمـام بها وقد رفدت مكتبـات تلـك الأماكـن بالكتـب النـادرة وخاصـة المخطوطـات واغلب مجاميعها تخـص الأديـان واللغـات والآداب والفلسـفة والتاريـخ ، بعضهـا كانـت تابعـة الى وزارة الأوقـاف (سـابقا) وبعضهـا تابعـة الى الشـخصيات وتعـد مـن المكتبـات الخاصـة واغلبهـا تضـم نـوادر المصـادر الـتي تصـل المكتبـات عـن طريـق التبـرع والاهـداء والوقـف وبعضهـا شـراء.

يعـدّ المركـز الوطـني للمخطوطـات مـن المكتبـات المتخصصة بالمخطوطـات بمختلـف الموضوعـات واللغـات وتضـم انـدر وانفس المخطوطـات ترجـع الى تاريـخ العـراق والامـة الاسلامية والـتي يبلـغ عددهـا نحـو 42.146 مخطوطـة. وقـد جمعـت تلـك المخطوطـات امـا بالشـراء او الاهـداء مـن المؤسسـات او الشـخصيات او عـن طريـق الاستيلاء والمصـادرة لبعـض المكتبـات اومـن الجوامـع والمـدارس الدينيـة.

الخاتمة :

وخلاصـة القـول مـن كل مـا تقـدم ان المشـهد المعلومـاتي في العـراق بعـد 2003 وحتـى يومنـا الحاضـر شـهد

قفـزات نوعيـة تسـتحق الوقـوف عندهـا ، فقـد تمكـن مـن احـداث تغيـيرات واضحـة في مجمـل الاداء المعلومـاتي

باختلاف وسائله ومؤسساته.

(ملاحظة للمحررين: لا مراجع متوفرة لهذا المقال)

التربية بواسطة وسائل الاعلام وتكنولوجيات الاعلام والاتصال في الجزائر الانجازات الكمية في مواجهة تحديات النوعية

أ.د.رضوان بوجمعة

مقدمة:

عرفت البشرية منذ القديم نقاشات فلسفية كثيرة حول قضايا المعرفةوالثقافة والحياة،كما عاشت صراعات اجتماعية وسياسية وأيديولوجية مختلفة،غالبا ما كانت مؤسسة التربية موضوع هذه النقاشات والصراعات، ولم يشد عصرنا عن هذه النقاشات والصراعات حول منظومات التربية ومؤسساتها، إلا أن مسألة الاتصال الجماهيري قد لعت، منذ العشرية الثانية من القرن الماضي على الأقل، دورا مركزيا في تضخيم هذه المسألة-أي، مسألة التربية - أو التقليل من أهميتها.

والأمر نفسه ينسحب، قليلا أوكثيرا، على المجتمع الجزائري، فقد عانى هذا المجتمع كثيرا من اتساع الأمية، بسبب الظاهرة الاستعمارية وآثارها السلبية بشكل خاص. إلا أنه سعى، منذ فجر الاستقلال،إلى بناء منظومة تعليمية ، تمثل هدفها المركزي في البداية في توسيع التعليم ونشره، وهو هدف يمكن القول أنه: تحقق نسبيا، وفقا لمؤشرات المعطيات الكمية المتوفرة؛ في حين أن تحدي الننوعية في هذه المنظومة التعليمية قد ظل قائما، خاصة في مجال اهتمامنا هذا، نعني في مجال إدخال التربية على وسائل الاعلام في منظومة التعليم ، واستخدام تكنولوجيات الاتصال الجديدة؛ حيث ظل مشروع رقمنة المدرسة تحديا قائما ينبغى رفعه منذ سنة 2001 وانشغالا أساسيا من انشغالات المنظومة التربيوية الجزائرية.الأمر الذي سنعرضه كما يلي: حيث سنبيّن كمّيا،من خلال بعض الأرقام والاحصائيات، مختلف المنجزات في مجال التكوين والتجهيز، المتعلق

125

باستراتيجية ادخال تكنولوجيات الاتصال الجديدة في منظومة التعليم - تكوين الأساتذة والتلاميذ على مختلف أنواع التقنيات الحديثة للاتصال - ولكن قبل ذلك ينبغي علينا، منهجيا، التوقف عند بعض المنطلقات النظرية، الخاصة بتطور مفهوم التربية عبر وسائل الاعلام، وبالعلاقة أيضا بين منظومة التربية ومنظومة الاعلام عموما.

التربية الاعلامية:تطور المفهوم وانفجار التقنية

يمكن أن يتحول مفهوم التربية عبر وسائل الاعلام لوحده إلى دراسة مستقلة، نظرا للنقاش الواسع الذي غذى الساحة الأكاديمية في علوم التربية وفي علوم الاعلام والاتصال، غير أن ذلك يمكن أن يخرجنا من عمق الاشكالية، لذلك سنكتفي باستعراض أهم المفاهيم الأساسية في هذا المقال وباستخلاصها.

فمن بين أهم التعاريف في هذا المجال، تلك التي انطلقت من وسائل الاعلام في مقاربة العملية التربوية، والتي أكدت أن التربية الاعلامية هي: عملية توظيف وسائل الاتصال بالطريقة مثلى من أجل تحقيق الأهداف التربوية المرسومة في السياسة التعليمية والسياسة الإعلامية للدولة، في حين تؤكد تعاريف أخرى أنها: عملية تهدف إلى تعليم التلاميذ والطلاب، وتدريبهم على التعامل مع محتوى الإعلام في الانتقاء والإدراك، بغية تجنب الآثار السلبية؛ مما يؤدي، مع تراكم التربية الاعلامية، إلى تشكيل وعي في التعامل مع الرسائل والصور الاعلامية. وقد شكل مفهوم التربية عبر وسائل الاعلام، مجالا واسعا للاهتمام من قبل مختلف المنظمات والهيئات الدولية، وتم انتاج عشرات التقارير في هذا المجال، فقد عرف تقرير توماس (1990)، مثلا، التربية الإعلامية بــــأنها: المقدرة على القراءة ومعالجة المعلومات، لكي تتم المشاركة بشكل كامل في المجتمع

في حين عرفها مـــؤتمر التربية من أجل عصر الإعلام والتقنية الرقمية (1999) بأنها: «التربية التي تختص في التعامل مع كل وسائل الإعلام والاتصال، وتشمل الكلمات والرسوم المطبوعة والصوت والصورة الساكنة والمتحركة التي يتم تقديمها عن طريق أي نوع من أنواع التقنيات». وهو التعريف الذي شمل التطورات الحاصلة في تكنولوجيات الاتصال الحديثة، خاصة وأن هذا التطور، أدخل تغييرات بنيوية على المنظومتين الاعلامية والتربوية على حد سواء؛ تغييرات زادت من التنافس والتسابق الحاصل بين منظومة الاعلام والاتصال ومنظومة التربية، وهو التنافس الذي سيؤدي إلى احتدام النقاش النظري والمفاهيمي، حول مفاهيم التربية والاعلام والتربية الاعلامية، مع تجاوز التعليم لحدود الزمان والمكان، خاصة مع تطور التعليم عن طريق الواب.

منظومتا التربية والاعلام في الجزائر: أو ثلاثية التنافس والتناقض والتجانس

عرفت الغالبية العظمى من المجتمعات اليوم اتساع التنافس بـل و حـتى التناقض في بعض المحطات، بين النظام التربوي و الإعلامي، حيث أفرز هذا التنافس تناقضات متشعبة في إدراكات الأفراد، وفي طرق تفكيرهـم. فإذا كان النظام التربوي يقوم على علـل التنافس في التحصيل و الانجاز، وعـلى التلقين وتعليم الفرد التفكير. فإن النظام الإعـلام يقـوم علـى الاتصال الجماهيري، الذي غالبا ما ينغلـق عـلى قيمة نشر الجديد، دون التوقف والتأمل في محتواه، مع تقديم بـرامــج الترفيهية المـمتعة، التي يسهل فهمها، بغض النظر عن ضعف الأسلوب أو ركاكة البنية اللغوية، و كل هـذه المعطيـات وغيرها تبـين، بوضوح، التناقض الموجود بين النظام التربوي و الإعلامي.

تناقض أفرز نوعا من الصدامية في العلاقة القائمة بين المؤسسات التربوية والإعلامية، وظهور تباين واضح بين الثقافة المدرسية التي تعتمد علـى معرفة ذات الطابع الأكاديمي، وبين الثقافة الإعلامية الـتي تروج لها وسائـل الإعـلام القائمة على الترويج والاثارة و الدعاية، وهي مسـتويات تبـرز بنيـة المؤسسـة الاعلامية في علاقتها بالمؤسسة التجارية و المؤسسة السياسية و الأمنية.

ورغم التناقض الموجود بـين بنيـتي التربيـة والاعلام، إلا أنه لا يمكن إغفال المجالات التجان س والتشابه بين الـمؤسستين التربوية والإعلامية، فالمؤسستان تؤديان عملهما في إطار عملية الاتصال، كما يسـاهم كل منهما في صيرورة التنشئة الاجتماعية للأفراد الذين يخصصون أوقاتا طويلة من حياتهــم في التعرض لوسائل الإعلام أو كمتعلمين في الأقسام الدراسية، رغم أن الكثير مـن المؤشرات أكدت منذ نهاية القرن الماضي، أن الطفل في فرنسا، مثلا، يقضي مـا معدله 1200 ساعة سنويا أمـام الشاشة، في حين يقضي معدل 900 ساعة سنويا فقط في مقاعد الدراسة.

فالعديد مـن الدراسات في علـم اجتماع الاتصال، وفي الدراسات الثقافية، تشدد عـلى أن تأثير وسائل الإعلام الجماهيرية في التكوين الثقافـي للأجيال الجديدة، وكذلك في تحديد أنماط سلوكها، وفي غرس القيم والعادات والاتجاهات، قـد تعاظم كثيرا في ظل التقدم متقنية الات صال والمعلومات، وازدحـام الفضاء بالأقمار الصناعية التي تبث برامجها دون انقطاع، الأمـر الـذي دعا الكثير مـن المتخصصين في القطاعين التربوي والاعلامي إلى تجاوز القطيعـة القائمة بين التر بوين والإعلاميين، والعمل على ارساء أسس التعاون في توظيف وسائل الإعلام في خدمة الأغراض التربو ية، وتـوظيف التربيـة في تفـعيل الرسائل الإعلامية.

وقـد وجـدت هـذه الدعوة صداهـا مع التطورات التقنية الحديثة، إذ ومع نهاية التسعينات

127

من القـرن المـاضي، عرفـت العلاقـة بـين المؤسسـتين التربويـة والاتصاليـة عهـد التجانـس،وأ صبحت وسـائل الإعـلام وتقنيـة المعلومات تستخدم فيصلب العملية التربوية،واستخدام المع لم الوسائط المتعددة وشبكة المعلومات الدولية، فيإعداد الخبرات التعليمية وتـوصيلها للطلاب، وأص بحا لتعليم عن بعـد والتعلم الإلكترونيو الجامعة الافتراضية، وكـذا المواقع التعليمية، مجالات مهمة تعتمدعليهاالمؤسسةالتربوية، وهو العهـد الـذي بـدأ في البلـدان المتقدمـة تكنولوجيا، وأصبح يشكل تحديـا حقيقيـا بالنسبة للبلـدان السـائرة في طريـق التنميـة، أو الناميـة الأخـرى، عـلى غـرار الجزائـر.

نسبة الأمية في الجزائرغداة الاستقلال تفوق86بالمائة

لا يمكـن فهـم واقـع التربيـة عـلى وسـائل الاعـلام في الجزائـر، دون أن نبـدأ مـن واقـع التعليـم وتاريخـه في الجزائـر، ففي هـذا البلـد الـذي اسـتقل عـن نظـام اسـتعماري عـرف بعنصريـة منظومتـه التعليميـة. كانـت تشـكل الأميـة فيـه عـام 1962 - سـنة التحـرر مـن الاستعمار الفرنسي- نسـبة تفـوق 86 بالمائة؛ وهـو معطـى أساسـي لفهـم نقص التربية عـلى وسـائل الاعـلام في المنظومـة التربويـة، ولفهـم النقائـص النوعيـة في إدراج تكنولوجيـات الاتصـال الجديـدة في منظومـة التعليـم. فقـد كان التعليـم سـنة 1962 محـدودا جـدا، إذ لـم يتجـاوز نسـبة 20 بالمائة مـن مجمـوع الأطفـال الذيـن بلغـوا سـن التمـدرس. كمـا ورثت الجزائـر هيـاكل اسـتقبال تربويـة قليلـة جـدا، مـع قلـة الإطـارات الجزائريـة وسـيطرة شـبه تامـة للغـة الفرنسـية، زاده انحصـار التعليـم في مناطـق محـدودة وعـلى طبقـات أو فئـات محـددة دون أخـرى ضعفـا مضاعفـا. الامـر الـذي سـعت الجزائـر المسـتقلة منـذ ذلـك الوقـت في تـدارك هـذا الوضـع التربيـوي، غـير المقبـول، باعتمادسياسـات بديلـة، وتدابـير إصلاحيـة مختلفـة.

ويمكـن تلخيـص أهـم محطـات هـذه السياسـات والتدابـير الإصلاحيـة، الخاصـة بالمنظومـة التربويـة في الجزائـر، في ثـلاث مراحـل، المرحلـة الأولى: وقـد امتـدت مـن 1962 إلى 1976، وتعد هـذه المرحلـة مرحلـة انتقاليـة سـادتها عـدة نقائـص؛ حيـث اقتـصرت عـلى إدخال تعديـلات تدريجيـة، تمهيـدا لتأسـيس نظـام تربـوي يسـاير متطلّبـات التنميـة. و كانـت أولويـة هـذه المرحلـة تعميـم التعليـم بإقامـة منشـآت تعليميـة وتوسـيعها للمناطـق النائيـة، والتعريـب التدريجـي للتعليـم، وقـد أدّت هـذه التدابـير إلى ارتفـاع نسـبة تمـدرس الأطفـال الذيـن بلغـوا سـن الدراسـة، إذ قفـزت مـن 20%، إبـان الدخـول المـدرسي الأول سـنة 1962، إلى 70% في نهايـة سـنة 1976. وامتـدت المرحلـة الثانيـة، التـي تلتهـا، مـن سـنة 1976 إلى 1999،

تنفيدا للأمر الصادر رقم: 35-76 المؤرخ في 16 أفريل 1976، الخاص بتنظيم التربية والتكوين بالجزائر. إذ أدخلت بموجب هذا الأمر إصلاحات على النظام التربوي غايتها مسايرة التحولات الاقتصادية والاجتماعية، وقد تجلت أولى ثمار هذه الاصلاحات، في تكريس الطابع الإلزامي للتعليم ومجانيه، حيث شرع في تعميم وتطبيق أحكام هذا الأمر ابتداء من السنة الدراسية 1980- 1981، وهو ما عرف بنظام "المدرسة الأساسية" ذات البعد العلمي والتكنولوجي.

أما المرحلة الثالثة فقد امتدت من سنة 2000إلى يومنا هذا، وهي فترة الإصلاحات الكبرى، وهي المرحلة التي تهمنا أكثر في سياق هذاه المقاربة، حيث تزامنت معها بداية استخدام تكنولوجيات الاتصال الحديثة، ومشاريع رقمنة المدرسة، بناء على توصيات الخبراء المشرفين على ورشات إصلاح المنظومة التربوية، الداعية إلى استخدام الوسائل التعليمية الحديثة في أداء المهمة التربوية وتعميمها.

التطورات الكمية وتحديات النوعية

لقد كان من الطبيعي أن تنعكس نسبة النمو الديموغرافي المرتفعةن نسبيا،في الجزائر، إضافة إلى مبدأ طيموقراطية التعليم في مضاعفة عدد الأطفال المتمدرسين بأكثر من عشر مرات؛ حيث بلغ عددهم، خلال العام الدراسي 2014- 2015، أكثر من 8 ملايين و 600 ألف تلميذ.

وارتفع عدد الناجحين في امتحان شهادة البكالوريا من 42 بالمائة سنة 1962 إلى 64،22بالمائة سنة 1976، وإلى 64،22 بالمائة عام 1979، لتصل نسبة 24،64 بالمائة عام 1999، وإلى ما يقارب 59 بالمائة عام 2012 . ولمواجهة هذا الارتفاع في عدد التلاميذ، كان من الطبيعي أن ترتفع أيضا نسبة توظيف الأساتذة بشكل كبير؛ إذ تضاعف العدد الإجمالي للأساتذة بـ 16 مرة، منذ 1962 إلى اليوم. مترجمة ذلك في رقم قدر بـ326 ألف عام 2000، منهم 170 ألف معلم ابتدائي، و101 أستاذ تعليم أساسي و55 ألف تعليم ثانوي. وغليه فقد قدرت نسبة التأطير على المستوى الوطني (عدد التلاميذ لكل أستاذ) بـ54،23 في الابتدائي و97،20 في المتوسط و16،10 في الثانوي.

كما يمكننا ان نسجل ملاحظة سوسيولوجية مهمة، في هذا السياق، وهي الارتفاع التدريجي لنسبة التأنيث في سلك التعليم، حيث سجّل خلال سنة 2010 2011 حوالي 130 امرأة مقابل 100 رجل، في مختلف الأطوار التعليمية، مقابل 89 امرأة سنة 2000

2001، ويتم تسجيل على التوالي 121 و149 و117 امرأة في الابتدائي، المتوسط والثانوي، مقابل 100 رجل، بعد أن كادت تكون منعدمة تماما غداة الاستقلال.

أما على صعيد الهياكل، فقد أنجزت الجزائر منذ 1962 إلى يومنا هذا، حظيرة تضمّ أكثر من 24.932 مؤسسة (مدارس ابتدائية، متوسطات وثانويات)، بعد أن كانت تقدّر عام 2000 بنحو 21 ألف مؤسسة تعليمية بمختلف أنواعها، مما يعادل فتح 355 مدرسة ابتدائية، 79 إكمالية (متوسطة) و32 ثانوية أو متقنة كلّ سنة.

الجدول (1): عدد المؤسسات التربوية في الجزائر من 1964 إلى 2000

طبيعة المؤسسات	1964	2000
المدارس الابتدائية	3050	19040
الثانويات	49	1218
المجموع	3099	20258

لكن هذه الأرقام، التي كثيرا ما شكلت مجالا لافتخار الرسميين الجزائريين، تخفي وراءها واقعاآخر، وهو واقع يتلخص في وجود أزمة نوعية التعليم في الجزائر، وهو ما دعا الكثير من المتخصصين في التربية في الجزائر للحديث عن وجود مدرسة مريضة و منكوبة من منظور النوعية هو التشخيص الذي فتح الباب لفتح ورشة الاصلاح سنة 2000، وهي الورشة التي كان من بين مقرراتها، تعميم تكنولوجيات الاتصال الحديثة في مختلف أطوار التعليم.

واقع تكنولوجيات الإعلام والاتّصال الجديدةفي جميع مستويات التعليم والتكوين الجزائرية

باشرت الجزائر منذ 2000 إصلاحات شاملة، وعميقة للمنظومة التربوية، وهي الاصلاحات التي انطلقت بعد العمل الذي قامت به اللجنة الوطنية لإصلاح المنظومة التربوية، و التي نصّبت يوم 13 ماي 2000 ،

وفي هذا الاطار، فتحت اللجنة عددا من الورشات، كـ»تكوين المكوّنين»، «التجديد الجذري للبيداغوجيا»، و»تقوية ودعم اللغة العربية»،و»ترقية اللغة الأمازيغية والتفتّح على اللغات الأجنبية»، «التربية المدنية والخلقية والدينية، من أجل تكوين مواطن يعتزّ بقيمه ووطنه ومتفتّح على العالم»، إلى جانب إدراج التكنولوجيات الجديدة للإعلام والاتصال في جميع مستويات التعليم والتكوين؛ وهو ما سيبرز فيما يأتي.كما وضعت

اللجنة عددا من المقترحات، أهمّها: تحسين مستوى تأهيل المعلّمين، مراجعة البرامج التعليمية، تحديد سياسة جديدة للكتاب المدرسي، إقامة نظام للتقويم، عصرنة تسيير المنظومة التربوية وإدخال التكنولوجيات الحديثة للإعلام والاتصال في المدرسة

ففيما يخصّ تحسين مستوى تأهيل المعلّمين، تمّ تصوّر سياسة جديدة لتكوين المكوّنين، ترمي إلى تلقين المعارف الأكاديمية والمهارات المهنية في آن واحد، أمّا فيما يتعلّق بمراجعة البرامج التعليمية، فتمّ إعادة النظر في مضامين البرامج التعليمية وطرق التعليم كلية لمواكبة تطوّر المعارف العلمية، التكنولوجية والبيداغوجية، قصد ضمان تفتّح المدرسة على العالم الخارجي الذي بات ضروريا، وكذا استجابة للحاجيات الجديدة للمجتمع الجزائري التي أفرزتها التحوّلات السياسية والاقتصادية والاجتماعية العميقة التي عرفتها الجزائر.

وخلصت اللجنة إلى أنّه من بين نشاطات الدعم التي تكتسي طابع الأولوية، تلك المتعلقة بالاستعمال العقابي لتكنولوجيات الإعلام والاتصال الحديثة، كسدّ أساسي لإصلاح المنظومة التربوية.

رقمنة المدرسة

لهذا كله و من أجل ضمان أحسن لتوظيف التكنولوجيا واستغلالها، أدخلت وزارة التربية في الجزائر، مقياس المعلوماتية، في إطار إصلاح المنظومة التربوية، حيث يتم تعليم المعلوماتية في كل المسار التعليمي للتلميذ.

ويؤكد الخطاب الرسمي و المقررات التربوية، أن التحكم في المعلوماتية يشكل هدفا استراتيجيا، وبأن القدرات المستهدفة من هذا تختلف من طور تعليمي إلى طور آخر، ففي التعليم الابتدائي مثلا، يستهدف هذا التعليم تمكين التلاميذ من التحكم في الوظائف الأساسية لجهاز الكومبيوتر، وبتمكينهم من أن يقوم بتحرير وثيقة إلكترونية. في حين وضع القائمون على شؤون التربية، هدف التعليم المعلوماتية في التعليم المتوسط، تمكين التلاميذ من معالجة و استغلال المعطيات: وهي القدرات التي يجب تطويرها في التعليم الثانوي، من أجل تحضير التلميذ لعالم الجامعة و البحث العلمي.

إدخال المعلوماتية في التربية، و تطوير التكنولوجيات الجديدة للاتصال، يشكل مجال استراتيجية«رقمنة المدرسة»»، «،وهي الاستراتيجية التي تنقسم إلى ثلاثة مستويات:e-Edu- cation التكوينوتجهيز المنشآت المدرسية و رقمنة المضامين البيداغوجية والإدارية،

ومن أجل تحقيق أهداف هذه الاستراتيجية، برزت خطة لتطبيقها، والتي نستعرضها فيما يأتي:

التكوين المستمر: رسكلة أكثر من 200ألف أستاذ

تم وضع برنامج تكوين لصالح الأساتذة في جميع أطوار التعليم، الابتدائي و المتوسط و الثانوي منذ سنة 2001، وهو البرنامج الذي يخص 50ألف أستاذ للتعليم الثانوي- من سنة -2001و2003، و أكثر من 18ألف أستاذ في طوري الابتدائي و المتوسط- من سنة 2003إلى2004.نجح القطاع فيالفترة الممتدة من 2006إلى 2008في تكوين و رسكلة أكثر من 102ألف أستاذ في الابتدائي، و 63ألف أستاذ في التعليم المتوسط، و36ألف أستاذ في التعليم الثانوي.

وقد تمحورت دورات التكوين هذه على أربعة مواد تعليمية منها: مدخل إلى استخدام التكنولوجيات الجديدة، وادراج قواعد التكنولوجياالجديدة، مع إدراج هذه الأخيرة في التعليم عن بعد.وهذه الأرقام من المتوقع أن تتضاعف بشكل كبير في غضون 2020، إذ من المحتمل أن يزداد التكوين ليتخصص أكثر ، خاصة و أن وزارة التربية لها مشروع استعمالاللوحات الذكية وتعميم استخداممختلف الوسائل التكنولوجية الجديدة في التعليم بمختلف أطواره.

تجهيز المنشآت المدرسية: كمبيوتر واحد لكل 15 تلميذ

خصصت وزارة التربية غلافا ماليا بقيمة 800مليون دينار، من أجل تجهيز المؤسسات التربوية بما يسمح لها ، بربط كل المؤسسات التربوية بشبكة «الأنترانت» و«الأنترنت»، وهو المشروع الذي تعول عليه كثيرا السلطات العمومية من أجل تحقيق ما تسميه بعصرنة منظومة التربية، خاصة فيما يتعلق بالتسيير الاداري و البيداغوجي، وسيتم تحقيق هذا المشروع على ثلاث مراحل: و تتعلق الأولى بربط وزارة التربية بكل المؤسسات التابعة لها، في حين تهدف المرحلة الثانية بربط ألفي ثانوية، و 5آلاف متوسطة،بينما تتعلق المرحلة الأخيرة بتعميم نسق «الأنترانت» و «الأنترنت» على كل المدارس الابتدائية- 15 ألف مدرسة ابتدائية.-وقد أكد مسؤولوقطاع التعليم في الجزائر، أن هذا المشروع يهدف إلى إدخال تقنية استخدام «الفيديو كونفيرونس»، حتي تتمكن مدارس جنوب الجزائر من الاستفادة من دروس مدارس الشمال، كما يسعى إلى تخزين المعلومة، بوضع كل الدروس والمحاضرات ورقمنتها وتسجيلها على موقع الـواب، ليتمكن التلاميذ والأساتذة من الاطلاع عليها.

وفي السياق الإحصائي نفسه، تجدر الإشارة إلى وجود68هيئة تربوية، في الوقت الراهن، تم ربطها بالموقع الرسمي للوزارة، كما تعرف نسبة الربط بشبكة الأنترنت 84بالمائة بالثانويات، و 77بالمائة في المتوسطات، و 23بالمائة فيما يخص المدارس الابتدائية.

ومن الواجب التنويه هنا، بأن امكانيات مادية كبيرة تم تجنيدها، من أجل تجهيز الثانوياتوالمتوسطات بمخابر المعلوماتية؛حيث تشير الأرقام الحالية إلى أنه يوجد معدل جهاز كمبيوتر واحد لكل 44تلميذ على مستوى الثانويات، و معدل كمبيوتر واحد لكل120تلميذا على مستوى المتوسطات،غير أن الأهداف التي يسعى المسؤولون لتحقيقها، على المدى القصير، هي كمبيوتر واحد لكل 15 تلميذ ثانوي، و كمبيوتر واحد لكل 30 تلميذا على مستوى المتوسطات، كما تهدف الخطة إلى ربط كل المؤسسات التربوية، على المدى القصير، بشبكة الأنترنت.

رقمنة المضامين البيداغوجية والادارية

ومن جانب آخر، فإن تكوين الموارد البشرية، لم يقتصر على الأساتذة فقط، بل شمل برنامج آخر لتكوين المفتشين، ومدراء المؤسسات التربوية و الاداريين، حيث تسعى هذه الخطة إلى وضع شبكة تربط المصالح المركزية بمختلف مديريات التربية، وهي العملية التي حققت تقدما كبيرا، كما تسعى هذه الخطة إلى ربط كل المصالح الادارية بمعاهد تكوين الأساتذة، بهدف الوصول، في النهاية، إلى رقمنةالمضامين البيداغوجية، وفي مقدمتها برامج التعليم.

وتعتبر هذه العملية مهمة على أكثر من صعيد، خاصة إذا ما علمنا أن قطاع التربية في الجزائر يوظف حوالي 650ألف شخص، من بينهم 400ألف أستاذ،يغطون بيداغوجيا نشاط 25ألف مؤسسة تربوية،إذ أن هذه الرقمنة ستخلق نوعا من المرونة في منظومة التعليم؛ وهو ما يمكن أن يساهم في إخراج المدرسة الجزائرية من ضعف مستوى التلاميذ، والنقص الملاحظ في التكوين، وهو ما قد ينتهي بتكوين جيد للأجيال القادمة. كما أن مسار الرقمنة سيساعد التلاميذ في صيرورة التكوين، وهو ما سيمكنهم من الاستفادة من مشروع المحفظة الرقمية، ليتمكن التلميذ من تفادي حمل أثقال المحفظة التقليدية الحالية،التي تفوق حمولتها الحالية، الـ 15 كغ من الكتب و الكراريس.

الخلاصة

يمكن التأكيد، في خلاصة هذه الورقة، أن التربية عبر وسائل الاعلام في الجزائر، لم تكن محط اهتمام كبير في منظومة التعليم، إلا ابتداء من نهاية التسعينيات من القرن الماضي، بسبب الظروف التاريخية و البنيوية التي عرفها المجتمع الجزائري، حيثكانت تشكل الأمية فيه عام 1962 -سنة التحرر من الاستعمار الفرنسي- نسبة تفوق 86 بالمائة، وهو معطى أساسي لفهم تخلف التربية على وسائل الاعلام في المنظومة التربوية، وكيف أن هذا الاهتمام ارتبط اليوم أكثر بإشكالية إدخال التكنولوجيات للاتصال في النسق التربوي.

ويصطدم هذا الاهتمام، اليوم بمجموعة من التحديات، أهمها نوعية التعليم، خاصة وأن الكثير من المتخصصين في التربية بالجزائر، يقرون بوجود أزمة عميقة في نوعية التعليم، متهمين المدرسة بأنها منكوبة ومريضة.

يوظف قطاع التربية في الجزائر اليوم حوالي 650ألف شخص، من بينهم 400ألف أستاذ على مستوى 25 ألف مؤسسة تربوية.لذلك فإن إدخال تكنولوجيات الاتصال الحديثة ستخلق نوعا من المرونة في منظومة التعليم، وهو ما يمكن أن يساهم كذلك في إخراج المدرسة الجزائرية من ضعف مستوى التلاميذ، و النقص الملاحظ في التكوين، وهو ما قد ينتهي بتكوين جيد للأجيال القادمة.كما أن مسار الرقمنة سيساعد التلاميذ في صيرورة التكوين، وهو ما سيعطيهم فرصة الاستفادة من مشروع المحفظة الرقمية، ليتمكن التلميذ من تفادي حمل أثقال المحفظة الحالية الحاملة لأكثر من 15 كغ من الكتب والكراريس.

غير أن إدخال التكنولوجيات لن يكون له أثرا كبيرا، لوحده، إذا لم يرفق بممارسة تربوية جديدة، وبخلق نشاطات تربوية أخرى، مصحوبة بديناميكية جديدة؛ ديناميكيةيجب أنتعبد طريق ايجاد مسار جماعي لبناء المعارف، هذا المسار الذي يلخص جيدا تحديات منظومة التعليم في الجزائر في علاقتها بالتربية عبر الاعلام، وعبر تكنولوجيات الاتصال الحديثة. تحديات النوعية التي تتجاوز لغة الكمبلغة الكيف.

أهم مراجع الورقة

ADEL, F. (2005). L'élaboration des nouveaux programmes scolaires in La refonte de la pédagogie en Algérie, Bureau International de l'éducation. Unesco. Ministère de l'éducation nationale. Algérie ; 2005, pp. 45-56.

CHINAPAH, V. (1997). Handbook on Monitoring Learning Achievement - Towards capacity building. UNESCO – UNICEF

DE KETELE, J.-M. & HANSSENS, C. (1999). L'évolution du statut de la connaissance. Des idées et des hommes : Pour construire l'avenir de la Wallonie et de Bruxelles. Louvain-la-Neuve : Académia – Bruylants.

DE KETELE, J.-M. (1996). L'évaluation des acquis scolaires : quoi ? pourquoi ? pour quoi ?, Revue Tunisienne des Sciences de l'Éducation, 23, p. 17-36.

GERARD, F.-M. & ROEGIERS, X. (1993 ; 2003). Des manuels scolaires pour apprendre. Bruxelles : De Boeck Université.

LE BOTERF, G. (1994). De la compétence : essai sur un attracteur étrange. Paris : Éditions d'Organisation.

PERRENOUD, P. (1997). Construire des compétences dès l'école. Paris : ESF.

REY, B. (1996). Les compétences transversales en question. Paris : ESF.
ROEGIERS, X. (2000). Une pédagogie de l'intégration. Bruxelles : De Boeck Université.

ROEGIERS, X. (2003). Des situations pour intégrer les acquis scolaires. Bruxelles : De Boeck.

ROEGIERS, X. (2004). L'école et l'évaluation. Bruxelles : De Boeck.

TAWIL, S. (2005). Introduction aux enjeux et aux défis de la refonte pédagogique en Algérie in La refonte de la pédagogie en Algérie, Bureau International de l'éducation. Unesco. Ministère de l'Education nationale. Algérie ; 2005, pp. 33-44.

أهم مراجع الورقة

TOUALBI-THAÂLIBI, N. (2005). Changement social, représentation identitaire et refonte de l'éducation en Algérie in La refonte de la pédagogie en Algérie, Bureau International de l'éducation. Unesco. Ministère de l'Education nationale. Algérie ; 2005, pp. 19-32.

فهد بن عبد الرحمان الشميمري:

التربية الاعلامية: كيف تتعامل مع الاعلام الرياض2010

التربية الاعلامية والمعلوماتية في المغرب

عبد الحميد النفيسي و ادريسية شويت

تسـاهم الصـور المنشـورة في وسـائل الاعـلام بقولبـة عمليـة الفهـم والتفسـير، والتفاعـل بين الأفـراد والأمـم والجماعـات في عالـم يتجـه أكـثر فأكـثر نحـو العولمـة. قـد تكـون الرسـائل الإعلاميـة مضـرّة، متضاربـة، أو مربكـة، وغالبـاً مـا لا تكـون مفهومـة بشـكل موحـد أو خاضعـة لتأثيـر الجماهيـر غيـر المتجانسـة الخاصـة بهـا. في هـذه الحـال، تصبـح التربيـة الإعلاميـة والمعلوماتيـة ضروريـة لتمكيـن الجماهيـر والسـماح لهـا بـأن تكـون بارعـة في الانتقـاد والحكـم الجيـد في تلقـي وتقييـم واسـتخدام المعلومـات ووسـائل الإعـلام. تتعـرض الأخلاقيـات الإعلاميـة للخـرق مـن قبـل الصحفييـن والمؤسسـات الإعلاميـة. ومـن شـأن هـذا الأمـر أن يؤثـر بشـكل كبيـر عـلى النـاس إن لـم يكونـوا مـن مستهلكي ثقافـة الإعـلام والمعلومـات. لهـذا السـبب، مـن المهـم أن نقـوم بتطويـر المهـارات النقديـة والتحليليـة العاليـة لـي نكـون مستهلكين مسـؤولين وفاعلين للمـواد الإعلاميـة ولـي نفهـم السـبيل للتخلـص مـن غمـوض ثقافـة الاعـلام والمعلومـات التـي تصـور الواقـع الاجتماعـي. تتمتـع التربيـة الإعلاميـة والمعلوماتيـة بمركـز مهـم جـداً وهـي مدمجـة في المناهـج التعليميـة في الكثيـر مـن الـدول المتقدمـة. إلا أنهـا غيـر معروفـة أو رديئـة المسـتوى في البلـدان الناميـة. ويتنـاول هـذا الفصـل حالـة التربيـة الإعلاميـة والمعلوماتيـة في المغرب؛ كمـا يسـلط الضـوء عـلى الخطـوات التـي اتخذتهـا جامعـة سـيدي محمـد بـن عبـد اللـه في هـذا المجـال.

تشـكّل كـلّ مـن وسـائل الإعـلام وتقنيـات المعلومـات والاتصـالات الجديـدة وسـيلة لتحقيـق التنميـة الاجتماعيـة والاقتصاديـة. مـع ذلـك، لا يمكـن أن تتحقـق الإمكانـات الكامنـة للتربيـة الإعلاميـة والمعلوماتيـة إن كان الأفـراد يفتقـرون للقـدرة عـلى الوصـول الى المحتـوى الإعلامـي وتحليلـه وتقييمـه وابتكـاره. وقـد بـدأت التربيـة الإعلاميـة والمعلوماتيـة تُعتبـر شـيئاً فشـيئاً المحـرك لاكتسـاب هـذه المهـارات والمعرفـة، وكعنـاصر إلزاميـة لكافـة مراحـل التعليـم

وكل فرد من أفراد المجتمع. إلا أن التربية الإعلامية والمعلوماتية لا تزال في بداياتها في الكثير من البلدان النامية وتواجه الكثير من التحديات. والهدف من هذا المقال هو دراسة حالة فن التربية الإعلامية والمعلوماتية في المغرب. وهو يتناول مسائل عدة على الشكل التالي: (1) يبين هذا الفصل كيفية التعريف بالتربية الإعلامية والمعلوماتية في المغرب؛ (2) ويسلط الضوء على الإجراءات التي اتخذها المغرب لتعزيز التربية الإعلامية والمعلوماتية بهدف إعداد المواطنين بشكل أفضل لعصر المعلومات، و (3) يهدف لإطلاع القارئ على الصعيدين الوطني والدولي على خطط العمل والمبادرات الرئيسية التي سيتم تنفيذها في المستقبل.

التربية الإعلامية والمعلوماتية في المغرب:

لا تزال التربية الإعلامية والمعلوماتية في المغرب في بداياتها، وليست مدرجة في مناهج النظام التعليمي. كما أنها ليست على جدول أعمال الناشطين وصانعي السياسات والمربين، كما أن الناس ليسوا على إطلاع عليها من أجل التفكير بها. بالنسبة الى الكثير من المغاربة، «التربية الإعلامية والمعلوماتية» تعني القدرة على القراءة والكتابة، وتفسير الرسائل المطبوعة. الا انه في عالم الوسائط المتعددة اليوم، لا يكفي تعليم هذا النوع من الثقافة فقط. نحن نعلم أن المعلومات حول ما يحدث في العالم تأتي إلينا ليس فقط من خلال وسائل الإعلام المطبوعة بل أيضاً من خلال الأصوات والصور القوية. بالتالي، فإن تزويد الأفراد بالمهارات والأدوات اللازمة لتقييم وفهم وتفسير محتوى الرسائل والأصوات والصور القوية التي توفرها الوسائط المتعددة بشكل نقدي قد أصبح ضرورة لا بد منها. في الواقع، تساهم تكنولوجيا المعلومات والاتصالات الجديدة والثقافة الإعلامية بتغيير حياة الناس وإعادة صياغة طريقة بناء المجتمعات على الصعيدين الوطني والدولي. لهذا، يتعيّن علينا تزويد أنفسنا بالمهارات اللازمة لمعرفة كيفية استخدام المحتوى الاعلامي والمعلوماتي في حياتنا.

دمج الدراسات الإعلامية في النظام التعليمي المغربي:

إدراكاً منها لأهمية الإنترنت في حياتنا اليومية، والتحديات التي يفرضها عصر المعلومات، أدخلت خطة الطوارئ المغربية للتعليم العالي في عام 2009 الدراسات الإعلامية والثقافة الالكترونية في المناهج الدراسية في كافة فروع اللغة الإنجليزية في كليات الآداب والعلوم الإنسانية في المغرب بهدف مساعدة الطلاب على فهم وظائف وسائل الإعلام وتأثيرها على المجتمع.

يتـم تدريس هـذه المـادة في الفصلين الدراسـيين 2 و 4، لتعريـف الطـلاب عـلى عالـم الإعـلام الجديـد والقديـم والثقافة الالكترونيـة (الانترنت). ويتمثل هـدف هـذه الـدورة في مسـاعدة الطـلاب عـلى فهـم وتعلـم سـير العمـل الإعلامي. هـذا يوفـر لنـا فرصة جيـدة لإدراج التربيـة الإعلاميـة والمعلوماتيـة في المناهـج الدراسـية لتمكين الطـلاب مـن تفسـير الرسـائل الإعلاميـة والمعلومـات والصـور التـي نواجههـا في حياتنـا اليوميـة بشـكل نقـدي.

تدريس التربية الإعلامية والمعلوماتية في كلية الآداب والعلوم الإنسانية سايس فاس: تجربة شخصية

عندمـا بـدأت تدريـس مـادة «مقدمـة في الدراسـات الإعلاميـة» في الفصـل الـدراسي الثاني والدراسـات الإعلاميـة والثقافة الإلكترونيـة في الفصـل الرابـع قبـل أربـع سـنوات، أعـرب طلابـي عـن اسـتيائهم مـن البرامـج الإعلاميـة المغربيـة، التـي تشـكل بحسـب تعبيرهـم، تهديـداً لهويتهـم وثقافتهـم. لهـذا، فـإن أول خطـوة قمت بهـا كانت دمـج التربيـة الإعلاميـة والمعلوماتيـة في المنهـج الـدراسي. وقـد سـاهمت التربيـة الإعلاميـة والمعلوماتيـة بإعطـاء قيمـة مضافـة إلى الدراسـات الإعلاميـة مـن خـلال تزويـد الطـلاب بالمهـارات التحليليـة لـي يصبحـوا مشـاهدين وقـراء ومسـتخدمي مسـؤولين لوسـائل الإعـلام المختلفـة ومحتـوى المعلومـات.

التربية الإعلامية:

تعرّف طلابي الى التربية الإعلامية من خلال فهم المفاهيم الأساسية التالية:

1. تتم صياغة الرسائل الإعلامية لتحقيق الربح والسلطة.

2. التفكير النقدي أساسي لتحديد المعتقدات الخاطئة التـي تتبناها بعـض المحتويات الإعلامية.

3. لوسـائل الإعـلام تأثيـر عـلى الأفـراد لأنهـا تسـاهم بتغييـر معالـم القيـم التـي يلتزمـون بهـا ووجهـات نظرهـم.

4. من المهم أن نطرح الأسئلة حول محتوى الرسائل الإعلامية على الشكل التالي:

من هو الجمهور المستهدف؟

ما هي التقنيات المستخدمة لإيصال معلومات محددة؟

ما هي القيم وأساليب الحياة التي يتمّ الترويج لها في هذه الرسالة؟

ما هي مصداقية المعلومات التي تنقل في رسالة معينة؟

5.   من المهم ألا يصبح المرء مدمناً على مصدر واحد للمعلومات بما ان وسائل الإعلام تستخدم طرقاً مختلفة لتقديم المعلومات المتعلقة بموضوع معين.

6.   من المهم أن نتخطى المظاهر وأن نتمكن من كشف الأحكام المسبقة والصور النمطية، والتشهير، والتلاعب، والتضليل أو تشويه المعلومات لأغراض محددة.

7.   كيف يمكن الاستثمار في الإعلام من أجل التنمية المستدامة والوصول الى عالم يسوده السلام؟

وقد ساهمت هذه المسائل بمساعدة طلابي على أن يدركوا لأول مرة أن هناك مهارات لا بد أن تؤخذ في الاعتبار عند قراءة الصحف المطبوعة، أو مشاهدة وسائل الإعلام وتصفح الإنترنت. وقد اعترف الطلاب بأن هذه المهارات قدمت لهم فرصة التعلم الانعكاسي لديناميات وسائل الإعلام الجماهيرية: طبيعة المشهد الإعلامي، وعملياته ووظائفه. وقد ساهم هذا الأمر بتعزيز وعيهم حول كيفية مساهمة الإعلام بوضع الأطر المرجعية للأفراد، وقيمهم، ومواقفهم وسلوكياتهم. كما قدمت لهم القدرة على الوصول الى المحتوى الإعلامي، وفك رموزه، وتقييمه وتفسيره إلى جانب الاستخدام المسؤول والمطّلع لكافة أشكال وسائل الإعلام، لكي يصبحوا بالتالي مستهلكين فاعلين ومسؤولين للمحتوى الإعلامي.

التربية المعلوماتية:

لم يتم دمج التربية المعلوماتية بالكامل في المناهج الدراسية في الجامعات المغربية. وتشمل التربية المعلوماتية المهارات المكتبية، الوعي بالحاسبات / الوعي التقني، ومهارات التفكير، الوعي البصري والوعي الثقافي؛ بالإضافة إلى مهارات البحث والتقييم للمصادر الإعلامية المطبوعة والمنشورة على شبكة الانترنت. إن التعرض لمجموعة متنوعة وغنية من مصادر المعلومات يتطلب اكتساب مهارات وكفاءات جديدة لتقييم المعلومات والمحتوى الإعلامي ويسمح بخلق قراء وباحثين ماهرين، قادرين على اتخاذ قرارات مطّلعة. قدمت هذه المهارات للطلاب الاطار المناسب لتعلم مهارات البحث والتقييم النقدي، والسعي، والتحقق واستخدام المعلومات في مجموعة متنوعة من الأشكال وفي سياقات مختلفة. وقد تعلّم الطلاب من خلال التربية المعلوماتية ما يلي:

140

1. تقييم قوة تأثير ومصداقية ودقة المواد المطلوبة في خلال إجراء البحوث الأكاديمية.

2. التشكيك بموثوقية المصادر على شبكة الانترنت لأنها لا تخضع للاشراف بقدر الموارد المتوفرة في المكتبة.

3. تحديد احتياجاتهم من المعلومات في الفضاء الإلكتروني؛

4. التحقق من دقة معلومة تمّ استقاؤها من الإنترنت؛

5. معرفة كيفية زيارة الموقع الالكتروني المناسب والمفيد؛

6. معرفة كيفية استخدام تكنولوجيا المعلومات والاتصالات على نحو فعال. من أبرز العقبات أمام كفاءة استخدام هذه التقنيات في البلدان النامية هو غياب التربية المعلوماتية.

اكتشف طلابي أن التربية المعلوماتية ساهمت بتمكينهم (1) ليكونوا باحثين ماهرين ومسؤولين في دراساتهم الأكاديمية؛ (2) في أن يكونوا مستهلكين فاعلين ومبتكرين للمعلومات؛ (3) لاستخدام المعلومات بشكل أخلاقي والمشاركة في بناء ثقافة السلام في مجتمعهم وفي المجتمع الدولي؛ و (4) لاستخدام تكنولوجيا المعلومات والاتصالات بفعالية وكفاءة.

التربية الإعلامية والمعلوماتية مجتمعة:

بعد تدريس التربية الإعلامية والتربية المعلوماتية كلّ على حدة في الفصل الثاني، اشتملت المادة التي قدمتها في الفصل الرابع بعنوان دراسات في الإعلام والثقافة الإلكترونية على مزيج من التربية الإعلامية والمعلوماتية مجتمعة، لأن كليهما يتضمن «دراسات في الإعلام» و «الثقافة الإلكترونية». لقد اغتنمنا الفرصة لكي نسلط الضوء على الواقع بأن منظمة الأمم المتحدة للتربية والعلم والثقافة (اليونسكو) قد تولت المبادرة في الجمع بين التربية الإعلامية والمعلوماتية وتشجيع عملية دمجها في النظم التعليمية كمجموعة من الكفاءات التي تهدف إلى تزويد الأفراد من كافة الأعمار والأجناس بالمهارات والكفاءات اللازمة لكي يكونوا أكثر مهارة في الانتقاد الحكم الجيد في تلقي، وتقييم، واستخدام المواد الإعلامية والمعلوماتية. إن مناهج اليونسكو الدراسية الخاصة بالتربية الإعلامية والمعلوماتية الخاصة بالمدرّسين، التي أطلقت في الملتقى الدولي الأول حول

141

التربية الإعلامية والمعلوماتية في 15 يونيو 2011، يضع المعلمين في صلب هذه العملية، من أجل تحقيق الأهداف الواردة في إعلان جرنوالد (1982) بشأن التعليم الإعلامي، وإعلان الإسكندرية (2005) وجدول أعمال اليونسكو باريس (2007).

من هنا، يمكننا أن نستنتج أن التربية الإعلامية والمعلوماتية لا تدرّس سوى في أقسام اللغة الإنجليزية في كليات الآداب. ومن الضروري أن يمتد تدريس تلك المادة الى كافة الكليات والمؤسسات. في هذه الحالة، ستكون التربية الإعلامية والمعلوماتية فعالة للمدرّسين وأولياء الأمور والشباب وصناع القرار، والكثيرين غيرهم. كما لا بد من التوضيح بأن اللغتين الرئيسيتين في المغرب هما العربية والفرنسية. الخطوة الأولى تقضي بترجمة الوثائق الرئيسية المتعلقة بالتربية الإعلامية والمعلوماتية إلى اللغة العربية من أجل السماح للجميع بالاستفادة من هذه المادة. بما أن التربية الإعلامية والمعلوماتية غير معروفة في المغرب، وإنطلاقاً من أهميتها بالنسبة الى الشباب وأولياء الأمور وكل مواطن، قررنا تنظيم مؤتمر دولي حول الموضوع من أجل تعريف الأكاديميين المغاربة به وتعزيز الوعي بين الأفراد بأهميته في حياتهم.

الأنشطة التي تضطلع بها جامعة سيدي محمد بن عبد الله في مجال التربية الإعلامية والمعلوماتية:

الملتقى الدولي الأول حول التربية الإعلامية والمعلوماتية:

تحت رعاية الملك محمد السادس، أُقيم الملتقى الدولي الأول للتربية الإعلامية والمعلوماتية من قبل مجموعة الأبحاث في الإعلام والثقافة والمجتمع. مختبر الخطاب، الإبداع والمجتمع: الإدراك والآثار؛ كلية الآداب والعلوم الإنسانية، سايس فاس؛ وجامعة سيدي محمد بن عبد الله، فاس، المغرب، ما بين 15-17 يونيو 2011 في كلية الطب والصيدلة في فاس، بالتعاون مع اليونسكو كشريك أساسي، والمنظمة الإسلامية للتربية والعلوم والثقافة (إيسيسكو)، ومكتب التربية العربي لدول الخليج، ورابطة الأمم المتحدة لتحالف الحضارات.

قادة المشروع:

وضع التصور الخاص بالمشروع من قبل كلّ من الدكتور عبد الحميد النفيسي، الرئيس، الملتقى الدولي للتربية الإعلامية والمعلوماتية، من كلية الآداب والعلوم الإنسانية، جامعة سيدي محمد بن عبد الله، فاس، المغرب؛ والدكتورة ادريسية شويت، نائب

الرئيس، الملتقى الـدولي للتربيـة الإعلاميـة والمعلوماتيـة، كليـة الآداب والعلـوم الإنسانيـة، جامعـة مـولاي إسماعيل، مكنـاس، المغرب.

الأساس المنطقي للملتقى:

أسباب الجمع بين التربية الإعلامية والمعلوماتية:

تنـاول الملتقـى كلاً مـن التربيـة الإعلاميـة والمعلوماتيـة لأنـه مـن الـضروري ان تكونـا متلازمتيـن في العصر الرقمـي والتقـارب بيـن وسـائل الاتصـال، مـن أجـل تحقيـق التنميـة البشـرية الكاملـة، وبنـاء مجتمعـات مدنيـة، وإرسـاء أسـس السـلام العالمـي والحـوار البنّـاء بيـن الثقافـات. وكان هـذا الملتقـى الأول مـن هـذا الحجـم منـذ أن بـدأت اليونسـكو المـزج بيـن هذيـن المفهوميـن بغيـة تمكيـن الجماهيـر مـن الاطـلاع عـلى وظائـف وسـائل الإعـلام وغيرهـا مـن مـزودي المعلومـات، والسـماح لهـا بـأن تكـون بارعـة في الانتقـاد والحكـم الجيـد في خـلال تلقـي وتقييـم واسـتخدام المـواد الإعلاميـة والمعلوماتيـة.

الأهداف

يهـدف الملتقـى الى مـا يـلي: (1) تعزيـز الوعـي والفهـم حـول أهميـة التربيـة الإعلاميـة والمعلوماتيـة في عصر المعلومـات والاتصـالات كشرط أسـاسي للتنميـة البشـرية والاقتصاديـة؛ (2) وضـع الخطـط لدمـج التربيـة الإعلاميـة والمعلوماتيـة في البرامـج التعليميـة الوطنيـة مـن اجـل تشـجيع تطويـر أفـراد المسـتخدمين والجماهيـر والمنتجيـن يتمتعـون بخـبرة في مجـال التربيـة الإعلاميـة والمعلوماتيـة ، وبالتـالي تحقيـق أقـصى قـدر مـن الإمكانـات الإعلاميـة والمعلوماتيـة في خدمـة الديمقراطيـة والعدالـة والنمـاذج الاقتصاديـة المسـتدامة والتطويـر في كافـة مسـتويات المجتمـع؛ (3) توعيـة المشـاركين بالقضايـا القانونيـة والسياسـية والاقتصاديـة والأخلاقيـة المرتبطـة بالتربيـة الإعلاميـة والمعلوماتيـة، ومناقشـة المقاربـات العلميـة لاسـتقاء المـواد الإعلاميـة والمعلوماتيـة، وتبادلهـا وتقييمهـا واسـتخدامها؛ (4) دراسـة المسـائل المفاهيميـة بشـأن التربيـة اللفظيـة والبصريـة والرقميـة؛ (5) تركيـز النقـاش عـلى التربيـة الإعلاميـة والمعلوماتيـة مـن خـلال وجهـات النظـر بيـن الثقافـات المختلفـة، والتعبيـر عـن مخـاوف، وانشـغالات وتطلعـات بلـدان الجنـوب والتشـديد عـلى أهميـة التعـاون ليـس فقـط بيـن الشـمال والجنـوب، بـل أيضاً بيـن دول الجنـوب نفسـها، مـن أجـل تشـجيع التربيـة الإعلاميـة والمعلوماتيـة، و؛ (6) التوصل إلى إعـلان فـاس حـول التربيـة الإعلاميـة والمعلوماتيـة ووضـع خطـة عمـل لهـذا الغـرض.

نتائج الملتقى: إعلان فاس حول التربية الإعلامية والمعلوماتية:

أصدر الملتقـى الـدولي الأول للتربيـة الإعلاميـة والمعلوماتيـة إعـلان فـاس حـول التربيـة الإعلاميـة والمعلوماتيـة. وقـد حـثّ المشاركون كلاً مـن اليونسكو، والمنظمـة الإسلاميـة للتربيـة والعلـوم والثقافـة (إيسيسكو)، ومكتـب التربيـة العربـي لـدول الخليـج،

وبرنامـج الأمـم المتحـدة لتحالـف الحضـارات، وغيرهـم مـن أصحـاب المصلحـة فـي كافـة أنحـاء العالم إلى مـا يلي:

1. إعـادة تأكيـد التزامهـم بالمبـادرات المتعلقة بالتربيـة الإعلاميـة والمعلوماتيـة للجميـع واعتبار هـذا الملتقـى الـدولي منصـة دوليـة حـول التربيـة الإعلاميـة والمعلوماتيـة.

2. تخصيـص أسـبوع، تحـت تسـمية «الأسـبوع الـدولي حـول التربيـة الإعلاميـة والمعلوماتيـة» بهـدف إبـراز قيمـة تعزيـز وتنفيـذ برامـج التربيـة الإعلاميـة والمعلوماتيـة حـول العالـم لجميـع المعنيـن. واقتـرح الاحتفـال بهـذا الأسـبوع مـا بـين 15-21 يونيـو مـن كل عـام.

3. دمـج التربيـة الإعلاميـة والمعلوماتيـة فـي المناهـج التعليميـة فـي أنظمـة التعليـم الرسمي وغيـر الرسمي، مـن أجـل (أ) ضمـان حـق كل مواطـن علـى الحصـول علـى هـذه التربيـة المدنيـة الجديـدة، (ب) الاستفادة مـن الأثـر المضاعف لقيـام المدرّسـين بتدريـب المتعلمين علـى التفكيـر النقـدي والتحليـل، (ج) تزويـد كل مـن المدرّسـين والمتعلمين بمهـارات التربيـة الإعلاميـة والمعلوماتيـة لبنـاء مجتمعـات متمكّنـة فـي مجـال التربيـة الإعلاميـة والمعلوماتيـة، الأمـر الـذي يمهـد الطريـق لمجتمعـات المعرفـة؛

4. إدراج إنتـاج وتوزيـع المحتـوى المقـدم مـن المسـتخدمين، وخاصـة المـواد الإعلاميـة التـي ينتجهـا الشـباب، كجـزء مـن الإطـار العـام للتربيـة الإعلاميـة والمعلوماتيـة؛

5. إجـراء البحـوث عـن حالـة التربيـة الإعلاميـة والمعلوماتيـة فـي مختلـف البلـدان، لـكي يتكمن خبـراء التربيـة الإعلاميـة والمعلوماتيـة والممارسين مـن تصميـم مبـادرات أكثـر فعاليـة؛

6. إجـراء متابعـة مناسـبة للمشـاورات الإقليميـة الخاصـة بتكييـف المناهـج الدراسـية الخاصـة بالتربيـة الإعلاميـة والمعلوماتيـة للمدرّسـين وتعزيـز التربيـة الإعلاميـة والمعلوماتيـة والحـوار بـين الثقافـات.

7. توسيع برنامج توأمة الجامعات والكراسي الجامعية لليونسكو و شبكة جامعات مبادرة تحالف الحضارات ـــــ اليونيسكو الـتي تعـنى بالتربية الإعلامية والمعلوماتية والحوار بين الثقافات لتشمل الجامعات الأخرى الـتي تمثل كافة مناطق العالم؛ وتشجيع إنشاء المعاهد أو المراكز الوطنية والإقليمية والدولية أو مراكز تبادل المعلومات حول التربية الإعلامية والمعلوماتية في كافة المناطق لدعم مبادرات التربية الإعلامية والمعلوماتية في كل أنحاء العالم. مما يجعل هـذه الشبكة القوة الدافعة لتعزيز التربية الإعلامية والمعلوماتية في كافة أنحاء المجتمعات ككل، والمساهمة بالتالي في بنـاء سـلام مستدام حـول العالـم.

8. تعزيز التربية الإعلامية والمعلوماتية من أجل تنمية الثقافات المحلية لتكون منصة للحوار بين الثقافات والمعرفة المتبادلة والتفاهم.

9. الحرص على أن تكون أخلاقيـات ثقافة الإعلام والمعلومات جزءاً لا يتجزأ من كافة المناهج الدراسية، ودعم القيم الأخلاقية المرتبطة بالاتصالات والمعلومات، ومقدمي المواد الاعلامية.

10. الموافقة على إنشاء معهد أو مركز اقليمي يُعنى بالتربية الإعلامية والمعلوماتية، من شـأنه أن يعمل تحت مظلة جامعة سيدي محمد بن عبد الله، فاس، المغرب، الـتي ستتعاون مـع هـذا المعهد أو المركز من أجـل تعزيز أهميتها الدولية في إطار منظمة شبكة جامعات مبادرة تحالف الحضارات ـــــ اليونيسكو الـتي تعـنى بالتربية الإعلامية والمعلوماتيـة والحوار بـين الثقافات.

11. عقد اجتماعـات سنوية للملتقى الـدولي للتربية الإعلامية والمعلوماتية لتوفير الفرصة لاستمرار التفاعـل حـول التربية الإعلامية والمعلوماتية عـبر الحـدود والثقافـات ومجالات الدراسة والممارسة المهنية. ومن المتوقع عقد الطبعة الثانية للملتقى الـدولي للتربية الإعلامية والمعلوماتية في عـام 2013. وسيتم تحديد الموعد المحدد بعد التشاور مـع جميع الشركاء.

ندوة دولية حول التربية الإعلامية والمعلوماتية على مستوى الجامعات:

في الذكـرى السنوية الأولى لإعلان فـاس حـول التربية الإعلامية والمعلوماتية، نظمت كلّ مـن مجموعة الأبحاث في الإعلام والثقافة والمجتمع. مختبر الخطاب، الإبداع والمجتمع: الإدراك والآثار؛ كلية الآداب والعلـوم الإنسـانية، سايس فاس؛ وجامعة سيدي محمد

145

بـن عبـد اللـه، فـاس، المغـرب، نـدوة دوليـة حـول «التربيـة الإعلاميـة والمعلوماتيـة علـى مسـتوى الجامعـات» مـا بيـن 20-19 يونيـو 2012 فـي كليـة الآداب والعلـوم الإنسـانية سـايس فاس، المغرب.

أهداف الندوة:

جمعـت النـدوة المدرّسـين والنشـطاء، والإعلاميـين والصحفيـين، وأمنـاء المكتبـات، والمحفوظات بهـدف تعزيـز الوعـي بيـن الطـلاب حـول الأهميـة الحيويـة للتربيـة الإعلاميـة والمعلوماتيـة فـي حياتهـم الأكاديميـة والمهنيـة. كمـا أكـدت علـى الفكـرة التـي تقـول، أنـه فـي عالـم يتحـوّل الى الرقمنـة علـى نحـو متزايـد، ونظـرا! لانفجـار المعلومـات، تشـكّل التربيـة الإعلاميـة والمعلوماتيـة الأسـاس للتعلـم طويـل الأمـد.

لمركز الإقليمي للتربية الإعلامية والمعلوماتية والحوار بين الثقافات:

يعمـل المركـز الإقليمـي للتربيـة الإعلاميـة والمعلوماتيـة والحـوار بيـن الثقافـات الـذي تمـت الموتفقـة علـى إنشـائه فـي إطـار إعـلان فـاس تحـت مظلـة جامعـة سـيدي محمـد بـن عبـد اللـه، فـاس، المغـرب، ويتعـاون مـع شـبكة جامعـات مبـادرة تحالـف الحضـارات ـــــ اليونيسـكو. وكان الهدف مـن المركز مـا يلي:

1. تعزيز التربية الإعلامية والمعلوماتية في المغرب والعالم العربي.

2. تسـليط الضـوء علـى الـدور الحاسـم الـذي يمكـن أن تلعبـه التربيـة الإعلاميـة والمعلوماتيـة فـي بنـاء ثقافـة السـلام مـن أجـل الحـوار بيـن الثقافـات والمعـارف المتبادلـة والتفاهـم بيـن الحضـارات؛

3. التأكيـد علـى أهميـة التربيـة الإعلاميـة والمعلوماتيـة لأغـراض التنميـة الاجتماعيـة والاقتصاديـة والثقافيـة؛

4. تعزيـز المبـدأ القائـل بـأن التربيـة الإعلاميـة والمعلوماتيـة هـي حـق أساسـي مـن حقـوق الإنسـان، ولا سـيما فـي العصـر الرقمـي الـذي يشـهد انفجـار المعلومـات وتقـارب تكنولوجيـات الاتصال.

5. تسـليط الضـوء علـى أهميـة التربيـة الإعلاميـة والمعلوماتيـة فـي البلـدان الناميـة وآثارهـا فـي عصـر مجتمعـات المعرفـة.

6. تعزيز دور الجامعات سواء كمراكز للمعرفة علم أو كناقلات للتنمية المستدامة.

ورش عمل حول التربية الإعلامية والمعلوماتية لمدرّسي المستقبل:

نظمت كلّ من مجموعة الأبحاث في الإعلام والثقافة والمجتمع. مختبر الخطاب، الإبداع والمجتمع: الإدراك والآثار ورشتي عمل للمربين الحاليين والمستقبليين ما بين 18-19 فبراير، 2013 و27-26 مارس، 2014 في كلية الآداب والعلوم الإنسانية، فاس، المغرب بالتعاون مع برنامج الأمم المتحدة لتحالف الحضارات (UNAOC)، وجامعة مولاي إسماعيل، بالمغرب، ومركز الدوحة لحرية الإعلام.

ورشة العمل الأولى حول التربية الإعلامية والمعلوماتية للمربين الحاليين والمستقبليين:

يعيش طلاب اليوم ويتعلمون في عالم دائم التغيير. وقد ساهمت هذه الورشة بتوفير الدعم للمدرّسين من أجل مساعدة الطلاب على التفكير النقدي حول استخدام وتقييم الكميات الهائلة من المعلومات المتاحة لهم من أجل حل المشاكل المرتبطة بواقع الحياة، وتزويدهم بالقدرات والمعارف التي ستكون حيوية لكي يعيشوا بشكل مثمر في القرن الحادي والعشرين.

كان الهدف من ورشة العمل الأولى هذه تدريب المدرّسين لكي يتمكنوا من تدريس التربية الإعلامية والمعلوماتية لطلاب

المدارس الابتدائية والثانوية. وقد هدفت ورشة العمل هذه إلى ما يلي:

1. تعريف المربين الحاليين والمستقبليين بأهمية التربية الإعلامية والمعلوماتية في العالم المتخم إعلامياً في القرن الحادي والعشرين؛

2. شرح العمليات الإعلامية الأساسية لهم؛

3. تعريفهم بمزوّدي المواد الإعلامية والمعلومات وعلى عالم تكنولوجيا المعلومات والاتصالات لكي يفهموا بشكل أفضل كيفية عمل الإعلام التقليدي والإعلام الجديد، ومدى تأثيرهما على الأفراد والمجتمع، وكيف يساهمان في تغيير وقولبة المواقف والسلوكيات.

4. التركيز على التحليل والتفكير النقدي لجعل المربين الحاليين مواطنين واسعي الاطلاع، ومستخدمين نشطين لوسائل الإعلام، وقادرين على قراءة ما بين السطور وفك رموز التلاعب بالمعلومات وتشويهها.

5. تعريفهـم بمـدى أهميـة التربيـة الإعلاميـة والمعلوماتيـة نظـرا لكميـة المعلومـات المتوفرة في المجتمع المعاصر. التعـرض لكـمّ كبير مـن المعلومـات لـن يولّـد مواطنـين مطّلعـين؛ بـل إنهـم بحاجـة إلى أن يتعلمـوا كيفيـة اسـتخدام تلـك المعلومـات بفعاليـة.

6. إن المجتمع القـادر عـلى الوصـول إلى المعلومـات وتقييمهـا واسـتخدامها وتوصيـل المعلومـات بشـكل فعّـال وكفوء هـو مجتمع يتمتع بثقافة الإعـلام والمعلومـات. عندمـا نـزوّد أولادنـا بما يلـزم مـن مهـارات الثقافـة الإعلاميـة، لا بـد أن يتمتـع المجتمـع بالثقافـة الإعلاميـة والمعلوماتيـة الواسـعة.

تنوعـت أوراق العمـل الـتي قدمـت خـلال هـذه الورشـة في مـواد المواضيـع المطروحـة، والتوجـه النظـري، والأسـلوب المنهجي. كما تـمّ طـرح عـدد مـن الموضوعـات والقضايـا الرئيسـية المشـتركة ومناقشـتها مـن قبـل مختلـف المتحدثـين وأفـراد الجمهـور.

ورشة العمل الثانية حول التربية الإعلامية والمعلوماتية:

النمـو السـريع لثقافـة الإعـلام والمعلومـات وتكنولوجيـا الاتصـالات وانفجـار المعلومـات جعل مـن الضروري تدريس التربيـة الإعلانيـة والمعلوماتيـة في المـدارس، لأن فئـة الشـباب هـي الأكـثر تأثراً بالمحتـوى الإعلامـي والمعلومـاني.

تعزيـز التربيـة الإعلانيـة والمعلوماتيـة بـين الطـلاب يتطلـب تمتع المدرّسـين بثقافـة الإعـلام والمعلومـات. في هـذا السـياق، خُصصت ورشـة العمـل الثانيـة لاستكشـاف الوحدات الرئيسـة لمنهـج التربيـة الإعلاميـة والمعلوماتيـة للمدرّسـين الـذي نشرته منظمـة اليونسـكو في عـام 2011. ويهـدف هـذا الكتيّـب الى تزويـد المدرّسـين بالمهـارات والمنهجيـة اللازمـة لتعليـم التربيـة الإعلاميـة والمعلوماتيـة في الصـف.

يوم دراسة حول التربية الإعلامية والمعلوماتية في عصر المعلومات:

نظمت كلّ مـن مجموعـة الأبحـاث في الإعـلام والثقافـة والمجتمع. مختبـر الخطـاب، الإبداع والمجتمـع: الإدراك والآثـار يومـاً دراسـياً حـول التربيـة الإعلاميـة والمعلوماتيـة في العـصر الرقمـي يـوم 20 فبرايـر 2014 في كليـة الآداب والإنسـان العلـوم فـاس، المغـرب.

جمـع يـوم الدراسـة المدرّسـين والباحثـين والناشـطين والمتخصصـين في المعلومـات والقيمـين عـلى المكتبـات مـن أجـل تعزيـز الوعـي بـين النـاس حول أهميـة التربيـة الإعلاميـة والمعلوماتيـة في العـصر الرقمـي.

إن الإنترنت وتكنولوجيا الاتصالات الأخرى هـو أعظم وسيلة لنقل المعلومـات الى جميع النـاس في العالم. كمـا أن المعلومـات التـي نتعرض لهـا عبـر شبكة الإنترنت تحـدد وتغيّر شـكل مواقفنـا، فهمنـا، وتفسيرنا ومعتقداتنـا، وآرائنا حـول العالـم. علـى الرغـم مـن أن الإنترنت وتكنولوجيا المعلومـات والاتصالات تشكّل وسائل لتحقيق التنميـة الاجتماعيـة والاقتصاديـة، ثمـة ايضاً كميـات غيـر مسبوقة مـن الأخطـاء والأحـكام المسبقة والصور النمطيـة والدعايـة والتشـهير، والتلاعـب، التضليل، والعديـد مـن أنواع تشـويه المعلومـات.

في هـذا السـياق، تصبح التربيـة المعلوماتيـة ضروريـة للسـماح للجماهير بالتمتع بالتفكير النقـدي والحكـم الجيـد لـدى تلقـي وتقيـم واستخدام المعلومـات؛ كمـا تسـمح لهـم بتطويـر المهـارات النقديـة والتحليليـة الضروريـة ليكونـوا مسـتهلكين فاعلـين ومسـؤولين للمعلومـات. وقد ناقش يـوم الدراسـة عـدداً مـن القضايـا الهامـة مثـل الجوانـب الرئيسـية للتربيـة الإعلاميـة، ودمـج التربيـة المعلوماتيـة في الفصول الدراسـية، ودور المواطنـين في العـصر الرقمـي، والوعـي الثقـافي والوعـي الحاسـوبي، والوعـي السـينمائي وثقافـة الأخبـار.

يوم دراسة حول الوعي الثقافي:

يـؤدي الاسـتخدام المتنامـي لتكنولوجيـا المعلومـات الى زيـادة الطلـب علـى البرامـج الـتي تعالـج التربيـة المعلوماتيـة والوعـي الثقـافي. ويُعتبـر مثـل هـذه البرامـج فائـق التطـور في الغـرب، بمـا ان نسـبة التعلّـم مرتفعـة في هـذه البلـدان. فضلاً عـن ذلك، تتمتع تلك الدول باسـتقرار اقتصادي وسياسي، الأمـر الـذي يوفر قاعدة متينة للتربيـة الإعلاميـة والمعلوماتية.

غيـر أن اسـتخدام تكنولوجيـا المعلومـات والاتصالات في البلـدان الناميـة معقـد للغايـة ويواجـه الكثيـر مـن العقبـات. إذ أن انتشـار الأميـة، وانعـدام الأمـن السـياسي، وعـدم الاسـتقرار الاقتصادي في العالـم العـربي، هـي عوامل تشـكل عائقـاً هامـاً أمـام قـدرة العـرب علـى أن يحققـوا إلمامـاً واسـعاً في مجـال الاعـلام والمعلومـات لأنـه مـن الصعـب تنفيـذ برامـج التربيـة الإعلاميـة والمعلوماتيـة.

إن الهدف من هذه الدراسـة حول الوعي الثقافي هو ذات شقين:

1. دراسة كيفية استخدام تكنولوجيا المعلومات والاتصالات بفعالية وكفاءة في الـدول العربية.

2. تعزيـز الوعـي حـول الحق في الوصـول إلى المعلومـات، وقيمة المعلومـات والحـق في حريـة التعبير.

3. نشر التربية الإعلامية والمعلوماتية لتطوير الثقافات المحلية ولتكون منصة للحوار بين الثقافات والمعرفة المتبادلة والتفاهم.

الخلاصة:

في السنوات الأخيرة، شكلت شبكة الإنترنت والتقنيات الشبكية الأخرى قضية رئيسية للتنمية في كافة أنحاء العالم. وقد أظهرت قدرتها على زيادة الإنتاجية والتنافسية في الاقتصاد، من أجل خلق طرق جديدة لتقديم الخدمات التعليمية والصحية، ولكي تكون القوى المحركة لتحديث الخدمات العامة. كما أنها تسهل الوصول السلس إلى المعلومات.

بسبب انفجار المعلومات، أصبحت التربية التربية الإعلامية والمعلوماتية ضرورة لا بد منها لمساعدة المواطنين على التعامل مع هذه المعلومات وتخصيصها لمنفعتهم الشخصية والأكاديمية والاجتماعية. وقد ركّز هذا الفصل على أهمية التربية الإعلامية والمعلوماتية في العصر الرقمي وسلّط الضوء على الخطط والإجراءات التي اتخذتها جامعة سيدي محمد بن عبد الله من اجل تعزيز التربية الإعلامية والمعلوماتية في المغرب.

نحن الآن بصدد إنشاء شبكة من الجامعات المغربية والعربية المهتمة بالعمل معنا كشركاء لتعزيز التربية الإعلامية والمعلوماتية في المغرب والمغرب العربي والمنطقة العربية. لكن، لا بد من الإشارة الى وجود تحديات كبيرة تواجهنا، أبرزها ما يلي:

1. نحن بحاجة إلى تكييف الإجراءات والأبحاث المرتبطة بالتربية الإعلامية والمعلوماتية لتتلاءم مع الظروف المغربية والعربية ولكي تساهم بأفضل طريقة في خدمة احتياجات الشباب المغربي وشعوب المنطقة.

2. إن نسبة الأمية في المغرب مرتفعة، وهذا ما يمنع الأفراد من الاستفادة من التربية الإعلامية والمعلوماتية. 3. ضعف إتقان اللغات الأجنبية وعدم وجود مراجع بالغة العربية حول التربية الإعلامية والمعلوماتية تشكل عائقاً حقيقياً.

4. لا تزال المكتبات في المغرب تعمل بالطرق التقليدية.

5. إن مستخدمي الإنترنت عاجزون عن الاستفادة بالكامل من هذه الوسيلة لأنهم غير ملمين بثقافة الإعلام والمعلومات.

المراجع:

آغر-غوتـا، ن. وآغر-غوتـا إي دي.. «اقتصـاد المعرفـة». في موسـوعة التعلـم المـوزع: أ. ديسـتيفانو، ك. إي. رودسـتام، وآر. جـي سـيلفرمان. لنـدن: منشـورات سـيج، 2003.

ألـواي، إن وي جيلبرت (1998). «ثقافة ألعاب الفيديو: اللعب بالذكورية والعنف واللـذة»، إس. هـوارد. «الاثـارة: الشـباب والإعـلام الإلكترونـي». لنـدن: «يـو سي إل بـرس»، ص: 114-95.

بـاري، دي. إس. (1999) «التربيـة علـى العنـف» في تأثيـر وسـائل الإعـلام الجماهيريـة، المسـائل الحالـة، لونغمـان.

س. بنتيفينيا. (2002) «السياسـة والإعـلام الجديـد.» في كتيب الإعـلام الجديـد، إل. آي ليفـرو وإس. لفينغسـتون، لنـدن: منشـورات سـيج، ص. 61-50.

بيرغر، آي. (2003) الإعلام والمجتمع: منظور نقدي. نيويورك: رومان وليتلفيلد للنشر.

دي. باكنغهام (2002). «الجيل الالكترونـي؟ الأطفال والإعـلام الجديـد». في كتيب الإعلام الجديـد، إل. آي ليفـرو وإس. لفينغسـتون، لنـدن: منشـورات سـيج، ص. 89-77.

دي. ديجلـر، وإل. باتـل (2000). إدارة المعرفـة في السـعي لتحقيـق الأداء: تحـدي السـياق تحسـين الأداء (طبعـة خاصـة). «آي إس بي آي» 39 (6)، يوليـو 2000. الرابـط الالكترونـي: www.ipgems.com/writing/kmcontext.htm .

جونتلت، دي. (2002) الإعلام، الجنس، والهوية: مقدمة. لندن: راوتليدج، 2002.

إل. جورمـان، ودي. ماكلين. (2003). الإعـلام والمجتمـع في القـرن العشـرين: مقدمـة تاريخيـة. المملكـة المتحـدة: بلاكويل.

إي. إس. هيرمـان، وآر. دبليـو ماكشـنسي (1997). الإعـلام العالمـي: المبشـرين الجـدد للرأسـمالية المؤسسـية. لنـدن: كاسـل.

دي. كيلـر (2002). «الإعـلام الجديـد والكفـاءات الجديـدة». في كتيب الإعـلام الجديـد، إل. آي ليفـرو وإس. لفينغسـتون. لنـدن: منشـورات سـيج، 2ص. 104-90.

دي. لامبرتـون، (2002). «اقتصاديـات الإعـلام والتغييـر الصناعـي». في كتيب الإعـلام الجديـد، إل. آي ليفـرو وإس. لفينغسـتون. لنـدن: منشـورات سـيج، ص. 349-334.

ش. موريـل، بي إتش سبيتزبـرغ، و جي كاي بـارج، (2007). «التواصـل الإنسـاني: الدافـع والمعـارف والمهـارات». كنـدا: «طومسـون ليرنـج» .

التربية الإعلامية والمعلوماتية في مصر

سامي طايع

مصر أو رسمياً جمهورية مصر العربية، دولة عربية تقع في الركن الشمالي الشرقي من قارة أفريقيا، ولديها امتداد آسيوي، حيث تقع شبه جزيرة سيناء داخل قارة آسيا. ويحدّ جمهورية مصر العربية كل من البحر الأحمر في الشرق، والبحر الأبيض المتوسط في الشمال. تتمتع مصر بأعلى كثافة سكانية في العالم العربي، حيث تجاوز عدد سكانها الـ 85 مليون (بحسب إحصائيات نشرت من قبل المركز الوطني للسكان، 2014)، يعيشون بشكل أساسي على ضفاف نهر النيل الذي يمتد بطول البلاد. وتشير التقديرات إلى أن 95 في المائة من السكان يعيشون ضمن مساحة 3 بالمائة فقط من الأرض. ويعيش في العاصمة القاهرة حوالي 18 مليون نسمة. تشهد مصر طفرة في أعداد السكان من الشباب، حيث يمثل الشباب الذين تقل أعمارهم عن 25 سنة نحو ثلث سكان البلاد، 17 مليون منهم هم من الطلاب في المدارس والجامعات.

التعليم في مصر إلزامي لجميع الأطفال الذين يرتادون المدارس الحكومية أو الخاصة من ستة الى اثني عشر عاماً، فيما توفر الحكومة التعليم المجاني تقريباً لكافة المستويات. وليس على الأولاد أن يدفعوا سوى مبلغ زهيد صغير من المال كرسوم (نحو 10 دولار في بعض الأحيان لكامل العام الدراسي)، يمكن ان يتم الاستغناء عنها إن كانوا لا يستطيعون تحمل هذه الرسوم. كما يتم توفير الكتب المدرسية مجاناً أيضاً. ويتم قبول الأطفال في المدارس الحكومية منذ سن السادسة. وهم يمثلون ما يقرب من 1.5 مليون طالب (بحسب تقديرات المركز القومي للسكان، 2014). أما المدارس الخاصة في مصر، فتتطلب تكاليف باهظة وقد يصل متوسط الرسوم فيها الى نحو 20 ألف دولار سنوياً، كما هي الحال في معظم المدارس الأمريكية والبريطانية في مصر، التي تقوم بتوفير تعليم ذي جودة. وتتميز معظم المدارس الحكومية بمستوى تعليمي رديء في غياب معلّمين مؤهلين تأهيلاً عالياً، كما تكون الصفوف مكتظة غالباً بالطلاب. وتتبع المدارس الخاصة والدولية النظم الأمريكية والبريطانية والفرنسية والألمانية في التعليم. ويقضي الطلاب المصريون عادة نحو 12 سنة دراسية إلزامية في المدرسة.

وسائل الإعلام في مصر:

تملك مصر مجموعة واسعة من وسائل الإعلام الحكومية والخاصة. ويتولى إتحاد الإذاعة والتلفزيون المصري (ERTU)، التابع لوزارة الإعلام، مهمة الاشراف على الإذاعة والتلفزيون ووضع الضوابط للأداء الاعلامي. توجد ثلاث شبكات قنوات للتلفزيون المصري تبث على المستوى الوطني وست محطات محلية. وتقوم القنوات الوطنية بالبث الى كافة انحاء البلاد بينما تتولى المحطات المحلية البث الى مناطق محددة مثل بعض المحافظات. القناة الثانية، وهي شبكة وطنية، تبث باللغة الإنجليزية بشكل أساسي بالإضافة الى الفرنسية. وتهدف الى خدمة المغتربين الذين يعيشون في مصر. كما توجد أكثر من 20 قناة تلفزيونية خاصة تتنافس أحياناً مع المحطات الرسمية (التي تديرها الدولة)، ولها نسبة مشاهدين أعلى من القنوات الوطنية. ويتعرض المشاهدون في العالم العربي الى المئات من القنوات الفضائية. بالإضافة إلى محطات التلفزيون، تمّ إحصاء ما لا يقل عن 696 قناة فضائية، منها 97 قناة حكومية، بينما بلغ عدد القنوات الخاصة 599 قناة. (جامعة الدول العربية، إحصائيات، 2014) 1. وتستخدم تلك القنوات 17 قمراً صناعياً تدور في مدار العالم العربي. وتضمّ الشبكات الحكومية 49 قناة شاملة تبث المزيج المعتاد من الأخبار ومواد التسلية، فيما تبث 48 قناة برامج متخصصة مثل التعليم أو الترفيه. كما يشاهد المصريون أيضاً العديد من القنوات الفضائية الأجنبية منها قنوات من أوروبا وأمريكا الشمالية وتركيا وغيرها. كما تملك مصر سبع شبكات إذاعية تجذب المستمعين من كافة انحاء البلاد. من هذه الشبكات، إذاعة «ما وراء البحار» overseas، التي تبث برامجها بأكثر من 40 لغة. كما توجد إذاعات محلية أخرى في كافة أنحاء البلاد بالإضافة الى إذاعات «إف إم» خاصة، تقوم ببث برامج التسلية الخفيفة والموسيقى في المقام الأول. وتستمع اليها فئة الشباب بشكل خاص.

ما خصّ وسائل الإعلام المطبوعة، توجد في مصر ثلاث دور نشر هامة تديرها الدولة، وهي تنتج العشرات من الصحف والمجلات باللغات العربية والإنجليزية والفرنسية والألمانية. كما تقوم الكيانات الخاصة و الأحزاب السياسية ايضاً بنشر الصحف مثل جريدة الوفد والأهلي. وتشير التقديرات إلى وجود أكثر من 600 صحيفة ومجلة في مصر، وفقاً للأرقام التي أصدرها المجلس الأعلى للصحافة عام 2011. لا بد من الإشارة الى أن إصدار الصحف الخاصة والصحف الحزبية السياسية تخضع لموافقة مجلس الأعلى للصحافة، وهو الجهة المنظمة لوسائل الإعلام المطبوعة. في ما خص الفن السابع،

إن امتداد صناعة السينما المصرية وانتشارها في العالم العربي يشبهان إلى حد كبير ما لدى هوليوود من انتشار في الغرب. وتحظى الأفلام والبرامج التلفزيونية المصرية بشعبية كبيرة، فيما تعتمد معظم القنوات التلفزيونية العربية على هذه البرامج. في ما يتعلق بوسائل الإعلام الأخرى، بلغت الاشتراكات في خدمات الهاتف المحمول ما مجموعه 125 في المائة من إجمالي سكان مصر، إذ يملك بعض المشتركين أكثر من خط واحد، فيما تجاوز عدد مستخدمي الإنترنت 40 مليون شخص (بحسب وزارة الاتصالات، 2013).

الشباب في مصر يعشقون مواكبة واستخدام التكنولوجيا الجديدة. وقد كانوا حريصين على استخدام الانترنت منذ عام 2002 عندما أطلقت وزارة الاتصالات مبادرة الانترنت المجانية لجميع المصريين. وفقاً للاتفاق بين وزارة الاتصالات وشركات مزودي خدمات الانترنت، بدأ تقديم خدمة الإنترنت بكلفة المكالمة العادية مع اقتسام تلك القيمة بنسبة 30% للمصرية للاتصالات و 70% لشركات تقديم خدمة الإنترنت. (مراد، 2002، ص. 76). في عام 2004، أطلقت الحكومة مبادرة الإنترنت عالي السرعة (ADSL)، مما جعل مصر تحتل المرتبة الأولى بين دول شمال أفريقيا والشرق الأوسط من حيث عدد مستخدمي الإنترنت. وسرعان ما أصبحت شبكات التواصل الاجتماعي وسيلة الاتصال الأكثر أهمية بين الشباب. (س. طايع، 2014).

منذ عام 2004، ازداد عدد النشطاء السياسيين الشباب والمدافعين عن حقوق الإنسان على الانترنت بشكل سريع، وتغير دور وسائل التواصل الاجتماعي. فأصبحت أدوات هامة لتعبئة الشباب ضد سوء السلوك وفساد الحكومة المخلوعة التابعة للرئيس حسني مبارك. أصبحت وسائل التواصل الاجتماعي أدوات مهمة وفعالة بسبب سرعتها وكفاءتها في تمكين التعبئة، وردود الفعل الفورية، واتخاذ إجراءات سريعة من قبل أعداد كبيرة من الناس في الاستجابة للقضايا الاجتماعية والسياسية. وقد ساهم التقارب بين وسائل الإعلام ووجود الوسائط المتعددة في كل مكان، بتغيير السيناريو والمشهد الطبيعي. بالنسبة إلى الناشطين من الشباب المصري داخل مصر وخارجها، وفرت وسائل التواصل الاجتماعي فرصة للتعبير عن آرائهم، والانضمام إلى الجماعات، والانخراط في مناقشات حول الأحداث الجارية والقضايا السياسية. وقد مهدت هذه المناقشات الطريق إلى أحداث الخامس والعشرين من يناير 2011، التي اتخذت شكل انتفاضات للاحتجاج على البطالة وارتفاع الأسعار والفساد.

وسائل التواصل الاجتماعي:

- سهلت الوصول إلى أعداد كبيرة من الناس وإبقائهم منخرطين في مناقشات حول القضايا السياسية.

- جعلت من الممكن المشاركة في المجموعات والمناقشات من دون الحاجة الى الكشف عن هوية الشخص. حصل ذلك في فترة دقيقة وحاسمة ، كانت فيه السلطات المصرية تولي اهتماماً وثيقاً بالأنشطة السياسية وفيما كان قانون الأحكام العرفية مفروضاً طيلة 30 عاماً. (شبيب وسهيل، 2011، ص 140).

- سمحت للشباب المصري بالمشاركة السياسية، الأمر الذي برز بشكل خاص في أبريل 2008. فقد أنشأ الناشطون المصريون صفحة على موقع فايسبوك للتخطيط وتنظيم إضراب عام للعمال في مصانع النسيج في المحلة الكبرى (محافظة شمال القاهرة احتجاجاً على غلاء المعيشة وسوء ظروف العمل ومطالبةً بزيادة الأجور. وبفضل استخدام وسائل التواصل الاجتماعي، شارك أكثر من 70 ألف متظاهر في التظاهرة التي أنهتها قوات الأمن بشكل حاسم باستخدام الغاز المسيل للدموع لتفريق المتظاهرين. تجدر الإشارة إلى أن عدد مستخدمي الإنترنت قفز من 1.5 مليون في عام 2004 الى 13.6 مليون مستخدم في عام 2008.

في عام 2009، قام طالب جامعي مصري شاب وناشط يدعى محمود الحيتة بانشاء حركة على موقع فايسبوك أطلق عليها اسم «البرادعي للرئاسة في مصر». وقد انضم عشرات الآلاف من الشباب المصريين إلى المجموعة التي تحولت إلى حركة شعبية لدعم وصول محمد البرادعي الى الرئاسة في مصر. وكان البرادعي ناشطاً سياسياً محبوباً جداً من الشباب. ترأس البرادعي الوكالة الدولية للطاقة الذرية (IAEA) لأكثر من ثماني سنوات، وعاد بعد تقاعده إلى مصر وقام بتشكيل حركة معارضة ضد نظام الرئيس مبارك. نجح البرادعي في حشد المؤيدين في أوساط الشباب الذين ضاقوا ذرعاً بالفساد وتدهور الأوضاع الاقتصادية. في عام 2010، أنشأ وائل غنيم، وهو ناشط مصري شاب آخر سبق أن عمل لدى موقع «جوجل»، موقعاً الكترونياً جديداً موالياً للبرادعي. وقد تجاوز عدد متابعيه الشباب 100 ألف شخص. عندما انشأ محمد البرادعي حساباً على موقع تويتر، نجح باستقطاب أكثر من 10 آلاف متابع في فترة قصيرة من الزمن (المرجع نفسه). في يونيو 2010، أطلق غنيم صفحة أخرى على موقع فايسبوك تحت عنوان «كلنا خالد سعيد»، في أعقاب قيام الشرطة المصرية بتعذيب شاب من مدينة الاسكندرية حتى

الموت. وتهدف الصفحة الى اقناع الناس على التمرد ضد وحشية الشرطة والفساد. ثم قام غنيم بتوسيع أنشطة الصفحة والمناقشات احتجاجاً على انتهاكات حقوق الإنسان التي تُرتكب في مصر وسوء سلوك الشرطة. وقد تخطى عدد متابعي الصفحة الربع مليون في سبتمبر 2010. عبر هذه الصفحة، قام المتابعون بتبادل الأخبار والمعلومات، ومشاركة الصور ومقاطع الفيديو دعماً للانتفاضة. وكان لتلك الصفحة تأثير تخطى أي وسيلة أو مصدر آخر للمعلومات في مصر. واعتمد المتابعون الشباب على هذا الموقع لتنظيم التجمعات والمظاهرات في الشوارع. عندما وصل عدد المتابعين الى 365 ألفاً، دعا هؤلاء إلى تظاهرات في الشوارع للتمرد على الظلم ووحشية الشرطة (ماسين، 2011، ص 19). وقد تجاوب الشباب مع تلك الدعوات بحماس شديد.

خلال الأحداث، قامت الحكومة المصرية بقطع الإنترنت ووسائل الاتصالات اللاسلكية (الهاتف المحمول) من 28 يناير الى 1 فبراير 2011، في اعتراف واضح بقوة وسائل التواصل الاجتماعي والإنترنت في تعبئة الشباب. وعلى الرغم من هذه التدابير، قفز عدد متابعي صفحة «كلنا خالد سعيد» على الانترنت من 365 الف إلى 640 الف متابع. بعد 25 يناير 2011، ارتفع عدد مستخدمي الإنترنت في مصر بمقدار 1.9 مليون في عام 2011 (طايع، 2014)،، ليصل إلى 23.1 مليون؛ فيما ارتفع عدد مستخدمي فايسبوك أيضاً من مليون إلى 5.2 مليون في تلك الفترة. في تلك الأثناء، ارتفع عدد مستخدمي تويتر في مصر من 26.800 إلى 44.200 في عام 2011. وبلغ عدد المشاهدات لصفحات الويب عبر موقع «يوتيوب» أكثر من 8.7 مليون صفحة، خلال الأسبوع الأخير من يناير 2011 (لو، 2011، ص.2).

التربية الإعلامية والمعلوماتية في مصر: مبادرات متأخرة -

لا تزال التربية الإعلامية والمعلوماتية في العالم العربي متخلفة عن الكثير من الدول الأخرى. وفي مطلع القرن الحادي والعشرين، بدأ طلاب الجامعات يتعرّفون الى هذا المفهوم. وقد حضر أكثر من 1200 مشارك دولي، بما في ذلك ممثلين عن منظمة الأمم المتحدة للتربية والعلم والثقافة (اليونيسكو) المؤتمر الذي نظمته مؤسسة «منتور» الدولية للتربية الإعلامية، والتي تولى رعايتها وأطلاقها المغفور له خادم الحرمين الشريفين الملك عبد الله بن عبد العزيز . وقد شارك الحضور، ومعظمهم من الميادين الأكاديمية ووسائل الإعلام، في الحدث الذي أدخل مفهوم التربية الإعلامية «الجديد» الى العالم العربي. في ذلك الوقت، لم يكن المفهوم الشامل للتربية الإعلامية والمعلوماتية معروفاً بشكل جيد بعد. بل كان استخدام تعبير التربية الإعلامية شائعاً

أكثر من استخدام التربية الإعلامية والمعلوماتية. وبعد هذا الحدث الإقليمي الهام، ظهرت بضع مبادرات في العالم العربي، قام بالترويج لها مكتب التربية العربي لدول الخليج، ومركز الدوحة لحرية الإعلام، وجامعات ومدارس الإعلام في منطقة الشرق الأوسط وأفريقيا.

في السنوات القليلة الماضية، أي منذ مطلع القرن الحادي والعشرين، حصلت بضع مبادرات مرتبطة بالتربية الإعلامية والمعلوماتية في مصر. من أبرز المبادرات الهامة التي تضمّنها الحدث، لا بد أن نذكر ما يلي:

1. إدراج التربية الإعلامية والمعلوماتية في المنهاج الدراسي في الجامعات المصرية.

2. تعريف الصحفيين الشباب والمتخصصين في المعلومات، والباحثين بالتربية الإعلامية والمعلوماتية.

3. إنتاج مجموعة مواد لتدريس التربية الإعلامية والمعلوماتية للجامعات في المنطقة.

4. تنظيم ورش عمل للتدريب على التربية الإعلامية والمعلوماتية للمدرّسين في المدارس الثانوية.

5. تنظيم ورش عمل تدريبية حول التربية الإعلامية والمعلوماتية لطلاب السنة الأخيرة في كلية الإعلام التابعة لجامعة القاهرة.

1 - إدراج التربية الإعلامية والمعلوماتية في المنهاج الدراسي في الجامعات المصرية:

في عام 2005، نظمت كلية الإعلام التابعة لجامعة القاهرة دورة تدريبية حول التربية الإعلامية والمعلوماتية للطلاب الجامعيين. وحذت بعدها الجامعات الحكومية والخاصة الأخرى حذوها. منذ عام 2000، أعتقد أنه تم تدريس التربية الإعلامية والمعلوماتية في الجامعات الحكومية التي يبلغ عددها 18 جامعة، والجامعات الخاصة التي يبلغ عددها 29 جامعة في مصر. بالإضافة إلى ذلك، تمّ وضع بضع أطروحات الماجستير والدكتوراه في مجال التربية الإعلامية والمعلوماتية.

2 - تعريف الصحفيين الشباب والمتخصصين في المعلومات، والباحثين بالتربية الإعلامية والمعلوماتية:

تماشيا مع سياسة «اليونسكو» لتعزيز التربية الإعلامية والمعلوماتية على الصعيد العالمي، نظمت جامعة القاهرة ورشة عمل للصحفيين الشباب والمتخصصين في

المعلومـات والباحثـين، بالتعـاون مـع جامعـة برشلونـة المستقلة (AUB)، بدعـم مـن «اليونسكو». كانـت ورشـة العمـل التـي استمرت ثلاثـة أيـام (مـن 14-17 فبرايـر 2013) مصمّمة أساسـاً لنحـو 25 مشـاركاً. إلا أن ازديـاد الطلـب مـن الفئـات المستهدفـة علـى مثـل ورش العمـل هـذه، دفـع بالمنظمـين الى توسيعها لاستيعاب 65 شخصاً مـن مختلـف الـدول العربيـة. وكان مـن بـين المتدربـين المشـاركين، شخصـين مـن أفغانسـتان وغانـا. ومـن أبـرز النتائـج التـي توصلـت اليهـا ورش العمـل، التغطيـة الإعلاميـة الواسـعة للحـدث وسـائل الإعـلام وذكـر التربيـة الإعلاميـة والمعلوماتيـة في كافـة وسـائل الاعـلام المكتوبـة والإذاعـة والتلفزيـون.

3 - إنتاج مجموعة مواد لتدريس التربية الإعلامية والمعلوماتية للجامعات في المنطقة:

قامـت جامعـة القاهـرة، بالتعـاون مـع جامعـة برشلونـة المستقلة (AUB) وبدعـم مـن مكتـب اليونسكو في القاهـرة، بإعـداد مجموعـة مـن المـواد التـي تهـدف إلى توفيـر المـوارد للإسـتخدام مـن قبـل أسـاتذة الجامعـات في تدريـس برامـج التربيـة الإعلاميـة والمعلوماتيـة في مختلـف المؤسسـات الحكوميـة والخاصـة.

وتشمل تلك المواد ما يلي:

- «لتربيـة الإعلاميـة والمعلوماتيـة والحـوار بـين الثقافـات (التنـوع الثقـافي والتربيـة الإعلاميـة والمعلوماتيـة؛ نمطيـة التفريـق، إعـادة بنـاء الصـور النمطيـة، والتعـاون الإعلامـي)؛

- الإعـلام الجديـد والشـباب (اسـتخدام وسـائل الإعـلام، ووسـائل التواصـل الإجتماعـي؛ المخاطـر والحسـنات) ؛

- التجارب العالمية في مجال التربية الإعلامية والمعلوماتية؛

- التربيـة الإعلاميـة والمعلوماتيـة: مناهـج للمدرّسـين (منهـاج «اليونيسكو»، منهـاج التربيـة الإعلاميـة والمعلوماتيـة حـول العالـم: دراسـات حالـة)؛

- مدخـل إلى التربيـة الإعلاميـة والمعلوماتيـة (التعريـف، منظـور تاريخـي، الإطـار العالمـي، التربيـة الإعلاميـة والمعلوماتيـة في التعليـم الرسـمي) ؛

- القيـم الإعلاميـة والتربيـة الإعلاميـة والمعلوماتيـة (تحليـل الأخبـار والترفيـه والدعايـة والإقنـاع السـياسي) ؛

159

- التربيـة الإعلاميـة والمعلوماتيـة في المدرسـة (لغـات ورمـوز جديـدة، وأماكـن جديـدة للتعلـم، نهـج جديـد للتعليـم، الكفـاءات في مجـال التربيـة الإعلاميـة والمعلوماتيـة) ؛

- تأثير حالة حرية التعبير وحرية الصحافة علـى التربيـة الإعلاميـة والمعلوماتيـة في بلـدان منطقـة الـشرق الأوسـط وأفريقيـا ؛

- 11 شريط فيديو تعليمي ؛

- قائمة بالموارد المتوفرة.

4 - تنظيـم ورش عمل للتدريب علـى التربيـة الإعلاميـة والمعلوماتيـة للمدرّسين في المدارس الثانوية:

قامـت كليـة الإعـلام بجامعـة القاهـرة، بالتعـاون مـع برنامـج الأمـم المتحـدة لتحالـف الحضـارات (UNAOC)، بتنظيـم ورشـة عمـل للمدرّسـين في المـدارس الثانويـة في مـصر استغرقت يومين (مـن 19-20 نوفمبر، 2103)، وحضرهـا نحـو 34 مشـاركاً مـن مختلف أنحـاء البـلاد. كما حـضر ورشـة العمل ايضاً ممثلـون عـن وزارة التربيـة والتعليـم، وتناولت مجالات مختلفـة مـن التربيـة الإعلاميـة والمعلوماتيـة. اشتمل اليـوم الأول علـى ثـلاث جلسـات حـول مفهـوم التربيـة الإعلاميـة والمعلوماتيـة، والتخطيـط لبرامـج التربيـة الإعلاميـة والمعلوماتيـة في المناهـج الدراسية (الاسـتراتيجيات والتحديـات).

وتضمـن اليـوم الثاني أربـع جلسـات. أولهـا عـن التربيـة الإعلاميـة والمعلوماتيـة ووسـائل الإعـلام التـي تمثل مختلف الثقافات. الجلسـة الثانيـة سلطت الضـوء علـى تطبيـق برامـج التربيـة الإعلاميـة والمعلوماتيـة في المـدارس. أمـا الجلسـة الثالثـة، فتضمنت إنتـاج المـواد الإعلاميـة الخاصة بالأطفـال، فيمـا تناولـت الجلسـة الرابعـة التدريـب والإنتـاج الإعلامـي الأساسـي. وفي الجلسـة الختاميـة، فتـح البـاب للنقـاش وأسـئلة المشـاركين، بالإضافـة الى اقتراحـات المشـاركين حـول كيفيـة تحسـين العمليـة التعليميـة في مـصر باسـتخدام برامـج التربيـة الإعلاميـة والمعلوماتيـة.

5 - تنظيـم ورش عمل تدريبية حول التربية الإعلامية والمعلوماتية لطلاب السنة الأخيرة في كلية الإعلام التابعة لجامعة القاهرة :

بالتعـاون مـع «فيلـم بيداجورجنـا» السـويد (وهي عضو مشـارك في برنامـج «توأمـة الجامعات» التابـع لليونسـكو، أو «يونيتويـن»)، تم إنشـاء شـبكة مـن الجامعـات في فـاس (بالمغرب) في عـام

160

2009. وتمثّل الهدف الرئيسي للشبكة في تشجيع التعاون بين الجامعات الأعضاء. وقد نظمت جامعة القاهرة ورشة عمل لمدة يومين لطلاب السنة الأخيرة، تدربوا في خلالها على التربية الإعلامية والمعلوماتية وإنتاج المواد الإعلامية، التي تمّ تقديم بعضها خلال «يوم التربية الإعلامية في السويد» في 29 يناير عام 2014. وقد لقيت المواد استحساناً جيدا من جانب الجمهور السويدي.

التحديات، التوصيات، ومستقبل التربية الإعلامية والمعلوماتية في مصر:

يقع التحدي الأبرز الذي يواجه التربية الإعلامية والمعلوماتية في مصر على عاتق صانعي السياسات. إذ لا توجد سياسة محددة بشأن هذه المسألة. حاول بعض العلماء والخبراء إشراك ممثلين عن وزارة التربية والتعليم ووزارة التربية والتعليم العالي في معظم هذه الأنشطة، إلا أنه تبيّن أن المشكلة والعقبات يتسبب بها كلّ من واضعي السياسات والعاملين في وزارة التربية والتعليم. أحد التحديات الأخرى يرتبط بانعدام الوعي بشأن التربية الإعلامية والمعلوماتية. من هنا تبرز الحاجة الى العمل بشكل وثيق مع الإعلاميين، بهدف تشجيعهم على نشر وبث مزيد من المعلومات حول هذه المسألة، والاشتراك معهم. كما يوجد أمل كبير بأن تحاول المنظمات الدولية، مثل اليونسكو وبرنامج الأمم المتحدة لتحالف الحضارات، التأثير على الحكومة المصرية من أجل اعتماد سياسات حول التربية الإعلامية والمعلوماتية.

المراجع:

- شبيب ن. ك، سهيل ر. م.، «أسباب مساهمة وسائل التواصل الاجتماعي في الثورة المصرية عام 2011»، المجلة الدولية لأبحاث الأعمال والإدارة (2.3، IJBRM)

- المجلس الأعلى للصحافة، (2011) الإحصاءات الصادرة عن وضع الإعلام في مصر،

- لو ل.ل. ، (2011) «الوحدة والصداقة واحترام الذات: تجربة طلاب الجامعات بالسنة الأولى في استخدام موقع فايسبوك، أطروحة دكتوراه غير منشورة: جامعة ولاية نيويورك.

- ماسين ر.، (2011) «تأثير استخدام موقع فايسبوك على تطوير العلاقات الشخصية بين طلاب الجامعات». أطروحة ماجستير غير منشورة: جامعة ولاية أوكلاهوما.

- وزارة الاتصالات، (2013) إحصاءات عن استخدام المحمول في مصر.

- مراد م. ، (2012) «استخدام المعلومات على الانترنت من خلال وسائل التواصل الاجتماعي وآثارها على الوعي السياسي لدى المصريين الشباب». المجلة المصرية للاتصالات. 42: 146-73.

- المركز القومي للسكان (2014)، إحصاءات عن عدد السكان، (القاهرة).

- طايع س.، (2008)، «الأطفال واستخدام وسائل الإعلام في العالم العربي: تحليل من المستوى الثاني» في جامعة كارلسون، وآخرون، «التمكين من خلال التربية الإعلامية: حوار بين الثقافات، ملحق من انتاج «نورديكوم».

- طايع س.، (2014)، «أثر وسائل التواصل الإجتماعي على المشاركة السياسية للشباب المصري». رسالة ماجستير غير منشورة، (القاهرة، الجامعة الأمريكية في القاهرة).

1 ملاحظات للمحررين: لم يتم العثور على المرجع المذكور

التربية الإعلامية والمعلوماتية من المنظور الأردني

يسار درة

تعرفت لأول مـرة عـلى مصطلح «التربية الإعلامية والمعلوماتية» خـلال مشاركتي في احـدى جلسـات المناقشـة مـع اليونسكو عـام 2012، فيما كنا نعمل عـلى تطوير أفكار لتنظيم سلسـلة مـن ورش العمل التدريبيـة الممولـة مـن الاتحـاد الأوروبي لتعزيـز التغطيـة الإعلاميـة للعمليـة الانتخابيـة في الأردن 1 بشكل دقيـق ومحترف. قبـل ذلك، كانت التربيـة الإعلاميـة والمعلوماتيـة بالنسبـة لي، مجـرد سلسـلة مـن القيـم والأهـداف الـتي يتـم تدريسهـا في مختلف المناهـج الإعلاميـة التدريبيـة ولا تشـمل صغـار طـلاب المدارس. امـا اليـوم، فقـد اصبح هـذا التعبيـر جـزءاً مـن المصطلحـات المستخدمـة مـن قبـل الموظفيـن والطـلاب في معهـد الإعـلام الأردني (JMI) وقـد اكتسـب مزيـداً مـن الزخـم، مـع تلقـي الطـلاب الدعـوة بشـكل منتظـم للمشـاركة في ورش عمل حـول موضوع التربيـة الإعلاميـة والمعلوماتيـة. كانت بـرامج التدريـب في معهـد الاعـلام الاردني تستهدف الصحفيـن في منتصف حياتهـم المهنيـة ومستخدمي وسـائل التواصـل الاجتماعـي مـن الشـباب. ويشـمل هـذا النـوع مـن التدريـب معظـم القيـم الـتي تنـدرج حاليـاً في خانـة التربيـة الإعلاميـة والمعلوماتيـة، إن لـم يكـن جميعها.

عـام 2013، اكتسـب هـذا التعبيـر وزنـاً وأهميـة أكـبر بالنسبـة لي. فقـد تلقيـت دعـوة مـن اليونسكو للمشـاركة في إطـلاق الشبكـة العالميـة للتربيـة الإعلاميـة والمعلوماتيـة في أبوجـا، نيجيريـا. (المنتـدى العالمي مـن اجـل إقامـة الشـراكات بشـأن التربيـة الإعلاميـة والمعلوماتيـة.) 2 المنتـدى ناقـش موضـوع «تعزيـز ثقافـة الإعـلام والمعلومـات كوسـيلة للتنـوع الثقـافي». شكلت العـروض والمناقشـات الـتي شـهدتها جلسـات المؤتمـر وخارجـه مفاجـأة سـارّة ومفيدة بالنسبـة لي، وكشـفت عـن مقدار العمـل الـذي لا بـد مـن الاضطلاع بـه في هـذا المجـال. للأسف، كانت هنـاك أولويـات تدريبيـة اخـرى أكـثر إلحاحـاً، بسـبب الثـورة التكنولوجيـة الـتي تشـهدها وسـائل الإعـلام، وعـدم توفـر منصـة للتربيـة الإعلاميـة

والمعلوماتيـة في الأردن، مـا جعـل الموضـوع يتحـول الى مجـرد طمـوح جـدي. اقتصرت مشاركتي في برامـج التدريـب المتعلقـة بالتربيـة الإعلاميـة والمعلوماتيـة في تلـك المرحلـة عـلى الترويـج للمفهـوم والتأكيـد عـلى الحاجـة الملحـة الى أن يتـم اعتناقـه مـن قبـل المدرّسـين وأولياء الأمـور. وانا أحـرص عـلى التأكيـد عـلى أهميـة هـذه المسألـة في كل مقابلـة، أو لقـاء أو كلمـة ألقيهـا أمـام الطـلاب والـزوّار في معهـد الإعـلام الأردني. منـذ أن بـدأت البحـث عـن الأدلـة عـلى وجـود التربيـة الإعلاميـة والمعلوماتيـة في الأردن، وقعـت عـلى كتيبـات التدريـب باللغـة العربيـة الخاصـة بتحالـف الحضـارات المنبثـق عـن الأمـم المتحـدة. كانـت مكتوبـة بشكل جيد باللغـة العربيـة السهلـة الاستخدام ولـم تكـن مختلفـة جـداً عـن الكتيبـات الـتي نستخدمهـا لتدريـب الصحفيـن الشبـاب إلا في كونهـا أكـثر شمـولاً واتسـاعاً.

مـن ناحيـة اخـرى، وإثر المقابـلات الـتي أجريتهـا مـع المدرّسـة غـادة قاقيـش، الـتي تشـارك حاليـاً في البرامـج التعليميـة حـول موضـوع التربيـة الإعلاميـة والمعلوماتيـة، ارتأيـت أن جوابهـا لا يمكـن أن يوصـف إلا بأنـه نـوع مـن الارتبـاط الشغـوف بهـذا الموضـوع. فهـي تـرى أن تلـك الكتيبـات ملائمـة للغايـة. ووصفـت السعـادة القصـوى بالنجـاح والرضـا الكبـير لـدى كلّ مـن المدرّسـين والطـلاب وأوليـاء الأمـور المشاركيـن في برامـج التربيـة الإعلاميـة والمعلوماتيـة الـتي تـشرف عليهـا. 3 عـلى الرغـم مـن غيـاب قاعـدة بيانـات وطنيـة أو مرجـع للحصـول عـلى معلومـات حـول برامـج التربيـة الإعلاميـة والمعلوماتيـة الـتي يتـمّ تنفيذهـا في الأردن، فـإن اليونيسكـو - عـمّان والمنظمـات غـير الحكوميـة الناشطـة قادتـني الى اكتشـاف أثـر عـلى وجـود عـدد محـدود مـن الأنشطـة والبرامـج الـتي يتـم تنفيذهـا في البـلاد.

ومـع أن وزارة التربيـة والتعليـم لا تنفـذ المناهـج التربويـة حـول التربيـة الإعلاميـة والمعلوماتيـة، إلا أن أحـد المؤشرات الايجابيـة كان تعليقـات مسؤولي الـوزارة الـتي ظهـرت في وسائـل الإعـلام عـام 2007، والـتي تدعـم برامـج التربيـة الإعلاميـة والمعلوماتيـة وقيمهـا. 4 وفي خـلال اتصالـي للاستفسـار عـن الموضـوع مـع الـوزارة، حصلـت عـلى ردود مشجّعـة، تـدلّ عـلى نوايـا إيجابيـة لناحيـة دمـج التربيـة الإعلاميـة والمعلوماتيـة في المناهـج التعليميـة لكـن مـن دون وضـع موعـد محـدد. 5

دمج التربية الإعلامية والمعلوماتية في المناهج

خـلال السنـوات القليلـة الماضيـة، تـم تنفيـذ عـدد مـن مبـادرات التدريـب الناجحـة في مجـال التربيـة الإعلاميـة والمعلوماتيـة. وفي مايـو مـن عـام 2013، تعاونـت اللجنـة الوطنيـة التابعـة لليونسكـو ومركـز الإعلاميـات العربيـات بهـدف دمـج التربيـة الإعلاميـة والمعلوماتيـة

في المناهج المدرسية الأردنية من خلال تزويد المدرّسين والطلاب في المدارس الثانوية بالتدريب اللازم من اجل جمع المعلومات وتحليلها واستخدامها. 6 استهدف المشروع 40 طالباً من الذكور والإناث، تتراوح أعمارهم بين 16 و 17 عاماً من أربع مدارس من شبكة المدارس المنتسبة لليونسكو يمثلون المناطق الشمالية والوسط والجنوبية من الأردن. المشروع، الذي حمل رسمياً عنوان «دمج التربية الإعلامية والمعلوماتية في المدارس الأردنية»، كان يتألف من مرحلتين. المرحلة الأولى تتضمن تدريب المدرّسين الذين سيشاركون في المشروع، تليها مرحلة ثانية قام خلالها المختصون والمدرسون بتزويد الطلاب بالتدريب العملي في مجال مهارات الكتابة الصحفية، وتقنيات المناقشة، والبحث على الإنترنت، وتطوير الموقع الالكترونية، وإدارة ونشر المعلومات من خلال الأدوات الإعلامية الحديثة.

كان الهدف من المشروع إثبات وجود بعض النشاط في مجال التربية الإعلامية والمعلوماتية وتسليط الضوء على هذا الموضوع من أجل مساعدة المسؤول عن إعداد المناهج على اعتماده ضمن المناهج الدراسية الأردنية، بحيث يتم تدريسها بشكل مستدام ومؤثر. وقد حظي المشروع بتمويل من الوكالة السويدية للتعاون والإنماء الدولي (SIDA) تحقيقاً لهدفه المتمثّل في تعزيز بيئة مؤاتية لحرية التعبير، مع التركيز بشكل خاص على المنطقة العربية. الذروة كانت الحدث الذي أقيم بمناسبة اختتام البرنامج، حيث تنافس فريقان في حوار مفتوح حضره كبار المسؤولين من وزارة التربية والتعليم ومراقبين وممثلي المنظمات غير الحكومية، وأفراد الجمهور. كشاهد على الحدث، لاحظت ان الحماس الذي تميز به المدرسون والمدربون والطلاب والحضور يؤكد على أهمية التربية الإعلامية والمعلوماتية بالنسبة للمسؤولين في الوزارة الذين يشاركون في هذا الحدث وبالنسبة للجمهور بشكل عام. وساهم النجاح الذي تحقق، في إبراز الأثر الإيجابي لهذا الحدث على الطلاب الذين شاركوا في التمرين، والذين أظهروا درجة عالية من الانفتاح والتسامح في مهارات المناظرة.

التدريب وورش العمل في مجال التربية الإعلامية والمعلوماتية

امتدت جهود اليونسكو لتشمل تدريب الصحفيين والناشطين الشباب عبر وسائل التواصل الاجتماعي بالاشتراك مع معهد الإعلام الأردني في إطار مشروع يهدف لتحسين نوعية التغطية الإعلامية للانتخابات البرلمانية عام 2013. وقد ركزت ورش العمل المختلفة، المموّلة من الاتحاد الأوروبي، على تدريب الصحفيين في مجال التغطية

الإعلامية المستقلة للانتخابات. وقد اشتملت الورش على مواضيع أساسية مثل فهم قوانين الانتخابات الأردنية، ومراجعة للانتخابات والممارسات الديمقراطية في كلّ من مصر ولبنان. وركز التدريب أيضاً على إجراء مقارنة بين قوانين الانتخابات في الأردن وبين المعايير الدولية، بالاضافة الى الانتخابات من منظور يراعي الفوارق بين الجنسين، والمبادئ التوجيهية للتغطية المستقلة والمحترفة للانتخابات.

بالنسبة الى النشطاء الشباب في المحافظات، ركزت ورش العمل على الكتابة الأساسية للأخبار وغيرها من المهارات الصحفية في مجال تغطية الانتخابات، وتقنيات إجراء المقابلات، والتأكد من مصداقية بيانات المرشحين الانتخابية، والتي تتطلب مهارات البحث الأساسية للمساعدة في طرح الأسئلة الموثوقة والذكية. كما اشتمل التدريب على جلسة عصف ذهني لتبادل الأفكار مع المشاركين وساعدهم على التركيز على الأولويات الملحة في المجتمعات التي ينتمي اليها كل منهم. وتولى شركاء آخرون المشاركة في مختلف مكونات المشروع مثل شبكة «إعلاميون من أجل صحافة استقصائية عربية («أريج» وشبكة الإعلام المجتمعي (CMN)، وهي مؤسسة إيرلندية غير ربحية تهدف إلى رفع مستوى التعاون داخل المجتمع الواحد، والى تحفيز تنمية الاتصالات بين المواطنين فيه. هذا الجهد المشترك أعطى زخماً للتغطية المستقلة والمحسّنة للانتخابات بطريقة أكثر احترافية مما كانت عليه في الانتخابات السابقة. 8

كما شارك تحالف الحضارات المنبثق عن الأمم المتحدة ايضاً في أنشطة التدريب في الأردن من خلال ورشة عمل امتدت على مدى يومين خلال أبريل من عام 2013. وقد تناولت الورشة، التي استضافها معهد الاعلام الاردني، موضوع «الأدوات الرقمية لجمع الأخبار وإعداد التقارير عبر الثقافات»، بمشاركة مجموعة من المحررين والصحفيين والمدونين من منطقة الشرق الأوسط وشمال أفريقيا. هذه الورشة، التي تأتي في إطار التعاون بين جوجل والأمم المتحدة لتحالف الحضارات وبالاشتراك مع معهد البنك الدولي، ساهمت بخلق البيئة المناسبة وسمحت للمشاركين بالتفاعل واكتساب المهارات الجديدة واستخدام الأدوات اللازمة التي تُعزز من قدراتهم على التواصل عبر الثقافات. وقد تعلّم المشاركون العديد من المهارات والمناهج التكميلية في مجال صحافة الانترنت باستخدام أدوات جوجل، وخرائط جوجل، والرسوم البيانية والتصفح المتقدم ومهارات البحث. 7 كانت تجربة تعليمية جيدة نظراً لوجود عدد كبير من المتحدثين الخبراء والمدربين الذين قاموا على مدى يومين بادخال المهارات والأدوات الجديدة التي يمكن للمشاركين الاستفادة منها ونقلها إلى زملائهم والمتدربين. 8

166

بيـد أن برنامـج التدريـب الأكـثر شمـولاً والأطـول مـدة في الأردن والـذي يتمحـور حـول التربيـة الإعلاميـة والمعلوماتيـة ، حصـل عـام 2006 في إطـار مشـروع تطويـر «التعليـم عـبر الصحافـة» (NIE). وقـد تـولى تنفيـذ البرنامـج، الـذي تدعمـه مؤسسـة «نورسـك سكوج» لصناعـة الـورق الـتي تتخـذ مـن النرويـج مقـراً لهـا، الاتحـاد العالمـي للصحـف وناشـري الأنبـاء (WAN-IFRA). كمـا اشـترك مركـز حمايـة وحريـة الصحفيـين في الأردن (CDFJ) مـع وزارة التربيـة والتعليـم الأردنيـة وكلّ مـن جريـدة الـرأي اليوميـة، وجريـدة الدسـتور اليوميـة، وجريـدة الغـد اليوميـة، في تنفيـذ برنامـج التربيـة الإعلاميـة والمعلوماتيـة الأكـثر جديـة حـتى الآن، بالتعـاون مـع شـركة زيـن للاتصـالات المحمولـة. وقـد تـم اختيـار عشـرين معلمـاً ومعلمـة مـن 25 مدرسـة مشـاركة في المرحلـة التجريبيـة الأولى مـن المشـروع (اختـارت خمـس مـدارس مغـادرة البرنامـج، مـا يـترك 20 عضـواً فاعـلاً). خضـع المدرّسـون للتدريـب طـوال ثلاثـة أيـام عـلى اسـتخدام الأدوات الـتي تـولى إعدادهـا الاتحـاد العالمـي للصحـف وناشـري الأنبـاء WAN-IFRA . وقـد خصصـت فـترة أسـبوعية لبرنامـج «التعليـم عـبر الصحافـة» (NIE) في كل مـن المـدارس العشـرين المشـاركة في البرنامـج. وتولـت الصحـف تزويـد المـدارس بنسـخ يوميـة للاسـتخدام مـن قبـل الطلبـة المشـاركين في صفـوف «التعليـم عـبر الصحافـة». وقـد أُنشـيء «نـادي الصحافـة» في كل مدرسـة مـن المـدارس، وأصبـح إعـداد صحيفـة جداريـة ونشـرة اذاعيـة صباحيـة عـن شـؤون المدرسـة جـزءاً مـن مسـؤوليات النـادي.

في إحـدى مـدارس الفتيـات المشـاركة في عمـان، عمـدت الطالبـات الى شـراء كامـيرا فيديـو وبـدأ إنتـاج أشـرطة الفيديـو عـلى الفـور. الأشـرطة تناولـت موضوعـات عـدة، بـدءاً مـن موضـوع التحـرش بالفتيـات وصـولاً إلى قضايـا أخـرى ذات الصلـة بالجنسـين. وقامـت مدرسـة أخـرى بتأليـف «نشـيد الصحافـة» المميـز. كان الحمـاس شـديداً وتحسّـن معـدل التقـدم في التعلّـم لـدى الطلاب المشـاركين بشـكل كبـير، بحسـب المقابـلات الـتي أجريـت مـع أوليـاء الطـلاب بعـد انتهـاء البرنامـج. كمـا نظـم الاتحـاد العالمـي للصحـف وناشـري الأنبـاء (WAN-IFRA) برنامجـاً لتدريـب المدربـين يسـتهدف المدرّسـين بشـكل خـاص. وعقـد المدربـون الجـدد ثمـاني حلقـات عمـل، حضرهـا المدرّسـون مـن مناطـق مختلفـة في الأردن. كانـت المواضيـع المعـدّة للتدريـب مسـتمدّة مـن القضايـا المحليـة. وقـد تعـاون ثلاثـة مدرسـين عـلى كتابـة دليـل «التعليـم عـبر الصحافـة» (NIE)، الـذي تـم توزيعـه عـلى المدرّسـين. ردة فعـل بعـض الطـلاب الذيـن شـاركوا في البرنامـج، كمـا نقلهـا تقريـر الفيديـو الـذي أنتجـوه، أشـارت الى تنامـي حـسّ الفضـول لديهـم والشـعور بالنضـج، نتيجـة لتبـادل منتـج أو سـلعة كانـوا يعتبرونهـا مـن المجـالات الخاصـة بالبالغـين. وقـال أوليـاء الطـلاب المشـاركين في البرنامـج أن

أولادهـم نضجـوا، فيمـا اشـار منسّـق البرنامـج، غيـث شـقيري، أن مهـارات القـراءة لديهـم. قـد تحسّـنت ايضـاً. مـن جانبهـا، قالـت ارالـين ماكمايـن، منسّـقة المشـروع لـدى الاتحـاد العالمـي للصحـف وناشـري الأنبـاء (WAN-IFRA): «مـا بـدأ مـع 25 مدرسـة حكوميـة داخـل عمـان وفي ضواحيهـا قـد توسّـع الآن ليصـل إلى 170 مدرسـة حكوميـة وخاصـة في كافـة أنحـاء الأردن.» بحلـول عـام 2010، كان أكثـر مـن 6،000 صـف دراسـي ينفـذ برنامـج «التعليـم عـبر الصحافـة». كمـا شكّـل المشـروع فريقـاً وطنيـاً مؤلفـاً مـن المدرّسـين القادريـن عـلى تدريـب زملائهـم في مجـال «التعليـم عـبر الصحافـة». وقـد أصبحـت اثنتـين مـن هـذه المجموعـة مـن المدرسـين، وهمـا رجـاء الخطيـب وغـادة قاقيـش، سـفيرتي الاتحـاد العالمـي للصحـف وناشـري الأنبـاء (WAN-IFRA) في مجـال التعليـم، وتولتـا شرح «التربيـة عـبر الصحافـة» الى المـدراء الإعلاميـين الذيـن يشـاركون في المنتـدى العـربي للصحافـة الحـرة الـذي ينظمـه الاتحـاد العالمـي للصحـف وناشـري الأنبـاء. قال المديـر التنفيـذي لمركـز حمايـة وحريـة الصحافيـين نضـال منصـور الـذي يتـولى تنفيـذ المشـروع: «لم يعـد اسـتخدام وسـائل الإعـلام مُقتصـراً عـلى السياسيـين والسياسـة. بـل إن جميـع النـاس يسـتخدمون وسـائل الإعـلام كمصـدر للمعرفـة والانخـراط في المشـهد السـياسي. لقـد أصبحـت وسـائل الإعـلام موجـودة الآن في كل مـكان - في المنـازل والمقاهـي، في العمـل - وينبغـي أن تكـون موجـودة أيضـاً في المـدارس وداخـل الصفـوف.» 9

كانت المـدارس الخاصـة المسـتفيد الرئيـسي عـلى المـدى الطويـل مـن البرنامـج. فقـد أدخلـت كافـة المـدارس الخاصـة الكـبرى تقريبـاً صفـوف التربيـة الإعلاميـة والمعلوماتيـة الى مناهجهـا التعليميـة وهـي تظهـر التزامـاً كبـيراً حيـال اسـتدامتها وقيمهـا. تشـكّل مدرسـة «اليوبيـل» أحـد نمـاذج النجـاح في مجـال تنفيـذ برامـج التربيـة الإعلاميـة والمعلوماتيـة في الأردن. وقـد تبنّـى الموظفـون المثـل العليـا والفكـرة المرتبطـة بالبرنامـج، فيمـا لاحظـوا تحسّنـاً ملحوظـاً في كلٍّ مـن مهـارات القـراءة لـدى الطـلاب، والمعرفـة العامـة والتفكـير النقـدي، بحسـب مـا أوردت مدرّسـة التربيـة الإعلاميـة والمعلوماتيـة غـادة قاقيـش. لهـذه الغايـة، تسـتخدم المدرسـة مجموعـة متنوعـة مـن الأدوات لتعزيـز مبـادئ التربيـة الإعلاميـة والمعلوماتيـة. كمـا تدعـم وتشـجع الأنشـطة الموسـيقية والمسرحيـات المدرسيـة الـتي تسـمح للطـلاب باكتسـاب فهـم عميـق لمختلـف أشـكال التعبـير. خـلال انتخابـات مجلـس الطلبـة في سبتمبر عـام 2014، قـام الطـلاب بتنظيـم محـاكاة لأنشـطة حملـة انتخابـات حقيقيـة. وفي اطـار تلـك الحملـة الافتراضيـة، نـشر المرشـحون بياناتهـم وشـاركوا في مناقشـات جديـة وناضجـة لـشرح أو الدفـاع عـن خطـط العمـل الـتي أعلنـوا أنهـم سـيعتمدونها في حـال انتخابهـم.

وقد تمّ نشر الإعلانات والملصقات التي تحمل الشعارات الانتخابية في كافة أنحاء المدرسة. ودعي أولياء الطلاب بصفة مراقبين لضمان نزاهة العملية الانتخابية. 10 وقد تولّت مدارس خاصة أخرى تنظيم ممارسات مماثلة بنجاح. إلا أن الغالبية العظمى من المدارس وخاصة في المناطق النائية من البلاد بالكاد تستطيع أن تقدم الخدمات الأساسية للطلاب، نظرا لمحدودية الموارد والتوسع السريع في عدد الطلاب الذي فرضه النمو السكاني غير المسبوق وتدفق اللاجئين من سوريا.

برنامج التمكين الديمقراطي

بحكم موقعه ومركزه الجيواستراتيجيين غير المستقرين، يعتبر الأردن شديد التأثر بالتطورات الحاصلة في البلدان المجاورة، والتي يمكن أن يقال عنها في هذه المرحلة من التاريخ، أنها غير مستقرة ومتقلبة الى حد خطير. إن تدفق اللاجئين المستمر، الذين يختلف عددهم بين يوم وآخر ووفقاً لكيفية إجراء الحسابات، يزيد على 614 ألفاً للمسجلين منهم، بحسب المفوضية العليا لشؤون اللاجئين التابعة للأمم المتحدة. وقد استقرت كبيرة أعداد غير مسجلة منهم خارج مخيمات اللاجئين في المدن والقرى. وقد عانت المدارس الواقعة شمالي الأردن على مقربة من الحدود السورية، بشكل كبير. ويعود السبب وراء ذلك إلى أن بنيتها التحتية ومواردها لم تكن مصمّمة لتحمل مثل هذا الإنفجار السكاني. 11 الموارد المحدودة أصلاً استنفدت إلى أقصى الحدود، الأمر الذي أدى الى تغيير الأولويات وتحويل الانتباه إلى القضايا اليومية المتعلقة بالبقاء على قيد الحياة. إلا أن مبادرة كبرى من صندوق الملك عبد الله الثاني للتنمية // http: www.kafd.jo أطلق عدداً من البرامج التي تتلاق أهدافها مع أهداف التربية الإعلامية والمعلوماتية. وتشمل أنشطة الصندوق أندية الحوار والمناظرة في المدارس، وبرامج التمكين الديمقراطي، والمواطنة المسؤولة من خلال المشاركة الفعالة، وتبني مقاربات منفتحة نحو الثقافة والفنون والفلسفة، التي كانت تعتبر من الكماليات التعليمية اللازمة في السنوات الأخيرة. وبحسب مديرة برنامج التمكين الديمقراطي يسر حسان، شارك 1،800 طالب وطالبة تتراوح أعمارهم بين 14-17 عاماً في أندية الحوار والمناظرة. وارتكز البرنامج التجريبي، الذي شمل 92 مدرسة، على سلسلة من المبادئ التوجيهية التي تم التوصل اليها بعد 23 جلسة من العصف الذهني مع المدرّسين. هذا وقد دعمت وزارة التربية والتعليم المشروع التجريبي من خلال تخصيص حصتين دراسيتين أسبوعياً، طيلة فصل دراسي كامل. وقد تمحورت حول قيم التسامح والمناقشة الفكرية

169

المستنيرة، والنقاش الهادف، وكان التركيز على الخلاف والمعارضة البناءة مستنداً الى مواقف مبنية على اسباب وجيهة، وليس على مجرد انطباعات، أو إشاعات، أو على التصوير الواقعي لحياة الشعب. كما استهدف البرنامج 6.500 طالب من ذوي المهارات الضعيفة في القراءة خلال الفترة نفسها وحقق نتائج مرضية.

خلال صيف عام 2014، ساهم 44 مخيماً صيفياً لوزارة التربية والتعليم بتوفير بيئة صحية تسمح للشباب بمناقشة قضايا واسعة النطاق. وقد بحثوا مجموعة من المواضيع التي تراوحت بين القضايا المحلية الملحة في إطار تعزيز الممارسات الديمقراطية وصولاً الى المواضيع الثقافية الشاملة مثل الشعر والموسيقى والفنون. شارك 1.320 طالباً في المناقشات خلال الصيف. وقدمت هذه التجربة لمسؤولي البرامج فرصة ثمينة للتعرف الى القضايا التي تهمّ الطلاب وتشكل مؤشراً للتخطيط لأحداث مماثلة في المستقبل لتحقيق أهداف البرنامج. على غير عادة، وجد الطلاب من يصغي بانتباه إلى ما كانوا يقولونه، بدلاً من أن يشكلوا الطرف المتلقي في المحاضرات التي يلقيها البالغون. وشعر كثيرون منهم بدرجة من الرضا فيما شعر آخرون بالسلطة، بعدما تعرفوا الى حقوقهم. ورأى آخرون ان التجربة قد حولتهم إلى راشدين مسؤولين، قادرين على المشاركة في صنع القرارات التي تؤثر على حياتهم عند انتخاب المرشحين الأكفاء لتمثيلهم في المجالس المحلية والبلديات. في إطار البرنامج نفسه، أطلقت مبادرات أخرى مثل مهرجان «خان الفنون» الثقافي، الذي يهدف إلى تعزيز التقدير للفن. وقد دُعي عدد من الفنانين والشعراء والموسيقيين من أجزاء مختلفة من البلاد والمنطقة للمشاركة. وقد نقل الشباب الذين يعيشون في المناطق النائية من البلاد، والعاجزين عن المشاركة بواسطة الباصات من مدنهم وقراهم لحضور فعاليات هذا المهرجان الثقافي والتفاعل مع الشباب من مختلف أنحاء البلاد.

ومن النشاطات الجديدة الأخرى، مهرجان «الحكواتي»، الذي يشكل البيئة المواتية لذوي مهارات السرد المميزة للترفيه عن الجمهور وسرد قصص من التراث أو الارتجال وابتكار القصص المرتكزة إلى مواضيع تراثية. شهدت تلك الفعاليات حضوراً كبيراً وقد أقيمت في أماكن مشهورة ومقصودة في العاصمة والتي تجذب فئة الشباب. وقد خلقت الأحداث والأنشطة أجواء إيجابية، تمكن الناس في خلالها من التواصل من خلال وسيلة لطالما كانت من اختصاص شاشة التلفزيون. في تجربة جريئة أخرى، تم إنشاء «ركن المتحدثين» في جامعة الهاشمية في الزرقاء. كما أطلق الطلاب مدوّنة خاصة بهم. كان

يتـم الاعـلان عـن المواضيـع فـي المدوّنـة، وكان الطـلاب يتجمعـون مـرة بالاسبوع ويتحدثون بحريـة الى حشـد مـن المسـتمعين الفضوليـين فـي «ركـن المتحدثـين». وقـد اكتسـب هـذا الحـدث زخمـاً قويـاً وأصبـح سـمة منتظمـة للحيـاة الطلابيـة فـي الجامعـة. هذا الركن سـاهم بتطبيـق مبـدأ حريـة التعبيـر، وتشـجيع النقـاش المنفتـح وتعزيـز جـو مـن التحديـات الوديـة بـدلاً مـن العنـف والمواجهـة، وهـي الآفـة الـتي ألمّـت ببعـض الجامعـات فـي السـنوات الأخيـرة وأسـفرت عـن خسـائر متفرقـة فـي الآرواح. 12

المنظمات غير الحكومية وتعزيز التربية الإعلامية والمعلوماتية

عـلى جبهـة المنظمـات غـير الحكوميـة، يتـم اجـراء الأنشـطة بشـكل منتظـم. للأسـف، لا توجـد اسـتطلاعات للـرأي أو بيانـات متاحـة حـول عـدد الأنشـطة، وطبيعتهـا الدقيقـة، أو عـدد المشـاركين. مـع ذلـك، الأمـل قـوي بـأن يـؤدي العمـل الـذي أجـراه مركـز المعلومـات والبحـوث - مؤسسـة الملـك الحسـين (IRC)، وصنـدوق الملـك حسـين للتنميـة عـلى المسـح الوطنـي للشـباب فـي الأردن، بدعـم مـن صنـدوق الأمـم المتحـدة للطفولـة (اليونيسـيف)، الى توفـير ضمـان جـودة الأبحـاث الـتي أجريـت، بعـد اكثـر مـن عـام مـن مجموعـات التركيـز وعمليـة ايجـاد ادوات المسـح الدقيقـة. وسـيتم توفـير أدوات المسـح مـن قبـل دائـرة الإحصـاءات العامـة فـي الأردن: وتهـدف هـذه المسـاهمة الهامـة الى توفـير معلومـات موثوقـة وتمثيليـة حـول المشـاكل المتنوعـة الـتي تواجـه الشـباب الأردنـي اليـوم. وقـد أعيـد تطويـر تلـك الأدوات بشـكل يأخـذ فـي الاعتبـار «العالـم بعـد الربيـع العـربي». بالتـالي، كان مـن المفـترض ان يقـدم هـذا المسـح رؤى تحليليـة حـول المشـاركة المدنيـة للشـباب، والوعـي السـياسي، والاسـتعداد للوظيفـة بعـد التحصيـل العلمـي، بالإضافـة الى عناصـر أخـرى تتعلـق بتطلعاتهـم، وتصوراتهـم، والفـرص المتوفـرة لهـم فـي عالـم اليـوم. 13

مـن المنظمـات غـير الحكوميـة المبتكـرة والفعالـة هـي MO7AKA أي «قـادة الغـد»، وهـي منظمـة مسـتقلة غـير ربحيـة يقودهـا الشـباب، وهي تنشـط منـذ عـام 2007 فـي الأردن وإقليميـاً. فـي غيـاب سياسـة وطنيـة أو برنامـج فـي مجـال التربيـة الإعلاميـة والمعلوماتيـة، تعمـل المنظمـة بنشـاط عـلى تنفيـذ المبـادرات المختلفـة الـتي تقـدم عـدداً مـن أهـداف التربيـة الإعلاميـة والمعلوماتيـة. مـن أبـرز المبـادرات الـتي أطلقتهـا منظمـة «قـادة الغـد»، مبـادرة «فضفـض» 14، والـتي يمكـن ترجمتهـا بشـكل تقريـبي إلى «عـبّر عـن إحباطـك» ومبـادرة «محـاكاة» (وهـي عبـارة عـن خلـوة تدريبيـة تعتمـد اسـلوب المحـاكاة و لعـب الادوار). «فضفـض» هـي مبـادرة موجّهـة للشـباب، توفـر منصـة مفتوحـة، متواضعـة وحـرة لتشـجيع المواطنـين للتعبـير عـن

آرائهـم بشـكل خـلاق حـول القضايـا الحساسـة علـى أوراق بيضـاء في الأماكـن العامـة. ومـن خـلال إعـادة تغريـد تلـك الآراء إلـى صنـاع القـرار والخبـراء والمسؤوليـن، يسـاهم المواطنـون في ردم الهـوة بيـن المجتمعـات المتصلـة وغيـر المتصلـة بالانترنـت، ومسـاءلة صنـاع القـرار، وإبقـاء الخبـراء علـى اتصـال مـع القاعـدة الشـعبية. كمـا يتولـى المواطنـون أيضـاً توثيـق الآراء العامـة، وتحليلهـا وكتابـة البحـوث والتقاريـر العلميـة والنوعيـة. أمـا مبـادرة «محـاكاة»، فهـي مبـادرة إبداعيـة تقـوم بإشـراك الشـباب في تجربـة قويـة وغامـرة تعـزز تفكيرهـم النقـدي وقدرتهـم علـى حـل المشـكلات الحرجـة مـن خـلال أسـلوب المحـاكاة ولعـب الأدوار. وتوفـر هـذه المبـادرة تجربـة مثيـرة حـول قضايـا حقـوق الإنسـان والمواضيـع الاجتماعيـة والسياسـية المثيـرة للجـدل في بيئـة غيـر تقليديـة. 15

في أكتوبـر عـام 2014، قـام معهـد الاعـلام الاردنـي بتدريـب 30 طالبـاً شـاباً في إطـار برنامـج ممـوّل مـن مؤسسـة نهـر الأردن علـى سـبل الاسـتخدام الأساسـي لوسـائل التواصـل الاجتماعـي ومهـارات الصحافـة. وقـد تضمـن التدريـب عـدة مكونـات تتفـق مـع ثقافـة التربيـة الإعلاميـة والمعلوماتيـة. وتلقـى المشـاركون الذيـن جـاؤوا مـن المجتمعـات النائيـة تدريبـاً مكثفـاً في مجـال التفكيـر النقـدي، وتقييـم مصـادر الإعـلام والمعلومـات ومهـارات السـرد، التـي سـمحت لهـم بإنتـاج تقاريـر أساسـية باسـتخدام هواتفهـم النقالـة، بالإضافـة إلـى عـروض شـرائح بسـيطة ونشـر التدوينـات حـول قضايـا مجتمعيـة. وركـز البرنامـج أيضـاً علـى ثقافـة الانتخابـات والديمقراطيـة وكيفيـة تقييـم الشـؤون البلديـة المحليـة والكتابـة عنهـا. في سـياق الزيـارة، زار المشـاركون في البرنامـج صحيفـة ومحطـة تلفزيـون ومنشـأة كمبيوتـر وتكنولوجيـا المعلومـات متطـورة حيـث يتـم تصميـم ألعـاب الفيديـو. والأمـل قـوي بـأن يسـمح مثـل هـذا البرنامـج بتمكيـن المشـاركين وتعزيـز وعيهـم بالمشـاكل المحليـة في مجتمعاتهـم وتمكينهـم مـن كتابـة المدونـات وإعـداد تقاريـر علـى وسـائل التواصـل الاجتماعـي. وقـد أطلـق معهـد الاعـلام الاردنـي، بالتعـاون مـع مؤسسـة «صحفيـون مـن أجـل حقـوق الإنسـان» الكنديـة (JHR)، المشـروع الـذي حمـل عنـوان «تعزيـز الحـوار العـام حـول قضايـا حقـوق الإنسـان»، الـذي أقيـم في عمـان. ويتضمـن المشـروع، الـذي يحظـى بدعـم مـن مبـادرة الشـراكة الأمريكيـة الشـرق أوسـطية (MEPI)، توجيـه وتدريـب الصحفييـن وطـلاب الصحافـة، وممثلـي منظمـات المجتمـع المدنـي علـى اسـتخدام قـوة البيانـات لجعـل هـذا الحـوار أكثـر فعاليـة واطلاعـاً. ويهـدف البرنامـج، الـذي صممتـه وتديـره مؤسسـة «صحفيـون مـن أجـل حقـوق الإنسـان» الكنديـة الرائـدة (JHR)، والـذي يتولـى معهـد الاعـلام الاردنـي تنفيـذه، الـى إشـراك شـريكين محلييـن آخريـن همـا: شـبكة الإعـلام المجتمعـي (CMN)، وهـي منظمـة

16 كما ستساهم مشاركة معهد الاعلام الاردني في تنفيذ هذا البرنامج بإعطاء الزخم لقيادتها حملات التربية الإعلامية والمعلوماتية جنباً إلى جنب مع شركائها الفاعلين. هذا وسيساهم إطلاق الموقع الإلكتروني لمرصد مصداقية الإعلام «أكيد»، بدعم من صندوق الملك عبدالله الثاني للتنمية، بتزويد عدد أكبر من الطلاب والصحفيين بالأدوات والمهارات اللازمة لتعزيز برامج التربية الإعلامية والمعلوماتية المستقبلية. وقد ساهم الموقع بالفعل بخلق ثقافة الوعي بالحاجة الى المساءلة، وحق الوصول إلى المعلومات، وتطبيق المعايير المهنية في مجال تحليل المحتوى، مما يسهم في رفع معايير الإعلام ويؤكد أهمية الممارسات الصحفية الجيدة. 17

توصيات

في ظل المناخ الحالي البغيض السائد في المنطقة، والذي يتم فيه القاء اللوم على فشل نظم التعليم في معالجة قضايا التعددية، وحرية التعبير، وحق الوصول الى المعلومات، يتحتم على وزارة التربية والتعليم دمج برامج التربية الإعلامية والمعلوماتية في المناهج التربوية على سبيل الأولوية. إن مثل هذه الخطوة، إذا كانت مصحوبة بحملة واضحة في وسائل الإعلام الوطنية تشرح ميزات التربية الإعلامية والمعلوماتية وتأثيرها على الشباب في إطار تشجيع التوافق وتخفيف التوتر، ستساهم بإعداد الشباب للعب دورهم في نشر الديمقراطية بالمجتمع. هذا وسيساهم تنظيم حملة قوية لتشجيع الآباء ومنظمات المجتمع المدني على دعم برامج التربية الإعلامية والمعلوماتية بتسريع تنفيذ مثل هذه البرامج وتشجيع اعتمادها من قبل المدرّسين والمدارس. سيظهر تأثير مثل هذه البرامج في تحسين مهارات القراءة وتوسيع الآفاق وتشجيع التفكير النقدي وتطوير العقل الفضولي. كما سيعزز قبول الاختلافات في الرأي، وتشجيع التعبير الحرّ غير المقيّد واحترام حقوق الإنسان. بالتالي، سيكون معهد الإعلام الأردني، ونقابة الصحفيين الأردنيين، والإدارات الإعلامية في الجامعات والمدارس الخاصة التي تطبق بالفعل برامج التربية الإعلامية والمعلوماتية، وكذلك المنظمات غير الحكومية واليونسكو، شركاء طبيعيين في مثل هذا المسعى. سيساهم هذا المسعى الموحد بدعم جهود وزارة التربية والتعليم في تقديم برامج التربية الإعلامية والمعلوماتية وتوفير الاعتمادات المالية الإضافية الضرورية لهذه الغاية. لا بد من حشد وسائل الإعلام الوطنية، مثل الصحف الرئيسية، والمواقع الإخبارية ووسائل التواصل الاجتماعي، ومحطات الإذاعة والتلفزيون، من أجل توفير العرض المستدام والدعم للمشروع.

173

تقدم المناهج والوحدات التعليمية الخاصة بتحالف الحضارات التابع للامم المتحدة موارد غنية وجاهزة للاستخدام لصالح المدارس والمدرّسين. في المناطق ذات الاتصال المحدود، يمكن دعوة المنظمات غير الحكومية والمتطوعين من المجتمع المدني للمساعدة. ينبغي الا تشكل التغطية الضعيفة للانترنت في بعض المناطق ذريعة لتأخير اتخاذ القرار لتسريع إدخال برامج التربية الإعلامية والمعلوماتية الى المدارس وترسيخها. تجدر الاشارة الى ان الأزمة الحالية في الشرق الأوسط تعطي زخماً وإلحاحاً لدفع صناع القرار والجهات المانحة الرئيسية المهتمة بتحقيق السلام والاستقرار في المنطقة الى دعم هذه الخطة.

ستكون هناك حاجة لمعالجة مسألة برامج تدريب المدربين والبرامج التدريبية الموجّهة للمدرّسين والإداريين. لا يوجد نقص بالوسائل المبتكرة من اجل تحقيق نتائج ملموسة. ينبغي وضع المعايير لتقييم نتائج وتأثير البرنامج في الوقت عينه. ينبغي دعوة المدارس التي تتمتع بتجربة مثبتة في مجال التربية الإعلامية والمعلوماتية الى تبادل تجاربها والمساهمة بخبراتها في تطوير المشروع وتنفيذه. لا بد من الاشادة بإنجازاتهم ومنحها الدعاية الكافية والتقدير من قبل وسائل الإعلام المحلية والمجتمع المدني. وينبغي تعريف الجمهور بقيمة الجهود الرائدة التي قاموا بها من أجل منحهم المزيد من التشجيع والحوافز لترسيخ البرامج الحالية وتوسيعها.

أن إعداد منصة للتدريس الرقمي لبرامج التربية الإعلامية والمعلوماتية من قبل وزارة التربية والتعليم سيشكل وسيلة فعالة من حيث التكلفة لإطلاق البرنامج. ومن شأنه أن يوفر الموارد الضرورية لتنفيذ هذا البرنامج بكفاءة، من خلال توفير المواد التعليمية اللازمة للمدارس بسهولة في كافة أنحاء البلاد. من شأنه أن يساعد أيضاً المشرفين على البرنامج على قياس وتقييم تأثيره، وعلى توفير آلية لاستقصاء التعليقات والاقتراحات البناءة من الطلاب والمدرّسين. وسيتم اختيار مواضيع النقاش الخاصة بالطلاب بعناية وستكون مصممة لتنشئة جيل الشباب وصياغة الأسئلة التي تثري معلوماتهم وتوسّع آفاقهم. كما أن مهارة صياغة الأسئلة ستخلق الوعي بشأن العقبات التي يتسبب بها كلّ من التعنت والكراهية والتعصب الأعمى.

النشرة الاذاعية المدرسية اليومية، التي تشكّل جزءاً من نظام حياة الطلبة الأردنيين، هي فرص ينبغي ألا تفوتها الوزارة لتعزيز التربية الإعلامية والمعلوماتية. إنها فرصة لدمج قيم التربية الإعلامية والمعلوماتية في محتوى النشرة الاذاعية المدرسية مع

لدمـج قيـم التربيـة الإعلاميـة والمعلوماتيـة في محتـوى النشـرة الاذاعيـة المدرسـية مـع المحتـوى الـذي يهـدف الى الإطـلاع والتحفيز والإلهام بواسـطة روايـات تسـاهم باطـلاق العنـان للخيـال. يمكـن تخصيـص المـوارد بشـكل يسـمح للمـدارس بالوصـول الى الأفـكار والمـواد الجديـدة للنشـرات الاذاعيـة اليوميـة التـي تتمحـور بشـكل خـاص حـول حقـوق الإنسـان، وحريـة التعبيـر، ونعمـة التعدديـة والمواطنـة المسـؤولة.

كما ان توفيـر صيغـة ديناميـة جديـدة لهذه النشـرات الاذاعيـة والتي تدمج المحتـوى المستمّد مـن مناطـق مختلفـة مـن البـلاد، ومـع التربيـة الإعلاميـة والمعلوماتيـة بشـكل خـاص، مـن شـأنه أن يحول هـذه التشـرات إلى عامـل تغييـر، نأمـل أن يسـاهم برسـم الطريـق للأجيـال الشـابة للعيـش بسـلام وتناغـم مـع أنفسـهم، مـع «الآخـر»، ومـع بقيـة العالـم.

ويسـاهم تقريـر نشـرته صحيفـة الـراي الوطنيـة اليوميـة بتاريـخ 4 اوكتوبـر 2014 18 عـن حالـة التعليـم في الأردن بإلقـاء الضـوء عـلى التحـدي الهائـل الـذي يواجـه الأردن في التعامـل مـع الحاجـة المتزايـدة الى المـدارس والمـوارد التعليميـة.

ملاحظات ومراجع

1) http://www.unesco.org/new/en/media-services/single-view/news/unesco_
and_partners_launched_global_alliance_for_partnerships_on_media_and_infor-
mation_literacy/back/18256/#.VC2LBL6OlBs

2) http://www.unesco.org/new/en/communication-and-information/media-de-
velopment/media-literacy/mil-events/global-forum-for-partnership-on-mil-gfp-
mil

3) رّسة غادة قاقيش

4) رقم العدد صحيفة الشرق الأوسط، http://classic.aawsat.com/details.asp?section
9159 تاريخ 26 ديسمبر 2003

6) http://www.unesco.org/new/en/amman/about-this-office/single-view/news/
integrating_media_and_information_literacy_into_jordanian_schools/#.VC8MN-
r6OlBs

7) http://www.unesco.org/new/en/amman/about-this-office/single-view/news/
unesco_and_jmi_hold_training_workshop_for_journalists_on_independent_me-
dia_coverage_of_elections/#.VBSL9Uvx9Bs

8) http://www.unaoc.org/2013/04/google-the-united-nations-alliance-of-civili-zations-and-the-world-bank-institute-jointly-organized-a-unique-digital-journalism-training-for-arab-media-professionals

9) http://www.wan-ifra.org/articles/2011/01/09/jordan-marks-fifth-year-of-using-newspapers-in-class

10) http://www.jubilee.edu.jo

11) http://www.fletcherforum.org/2014/04/07/siam

12) http://www.kafd.jo/node/77

13) http://www.kinghusseinfoundation.org/index.php?pager=end&-task=view&type=news&pageid=200

14) www.fadfed.org

15) http://www.youtube.com/watch?v=ZuwWobdx_4g

16) http://www.jmi.edu.jo/en/details/3069/The-Announcement-of--Launching-Expanding-Public-Dialogue-on-Human-Rights-Issues-Project

17) http://www.akeed.jo

18) http://www.alrai.com/article/673265.html

مقرر «ثقافة الإعلام والمعلومات» بسلطنة عمان

نايفة بنت عيد سليم

«في الوقت بدأ فيه المجتمع والشعوب يشعرون على نحو متزايد بأهمية دور وسائل الإعلام في العصر الحديث، من المهم جداً تطوير الإعلام العماني للإضطلاع بمهمته في تطوير قدرات المواطنين وتوعيتهم بشأن دورهم الأساسي في بناء دولتهم.» *

في بعض الحالات، قد تكون المعلومات غير معلنة كما انها قد تكون مكلفة للنشر، أو صعبة التفسير (شينيك وريان، 2008).

تلعب المعلومات دورا مهما في تقوية وتعزيز القرارات التي يتخذها صانعو القرارات ، ودون توفر المعلومات المناسبة للصاحب القرار المناسب في الوقت المناسب يعد اتخاذ القرار في غير محله الصحيح؛ ذلك أن اتخاذ القرارات لم يعد يعتمد على الخبرة أو الحدس بل على توفر المعلومة الموثوقة من مصادرها المتنوعة. وفي العصر الحالي الذي نعيشه ويعرف بعصر انفجار المعلومات لا تستطيع أي مؤسسة بأي حال من الأحوال أن تستغني عن مصادر المعلومات الحديثة، بل على العكس تتبارى معظم المؤسسات في توفير المكتبات ومراكز المعلومات بمؤسساتها حرصا على توفير وإيصال مصادر المعلومات الدقيقة والمناسبة لأصحاب القرار وجميع المستفيدين من المؤسسة.

بحسب الاتحاد الدولي لجمعيات ومؤسسات المكتبات (إفلا)، يتم الوصول الى المعلومات المنشودة من خلال ثلاث خطوات: 1) الملاحظة والتجربة 2) الحوار والمحادثة والاتصال مع أشخاص آخرين 3) التشاور مع مؤسسات ذاكرة المعلومات أو الحافظة لها وهي مراكز ومؤسسات المعلومات بالإضافة الى المكتبات. (إفلا 2014). ولفترة ليست ببعيدة ظلت المعلومات الدقيقة والمهمة سرا على المواطن على الرغم من أهمية المعلومات بالنسبة لذلك المواطن خاصة ما تعلق منها بالصحة وبالاستهلاك وبالرواتب. وكان عدم

اطلاع المواطن على المعلومات المهمة حاجزا، لعدم الثقة في السلطات العليا. ولم يكن المواطن يحق له التعبير بحرية عن كل ما يجول في خاطره. إلا أن تطور تكنولوجيا المعلومات والاتصالات والتدفق الهائل للمعلومات جعل من السهل على أبرز الفاعلين في المجتمعات المدنية تبادل المعلومات مع بعضهم البعض. وقد تحدث السلطان قابوس عن هذا الأمر في مجلس عمان في نوفمبر عام 2008، حين قال: «لقد أصبحت تكنولوجيا المعلومات والاتصالات المحرك الأساسي لدفع التنمية في الألفية الثالثة. لهذا السبب ركزنا اهتمامنا على ايجاد استراتيجية وطنية لتطوير مهارات المواطنين وقدراتهم في هذا المجال، بهدف دفع الخدمات الحكومية الالكترونية قدماً. »

ومع قدوم الربيع العربي لمعظم الدول العربية وقيام المواطنين في تلك الدول بتطبيق ما يرونه حقا مكتسبا في التعبير بكل حرية عن آرائهم تجاه الحكومات وتجاه لقمة العيش، لم يعبروا عن الحقوق المشروعة بطريقة ممنهجة صحيحة؛ فبدلا من أن تصبح تلك الآراء تعبيرا عن الحقوق تحولت إلى تطاول طال الأخضر واليابس، كما لحظ «كالكنز (2013). فهو يعتبر أن «الربيع العربي» قدم للعرب أول فرصة منذ عقود ليكون صوتهم مسموعاً، إلا أن إنشاء الحكومات والدساتير الجديدة لا يزال قائما وتواجه بلداناً عدة ردود فعل عنيفة فيما يتعلق بحرية التعبير. إن الطريقة الصحيحة لمد وتزويد المواطن والمستفيد من الحكومات على حد سواء بالمهارات والمعلومات بطريقة صحيحة وفعالة يسمى ب«ثقافة الإعلام والمعلومات». كيف ولا وهي تتكون من المعرفة والسلوكيات كما تشتمل المهارات اللازمة للمعرفة على:

1) المعلومات التي نحتاج إليها
2) متى نحتاج إليها
3) وكيف ومن أين نحصل عليها
4) كيفية تحليل ونقد وترتيب تلك المعلومات بعد الحصول عليها
5) والأهم من كل ما سبق كيفية استخدام تلك المعلومات بطريقة أخلاقية.

إن مفهوم « ثقافة الإعلام و المعلومات» لا يقف عند تكنولوجيا المعلومات والاتصالات بل يتخطاها ليشمل التعلم والتفكير النقدي ومهارات التحليل والتفسير خارج وداخل نطاق التعلم والتعليم. وبالنسبة لأشكال ومصادر المعلومات فإن المفهوم يشمل كل أشكال المعلومات الشفهية والمطبوعة والرقمية ومصادرها المختلفة (إفلا، 2014؛ فان دي فورد، 2010). ومن أجل مساعدة الدول العربية منها والأجنبية على تعلم وتطبيق

«ثقافـة الإعـلام والمعلومـات» بطريقـة صحيحـة وتمكيـن المواطنيـن مـن تعلـم وكسـب «ثقافـة الإعـلام و المعلومـات»- قامـت اليونسكـو (منظمـة الأمـم المتحـدة للتربيـة والعلـم والثقافة) بإعـداد مقـرر يسـمى « ثقافـة الإعـلام والمعلومـات» يغطـي الآتي:

أساسيات ثقافة المعلومات

1) تعريف وتفصيل الحاجة إلى المعلومات

2) تحديد موقع المعلومات والوصول إليها

3) تقييم المعلومات

4) تنظيم المعلومات

5) استخدام المعلومات مع احترام الأخلاقيات

6) إيصال ونقل المعلومات

7) استخدام مهارات تكنولوجيا المعلومات والاتصالات في معالجة المعلومات

أساسيات ثقافة الإعلام

1) فهم دور ووظائف الإعلام في المجتمعات الديموقراطية

2) فهم الظروف التي تتمكن وسائل الإعلام من وظائفها من خلالها

3) تقييم محتوى الإعلام نقديا على ضوء وظائف الإعلام

4) التعامل مع وسائل الإعلام للتعبير عن الذات والمشاركة الديموقراطية

5) مراجعـة المهـارات اللازمـة، بمـا في ذلـك تكنولوجيـا المعلومـات والاتصـالات، لإنتـاج المضمـون الإعلامـي مـن قبـل المستخدمين.

تهدف هذه المقالة إلى إلقاء الضوء على النقاط الاتية:

1) الإعلام والمعلومات بسلطنة وعلاقته بمقرر «ثقافة الإعلام و المعلومات»،

2) وزارة التربية والتعليم و دورهما في مبادرات غرس «ثقافة الإعلام والمعلومات»،

3) مؤسسات وزارة التعليم العالي وثقافة الإعلام والمعلومات،

4) التعرف على مقرر «ثقافة الإعلام والمعلومات»،

5) الإنتاج الفكري العربي و «ثقافة الإعلام والمعلومات»،

6) التقـارب بيـن مقـرر « ثقافـة الإعـلام و المعلومـات» وبيـن مقـررات جامعـة السـلطان قابـوس.

179

الإعلام والمعلومات بسلطنة وعلاقته بمقرر «ثقافة الإعلام و المعلومات»

تكاد لا تخلو دولة عربية من وزارة إعلام وأخرى لها علاقة بالمعلومات والثقافة وهاتان الوزارتان في معظم الدول هما وزارتان مستقلتان؛ فعلى سبيل المثال في المملكة العربية السعودية تسمى وزارة الثقافة والإعلام، وفي دولة الإمارات تسمى وزارة الإعلام والثقافة، بينما في قطر نجد منحى آخر في تسمية الوزارة حيث تسمى وزارة الثقافة والفنون والتراث، وفي مملكة البحرين تسمى بوزارة الثقافة، أما في سلطنة عمان فهناك وزارة للإعلام ووزارة أخرى تسمى وزارة التراث والثقافة، كما توجد هيئة لتقنية المعلومات وتتمثل رؤيتها في «تحويل سلطنة عُمان إلى مجتمع معرفي مستدام من خلال الاستفادة من تقنيات المعلومات والاتصال لتعزيز الخدمات الحكومية وإثراء قطاع الأعمال وتمكين الأفراد. »

ومهما تعددت واختلفت أسماء تلك الوزارات والهيئات بسلطنة عمان فإن هدفها النهائي هو تزويد المواطن والمقيم بالمعلومات الصحيحة والدقيقة كما يفترض أنها تقوم بتهيئة الأشخاص لكيفية التعامل مع المعلومات وكيفية النقد والتحليل البناء لكل معلومة يتم الحصول عليها. وبمراجعة متفحصة ودقيقة لكل المقترحات والمبادرات التي أطلقتها الوزرات السالفة الذكر (وزارة الإعلام ووزارة التراث والثقافة وهيئة تقنية المعلومات)، تبين أن أيا منها لم تقم سابقا بتقديم مقترحات لتبني مقرر ممنهج يتعلق ب«ثقافة الإعلام و المعلومات». ويعتبر تزويد المواطن بثقافة الإعلام والمعلومات حقا إنسانيا مكتسبا لكل مواطن وهو من الحقوق المدنية الجديدة التي بدأت تظهر في الآونة الأخيرة ودعمها تطور الرقمية والتكنولوجيا. وتبرز أهمية هذا المقرر في دعوته للدمج الاجتماعي وتجسير الفجوة المعلوماتية بين الفقراء والأغنياء (إفلا، 2014).

وزارة التربية والتعليم و دورهما في مبادرات غرس «ثقافة الإعلام والمعلومات»

بالإضافة إلى وزارة الإعلام ووزارة التراث والثقافة وهيئة تقنية المعلومات يجب ألا نتغتضى عن دور ومهمة مؤسسات التعليم التي تكمن في تزويد المدرجين تحت مظلتها بالمهارات المرتبطة ثقافة المعلومات والاتصالات، وبالتحديد اين يمكن إيجاد مصادر المعلومات وكيفية اختيارها.

وفي حالة عدم طرح مقرر لثقافة الإعلام والمعلومات في المراحل التربوية والتعليمية الأولى للطفل يفترض أن يكون هذا المقرر بين وحدات الخطة الدراسية لطلبة المراحل

الجامعية الأولى لا العليا؛ ذلك أن المقرر يفضل أن يرافق الطالب من مراحله الدراسية الأولى ولا يحبذ أن يؤخر. على الرغم من خلو المقررات الدراسية لوزارة التربية والتعليم من مقرر يعني ويعالج قضايا ثقافة الإعلام والمعلومات -وربما كان ذلك لعدم تطابق مفرداته مع أي مقرر دراسي- إلا أن مؤسسات ومدارس وزارة التربية و التعليم مزودة بما يسمى مراكز مصادر التعلم وهي في مقابل المكتبة المدرسية.

منذ أن تولى حضرة صاحب الجلالة لمقاليد الحكم في البلاد، أولى جلّ اهتمامه للتعليم وتطويره وتحديثه، وكان من ضمن العناصر التي اهتم بها جلالته -حفظه الله!- إنشاء المكتبات المدرسية. فارتفع عددها من تسع مكتبات عام 1977، إلى 134 مكتبة مدرسية عام 1990، في جميع محافظات وولايات السلطنة (وزارة التربية والتعليم،1990). وفي العام الدراسي (1998/1999) طبقت وزارة التربية والتعليم نظام التعليم الأساسي في 17 مدرسة، وهذا النظام يهدف إلى إحداث نقلة نوعية في التعليم، وضمان جودة مخرجات العملية التعليمية ومواكبة الانفجار المعرفي والتطور التقني الهائل (الهنائي،2007*). وشمل تغير نظام التعليم جميع نواحي النظام التعليمي كما تضمن نظام التعليم الأساسي تخصيص مركز لمصادر التعلم بكل مدرسة ليكون بديلا عن المكتبة التقليدية وموفرا بيئة تقنية راقية ومصادر متنوعة وكافية للمعلومات. ويفترض إذا كانت مفردات مقرر «ثقافة الإعلام و المعلومات» لا تتطابق مع مقررات وزارة التربية والتعليم -وذلك لشمول مقرر «ثقافة الإعلام والمعلومات» لبرامج الإعلام و المعلومات- أن تقوم مراكز مصادر التعلم بتقديم ذلك المقرر، لأنها المكان الذي له علاقة بالمعلومات. ولكن ينبغي أولا طرح المقرر وتبنيه من قبل وزارة التربية والتعليم. يلاحظ من أساسيات مكوني ثقافة الإعلام والمعلومات، اللذين ذكرا سابقا أنهما يساعدان الأفراد على التعامل بفعالية مع المعلومات كما يساعدان على تكوين صورة واضحة صادقة عن الإعلام، لأن هذا المقرر يركز على تزويد الأفراد بالمهارات سواء أكانت التكنولوجية أو مهارات تقييم وتنظيم واستخدام المعلومات، وكل ذلك مع احترام الأخلاقيات التي لا نركز عليها كثيرا في تعاملنا مع المعلومات. إذ قامت الباحثة بدراسة عن أخلاقيات طلبة المرحلة الجامعية الأولى في تعاملهم مع الأنترنت، وتبين أنهم على رغم علمهم بأن بعض الأخلاقيات لا يجوز تخطيها كتبادلهم لأرقامهم السرية اللازمة للدخول إلى شبكة الإنترنت، إلا أنهم لا يبالون بذلك (سليم،2013).

181

مؤسسات وزارة التعليم العالي وثقافة الإعلام والمعلومات

واذا لـم تكـن مراكـز مصـادر التعلـم التابعـة لـوزارة التربيـة و التعليـم تقـدم هـذا المقرر، يفضل أن تكون جامعـة السلطان قابوس -وهي الجامعة الحكومية الوحيدة- أو الجامعـات الخاصة كجامعة صحار، وجامعة نزوى، وجامعة ظفار أو الجامعة الألمانيـة للتكنولوجيا أو مؤسسات التعليم العالـي الأخرى ، هـي الـتي تطرح هـذا المقرر ضمـن خططها الدراسية، ويفضل أن يكون هـذا المقرر متطلبا لـكل طلبة الجامعـات.

وتمت مراجعـة الخطـط الدراسية لتلك الجاعـات. وقام القسمان بطـرح مقررات لهـا علاقـة بالإعـلام والمجتمع والإعـلام والتكنولوجيا. عـلى سبيل المثال يطـرح قسم الإعـلام بجامعـة السلطان قابوس المقررات الآتيـة :

الجـدول (1) : مقررات قسـم الإعـلام بجامعـة السـلطان قابوس الـتي لهـا علاقـة بثقافة العـلام والمعلومات

م	اسم المقرر	الفصل الدراسي	الساعات المعتمدة
1	الخبر في وسائل الإعلام	2	3
2	تكنولوجيا الإذاعة و التلفزيون	4	3
3	أخلاقيات العمل الإعلامي والتشريعات	7	3

الجـدول (2) : مقررات قسـم الصحافـة والإعـلام بجامعـة السـلطان صحـار الـتي لهـا علاقـة بثقافة العـلام والمعلومـات

م	اسم المقرر	الفصل الدراسي	الساعات المعتمدة
1	الإعلام والمجتمع	2	3
2	المؤسسات ودور العلام في المجتمع	2	3
3	وسائل الاتصال والإعلام الجديد والمجتمع	2	3

أما بالنسبة لقسـم دراسـات المعلومـات بجامعـة السلطان قابوس فهـو يطرح مقررا بعنوان الوعـي المعلومـات، ولكـن مـا يؤسف لـه أنـه عـلى الرغـم مـن أهميـة هـذا المقـرر ودوره في تعريف الطالب كيفية الوصول إلى المعلومـات، وتنظيمهـا، وتقييمهـا، واستخدامها عـبر الأنواع المختلفة للمصـادر- إلا أنه تم طرحـه مقررا اختياريـا لطلبة الجامعـة، أي لمن أراد

التسجيل في المقرر، والمفترض أن يكون هذا المقرر إجباريا لكل طلبة الجامعة خاصة أنه يتعلق بالمكون الثاني لثقافة العلام والمعلومات.

قام محمد (2008) بدراسة استعرض فيها بعض النماذج لجامعات تدرس مهارات الوعي المعلوماتي ضمن مقرراتها الدراسية منها جامعة Maricopa، وجامعة Dakota State، وجامعة Oregon State في الولايات المتحدة الأمريكية. وإذا ما نظرنا لجهود هذه الجامعات يتضح لنا حرصها المتواصل على إدراج مهارات الوعي المعلوماتي ضمن الخطة التدريسية ويلزم الأساتذة بالتعاون مع اختصاصي المعلومات في تدريسها للطلاب بالطريقة الفعالة.

عليه لا يوجد مقرر فعلي ينقل لكل طلبة جامعة السلطان قابوس أو طلبة الجامعات الأخرى الخاصة، مكونات مقرر «ثقافة الإعلام والمعلومات»؛ فالمقررات التي تطرح في قسم الإعلام أو التي بقسم دراسات المعلومات بجامعة السلطان قابوس تعالج قضايا كل تخصص منفرد، ولا يوجد مقرر يجمع مكونات وقضايا المكونين.

التعرف على مقرر «ثقافة الإعلام والمعلومات»

بدأت معرفة الباحثة بمقرر «ثقافة الإعلام والمعلومات» عام 2011، عندما حضرت الباحثة الملتقى الدولي الأول حول وسائل الإعلام ومحو الأمية المعلوماتية، الذي نظمته اليونسكو بالتعاون مع المنظمة الإسلامية للتربية والعلوم و الثقافة (أيسيسكو)، ومكتب التربية العربي لدول الخليج في فاس، في المغرب.

تم خلال الملتقى توزيع المقرر المقترح على المعلمين. ويرطز المقرر على محاور الإعلام والمعلومات خاصة ما تعلق منها بفهم دور ووظائف الإعلام في المجتمعات الديموقراطية، وتقييم محتوى الإعلام نقديا على ضوء وظائف الإعلام، والتعامل مع وسائل الإعلام للتعبير عن النفس، والمشاركة الديموقراطية. كذلك من الجيد وجود مقرر مدروس بكل عناية، يعالج استخدام مهارات تكنولوجيا المعلومات والاتصالات في معالجة المعلومات؛ فنحن نحتاج فعليا إلى أن يكون معلمونا وطلبتنا على وعي بطرق المعلومات ومصادرها وطرق إيصال ونقل المعلومات وتبويبها وتقييمها، وأهم من ذلك كيفية مراعاة الجوانب الأخلاقية في استخدام المعلومات. مع الأسف لم أستطع بوصفي باحثة مهتمة بعناصر وأساسيات الإعلام والمعلومات، إنجاز أبحاث تتعلق بالمقرر، ولكنني تعرضت بأحد أبحاثي لبعض الجوانب، كجانب الأخلاقيات في التعامل

مـع الإنترنـت، وبحـث آخـر لسـلوكيات طلبـة المرحلـة الجامعيـة الأولى في التعامـل مـع المعلومـات في عصـر التقنيـة المتغيـر.

الإنتاج الفكري العربي و «ثقافة الإعلام والمعلومات»

مـع الأسـف لا يتضمـن الإنتـاج الفكـري العربـي أيـة كتابـات تتنـاول هـذا المقـرر والأساسـيات والمكونـات التـي يضمهـا. ولـم تجـد الباحثـة إلا مؤتمـرا عقـد في دولـة قطـر في العـام 2013، أوصـى بتدريـس الثقافـة الإعلاميـة السـليمة في مختلـف المناهـج الدراسـية، ومـد الأجيـال الناشـئة بمـا يمكنهـا مـن تفـادي سـلبيات الإعلام .

التقارب بين مقرر « ثقافة الإعلام و المعلومات» وبين مقررات جامعة السلطان قابوس

بمـا أن جامعـة السـلطان قابـوس هـي الجامعـة الحكوميـة الوحيـدة بسـلطنة عمـان، وهـي الوحيـدة التـي تضـم قسـما لدراسـات المعلومـات، ولأن قسـم دراسـات المعلومـات يطـرح مقـررا يسـمى «الوعـي المعلومـاتي»- ينبغـي التقريـب بـين محتويـات المقرريـن.

" مقـرر «ثقافـة العـلام والمعلومـات» مقـررا شـاملا لمكونـات تخصصيـن همـا الإعلام والمعلومـات؛ ومـن ثـم تبنـي مثـل هـذا المقـرر بعـد «تَعْمِينـه» أي جعلـه يناسـب واقـع وطبيعـة المجتمـع العمـاني، يعـد مكسـبا علميـا للطلبـة وللمجتمـع، كيـف ولا وبتطبيقـه سـيحصل المجتمـع عـلى خريـج واع بالمعلومـات والإعلام وقضاياهمـا.

التوصيات:

بناء على كلّ ما سبق، توصي الكاتبة بما يلي:

1. تطبيق مقرر «ثقافة الإعلام والمعلومات»

2. يفضل إدراج المقرر ضمـن خطـط ومقـررات وزارة التربيـة والتعليـم ولكـن عـلى مسـتوى مبتـدئ للطلبـة في المراحـل التعليميـة الدنيـا ، ثـم التوسـع في المقـرر عندمـا يلتحـق الطالـب بالدراسـات الجامعيـة.

3. إضافـة المقـرر للخطـط الدراسـية لجامعـة السـلطان قابـوس بجعـل المقـرر متطلبـا إجباريـا لـكل طلبـة الجامعـة حتـى نضمـن انتقـال المعـارف والمهـارات إلى كل منتسـبي الجامعـة.

المراجع العربية:

جامعة الملك عبدالعزيز. (2014). كلية الاتصال والإعلام. متاح في .http://fcm.kau.edu
sa/Default.aspx?Site_ID=325&Lng=AR تاريخ الزيارة 28 أكتوبر 2014.

الجزيرة .نت. (2014). توصية بإدراج الثقافة الإعلامية بمناهج التعليم. متاح في //http:
www.aljazeera.net/

سليم ، نايفة بنت عيد. (2013/2014). أخلاقيات طلبة المرحلة الجامعية الأولى بجامعة
السلطان قابوس بسلطنة عمان في التعامل مع الانترنت و توظيفهم الإيجابي لها في التعليم.
مجلة مكتبة الملك فهد الوطنية، 20(1)، 239-306. تصدر عن طريق مكتبة الملك فهد
الوطنية ،المملكة العربية السعودية. متاح ف
http://www.kfnl.org.sa/ ي

عمان الرقمية. (2014). رؤية ومهمة هيئة تقنية المعلومات. متاح في _gov.om/ITAPortal
AR/ITA/ITA_Vision_Mission.aspx?NID=3

عمان. وزارة التربية و التعليم .(1990). واقع المكتبات المدرسية في سلطنة عمان.
محمد، مها.(2008). أبعاد الوعي المعلوماتي لدى طالبات الدراسات العليا في تخصص
المكتبات والمعلومات بالجامعات السعودية: دراسة لواقعها واتجاهاتها المستقبلية. جامعة
الأمام محمد بن سعود السعودية.

اليونسكو. (2011). معرفة أساسيات المعلومات والإعلام :منهاج للمعلمين. ويلسون، س.
وغيره. متاح في: http://unesdoc.unesco.org/images/0019/001929/192971a.pdf

المراجع الأجنبية:

Calkins, A. (2013). A Rude Awakening: Free Speech and the Arab Spring. The
Vanderbilt Political Review. Available at http://www.vanderbiltpoliticalreview.
#/com/a-rude-awakening-free-speech-and-the-arab-spring-2

College of Arts and Social Science. (2015). Mass Communication. http://www-
dev.squ.edu.om/cass/Departments/MassCommunication.aspx

Dhofar University. (2015). Academic programme. Available at http://www.du.edu.om/index.php?lang=en&name=College%20of%20Arts%20and%20Applied%20Sciences%20%28CAAS%29&itemid=28

IFLA. (2014). IFLA Media and Information Literacy Recommendations. Available at http://www.ifla.org/publications/ifla-media-and-information-litera-cy-recommendations.

Information Technology Authority: Sultanate of Oman. (2013). Sultanate of Oman progress report on the information society 2003-2013. Available at http://www.itu.int/wsis/review/inc/docs/rcreports/WSIS10_Country_Reporting-OMA.pdf

Information Technology Authority: Sultanate of Oman: eOman. (2015). Vision and Mission. Available at http://www.ita.gov.om/ITAPortal/ITA/ITA_Vision_Mission.aspx?NID=3

German University of Technology in Oman: GUtech. (2015). Available at http://www.gutech.edu.om/Default.aspx#

Shinnick, E. & Ryan, G. (2008). The Role of Information in Decision Making. Source title: Encyclopedia of Decision Making and Decision Support Technologies. Pennsylvania & London: Ideas Group Reference.

Sohar University. (2013). Faculty of English & English Language Studies. Available at http://www.soharuni.edu.om/fels/index.php/en/component/content/article?layout=edit&id=56-

Sultanate of Oman: Ministry of Information. (2015). Available at http://www.omaninfo.om/english/

Van de Vord, R. (2010). Distance students and online research: Promoting information literacy through media literacy. The Internet and Higher Education, 13(3), 170-175. Available at http://ac.els-cdn.com/S1096751610000266/1-s2.0-S1096751610000266-main.pdf?_tid=f1c99c30-5b4a-11e4-855e00000aab0f02&acdnat=1414133997_faa53a6d20095afe5261dbf9c8ef116c

University of Nizwa: College of Arts and Sciences. (2015). Departments. Available at http://www.unizwa.edu.om/index.php?contentid=283&lang=en

ملاحظات:

*) ملاحظة للمحررين: لم يتم العثور على المرجع المذكور

186

التربية الإعلامية والمعلوماتية من المنظور اللبناني

ماجدة أبو فاضل

هـل يفهـم مسـتهلكو الإعـلام ومنتجـوه في منطقـة الـشرق الأوسـط وشـمال أفريقيـا عـلى إختلافهـم وعـبر منصـات غـير متناهيـة مـا يقومـون بـه ومكانتهـم في المخطـط الشـامل للأمـور؟

هـل تكـرّس الجماعـات المختلفـة والأفـراد بعضـاً مـن الوقـت لتفكيـك الرسـائل والعمليـات ومخرجـات وتداعيـات التفاعـل والتكامـل والتقـارب والكـمّ الهائـل مـن الاتصـالات الـتي ترتـدي باسـتمرار أشـكالاً جديـدة بسـرعة بالـكاد نتمكـن مـن مواكبتهـا؟

ن الأمـر مذهـل للغايـة، مثـل مـورك مـن كوكـب «أورك»، الشـخصية التلفزيونيـة الشـهيرة الـتي لعـب دورهـا الكوميـدي الأمـريكي روبـن ويليامـز، الـذي يُنسـب اليـه بعـض الفضـل في تمهيـد الطريـق لعـادات الاسـتهلاك الإعلامـي المختصـرة في السـبعينات. وعنونـت صحيفـة «بزنيـس إنسـايدر» أحـد مقالاتهـا: «روبـن وليامـز كان نـبي عـصر الإنترنـت، عـن غـير قصـد»، تتحـدث فيـه عـن تأثـير ويليامـز الحمـاسي والسـاحر علينـا 1. وبحسـب الكاتـب آرون غيـل، فـإن روبـن وليـام سـاهم برسـم مسـار الثقافـة؛ وكان أسـلوبه في الاسـتعارة أو مـا يُعـرف بـ«القطـع والتلصيـق»، يعكـس طريقـة تعامـل مغـني الـراب مـع العينـات الموسـيقية؛ ومثلهـم، كان يقـع أحيانـاً في المتاعـب بسـبب اسـتعارته للمـواد. وقـال غيـل في مقالتـه: «اليـوم، عندمـا نعـود بالذاكـرة الى الفـترة الماضيـة - نحـن الذيـن نعـاصر تقنيـات النطـاق العريـض ووجـود التطبيـق المناسـب لذلـك، تويـتر و«المنتديـات الفرعيـة» والمشـاهدة المسـتمرة والتنقـل بـين القنـوات والصـور الرمزيـة (الإيموجـي) وتطبيـق «جوجـل نـاو» والقـدرة عـلى الوصـول الى كل شيء عـلى الفـور في كل مـكان وفي كل الأوقـات - يمكننـا ان نفهـم مـن ايـن أتى، ونقـرّ بفضلـه ونتعـرف عـلى علامـات التحذيـر الـتي كان يطلقهـا.» وعندمـا إنتـشر خـبر انتحـار

وليامـز في أغسطس عـام 2014، سـارع كلّ مـن وسائل الإعلام وصحفي الانترنت في كافة أنحـاء العالم الى نقل الخبـر... الكثير منهم بشكل سـيئ للغايـة 2. وفي اليوم التالي، عـزز موقع تلفزيون المستقبل في لبنان مـن حدة النقاش عبـر نشـره صورة تظهـر فيها صـورة لـجثة 3 زعم الموقع أنها تعود للممثل الراحل ويليامـز، تظهـر فيها علامـات الحـزام الـذي استخدمه لشـنق نفسـه حـول العنق؛ صـورة اشـارت عـدة مواقع أخـرى في وقت لاحق انها مزيفة 4. مثل هـذه المشاهد وغيرها مـن الانتهاكـات السابقة دفعـت بالكاتـب للإهتمام بأخلاقيات الإعلام (أو عـدم توافرها) في تسعينيات القرن الماضي، حيث دأب عـلى شرح دور وسائل الإعـلام ونفوذهـا، وبرهـن كيف يمكن اسـتخدام وسائل الاعـلام لإشراك المواطنيـن بشكل أفضل وجعلهـم أكثر تسامحاً، بالإضافة الى تطويـر الوعي بشـأن الحاجـة إلى التربيـة الإعلاميـة والمعلوماتيـة عـلى كافة الجبهـات.

التسلسل الزمني للتربية الإعلامية والمعلوماتية في لبنان:

مـن خـلال عملـي كأسـتاذة ومنسقة برنامـج الصحافـة ومديـرة المطبوعـات ومديـرة معهـد الصحافيين المحترفين في الجامعة اللبنانيـة الأميركيـة (العمل في المجالات الثلاثة)، شـاركت في تجربـة تبـادل أكاديميـة وصحافيـة افتراضيـة بيـن الثقافات مـع الأستاذ والطلاب في كليـة الصحافـة بجامعة ميسـوري. حملت النـدوة عنوان «تدويل منهج الصحافة باسـتخدام تكنولوجيا التعليـم عـن بعد: مـشروع تجريبـي بيـن الجامعـة اللبنانيـة الأميركيـة وجامعـة ميسـوري، كولومبيا (كليـة ميسـوري للصحافة). يمكن إيجاد ورقة عمل حـول هـذه النـدوة عـلى الرابط التالي عـلى الانترنت 5. كانت تجربـة غنيـة في مجـال التواصـل بيـن الثقافـات، والقيـم، والأخبار الهامـة، واستخدام التكنولوجيا الناشئة (خصوصاً الإنترنت في لبنـان) ومعرفـة مـا هـي الأمور التـي تهمّ أشخاصاً يعيشون عـلى قارتين مختلفتين في بيئة الإعـلام.

لنعـد بسرعـة الى الـوراء، الى العـام 2002، عندمـا قمت بدراسـة كيفيـة تعاطـي وسـائل الإعـلام في لبنـان والـشرق الأوسط وتغطيتهـا لهجمـات الحـادي عـشر مـن سبتمبر / أيلـول 2001 عـلى الولايـات المتحدة في مقالـة صـدرت في عـدد ربيع عـام 2002 مـن مجلة «-Leba non Journalism Review» (المنحلة) بعنوان «فكروا بالأولاد لـدى كتابتكـم ذلك المقال: هـل تستحق الصـور المفضّلة كلّ هـذا العنـاء؟» 6

الجميـع، كبـاراً وصغـاراً، مسـمّراً أمـام شاشـات التلفاز، يشـاهد لحظات اصطـدام طائرات ركاب ببرجي مبنى مركز التجارة العالمي في نيويورك، ومبنى البنتاجون في واشنطن وسقوطها

ا في أحد الحقول خارج بيتسبرغ ، بنسلفانيا، يوم الحادي عشر من سبتمبر 2001.

كانت ردود الفعل متباينة، إلا أنها غالباً ما كانت ترتكز على تجاربهم الخاصة مع برامج التلفزيون العنيفة، وأفلام هوليـوود البطولية، أو ألعـاب الفيـديو الخياليـة أو ألعـاب الكمبيوتر. لكن عندمـا بدأت حقيقـة الأمـور تتوضـح، بفضل الإعـادات الـلا متناهيـة للمشاهد والصـور المروعـة، بدأ الخـوف والشـك يسـيطران أيضاً. 7

في مايـو / أيـار عـام 2004، قـدم هـذا الكاتب ورقـة عمل بعنوان «التربيـة الإعلاميـة: الوعي مقابـل الجهـل» في إطار النـدوة التـي نظمهـا المعهـد السـويدي في الإسـكندرية، مصـر، بعنـوان: «الشباب والإعلام». 8 في إطار تلك الورقة، سألت عما إذا أدرك الأولاد مـا تلقـوه مـن معلومـات، عمـا إذا قامـوا بتقييـم المحتـوى، وإذا سـاعدهم أهلهـم أو أسـاتذتهم في اختيـار البرامـج، أو إذا سـمحوا للشباب بـأن يحكمـوا بأنفسـهم مـا هي المـواد المناسـبة للقـراءة أو الاسـتماع أو المشـاهدة أو التصفـح .

إن الرسـائل المموهـة التـي يتـم إدراجهـا في البرامـج قـد تؤثـر علـى أنمـاط الشـراء. الحلقـات المليئـة بالصراعـات أو ألعـاب الفيـديو يمكـن أن تحـرض علـى العنـف وتـؤدي إلى السـلوك العـدواني. حتـى المسلسـلات التـي تبـدو بريئـة في الظاهـر قـد تدفـع الشباب الى الخلـط بيـن الخيـال والواقـع. بالنتيجـة، فـإن الاستهـلاك السـاذج للأخبـار ومـواد الترفيـه، وحتـى «التعليـم الترفيهـي» الأكثـر شـعبية يمكـن أن تسـهم في خلـق مجتمعـات مفككـة وأفـراد مضطربيـن، أو، علـى أقـل تقديـر، الى خلـق ارتبـاك حـول كيفيـة التفاعـل مـع الرسـائل المتنافـرة التـي تكتسـح مشـاعرنا الحسـية.

قـد يكون اذاً مـن المفيـد ان نستكشف عالـم التربيـة الإعلاميـة مـن أجل مسـاعدة الشباب - وذويهـم ومعلميهـم ومرشـديهم - علـى فهـم تأثيـر وسـائل الإعـلام عليهـم وكيـف تسـاهم بتشـكيل قيمهـم ووجهـات نظرهـم . 9

في نوفمبر 2004، ألقيت محاضـرة بعنوان «الشباب اللبناني والإعلام: التأثيرات الاجتماعيـة والسياسـية» في إطار «حـوار وسـائل الإعـلام العربيـة الألمانيـة» في مؤتمـر نظمتـه وزارة الخارجيـة الألمانيـة ومعهـد الشـؤون الخارجيـة والثقافيـة في برليـن.

كتب أستاذ الإعلام اللبنـاني والمحلـل جـان كـرم: «في أي بلد، عندمـا تكون الدولـة شـريكاً أساسـياً في وسـائل الإعـلام، أو مرتبطـة بهـا بشـكل أو بآخـر، لا يوجـد أمـل في أن تتمكـن وسـائل الإعـلام الليبراليـة مـن العمـل.»

وأضاف أنه بغض النظر عن مواقف الدولة الليبرالية والمنفتحة والديمقراطية، لا يوجد أمل في أن تتخلى عن موقفها المهيمن، لا سيما عندما تشعر بأن خططها السياسية أو الاقتصادية أو الدبلوماسية مهددة من حرية التعبير الشرعية التي يتمتع بها كل صحافي . (وسائل الإعلام في حالة غليان، جان كرم، النهار، 29-10-2004).

وقد نشر مركز «نورديكوم» في السويد هذا المقال كفصل في كتاب بعنوان: «في خدمة الشباب؟ دراسات وتأملات في وسائل الإعلام في العصر الرقمي» في سبتمبر عام 2005. 10 عاد هذا الكاتب ليعالج هذا الموضوع مجدداً في محاضرة بعنوان «المعوقات وآراء المرأة والشباب في منطقة الشرق الأوسط وشمال أفريقيا» ألقاها في خلال الندوة / ورشة العمل «الإعلام والمرأة والشباب في منطقة الشرق الأوسط وشمال أفريقيا» التي نظمتها مركز «أولوف بالم» الدولي في المعهد السويدي في الإسكندرية، مصر في فبراير عام 2005.

في مارس عام 2007، قدمت ورقة بحثية خلال مؤتمر الأونيسكو الإقليمي لدعم محو الأمية الإعلامية في العالم الذي عقد في الدوحة بقطر تحت عنوان «التربية الإعلامية: أداة لمحاربة الصور النمطية وتعزيز التفاهم بين الثقافات». 11

لقد شهدت التربية الإعلامية والتوعية إهمالاً طويل الأمد في العالم العربي، الأمر الذي غالباً ما يؤدي إلى عواقب سلبية ويزيد من خطورة الوضع المتفجر الناجم عن الاضطرابات السياسية والاقتصادية والاجتماعية، وعن غياب القيادة. كما أن موضوع التربية الإعلامية كمادة تدريس منظّمة نادراً ما كان يُدرّس في المدارس، وغالباً ما كانت تتم الاشارة اليها بواسطة مصطلحات غامضة في إطار مواد التدريس الجامعية التي تعجز عن معالجة سبب وجود وسائل الاتصال الجماهيري، وأنظمة الدعم المالي الخاصة بها والتأثيرات المختلفة التي يمكن أن تجعل منها «أسلحة للخداع الشامل».

إن مفهوم التفكير النقدي الذي يشكل جزءاً من التربية الإعلامية يبدو غريباً بالنسبة الى الشباب الذين اعتادوا على نظام ثابت من التعلم عن ظهر قلب والدروس التحضيرية السلبية. يبدو الأمر واضحاً بشكل خاص في المدارس التي تتبع الأنظمة التعليمية الفرنسية والعربية حيث لطالما كانت فكرة مساءلة السلطة بمثابة لعنة. كما عجزت الأنظمة التعليمية البريطانية والأمريكية في بعض الأحيان عن بلوغ أهدافها المعلنة في مجال التعلم والاستجواب الفعالين.

وفي معرض تعليقه على الأمر، أشار رجا كمال، عميد تنمية الموارد في كلية هاريس للسياسات العامة في جامعة شيكاغو، إن أداء التعليم العالي في العالم العربي كان غير كافٍ، وأنتج خريجين يواجهون صعوبة في الاندماج في الاقتصاد العالمي واستيعابه. وقال: «إن الغالبية العظمى من الجامعات العربية تعلّم طلابها ما ينبغي أن يفكروا به بدلا من كيفية التفكير.» وأضاف: «ما لم تتغير هذه العقلية سريعاً، فالأمل ضئيل في تحقيق التقدم.» (كمال، 2007). وحثّ كمال الدول العربية على إدراج التعليم العالي في مشاريع التخطيط الاستراتيجي، وخلق شراكة بين القطاع الخاص والمدرّسين. 12

في يناير من عام 2008، قدم هذا الكاتب ورقة عمل في إطار أحد المؤتمرات باليونسكو حول التنوع الثقافي والتعليم بعنوان «تعزيز القدرات الحرجة ومكافحة وجهات النظر احادية الجانب: إيجاد أرضية مشتركة ومواضيع ملائمة للتعليم من خلال التنوع الثقافي – أبعاد تعليم الصحافة والتدريب».

«تبرز الصور النمطية وسوء التفاهم في حال وجود نقص في المعلومات، أو عندما يتم تشويه المعلومات ونقلها بشكل سيء، أو عندما تكون هناك سوء نية أحياناً. لهذه الغاية، نحتاج الى تعليم إعلامي متين والى تربية إعلامية مناسبة، وكذلك الى البحث الكافي والمثابرة والصبر وروح المغامرة والاستعداد للنظر والتفكير على غير العادة.»

في هذا السياق، تم وضع تقرير حاسم بناء على الحدث الأول الذي أقيم في برشلونة، اسبانيا وأطلق خلال منتدى الأمم المتحدة لتحالف الحضارات في ريو دي جانيرو، البرازيل في مايو 2010. وقد أدرجت توصيات المؤلف التي خلّص اليها في ورقة عمل المنتدى الأول في التقرير. 13 مذاك الحين، ألقيت محاضرات عدة عن الموضوع وأقمت ورش عمل حول التربية الإعلامية والمعلوماتية في لبنان وقطر والمغرب وتونس واليمن. لا بد من الإشارة الى أن الكثير من الاشخاص في أماكن أخرى في لبنان قرروا أن يسيروا على هذا النهج. فأنشأت الجامعة الأميركية في بيروت أكاديمية التربية الإعلامية والمعلوماتية الرقمية في بيروت 14 جمعت عدداً من المشاركين والمتحدثين من مختلف أنحاء العالم العربي وخارجه. ألا أن جهودها لا تزال تحتاج أن تترجم من خلال تنفيذ برنامج مستدام وقابل للتطبيق تشارك فيه كافة المؤسسات التعليمية في البلاد وباللغات الثلاث الرئيسية. مدرسة «انترناشيونال كولدج» («آي سي») 15، وهي مدرسة ابتدائية وثانوية خاصة لها فرعين في كلّ من بيروت ومنطقة عين عار، لبنان، كانت من ابرز من حرص على تبني مفاهيم التربية الإعلامية والمعلوماتية وممارساتها. وقد خضع المدرّسون والمنسقون

ورؤساء الأقسام في تلك المدرسة الى تدريب أولي في مجال التربية الإعلامية والمعلوماتية، لكنهم لا يزالون بحاجة إلى التعمّق أكثر في هذا الموضوع. وفي ما يتعلق بالطلاب، وضعت مدرسة «آي سي» ما أسمته بـ«اتفاقية المواطنة الرقمية المسؤولة» للطلاب في المرحلة الابتدائية، والمتوسطة والثانوية ، تركز على احترام وتثقيف وحماية أنفسهم والآخرين. 16 ويتوقع من الطلاب التوقيع على هذه الاتفاقية التي تنطوي على قواعد السلامة على الإنترنت والمواطنة الرقمية مع ذويهم، في محاولة لخلق الوعي وتعزيز مسؤولية الطلاب لدى استخدام الانترنت. ولا بد من اعتماد نموذج مماثل في انحاء البلاد.

من جهة اخرى، قامت مطرانية بيروت للروم الاورثوذوكس باعتماد الكتب الرقمية في الصفوف، بدلاً من الورقية الثقيلة الوزن، في إطار المشروع الذي أطلقته مجموعة المدارس الأرثوذكسية في لبنان 17التي تضمّ ثلاث مؤسسات تعليمية. 18 تشتمل سلسلة الكتب الرقمية التي قام بتطويرها عدد من التربويين المدرسين في كلّ من مدرسة البشارة الأرثوذكسية بيروت وثانوية السيدة الأرثوذكسية ومدرسة الثلاثة أقمار، على مواضيع مختلفة مثل الادب العربي والعلوم الاجتماعية والادب الانكليزي والادب الفرنسي والرياضيات والعلوم للصفوف الابتدائية الثلاثة الأولى. 19 يحتاج الطلاب الى إحضار أجهزتهم اللوحية الخاصة (كأجهزة الآيباد وغيرها). لكن لا توجد إشارات كثيرة على أن مهارات التفكير الناقد التي يتدربون على استخدامها تشمل فك رموز الرسائل الإعلامية. ويبدو أن سلسلة الكتب الرقمية تركز أكثر على تطوير مهارات تكنولوجيا المعلومات والاتصالات لاستكمال عملية التعلم بدلاً من التعمّق في عالم الرسائل الرقمية والوسائط المتعددة.

من جهة أخرى، قامت أحدى الصحف اليومية «النهار» 20 بإنتاج ملحقات خاصة بالأولاد والشباب لبعض الوقت - كما فعلت بضع وسائل إعلام مطبوعة أخرى - وشاركت لفترة وجيزة في تجربة متواضعة مع الرابطة العالمية للصحف وأخبار الناشرين (WAN-IFRA) تحت عنوان: «الصحف في التربية والتعليم». 21 إلا ن الخطة لم تذهب بعيداً ولم يُكتب لها الاستمرار.

في مايو 2012، أعلن وزير التربية والتعليم العالي في ذلك الوقت حسان دياب ووزير الاتصالات السابق نقولا صحناوي عن توفير حواسيب لوحية لطلاب الصفين العاشر والحادي عشر في المدارس الحكومية بهدف تحسين المناهج وتطوير النظام التعليمي في

البلاد. وكانت وزارة التربية والتعليم العالي قد تلقت هبة أولية من 1،500 جهاز ستكون بمثابة عينات اختبار في المدارس العامة والخاصة. كما وضعت الوزارة أيضاً برنامجاً خاصاً للتربية الإعلامية والمعلوماتية يهدف الى إنشاء شبكة لخدمة المدارس في كافة أنحاء البلاد. (وزارة التربية والتعليم العالي 2012). لكن لم تُعرف معلومات كافية حول هذا المخطط.

إلا أن مجلس الوزراء اللبناني هذا (والوزارة) قد تغير، وعرفت الحياة السياسية في لبنان الكثير من العقبات، كما تأثر الوضع الأمني سلباً، ومذاك الوقت، يشهد النظام التعليمي المدرسي بقيادة نقابة المعلمين موجة من الإضرابات والعراقيل والتعطيل المدرسي، مما تسبب بإيلاء اهتمام ضئيل الى ما يمكن اعتباره ذات أهمية ثانوية. بالإضافة الى ذلك، واجهت الخطة الطموحة لتعزيز التربية الإعلامية والمعلوماتية سلسلة من مع العقبات المتكررة والسخيفة مثل انقطاع التيار الكهربائي المزمن والنقص في الطاقة وبطء خدمة الإنترنت على الرغم من المزاعم الرسمية التي تؤكد توفير خدمة الخطوط الاشتراك الرقمية غير المتماثلة («آي دي إس إل»). للأسف، فإن ثقافة التربية الإعلامية والمعلوماتية لم تنتشر بشكل كافٍ حتى الآن في المؤسسات التعليمية في لبنان في المستويات الابتدائية والمتوسطة والثانوية والجامعية. كما أنه لم يتم بعد إشراك ذوي الطلاب بالكامل في هذه العملية. ولم تخصص الحكومة الموارد الكافية لتوفير برامج التربية الإعلامية والمعلوماتية في كافة المدارس العامة. الأهم من ذلك، لم يصبح المحتوى والمواد الخاصة بالتربية الإعلامية والمعلوماتية متوفرين على نطاق واسع باللغة العربية (اللغة الرسمية للبلاد)، او باللغة الفرنسية والإنجليزية في المدارس التي تُدرّس المناهج الفرنسية والانكليزية، وإلى حد أقل، باللغة الأرمنية، وهي لغة أكبر أقلية في البلاد.

الخاتمة:

كيف يمكننا المساهمة في التربية الإعلامية والمعلوماتية في لبنان؟ تشكل الألعاب إحدى الوسائل التي يمكن ان توجّه طاقة الشباب وهي صناعة مزدهرة تلبي كافة الأذواق. وتُستخدم الألعاب، وخاصة الألعاب الإلكترونية والافتراضية، في التعليم من اجل تدريس المهارات الحياتية، والرياضيات، والعلوم، واللغات، ومجموعة كبيرة من المواضيع، سواء كبرمجيات مستقلة وعلى شكل تطبيقات. وبحسب الخبراء، إن كنتم.

تريدون أولاداً «أفضل تكيفاً»، فإن ساعة من ممارسة ألعاب الفيديو يومياً (وليس أكثر) قد تكون مفيدة.

«خلصت دراسة حديثة أجرتها جامعة أوكسفورد الى أن ممارسة الأطفال لألعاب الفيديو قد يكون في الواقع مفيداً لنمو الطفل، لكن فقط إذا لعب الأطفال لأقل من ساعة في اليوم. وأشارت الأبحاث التي قام بها الدكتور أندرو برزبلسكي، استاذ علم النفس التجريبي أن الشباب الذين مارسوا ألعاب الفيديو لبضع ساعات فقط في الاسبوع كانوا أفضل تكيفًا، وأكثر اهتماماً برفاهية أقرانهم ويظهرون مشاكل سلوكية أقل في الإجمال.» 22

إلا أن هناك ايضاً أنواعاً سيئة من الألعاب و»التطبيقات» تركّز بشدة على العنف والحروب، والسلوك المنحرف. مع انتشار الحروب المشتعلة في كافة الدول العربية وفي وقت يسود عدم الاستقرار في لبنان، من المهم أن نثبت للشباب الشديد التأثر بأن الألعاب التي ترتكز على الصراعات ليست بالضرورة أمثلة جيدة يمكن الاقتداء بها. كذلك، يمكن أن تكون للرسوم المتحركة، وهي نموذج آخر يعشقه كلّ من الصغار والكبار، دور فعال وحيوي في تعزيز الصور النمطية واستمرارها، وفي نشر الصور الإيجابية والسلبية، وتحفيز الأفعال وردود الأفعال. السر يكمن في الاستفادة من النواحي الإيجابية.

في السابق، كان لأسلاف الرسوم المتحركة، وأعني بذلك الكتب المصورة، تأثير مماثل على القراء الذين كانوا احياناً يخلطون بين الخيال والواقع. ولا تزال الكتب المصورة نوعاً من وسائل الإعلام الشعبية، ويمكن استخدامها لإحداث تأثير جيد في مجال التدريس والتعليم. تجدر الإشارة الى أن الكتب المصورة متوفرة في لبنان باللغات الثلاث، العربية والفرنسية والإنجليزية، إلا أنه يمكن إيجاد مثل هذه المنشورات بلغات أخرى ايضاً. ادمجوا الإغراء الذي تشكله الإعلانات عبر مختلف المنصات وقوتها في التأثير بالسلوك، سترون أن هذا المزيج سلاح ذو حدّين - ويستطيع لأن يوجّه الرسائل الإيجابية والسلبية على حد سواء. أضيفوا الملصقات ولافتات الشوارع، ستشعرون انكم تغرقون تحت الكمّ الوافر منها. الصحف والمجلات ليست مهيمنة بقدر وسائل الإعلام الرقمية والمتنقلة والاذاعة تلعب دوراً ثانوياً مقارنة بالمحتوى الصوت والفيديو عبر الإنترنت. أما التلفزيون، فقد وَصف فيما مضى بأنه «جليس الأطفال» في وقت كان الأهل يسعون لتهدئة أطفالهم. إلا أن أهميته تراجعت منذ بعض الوقت لصالح وسائط البث المتنقّلة والانترنت، حيث المحتوى المقدم من المستخدمين شامل وموجود في كل مكان. في بيئة الخلط الموسيقي الهجين وتوزيع المحتوى عبر وسائط عدة، من السهل أن يغفل المرء

عـن الأخـلاق وآداب المهنـة، وحقـوق الطبـع والنـشر وانتهـاكات الخصوصيـة. لطالـما واجـه اللبنانيـون صراعـاً طويـل الأمـد مـع قوانيـن حقـوق التأليـف والنـشر والعلامـات التجاريـة المسجلة. بـل ويتجاهلونهـا بالكامـل. لا بـد مـن الإشـارة الى أن فهـم كل هـذه المفاهيـم والممارسـات والطريقـة الأمثـل لخـوض هـذا المجـال المتقلـب قـد أصبـح أساسـياً في القـرن الحـادي والعشريـن المعولـم.

في لبنـان، ترتبـط التربيـة الإعلاميـة والمعلوماتيـة بالتعليـم والتربيـة والديـن والإعـلام بالمعنى العـام. وغالبـاً مـا يتـمّ إدخـال المعلومـات كعامـل مسـاعد، فيـما تلعـب التكنولوجيا دوراً داعمـاً. إن تطبيـق البرامـج التـي تعـزز المعرفـة الرقميـة إلى جانـب التربيـة الإعلاميـة يتطلـب الكثيـر مـن الجهـد والعمـل الحثيـث. ونظـراً للموقـع الجغـرافي للبـلاد، ثمة ضرورة ملحـة لتوفيـر محتـوى أكثـر عمليـة باللغـة العربيـة، إلى جانـب إنتـاج المـواد باللغتيـن الفرنسيـة والإنجليزيـة لتلبيـة احتياجـات ومتطلبـات المجموعـات الفرعيـة المختلفـة. في غضـون ذلـك، يقـدم أسـتاذ التربيـة في جامعـة ديـربي في بريطانيـا، دنيـس هايـز، رأيـاً مناقضـاً لمـا كنـا نسـمعه وننصـح بـه طـوال سـنوات عـدة. وفي إحـدى التدوينـات بعنـوان «لنكف عـن محاولـة تعليـم التفكيـر النقـدي للطـلاب»، يقتـرح هايـز أن المفهـوم ليـس مهـارة. هـذا يعنـي أن التلقيـن والنظريـات النقديـة لا تتفـق مـع قواعـد النقـد النزيـه. 23

«في الحقيقـة، لا يمكـن تعليـم النـاس أن يكونـوا ناقديـن مـا لـم يكن المـرء بنفسـه ناقـداً. هـذا يتطلـب أكثـر مـن مجـرد الطلـب مـن الشـباب أن «ينظـروا بشـكل ناقـد» الى الأمـور، كما لـو كانـت الانتقـادات مهمـة آليـة.

كمدرس، يجب ان تتمتع بـروح النقـد. هـذا لا يعنـي التذمـر باسـتمرار مـن سياسـات التعليـم السـائدة التـي لا تـروق لـك أو الإيحـاء الى الطـلاب بمـا ينبغـي أن يفكـروا بـه. هـذا يعنـي قبـل كل شيء أم تتمكـن مـن الانخـراط فـي محادثـة عميقـة. هـذا يعنـي ايضـاً الحـوار والمناقشـة بالارتكـاز عـلى معرفـة واسـعة - وهـو أمـر غائـب بشـكل شـبه تـام في عالـم التعليـم. كما ينبغـي أن يحصـل في الأماكـن العامـة، مـع الآبـاء والأمهـات وغيرهـم ممـن ليسـوا معلميـن، وليـس فقـط في الصفـوف أو قاعـات الأسـاتذة.»

بنـاء عـلى ذلـك، سـيطلب هـذا المؤلـف مـن القـراء التفكيـر بالمسـألة، والانخـراط في محادثـة عميقـة ومناقشـة الأمـر في الأماكـن العامـة، وإشـراك الآخريـن فـي محاولـة لخدمـة التربيـة الإعلاميـة والمعلوماتيـة بشـكل أفضـل.

195

المصادر والمراجع

أبو فاضل، م. و جافكي، ر. / «تدويـل منهـج الصحافـة باسـتخدام تكنولوجيـا التعليـم عـن بعـد: مشـروع تجريبـي بيـن الجامعـة اللبنانيـة - الأميركيـة وجامعـة ميسـوري - كولومبيـا (كليـة ميسـوري للصحافّة). أعـدت للمؤتمـر السـنوي الرابـع للجمعيـة العربيـة الأميركيـة لأسـاتذة الاتصال (أوسـاس) (AUSACE)، بيـروت، لبنـان، أكتوبـر 26-29، 1999.»
http://ipj.lau.edu.lb/outreach/1999/ausace/ausace1.php

أبـو فاضـل، م. / «فكـروا بالأولاد لـدى كتابتكـم ذلك المقال: هل تسـتحق الصـور المفضّلة كلّ هـذا العنـاء؟» مجلـة «Lebanon Journalism Review»، ربيـع عـام 2002.
http://ipj.lau.edu.lb/outreach/2002/03_ljr/ljrspring2002.php

أبـو فاضـل، م. / «التربيـة الإعلاميـة: الوعـي مقابـل الجهـل» ورقـة عمـل فـي إطـار نـدوة «الشـباب والإعـلام» التـي نظمهـا المعهـد السـويدي فـي الإسـكندرية، مصـر.
http://ipj.lau.edu.lb/outreach/2004/05_youth/media_literacy.pdf

أبـو فاضـل، م. (2006)/ «الشـباب اللبنانـي والإعـلام: التأثيـرات الاجتماعيـة والسياسـية». فـي كتـاب بعنـوان لـكلّ مـن و. كارلسـون و س. فـون فيلتزيـن: «فـي خدمـة الشـباب؟ دراسـات وتأمـلات فـي الإعـلام فـي العـصر الرقمـي». الكتـاب الحـولي 2005 / 2006. المركـز الـدولي لتبـادل المعلومـات حول الأطفال والشـباب والإعلام التابع لمركـز «نورديكـوم»، جامعـة «جوتنبرج»، السـويد. متوفـر عـلى الرابـط التـالي: www.nordicom.gu.se

أبـو فاضـل، م. / «التربيـة الإعلاميـة: أداة لمحاربـة الصـور النمطيـة وتعزيـز التفاهـم بيـن الثقافـات». ورقـة بحثيـة أعـدّت لمؤتمـر الأونيسـكو الإقليمـي لدعـم محـو الأميـة فـي العالـم، الدوحـة، قطـر، مـارس 2007.
http://unesdoc.unesco.org/images/0016/001611/161157e.pdf

أبـو فاضـل، م. / «تنفيـذ برامـج التربيـة الإعلاميـة»، تقريـر اليونسـكو العالمـي: الاسـتثمار فـي التنـوع الثقـافي والحـوار بيـن الثقافـات، منظمـة اليونسـكو، باريـس، فرنسـا. متوفـر عـلى الرابـط التـالي:
http://unesdoc.unesco.org/images/0018/001852/185202e.pdf

وزارة التربيـة والتعليـم العالـي في لبنـان (2013): «كتـاب يوثّـق إدارة الوزير الاستاذ حسـان ديـاب في وزارة التربيـة والتعليـم العالـي»، الطبعـة الأولى، ص. 127-124.

https://www.linkedin.com/profile/view?trk=nmp_pymk_name&auth-
Token=ME-V&authType=name&id=325913617

غيـل، آ. / «روبـن وليامـز كان نـبي عـصر الإنترنـت، عـن غـير قصـد»، صحيفـة «بزنيـس إنسـايدر»، 12 أغسطس 2014.

http://www.businessinsider.com/robin-williams-internet-prophet-2014-8

هايز، دنيس / «لنكف عن محاولة تعليم التفكير النقدي للطلاب» المحادثة. 9 أغسطس 2014.

http://theconversation.com/lets-stop-trying-to-teach-students-critical-thinking-30321

هونجـو، إتـش./ «توقفـوا عـن نـشر صـورة روبـن وليامـز الميـت»، «انـتي فـيرال غوكـر». 13 أغسـطس 2013.

http://antiviral.gawker.com/stop-sharing-that-fake-robin-williams-death-photo-
1620835563/+leahfinnegan?utm_campaign=socialflow_gawker_twitter&utm_
source=gawker_twitter&utm_medium=socialflow

مدرسة «انترناشيونال كولدج» ، لبنان. «اتفاقية المواطنة الرقمية المسؤولة».
http://cld.bz/bookdata/uFKqVZt/basic-html/page40.html

و

http://cld.bz/bookdata/SOlKqHt/basic-html/page50.html

«روبن وليامز: الإعلام يتجاهل مبادىء الانتحار» المدونة الإعلامية، 13 أغسطس 2014.
http://www.themediablog.co.uk/the-media-blog/2014/08/robin-williams-newspa-
per-coverage.html

«أول صـورة بعـد انتحـار روبـن وليامـز»، تدوينـة بالعربيـة وصورتـين عـلى موقـع تلفزيـون المسـتقبل ، لبنـان، 13 أغسـطس 2014.
http://www.futuretvnetwork.com/node/106731

فنسنت، جيمـس / «هـل تريـدون أطفـالاً أفضـل تكيفـاً؟ سـاعة مـن ممارسـة ألعاب الفيديـو يوميـاً (وليـس أكـثر) قـد تكون مفيـدة»، صحيفـة «اندبندنت»، 4 أغسـطس 2014.
http://www.independent.co.uk/life-style/gadgets-and-tech/gaming/want-better-ad-
justed-children-an-hour-of-video-gaming-a-day-and-no-more-might-help-9645834.
html

الرابطة العالمية للصحف وأخبار الناشرين(WAN-IFRA) : «الصحف في التربية والتعليم».
http://www.wan-ifra.org/microsites/youth-engagement-news-literacyprogram

1 . http://www.businessinsider.com/robin-williams-internet-prophet-2014-8

2 . http://www.themediablog.co.uk/the-media-blog/2014/08/robin-williams-newspa-
per-coverage.html

3 . http://www.futuretvnetwork.com/node/106731

4 . http://antiviral.gawker.com/stop-sharing-that-fake-robin-williams-death-pho-
to-1620835563/+leahfinnegan?utm_campaign=socialflow_gawker_twitter&utm_
source=gawker_twitter&utm_medium=socialflow.

5 . http://ipj.lau.edu.lb/outreach/1999/ausace/ausace1.php

6 . http://ipj.lau.edu.lb/outreach/2002/03_ljr/ljrspring2002.php

7 . المصدر نفسه

8 . http://ipj.lau.edu.lb/outreach/2004/05_youth/media_literacy.pdf

9 . المصدر نفسه

10 . http://www.nordicom.gu.se/en/publikationer/service-young-people/le-
banese-youth-and-media-social-and-political-influences

11 . http://unesdoc.unesco.org/images /0016/001611/161157e.pdf

12 . المصدر نفسه

13 . Abu-Fadil, M. (2009)

14 . https://www.facebook.com/mdlab.aub

15 . www.ic.edu.lb

16 . http://cld.bz/bookdata/uFKqVZt/basic-html/page40.html
http://cld.bz/bookdata/SOIKqHt/basic-html/page50.html I

17 . http://www.eduvation.edu.lb

18 . http://www.dailystar.com.lb/News/Lebanon-News/2015/Apr-10/293984-
textbooks-at-eduvation-school-network-go-high-tech.ashx

19 . http://www.lorientlejour.com/article/929878/le-cursus-scolaire-libanais-adapte-
sur-support-numerique.html

20 . www.annahar.com

21 . http://www.wan-ifra.org/microsites/youth-engagement-news-literacy

22 . http://www.independent.co.uk/life-style/gadgets-and-tech/gaming/want-better-
adjusted-children-an-hour-of-video-gaming-a-day-and-no-more-might-help-9645834.
html

23 . http://theconversation.com/lets-stop-trying-to-teach-students-critical-
thinking-30321

تمكين الاطفال والشباب في تونس
الدمج بين الإعلام والتعليم

كارميلا فلويد وغابرييلا ثينز

تونس، في صباح أحد ايام فبراير 2014. كانت أولى خيوط أشعة الشمس الدافئة تحاول اختراق الضباب، وكان الهواء بارداً للغاية. في تلك اللحظات، كانت كافة القنوات الإخبارية تحيي الذكرى السنوية الأولى لاغتيال شكري بلعيد، السياسي العلماني الذي قتل في الشارع أمام منزله في تونس في العام السابق، يوم 5 فبراير، 2013. كان التوتر سيد الموقف... أو ربما كان هذا الشعور وليد مخيلتنا؟ لأننا كنا نعلم جيداً أن تونس وتونس العاصمة - تلك المدينة النابضة بالحياة التي يعيش فيها الملايين من السكان الذين يشكلون مزيجاً من العالمين الجديد والقديم؛ ويجمعون بين التقاليد والحداثة - قد عانت أكثر مما يعتقد المرء أنه ممكن في غضون بضع سنوات فقط. كنا فريقاً صغيراً من المدربين الإعلاميين في طريقنا إلى بلدة بني خالد الصغيرة التي تبعد مسافة ساعة بالسيارة عن مدينة تونس، حيث من المقرر ان نبدأ بعقد أول سلسلة من ورش العمل حول التربية الإعلامية والمعلوماتية. وبعدما كان مشروعنا، الذي يحمل شعار مر» مجرد حبر على ورق منذ عام 2011؛ كنا الآن، في فبراير عام 2014، على وشك النزول فعلياً على الأرض في محاولة لتطبيق الأفكار والمفاهيم عملياً لأول مرة .

كان من المقرر ان نلتقي في فترة ما بعد الظهر بالأولاد والشباب الذين يرتادون مركزاً للشباب المحلي، لمنحهم دورة مكثفة في التربية الإعلامية والمعلوماتية. قبل ذلك، كنا قد عقدنا جلسة صباحية مع مجموعة من قادة الشباب الذين يعملون في المركز. لكن السيارة التي كانت تقلّنا كانت لا تزال تتحرك ببطء شديد خلال ساعة الذروة وسط مدينة تونس حيث كانت الأرصفة تعجّ بالناس. شاهدنا عدداً من الجنود وضباط الشرطة بكامل عتادهم المخصص لمكافحة الشغب، ومررنا امام أحد المباني الحكومية تحيط به الأسلاك الشائكة والدبابات. ما لم نكن نعرفه في تلك اللحظات، أنه وقبل بضع

ساعات فقط، على مسافة بضعة كيلومترات، تم «تفجير» خلية إرهابية – بالمعنى الحرفي. بالتالي، لم يكن ذلك التوتر السائد مجرد وهم. في نهاية الأمر، تمكنا من الخروج من وسط المدينة المكتظ بالناس وانطلقنا في شوارع ضيقة ومتعرجة. فعلى الرغم من أن وسط مدينة تونس يتميز بالتصميم الطبيعي للمدن الحديثة، ثمة تناقضات كبيرة بين وسط المدينة وبين الضواحي والريف. بعد ساعة أمضيناها على الطرقات العامة الوعرة، بلغنا أخيراً بلدة بني خالد واوقفنا السيارة بجوار احد المباني الذي تغطي جدرانه الخارجية كمية من الكتابات والنقوش وسط الشوارع المزدحمة. كنا في الوقت عينه متوترين ومتحمسين لبدء العمل. لكن قبل ان نبدأ، لا بد من كلمة عن تونس وخلفية هذا المشروع.

لماذا تونس؟

شهدت تونس انطلاقة أحداث ما عُرف بـ«الربيع العربي». في ديسمبر من العام 2010، أضرم البائع المتجول محمد البوعزيزي النار في نفسه عند ولاية سيدي بوزيد، وهي بلدة صغيرة في وسط تونس، احتجاجاً على مصادرة بضاعته. وقد وُصفت تلك اللحظة بأنها الشرارة الأولى التي أشعلت لهيب الانتفاضات في تونس، ثم في مصر وليبيا.

عواقب الثورة من المنظور الإعلامي تكاد تكون مستحيلة الفهم.

تصوروا هذا: اضطر النظام الذي يسيطر من دون ضمير وازع على وسائل الإعلام الى التخلي عن السلطة. قبل الثورة، كانت الرقابة امراً شائعاً. وغالباً ما كان الصحافيون يتعرضون للمضايقات.i للمرة الأولى، خلال الثورة، نزل الصحفيون التونسيون الى الشوارع ونقلوا الأحداث مباشرة من أرض الحدث، ما سمح للجمهور بالتعبير عن رأيه من دون أي رقابة. ومع سقوط النظام، ألغيت وزارة الإعلام، التي كانت فيما مضى أداة مثيرة للخشية للسيطرة الإعلامية؛ الأمر الذي شكّل انطلاقة لحرية التعبير. ومع هذه الحرية، ولدت اعداد كبيرة من المحطات الإذاعية الجديدة والقنوات التلفزيونية تبعتها المواقع الاخبارية على الانترنت، في حين أعادت المحطات الحكومية تنظيم نفسها، وبدأ التداول اللامتناهي للمعلومات والأخبار من خلال المواقع الاخبارية على الانترنت والشبكات الاجتماعية. إلا أن الناس شعروا بالملل، بعدما زال ذاك الشعور الأول بنشوة الحرية. ومع أن وسائل الإعلام المملوكة للدولة التي تحولت إلى شبكات عامة كانت تسعى بشكل يائس لإقناع الجماهير بأنها تغيرت، إلا ان الكثيرين لا يزالون يعتبرونها جزءاً من النظام القديم. وبما أن كافة وسائل الإعلام التونسية السائدة كانت في وقت

من الأوقات على صلة وثيقة، إلى حد ما، بنظام بن علي المخلوع، بقي الناس على حذرهم. وغمرت الشائعات وسائل الإعلام، بسبب رغبة جميع الأطراف في اعطاء آرائهم الخاصة عن الماضي والحاضر. وفي وسط الاضطرابات، نجد مجموعة من السكان الشباب – نصف التونسيين على الأقل هم دون العشرين من العمرii. نشأوا على التعاليم التي تقول ان بعض القوانين تطبق في هذا المجال، ليتعلموا لاحقاً أن ذلك لم يعد مهماً. إلى من ينبغي ان يصغي المرء، وبمن يستطيع الوثوق؟

– نصف التونسيين على الأقل هم دون العشرين من العمرii. نشأوا على التعاليم التي تقول ان بعض القوانين تطبق في هذا المجال، ليتعلموا لاحقاً أن ذلك لم يعد مهماً. إلى من ينبغي ان يصغي المرء، وبمن يستطيع الوثوق؟

بحسب دراسة اجراها كلّ من مركز جيرهارت للعطاء الاجتماعي والمشاركة المدنية والمجلس الثقافي البريطاني، ما زالت وسائل الإعلام في تونس ما بعد الثورة تعتبر إلى حد كبير من قبل الشباب على أنها «تجارية وشديدة التلاعب، تحركها أجندات مختلفة بدلاً من أن تحركها الحقيقة»، وأنها «تفتقر الى المهنية ومسؤولة عن نشر الأخبار الزائفة». وعلى الرغم من الدور الإيجابي الذي لا يمكن إنكاره الذي لعبته وسائل الإعلام الاجتماعي في الثورة، تشير الدراسة إلى أن التصور السائد حالياً بين الشباب هو أن نفوذها قد تحول من ايجابي الى سلبي: «مع أن وسائل الاعلام الاجتماعي قد ساهمت في زيادة الوعي بين الناس في السابق، يعتبرها الكثيرون الآن أداة غير عملية لتعزيز الانقسامات ونشر الشائعات. كما أدى الاستخدام الحالي لوسائل الإعلام الاجتماعي في التعبئة السياسية بمزيد من التنميط والتلاعب؛ الأمر الذي حمل العديد من المشاركين الذين شملتهم الدراسة الى الظن بأن دورها الثوري قد يكون انتهى. « ومع ذلك، وعلى الرغم من تلك المخاوف، يبدو أن هناك موقف إيجابي شامل وحذر بين المستجيبين الشباب الذين شملتهم الدراسة تجاه وسائل الإعلام وحرية التعبير التي بدأت تشهدها. وتعتبر شريحة الشباب هذه التغييرات مهمة وإيجابية، وهناك قناعة ثابتة بامكان استخدام وسائل الاعلام كأداة للديمقراطية iii. هذا يعني ارضاً خصبة لمشروع التربية الإعلامية والمعلوماتية. كان المشروع الذي يوشك الشركاء التونسيون والسويديون على الشروع فيه في فبراير عام 2014 واسع النطاق. كنا قد قررنا في وقت سابق أن نضمنه بناء القدرات، ليس فقط للشباب والمربين بل ليشمل أيضاً المنتجين الإعلاميين. ويتمثّل الهدف النهائي للمشروع بتفعيل دور الأطفال والشباب ومنحهم إمكانية إيصال صوتهم في المسائل المرتبطة بحقوق الإنسان وتونس الديمقراطية. لتحقيق هذا الهدف، نحن

203

نعتبر أنه من الضروري أن يتم تدريس أساسيات التربية الإعلامية والمعلوماتية للبالغين أيضاً - المعلمين وقادة الشباب والأهل. أضف إلى ذلك، كنا مصممين على الوصول إلى الأشخاص المسؤولين عن انتاج المواد الإعلامية: أي الصحفيين والمحررين ومدراء غرف الأخبار والمنتجين التلفزيونيين والمدوّنين. يتعين على تلك العوالم أن تلتقي من أجل تعزيز الاندماج والإثراء المتبادل للمعارف والأفكار والرؤى.

برأينا، ينبغي على المنتجين الإعلاميين الإصغاء إلى الأطفال والشباب وإشراكهم في عمليات الإبداع. هذه الطريقة ستسمح لوسائل الإعلام بأن تصبح أكثر أهمية بالنسبة للشباب وتشجع مشاركتهم في مجتمع ديمقراطي. ببساطة، إن نشرت وسائل الإعلام رسالة مغرضة من دون التحقق من المصادر - وقامت بتعزيز الصور النمطية، من دون أي مبالاة بجمهورها - هل يهم إن اضطلع الشباب بأساسيات التربية الإعلامية؟ العكس صحيح أيضاً: كيف يمكن لوسائل الإعلام أن تتطور إن لم يكن الشباب من كافة الفئات يتمتعون بالمهارات اللازمة لـ«قراءة» وسائل الإعلام وعناوينها الفرعية؟

مواجهة الواقع:

بالعودة إلى بني خالد، حيث كنا واقفين عند زاوية الشارع بحثاً عن مدخل مركز الشباب، يرافقنا المترجم الذي يتولى مهمة ترجمة الحديث من الإنجليزية والفرنسية إلى اللهجة العربية المحلية (أو ما يُعرف باللغة العامية «الدارجة») التي يستخدمها معظم المراهقين في هذه المنطقة. نادتنا مجموعة من الشباب وأرشدتنا الى المدخل. قال لنا أحدهم: «أنتم من السويد، اليس كذلك؟ أهلاً بكم!» في المركز، كانت مجموعة من قادة الشباب في انتظارنا، حيث قدموا لنا الشاي والكعك المحلى وطرحوا علينا الكثير من الأسئلة. قمنا بالإجابة على اسئلتهم وطرحنا الأسئلة من جانبنا، الأمر الذي سمح لنا شيئاً فشيئاً بتكوين صورة عن آرائهم، ومعرفتهم ووعيهم الإعلامي بشكل عام وعن التربية الإعلامية والمعلوماتية بشكل خاص.

تجدر الإشارة إلى أن المركز في بني خالد هو واحد من أكثر من 300 موقع مماثل في كافة أنحاء البلاد والتي تم إنشاؤها خلال نظام بن علي وكانت تُستخدم أحياناً من قبل الحزب الحاكم في سبيل الدعاية والترويج. ومنذ مايو عام 2011، أصبحت تلك المراكز خاضعة من الناحية القانونية للمرسوم الثوري الذي يمنح المراكز مزيداً من الحرية إزاء الحكومة. ووصف قادة الشباب منطقتهم بأنها «غير حصينة من الناحية الاجتماعية»، وهي منطقة صناعية وريفية تتميز بنسبة عالية من البطالة. وقد أخبرنا

مدير المركز بأن الكثيرين، وربما الأغلبية من الأطفال والشباب الذين يستخدمون المركز، يتحدرون من عائلات فقيرة ويواجهون الكثير من المشاكل منها الفقر والمخدرات والعنف المنزلي. وقد ناقشنا مع هؤلاء كيف يقوم الشبان الذين يستفيدون من رعايتهم باستخدام وسائل الإعلام ويتأثرون بها. تحدثنا عن وسائل الإعلام الاجتماعي والصور النمطية بين الجنسين والتسييس. كان قادة الشباب منفتحين للغية وفائقي الذكاء. جميعهم كان متحمساً لقضية دعم الشباب في المركز، لكنهم كانوا يشعرون أنه ليس للأطفال والشباب صوت في وسائل الإعلام السائدة. بحسب قولهم، فإن القيود المالية تحدّ من وصول الشباب في بني خالد الى وسائل الاعلام الاجتماعي، التي شكلت منصة كان للشباب التونسي دوراً نشطاً فيها. اعتبر كافة قادة الشباب أن القضايا المتعلقة بالإعلام مهمة جداً في تونس اليوم، لكنهم أشاروا إلى أن مفهوم التربية الإعلامية والمعلوماتية غير معروف تقريباً في المدارس ومراكز الشباب، وفي المعهد العالي للتنشيط الشبابي والثقافي في بئر الباي، حيث يحصل كافة قادة الشباب في تونس تقريباً على شهاداتهم في الترفيه الشبابي والقيادة. قبيل وقت الغداء، قمنا بجولة في المركز الصغير وعلى غرفه الخالية لكن الزاهية الألوان. خلال تلك الجولة، أخبرنا قادة الشباب بفخر عن أحدث مشروع يخططون له: محطة إذاعية عبر الإنترنت تبثّ إنطلاقاً من مركز الشباب محتوى إعلامي يتولى الشباب أنفسهم إنتاجه وتقديمه. زرنا ايضاً الاستوديو الصغير المؤقت وطلبوا رأينا بما رأيناه.

كانت هذه زيارتنا الأولى إلى مركز تونسي للشباب ولم ندرك مدى التقدم الذي احرزوه في بني خالد مقارنة مع الكثير من المراكز الأخرى في مختلف أنحاء البلاد. كنا نجهل مقدار الحواجز التي تواجه مشروع إذاعة غير تجارية، وعلمانية وغير سياسية يشارك فيها الشباب. لم ندرك كل هذه الأمور سوى لاحقاً، بعدما سافرنا إلى أنحاء أخرى من البلاد، والتقينا المزيد من الناس وزرنا مراكز الشباب الأخرى التي بالكاد تملك أي معدات أو الحيز. كانت الحماسة لاحداث التغيير وتمكين الشباب واضحة في كل مكان. لكن التمكن فعلياً وعملياً من منح الأطفال والشباب الفرصة للتعبير عن آرائهم على الهواء كان امراً نادراً. بعد الظهر، التقينا بالشباب للمرة الأولى. كنا قد طلبنا اللقاء بمجموعة من 15 شخصاً، لكن ما لا يقل عن 30 شاباً وشابة، تتراوح أعمارهم بين 20-12 كانوا بانتظارنا بكل حماسة في قاعة كبيرة متعددة الاستخدامات يتم فيها إعطاء الدروس ما بعد المدرسة ودروس الرقص وعروض الراب. استمر توافد الشبان طوال فترة بعد الظهر من اجل المشاركة في ورشة العمل، إذ أغلقت المدارس ابوابها وتناقل

الجميـع الخبـر بـأن ثمـة مـا يحصـل فـي المركـز. بدأنـا بالأساسـيات. ومـن خـلال النشـاطات التعليميـة التفاعليـة البسـيطة، تعرفنـا الى كيفيـة تعريـف الشـباب لوسـائل الإعـلام ومـا تعنيـه لهـم. كان بعـض المراهقيـن سـناً يملكـون هواتـف محمولـة بسـيطة وزهيـدة الثمـن، لكنهـم تمكنـوا مـن اسـتخدامها للولـوج الى مواقـع مثـل موقـع التواصـل الاجتماعـي «فيسـبوك» و«جوجـل». كانـوا ايضـاً يسـتخدمون أجهـزة الكمبيوتـر القليلـة الموجـودة فـي مركـز الشـباب لمشـاهدة مقاطـع الفيديـو عبـر «يوتيـوب»، أو يقصـدون أحـد مقاهـي الإنترنـت المحليـة. قلـة منهـم كانـوا يملكـون أجهـزة الكمبيوتـر فـي المنـزل. اختتمنـا ورشـة العمـل ذاك اليـوم، علـى أن تكمـل فـي اليـوم التالـي. وكـم كانـت مفاجأتنـا كبيـرة عندمـا وصلنـا الى المركـز ورأينـا الشـبان ينتظـرون بالصـف فـي الخـارج. أكثـر مـن 60 شـاباً وشـابة، تزاحمـوا فـي تلـك القاعـة وجلسـوا الى الطـاولات وحتـى علـى الارض، أو اتكـأوا علـى طـول الجـدران. قـال أحـد قـادة الشـباب واصفـاً هـذا المشـهد: «إنهـم متعطشـون للمعرفـة، للتعـرف الى كل مـا هـو جديـد». كان الأمـر شـاقاً بعـض الشـيء - لأنهـا أكبـر مجموعـة مـن الشـبان سـبق لأي منـا أن عمـل معهـا باسـتخدام الأنشـطة التعليميـة التفاعليـة. بدأنـا اولاً بتمريـن «إحصـاء الـرؤوس»، وقمنـا بتقسـيم الشـباب إلى مجموعـات أصغـر وطلبنـا منهـم إحصـاء عـدد النسـاء والرجـال، وكذلـك الأطفـال والشـبان فـي مجموعـة مـن الصـور التـي نشـرت خـلال الأسـبوع فـي الصحـف المحليـة والوطنيـة. لـم نسـتغرب بـأن نكتشـف أنـه ليـس هنـاك عمليـاً أي ذكـر للنسـاء والأطفـال فـي الأخبـار، فـي حيـن بـدا ذكـر المراهقيـن أكثـر وضوحـاً، لكـن فقـط بالإشـارة اليهـم كضحايـا أو كجانحيـن. كنـا كمدربيـن نتوقـع هـذا الأمـر، بعدمـا أظهـرت الدراسـات علـى مـدى سـنوات أن هـذه النسـبة تتكـرر فـي كافـة أشـكال وسـائل الإعـلام فـي أنحـاء العالـم تقريبـاً. لكـن الشـبان المشـاركين فـي الورشـة فوجئـوا بالأمـر وغضبـوا. «لـم لا يوجـد اي شـيء عنـي؟ أو عنـا؟» سـؤال طرحتـه فتـاة شـابة، بعدمـا اكتشـفت للمـرة الأولـى أنهـا وأقرانهـا، وخاصـة الفتيـات، انـه لا يوجـد تقريبـاً أي ذكـر لهـنّ تقريبـاً فـي وسـائل الإعـلام. خـلال يـوم اسـتراحتنا، ركزنـا علـى الاسـتفادة مـن مشـاعر الغضـب والإحبـاط للتصـرف فـي هـذا الشـأن. قمنـا بتجربـة الأنشـطة المختلفـة؛ مثـل كتابـة العناويـن والعناويـن الفرعيـة او شـرح الصـور؛ تحليـل التعليقـات التـي تنشـر عبـر مواقـع التواصـل الاجتماعـي وأشـرطة الفيديـو القصيـرة؛ إنشـاء غرفـة التحريـر وهميـة؛ والسـماح للمراهقيـن بالتخطيـط لبرامجهـم الاخباريـة الخاصـة. بعـد ذلـك، كنـا منهكيـن لكـن ممتلئيـن بالحمـاس والمعرفـة الجديـدة. شـعرنا أننـا نسـير فـي الطريـق الصحيـح.

جهد مشترك:

جاءت فكرة إطلاق مشروع للتربية الإعلامية والمعلوماتية في تونس من المركز الإفريقي لتدريب الصحافيين والاتصاليين (CAPJC). خضع المركز، الذي احتفل بالذكرى السنوية الثلاثين لتأسيسه عام 2013، إلى عملية إصلاح شامل بعد الثورة. وتم تعيين القيادة الجديدة بعد الاطاحة بالرئيس في عام 2011، بهدف إعادة هيكلة وتطوير المؤسسة وخدماتها لتتمكن من تلبية الاحتياجات والتحديات التي تواجهها وسائل الإعلام التونسية القائمة والناشئة. وأدرك المركز منذ البداية أهمية تمكين الشباب التونسي المستهلك للإعلام من خلال برامج التربية الإعلامية والمعلوماتية، فدخل في شراكة مع مكتب تطوير الإعلام في الإذاعة السويدية (SR MDO vi). مكتب تطوير الإعلام في الإذاعة السويدية هو جزء من الإذاعة السويديةvii، وهي اذاعة حكومية بقيت لعدة سنوات المؤسسة الأكثر ثقة في نظر الجمهور السويدي. viiiويتمتع مكتب تطوير الإعلام في الإذاعة السويدية بنحو 20 عاماً من الخبرة في مجال التعاون الإنمائي في آسيا وأفريقيا، وهو قادر على توفير الكفاءات والخبرات للتدريب الصحفي والتطوير الإعلامي من كافة المؤسسات الحكومية في السويد: الإذاعة السويدية، التلفزيون السويدي ix، والمؤسسة التعليمية السويدية x. تجدر الإشارة إلى أن المهمة التي تسعى المؤسسة التعليمية السويدية لتحقيقها هي العمل بشكل ناشط لتعزيز التربية الإعلامية والمعلوماتية. وهي تنتج سنوياً العديد من البرامج التعليمية وبرامج المعرفة العامة ومجموعة من الوسائط التعليمية المتعددة لقطاع التعليم، من مرحلة ما قبل المدرسة إلى المدرسة الثانوية. وقد نجحت بشكل خاص في مدّ الجسور بين وسائل الإعلام والمدارس. المؤسسة التعليمية السويدية هي أيضاً جزء من شبكةxi وطنية تعمل على تنفيذ برامج التربية الإعلامية والمعلوماتية في النظام التعليمي.

هذا ويشكّل التعاون مع الشركاء الدوليين جزءاً هاماً من إعادة هيكلة المركز الإفريقي لتدريب الصحافيين والاتصاليين (CAPJC). ويعمل المركز ايضاً مع منظمة دعم الإعلام الدولي (IMS)، في الدنمارك، وهي منظمة غير ربحية تهدف إلى تعزيز قدرات وسائل الإعلام للحد من النزاعات وتعزيز الديمقراطية وتسهيل الحوار. من شركاء المنظمة ايضاً أكاديمية «دويتشه فيله»، المنظمة الألمانية الرائدة في مجال تطوير وسائل الإعلام الدولية؛ ومؤسسة فريدريش ناومان، وهي مؤسسة ألمانية تدعم المشاريع في مجال حقوق الإنسان، وسيادة القانون والديمقراطية. بالإضافة إلى ذلك، تجدر الإشارة إلى أن

المركـز الإفريقـي لتدريـب الصحافييـن والاتصالييـن (CAPJC) مسـؤول عـن برنامـج تمويـل الاتحـاد الأوروبـي لدعـم وسـائل الإعـلام فـي تونـس، xiiجنبـاً إلـى جنـب مـع المركـز الأوروبـي للصحافـة فـي ماسـتريخت وغيـره مـن الشـركاء التونسـيين. ويهـدف البرنامـج، الـذي يمتـد علـى مـدى ثـلاث سـنوات، إلـى تعزيـز دور الصحفييـن ووسـائل الإعـلام فـي تونـس وقدراتهـم المهنيـة مـن خـلال تعميـق العلاقـات بيـن وسـائل الإعـلام وهيئـات التنميـة الاجتماعيـة والاقتصاديـة والمجتمـع المدنـي. ويمكـن لبرامـج التربيـة الإعلاميـة والمعلوماتيـة أن تلعـب دوراً هامـاً أيضـاً فـي هـذا المجـال. وقـد تولـى المركـز الإفريقـي لتدريـب الصحافييـن والاتصالييـن (CAPJC) ومكتـب تطويـر الإعـلام (MDO) تصميـم مشـروع التربيـة الإعلاميـة والمعلوماتيـة معـاً كأداة لتحقيـق الديمقراطيـة وتمكيـن الشـباب، بالارتكـاز علـى تجاربنـا وخبراتنـا المختلفـة. وقـد سـبق للأشـخاص الرئيسـيين المشـاركين فـي المشـروع أن سـاهموا بوضـع وإدارة مشـاريع أخـرى فـي مجـال التربيـة الإعلاميـة والمعلوماتيـة الدوليـة فـي فلسـطين وروسـيا البيضـاء علـى سـبيل المثـال. كذلـك، اسـتمد البرنامـج الإلهـام مـن مختلـف مشـاريع التربيـة الإعلاميـة والمعلوماتيـة الوطنيـة والدوليـة فـي السـويد، بمـا فـي ذلـك الحملـة الوطنيـة الناجحـة التـي سـاهمت بمكافحـة الأفـكار النمطيـة بيـن الجنسـين وعـززت المشـاركة المدنيـة للمراهقـات فـي كافـة أنحـاء السـويد فـي عـام 2005. ويسـتهدف البرنامـج، الـذي تتولـى تشـغيله بشـكل مشـترك كلّ مـن وزارة الشـؤون الاجتماعيـة السـويدية وشـبكة مـن المنظمـات غيـر الحكوميـة ووسـائل الإعـلام، المعلميـن وطـلاب المرحلتيـن المتوسـطة والثانويـة، ووسـائل الإعـلام، مـن خـلال إجـراء ورش العمـل وإطـلاق حملـة توعيـة عامـة. وتقـوم الوكالـة السـويدية للتعـاون الإنمائـي الدولـي xiii («سـيدا») بتمويـل المشـروع الـذي ينفـذه المركـز الإفريقـي لتدريـب الصحافييـن والاتصالييـن (CAPJC) ومكتـب تطويـر الإعـلام فـي الإذاعـة السـويدية (SR MDO) فـي تونـس، وذلـك تماشيـا مـع اسـتراتيجية الحكومـة السـويدية لتقويـة التعـاون الإنمائـي مـع الشـرق الأوسـط وشـمال أفريقيـا xiv: مـن خـلال تعزيـز الديمقراطيـة واحتـرام حقـوق الإنسـان؛ وتعزيـز التنميـة المسـتدامة التـي تعمـل علـى تحسـين ظـروف السـلام والاسـتقرار والحريـة فـي المنطقـة. وتوفـر وكالـة «سـيدا» الدعـم فـي منطقـة الشـرق الأوسـط لمجموعـات المجتمـع المدنـي التـي تعـزز الديمقراطيـة وحقـوق الإنسـان مـن خـلال وسـائل الضغـط، وبنـاء الـرأي ومـن خـلال وسـائل الإعـلام والصحافـة المسـتقلة.

الدمج بين الإعلام والتعليم :

بعـد التدريـب في بـني خالـد، أقيـم الكثيـر مـن ورش العمـل في مراكـز أخـرى لدعـم الشباب. وتمّ أيضاً تنظيم الندوات واللقاءات في تونس وضواحيها بهدف إنشاء شبكة للتربيـة الإعلاميـة والمعلوماتيـة مـع مختلـف الفاعليـن المتحمسيـن بشـأن تمكيـن الشباب في الإعـلام، بمـا في ذلـك المدونيـن وصانعـي السياسـات والناشطين الاجتماعيـن وأساتذة الجامعـات ومنتجـي الأفـلام والصحفييـن والمعلميـن والفنانيـن. وعقـدت اجتماعـات أيضـاً مـع المؤسسـات والمنظمـات الدوليـة والمحليـة العاملـة في تونس.

في أبريـل 2014، نظـم كلّ مـن مكتـب تطويـر الإعـلام في الإذاعـة السويديـة (SR MDO) والمركـز الإفريقـي لتدريـب الصحافييـن والاتصالييـن (CAPJC) سلسـلة ثانيـة مـن ورش العمـل في مجـال التربيـة الإعلاميـة والمعلوماتيـة. وكان الهـدف هـذه المـرة أن تشـمل تلـك الـورش الإعلاميـن، وبشـكل خـاص المنتجيـن العامليـن في مجـال التلفزيـون والراديـو، كمشاركيـن فاعليـن. عندمـا وصـل أعضـاء الفريـق مـن السـويد إلى تونس في شـهر أبريـل، كان المنـاخ السياسي قـد هـدأ. وكانـت المقاهـي في الشـوارع تغـصّ بالنـاس مـن كافـة الأعمـار؛ نسـاء ورجـال، فتيـان وفتيـات... يتبادلـون الأحاديـث ويتجادلـون ويبتسـمون. كان الدسـتور الجديـد قـد دخـل أخيـراً حيـز التنفيـذ، واعتبـره الجميـع في كافـة أنحـاء العالـم فريـداً مـن نوعـه، وتطلعيـاً وتقدميـاً. عنـد هـذا الحـد، أصبحـت بعـض تلـك الأجـزاء مـن البـلاد التـي سـبق أن نصحونـا بالعـدول عـن زيارتهـا قبـل شـهرين فقـط، مفتوحـة أمامنـا الآن. في إطـار تلـك السلسـلة مـن ورش العمـل، طُلـب مـن المنتجيـن والصحفييـن إعـداد مجموعـة مـن أشـرطة الفيديـو القصيـرة التـي تركـز عـلى الشـباب ووسـائل الإعـلام في تونس، مـن خـلال عمليـة التعلـم التشـاركية. وعقـدت حلقـات العمـل في تونس وصفاقـس، وكان عـلى الإعلاميـن أن يعملـوا بشـكل وثيـق مـع قـادة الشـباب والأطفـال والمراهقيـن. كانـت العنـوان الأبـرو لتلـك الحلقـات الإدمـاج والتعـاون والابتـكار. أقيمـت ورشـة العمـل الأولى في تونس في مركـز التدريـب التابـع للمركـز الإفريقـي لتدريـب الصحافييـن والاتصالييـن (CAPJC). وقبـل أن نتـرك للصحفييـن مهمـة اختيـار القصـص ومباشـرة العمـل عليهـا، قمنـا بتزويدهـم بأساسـيات التربيـة الإعلاميـة والمعلوماتيـة، باسـتخدام الأنشـطة التعليميـة نفسـها التـي نفذناهـا في فبرايـر 2014 مـع قـادة الشـباب والشـباب أنفسـهم في مراكـز الشـباب في بـني خالـد وخارجهـا. عندمـا نقّـذ الصحفيـون نشـاط «عـدّ الرؤوس»، الـذي مـن خلالـه يتولـون إحصاء عـدد الذكـور والإنـاث، والأطفـال والبالغيـن في وسـائل الإعـلام، فوجئـوا بالنتيجـة واسـتفزتهم تمامـاً كتلـك

الفتاة البالغة من العمر 15 عاماً التي كانت جالسة على الأرض في مركز الشباب في بني خالد. وقد تساءل أحد الصحفيين: «ما هذا؟» بالإشارة الى النتائج التي تمّ تدوينها على اللوح. «هل يحق فقط للرجال في منتصف العمر أن يظهروا في الإعلام؟» كنت قد دعونا قادة الشباب والشباب الذين شاركوا في ورش العمل في بني خالد في فبراير للقاء المنتجين الإعلاميين في تونس. وفي تلك اللحظة بالذات، ظهر الجانب العملي للتربية الإعلامية والمعلوماتية واضحاً لنا جميعاً في الفريق المنفذ للمشروع: عندما يقوم المنتج الإعلامي بإشراك الجمهور من شبان وشابات في العملية الإبداعية، فإن هذا الأمر يؤثر على المنتج الإعلامي النهائي بطريقة إيجابية جداً. وأصبح فجأة للأطفال والشباب دور رائد في سرد القصص. لاحظ الصحفيون المشاركون أنها المرة الأولى التي يتحدثون فيها مع الشباب بدلاً من التحدث عنهم. تم تشكيل مجموعة مرجعية من الشباب الذين تمت دعوتهم لاحقاً من أجل تقييم أشرطة الفيديو القصيرة التي أنتجها المشاركون البالغون في حلقة العمل. وهنا، طُرحت كل الأسئلة الهامة: كيف تمّ وصف الأشخاص؟ ما الذي يقال وما الذي لا يقال؟ هل توجد رسائل خفية؟ وقد ساهم وجود الشباب وردود فعلهم بدفع الصحفيين للتساؤل أكثر عن عملهم وبطريقة جديدة.

بعد إنتهاء ورش العمل في تونس، انتقلنا إلى الجنوب وتحديداً الى صفاقس، ثاني أكبر مدينة في تونس. تجدر الإشارة الى أن صفاقس أكثر استقطاباً من تونس، وهي مركز لحركة يسارية قوية فضلاً عن العديد من الجماعات الاسلامية والمحافظة ذات النفوذ. هناك ايضاً عملنا مع الصحفيين المحليين، من الإذاعة والصحف المحلية، وقادة الشباب والشباب. قمنا نوعاً ما بتكرار التجربة التي قمنا بها في تونس؛ لكن هنا، أصبح كل شيء أكثر وضوحاً. وكانت آثار عقود من الرقابة وممارسة السلطة لا تزال ظاهرة في المؤسسات الإعلامية ومراكز الشباب. قال الصحفيون الذين عملنا معهم أنهم لم يجروا عملياً أي مقابلات مع الأطفال أو الشباب من قبل، لكنهم كانوا مستعدين للتغيير. وجاء كلامهم ليعكس ما قاله رئيس أكاديمية دويتشه فيله في تونس، روديغر ماك، في إحدى المقابلاتxv: «طوال 25 عاماً، لم يكن للصحافة وجود فعلي في تونس. كانوا (أي الصحفيين) يحملون الميكروفون لأولئك الذين في السلطة ويسجلون تصاريحهم، لكن ليس بالمعنى الصحفي، الذي يأخذ المشاهدين أو المستمعين في الاعتبار.»

210

التطلع إلى المستقبل

أسفرت ورش العمل التي عقدت في شهر أبريل عن عدة أشرطة فيديو قصيرة حول المواضيع الراهنة من منظور الشباب في صفاقس. وقد شعرت وسائل الإعلام المشاركة أنها تعلمت مهارات جديدة هامة، على الأقل من خلال التفاعل مع الشباب. من جانبهم، قال الشباب انهم شعروا بمزيد من الثقة في تبادل آرائهم وأفكارهم مع وسائل الإعلام. في الواقع، لم يشأ أي من المشاركين المغادرة بعد انتهاء ورش العمل، بغض النظر عن العمر، والخبرة أو الجنس. وقالت إحدى الشابات الصحافيات العاملة في الإذاعة: «اعتدنا أن نفعل الأشياء لأنه طُلب منا القيام بها. لكننا الآن نريد ان نجري اللقاءات والحوارات بشأن ما نقوم به ولماذا نقوم به. يجب أن نستمع الى بعضنا البعض.» بالنسبة لنا في الفريق، قدمت ورش العمل وما نتج عنها من أشرطة فيديو مدخلاً هاماً لاستمرار المشروع، بما أن أحد أهدافنا الرئيسية كان تطوير نهج ملائم محلياً ووسائل التربية الإعلامية والمعلوماتية التي تحتوي على أساليب ومواد التدريب، من خلال عملية تشاركية. وبالتالي، فإن السنة الأولى من الأنشطة – والتي تتضمن ورش عمل وندوات واجتماعات ودورات تدريبية للصحفيين - كان لها هدف مشترك؛ ألا وهو تحديد الاحتياجات المحلية وتجربة أنشطة التعلم المختلفة التي يمكن تضمينها في الحزمة التعليمية المكيّفة محلياً. ومع اقتراب العام الأول على المشروع من نهايته في شهر أغسطس عام 2014، شعرنا أننا وصلنا الى أبعد مما كنا نتأمل. كنا قد اجتمعنا مع المئات من الشباب وقادة الشباب والإعلاميين الذين ساعدونا على تصميم شكل المرحلة المقبلة، التي من المقرر أن تبدأ في عام 2015. معاً، وضعنا الخطوط العريضة للوسائل والمبادئ الإعلامية التوجيهية التي تناسب ظروف واحتياجات تونس والمشهد الإعلامي سريع التغير الخاص بها. وكان الشباب وقادة الشباب والمنتجين الإعلاميين قد شاركوا بفعالية في العملية الإبداعية، من خلال تحسين قدراتهم ومهاراتهم في الوقت نفسه.

وفيما نتطلع إلى المستقبل، يسعدنا أن نكون قد وضعنا الأساس لشبكة واسعة، تتضمن ممثلين عن المنظمات والمؤسسات الدولية والوطنية مثل اليونسكو xvi واليونيسيف xvii ومفوضية حقوق الإنسان xviii، ومعهد الصحافة وعلوم الأخبار IPSI) xix)، والجمعية التونسية لحقوق الطفلATDDE) xx)، وزارة الثقافة والشباب التونسية والمركز الوطني للتجديد البيداغوجي والبحوث التربوية (CNIPRE). على الرغم من قلة المشاريع

الأخرى في مجال التربية الإعلامية والمعلوماتية تعمل في تونس، تم تنفيذ العديد من المبادرات وأنشطة التطوير الإعلامي في تونس بعد الثورة. ويتطرق الكثير من تلك المشاريع أو يشتمل على جوانب التربية الإعلامية والمعلوماتية. على سبيل المثال، تولت منظمة «إنترنيوز»، وهي منظمة دولية غير ربحية، بتدريب الصحافيين الشباب والمدونين من خلال سلسلة من ورش العمل حول البرامج الحوارية السياسية، التي تغطي قضايا حقوق الإنسان من خلال التقارير الإذاعية، والصحافة الاستقصائية في التعامل مع الفسادxxi. هذا وقد قام معهد صحافة الحرب والسلام (IWPR) بدعم شبكة الإعلاميين الشباب التونسية (TYMN)، وهو مشروع يستغرق عامين بدأ عام 2011 وتضمن تدريب الصحفيين والمدونين الشباب وفقاً لأفضل الممارسات، فضلاً عن إنشاء مراكز الإنترنت كمراكز للنشر والتدريب، ومحطات الإذاعة المجتمعيةxxii. تم إطلاق مشروع تجريبي لتعزيز المواطنة وثقافة حقوق الإنسان عام 2012 بالتنسيق مع اليونسكو، ويضمّ ست وكالات تابعة للأمم المتحدة (مفوضية حقوق الإنسان، وبرنامج الأمم المتحدة الإنمائي، واليونسكو، وصندوق الأمم المتحدة للسكان، المفوّضية العليا للأمم المتحدة لشؤون اللاجئين، واليونيسيف) بالإضافة الى الحكومة التونسية، والمعهد العربي لحقوق الإنسان (AIHR) ومنظمات محلية غير حكومية. هذا المشروع كان يهدف لخلق نوادي التربية على المواطنة وحقوق الإنسان في سبع مناطق في تونس.

على الرغم من عدم وجود أي سياسات أو استراتيجيات وطنية في مجال التربية الإعلامية والمعلوماتية طور التطوير، كان هناك إجماع ساحق خلال كافة اجتماعاتنا وأنشطتنا بالحاجة إلى برامج التربية الإعلامية والمعلوماتية في المشهد الإعلامي الذي شهد تحولاً جذرياً في تونس ما بعد الثورة. وقد أعرب مسؤولون حكوميون أيضاً عن اهتمام قوي، خصوصاً أنهم أقروا بأن تعزيز قيم الديمقراطية يكمن في صميم التربية الإعلامية والمعلوماتية. هذا وقد تمّ التشديد على الحاجة الى التربية الإعلامية والمعلوماتية في خلال سلسلة من الإجتماعات مع الهيئة العليا المستقلة للإتصال السمعي البصريxxiii (HAICA))، وهي الهيئة الرئيسية في تونس، والتي تأسست في مايو عام 2013 لتنظيم القطاع السمعي البصري في البلاد. وذكرت الهيئة بشكل واضح، تماماً كما فعل كافة شركاؤنا الآخرون في تونس، أن جميع التونسيين وخاصة الأطفال والشباب، هم في حاجة ماسة إلى المهارات المناسبة من أجل تصفية وتحليل ومعالجة السيل اللامتناهي من الرسائل التي تملأ حياتهم اليومية. في هذا المشروع، نشعر بأننا قمنا بخطوة كبيرة إلى الأمام من خلال السماح بلقاء نوعي بين المنتج الإعلامي والمستهلك سيؤدي، من الناحية العملية، إلى خلق طرق جديدة في التفكير والعمل.

ملاحظات ومراجع:

1. http://en.rsf.org

2. http:// ww.unicef.org/infobycountry/Tunisia_statistics.htmlw

3. دراسة بحثية: الوعد الثوري: التحوّل في مفاهيم الشباب في مصر وليبيا وتونس. مركز جيرهارت للعطاء الاجتماعي والمشاركة المدنية والمجلس الثقافي البريطاني http://www.britishcouncil.org/sites/britishcouncil.uk2/files/revolutionary-pro-mise-summary_0.pdf

4. إريك تشرشل: تقرير: عمل الشباب في تونس ما بعد الثورة (2013)، «يوروميد». http://euromedyouth.net/IMG/pdf/youth_work_in_tunisia.pdf

5. http://whomakesthenews.org

6. http://www.srmdo.se

7. http://www.sverigesradio.se

8. تنشر سنوياً من قبل «ميدي أكاديمين» وجامعة «جوتنبرج»، السويد لقياس ثقة الجمهور بوسائل الإعلام المختلفة والشركات والمؤسسات الخاصة، منذ عام 1997.

9. http://svt.se

10. http://www.ur.se

11. http://mik.statensmedierad.se

12. http://www.capjc.nat.tn/index.asp?pld=75

13. http://www.sida.se

14. الاستراتيجية الإقليمية للوكالة السويدية للتعاون الإنمائي الدولي («سيدا») مع الشرق الأوسط وشمال أفريقيا (2010-2015). http://www.government.se/sb/d/574/a/156049

15. http://www.dw.de/interview-r%C3%BCdiger-maack-head-of-dw-akade-mies-tunis-office/a-17017431

16. http://www.unesco.org/new/en/unesco/worldwide/unesco-regions/arab-states/tunisia

17. http://www.unicef.org.tn

18. http://www.ohchr.org/EN/countries/MENARegion/Pages/TNIndex.aspx

19. http://www.ipsi.rnu.tn/

20. http://www.enfant.tn`

21. التربية الإعلامية 2.0: عيّنة من البرامج حول العالم. تحديث مركز المساعدة الإعلامية الدولية. نوفمبر 2013. تقرير «إنترنيوز». https://internews.org/sites/default/files/resources/CIMA-MediaLitera-cy_2_0-11-21-2013.pdf

22. http://haica.tn

·